Fifth Edition

FLASHBACK
A Brief History of Film

LOUIS GIANNETTI
Case Western Reserve University

SCOTT EYMAN

PEARSON
Prentice
Hall

Upper Saddle River, New Jersey 07458

Library of Congress Cataloging-in-Publication Data

Giannetti, Louis D.
  A brief history of film / Louis Giannetti, Scott Eyman.—5th ed.
    p. cm.
  Includes bibliographical references.
  ISBN 0-13-187457-8
  1. Motion pictures—History.   I. Eyman, Scott   II. Title.
  PN1993.5.A1G54 2006
  791.43'09–dc22
      2005014349

Executive Editor: Deirdre Anderson
Editorial Director: Leah Jewell
Editorial Assistant: Christina Walker
Marketing Manager: Kate Stewart
Marketing Assistant: Kara Pottle
Manufacturing Buyer: Brian Mackey
Cover Design: Laura Gardner
Composition/Full-Service Project Management: Pine Tree Composition
Printer/Binder: Bind-Rite Graphics
Cover Printer: Phoenix Color Corp.
Text Typeface: 10/12 Baskerville

Pearson Education LTD., London
Pearson Education Singapore, Pte. Ltd
Pearson Education, Canada, Ltd
Pearson Education–Japan
Pearson Education Australia PTY, Limited

Pearson Education North Asia Ltd
Pearson Educación de Mexico, S.A. de C.V.
Pearson Education Malaysia, Pte. Ltd
Pearson Education, Upper Saddle River, New Jersey

10 9 8 7 6 5 4 3 2 1
ISBN: 0-13-187457-8

This book is in memory of Marilyn Nank Eyman and Vincenza Giannetti,
who took us to the movies for the first time,
and who loved them, and their sons, very much.

Contents

Preface

WE SET OUT TO WRITE A REALLY BRIEF BOOK. Just the basics, no frills. After considerable deliberation, we finally decided on a mechanical form of organization by decade. We then proceeded to cheat left and right, cramming major figures and film movements into their decade of greatest influence or prestige. Here, then, is a bare-bones history of fiction movies, copiously illustrated with photos, many of them rarely reprinted. Since this book was written primarily with an American audience in mind, we have emphasized the American cinema. Eclectic in our methodology, we have adhered to a broad consensus tradition of film history and criticism; except for a humanist bias, we have had no theoretical axes to grind. Nor have we attempted to dazzle the reader with a fresh array of jargon; the text is in plain English, with essential terms in **boldface** to indicate that they are defined in the glossary. Our main concern has been with film as art, but when appropriate we also discuss film as industry and as a reflection of popular audience values, social ideologies, and historical epochs. History books are filled with value judgments, and this one is no exception. We have not hesitated to call a bomb a bomb. On the whole, however, our attitude has been similar to that of André Breton, the founder of the surrealist movement, who said, "The cinema? Three cheers for darkened rooms."

Acknowledgments

We gratefully acknowledge the input received from the following reviewers of the mansucript: Douglas F. Rice, California State University of Sacramento; Christopher R. Young, University of Michigan at Flint; Roger Vaccaro, SJRCC; and Robert Hoskins, James Madison University. And also Web Survey respondents, David Allen, Midland College; Terry Bales, Santa Ana/Santiago Canyon Colleges; Bob Baron, Mesa Community College; Sharon Bolman,

University of Advancing Technology; Doyle Burke, Mesa Community College; Tim Cavale, John Jay College; Peter Condon, Keene State College; Robert Darden, Baylor University; Stefan Hall, Bowling Green State University; John Lee Jellicorse, UNC Greensboro; Bob Jordan, San Diego State University; Kenneth Kaleta, Rowan University; Steve Keeler, Cayuga Community College, Barbara Keyser, Baruch College; Sharon Kleinman, Quinnipiac University; Bobbie Klopp, Kirkwood Community College; Arthur Lizie, Bridgewater State College; Gary Martin, Cosumnes River College; Robin McKell, Columbus College of Art and Design; John Murphy, Youngstown State University; Bruce Nims, USC Lancaster; Elizabeth Nollen, West Chester University; Kenneth Nordin, Benedictine University; Heather Polinsky, Central Michigan University; Rashna W. Richards, University of Florida; Luther Riedel, Mohawk Valley Community College; Randy Roberts, Purdue University; Jack Ryan, Gettysburg College; Susan Scrivner, Bemidji State University; Joseph Sierra, Pasadena City College; Michael Soderlund, Central Lakes College; Fred Svoboda, The University of Michigan-Flint; Paddy Swiney, Tulsa Community College; Ed Thompson, UMass Dartmouth; and Ken White, Diablo Valley College.

Others who have helped us include Jonathan Forman of Cleveland Cinemas; Marcie Goodman of the Cleveland Film Society and International Film Festival; and Patty Donovan of Pine Tree Composition.

LOUIS GIANNETTI
SCOTT EYMAN

About the Authors

LOUIS GIANNETTI is a Professor Emeritus of English and Film at Case Western Reserve University in Cleveland. He has taught courses in film, literature, writing, drama, and humanities. In addition to being a professional film critic for several years, he has also written about movies for a variety of scholarly journals. His other books include *Godard and Others: Essays on Film Form, Masters of the American Cinema,* and *Understanding Movies,* which is currently in its 10th edition. Professor Giannetti is the father of two daughters, Christina and Francesca. He lives in Shaker Heights, where he spends an inordinate amount of time tending his Japanese-style garden, to make sure it keeps that natural look.

SCOTT EYMAN'S *Print the Legend,* the authorized life of John Ford, was named one of the Best Books of 1999 by the *Los Angeles Times.* He won awards for his journalism, criticism, and television writing. His other books include *Five American Cinematographers, Mary Pickford: America's Sweetheart, Ernst Lubitsch: Laughter in Paradise, The Speed of Sound: Hollywood and the Coming of Talkies,* and most recently, *Lion of Hollywood: The Life and Legend of Louis B. Mayer.* He writes frequently for the *New York Observer* and lives in West Palm Beach with his wife Lynn, and an assortment of animals who love the movies too.

Flashback

1

Beginnings

Young man, you can be grateful that my invention is not for sale, for it would undoubtedly ruin you. It can be exploited for a certain time as a scientific curiosity, but apart from that, it has no commercial value whatsoever.
—AUGUSTE LUMIÈRE, 1895

Museum of Modern Art

Timeline: 1870–1908

1871
U.S. population: 39,000,000

1874
First Impressionist painting exhibition, Paris

1876
Alexander Graham Bell invents the telephone

1877
Thomas Edison invents the phonograph

1879
Hendrik Ibsen's "scandalous" play, *A Doll's House*

1880
Thomas Edison and Joseph Swan independently devise the first practical electrical lights

1885
George Eastman manufactures coated photographic paper

1888
George Eastman perfects Kodak box camera

1893
Art Nouveau movement in Europe

1895
Marconi invents radio telegraphy

1900
Sigmund Freud's *The Interpretation of Dreams* published

1901
Death of Britain's Queen Victoria

1901–1909
Theodore Roosevelt (Republican) U.S. President

1903
Henry Ford founds Ford Motor Company

1906
Ruth St. Denis introduces modern dance

1907
First Cubist art exhibition, Paris

1908
General Motors Corporation established

Early experiments in motion picture technology. Eadward Muybridge's sequential still photographs, 1870s. The Zoetrope. Thomas Edison and William Dickson. First Kinetoscope parlor opens in 1894. Auguste and Louis Lumière open a projected motion picture parlor in Paris, 1895. Vitascope parlor opens in New York City, 1896. The fantasy films of Georges Méliès: early 1900s. Edwin S. Porter's *The Great Train Robbery* (1903), the first western. The Nickelodeon era begins, 1905. France's Max Linder: the screen's first important comedian. Movies acquire pretentions: the French *film d'art,* 1908.

O F ALL THE PECULIAR SPECIES of holy madmen that dot the history of the cinema, none was holier or, arguably, madder than Henri Langlois, founder and major domo of the Cinémathèque Français. It was Langlois's contention that, like the continent of North America before Columbus, which geographers knew had to be there, the movies always existed; they were just waiting to be invented. Even though the mechanical means that would make pictures move had to wait several thousand years, a Renaissance, and an Industrial Revolution before the mechanics could be perfected, the need was always there—man's need to study himself and the world around him *directly,* as he actually moved, as the world he lived in really looked.

Who invented the movies? Well, as Peter Sellers's Inspector Clouseau said when confronted with murder, "I suspect everyone . . . and I suspect no one." The mechanical development of cinema was the end result of several dozen men, American, British, and French, who took moving pictures from the realm of a Platonic ideal to that of a sophisticated art form within the space of a single generation—the only true miracle of the movies.

Begin then in the Renaissance, as Leonardo Da Vinci, the genius of his age, writes in *Trattato della pittura* of his desire for a painting to be a living thing. Film historian Terry Ramsaye said of Da Vinci, "He took life apart in search of its secrets, taking apart bodies, observing executions."

The science of optics evolved and brought with it the magic lantern, a simple projection device for slides. That inveterate diary keeper, Samuel Pepys, in an entry dated August 19, 1666, wrote of a visitor who brought with him a new marvel, "a lantern with pictures in glass to make strange things to appear on a wall, very pretty." Mr. Pepys purchased a trick lantern, a projector that showed pictures on a wall. All that remained was to make what was cheerfully called "white magic" come alive. Fade out.

Fade in, to 1872. Leland Stanford, governor of California, insists that a horse in full stride takes all four feet off the ground. Preposterous, says Mr. Stanford's opposition. Twenty-five thousand dollars of Stanford's money backs up his conviction. He hires Eadward Muybridge, a San Francisco photographer, to prove his point. Muybridge sets to work, but his research into the problem is temporarily interrupted when he murders his wife's lover and is adjudged innocent by reason of temporary insanity. Aside from that unfortunate occurrence, he works diligently. After many unsuccessful experiments, Muybridge mounts a line of cameras alongside the racetrack and trips the shutters with electromagnets as a horse and rider gallop down the track and over a short hurdle. The pictures prove conclusively that, yes, a horse does take all four hooves off the ground while galloping **(1–1).** Leland Stanford is $25,000 richer.

These sequential photographs of a horse in motion fascinated Jean Louis Meissonier, a Parisian painter. He set about converting the Muybridge photographs into a series of silhouettes for a projecting Zoetrope, a revolving disc holding the transparencies and lit from behind. In front of that disc was mounted another opaque disc with slots cut into it. This slotted disc revolved in the direction opposite of the picture disc, helping to provide the all-important persistence of vision. (*Persistence of vision* is the phenomenon whereby the eye "remembers" what it has just seen even after the object has disappeared. Try looking at a light, then closing your eyes. The length of time this afterimage lasts averages only a tenth of a second, but that's just long enough to create the illusion of continuity. This same principle is what makes movies possible.)

Although it could be seen only by a few people, the illusion of a horse galloping and jumping was revelatory. In East Orange, New Jersey, Thomas Edison was pridefully working on perfecting his favorite of all his inventions, the phonograph. News of the work being done by Meissonier found its way to Edison. Taking over these European modifications of Muybridge's photographs and other concurrent experiments in the projection of sequential photographs, Edison assigned William Dickson, a bright, twenty-four-year-old assistant, to the project of developing a machine that could visually accompany his beloved phonograph.

For over two years, Dickson worked. Nothing much resulted. He and his employer tried and discarded dozens of alternative methods. When they finally designed a machine that they thought might work, they were stymied. What were the pictures to be on? Cardboard? A concurrent invention came to the rescue. Edison

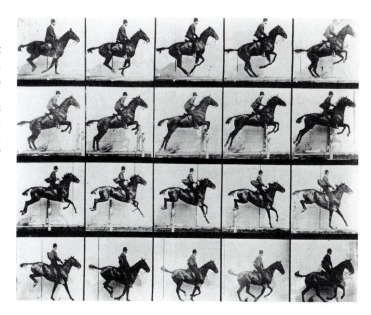

1–1. *Horse Jumping* (circa 1877), *sequential photographs by Eadward Muybridge.*
Muybridge lined up twenty separate cameras to get these photographs. If he had been able to put each separate photo on a clip card or flexible-base film, he would have had a motion picture. As it happened, Muybridge had no interest in movies as such. He stayed with his sequential photos even after others moved on to discover a film on which such photos could be printed and then projected for audiences.   (*Museum of Modern Art*)

heard that George Eastman had devised a flexible film base covered with a photo-graphic emulsion. Edison ordered a sample, looked at it, and turned to Dickson. "That's it," he said. "We've got it. Now work like hell."

Dickson worked and came up with a machine that definitely worked, after a fashion. But Edison was an inventor of machines and did not have faith in motion pictures as a mass medium. He also had a knack of making successes out of other people's failures. A superb conceptualist and equally superb synthesizer, Edison's pattern of supervising the efforts of a large and creative staff, and then cheerfully appropriating the results as his own, helped to obscure the fact that no basic part of the Edison invention was actually Edison's invention. Perfect-ing a projector so that a mass of people could enjoy the astonishing effect of mov-ing pictures would, Edison firmly believed, burn out the public's interest in the novelty.

Edison instead opted for a machine on which only one person at a time could watch the film. It was a peep show at a penny a shot and it was called a **Kinet-oscope**—a continuous loop of film that passed over a series of rollers and in front of a lens **(1–2).** The spectator had to stoop to look through the viewer. The Kineto-scope was patented in August, 1891. When Edison was asked if, for an extra $150, he wished to take out a copyright that would cover England and France, he de-murred, saying "It isn't worth it." With his patent in his pocket, Edison concen-trated on more pressing matters. He was particularly intent on new projects like the electric storage battery, an iron-ore separator, and a talking doll.

In 1893, an entrepreneur named Norman Raff heard that the Kinetoscope invention was lying fallow in the New Jersey workshop, and he pressed his way into a partnership with the nonplussed Edison. Under Edison's name and Raff's manu-facture, the first Kinetoscope parlor opened in April, 1894, at 1155 Broadway. Each of the ten machines wholesaled for $350. The parlor was an instant sensation. Pa-trons paid a 25 cent admission charge, while an attendant switched on each ma-chine as the customers passed down the row. Edison soon devised a nickel-in-a-slot attachment to lower the overhead and increase the takings.

1–2. The simple and foolproof workings of a Kinetoscope.
The film wound around a series of rollers in an end-less loop. A crude, prefocused glass fixed the image on the glass through which the viewer observed the film, while the spinning shutter between the lamp and the glass provided the necessary persistence of vision. *(Museum of Modern Art)*

1–3. Kinetoscope parlor (circa 1895).
The viewer paid the attendant 25 cents; the attendant then switched on the machine; the viewer looked through the slot on the top of the machine; patrons went right down the line of machines to catch up on all the latest releases. The essential innocuousness of the subject matter helped kill the novelty of the peep show device. Besides, the all-important communal element of a shared experience was missing—but not for long.   *(Museum of Modern Art)*

As Edison built a studio to begin supplying films for this back-door sensation, other parlors opened in Chicago, San Francisco, and Atlantic City, and all met with tremendous public popularity. Other people in other countries paid their nickel, looked at Mr. Edison's machine, and saw that it was good. They also saw that it could be better. Competition began, and the race was on. Storefront theaters opened in St. Petersburg in Russia by May, 1896.

Meanwhile, Norman Raff began to realize that a machine that threw pictures on a wall was the next logical step, whether Edison liked it or not. At about the same time, Edison's employee William Dickson quit and threw in his lot with the Latham family, a father and two sons who likewise believed that a projecting machine was of vital importance.

There were two main obstacles. First, films had to be lengthier. Until then, movies lasted only thirty seconds or so, because the fierce jerking movement of the

1–4. Edison's Black Maria studio, in East Orange, New Jersey (circa 1895).
The Black Maria was mounted on a turntable, the better to catch the sun that was let in through a hinged roof. The operator of the ungainly, almost immobile Edison camera was located in the cubicle on the right, while vaudeville or circus performers did their turns in front of the rear wall. Produced at the rate of one or two a day, the specialty scenes shot at the Black Maria fed Kinetoscopes all over America.   *(Museum of Modern Art)*

feed mechanism tended to break filmstrips that were more than fifty to a hundred feet long. Second, there was the problem of intermittent movement. To photograph movies, it was necessary to stop each **frame** for a fraction of a second to allow the light passing through the lens to impress its image on the film. If only the Lathams could figure out a way to do that in a projecting machine. . . .

Within the space of three years, all the basic problems were solved. The Lathams came up with the simple alternative of leaving slack in the film at the top and bottom of the film gate; this loop took the stress off the tightly threaded ribbon of celluloid. Another inventor, named Thomas Armat, made the vital connection that what the camera did to hold the film stationary while the images were being photographed could be repeated in the projection mechanism itself. In September, 1895, in Atlanta, Georgia, Armat and a partner demonstrated a projector that worked, however crudely. That was a magic year, for three months later the brothers Lumière—Louis and Auguste—opened a picture parlor in Paris.

By that time, William Dickson was inventing another kind of machine entirely, a new kind of peep show designed to evade Edison's patents. The film was photographed in the usual manner, but each frame was printed on an individual

1–5. *The Arrival of a Train* (France, 1895), *directed by Louis and Auguste Lumière.*
A prime example of what early films were: a snapshot service for the family of humanity. In the earliest days, the camera never changed from a single-**take** grainy black-and-white image. Patrons of the early movies couldn't help but be startled as the train moved toward the camera—toward *them*. This was no painted flat, no stage illusion or obviously artificial Méliès construct. Nor did the audience have the comfort of placing themselves out of harm's way, as they would have been able to do if they were standing on a real station platform. No wonder people panicked. Realistic but not real, bigger than life but capable of capturing the smallest nuance, the movies were a revelation even to sophisticates. *(Museum of Modern Art)*

piece of cardboard and mounted consecutively on a wheel. When the wheel was cranked, the cards clicked past and the figures moved. The machine was called a Mutoscope. It worked on cardboard, but it worked. Essentially, it was a mechanized flip-card device, but it was a particularly durable, charming variation on a theme. Mutoscopes are still in use in amusement parks and arcades.

The snowball continued to gather momentum. Raff was still insisting on a projecting Kinetoscope; Edison was still not interested, but Armat had one. Raff and Armat joined forces and marketed the latter's machine, paying Edison a fee for the use of his name, which gave them a credibility they would otherwise lack. Their advertising billed it as "Edison's latest marvel, the Vitascope," and it premiered at Koster and Bial's music hall in New York on April 23, 1896. In all essential respects, the Vitascope was the prototype for the modern movie projector.

The screen at Koster and Bial's was twenty feet wide, and the program included an excerpt of a prize fight, several dance acts, and the surf at Dover, England, which the audience took for the Jersey coast. When the waves broke over the rocks, splashing spray toward the camera, there was a brief flurry of panic in the front rows, a reaction that was to be repeated for several years in theaters across the world whenever an object came close to the camera.

As good as the Vitascope was, the best equipment of the day was being manufactured in France by Louis and Auguste Lumière, who pioneered the moving snapshots that formed the basis of this parlor amusement (1–5). From the beginning, the Lumière brothers sent their light, hand-cranked projectors into middle Europe, Russia, and even the Far East, showing audiences films of people doing what people do: thirty seconds of a train pulling into a station, a minute of a happy couple (Louis Lumière and his wife) lovingly feeding their baby, followed by three old men (Lumière's father and two cronies) playing cards. The Lumière brothers followed Shakespeare's dictum to "hold a mirror up to nature" when they ventured into newsreel production. In June, 1895, Louis Lumière had photographed the members of the Photographic Congress disembarking from a gangplank at Neuville-Sur-Saone. That same night, Lumière showed the film to the suitably impressed Congress.

All this open-mouthed wonder might seem naive today, but nobody had ever seen a picture move before. Motion picture pioneer Albert Smith, who would cofound Vitagraph, one of the early giants of the movie industry, judged it all correctly when he wrote, "It was motion alone that intrigued the spectators." It really didn't make much difference what was moving or why.

The motion picture was an invention with many inventors. Dickson's contribution has certainly been undervalued even as Edison's was overrated. All either of them really did was design a machine through which film could pass. The film itself had been invented by George Eastman. The gears that were used for the stop-and-start movement necessary to imprint an image on each frame were essentially

1–6. *The Kiss* (U.S.A., 1896), *with May Irwin and John Rice, released by Edison.*
This movie runs about a minute and involves little more than John Rice smoothing his voluminous mustache and launching his lips onto those of his costar. It is, in fact, a scene from a popular play of the day. Two things about the movie startled audiences. First, the closeness of the people—strictly speaking, the entire film, such as it is, is one long **medium shot.** Second, the lasciviousness of the kiss itself. Seen today, the lasciviousness stems from the fact that May Irwin seems to be talking throughout the kiss. *(Museum of Modern Art)*

1–7. *A Trip to the Moon* **(France, 1902),** *directed by Georges Méliès.*
The man in the moon is unceremoniously introduced to explorers from earth. The rocket is painted cardboard, the face peering out from the moon appears to be covered with thickened shaving cream. The means are naive, almost gauche, but the effect is charming, like a primitive painting come to life—its sole intent to delight and amuse. *(Museum of Modern Art)*

borrowed from clock movements. It was all a matter of putting the pieces together, with men like Armat and even the murderous Eadward Muybridge contributing to the shape and placement of each piece within the jigsaw puzzle.

News of the Koster and Bial's show traveled fast. Exhibitors in England and France contracted for "Edison's Vitascope," while demand for the little scenes that were its *raison d'être* began to accelerate. Vitascopes, as well as competing machines like Lumière's Cinématographe, began to be an accepted part of vaudeville programs across the country. This was a mixed blessing. As Terry Ramsaye observed, vaudeville served to keep the film alive and slowly evolving, but it also enslaved and cheapened movies until they were known merely as "chasers," marking the end of the show and clearing the house for the next performance.

Also, there were only so many times even the most voraciously curious spectator could view the little fragments of reality that the Vitascope and its competition could supply. What the movies needed was something more than white magic. They needed storytelling, a method of involving the audience for periods longer than a minute. They got it from, of all people, a French magician, Georges Méliès, and an American who had been an able-bodied seaman, Edwin S. Porter.

Georges Méliès (1861–1938) had understudied the famed magician Robert Houdini in Paris and seized upon films as a new vehicle for illusion. Beginning in 1896 and continuing until just before World War I, Méliès wrote, directed, designed the scenery for, and often acted in some five hundred enchanting little films. His stage presentations concentrated on fantastic narratives in never-never-land settings, usually combining elaborate stage scenery with lantern-slide projections. In his glass-enclosed studio, Méliès turned out the cinematic equivalent of those presentations, tableaux fantastiques **(1–8),** whose increasing length allowed more room for the often brilliant use of **fade-outs, dissolves,** and **double exposures.** Many of Méliès's techniques were the results of a propitious accident. Photographing a scene on a Paris street, his camera jammed and stopped. He cleaned out the mechanism and started cranking again. When he printed the film, a bus was suddenly transformed into a hearse. Somewhere in Méliès's head, a light bulb switched on and **special effects** were born.

In *The Damnation of Faust* (1898), Méliès proudly showed off his set-designing magic in a complicated sequence of Faust's descent into hell. Méliès's intricately painted stage flats slide away to reveal even more intricately painted scenery behind them. He did this not once but nearly a half-dozen times. The effect is purely theatrical, but Méliès's pride in his craft is so tangible, and the effect so innocently pleasurable, that quibbles are soon swept away. No one else was making movies that were quite so ambitious, or quite so charming.

A staple of Méliès's work is an oddly childlike ghoulishness. In *The Terrible Turkish Executioner* (1904), a man wielding a gigantic scimitar beheads four men with one swooping stroke. He throws their heads into a barrel, but one head unaccountably floats out and reattaches itself to its body. The now-whole prisoner helps reassemble the others. They turn on their executioner and cut him in half with his own sword. His upper torso flops around on the ground like a dying fish and tries to join with his lower half. He finally succeeds and chases the four men. A small ballet troupe (a Méliès trademark) dances out from the wings. Everyone smiles.

Méliès gradually increased the complexity of his films, working his way up to spectaculars that were a full reel (ten minutes or so) in length. Films like *The Conquest of the Pole* (1912) had several dozen scenes and more elaborate effects, requir-

1–8. *The Merry Frolics of Satan* **(France, 1906),** *directed by Georges Méliès.*
Fueled by an imagination of remarkable innocence, Méliès made films out of cardboard and paint that seem like the dreams of a creative child: primal, pure, startling imagery completely free of literary or social sophistication. It was, apparently, an authentic projection of Méliès's personality. When times changed, he was unable to change with them, but instead continued to turn out his little one-reel fantasies until he was overtaken by bankruptcy.   *(Museum of Modern Art)*

ing considerable virtuosity, but Méliès's touch was as light, as fantastically literal, as ever. A fat woman falls out of a balloon, is impaled on a church spire, and explodes like an overinflated balloon. When the explorers are attacked by the Giant of the North Pole, a sort of large Old Man Winter, they pelt him with snowballs until he spits out the explorer he had previously eaten. The expectorated explorer picks himself up and hustles away. No harm done.

Méliès's benign fantasies began to decline in favor by 1910. Films were becoming more dramatically complicated, and the Frenchman's combination of pure fantasy and the theatrical proscenium seemed passé. The outbreak of World War I ruined this great primitive artist's career. Late in life, Méliès and his second wife were discovered selling toys and candy in a Paris kiosk. The government pensioned him off and admitted him to the Legion of Honor. But in his early days, Méliès's influence was strong, especially in America, where his films were popular enough to warrant wholesale duping (unauthorized copying, followed by exhibition of the bootlegged copies) and even outright imitation.

The Dream of a Rarebit Fiend (1906) is an entertaining Edison production wherein an orgy of eating and drinking leads a top-hatted toff on a **surrealistic** walk home, during which hand-held, weaving views of a city are superimposed over him as he holds on to a street lamp that sways like a clock pendulum. Once the *roué* manages to get to bed, the furniture begins to rearrange itself. Cut to a split-screen shot of devils dancing above the actor's head. The film then cuts to an artful **miniature** of the bedroom set, as the bed whirls furiously, shakes and twirls à la *The Exorcist*. The bed ends this St. Vitus dance by launching itself through the window, flying over the city in double exposure. For all its camera trickery and fanciful imagery, *The Dream of a Rarebit Fiend* eschews the painted scenery of Méliès and as a result seems less magical, more realistic. And more profitable as well. At this stage in film history, prints were sold outright to exhibitors. *Rarebit Fiend* cost $350 to produce and sold $30,000 worth of prints.

1–9. *Pipe Dreams* **(U.S.A., 1903),** *produced by Edison.*
Here we see the influence of Georges Méliès on American film production. Although **matte shots** (in which two or more separate pieces of film are combined on one piece) existed at this time, they were difficult to achieve. Phantasmagorical effects like these tended to be created "in the camera." The actress smoking the cigarette—a daring act in itself in 1903—would go through the desired actions and reactions against a black backdrop. The film would be rewound and the other performer in the scene would then be photographed at a different **angle.** If the two images were lined up correctly, the illusion worked, producing a "realistic" fantasy world. *(Museum of Modern Art)*

The Dream of a Rarebit Fiend was directed by Edwin S. Porter (1869–1941), one of the most mystifying of all early filmmakers. A sailor and an electrician, Porter spent his early career at Edison's studio as an unpretentious jack-of-all-trades cameraman—who, in those days, was usually the director as well. Unwittingly, Porter seems to have stumbled on the basic alphabet of film.

In 1903, Porter made *The Great Train Robbery*, which took a few more steps in evolving a film grammar **(1–10)**. A western filmed in New Jersey, *The Great Train Robbery* is one reel of action, violence, frontier humor, color (in the form of hand-tinting), special effects (a very effective **matte shot** of a train passing as seen through a stationhouse window), and, as a final fillip, a full-screen **closeup** of a bandit firing his pistol at the audience. Viewed today, the movie seems competent but unremarkable. But consider: In fourteen **scenes,** Porter told a (comparatively) complicated story and told it *visually,* with virtually no **titles.** In exterior scenes,

1–10. *The Great Train Robbery* **(U.S.A., 1903),** *directed by Edwin S. Porter.*
Porter's film liberated movies from the realm of thirty-second playlets of vaudeville headliners. The train is a real train, the costumes and scenery well chosen (considering the film's New Jersey locations), and Porter's camera angles tend to emphasize the realism of the exteriors. *The Great Train Robbery* was not only the most famous film produced by Edison studios, it was also the single most famous American movie until it was displaced twelve years later by *The Birth of a Nation.* *(Museum of Modern Art)*

Porter had his actors move not just from stage left to stage right, but away from and toward the camera. In one scene, Porter mounts the camera on top of a moving train; in another, the camera **pans** with the escaping bandits. For what it is, not to mention what it was, *The Great Train Robbery* is a supple, perfectly articulated piece of filmmaking, and it made Porter the leading filmmaker of his day.

All over America and the world, exhibitors clamored for prints of the film, the prime mortgage-lifter of its era and a factor in the explosion of the **nickelodeons** that occurred around 1905. (*Odeon* is Greek for "a hall of music," *nickel* is what it cost to get in.) By 1907, there were three thousand nickelodeons in America **(1–11)**. There was no better place for this classically democratic phenome-

1–11. Nickelodeon (circa 1905).

As movies like *The Great Train Robbery* lifted film out of the realm of the peep shows, Kineto-scope parlors gradually converted into nickelodeons—about an hour's worth of short films for a nickel. Most nickelodeons were located near large working- or middle-class populations. Overhead was low, turnover was high. Theatrical empires like that of the Warner Brothers began in modest theaters like these. By 1920, the nickelodeon had evolved into movie palaces that thrived in large metropolitan areas, opulently appointed downtown theaters seating as many as five thousand people. After thirty more years, the moviegoing population shifted away from downtown toward suburbia, and downtown theaters were gradually replaced by shopping mall multiplexes—small, narrow, uniformly forgettable. In seventy-five years, movie exhibition had come full circle. *(Museum of Modern Art)*

non. Here, immigrants who couldn't speak English and illiterate laborers attended a new invention, learning about their new land and its customs, transported by the magic of storytelling drama for the first time in their lives, many of them learning English bit by bit, word by word in the bargain. For millions, the movies were art, science, and schooling all in one.

Though Porter led the league by many lengths, his intuitive grasp of screen technique never grew much beyond *The Great Train Robbery*. In 1912, he became director-general for Famous Players–Lasky, the forerunner of Paramount Pictures. Here he directed a series of stately short features that consisted almost entirely of static tableaux of, well, Famous Players in Famous Plays. Porter's camera was invariably in the position of a spectator in the first five rows of a theater, a fatally passive observer. It was as if one man had collaborated on the invention of the alphabet, had been able to type out "The quick brown fox jumped over the lazy dog," and then, with the whole world watching, was resolutely unable to extend this infinitely adaptable resource to encompass anything more articulate or profound.

Obviously, Porter was an instinctive talent, one who shot and **edited** his films the way he did because it seemed the best way to tell a story. As critic William K. Everson noted, Porter "saw films in terms of plot, not people." But as cinema evolved into a medium of character development, people like Porter were left behind. He retired from Famous Players–Lasky in 1915 and went to work for the Simplex projector company, whose machines have always been among the most reliable available to exhibitors. He spent the remainder of his life inventing and tinkering with the machines he felt most comfortable with.

It was Porter and Méliès who together can be said to have recognized, if not utilized, practically everything that filmmakers have been refining ever since. It's no accident that in the pre–World War I era, America and France had the most vital filmmaking by far. France, under producers like Charles Pathé and Leon Gaumont, recognized and supported filmmaking by establishing a frankly commercial base for it, despite the fact that the American Edison and many others were convinced that the peep show fad would soon pass. It certainly would have, had it not been for more farsighted entrepreneurs.

In France, the great comedian Max Linder (1883–1925) began making films in 1905, and his smooth, eternally elegant savoir-faire made him the first great comedy star. Dapper and delicate, Linder worked completely in screen terms, and then some. In *Max Takes Quinine*, Linder, entangled in a tablecloth, notes an onrushing policeman and flicks the cloth at him as if he were a bullfighter and the policeman a bull. Lightning transpositions like that mark Linder as a clear predecessor to the great Charlie Chaplin, who went Linder one better by turning the joke on its head: Instead of Linder's aristocrat, always skating along the thin edge of disaster but invariably finding a way to maintain control, Chaplin created a shabby tramp every bit as incapable of defeat.

On the other end of the French film spectrum, the Film D'Art was formed in 1908. Actors from the Comédie Française, composers like Camille Saint-Saëns, and writers like Edmund Rostand all banded together for the express purpose of producing *art*. It was farewell to cheap tent shows and nickelodeons, hello to film as a tributary to theater. As an attempt to elevate films, it was doomed to failure, although the Film D'Art did meet with an initial, somewhat fluky period of success. For example, Sarah Bernhardt's *Queen Elizabeth* (1912) swept Europe and America, leading otherwise canny producers like Adolph Zukor and Samuel Goldwyn to

1–12. *The Count of Monte Cristo* (**U.S.A., 1912**), *with James O'Neill (left front), directed by Edwin S. Porter.*
The set had wooden planks on the floor so the actors wouldn't step out of the sightlines of the frame. The scenery and props—doors, stone arch, wine casks in the back room, the back room—are painted. The main value of a movie like *Monte Cristo* is that it gives a good idea of what popular melodrama was like during the late nineteenth century—and what James O'Neill's son Eugene was rebelling against when he became the first great American dramatist.   *(Famous Players–Lasky)*

launch American versions of the Film D'Art. The results were artistically negligible and financially disastrous, for once the novelty value wore off, the middle-class intelligentsia dropped these bastard crossbreedings and went back to the live theater. Hardcore movie fans never cared a whit for such pictures in the first place.

In Russia, efforts were turned toward imitating the French, except for Ladislas Starevitch, a sort of mutated Méliès, who launched a lovely series of elaborate puppet films in 1913. Italy was specializing in heavy historical spectaculars (**1–13**),

1–13. *Cabiria* **(Italy, 1913),** *directed by Giovanni Pastrone.*
The acting in the early Italian spectaculars has been described as being like the moment after somebody shouts "Fire!" in a crowded theater. Subtlety, in short, was not their strong point.
(Museum of Modern Art)

and Germany, which along with America was to provide the most fertile cinema of the postwar era, was existing mainly as a conduit for Danish movies.

Except for isolated cases like Linder's, after slightly more than ten years of public existence, the cinema was completely without stars, and usually without stories. White magic now existed; what was needed was a new format for its tricks, and magicians whose vision matched the medium's capabilities. What saved the movies was the fact that they are a medium particularly suited for storytelling. All that was needed was one master storyteller to make the movies come completely, compellingly alive.

FURTHER READING

BARDECHE, MAURICE, and ROBERT BRASILLACH. *The History of Motion Pictures.* New York: Arno Press, 1970. (Originally published in 1938.) Rampantly opinionated but valuable and readable early history by two French cinéastes.

BARNOUW, ERIC. *The Magician and the Movies.* New York: Oxford University Press, 1981. An overview of how Méliès, Houdini, and other professional magicians used film as a medium for their illusions.

COOK, DAVID A. *A History of Narrative Film.* New York: Norton, 1990. A comprehensive, well-documented world film history.

HAMMOND, PAUL. *Marvelous Méliès.* New York: St. Martin's Press, 1975. A good study of the underrated French filmmaker.

JACOBS, LEWIS. *The Rise of the American Film.* New York: Columbia University Teachers College Press, 1939. A classic, scholarly study.

MACGOWAN, KENNETH. *Behind the Screen.* New York: Delacorte Press, 1965. An able, informative history of the movies, written by a man who later became a distinguished producer of films.

MAST, GERALD and BRUCE F. KAWIN. *A Short History of the Movies.* New York: Macmillan, 1992. A well-written, comprehensive world history of film.

QUIGLEY, MARTIN, JR. *Magic Shadows*. Washington: Georgetown University, 1948. The story of the origin of motion pictures, from ancient Greece to the late nineteenth century.

ROBINSON, DAVID. *The History of World Cinema*. New York: Stein and Day, 1973. Entertaining jog through film by the always lucid English critic.

SLIDE, ANTHONY. *Aspects of American Film History Prior to 1920*. New York: Scarecrow Press, 1978. A forbiddingly formal title conceals an entertaining series of essays on esoterica of the early days of movies.

2

Griffith and His Contemporaries: 1908–1920

You're too little and too fat, but I might give you a job.
—Biograph director-general D. W. GRIFFITH to a young
Canadian actress named MARY PICKFORD

Museum of Modern Art

Timeline: 1908–1920

1908
Ford Motor Company produces first Model T—15 million eventually sold

1908–1914
Nearly 10 million immigrants enter the United States, mostly from southern and eastern Europe

1913
Igor Stravinsky's revolutionary *Rite of Spring* ballet, Paris

1913–1921
Woodrow Wilson (Democrat) U.S. President

1914–1918
World War I—63 million forces mobilized; 10 million killed; 21 million wounded

1915
Beginning of Jazz craze in New Orleans
Margaret Sanger jailed for writing about birth control

1917
United States enters World War I, emerges as the most powerful nation in the world
Bolshevik Revolution overturns Czarist regime in Russia

1918
U.S. population: 103 million

1918–1920
Worldwide influenza epidemic kills 22 million

1919
Beginning of Prohibition of alcohol in United States

1920
Women given right to vote in United States

The nickelodeon era—an art for the masses. Cinema's first genius: D. W. Griffith. Griffith's Biograph shorts: 1908–1913. Evolving a film grammar: the art of editing. The Griffith stable of actors and technicians. Lillian Gish: the screen's first great actress. Attempt by the Patents Company to monopolize motion picture production. The first moguls: Carl Laemmle, William Fox, and Adolph Zukor. Griffith's *The Birth of a Nation* (1915), the screen's first feature film masterpiece. Racial controversy. Griffith's monumental *Intolerance* (1916) introduces thematic editing. The westerns of William S. Hart. Thomas Ince, the founder of the American studio system. Early works of Cecil B. De Mille, showman. Mack Sennett establishes the Keystone Studio, specializing in slapstick comedies. Early screen clowns: Mabel Normand and Fatty Arbuckle.

IF THE STANDARD TRUISM ABOUT AMERICA being a nation of immigrants is even close to the truth, it was never more so than in the years before World War I. In Europe, royalty was living out the last moments of what social historian Frederic Morton called "A Nervous Splendor." In America, the upper and middle classes alike were enjoying what Mark Twain had rightly called "The Gilded Age." Under a succession of presidents frankly powerbrokered by kingmakers like Marcus Hanna, American industry and its gospel of the dollar began to spread across the world, even as the country fell into an aesthetic trough. The theater was moribund, subsisting on threadbare melodramas as vacuous as they were popular, marking time until Eugene O'Neill's poetically morbid meditations on human frailty made later writers like Tennessee Williams, Arthur Miller, and Edward Albee possible.

In literature, one of the greatest American writers of the nineteenth century, Mark Twain, had long since faltered, his genius eroded by bitterness and despair. A young writer named Booth Tarkington was mining similar material with his nostalgic stories of midwestern boyhood. Later, a more mature Tarkington wrote penetrating novels of middle-class delusions, two of which, *Alice Adams* and *The Magnificent Ambersons,* would win Pulitzer Prizes and be made into superb movies. But that lay in the future. In the **nickelodeon** era, movies were closer to ten-minute précis of *Classics Illustrated* versions of literary works.

Nickelodeons were coining money with shows lasting between a half hour and an hour. Programs included a few one-reel shorts with some sing-along songs illustrated by hand-colored lantern slides, interspersed between the movies. Why change? By 1910, the peak of the craze, ten thousand nickelodeons were attracting 26 million people every week. Gross receipts for the year totaled $91 million, most of it from the pockets of immigrants, the working class, or the unemployed. This was not so much because the infant industry wanted that audience, but rather because the middle and upper classes wouldn't have been caught dead in a disreputable nickelodeon.

Consider the environment. A nickelodeon was generally a converted storefront or a dance hall with cheap folding chairs rented from undertakers. A white sheet or square of muslin served as a screen. The projection booth was often enclosed in a homemade hut of galvanized tin. The heat it radiated—as well as the heat from the hundreds of warm bodies that thronged into the narrow, confining theaters—made a nickelodeon a potentially rank experience. Enterprising owners sought to counter the olfactory threat by spraying cheap perfume between shows.

2–1. Publicity photo of (left to right) Cecil B. De Mille, D. W. Griffith, and Mack Sennett (circa 1926).
These three men (in addition to Thomas Ince) were the most important to the development of the American film as art and industry. De Mille's sensational subjects and artful lighting and direction produced films of enormous popularity, helping to give movies the mass audience base that made the studio system possible. Griffith's poetry and spectacles centered on attractive leading players whose popularity cemented the star system, while his techniques served as primers for other directors. Sennett's dizzyingly fast, somewhat mechanical comedies crossbred French comic traditions with the indigenous American love of violence and slam-bang action. *(Museum of Modern Art)*

It was no wonder that the movies were considered coarse and distasteful by those more attuned to the opera or to the tragedy and melodrama of the stage. As late as 1913, no movie theater was allowed within two hundred feet of a church. And still, moviegoing expanded exponentially, becoming the first national group experience. As Kevin Brownlow commented, the nickelodeons "offered in one program the same kind of fare as vaudeville, the same thrills as melodrama, potted culture from the art galleries and the legitimate stage, action from the ballpark and boxing ring together with glimpses of foreign countries which could only be duplicated by travel. And, on top of all this, topical items of sensational journalism. . . . And all it cost was a nickel."

At the same time that the audience base was first forming and broadening, the industry itself was being torn by the most savage legal, creative, and commercial buccaneering in its entire history. At the beginning of the nickelodeon era, the leading companies were Biograph, Vitagraph, Edison, and Kalem; they all operated out of New York or nearby New Jersey. A scant ten years later, all but Vitagraph were dead and buried, pushed aside by their own passivity and lack of foresight.

2–2. *The Perils of Pauline* (U.S.A., 1914), *with Pearl White, directed by Donald MacKenzie and Louis Gasnier.*
The serial was a staple of second- and third-run theaters for forty years. Until episodic television and rising costs replaced it, the serial evolved rather methodically, from self-contained weekly stories like *The Perils of Pauline,* to the "cliffhangers" of several years later. Pearl White was a spirited, reasonably attractive actress who had been in films for several years, but this, her first serial, cemented her career and fame. She encored the simple good-guys-in-perennial-peril-from-the-bad-guys some half dozen times before retiring to France in the mid-1920s. A host of less popular stars repeated the pattern for the serials' predominantly juvenile audiences.
(Pathé Films)

They refused to move with the times. Historian Terry Ramsaye reported a typical remark by Kalem's Frank Marion: "These long pictures . . . tie up a lot of money and you have to take a chance. We'll keep Kalem going as long as the short picture lasts and then we'll quit."

The story of the transition of movies from transient amusement to an abiding weave in the national fabric is the story of a handful of people, chief among them a lean, hawk-nosed Kentuckian named DAVID WARK GRIFFITH (1875–1948). Griffith steadfastly followed a nebulous vision of what this glorified toy might become. To paraphrase historian Lloyd Morris, Griffith and his contemporaries had no great respect for the medium they were working in, but their temperaments compelled them to treat it as if it was an art. The result was that they made it one.

At the age of thirty-two, Griffith did not seem to be going anywhere, a fact that was not lost on him. A modest failure as a writer and stage actor, he was the son of a Kentucky colonel, a veteran of the Confederacy who had fallen on hard times after Appomattox and had been unable to recoup his fortune. But despite the comparative impoverishment of his family and the limitations imposed on him by a sixth-grade education, David Griffith carried himself with a lordly grace and had long since cultivated a mien of reserve and dignity born of an innate shyness. He was the sort of man who withheld a central part of himself even from his friends.

Like most theatrical people, Griffith had nothing but contempt for "the flickers." Still, a job was a job, five dollars a day was five dollars a day. In 1907, while at liberty in New York, Griffith obtained some acting work at the Edison studios. He appeared in Edwin S. Porter's *Rescued from an Eagle's Nest,* a film as silly then as it is now. Griffith, arms flailing in the manner that made him such an abysmal actor, does embarrassed battle with a stuffed turkey that, the scenario insists, has snatched a baby.

Griffith's future was manifestly not as a performer, but he nonetheless acted in a few films for the American Mutoscope and Biograph Company, popularly known as Biograph, which was located in an unprepossessing brownstone at 11 East 14th Street. Eager to pick up some extra money, Griffith sold a few stories to the company, who then asked him to try his hand at directing so they could better meet the burgeoning demand for films. Griffith, sensitive to the failure that he had experienced and not eager to repeat it, extracted a promise that, if he failed at directing, Biograph would still employ him as an actor and writer. They agreed. Over dinner, a taciturn staff cameraman named Billy Bitzer gave Griffith a quick primer on how to direct a movie.

Griffith's first film, *The Adventures of Dolly,* about a chubby little girl kidnapped by gypsies, was released on July 14, 1908. In and of itself, the picture was nothing special, but it was made cleanly and within budget. Griffith went to work at Biograph as a contract director, still vaguely contemptuous of the movies, a discontent that carried within it a complete disregard for all the accepted rules of "proper" filmmaking of the day. There were several unwritten doctrines whose effect was to make movies almost exactly like the live theater as viewed from front row center: Actors had to be shown full figure, and cutting was to be reserved primarily for scene changes.

Griffith's sensibility was profoundly romantic. He had been influenced by the novels of Dickens, with their fragile, flowerlike heroines, upstanding heroes, and malignant villains—characters whose actions were constantly being interrupted by other characters' actions, paralleling and crossing each other in furious finales. Instinctively, Griffith knew that there was no reason why movies could not emulate their cultural betters, so he turned his peculiarly American genius to the problem. Like Edison, Henry Ford, or, later, Walt Disney, Griffith lacked an enriching education, had no particular interest in the theory behind his efforts, and lacked the ability to articulate how, why, and where those instincts were taking him. But none of that mattered. Griffith knew how to make movies *work*.

He didn't do it all at once. Grinding out at least two pictures a week left little time for lavish displays of experimentation. Mostly, Griffith moved slowly, introducing a camera experiment in this film, a lighting experiment in that film. But he didn't move so slowly that nobody noticed. By 1912, a survey in the trade magazine *Moving Picture World* noted disapprovingly that Griffith's one-reeler, *The Sands of Dee,* contained sixty-eight **scenes** when a half dozen competing firms used only from eleven to forty-six in their films. It was a wonder audiences could walk out of a theater unaided after all that fragmentation and excitement!

Griffith's *The Lonedale Operator* (1911) is a simple story about robbers laying siege to the heroine in her house while her husband rushes to get there before the

2–3. *The Birth of a Nation* (U.S.A., 1915), *with Mae Marsh, directed by D. W. Griffith.*
After Lillian Gish, Marsh was Griffith's most expressive actress. Where Gish worked with her entire body, Marsh's main instruments were her eyes and hands. Where Gish seemed an ageless young woman, Marsh's pixie features seemed to categorize her as an adolescent. Where Gish had a core of strength, Marsh had a quality of worn desperation. Perhaps her finest performance is in the modern story from *Intolerance* (1916), which Griffith released in an expanded version three years later as *The Mother and the Law.* *(Museum of Modern Art)*

bad guys can get to his beloved. The film contains nearly a hundred **shots.** By isolating the robbers, the heroine, and the husband into separate locations, then rapidly cutting between them, Griffith discovered the main cinematic means of creating and building tension. He then intensified the emotion by moving his camera closer to Blanche Sweet's terrified heroine.

The switch from the static to the mobile was far from Griffith's only innovation. He took devices that other filmmakers used only from plot necessity—a **closeup** of a letter or of a hand reaching into a drawer to extract a gun—and began using them as a regular tool of his trade. Instead of the flat stage lighting that emphasized the painted scenery of other directors' films, Griffith experimented with naturalistic light sources—fireplaces, windows—more realistic sets, and increased use of locations.

Rather than the crude, lumbering gesticulations of the stage-trained actors who were the staples of early films, Griffith began using youthful newcomers untrammeled by years of barnstorming and Emphasized Representation. "On Mondays," wrote Mary Pickford, "we would rehearse. Mr. Griffith would call the company around him and assign our parts. . . . The story would be written or built up. Tuesdays we took interior scenes and Wednesdays we took exteriors." This was a fairly normal production pace for the period, although both Kalem, whose films are among the most picturesquely pleasant of the early days, and Broncho Billy Anderson, the first Western star, regularly ground out films in a single day.

Griffith's achievements in these years were not merely technical. Rather, technique served his passion for the gesture, the moment that would reveal a human soul. In *The Mothering Heart* (1913), Lillian Gish plays a young wife whose child has just died because of the neglect of her husband. Stunned to the point of catatonia, she wanders alone in a garden. Suddenly, she picks up a dead branch and begins thrashing madly at the foliage around her, the explosion of motion betraying the sublimated, seething emotion, a woman overcome by death trying to destroy the strong green life around her.

At other times, a revelation was made explicit by the director, not the character. Griffith's *A Corner in Wheat* (1909) is ten minutes of perfection, a canny amalgamation of two works by the influential American novelist and journalist Frank Norris **(2–4)**. Anticapitalist in theme, it is lovingly photographed by Bitzer with a pastoral gentleness worthy of Corot or Millet. In one sequence, Griffith shows a lavish banquet thrown by a profiteering grain speculator, then cuts directly to a motionless tableau of farmers standing in a bread line, the victims of the tycoon's feast starkly frozen in their misery.

Joseph Henabery, an actor and assistant to Griffith, echoed the opinions of his contemporaries when he said that

> Griffith was an inspiration . . . . He was the first man to realize that a good story depends on characters that are well developed and interesting. Our early pictures were crude and elementary; two people would meet and you

2–4. *A Corner in Wheat* (**U.S.A., 1909**), *directed by D. W. Griffith.*
Griffith used this shot as a **freeze frame** and contrasted it with the bountiful banquet set by a grain tycoon. Although the movie was only a standard one-reeler as far as Biograph was concerned, shot in the usual two or three days, Griffith took his pains. Note the authenticity of the costumes and the bedraggled, believably haggard faces of the actors representing members of the working class. Details like these set Griffith Biographs apart from the competition. *(Museum of Modern Art)*

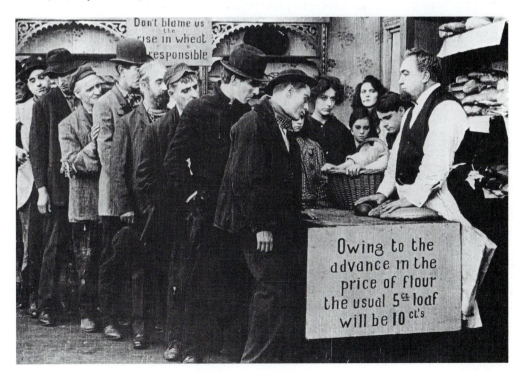

knew nothing whatever about them as people—where they came from, what they were, whether they liked limburger cheese or ladyfingers. They were just impersonal puppets. But Griffith made sure you knew his characters. He'd begin by saying, "Now, what does a woman do who takes care of a family?" And he might show her on a porch and she'd be husking corn, and with little details he would get you to feel the character—"That's my mother," you'd think.

In combining such diverse methods as **parallel editing,** frequent closeups, a superb sense of locations and of landscapes, and the use of objects to synopsize and define character, in creating what amounted to a personal style, Griffith was foraging in completely uncharted territory and doing it against the tacit wishes of his employers.

In 1908, Biograph had joined with Edison, Vitagraph, Selig, and five other companies to form the Patents Company. With Edison's U.S. patents as their legal justification, they sought to levy a weekly tariff of two dollars on every theater that showed their films, in addition to film rentals. They also sought to halt anybody from making or exhibiting films other than their own. Enforcing these demands was difficult, but the Patents Company signed a contract with George Eastman for the exclusive rights to his output of film stock. Not content with declaring war, the trust was now trying to strangle all those companies not allied with them.

By 1910, over half of the ten thousand nickelodeons were in the fold of the Patents Company; the license fee alone was bringing in $1,250,000 yearly. The in-

2–5. *Orphans of the Storm* (U.S.A., 1921), *with Lillian Gish, directed by D. W. Griffith.*
Piquant, often playful, always persecuted but with undreamt of reserves of strength, Gish (1893–1993) was Our Lady of Constant Sorrow to a generation of filmgoers. Among silent screen leading ladies, she was the only one who could legitimately lay claim to the title great actress. A relationship of ambiguous intensity with her mentor, Griffith, made her the perfect transmitting medium for his view of femininity—and, for Griffith, his view of woman was his view of the world. It was a partnership whose revelations of dignity, truth, and inescapable pain would not be matched for over forty years, until the partnership of Ingmar Bergman and Liv Ullmann. *(United Artists)*

dependents (the trust called them "pirates") were led by the feisty, flamboyant Carl Laemmle, later to found Universal, and by William Fox. They fought brilliantly, first cutting a deal with Lumière in France for the supply of raw film, then prodding the U.S. government to institute antitrust action against the Patents Company. While the lawyers argued, the Patents Company sent enforcers to engage in the strong-arm destruction of whatever independent equipment could be found. The only alternative was to go where the Patents Company would have a hard time finding them, far away from New York or New Jersey. The independents looked at the map and noted that the farthest continental point from New York was California, at that time a rare location site. They began to pack their bags and whatever cameras hadn't been hammered into shards by the Patents Company thugs.

It was the height of irony that the great innovator of film found himself working for a retrograde company that was doing everything possible to maintain the status quo. Biograph even kept the names of the actors in their films a secret, in a hopelessly vain effort to prevent the emergence of stars, whose renown would cause them to ask for more money, which would in turn divert power from the business end to the creative end.

Anonymous or not, what creativity Griffith had gathered! A bright, acquisitive, ambitious little girl from Toronto named Mary Pickford; Henry B. Walthall, a Southern gentleman with a saintly face and a whisper-soft acting style; a sensitive juvenile, Robert Harron; Lillian and Dorothy Gish, a pair of sisters from Springfield, Ohio—the latter a light, giddy Ariel; the former pensive, with the face of a Raphael Madonna.

By 1913, Griffith had directed around four hundred fifty short films for Biograph. The company actively resisted his demands to increase the length of his pictures, not to mention his demands for part ownership of the company he had single-handedly raised to preeminence. What Griffith had done in five years' time was to change the way films were made and watched. He had taken an uninflected, objective medium that merely recorded an actor's stage performance or scenes like a train pulling into a station and had transformed it into a subjective medium of individual observation and opinion.

Griffith left Biograph and joined Mutual, directing a series of **programmers** while formulating plans for the film he had long since promised himself he would make: the story of the Civil War, told from a frankly partisan, Southern viewpoint as he had heard it detailed at his father's knee. For his source material, he turned to a popular novel of 1905, later a successful play, *The Clansmen,* by the Reverend Thomas Dixon. On July 4, 1914, with a cast drawn almost completely from actors who had loyally followed him from Biograph and with financing that was scraped up as they went along, Griffith began production of the longest movie made in America up to that time. It was a film on fire with his own special qualities of passion and tenderness, a picture that, in Kevin Brownlow's words, fired the starting gun for the American cinema: *The Birth of a Nation.*

While Griffith was in his prime, a fount of energetic creativity, he had only nominal competition. He led; others followed. The canny producer Adolph Zukor had struck gold with the importation of Sarah Bernhardt's film, *Queen Elizabeth,* produced in France by the Film D'Art (see Chapter 1). Zukor launched a similar, homegrown series: America's most famous stage actors in the roles that made them famous. Among others, James K. Hackett made *The Prisoner of Zenda* and James O'Neill (father of Eugene) starred in *The Count of Monte Cristo* (see **1–12**). The latter was directed by the redoubtable Edwin Porter, and they were all slavish

2–6. D. W. Griffith and Billy Bitzer on location for
Way Down East (U.S.A., 1920).
For over fifteen years, Bitzer was Griffith's strong right arm,
a superb technician continually devising ways and means to
put on film what existed only in the director's imagination.
Griffith was an early believer in what has come to be known
as creative tension—subtly placing actors in competition
with actors, crews in competition with crews. Bitzer re-
sented ceding a portion of his authority to Hendrick Sartov
when Griffith brought Sartov's expertise in **soft-focus** and
closeup photography to the production of *Broken Blossoms*.
The Griffith–Bitzer partnership foundered in the mid-
1920s, although the two men remained fond of each other.
Griffith continued placing his trust in the very finest cameramen, artists like Karl Struss and Joe Ruttenberg, superior
stylists in the assured Hollywood manner. But even they
could only expand on what the stubby little German had
created under the tactful but domineering pressure exerted
by Griffith.   *(United Artists)*

imitations of the stage, complete with painted scenery, entrances and exits, and actors reproducing the performances that they had given on the stage. Seen today,
they are incomprehensibly dull; seen in context with *The Birth of a Nation*, made
only a year or two later, they seem antediluvian.

Even today, seen in a good print with an appropriate musical score, *The Birth
of a Nation* is a potent picture. Despite its iconoclastic and outrageously racist politics, the breadth and perfection of its battle scenes—like newsreels of the Civil
War—and the surefire melodrama of a ride-to-the-rescue climax are all executed
with unsurpassed panache by Griffith. For audiences of 1915, it was as if they had
never seen a movie before and, in truth, they hadn't—not a movie like *The Birth of
a Nation*. Three hours long, Griffith's first feature masterpiece is a panoramic history of the Civil War and its aftermath as reflected by two families, the Stonemans
of the North and the Camerons of the South. The eldest Cameron son founds the
Ku Klux Klan and makes the streets of the vanquished South safe from the ravish-
ments of wild-eyed Negroes and white carpetbaggers.

The Birth of a Nation—the film was shot and previewed under its original title
of *The Clansmen*—has long been something of an embarrassing conundrum for
critics. The movie was often denounced and boycotted in various northern cities.
Can something artistically first rate be a political and sociological embarrassment?
Provisionally, yes. "Provisionally" because, while Griffith's film is frankly told from a
Southern viewpoint, as a Southerner Griffith was actually something of a liberal—
for his day. But he understood blacks only as a liberal nineteenth-century Southerner understood them: Negroes who were faithful loyalists to their former masters
were accorded respect and affection; blacks who were not loyalists were, by defini-

tion, slavering thugs with dangerous urges toward white women. Griffith's treat-ment of the race conflict and the Ku Klux Klan occupies the second half of *The Birth of a Nation* and, to modern eyes, may appear insupportable. But a measure of his restraint can be gauged by scanning his source material, an indescribably pur-ple, extended rape fantasy whose author saw African-Americans as completely sub-human creatures who had to be either subjugated or exterminated.

Looking beyond the ever-widening social gulf between modern attitudes and those that were the norm in 1915, *The Birth of a Nation* remains a remarkable achievement. It is a film whose firestorm success—an investment of less than $110,000 yielded returns of ten to fourteen million dollars—provided ringing affir-mation that the cinema was, commercially, a sleeping giant, newly sprung to its feet. Aesthetically, moreover, the movies could now go anywhere the human mind could conceive.

One of Griffith's most astonishing gifts was his ability to make intimate epics. Battle scenes aside, the moments one remembers in *The Birth of a Nation* are the small ones: Lillian Gish emerging from a hospital visit where a sentry, gasping at her in unalloyed ecstasy, sighs in doglike devotion; a title proclaiming "War's

2–7. *The Birth of a Nation* (**U.S.A., 1915**), *with Henry B. Walthall (center being carried), directed by D. W. Griffith.*

The battle scenes of this film are often singled out, but it is a mark of the movie's quality that there are a half dozen memorable scenes of human interaction as well. Griffith and Billy Bitzer studied Civil War photographs and sought to reproduce the same look of dusty, fly-infested trenches where ragged, raw-boned men died. Helped by the razor-sharp focus and multitudi-nous shades of gray that could be captured on the early orthochromatic film stock, Griffith and Bitzer succeeded. The only sound film to approach the visual accuracy of Griffith was John Huston's *The Red Badge of Courage* in 1951.   *(Epoch Releasing)*

Peace," followed by a medium closeup of a dead soldier, young, unshaven, and as terribly still as one of the dead in the war photographs of Brady or Gardner.

Or, most movingly, the oft-cited scene in which Henry Walthall, in one of the delicate, understated performances that Griffith habitually coaxed from his male leads, returns home to the South after Appomattox. He finds a devastated house. His younger sister runs out to meet him. They look at each other for what seems forever. She notes his tattered uniform; he notes her use of cotton wool to imitate ermine. She begins to cry and he holds her, kissing her hair, a mournful, faraway look in his eyes. The shot changes and Walthall and his sister walk up the steps to the house as two arms reach out from behind the door, the unseen mother enfolding her children, welcoming the hunter home from the hill. The scene graphically demonstrates Griffith's main strength: a profound tenderness that transcends ideologies or political orientation. One doesn't have to be a Southern apologist or a racist to be moved by much of *The Birth of a Nation;* one has only to be a human being.

The furor and success of *The Birth of a Nation* caught Griffith completely unaware. He had already completed what was meant to be a modest programmer before the Civil War picture opened. Looking with a dispassionate eye at what he was calling *The Mother and the Law,* and deeply wounded by the cries of "racist" that had greeted the release of *The Birth of a Nation,* Griffith resolved to face the challenge of what he was going to do next by facing it head on. Elsewhere, the film industry was breaking wide open. The year 1915 had brought the beginning of the end of the Patents Company, as the government enjoined it from enforcing its interlocking agreements, in effect gutting it. Heads in the sand, the Patents founders refused to believe that times were changing—indeed, had already changed. Vitagraph's Albert Smith defiantly declared that the one- and two-reel film was the foundation of the industry and, as far as Smith was concerned, always would be.

With financiers waving money at him, Griffith made what was probably a psychological error: He tried to top himself. He surrounded *The Mother and the Law* with three other stories—the massacre of the Huguenots by the Catholics in sixteenth-century France, the fall of Belshazzar's Babylon, and, just for good measure, the story of Christ. All four stories were partially linked by titles and, more importantly, by the symbolic image of Lillian Gish gently rocking a cradle, an image Griffith took from Whitman: ". . . out of the cradle, endlessly rocking, Uniter of here and Hereafter."

Griffith took eighteen months to make his film, as usual working completely without a script, spending half a million dollars of other people's money. Griffith called his film *Intolerance.* Moving far beyond what even he had done, he refused the easy alternative of telling the four stories of the film consecutively. Rather, he opted to tell them concurrently. As he put it, "The stories will begin like four currents looked at from a hilltop. At first, the four currents will flow apart, slowly and quietly. But, as they flow, they grow nearer and nearer together, and faster and faster until the end, in the last act, they mingle in one mighty river of expressed emotion."

In other words, Griffith **cross-cut** from exposition of one story to the exposition of another story, development to development, and, breathtakingly, from climax to climax. Toward the end of the film, some of the shots last all of eight **frames,** or less than half a second at the correct projection speed. Without fanfare or weighty intellectual justification, Griffith was making an unparalleled experiment in film form. In his use of a near-subliminal stream-of-consciousness flow,

2–8. Publicity photo of D. W. Griffith directing *Intolerance* from the basket of a balloon. (The banner at left is a fragment of the film's original title, *The Mother and the Law*.) Below, the Babylonian set from *Intolerance* (U.S.A., 1916).

Produced for something more than $400,000, *Intolerance* failed at the box office, forcing Griffith to spend the rest of his professional life backtracking. The Babylonian set alone cost more than all of *The Birth of a Nation* had a year and a half earlier. Aided by an unsung genius of a set designer named Walter Hall, Babylon was built as a series of parallel planes that stretched on for more than a quarter of a mile. With the help of director Allan Dwan, a former engineer turned director then working on the same studio lot, Griffith even devised the early equivalent of a camera **crane.** The camera was mounted on top of a specially built elevator that was in turn constructed on top of what amounted to a railroad flat car, complete with tracks. As the car rolled toward the set, the elevator descended. In the movie, the audience floats toward Babylon's barbaric splendor as if in a dream. *(Museum of Modern Art)*

Griffith was coming very close to a replication of the workings of the human mind and imagination itself.

Intolerance cunningly balances spectacle and intimacy. The Babylonian sequence is mostly for show, although Constance Talmadge's rowdy Mountain Girl is a delight. The reconstituted *The Mother and the Law,* a story of labor, domestic troubles, and would-be reformers, is more nuanced, which intensifies the anguish of Mae Marsh as her child is taken away from her, or the piteous look of fear in Bobby Harron's eyes as he is led to the gallows for a murder he didn't commit. The French episode is visually sumptuous, but it and the scanty biblical episode pale next to the barbaric grandeur of the ancient tale and the tensile desperation of the modern story.

The film was three hours and ten minutes long. Of course it failed. Many theories have been advanced for the resounding financial failure of *Intolerance.* They range from the film being ahead of its time to audiences not being able to follow the plot. While *Intolerance* was indeed ahead of its time, audiences had no problems following Griffith's machine-gun editing in *The Birth of a Nation* and would have had to suffer a massive IQ relapse to be confused by its application in *Intolerance.* Likewise, the four separate narrative lines may be unusual, but they're certainly not difficult to grasp.

No, *Intolerance's* great flaw was probably a simple question of bad timing. When Griffith began the film in 1915, America was awash in pacifist sentiment. Europe may have been crumbling, but that wasn't our problem. Woodrow Wilson had been elected president on a peace platform. But by the time the film was released, in the latter part of 1916, war was obviously inevitable, and much of America was getting rather fond of the idea of going "Over There" and giving the Kaiser what was coming to him. And here was Griffith, preaching love, tolerance, and the uselessness of war.

In a grand gesture that was typical of his odd combination of hubris and honor, Griffith personally assumed all the debts of *Intolerance's* failure, which not only included its negative cost but the enormous expense of its road-show engagements as well. It was the height of irony that while the burden of these and other debts were a crushing weight that Griffith could never completely escape, *Intolerance* and *The Birth of a Nation* proved to the world film industry that the time of small film companies, small individual profits, and small thinking was becoming passé. What lay in the future was high finance and a corporate system. Irony upon irony: There was no possible way a self-taught individualist like Griffith could function as a cog in such a system. Before that attempt would end in disaster, however, there were still some moments of glory for the colonel's son.

In 1919, he directed *Broken Blossoms* in eighteen days, spending only sixty thousand dollars. There are those who would gladly trade all of Griffith's moralistic symphonies for this one chamber piece of gentleness and pity. *Broken Blossoms* tells the story of the brutalized child of a boxer. Stumbling through the streets of Limehouse after a beating, she is discovered and cared for by an immigrant Chinese named Cheng Huan. After he nurses her back to health, their innocent idyll is destroyed when the boxer discovers where his daughter has been living: He assumes miscegenation. He drags her home and beats her to death. Discovering her body, Cheng Huan kills her father and then commits suicide while "all the tears of the ages rush over his heart."

(A word about Griffith's subtitles: Generally, they're terrible, florid, and pseudopoetic. But, as Andrew Sarris has observed, the first scene between Gish and

Barthelmess in *Broken Blossoms* is invariably "explained" and often judged on the basis of the dime-magazine titles that are interspersed with it. However, in the scene itself, the interaction between two great actors would be beyond the descriptive powers of most novelists. Ultimately filmmakers, especially silent filmmakers, must be judged by the pictures and emotions they create, not the words they use.)

To this fragile, grim fairy tale, Griffith imparted a remarkable sense of mood and visual poetry and mixed in two performances of purity and the most delicate sincerity from Lillian Gish and Richard Barthelmess. Except for some atmospheric shots of Chinese junks crossing a river in the moonlight and some breathtaking shots of the Limehouse slums cloaked in a shifting river mist, the film is entirely a studio product, and as such it deeply influenced a generation of European and domestic filmmakers.

After *Broken Blossoms,* Griffith's only critical and popular success was *Way Down East* (1920), a ridiculous old play made less ridiculous by a superior performance by the redoubtable Gish and some of Griffith's most spectacular cutting. In the film's climax, Gish, marooned on an ice floe that's drifting toward the edge of a waterfall, is rescued by Barthelmess even as they are going over the precipice.

The close relationship between Griffith and Gish extended past that of director and actress at least to the realm of confidants, the director relying on her opinions and invariable good judgment. In 1920, awash in plans to open his own studio at Mamaroneck, New York, but still responsible for the supervision of a slate of program pictures, Griffith asked Gish to direct *Remodeling Her Husband,* a light comedy vehicle for her sister Dorothy that is, unfortunately, no longer extant. Although

2–9. *Broken Blossoms* (**U.S.A., 1919**), *with Richard Barthelmess, directed by D. W. Griffith.*

Whenever possible, Griffith had his actors incarnate their characters physically as well as emotionally in a subtle variation of the Del Sarte school of acting, which was in vogue in the late nineteenth century. Barthelmess's tentative, delicate pose against the rough stone wall captures much of the character's gentle stoicism. An extremely fine actor, Barthelmess left Griffith in 1920 and formed his own company, which immediately scored one of the decade's major successes with *Tol'able David* (1921). Henry King's film was full of quiet observational detail and evocative photography of the Kentucky hill country and was much admired by Soviet directors like Pudovkin. Although unfairly forgotten today, Barthelmess was one of the leading stars of his era, and Griffith never found a leading man to equal him. *(United Artists)*

modestly successful, it was an experience the elder sister had no desire to repeat. For one thing, the film caused stress between the two sisters; for another, as she explained it, "directing is no job for a lady."

In Mamaroneck, where he had also made *Way Down East,* Griffith made the almost entirely satisfactory *Orphans of the Storm* (1921), very much the mixture as before but energized with undiminished vitality and brio. The story was a Dickensian saga of the French Revolution with a patented ride to the rescue by Danton himself. As in many of his major films, Griffith experimented with the frame size of the image itself, **masking** off the top and bottom of the frame in several shots, leaving the center section in a ratio identical to that of CinemaScope. Griffith's experiments were almost certainly the genesis for Abel Gance's Polyvision of a few years later.

In scenes depicting the Revolution, Griffith took one shot from a balcony, with a hat and coat casually thrown on a settee in the foreground of the shot, as if the occupant of the balcony had just left the frame because of the street riot raging in the background. The effect is of a startling immediacy, history observed.

But Griffith was being hamstrung by his own terminal lack of business acumen. Struggling under a large studio overhead and with an indifferent box office response for the pictures after *Way Down East,* he was soon mortgaging each newly completed film to get money to make his next one. In deeper and deeper to the banks, his confidence faltering, Griffith was forced to give up his beloved Mamaroneck studio and go to work for Paramount. His judgment was no longer as certain as it had been before. A film like *America* (1923) is as beautifully mounted as anything Griffith ever made, but it is oddly hollow at its center, hampered by stolid leading players and a mechanical lack of conviction in the direction.

More than he probably wished to admit, Griffith had been hurt by allowing—encouraging actually—Lillian Gish to leave his stewardship. He replaced her with Carol Dempster, whose talent was elusive and whose appeal was nonexistent. A few unsuccessful, indifferent pictures later, Griffith was back at United Artists, but under very different circumstances than eight years before, when he had been a founding partner. This time he was an employee making an employee's films.

Sound didn't really seem to faze him. His first talkie, *Abraham Lincoln* (1930), contains fine things, kinetic and deeply felt moments. Nobody with a feeling for motion picture history can fail to be moved by the presence of old Griffith actors like Henry B. Walthall, once again called upon to play a gracious Southern officer. But one disastrous film later, Griffith entered an embittered, often alcoholic exile from which he never escaped. He died in 1948, a gray ghost on the edges of a town that could never have been built without him.

After the mid-1930s, Griffith was condescended to as the Last Victorian, a charge made superficially convenient by his own aloof nature and erratic career. At least one of his productions, *Dream Street* (1921), may be the worst film ever made by a great director, and, to echo James Agee, even in Griffith's best work there is enough that is foolish or sentimental to enable the ignorant to ignore the far more meaningful moments of volcanic emotion, purity of expression, and formal genius.

But Griffith gives much more than he takes. He gave the nascent movie industry the capacity to make more money than it had previously dreamed existed. More importantly, Griffith showed the world on what scale a movie could be made. *Intolerance* proved that a movie could re-create an entire lost world; *Broken Blossoms* proved that a movie could capture and define two human souls. In a very real sense, D. W. Griffith put the movies inside us, personalizing them and forcing us to care about his characters and their problems.

Part of the problem was a misperception by the public—and probably by Griffith himself—of his gifts. Acclaimed a realist because of the comparatively restrained acting in his films (which was "realistic" only when compared to the melodramatics that prevailed before him), he was actually almost pure poet and dramatist. Clinical documentation interested him not at all. His editing techniques are almost completely concerned with creating an emotional reaction. His acting was actually quite stylized, but stylized for the screen, not molded around the outmoded precepts of the stage. Griffith's poetic approximations of naturalism penetrated to deeper truths than a realist's objective recordings ever could. Hence his preference for generalized identities for his characters, who are as likely to be identified as "The Boy" or "The Mountain Girl" as they are by specific names.

Naive? Yes. Pretentious? Certainly. But magnificently audacious as well. This was no small man. Lillian Gish said it best: "To us, Mr. Griffith was the movie industry. It had been born in his head."

Although Griffith was without peer, he was not completely without competition. Almost forgotten today, THOMAS INCE (1882–1924) was commonly regarded, especially by the French, as a superb primitive poet, although much of Ince's standing derived from the fact that he was a notorious credit hog, usurping the writing and directing title of any film he produced that particularly pleased him. In a sense, Ince was entitled to this cinematic privilege, for he was the largely uncredited originator of what would come to be known as the Hollywood studio system, the main component of which, as far as Ince was concerned, was the story. Ince personally edited every script, breaking it down into individual shots with very specific instructions as to the action each shot should contain. The finished script, stamped "Produce Exactly as Written," would then be parceled out to a director, with Ince editing the finished film.

Ince's standing began to decline in the latter part of the teens, as his cut-and-dried techniques and lack of popular stars exposed his formulaic, assembly-line methods. Also, aside from Hart and, briefly, Henry King, no top-rank director worked for Ince, a producer who rendered direction superfluous. Compare this to Griffith, whose benevolent rule-by-example attracted such future directorial luminaries as Erich von Stroheim, Raoul Walsh, Tod Browning, Sidney Franklin, Allan Dwan, and John Ford, Griffith's only competition as the premier folk poet of the cinema. Ince's studio and renown died when he did, but his systematized production methods, with writers and directors interchangeably serving at the pleasure of a controlling producer, would flourish under the aegis of Irving Thalberg and Metro-Goldwyn-Mayer and continues into the present day.

Griffith's main critical competition as a producer-director of dramas was CECIL B. DE MILLE (1881–1959), whose early masterpiece, *The Cheat* (**2–11**)**,** was hailed by European critics as a breakthrough in artistic **mise en scène.** The film also features a sadistic sensuality that would come to be recognized, in a somewhat heavier, more obvious form, as a basic element of De Mille's films. It is no longer fashionable to admire De Mille. The blatancy of his later spectacles and his uninhibited right-wing politics have been found by several generations of American critics to be nearly as offensive as a half century of nearly unbroken financial success.

2–10. *Tumbleweeds* **(U.S.A., 1925),** *with William S. Hart, directed by King Baggott.*
Hart was not the first western star nor even the most influential, but he was certainly the most serious about the west. His films are intensely realistic in terms of sets and costumes, intensely romantic, even sentimental, in terms of character. Hart's austere, silent, lonely man who felt things too deeply to be cheaply confessional would be elaborated upon by John Wayne and John Ford, but it was Hart's basic creation, his projection of the way a man had to be if he wanted to survive in a hostile land.   *(United Artists)*

But, at least in his early days (1914–1920) and intermittently thereafter, De Mille was a director of forceful style and some courage, opening up movies to more provocative subject matter in both drama and social comedies. De Mille also provided new standards for artistic productions, with art direction and photography carefully modeled on artists that had enthralled him as a child, like Doré and Rembrandt.

De Mille's greatest gift, aside from an uncanny instinct for popular taste, was his storytelling. A good De Mille film is akin to listening to a saga told by a literal-minded, vigorous grandfather with a remarkable gift for elaboration. De Mille's bread and circuses could be gauche and absurd, but he never dropped a stitch in a story. Critic Carlos Clarens has noted that De Mille's characters did not function as metaphors, had no inner lives or deep meaning, but were still compelling precisely because of their vivid behavioral coloring and De Mille's perpetually forward narrative. His genius for external drama, so obvious in all of his later films, disguised the fact that he was more than a maker of garish comic books sprung to life.

While Griffith and his confreres were developing indigenous forms, comedy was being transplanted from France and being given a distinctly domestic twist.

2–11. *The Cheat* **(U.S.A., 1915),** *with Fannie Ward and Sessue Hayakawa, directed by Cecil B. De Mille.*
This film deals with a sophisticated story of a spoiled society butterfly who agrees to give herself to a wealthy Oriental in return for a much-needed loan, then reneges. Enraged, he brands her as if she were a piece of livestock. De Mille incorporated stage techniques like the use of scrim curtains and dramatic lighting effects, but it was his touches of psychosexual realism that made the film a critical revelation and a public sensation. Hailed by the French as a masterpiece, *The Cheat* was soon forgotten as De Mille embarked on the series of naughty sex dramas and the more successful biblical spectacles that made his name and fortune. Nonetheless, the movie remains an important achievement, far ahead of its time, and a landmark of early American cinema.   *(Lasky)*

The progenitor of much madness, the owner of the grand title King of Comedy was a burly, grumpy Canadian boilermaker named MACK SENNETT (1880–1960). Sennett had apprenticed under Griffith as a bit actor around the Biograph Studio and was possessed by the odd idea that cops and other keepers of dignified social order, taken as a group, were funny.

Griffith, rarely noted for a sense of fun, let alone a sense of humor, ignored his adoring protégé. One day, Sennett's badgering paid off: Griffith directed a one-reeler called *The Curtain Pole* (1908), a trifle about just how much havoc an unknowing, bumbling klutz, armed only with a curtain pole, can wreak on an entire town. The film is interesting on several counts. The star of the film was Mack Sennett. It's also quite funny, building to a classic "rally," comic incidents piling up, involving more and more people until what looks like the entire population of a small community—with mayhem on their minds—is chasing the clumsy owner of the curtain pole.

By 1913, with a small grubstake from the New York Motion Picture Company, the backers of Tom Ince's company, Sennett founded the Keystone Studio. He staffed it with a small troupe of raffish small-part players who had felt stultified by the high literary tone of Biograph under Griffith, most notably a piquant, high-spirited artist's model named Mabel Normand.

The success of the Keystone Studio was immediate. Sennett's unsophisticated humor struck wildly responsive chords in still-unsophisticated audiences **(2–12).** The Keystone films were basically domestic versions of the broadest French farces, populated by character types—the Unfaithful Wife, the Unfaithful Husband—who flew through stock situations at top speed. People hid under beds, doors flew open and slammed shut, but it was farce as it might be performed in a barnyard by circus clowns out of makeup—all action, exaggeration, and speed. (Sennett's films were the only silent movies that were purposely photographed so as to move throughout

2–12. *Tillie's Punctured Romance* (**U.S.A., 1914**), *with Charlie Chaplin and Marie Dressler, directed by Mack Sennett.*
A typical example of the manic acting style Sennett imposed on everyone, even actors as intelligent as Chaplin and Dressler. If a Sennett actor wished to indicate imminent movement, he would throw his arm out at an 80-degree angle, point, turn to the camera, and mouth "I'm going over there," then stalk off. No wonder Chaplin was uncomfortable at Keystone. As he would write later, such circus-clown acting resolutely prevented any kind of character development, and inexperienced as he was, he knew instinctively that nothing transcended character.
(Keystone Studio)

at a faster-than-life speed. Other silent films that seem to be moving fast do so only because they are being improperly projected at twenty-four frames a second, the speed that became necessary for the correct reproduction of sound when talkies came in.)

Mostly, Sennett's actors were defined by their physical characteristics, nothing more. There was the juvenile lead, the funny fat man (the admirably nimble and adept Roscoe Arbuckle), the cross-eyed man (the less admirable Ben Turpin), and so on. Sennett's comics were the sort who did funny things rather than the sort who did things funny.

Seen today, Sennett's films are unutterably crude, seeming to derive from some time before the dawn of civilization. Europe adored them, of course, because Sennett seemed to prove their patronizing, affectionate feelings for Americans as glorious savages. Sennett's movies are indeed robust, exhausting blurs of movement. More to the point, they are not very funny. Several hours of Keystone comedies can be sat through without much more than a few mild chuckles.

Sennett's was a case of the right man being in the right place at the right time. His movies were as mechanical at the end of his career as they were at its height. (A series of four shorts with W. C. Fields made in the early thirties should be excepted, as they are atypically personal, shaggy-dog movies that clearly owe

2–13. *Fatty and Mabel Adrift* **(U.S.A., 1916),** *with Roscoe "Fatty" Arbuckle and Mabel Normand, directed by Arbuckle.*
Normand, sometimes a spunky tomboy, sometimes sweetly feminine, sometimes both in the same scene, was the screen's first important comedienne, with a vivacious grace and sweetness that were, in Sennett's words, "as vivid as summer lightning." Arbuckle, her partner in dozens of films, had a similar humanity and a deft, expert way with gags and props. He was a sophisticated director in the bargain. Both were among the most universally beloved people in the early movies. But in 1921, Normand's career was damaged and Arbuckle's destroyed by separate scandals, of which both were innocent. Both died prematurely, Normand in 1930, Arbuckle in 1933. Both were figures of tragic dimensions.   *(Triangle)*

more to Fields than to Sennett.) But with all his limitations, what an eye Sennett had for talent! With the exception of Stan Laurel and Buster Keaton, every major comic of the silent screen worked for Sennett at the beginning of their movie careers, not to mention the occasional ingenue who would evolve into something considerably grander—Gloria Swanson and Carole Lombard, among others.

The problem with superlative talent is that it always is original, always moves inexorably to express itself, and there was very little room in Sennett's frenetic hurly-burly for individuality. Premier talents like Arbuckle, Harold Lloyd, and, supremely, Charlie Chaplin, moved on to greener pastures and more freedom as soon as was practicable. Mabel Normand left, came back, left again, then came back again, but her semienduring professional relationship with Sennett was mostly the result of their tempestuous private relationship. Sennett did attempt to modify his style when he signed up Harry Langdon in the mid-1920s, making a notable effort to slow the films down to accommodate Langdon's snail-like thought processes. But by then, while Sennett and his films were still making money, audiences were increasingly turning to the character-oriented comedies coming from the Hal Roach studios, with stars like Laurel and Hardy and Charlie Chase.

Sennett went into bankruptcy in 1935. In Walter Kerr's felicitous phrase, the King of Comedy was more the "Carpenter of Comedy. He built the house. It is hard now to believe that he ever entertained friends in it." But by 1920, Sennett, as well as Griffith and Ince, had done their best work. It was time for their insights and innovations to be adopted and utilized by others. The torch was about to be passed.

FURTHER READING

BALSHOFTER, FRED, and ARTHUR MILLER. *One Reel a Week.* Berkeley and Los Angeles: University of California Press, 1967. An evocative if not always completely reliable account of the patent wars and early filmmaking days in New York, New Jersey, and Hollywood by two men who were there.

BROWN, KARL. *Adventures with D. W. Griffith.* New York: Farrar, Straus and Giroux, 1973. Perhaps the single most valuable first-person account ever written about Griffith, by his assistant cameraman. A wise, witty, informative book.

GEDULD, HARRY, ed. *Focus on D. W. Griffith.* Englewood Cliffs, N.J.: Prentice-Hall, 1971. A useful collection of both period and modern articles and documents.

HANSEN, MIRIAM. *Babel and Babylon: Spectatorship in American Silent Film.* Cambridge: Harvard University Press, 1991.

KOSZARSKI, RICHARD, ed. *The Rivals of D. W. Griffith.* Minneapolis, Minn.: Walker Art Center, 1976. A good introduction and series of essays on Griffith and his contemporaries that puts the achievements of "The Master" in a broader context.

O'DELL, PAUL. *Griffith and the Rise of Hollywood.* South Brunswick, N.J.: A. S. Barnes, 1970. A sharp, critically valuable analysis of pre-1920 Griffith.

RAMSAYE, TERRY. *A Million and One Nights.* New York: Simon & Schuster, 1964. (Originally published in 1926.) The definitive, exhaustively detailed history of the first thirty years of film, told mostly from an industrial and business viewpoint.

SCHICKEL, RICHARD. *D. W. Griffith: An American Life.* New York: Simon & Schuster, 1984. The best single-volume biography.

SLIDE, ANTHONY. *Early American Cinema.* South Brunswick, N.J.: A. S. Barnes, 1970. A worthy companion piece to the O'Dell book, by a noted film scholar.

WAGENKNECHT, EDWARD, and ANTHONY SLIDE. *The Films of D. W. Griffith.* New York: Crown Publishers, 1975. A difficult, sprawling job well done, although lacking sufficient detail on the Biograph years.

3

American Cinema in the 1920s

Silent films got a lot more things right than talkies.
—STANLEY KUBRICK

Timeline: 1920–1929

1920

U.S. population: approximately 107 million

1921

Warren G. Harding (Republican) U.S. President (1921–1923); beginning of boom years on Wall Street
Violent Ku Klux Klan activities throughout South

1922

Eugene O'Neill wins Pulitzer Prize for drama

1923–1929

Calvin Coolidge (Republican) U.S. President

1925

F. Scott Fitzgerald's novel *The Great Gatsby* defines the Jazz Age—an era of glamour, creativity, and excess
Scopes Trial—biology teacher convicted of violating Tennessee's law forbidding the teaching of evolution
Charleston craze sweeps the United States; revolution in female fashions: lean bodies, short skirts, cropped hair, and lots of attitude

1926

First jazz recordings of Duke Ellington and Jelly Roll Morton; African-American culture at its zenith with the famous Harlem Renaissance
The Black Pirate is the first major studio production in Technicolor

1927

Lindbergh's rickety monoplane, "The Spirit of St. Louis," crosses Atlantic: New York to Paris nonstop in 33½ hours

1929

Herbert Hoover (Republican) U.S. President (1929–1933)
William Faulkner's landmark novel *The Sound and the Fury* published
Opening of the Museum of Modern Art, New York City
Wall Street crashes, ushering in the Great Depression, which soon spreads worldwide

Hollywood, the place. The great clowns: Chaplin, Keaton, Lloyd, Langdon, Laurel and Hardy. The Chaplin craze. Charlie the tramp. The frozen beauty of Buster Keaton. Harold Lloyd and the era of the "go-getter." The star craze. The royal couple of Hollywood: Mary Pickford and Douglas Fairbanks. Erich von Stroheim and the lure of Europe. The sophisticated "Continental" comedies of Ernst Lubitsch. More European emigrés: Mauritz Stiller, Emil Jannings, Pola Negri, Greta Garbo, and F. W. Murnau. The exotica of Josef von Sternberg. The expressive art of King Vidor. The talkie revolution: Warner Brothers' *The Jazz Singer*. End of a Golden Age.

By 1920, AMERICAN FILM PRODUCTION was centered in and around Hollywood. While movies were still being made in New Jersey and Paramount would open a studio complex in the Long Island suburb of Astoria, the only filmmaker of importance to be headquartered in the East was D. W. Griffith, whose isolation at Mamaroneck would soon be reflected in a mostly lackluster series of films.

In Hollywood, the population had grown from 5,000 to 36,000 in ten years; by 1930, it would be 157,000. Twenty Hollywood studios were churning out features and shorts for a weekly audience of forty million people. The demand for movies was so incessant that most theaters which weren't downtown movie palaces changed their features at least two, sometimes three times a week.

The town from whence this ocean of celluloid flowed was very much betwixt and between, half booming company town, half sleepy rural hamlet, a place where actors making three thousand dollars a week could build sumptuous castles on hillsides that overlooked avocado and orange groves, not to mention a few oil wells.

For the people across America, where the population was much less centered in urban areas than it is now and where rural values still predominated, Hollywood and its films seemed impossibly glamorous and, perhaps, just a little dangerous and wicked; hence the widespread public revulsion over the rash of scandals that hit the movies in 1921–1922: the drug-related death of popular leading man Wallace Reid, the unsolved murder of director William Desmond Taylor, and the Roscoe Arbuckle rape/murder trial.

And yet, the writing of F. Scott Fitzgerald, Sinclair Lewis, and, later in the decade, Ernest Hemingway declared open war on the cozy morality and cloistered sensibilities still hanging on from the nineteenth century. Hollywood, no less than the rest of the country, was split down the middle, a division that would lessen as the decade wore on, as the influence of Griffith waned and the influence of the more culturally sophisticated European filmmakers like F. W. Murnau increased.

There was only one absolute: money, and large amounts of it. While costs increased throughout the decade, so did grosses. A hit film like Harold Lloyd's *Safety Last* (1923) cost $120,963 and grossed $1,588,545, with Lloyd receiving 80 percent of the profits. Fortunes were made, great companies like Metro-Goldwyn-Mayer and Warner Brothers were incorporated, and a profound allegiance between an audience and an industry was being formed. And, as art and commerce mingled, with less of an emphasis on the latter than would be the case in future years, great films were made. Fluid, astonishingly adept at telling a story in pictures, silent films were an art that, by the end of the 1920s, had perfected itself.

For modern audiences, silent dramas tend to require some conditioning. For one thing, more attention must be paid to a silent film than to a talkie. Plot points and details of characterization have to be closely observed or the film makes no sense. This added concentration takes its toll, and a double feature of silent films, even if properly scored, is a much more tiring experience than two back-to-back talkies.

But silent comedies require little more than an open mind and an attentive intelligence. The ruling triumvirate of Chaplin, Keaton, and Lloyd, along with aspirants like Raymond Griffith (whose character of a sly boulevardier owed much to Max Linder), Harry Langdon, Stan Laurel, and Oliver Hardy, combined to create a self-contained comic environment that was largely lost when talkies arrived.

The soil from which this fine, rare flower grew was vaudeville, or, as it was known in England, the music hall, a series of individual acts lasting fifteen to

3–1. *Angora Love* **(U.S.A., 1929),** *with Stan Laurel and Oliver Hardy, directed by Lewis R. Foster.*
The perfection of Laurel and Hardy, their uncanny symmetry, is reflected in their still photos as much as their intricate gag structures. Unlike most comedians, the effectiveness of whose gags is at least partly dependent on surprise, Laurel and Hardy made a virtue of repetition and obviousness. They showed you what was going to happen, introduced a moment of Ollie's vast self-confidence or Stan's equally vast dimness, then inflicted the gag on themselves. Their basic likability invited us, made accomplices of us; and by tipping us off, they didn't depress our interest but rather heightened our anticipation. Unlike the comedy teams that followed them, they were both superb comedians, not just a prosaic combination of a comic and a straight man. Moment for moment, scene for scene, in terms of pure laughter, Laurel and Hardy were probably the funniest men who ever made movies. *(Metro-Goldwyn-Mayer)*

twenty minutes apiece. Performers rarely interacted on stage but simply followed one another, with an emphasis on variety. Vaudeville featured jugglers and song-and-dance performers, but every bill had at least one comic, often two, working not so much in the arena of jokes as that of character. Acts were rarely written down but were developed by a process of accretion, performance by performance, audience by audience, five and six shows a day. Working this way, a performer developed an almost infallible sense of how to project a character, stage a gag, create a moment. By the time a performer graduated from this rigorous basic training, there was very little else he or she needed to learn about the art of making people laugh.

Major Filmmakers

It was while working in just such an environment that a young English comedian named CHARLES SPENCER CHAPLIN (1889–1977) was seen by Mack Sennett. Although only twenty-four at the time, Chaplin was a well-known performer, mostly because of his stage portrayal of a rude, obstreperous drunk. It was a convincing portrait because he'd drawn it from life. Chaplin's father, himself a music hall entertainer of some note, had drunk himself to death at the age of fifty-two. Even before that, Chaplin's mother had gone mad, exhausted by attempting to raise Charlie and his half-brother Sydney on hopelessly insufficient means. For a time, little Charlie lived on the streets of London. He and his brother were put in an orphanage, a common placement for indigent children at that time. Their mother recovered somewhat, although she was never even remotely a whole person again, and her children were released into her care. A sense of deprivation and the helplessness of poverty would last all of Chaplin's life.

It was Syd Chaplin who first entered show business and promoted his more talented younger brother, who by 1913 was a headliner. Sennett, always on the lookout for new talent, expressed his enthusiasm for the young comic and hired him for $150 weekly. Chaplin finished his tour with the vaudeville troupe in late November, arriving at the Keystone studio in the first week of December, 1913. He was a year and a half away from being the most famous man in the world.

Initially scared, then bewildered, then contentious, Chaplin was by temperament as well as training hopelessly opposed to the Keystone style of running around and falling down. Nevertheless, he tried to be a good soldier and in his first film, the not inaptly titled *Making a Living* (1914), costumed in an odd frock coat, top hat, and dangling villain's mustache, he ran around and fell down with the best of them. Even here, however, he added fizzy little bits of business that are pure Chaplin: A celluloid cuff loosens and begins to fall, but Charlie lifts his cane, causing the cuff to slide back into place. The moment takes longer to describe than it does to happen, but, along with Mabel Normand, Chaplin was the only Keystone performer capable of such detailed grace notes.

Chaplin assembled the tramp costume from odds and ends in the dressing room. It was all very improvisational, yet he responded to the costume's possibilities immediately, as did audiences. By the end of his year at Keystone, he had made thirty-five short comedies and Sennett's *Tillie's Punctured Romance,* a film whose main distinction is its status as the first feature comedy.

In 1915, Chaplin joined Broncho Billy Anderson's Essanay company for ten times his Keystone salary. He rattled off fifteen more films, then signed with Mutual for ten thousand dollars weekly. Business was good and so were the films. Chaplin seemed unstoppable, spraying his genius as if it were a geyser that had been bottled up for too long by poverty and insecurity. The comic invention was and is prodigious, not just in terms of quality but quantity. In these early films, Chaplin is doing something almost every second, yet he doesn't seem oppressively "busy." As an actor, he was compact, sly, never seemed to be pushily presenting a scene to the audience. Comedy was something you caught him at.

In *The Pawnshop,* one of the playful twelve films Chaplin made at Mutual in 1916–1917, regular foil Albert Austin brings in an alarm clock and asks handyman Charlie, filling in as a clerk, what he'll give him for it. Chaplin looks at the man doubtfully. He is shabby, as is Charlie, but he lacks jauntiness, which Charlie never does. Charlie turns his attention to the clock, tapping its back with two fingers as if he were a doctor investigating a nasty chest cough. He takes out a stethoscope, listens carefully, doesn't seem to like what he hears. Out comes the drill, then a can opener. A closer examination tells him that the situation is so dire that only emergency surgery can save the patient. He starts pulling out the works of the clock with a pair of pliers, then examines what's left with a jeweler's loupe. He dumps the works on the counter where, like worms, they begin wriggling around. A couple of squirts of oil calms the metal mass down. He sweeps the dead metal into the hollow clock shell, and with the professional grief of a doctor who was, alas, called into the case too late, he hands the hapless Austin back the fragments of his clock.

Chaplin has not merely transformed himself into several roles, he has transformed an inanimate object as well, delicately crossbreeding his own subtle play with a lusty variation on the basic comic principle of destruction. Such transpositions became a Chaplin staple, the most famous being the scene in *The Gold Rush* (1925), in which Charlie spears a couple of dinner rolls on forks. The camera is looking down at him slightly, and with the outline of his body blacked out by the careful lighting, Chaplin manipulates the rolls as if they were the feet supporting his comically oversized head, doing a little slip-and-slide soft shoe. As with practically every moment of Chaplin, it is a dance.

Comic devices and jokes as such were just means to an end for Chaplin, a way of holding the mirror up to life. No wonder he succeeded so gloriously so quickly. All about him, actors and comedians were performing in the manner of exuberant children, and here, finally, was a man psychologically incapable of being that frivolous. His childhood had given Chaplin the truth about much of life, and he was determined to filter that truth through his character. Reality became the center of Chaplin's art. In the midst of the chaotic flailing arms and cartoonish uproar that were endemic to the comedies of his time, Chaplin dared to walk in casually and whisper, to portray a recognizable human being that everyone could recognize as a kindred soul.

Worldwide success never isolated Chaplin from the emotional basis of his work. In all his features of the twenties—*The Kid* (1921), *The Gold Rush* **(3–2),** *The Circus* (1928), and *A Woman of Paris* (1923), a quietly brilliant psychological drama that he wrote and directed but did not star in—he delved ever more deeply into the pain attendant to being human, to love more than you are loved, to have those things you value most torn away, to be ignored when you deserve to be noticed, to be forever isolated in a world where everyone else seems to be happily making contact. And, recognizing all that, to never give in to despair or hopelessness, to always carry on.

Never shrinking from where his instincts led him, Chaplin reached his apotheosis with a silent film made several years after silents were dead. *City Lights* (1931) is his most methodical, rigorously perfect film and one of the most freezingly melancholy of all comedies.

In *City Lights* (1931), the tramp risks everything to help a blind girl who lives in poverty. He cleans the streets, he boxes and gets knocked out, and he endures the schizophrenic attentions of an alcoholic millionaire who adores the tramp and gives him money when he's drunk and completely ignores him when he's sober. Near the end of the film, the tramp is sent to jail after the (sober) millionaire mistakes him for a thief, but not before Charlie gives the blind girl enough money for an operation to restore her sight.

Released from jail six months later, an extremely bedraggled tramp walks down the street, pauses to pick up a flower lying in the gutter, and sees the girl he loved and sacrificed for through the window of her newly opened flower shop. He beams with pleasure, but she sees only a funny-looking tramp and laughs.

Feeling sorry for him, she walks out into the street to give him some money. It is only when she presses the money into his hand that she recognizes the feel of the man who had befriended her when no one else would.

Chaplin's camera exchanges emotionally intense closeups of the two. The girl is initially confused, then moved, the tramp hesitant but serenely pleased. Finally,

3–2. *The Gold Rush* (**U.S.A., 1925**), *with Charles Chaplin, directed by Chaplin.*

The Tramp has invited some girls that he hopes will become his friends to a New Year's party. He slaves for weeks to earn the money for favors and presents. But the girls never really intended to come to the party; Charlie is stood up, and as the celebrants of the ramshackle gold rush town greet the new year in the warmth and conviviality of the saloon, the Tramp stands alone in his little hut, sadly listening to the distant strains of "Auld Lang Syne." This is apparently impossible material for a comedy, but Chaplin was more than a comedian and *The Gold Rush* is more than a comedy. It deftly alternates sequences of comedy and drama, acceptance and rejection, cold and warmth, effectively simulating the ebb and flow, the pleasures and pains of life itself. Unlike Griffith or Ingram, whose thematic inspiration often came secondhand from literature or the theater, Chaplin aimed to synthesize experience itself, which accounts for the astonishing, timeless directness of his art. Chaplin made more perfect films than *The Gold Rush*, but he never made one that was more human or poignant. *(United Artists)*

we see the tramp's face frozen in a mixture of joy and fear. She can see him now, as he wished, but now that she can see him, how can she possibly love him? It is on this closeup that Chaplin's greatest achievement fades out. Although Chaplin owed much to many, to the music hall, to the ragged street buskers he observed as an impoverished child, to the casual elegance of Max Linder, to the shabby ragamuffin charm of Mabel Normand, the credit for the synthesis that resulted in his protean career must go to Chaplin himself, for it was he who forged the all-important link that reflected the mingled joy and absurdity of life itself.

In the eyes of posterity, Chaplin's only serious challenge has come from BUSTER KEATON (1895–1966), whose dry, sardonic, analytically abstract humor is much more in tune with modern sensibilities than Chaplin's open vulnerability. Keaton's clear-eyed objectivity was formulated early, as he traveled around America with the rough-and-tumble family vaudeville act headed by his father, Joe, a heavy drinker who occasionally became abusive. A child star, Keaton gained fame for his impassivity in the face of the spectacular falls he could take on stage.

By 1917, the stage was serving as a direct conduit to the screen, and Keaton was no exception, even taking a pay cut to work as a second banana to Roscoe Arbuckle, newly freed from Keystone. Arbuckle and Keaton became the best of friends and, surprisingly, even meshed together well on screen, the stoic Buster serving as a contemplative *yin* to Arbuckle's more expressive *yang*. Still, Keaton's essential stillness began to assert itself, and after World War I he got the opportunity to make his own two-reel comedies, taking over Arbuckle's unit after Arbuckle was promoted to features. From the beginning, Keaton was clearly a screen original. His character was earnest, hardworking, and resolutely unable to assimilate the reality around him, a perfect stranger in a strange land.

Unlike Chaplin, whose development was a methodical process of growth, Keaton seemed to grasp his own and the medium's possibilities immediately. He also had a way of devising perfect visual metaphors for his invariably besieged character. In *Seven Chances* (1925), Keaton's producer handed him a formula stage farce whose plot posited a single man needing to be married by a certain time in only a few days in order to inherit a million dollars. But Keaton managed to turn it into something completely, deliciously his.

Through the usual complications of farce, several hundred women show up at the church. Since Keaton can't marry them all, he doesn't marry anybody. Angered, they take off after the man who has so grievously misled them. Through the streets, intersections, and junkyards of the city, they chase him, several hundred women in bridal gowns, a mobile nightmare in white pursuing one lone, increasingly desperate figure.

The chase continues into the countryside, where Keaton, rushing down a mountainside, accidentally dislodges a few rocks, which dislodge some larger rocks, which bang into some boulders, which also start to rumble downhill.

Soon, virtually an entire mountain of rock is hurtling down on Buster, who makes a valiant stand and attempts to dodge them, getting flattened several times for his trouble. The sequence is pure Keaton in both imagery and point of view: Not only are livid hordes after him through no fault of his own, it seems that God himself wants to get in on the punishment.

In *The General* (1926), Keaton's most famous feature, a Union officer orders a locomotive across a bridge dangerously weakened by fire, asserting that the bridge is strong enough to hold. Halfway across in a spectacularly beautiful shot, the

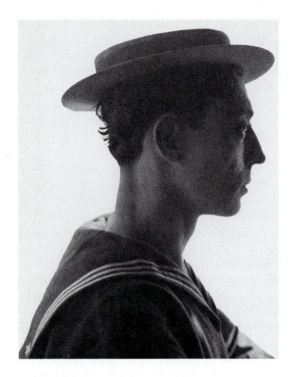

3–3. *The Navigator* **(U.S.A., 1924),** *with Buster Keaton, directed by Keaton and Donald Crisp.*
Keaton was the most unconsciously cerebral of the great comedians. His films are as gravely beautiful as he is, have the same planed, precise features. Most of his movies are so solidly structured that they could have been made as straight dramas, and Keaton could surely have directed them as such. His camera was always in the right place, his directorial style fluid yet unobtrusive, his films sometimes too brilliant and clever to be truly funny. His career was effectively ended by alcohol and studio regimentation by the time he was in his early thirties.   *(Metro Pictures)*

bridge gives way, and like a falling dinosaur, the train majestically collapses into the river below. Keaton holds on the spectacle for a moment—the shot was not faked, for the Keaton unit actually dumped an antique locomotive into Oregon's McKenzie River. Then he cuts to a **reaction shot** of the incomparably wrong officer—or, rather, a nonreaction shot, for the officer's face is almost as impassive as Keaton's would be, except for a slightly stunned look around the eyes. Somewhat weakly, he waves his troops forward with the air of a man who has just become aware that it's not going to be a good day.

As undemonstrative in life as he was in his work, Keaton was undone by his marginal position within the industry. He was never particularly commercial—certainly not when compared to the immediate competition of Chaplin and Lloyd. Even an effort as fine as *The General* lost money and garnered mediocre reviews. In 1928, Keaton's producer and brother-in-law, Joseph Schenck, sold Keaton's contract to MGM, where his morose character was smoothed out, the films glossed up, and the grosses quadrupled. A despondent Keaton went into a tailspin of drinking from which he didn't recover for nearly fifteen years. With the exception of *The Cameraman* (1928), his first film for MGM, Keaton's later movies are various shades of terrible, as are the cheap two-reelers with which he was forced to occupy himself until the 1950s, when a wonderful guest appearance in Chaplin's *Limelight* (1952) led to a gradual revival of interest, especially in Europe.

By the early 1960s, Buster Keaton had all the work he could handle. His films had been restored and were once more being shown, enjoyed, and, oddly (at least so far as their creator was concerned), analyzed. The quiet little man with the yearning eyes had finally won.

HAROLD LLOYD (1893–1971) always won, which is a partial explanation for his enormous popularity during the optimistic twenties and the steely condescension

3–4. *Never Weaken* **(U.S.A., 1921),** *with Harold Lloyd, directed by Fred Newmeyer.*
Although Lloyd, to quote the title of one biography, is usually thought of as "the man on the clock" teetering on tall buildings in mortal peril, he actually made only three such movies. But they were so successful and the appearance of danger so convincing that they entered popular mythology. Such scenes actually weren't very dangerous. The "buildings" Lloyd was trapped on were actually false fronts that were constructed on the roofs of authentic office buildings. Although Lloyd could not have fallen more than fifteen feet, with the proper camera angles the illusion was—and is—perfect, a fine example of the painstaking care and technical expertise of silent films. Talkies tended to slough off similar scenes via less authentic—and less expensive—rear projection. *(Pathé Films)*

of critics ever since. Reflexively, Lloyd is bracketed with Chaplin and Keaton, but without enthusiasm, let alone analysis. After Lloyd's death, his films were purchased for reissue, recut, horribly scored, and thoroughly devalued. Yet when seen in a complete print before a receptive audience, the basic sweetness of Lloyd's character, his gallant, dogged personality, unfailingly assert themselves and the films spring to life **(3–4).**

Alone among his contemporaries, Lloyd never really had much theater experience. He was a creature of the movies almost from the beginning and had to serve a long and painstaking apprenticeship in the art of making people laugh. His first starring films were in 1915, cheap, low-comedy one-reelers in which Lloyd did what amounted to a mediocre Chaplin imitation. Lloyd's character, named Willie Work, evolved into another one called Lonesome Luke. Hyperactive, adept at his gags, totally without personality, Lloyd nonetheless achieved a modicum of success, even though he realized the essential worthlessness of what he was doing.

One day in 1917, Lloyd drifted into a Los Angeles theater and saw a film about a fighting parson who wore tortoise-shell glasses. Lloyd liked the passive image the glasses provided, and over the objections of Pathé, his distributor, who didn't want to interfere with a sure thing, Lloyd introduced what he always referred to as "The Boy" or "The Glasses Character." "The Boy" embodied much of Lloyd's own quiet decency. Audiences looked him over and decided they liked what they saw. Building his career and audience reel by reel, by 1922 Lloyd was America's favorite projection of itself, gracefully inhabiting what Walter Kerr has called "the myth of the Good American." He was the incarnation of the go-getter ideal of the 1920s.

Films like *Safety Last* (1923), *The Freshman* (1925), and *Girl Shy* (1924) are hymns to spunk, the middle-class values of home, hearth, and One True Love, and a basic philosophy of Never Say Die. Some critics have accused Lloyd of aesthetic shallowness, saying that he lacked Chaplin's poetry or Keaton's stark, surrealistic vision of life. But there are different kinds of poetry and many paths to paradise. One would be hard pressed to find a more poetic moment in silent movies than in

3–5. *Why Worry?* (U.S.A., 1923), *with Harold Lloyd and John Aasen, directed by Sam Taylor and Fred Newmeyer.*
Lloyd was similar to Douglas Fairbanks and Mary Pickford in that he, not the director or studio, was the controlling force behind his films. Spunky, vigorous, entirely American, particularly adept at acting scenes of embarrassment or humiliation, Lloyd tended to prefer his films to be realistically plotted, with the gags arising out of a sound story structure. *Why Worry?* is a delicious exception, as Lloyd plays an indolent playboy who stumbles into the middle of a South American revolution and makes a faithful, devoted retainer out of a crazed giant by the simple expedient of pulling the bad tooth that's put the giant in such a dreadful humor in the first place. *(Pathé Films)*

Lloyd's *The Kid Brother* (1927), one of his finest films. Harold—Lloyd was always named Harold in his films—has just met The Girl for the first time. She bids him farewell and disappears over a hill. Suddenly panicked, realizing he doesn't even know her name, Harold climbs a tree, the camera rising with him until his higher **angle** once more brings her into view. He calls out to her; she gives him the desired information and once more disappears. Harold is struck by another thought and begins climbing again, the camera **craning** up ever higher. This time he finds out where she lives. She walks over the next rise and one more time he climbs, the camera going up to what seems a precipitous height. What does he so desperately need to say to her? "Goodbye," the title tells us. Aside from the narrative cleverness and intrinsic charm and beauty of the scene, the ascending camera is a perfect equivalent of Lloyd's rapture at the girl's beauty. Movement and meaning are united by an expressive camera.

Talkies did Harold Lloyd no favors. His go-getter impulses seemed anachronistic and even vaguely insulting when contrasted with the social disintegration that was everywhere during the Depression. Unlike Chaplin, Lloyd seemed oblivious to social undercurrents; unhappy endings made him nervous. His irrepressible cheerfulness and optimism made him seem out of touch. He attempted to salvage his career with the same resourcefulness he showed on the screen, trying the new genres of political comedy à la Frank Capra with *The Cat's Paw* (1934) and screwball comedy with *The Milky Way* (1936), but it was too late in the day. Lloyd entered a forced retirement in 1938.

The case of the Vanishing Career also struck HARRY LANGDON (1884–1944), except where Lloyd's career lasted well over ten years, with a five-year addendum at the end for the gradual loss of his audience, Langdon's starring career encompassed all of four years. Beginning with Mack Sennett in 1924, Langdon achieved fame in two years, left Sennett to make features at First National in 1926, and made two critical and commercial successes in one year. But by late 1928, First National had canceled his contract to no public protest whatever.

For those two years, Langdon could do no wrong. *Tramp, Tramp, Tramp* (1926), *The Strong Man* (1927), and *Long Pants* (1927) were smash hits **(3–6).** Sennett declared Langdon and his **persona** of an overgrown baby to be a more fascinating comic talent than Chaplin, to whom the New York critics regularly compared him. A great deal of speculation has centered on Langdon's precipitous fall, much of it customarily attributed to his disastrous decision to fire directors Frank Capra and Harry Edwards and take control of his own films. Referring to the three commercial disasters that followed, Harold Lloyd said, "Langdon couldn't do his own work."

But the fact remains that two of the three films that Langdon directed himself—*Three's a Crowd* (1927), *The Chaser* (1928), and the lost *Heart Trouble* (1928)—while unquestionably odd and sometimes downright bizarre, are not all that inferior to the films that preceded them. It is more likely that the public simply grew tired of Langdon's one-note winsomeness.

Langdon's character was unusual enough, but that's as far as it went. The world around him was the usual silent comedy world of glowering heavies, lid-fluttering leading ladies, and sultry vamps. Once the initial curiosity value of Langdon's character wore off, there wasn't much left to look at. The four-year rise and fall of the little man from Council Bluffs, Iowa, bore all the hallmarks of nothing more than a fad, quick to bloom, quick to die. Langdon spent the rest of his life

3–6. *The Strong Man* **(U.S.A., 1927),** *with Harry Langdon, directed by Frank Capra.*
For one brief, shining hour, Langdon threatened the heretofore uncontested throne of Chaplin himself, at least among critics. His character was essentially that of a presexual adult baby and his reaction to absolutely anything could be described by the adjective "tentative." Soon after *The Strong Man*, Langdon fired the young Frank Capra and began to direct himself, meeting with critical and commercial disaster. Not that the results completely deserved it. A film like *Three's a Crowd* (1927) is not without interest. As James Agee wrote, "Langdon had one queerly toned, unique little reed. But out of it he could get incredible melodies." *(First National Pictures)*

appearing in cheap two-reelers interspersed with writing assignments for Laurel and Hardy. He never knew what hit him.

But of all the silent movie stars it was Douglas Fairbanks and Mary Pickford who best personified their era, its ascent from primitivism into aesthetic accomplishment, from a disreputable peep show to a multimillion-dollar industry. DOUGLAS FAIRBANKS (1883–1939) was a Broadway juvenile of some success and no particular acting distinction who came to films in 1915. He became a star in a series of light situation comedies that were equal parts satire of current fads and events, frequently laborious; and acrobatic flights of fancy from the star, usually delightful. Where the stage had weighed him down with mundane requirements like plot, films distilled the essence of Fairbanks, a rambunctious ten-year-old boy who had unaccountably been placed in the body of a mature athlete and gymnast.

In 1920, already his own producer, Fairbanks decided to pursue a personal fantasy and make a swashbuckling adventure film, long before such a thing existed as an entertainment staple. The result was *The Mark of Zorro* (1920), whose considerable success proved that Fairbanks's fantasies were the audience's as well. He spent the rest of the decade turning out a film a year, many partially authored by

3–7. *The Thief of Bagdad* **(U.S.A., 1924),** *with Douglas Fairbanks, directed by Raoul Walsh.*
Lithe, superbly conditioned, exuberantly athletic, eternally optimistic, Fairbanks in the 1920s created the genre of costume adventure and featured trajectories of movement that, as this photo suggests, are close to ballet. After 1919, he was his own producer and maintained the highest standards of quality and craftsmanship. Until age, something of a midlife crisis, and changing audience tastes of the 1930s conspired against him, Fairbanks was the ideal actor-producer. *(United Artists)*

himself, each one painstakingly hand-crafted but still luxuriant with exuberance and good humor (**3–7**). As with his close friend and partner in United Artists, Charlie Chaplin, Fairbanks was the sole authority on his pictures, even though he took official directorial credit only once in his career.

MARY PICKFORD (1893–1979), Fairbanks's wife from 1920 to 1935, began her career as a child actress and soon developed her basic character, a girl combining the resilience of a tomboy with a genuine feminine winsomeness. At her best, working for Marshall Neilan or Maurice Tourneur in films like *Stella Maris* (1918), Pickford was a remarkable dramatic actress with an unerring sense of *line,* of how to create a character with a minimum of apparent effort. As it happened, both she and her audience seemed more comfortable with her somewhat coy, overemphatic comedies.

More than any other star, the flow of Pickford's career paralleled the evolution of the movies themselves. In 1909, a plump teenager, she had gone to work at Biograph for five dollars a day. Ten years later, she owned her own studio, earned around a half-million dollars a year, and had just helped form United Artists. Her marriage to Fairbanks carried the symmetry of a happy ending to a well-told story. Together they were as close to a royal couple as Americans would ever see, and Pickford played up to that image by concentrating on essentially stock parts left over from Victorian literature and stage conventions, films whose main distinction was the Madonna sweetness she brought to them (**3–8**).

3–8. *Sparrows* (U.S.A., 1926), *with Mary Pickford, directed by William Beaudine.*
Pickford was called America's Sweetheart, and it was not an empty publicity phrase. Audiences weren't just fascinated by celebrities of the 1920s, they genuinely loved them, and no one was loved more than Mary Pickford. Like some kinds of love, it must have been a trifle suffocating for her. Her audience didn't want to see her play grown women. She therefore tended to play about half her actual age.   *(United Artists)*

In their time, Pickford was considered the artist, Fairbanks the entertainer, but time, if not exactly reversing the judgment, has firmly relegated Pickford's work to the status of period pieces that need some degree of social context. Fairbanks's best films, however—*The Mark of Zorro, The Thief of Bagdad* (1924), *Don Q, Son of Zorro* (1925), and *The Iron Mask* (1929)—can be viewed with as much pure innocent pleasure today as they were sixty years ago. Even when he was making million-dollar productions, with sets, costumes, and pageantry that threatened to become oppressive, Fairbanks could make a scene effervesce just by entering it **(3–9).**

Pickford and Fairbanks made only one film together, an enjoyable talkie version of *The Taming of the Shrew* (1929), memorable for Fairbanks's randy, charming Petruchio. Even then, however, age was conspiring against both of them. Most of Fairbanks's talkies are the obvious products of a man who has lost interest, although *The Private Life of Don Juan* (1934), his last film, does resonate with intimations of an aging man's sense of regret. Pickford won an Academy Award for *Coquette* (1929) but gave up her career just four years later after making one of her best films, *Secrets* (1933), the financial failure of which impelled this always discerning businesswoman into an unfortunately premature retirement.

The 1920s were the last years when movies, generally speaking, could be considered a director's medium. Star directors like Rex Ingram maintained absolute

3–9. *The Gaucho* (**U.S.A., 1927**), *with Douglas Fairbanks, directed by F. Richard Jones.*
Art direction as psychology. Fairbanks was a small man (five feet eight inches), and in this scene of imprisonment the set makes him look even smaller, less significant—note the oversized bed. Fairbanks's reaction is one of cavalier unconcern, and he escapes with hardly an effort. The set's purpose is thus to condition the audience, not the character. Clearly, anybody who can escape from such intimidating surroundings must be a very remarkable fellow. *(United Artists)*

control over their work, just like the Spielbergs and Scorseses of today. But even second-string talents like James Cruze, Henry King, Herbert Brenon, or George Fitzmaurice accrued prestige and something close to *carte blanche* so long as budgets were observed.

Ironically, it was ERICH VON STROHEIM (1885–1957), a director who greatly increased the latitude for serious filmmakers, who was also responsible for shifting the balance of power from the creative to the business end, precisely because of his cavalier disregard for budgets. A Viennese emigré and a former assistant director to D. W. Griffith, von Stroheim specialized in elaborate portrayals of a Europe in the last stages of decay. At heart, his films were mordant melodramas, but with such flashes of wit, atmosphere, audacious sexuality, and starkly observed realism that the often silly stories were transcended and transformed. Two of von Stroheim's best films, *Foolish Wives* (1921) and *The Wedding March* (1928), bookended the decade, the first diabolically sardonic, brilliantly observed and photographed, the second romantic and full of a longing for love so far lost that it can never be regained.

Even people who loathed von Stroheim's films acknowledged his genius—Louis B. Mayer was one—but von Stroheim's fabulous re-creations of a nineteenth-century world he, a poor tailor's son, could only have known from very far outside entailed a near psychotic disregard of time and money. *Foolish Wives* was in production for a full eleven months and cost either $735,000 (von Stroheim's figure) or $1,103,736 (Universal's figure). Either way, it was an outrageous sum of money for the time, and the outrage didn't stop there. Von Stroheim's **final cut** of the film

59

3–10. *The Four Horsemen of the Apocalypse* (**U.S.A., 1921**), *with Rudolph Valentino, directed by Rex Ingram.*

The scene is a low-life dive in Argentina, and Valentino, up to that point in his career a bit-part player specializing in gigolos, dances a tango. It was at that moment that he became a star and the picture became the smash hit of its year, catapulting its director into the front rank of Hollywood talent. Such was Ingram's prestige that Metro financed him in building his own studio at Nice, in the south of France, where, when not writing, sculpting, or drawing, he would make movies of increasing exoticism and visual beauty. They were also oddly static and remote, possibly because of Ingram's tendency toward tableaux and a dislike of intense **closeups.** Still, Ingram was among the silent screen's finest pictorialists, as this photo shows. It would remain for Josef von Sternberg to make the nebulous connection between the splendor of a set as a corollary to his characters' souls.   *(Metro Pictures)*

ran eight hours. Not surprisingly, the studio cut it to three and a half. *The Wedding March* likewise cost a million dollars before production was halted approximately two thirds of the way through the script. Von Stroheim edited the material down to eleven hours and then decided to cut it into two films instead of one.

This refusal to abide by the financial and practical realities of a commercial art form doomed von Stroheim's career and hamstrung others as well (**3–11**). One of the seminal historical developments in Hollywood came in 1923, when von Stroheim, already overbudget after two months of shooting on a film called *Merry Go Round,* was fired by Universal's production chief Irving Thalberg, who replaced him with a contract nonentity. The decision was indefensible from a creative point of view, as Thalberg well knew, but it made fine financial sense indeed. Experimentation and art with a capital *A* had their modest place in the filmmaking enterprise, especially if done on a low budget. Thalberg was to prove he was not insensible to outright experimentation by his backing of such frankly uncommercial films as *The*

Crowd and *Freaks*. But when von Stroheim's costs made even a modest return on large investments impossible, he was banished. He had to move to Europe to find work, and even then only as an actor.

Von Stroheim's career, with its recurring obsessions with sex, sadism, the impossibility of lasting love, and the venality of humankind, would qualify him as the Marquis de Sade of cinema were it not for his humor and humanity. No matter how loathsome they might be in the light of conventional morality, von Stroheim's characters are fascinating and often likable because they have size and stature. Whatever their other failings, they are not hypocrites. As critic Jonathan Rosenbaum has noted, in their accumulation of behavioral detail and as overt analyses of social and psychological textures, von Stroheim's films come very close to the best nineteenth-century novels.

3–11. *Greed* **(U.S.A., 1924),** *with Zasu Pitts and Gibson Gowland, directed by Erich von Stroheim.*

When it suited his purposes, Stroheim was a realist in the tradition of Zola, painstakingly recording the quirks and foibles of his characters. *Greed*, his most generally admired work, was an extreme effort, as he attempted to film Frank Norris's novel *McTeague* paragraph by paragraph, detail by detail. This resulted in an art film that was, to say the least, overlong. Exhibit A in the case of materialistic Hollywood against the Artist of Integrity, or so von Stroheim's die-hard supporters would have it. Here, a wedding attended mainly by transplanted Germans provides the director with a chance to document the dubious table manners of the lower middle class at the turn of the century.   *(Metro Pictures)*

Hollywood had to supply a seemingly endless amount of product, and the studios were always looking for fresh talent for both behind and in front of the cameras. It was only natural that they began to go on periodic raiding parties. The first to arrive and probably the most successful of all the emigré directors were Germans. Mary Pickford brought Ernst Lubitsch over in 1923, but he and his putative sponsor only made one picture together, *Rosita*. They discovered that artistically they lived in two different worlds. Pickford was a classicist, a devout believer in story and performance. For Lubitsch, the best story was often the slightest, where a silken, sly double entendre with a closed door or an off-screen sound could get a bigger laugh than any actor.

A genius of innuendo, a crafty careerist, Lubitsch immediately assumed the role he instinctively felt Americans expected of a European, the naughty sophisticate. In a series of social comedies for Warner Brothers, most of which took their

3–12. *The Scarlet Letter* (**U.S.A., 1926**), *with Henry B. Walthall and Lillian Gish, directed by Victor Seastrom.*

By the time she made *The Scarlet Letter,* time and tide were both running against Lillian Gish, for it was the era of the flapper, of the carefree Clara Bow. At Gish's own studio, the exotic Greta Garbo was the new sensation. At the age of thirty-two, Lillian Gish was about to be fobbed off as a prissy antique, in spite of the fact that she was doing some of her finest work. Gish insisted on the Swedish emigré Seastrom as director because she believed his Scandinavian temperament was aptly suited to Hawthorne's powerful morality tale of Puritan repression. Gish proved to be as astute a production executive as she was an actress. *(Metro-Goldwyn-Mayer)*

blasé attitude from Chaplin's *A Woman of Paris*, Lubitsch satirized sex, fidelity, and bad faith in intimate relations. Mostly, Lubitsch appreciated elegant manners.

The Swedish cinema was very nearly decimated by the departure of art director Sven Gade, directors Victor Seastrom (1879–1960) and Mauritz Stiller (1883–1928), and leading man Lars Hanson (1887–1965). When Stiller set sail for America, he was accompanied by his protégée and leading lady, a tall, somewhat horsy young actress who photographed like a goddess from Olympus—Greta Garbo, née Gustafson. Stiller's protégée did better than he did. Driven, high-strung, he was fired by MGM after ten days' shooting on his first picture. He went over to Paramount and made the intense *Hotel Imperial* (1927) with Pola Negri. Stiller made one more film in the town that he felt had betrayed him. Then, a sick, defeated man, he went back to Sweden to die.

Of the Swedish enclave, it was Seastrom who seemed to acclimate himself most comfortably, successfully directing stars as varied as Lon Chaney, Garbo, and Lillian Gish. Seastrom's films were notable for their unrelenting psychological intensity and painstaking character development that never became mere clinical observation **(3–12)**. This avuncular, well-liked man appears to have been one of those lucky people who could achieve success at whatever they turned their hand to. Shortly before his death, Seastrom starred in *Wild Strawberries* (1957) for his friend and idolater Ingmar Bergman. The undemonstrative but palpable humanity that Seastrom achieved in his directing was revealed to be a function of his own personality, as he provided the vital spark for one of the normally dour Bergman's warmest works.

By the mid-1920s, studios like Universal and Fox, which frankly lacked the resources of MGM or Paramount, would hire "prestige" directors for the express purpose of pleasing the critics and thus justifying the wealth and influence that the standard Hollywood fodder brought them. William Fox, who subsisted largely on the hugely popular westerns of Tom Mix, went shopping and came back with the most influential and, with the exception of Lubitsch, the most talented of the foreign directors, F. W. Murnau (1888–1931).

Murnau was fresh from the worldwide success of *The Last Laugh* (1924). That film's mobile camera and stylized **mise en scène** helped wean the American film industry away from Griffith-inspired rural romances, with their vigorous style and empathetic star performances. The marriage between Fox and Murnau did not seem to be destined for permanence, and indeed it ended badly. For his first project, Fox offered Murnau *carte blanche* in addition to a four-year contract that started at $125,000 for the first year and went up to $200,000 for the last year—more than the entire cost of *The Last Laugh*. Murnau hastened to sign the contract, finished up his adaptation of *Faust* (1926), and set sail for America.

The first film he made for Fox was *Sunrise* (1927). Setting out to make nothing less than a work of art, Murnau succeeded completely, with the aid of two great American-trained cameramen, Charles Rosher and Karl Struss. Murnau used an anecdotal story of great simplicity—a man, embroiled in an illicit affair, determines to kill his wife, then relents. Murnau produced the film with some of the most complex technique of the period, never swamping the story or turning it into an empty exercise in style. All the sets, interior and exterior, had floors that sloped slightly upward as they receded. Interior ceilings had artificial perspectives; light bulbs in the foreground were physically bigger than the light bulbs in the background. Small figures in the background of the city sets were midgets. All this combined to produce visuals with an amazing sense of depth. But Murnau didn't stop there. He coaxed moving performances from his two stars, Janet Gaynor and George O'Brien, who were only pleasant actors for other directors.

Sunrise actually had no set budget, so it naturally cost too much for it to make a profit. But it brought William Fox the prestige he had sought. With *Sunrise,* Murnau seemed to have exhausted himself, for his succeeding films, *The Four Devils* (1928) and *Our Daily Bread* (1930), seemed to be excessively safe choices. Opinions have to be hedged, however, because *Four Devils* is a lost film, and there is some question of studio interference on the surviving version of *Our Daily Bread.*

Ironically, Murnau was already tiring of the lavish studio productions he had eagerly sought only a few years before. Finishing up his contract with Fox, he bought a yacht, formed a partnership with documentarist Robert Flaherty **(3–13),**

3–13. *Nanook of the North* (**U.S.A., 1921**), *directed by Robert Flaherty.*
For the sake of historical convenience, Flaherty has come to be known as the father of the documentary, a half-truth if ever there was one. Flaherty never simply reproduced an environment or its people on film for didactic or informational reasons. Rather, his method was to immerse himself in a culture, get to know the people and their ways, and only then to begin filming, adding incident and drama as if they were pearls on a string, ultimately improvising a sort of mythical essence of humans interacting with a specific natural order. The success of *Nanook* prompted offers from studios, the results of which tended to be a disappointment for both parties. A pantheistic poet, something of a dreamer, Flaherty preferred working methods that were frankly impossible for the studio system to countenance. In nearly thirty years of work, this one-of-a-kind genius completed only five feature-length films.   *(Pathé Pictures)*

3–14. *Sunrise* **(U.S.A., 1927),** *directed by F. W. Murnau.*
By the mid-1920s, Hollywood technicians were capable of creating whatever kind of world was called for, as in this authentic if stylized amalgam of American and European cities for Murnau's great film poem, a set that is at once artificial and realistic.   *(Fox Film Corporation)*

and set sail for the South Seas. Here they filmed *Tabu* (1931), a native idyll with a tragic ending that is a typical Murnau film in its celebration of love, but with oppressive Germanic overtones of a hostile fate more typical of Fritz Lang. *Tabu* is the most sensual of Murnau's films, more relaxed and less formal than *Sunrise* **(3–14),** which aside from its American stars might as well have been made in Germany. *Tabu's* greatness is attributable to Murnau, for he and Flaherty came to an amicable parting of the ways early on in the production. It is hard to imagine how Flaherty's humanistic optimism could ever have coexisted with Murnau's humanistic fatalism. Unfortunately, Murnau never lived to see *Tabu* receive the success it deserved. A week before its premiere, on March 11, 1931, he was killed in a car accident. Murnau was a visionary, a mystic, a theoretician who was also a profoundly gifted artist, a maker—in Fritz Lang's words—of "animated ballads." His early death was as grievous a loss as any in the history of film.

While there is almost universal critical agreement about Murnau, the work of Josef von Sternberg (1894–1969) still arouses controversy. He is thought by some to be an erotic fantasist of the highest order. Others consider him a flamboyantly phony purveyor of kitsch and point to his elaboration on the name he was born with in the Vienna ghetto—Jonas Sternberg—as a vain attempt to emulate the aristocratic pretensions of von Stroheim. At the very least, von Sternberg was an original. Even friendly biographers refer to his "bizarre personality," which can be distilled as a consistent, concerted effort to make himself as arrogant and indifferent to the emotional and practical needs of his actors and technicians as possible. The list of people who disliked him is lengthy. Actors like William Powell, having suffered under him once, made it a point to have clauses inserted in their contracts that under no circumstances would they work for him again.

Although he achieved his greatest fame during the 1930s with his discovery and protégée Marlene Dietrich, most of his best work was silent: *Underworld* (1927), *The Docks of New York* (1929), and, supremely, *The Last Command* (1928). Von Sternberg's films tended to center on women whose knowledge of themselves and their sexuality made them infinitely attractive and infinitely dangerous to the males of the species, who are more controlled by their ego and pride. For von Sternberg, love can either ennoble or destroy, often ennoble *then* destroy. It all depends on the luck of the draw.

Actually, von Sternberg probably should have been a painter, for, with the exception of *The Blue Angel* (Germany, 1929), he couldn't tell an effective story. A talkie like *The Scarlet Empress* (1934) carries more titles for purposes of exposition and story clarity than most silent films. But then von Sternberg was the first to admit that story as such meant nothing to him. If he was anything, this diminutive man was an explorer of the baroque in human behavior, an investigator of light and of the many ways men choose to destroy themselves.

He certainly was a kind of artist, struggling to find corollaries for his characters in the settings around them, trying to indicate their emotional state not by words (most of von Sternberg's characters hide their passions behind a blasé attitude, just as their creator did) but by the slash of shadow on a face or by the animation of what critic John Baxter calls "the dead space" that separated the camera from its subject and the subject from the background. Where most directors were content with leaving such space as clear as possible, von Sternberg, the cinema's most rarefied lapidary, interspersed nets, balloons, veils, grotesque statuary—anything and everything to intrigue the eye and create a specific spiritual atmosphere to make his images come alive. Emotionally, his films are repressed, suggesting much, saying little; visually, they are wildly ornate.

His career is the ultimate triumph of conspicuous style over sublimated substance. Even though he made sixteen talkies as opposed to only six released silents, his career made no concessions to sound. His sound pictures are essentially silent films overlaid with fragmentary, allusive dialogue. In some deep, instinctual way, von Sternberg must have sensed his own capacity for capricious self-destruction, for his films constitute a prophetic autobiography. After 1935 and his final collaboration with Dietrich, von Sternberg's career crumbled. By 1946, he was working as an uncredited assistant to King Vidor on *Duel in the Sun*, disenfranchised from his profession, only his pride intact—like one of his own ruined characters.

For KING VIDOR (1896–1983), von Sternberg's fall from grace and status must have constituted the sound of a faintly tolling bell. They were contemporaries, both coming to public attention in the mid-1920s, both achieving fame for their innovative ideas about film, both firmly installed as artistic house directors at their respective studios, von Sternberg at Paramount, Vidor at MGM. A Texan with an inquiring curiosity about art and religion, King Vidor gained notice with *The Jack Knife Man* (1921), a rural melodrama of the Griffith school. He began moving toward his own style with *Wild Oranges* (1924), a romance set in a moss-hung bayou illuminated by what would come to be recognized as Vidor's arrhythmic, propulsive energy.

Vidor came to fame, as well as a measure of fortune, with *The Big Parade* (1925), a triumph whose comparative **realism** proved to be somewhat misleading, for Vidor evolved into a director much given to stylization, not to mention bursts of outright **expressionism.** He was one of the most musical of all directors in the sense that the rhythm of his **editing** and the movement of his actors were analogous to the dramatic progression of musical notes.

Vidor's *The Crowd* **(3–15),** one of the finest of silent films, is unusual in that unlike other late silent masterpieces such as *Sunrise* or *The Last Command,* it is not a simple story elegantly told, but a complicated social fable with profound implications. *The Crowd* is one of the few films of the period to deal with something approaching real life, although a remarkable, practically forgotten MGM film of 1927, *Man, Women and Sin,* does predate it in its concerns with working-class pressures and a sensitive, well-meaning, but fatally passive man in over his head, buffeted by forces he can barely ascertain, let alone control.

3–15. *The Crowd* (U.S.A., 1928), *directed by King Vidor.*
Vidor's set is a perfectly geometrical realization of a man's isolation. That this movie is an enduring masterpiece is irrelevant; even mediocre silent films generally gave their audiences something good to look at. *(Metro-Goldwyn-Mayer)*

The Crowd is about the process of coming to terms with limitations both internal and external. When John Sims is born on July 4, 1900, his father is convinced of his future greatness, a conclusion shared by John when he arrives in New York to claim his birthright at the age of 21. He finds a job, a girl, dreams of an ideal home, a perfect life. Reality begins to intrude as he and his wife find themselves in a cramped tenement, John trapped in a stagnant job, his life gradually being eroded by regret and bitterness. Finally, devastated by the death of his daughter, he realizes how tenuous life's delicate balance really is and how hard it is to survive in a monolithic world, which is brilliantly characterized by vast, impersonal sets and a few key scenes of faceless, onrushing masses. At the end, Sims and his wife sit in a theater, laughing at an unfunny clown act, trying to convince themselves that with lessons learned and painful adjustments made they might still be able to have a life together. The camera, mounted on an overhead trolley, pulls away quickly, back, back, until Sims and his wife are just dots among other dots, lost forever in the crowd they cannot escape.

Vidor's later career was impressive, if sometimes spotty—the delirious sexuality of *Duel in the Sun* and *Ruby Gentry* (1952); the painstaking, coolly impassioned

3–16. Production photo of *Show People* (U.S.A., 1928), *with Marion Davies, directed by King Vidor.*
A witty satire on Hollywood pretensions and mores of the period, *Show People's* behind-the-scenes situations give it an added archaeological interest today. Note the adjacent sets, which allowed two or more pictures to be shot at the same time. At the far right is a portable organ for music, which helped the actors better communicate the mood of the scene.   *(Metro-Goldwyn-Mayer)*

The Citadel (1938); a fine *War and Peace* (1956), which was marred only by miscasting; and the florid, rather demented *The Fountainhead* (1949). Aside from the increasing emphasis on hothouse sex, all these movies offered variations on a theme Vidor would never state as cogently as in his great silent works—the restless search for a peaceful place to come to, within society, and within oneself.

Talkies

By 1927, the silent film was a mature art form, as such films as *Wings* (**3–17**), *The Last Command, The Crowd,* and *The Wedding March* conclusively proved. With its own style and storytelling conventions, its own sense of wonder, an art had been forged out of a parlor amusement. Even ordinary actors seemed more than that when effectively presented in a silent film because their own specific identity was somewhat nebulous. The audience, swayed by the continuum of the story, guided by the music of the orchestra underlining emotions, projected their own feelings onto the actors and thus participated in a communal dream state. In the words of critic Alexander Walker, "The silent stars were mythic figures, not quite human because they didn't speak yet, giving emotions a human shape." Silent films were actually a blending of several arts—photography, lighting, music, acting—molded together so as to arouse emotion. Though voiceless, the silent film was understood everywhere, was intelligible in all languages. It was a universal art.

3–17. *Wings* (U.S.A., 1927), *directed by William A. Wellman.*
Coming at the tail end of the cycle of films about World War I, and hampered only slightly by a predictable story, *Wings* transcended its genre and period because of the astonishing, epic sweep given it by its sadly underrated director, himself a veteran of the Lafayette Flying Corps in the war he so grandly re-created.   *(Paramount Pictures)*

Enter Jack, Harry, Albert, and Sam Warner, who had incorporated in 1923 as Warner Brothers and become a moderately successful company whose principal asset was Rin Tin Tin. Warner Brothers had produced *Don Juan,* a John Barrymore swashbuckler that premiered on August 6, 1926. A Fairbanksian delight, *Don Juan* came complete with a musical score that had been recorded on large wax discs and accompanied the feature in fair synchronization. The device was called Vitaphone and was a sensational success. *Don Juan,* along with a series of shorts with **synchronous sound** likewise recorded on discs, ran for nearly eight months at New York's Warner Theater.

Back in Hollywood, nobody thought too much about all this. Movies with sound had been around almost as long as movies had been. D. W. Griffith's *Dream Street* had talkie sequences included in it at the time of its New York premiere in 1921. But the public had always turned its back, partly because the various systems weren't really perfected, partly because people liked silent films the way they were. The audiences weren't the only ones. Before they had made *Don Juan,* the brothers Warner had been discussing the application of the new Vitaphone, mostly in terms of canned concerts or vaudeville for towns too small to have a legitimate theater.

"But don't forget," said Sam Warner, "you can have actors talk, too." "Who the hell wants to hear actors talk?" shot back Harry. But Harry Warner was over-looking that in the five years since *Dream Street,* an invention called radio had swept over America much as television would twenty-five years later. The public went mad for sound, music, voices. *Don Juan* forced Warners' stock upward, from fourteen

3–18. Publicity photo of Clara Bow (circa 1926).
Bow, a working-class girl from Brooklyn, achieved major stardom in films like *It* and *Wings* (both 1927). She was a distinct contrast to the demure tradition of silent film leading ladies. Bow's character liked men a lot, didn't even mind being kissed or thought loose—if it was for the good of the man she really loved. At heart, she was still the dutiful girl next door, but she represented a far less idealized view of femininity than did Pickford or Gish. Wild and reckless in real life, Bow, "The It Girl," was popularly regarded as the incarnation of the Jazz Age flapper. Like many high-livers of her generation, she crashed badly. Emotional difficulties, scandals, and a serious weight problem all put her out of the movies by 1934. Her career from start to finish barely encompassed ten years. *(Paramount Pictures)*

dollars a share before the premier to fifty-four dollars by the end of August. The second Vitaphone presentation didn't open until October: Syd Chaplin in *The Better 'Ole*. On the bill of talking shorts preceding the feature was America's leading musical comedy and recording star, Al Jolson. The program was another hit, and Jolson's three songs were bigger than that. Here was America's favorite popular singer, who made five thousand dollars a week, and the public could see him for the price of a movie, albeit a reserved-seat movie.

The wedge began to widen. Fox bought into a sound system wherein the sound was recorded on the film itself, which offered obvious advantages over the cumbersome, hard-to-synchronize disc system Warners was using. The Fox newsreel, rechristened Fox Movietone, featured Charles Lindbergh's takeoff from New York en route to Paris and world fame. The dim misty morning and the thin, ratchety buzz of Lindbergh's fragile single-engine plane thrilled audiences and made the muddy half-tone newspaper photographs of the day seem passé. Sound made things more immediate, made it seem as if it was happening *now*.

In Hollywood, Warner Brothers decided to drop the other shoe. They put into production *The Jazz Singer* (3–19), a story of the difficult ethnic assimilation of a Jewish cantor's son. The star was Al Jolson. Even then, the Warners were hedging their bets, for *The Jazz Singer* was designed and shot as a silent film with sound sequences, which were supposed to consist only of Jolson singing, nothing more. But the excitable, energetic Jolson wasn't satisfied with just singing. In the film's first musical interlude, after singing an unmemorable sob-song called "Dirty Hands, Dirty Feet," Jolson ad-libs, "Wait a minute, wait a minute. You ain't heard nothin' yet" and proceeds to prove it by launching into "Toot, Toot, Tootsie." There is only one other sequence in the film that features synchronized speech. In a scene between Jolson and his mother, he sings "Blue Skies," then, probably extemporizing, starts talking about how his success is going to affect her. "We're gonna move up in the Bronx. A lot of nice green grass up there. A whole lot of people you know. There's the Ginsbergs, the Guttenbergs, the Goldbergs. Oh, a lot of Bergs, I don't know them all." This loose babble goes on for another minute or so, while Eugenie Besserer, playing Jolson's mother, grows noticeably dazed, apparently having given up trying to figure out just where the scene is leading. The theme of Jewish assimilation presented by Jolson's hypnotically egocentric personality, and with sound yet, combined to make *The Jazz Singer* a spectacular success from its first performance in October of 1927. By January of 1928, as more theaters began wiring for sound at the not inconsiderable expense of twenty thousand dollars apiece, Warners was advertising that their "Supreme Triumph" was playing to a million paying customers a week.

From initial indifference, the competitors of Warners and Fox began to exhibit open alarm while at the same time stalling for time, convinced that sound was a temporary fad that wouldn't, couldn't render silent films obsolete. This was not a stance derived from aesthetic loyalty, but rather economic conservatism. Paramount owned five hundred theaters, MGM owned three hundred. To wire each of them for sound, in addition to outfitting the studios for recording, would entail a massive capital reinvestment.

But by midsummer of 1928, the handwriting was on the wall: Mediocre films with talking sequences were outgrossing the finest silent films. The studios moved and moved fast. They inspected their lists of contract directors and noticed that of the 157 directors working for the eight major studios, only 76 had had stage experience, which was thought to be an absolute necessity in the brave new world of

3–19. *The Jazz Singer* **(U.S.A., 1927),** *with Al Jolson, directed by Alan Crosland.*
It was for the clink of plates, the rattle of ice cubes, the sounds of a man singing, of two people talking, that silent films died. The audience had a choice and they freely chose talkies. For
75 percent of its running time, *The Jazz Singer* is a silent film, and a pretty good one, but Jolson's exuberance, fueled by one of the most all-encompassing egos in show business, transformed the occasional talkie sequences with an electrical charge that is still noticeable. *The
Jazz Singer* opened in October; by late summer of 1928 Hollywood was gearing up for the
mass production of talkies. The single most important transition in the still-young art form
had been effected with scarcely a whimper of protest from the public. For several years, until
talkies found their own rhythm, it seemed like a horrible mistake had been made.   *(Warner
Brothers)*

talkies. So, in addition to retooling the studios themselves, the majors plundered
New York for likely directorial, acting, and writing talent.

It seemed like a good idea, but it turned out to be an unfortunate return of
the Famous Players in Famous Plays delusion. Of the thirty-two actors Fox signed
for the talkies, the only ones to succeed were Paul Muni, Will Rogers, George Jessel
(a marginal success), and Louise Dresser; and both Rogers and Dresser already
had some success in silent movies. Loud camera noises forced the camera into a
soundproof booth, resulting in static shots and listless scenes. Suddenly, films
stopped dead while actors stiffly stood around a microphone hidden in a telephone, a plant, or a lamp and eee-nun-see-ate-ed oh so carefully. The movies had
stopped moving, partly out of laziness, partly because it was what the public
wanted, partly because the moviemakers didn't know any better. The novelty of dialogue—endless amounts of dialogue—began doing the job that expressive photography and pantomime had been doing.

But the public did want it. In 1929, the first year of talkie supremacy, Warners' profits were over seventeen million dollars, as opposed to just over two million
the year before. Paramount cleared fifteen million as opposed to eight, and Fox

3–20. Production photo from *Sparrows* (U.S.A., 1926), *with Mary Pickford, directed by William Beaudine.* Silent films were made in an atmosphere of sunshine and open air, a small group of people creating art unawares. Note the comparatively streamlined crew that could make a major production of a major star. To paraphrase ace camera-man John Seitz, sound changed films from an optical enterprise to an electrical one, and the innocent, *al fresco* atmosphere captured in this photo vanished like the cool dream of a hot summer night. *(United Artists)*

nine million as opposed to five. Leading silent directors like von Sternberg and Vidor bewailed the dying of silent films as an industry while they were still flourishing as an art. In a letter to a friend, F. W. Murnau managed to steer an intelligent middle course when he wrote, "The talking picture represents a great step forward in the cinema. Unfortunately it has come too soon: we had just begun to find our way with the silent film and were beginning to exploit all the possibilities of the camera. And now here are the talkies and the camera is forgotten while people rack their brains about how to use the microphone."

As salaried employees, even directors who were opposed to sound had little voice in the matter beyond struggling to make their talkies as much like silent films as possible. King Vidor's first talkie, *Hallelujah* (1929), was largely shot silent with the sound **dubbed** in later, which accounts for the picture's fluidity. Other directors adopted a more spiteful attitude. John Ford's early talkie, *Salute* (1929), is full of lackadaisical camerawork and inanely bad acting, flaws that are rare in the earlier or later films of that great director. Ford's contemptuous disdain for the new medium could hardly be more evident.

While the legend is that the shores of the Pacific were littered with the bodies of silent stars who couldn't make the transition, the truth is considerably less morbid. Major stars like Swanson, Garbo, Ronald Colman, Joan Crawford, Lon Chaney, and Richard Barthelmess, to name just a few, survived intact. True, foreign stars like Emil Jannings and Pola Negri did have to go back to Europe and their native languages, which was a loss. But supposed casualties like Fairbanks and Pickford were the victims of the calendar.

The fabled case of John Gilbert is attributable to the increased naturalism of talkies more than any vocal inadequacy. Gilbert, along with Valentino *the* romantic leading man of his era, has for years been labeled as having a ludicrously high-pitched tenor that set audiences pitching into the aisles with glee the first time they heard it. It's a funny story, invaluable for establishing silent films as some sort of prehistoric absurdity unworthy of serious consideration. It's also insupportable if Gilbert's talkies are experienced first-hand. Gilbert's voice was adequate, if somewhat actorish and breathy. What destroyed his career was nothing more than ignorance, his own, MGM's, and that of the entire industry. Quite simply, nobody realized that the game had changed in an essential way.

Talkies were less romantic than silents, more real; less utopian, more democratic; less behavioral, more psychological. Poor Gilbert, unthinking, unknowing, sailed into sound as if he were making a silent film—flaring his nostrils, ardently declaiming his lines. (When not controlled by a King Vidor or other first-rate directors, Gilbert tended to overact.) The headlong romantic ardor he projected as a matter of course was suddenly embarrassing to audiences who for so long had *felt* the emotion, not heard it boldly stated in a ludicrous series of "I love you's."

Gilbert tried to recoup in later films, modulating his style, but it was too late. When a star the stature of Gilbert fell, it was like the fall of an angel, awful and irrevocable. His confidence shattered, he drank himself to death by the age of forty-one. Gilbert's failure served final notice that talkies had not evolved out of silents but had sprung up alongside them, an initially half-witted hybrid that thrived in spite of itself, expanding voraciously and choking off the purer, more fragile strain of silent pictures, leaving no room in the garden for anything else.

Harry Warner had been very wrong. A lot of people wanted to hear actors talk.

FURTHER READING

AGEE, JAMES. "Comedy's Greatest Era," in *Agee on Film*. New York: Grosset and Dunlap, 1958. An essay tinged with literary genius by one of America's finest film critics.

BAXTER, JOHN. *The Hollywood Exiles*. New York: Taplinger, 1976. Readable, gossipy, informed survey of all the talented and not-so-talented emigrés who came to Hollywood to make films.

BROWNLOW, KEVIN. *The Parade's Gone By . . .* New York: Alfred A. Knopf, 1968. An indispensable tapestry of criticism, first-person reminiscence, and superb illustrations by the editor, director, and archivist largely responsible for the recent increased appreciation of silent films.

———. *Hollywood: The Pioneers*. New York: Alfred A. Knopf, 1979. An abridgment of the material included in Brownlow's excellent thirteen-part television series, this brief study provides a good overview, sharply reasoned and informed.

EYMAN, SCOTT. *Mary Pickford: America's Sweetheart*. New York: Donald I. Fine, Inc., 1990. A biography of the most powerful woman of the American silent era.

KERR, WALTER. *The Silent Clowns*. New York: Alfred A. Knopf, 1975. An analytical volume of superb illustrations with elegantly stated, though not always original, critical opinions.

PRATT, GEORGE C. *Spellbound in Darkness*. Greenwich, Conn.: New York Graphic Society, 1973. A valuable source book of contemporary reviews, feature articles, scripts, and other previously lost ephemera of the silent era.

TORRENCE, BRUCE T. *Hollywood, The First Hundred Years.* New York: New York Zoetrope, 1982. A mostly pictorial history of the changes and permutations in Hollywood as a geographic location.

WAGENKNECHT, EDWARD. *The Movies in the Age of Innocence.* Norman: University of Oklahoma Press, 1962. An affectionate reminiscence about silent films by a scholar who grew up with them.

WALKER, ALEXANDER. *The Shattered Silents.* New York: Morrow, 1979. Useful, savvy examination of the coming of sound by a solid critic and historian.

4

European Cinema in the 1920s

Without enthusiasm, there is no cinema, there are no films, there is nothing. There must be enthusiasm and it must be communicated like a flame—the cinema is a flame in the shadows. If one does not feel it, one cannot transmit it.

—ABEL GANCE

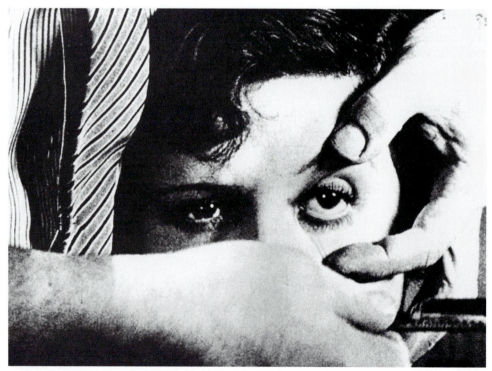

Raymond Rohauer

Timeline: 1920–1929

1920

Height of influence of German Expressionism in the arts

Gandhi emerges as India's leader for national liberation

1921

U.S.S.R. is the first country to legalize abortion

1922

Mussolini's Fascist troops march into Rome and form a new Italian government

Publication of T. S. Eliot's *The Waste Land,* the most influential poem of the Modernist movement

Publication of James Joyce's radically experimental novel *Ulysses,* Paris

1923

German crisis: rampaging inflation, widespread unemployment, and a paradoxical boom in the arts

1924

After years of experimentation in abstraction and formal expressiveness, Pablo Picasso is widely regarded as the towering genius of the modern art movement

Death of Lenin, leader of the Soviet revolution—he is eventually succeeded by the murderous Josef Stalin

1925

The Jazz craze sweeps Europe, especially Paris and Berlin

Paris exhibition ushers in the Art Deco era, which evolves into the sleek, streamlined style known as "Moderne"

1927

Burdened with crippling war reparations debt, Germany's economy collapses—strikes and riots ensue

1928

The landmark *Threepenny Opera* (text by Bertolt Brecht, music by Kurt Weill) creates a sensation in Berlin

1929

Widespread famine and disease in the U.S.S.R. as a result of Stalin's first Five-Year Plan

Nazi party gaining wider popularity in Germany

A world of ashes and diamonds: post–World War I Europe. The Soviet Revolution: a new art for a New Society. Pudovkin and Eisenstein: radical explorations in the art of editing and the craft of propaganda. Peasant poetry: Dovzhenko. Germany's golden age: expressionism and its discontents. Ernst Lubitsch, "The Griffith of Europe." Fritz Lang: nationalistic sagas and paranoid fables. The poetic studio world of F. W. Murnau. G. W. Pabst: a view from the Left. French cinema of rebellion: Dada and Surrealism. Jean Vigo and René Clair. The enthusiasm of Abel Gance. Gance's *Napoleon*. The subversive cinema of Luis Buñuel. Dark clouds gathering.

WHEN THE SMELL OF GUNPOWDER finally wafted away from Verdun and the rest of the European battlefields, all that was left was devastation, a society reeling from nearly ten million people killed. The United States had been comparatively untouched, losing only fifty-three thousand in casualties. For the American film industry, the war had been a temporary inconvenience, but in Europe the Indian summer of the Belle Epoque was irrevocably shattered. No more would ladies dangle their parasols by fragrantly sunny river banks while gentle impressionist artists like Renoir and Seurat created shimmering images of grace and beauty.

France and Germany were equally traumatized. The artists and filmmakers of each country set about dealing with a new world that had brutally revealed itself to them in ways that would have been unthinkable only a decade earlier. It seemed that all of Sigmund Freud's inferences about the dark side of the psyche were coming true: Artistic movements like **surrealism,** which had sprung from his theories, became the rage, especially in France. To the surrealists, the unfettered expression of the imagination had nothing to do with reason—it was nationalistic reason that had killed millions of people. German directors like Fritz Lang and F. W. Murnau, English artists like Alfred Hitchcock **(4–1),** and Soviet filmmakers like Eisenstein and Dovzhenko strove to express the workings of the subconscious, even during waking hours. Above everything else, they developed new ways of seeing.

Soviet Union

No country seemed less likely to make a strong recovery and develop a national cinema than the U.S.S.R., newly freed from the fumbling rule of the Romanovs, the last of whom, the remarkably dim Nicholas II, took a condescending interest in movies. Before the Revolution of 1917, spearheaded by a theoretician using the pen name Lenin (a far more discerning fan of film than the man he replaced), Soviet cinema was similar to American films of ten years before—one- and two-reel adaptations of classic native literature. Nevertheless, Russians loved movies, and in the years before the Revolution both the middle and upper classes patronized lavishly appointed theaters in Moscow and St. Petersburg. At that time, American films were largely unknown except for the popular **serials** of Pearl White.

4–1. *The Lodger* **(Great Britain, 1927),** *with Ivor Novello, directed by Alfred Hitchcock.*
Hitchcock is usually associated with an American style of filmmaking, but his earliest movies
look more German than anything. In place of the contemplative, methodical styles of German
directors, however, Hitchcock devised an allusive, suggestive camera shorthand that became
the *raison d'être* of every Hitchcock movie, beyond considerations of plot, character, or art direction. *(Gainsborough)*

4–2. *The Saga of Gösta Berling* **(Sweden, 1924),** *with Greta
Garbo, directed by Mauritz Stiller.*
Stiller (1883–1928) and Victor Sjöström, (1879–1960) were the
leading Swedish filmmakers in the early 1920s. Both emigrated to
Hollywood, where Sjöström, under the name of Victor Seastrom,
prospered (see **3–12**). Stiller was not so lucky, though his protégée
Garbo became one of the legendary stars of the American cinema.
He began his career adapting literary national epics like *The Saga of
Gösta Berling*. His earliest movies were noted for their full use of
landscape and psychologically based characters, but Stiller was most
comfortable working on a small scale. Over and above their nationalistic source materials, Sjöström and Stiller set the pattern for the future of Scandinavian cinema—the painstaking exploration of
rampant suffering brought on by the conflict between a severe
Protestantism and its constricting effect on the human instinct for
pleasure. *(Museum of Modern Art)*

With the Czar deposed, Lenin embarked on a program that would deemphasize Russia's feudal past and emphasize its present and future by explaining the theories of Marx and the strength of collective action. By November, 1918, Lenin had sent out the "Red Train," which traveled station to station along the Soviet Union's western front showing a film entitled *The October*, which had been put together by a theorist and filmmaker who called himself Dziga Vertov (1896–1954).

Concurrent with Vertov's work was that of Lev Kuleshov (1899–1970), who believed that the essence of cinema was **editing**—not the writing of a script or the photographing of actors, but the joining together of little pieces of film in combinations that the director had visualized in his mind. Kuleshov demonstrated: He took **shots** of Red Square and the American White House, individual **closeups** of two men, and a closeup of two hands shaking and cut them all together creating a continuous effect, an *impression* that all the action takes place at the same time, in the same place.

But it was Kuleshov's most famous experiment that revealed the all-important value of editing, not to mention subjectivity. He intercut a perfectly neutral closeup of an actor with a shot of a plate of soup; then the same closeup with a dead woman in a coffin; then with a little girl playing with a doll. Audiences raved about the actor's sensitive projection of hunger, grief, and paternal joy, his subtle shifts of emotion depending on what he was looking at. Kuleshov proved that the order of shots in a sequence influenced the perception and meaning of any given action.

The Soviets began to view film as something completely malleable—the favored term was "plastic." Their perceptions were further sharpened by the editing of Griffith's *Intolerance* (1916), which arrived in the U.S.S.R. after the war. They were especially attracted to the theme of the modern story, which deals with working-class life in peril from a hostile capitalist society. In many ways, the next ten years of Soviet filmmaking and writing were an attempt to objectify and intellectualize what Griffith had already accomplished on a purely instinctual basis.

The operative theory of Russian filmmaking was contained in a statement of Vsevelod Pudovkin (1893–1953): "The foundation of film art is *editing*." Not story, actors, human emotion, but editing. The Soviet theories were most instructive to filmmakers like Alfred Hitchcock, who adopted similar methods of manipulative cutting when it suited his purposes. The shower murder in *Psycho* (1960) is a sequence that Pudovkin and his colleagues would have applauded for its technical brilliance.

Although Pudovkin had been trained as a scientist, he was far from a clinical technician. His movies *Mother* **(4–3),** *The End of St Petersburg* (1927), and *Storm Over Asia* (1928) deal less with revolutionary abstractions than with eternal fables. His talent was essentially novelistic, for he concentrated on creating believable characters and telling stories with them. He eschewed the habit of other Soviet filmmakers, who chose nonprofessional actors, strong-featured "types" whose import and meaning could be captured in a single dramatic **closeup.** Rather, Pudovkin used less stereotypical faces and let the audience discover their common humanity during the course of the film.

SERGEI EISENSTEIN (1898–1948) was the logical culmination of a revolution stoked by intellectuals. He had been a stage director dabbling in revolutionary theater after an abortive stab as an engineer. From a comfortable, middle-class Jewish family, Eisenstein was bright, friendly, and ingenuous, a brilliant caricaturist who fell under the aesthetic influence of Meyerhold, who was to Soviet theater directors

4–3. *Mother* **(U.S.S.R., 1926),** *directed by V. I. Pudovkin.*
An adaption of Maxim Gorky's famous novel about the 1905 anticzarist uprising, *Mother* was an international success, establishing Pudovkin as a major Soviet filmmaker. Unlike Eisenstein, who was more interested in mass movements than individuals, Pudovkin—like his idol Griffith—emphasized the humanity of his characters, who are placed before a backdrop of epic events. Most movies of the Soviet golden age in the 1920s dealt with the 1917 Revolution, or precursors to it.   *(Museum of Modern Art)*

what Stanislavsky was to actors. Eisenstein's own early accomplishments were in the live theater.

Eisenstein's overriding principle was that of kineticism—of jagged, intense movement within the **frame** and in the cutting between shots. Movement was all. The only true sin was a static shot. Eisenstein made a promising debut with *Strike* (1925), an apprentice work that subsequently gave him the opportunity to make the official commemorative film for a partially successful revolution that had taken place in 1905. The script contained an episode about a mutiny on board the battleship *Potemkin,* but Eisenstein began altering the script and structuring the entire movie around the mutiny. It was eventually entitled *Potemkin* (1925), and it revolutionized the cinema. The port town of Odessa was the film's setting, and in scouting for locations, Eisenstein came upon a great flight of marble steps leading down to the harbor. Then and there, he determined to stage the film's major sequence— Cossack soldiers leading reprisals against a helpless populace—on those steps **(4–4).**

a

b

4–4 a & b. Two successive shots from the Odessa steps sequence of *Potemkin* (U.S.S.R., 1925), *directed by Sergei Eisenstein.*
A mother carries her wounded son up the steps while Cossacks prepare to fire another round on the panicked citizens below. Action, reaction. Eisenstein usually cut to **reverse angles** for different reasons than other filmmakers. Whereas most directors use reverse angles to reveal more information, Eisenstein cut for cutting's sake—to juxtapose purely formal elements, to create a sense of visual and kinetic clash, irrespective of the subject matter. The staccato collision of images set up the rhythm of his movies and was the prime tenet of his revolutionary aesthetic. Eisenstein's aim was not to define characters or even to tell a story—which he could do quite well when he wanted to—but to explore the outermost possibilities of film itself. Such modernist experiments in form were very much in the air during this era and could also be found in music (Stravinsky, Schoenberg), painting (Picasso, Braque), drama (Brecht, O'Neill), and literature (Joyce, Eliot).   *(Museum of Modern Art)*

Eisenstein's Odessa steps sequence is a powerful re-creation of what it's like to be caught in an explosion of random violence. The soldiers march down the stairs, and their movement is intercut with fleeing bodies, terrified faces. A soldier slashes angrily at the camera, and Eisenstein cuts to a tight closeup of an old woman with her face torn open. Winding through it all, a detail glimpsed as if out of the corner of a frantic eye, a baby carriage shakily bumps down the great steps, its wailing occupant heading for certain disaster, even as the soldiers continue their rigid, mechanical advance down the stairs. The sequence has been parodied many times, most recently in Brian DePalma's *The Untouchables* (1987).

After the massacre, the mutineers on board the *Potemkin* steam toward freedom, fully expecting to be fired on by other battleships. But the sailors on the other ships, heartened by the bravery of their comrades and sickened by the slaughter on land, refuse to shoot. United in their defiance and solidarity with their brother sailors, the crew of the *Potemkin* advances triumphantly, the keystone of the successful rebellion.

Eisenstein's editing in *Potemkin* was the most sophisticated cutting style yet developed in movies. Almost every moment of every action is broken up into a series of clashing shots. The film is given a needed grit by its photography, by Edward Tissé, who, significantly, began his career as a newsreel cameraman. Eisenstein's disjunctive editing was at least partly the result of necessity; the Soviets had primitive equipment, and camera dollies for tracking shots were virtually unheard of. One way to give a film a sense of movement was at the editing table. Later, when modern equipment was accessible, the Russians still avoided **tracking, panning,** and other camera movements because they believed that these techniques made the audience too conscious of the camera.

It was only natural that Eisenstein be handed the plum assignment of making one of two films to commemorate the tenth anniversary of the Revolution. The resulting movie was *October* **(4–5),** or, as it was called in America, *Ten Days That Shook the World,* a title cribbed from American John Reed's book of reportage on the same Revolution. Popular abroad, attacked at home, *October* seems strangely empty today. Its most famous sequence is a series of shots of Alexander Kerensky, the vacillating leader of a provisional government that preceded Lenin's. We see Kerensky climbing, endlessly climbing palace stairs, as Eisenstein intersperses titles sarcastically ridiculing Kerensky's presumptions of grandeur. The sequence is clever and beautifully shot, but it's also cheap and easy. Eisenstein allowed his art to be used for glib political gamesmanship.

The 1930s were a time of enormous frustration for Eisenstein. Six months in Hollywood produced two screenplays, which Paramount declined to make. An independent production in Mexico turned into a disaster when its backer, American novelist Upton Sinclair, withdrew his financial support after Eisenstein had exceeded his absurdly low budget three times over.

At home, he was deemed politically untrustworthy by the Soviet dictator Josef Stalin, an anti-Semite who regarded Eisenstein's homosexuality as additional proof of his dangerous instincts. One film, *Bezhin Meadow* (1937), was suppressed for political reasons and Eisenstein was forced to demean himself by publishing an apology, entitled "The Errors of *Bezhin Meadow.*" It was, in all senses, a film born under a dark star; the negative was destroyed during World War II. Surviving still photos suggest that Eisenstein was exercising the more reflective, lyrical side of his talent.

What was Eisenstein's great sin? "Formalism" was the name Stalin gave to it, which meant simply that he was ignoring the social needs of the masses for the sake of his self-expression. The director contented himself with teaching, and finally he managed to finish *Alexander Nevsky* (1938), a patriotic epic of fourteenth-century Russians repelling German invaders. The contemporary overtones were obvious to all (see Chapter 9). As a film, *Nevsky* is characteristic of the later Eisenstein: remote, sagaesque, with a resplendent battle scene enlivened by an impressive musical score by Sergei Prokofiev. Something was missing, however. Eisenstein's passion had been banked by too much inactivity, too many disappointments.

He completed two more movies before his premature death: *Ivan the Terrible, Part I* (1945) and its continuation *Part II* (1948). Beautifully composed but emotionally barren, Eisenstein's last work is often referred to as operatic, but as Pauline Kael has observed, if it's opera, it's opera without singers or drama, only music and settings.

There were other directors working in the Soviet Union. There had to be: Nine thousand movie theaters were operating in the country by 1928. Eisenstein's friendly

4–5. *October* (**U.S.S.R., 1927**), *directed by Sergei Eisenstein.*
Eisenstein was a supreme master of **mise en scène,** including actions and reactions within the same frame. In this shot, Lenin's lean forward is counterbalanced by the angle of the flag, while an artfully swirling blanket of smoke lends the Father of the Revolution the appropriate mythological quality. *(Sovkino)*

rival, Alexander Dovzhenko (1894–1956), was the Ukraine's resident agrarian poet. He entered films from painting somewhat late, at the age of thirty-two. Dovzhenko made a trilogy of ballads involving farms and farmers, spring plantings and autumn harvests, old people dying and children being born—Russian *Our Towns* fueled by revolutionary fervor and Dovzhenko's feeling for his native Ukraine.

His poetic sensibility is shown in *Arsenal* (1929), as he introduces his characters: "There was a mother who had three sons." The social milieu is sketched in equally brusquely: "There was a war." The director's free flow of images takes the place of conventional narrative and, in many cases, goes beyond that basic function. In *Arsenal,* a farmer is beating a horse out of frustration. When the animal turns and tells him, sensibly enough, "I'm not what you need to strike at," a chastened farmer quietly leads the horse away.

In Dovzhenko's *Earth* (4–6), a gently dying old man bites hungrily into a ripe apple, which led Ivor Montagu to write: "The key to all the poignance in Dovzhenko's films is death. Just that, the simplest thing of all. [But] death apprehended never as an end, a finish, dust to dust, but death as a sacrifice, the essential one, a part of the unending process of reviving life."

All these filmmakers were fervent supporters of Lenin's new Russia, but as the Revolution evolved, its foremost cinematic explicators were shunted aside and rendered impotent by the despot Stalin. Also, the naturalism of sound stifled them. Eisenstein's completed talkies are essentially silent films with the music used for dramatic inflection and coloring. They are impressive, but the components are painfully unintegrated.

4–6. *Earth* **(U.S.S.R., 1930),** *directed by Alexander Dovzhenko.*
The forceful, metaphoric compositional style of Eisenstein was freely adapted by Dovzhenko for his own more pastoral purposes. A blooming sunflower symbolizes the strong-featured Ukrainian woman next to it. *(Museum of Modern Art)*

This first generation of filmmakers, who had grown up watching movies, shared a scorching, revolutionary spirit that transcended geographical boundaries. After 1930, however, as Soviet home rule hardened, Russian films returned to their status of fifteen years before: fodder for the native audience only. This provinciality would continue until the late 1950s, when the cultural thaw that followed the death of Stalin slowly, very slowly, worked its way down to the film industry.

Germany

During this era, Germany had the only national cinema comparable to America's. Ironically, Germany's three leading filmmakers—Lubitsch, Murnau, and Lang—eventually emigrated to the United States. It was the Austrian Fritz Lang who most effectively captured the psychological mood of this as well as several succeeding eras. Of the chaotic period following World War I, he wrote: "Germany entered a period of unrest and confusion, a period of hysteric despair and unbridled vice full of the excesses of an inflation-ridden country. . . . Money lost its value very rapidly. The workers received their money not weekly but daily and even so . . . their wives could hardly buy a couple of rolls or half a pound of potatoes for a day's work."

In this atmosphere, **expressionism** flourished. Expressionism, as a theory of art, emphasized a given artist's emotional, intensely personal reactions; it was thus in contrast to the traditional view that an artist should strive faithfully to reproduce the natural appearance of the object or person being painted, sculpted, or written about. As adapted for film, expressionism concentrated on a heavy use of light and dark contrasts, exaggeration, tilted angles, a dreamlike atmosphere, and a distorting of the external world to reveal a given psychological state. German films of this era are united by their uncanny evocation of *stimmung*, an intense atmospheric mood at least partially attributable to the taste of most German directors for production completely within the studio, a method that lent their movies a unified, claustrophobic style.

German films of the 1920s generally fall into two categories, the epic and the intimate. The latter group were known as *kammerspiel*, intimate films of psychology rather than action. They tended to observe strict unities of time, place, and action. The best of them were written by Carl Mayer, whose scripts were impressionistic poems that make somewhat baroque reading but nonetheless provided the stimulus for fine films from directors as diverse as Murnau, Robert Wiene, and Walter Ruttman.

Isolated between the two poles of German cinema was the overt, virtually undiluted expressionism of *The Cabinet of Dr. Caligari* **(4–7),** the story of a madman's fantasies filmed with starkly artificial sets made up of cardboard backdrops or painted cubist shadows, which effectively suggested the disorientation of the storyteller's mind. "Film," said *Caligari's* designer Herman Warm, "must be drawings brought to life." The warped contortions of this film were matched by the warped contortions of its actors. The artificiality and limited storytelling potential of such purebred expressionism restricted its use. Despite its good reviews and acknowledged place in film history, *Caligari* proved to be something of a dead end. In modified form, however, expressionism exerted an enormous influence, especially in the American cinema of the 1940s.

The 1920s was to be the golden age of German cinema. The first German filmmaker to achieve success was also the first to depart for Hollywood. ERNST LUBITSCH (1892–1947), the canniest careerist of all his peers, left Germany in 1922, the vanguard of a tide of foreign filmmakers to flood Hollywood during the next

4–7. *The Cabinet of Dr. Caligari* **(Germany, 1919),** *with Conrad Veidt, directed by Robert Wiene.*
Unlike the murky film prints usually seen by audiences, this remarkably clear still photo shows just what a jerry-rigged, low-budget production *Caligari* really was. It is a classic example of turning limitations into virtues. Bare supplies of cardboard, plywood, and paint create a landscape of angular nightmares. Besides influencing filmmakers, *Caligari* established Veidt as a character star, who could suggest an elegant otherworldliness in movies like *The Beloved Rogue* and *The Man Who Laughs*. An anti-Fascist who left Germany with the rise of Hitler, Veidt thrived as an actor in England and America until his death in 1943.   *(Decla–Bioskop)*

twenty years. Lubitsch, a draper's son, began as an actor working for the revered stage director Max Reinhardt. From him the novice developed a sense of the intimate moment, of the value of underplaying. Lubitsch began his film career in 1913 as the star in a series of movies about an inept working-class pawn named Meyer. Relying mostly on Jewish stereotypes of the period, these pictures also served as an eerie ethnic counterpoint to the adventures of Chaplin's upstart happy wanderer and gave Lubitsch the opportunity to learn the technique of the camera thoroughly.

Lubitsch's first directorial success was *The Eyes of the Mummy Ma* (1918), derived in large part from the impersonal Italian spectaculars then enjoying a vogue. Lubitsch cut back on his acting and concentrated on directing, continuing in the vein of historical spectaculars—but spectaculars with a difference. Refining his style, paying close attention to the acting, Lubitsch directed movies like *Passion* (1919) and *The Loves of Pharoah* (1922), which earned him the title of "The Griffith of Europe." At the same time, he launched a series of satirical, sophisticated come-

4–8. *Madame Dubarry* **(Germany, 1919)**, *with Pola Negri, directed by Ernst Lubitsch.*
A good example of the American influence on the European cinema. Expressionist introspection would never be for Lubitsch; bread, circuses, and spectacle in the Griffith–DeMille manner were. Lubitsch's historical spectaculars proved quite profitable, much more so than the austere critics' favorite, *The Cabinet of Dr. Caligari*. Even the more commercial *The Last Laugh* was only a moderate success financially, compared to Lubitsch's film. Because Lubitsch's sensibility seemed so palatable to American audiences, he departed for the United States. In America he avoided epic materials, concentrating instead on sophisticated comedies of manners, sparkling sexual roundelays, which were his true métier. They were also much less successful commercially, a bit highbrow.   *(UFA)*

dies of manners, which were not widely distributed outside Germany but were to form the foundation for the rest of his career.

Lubitsch's spectacle films were highly popular for the wit with which he portrayed remote historical personages like Madam Dubarry **(4–8).** But in his less famous comedies of manners, not to mention his considerably more distinguished Hollywood comedies of the 1930s and 1940s (see Chapter 6), there was a profound, almost mournful seriousness underneath all the mittel-Europa vaudeville.

Unlike Lubitsch, who concealed his seriousness behind a slyly comic exterior, FRITZ LANG (1890–1976) was always among the most earnest of filmmakers. He began his career with novelettish thrillers like *The Spiders* (1919) and *Dr. Mabuse, The Gambler* (1922), which dealt with larger-than-life criminal masterminds who inhabit anarchic environments and jagged, expressionist sets. They are movies distinguished by their discomforting mood and by the uncompromising sense of conviction the director brought to them, a prime feature of all his work.

Lang evolved into more folkloric movies with his two-part retelling of the Germanic saga of Siegfried. The first film, *Siegfried* **(4–9),** is a majestically evocative, methodically detailed re-creation of a world before time began, where Aryan gods do battle with dragons. Lang makes the film a study in symmetry, a vast, inexorably grand construct that leads to the massive bloodletting of *Kriemhild's Revenge* (1924, but not released in America until 1928). It is as true a *Götterdämerung* as was ever put on film, as well as an unintentional prophecy of the end of the Nazi movement in fire and blood.

Ironically, although the films were often bracketed in the public mind with Wagner's operas and *Siegfried* was reissued under Hitler with a musical accompani-

4–9. *Siegfried* **(Germany, 1924),** *with Paul Richter, directed by Fritz Lang.*
A typically majestic composition from Lang's two-part retelling of the German national myth. The studied artificiality created in the studio provides a sense of a total environment that could not have been captured so effectively on actual locations.   *(UFA)*

ment drawn from the work of the anti-Semitic composer, Lang loathed the music and, in making the films, overtly ignored Wagner's librettos, going to the original ancient German myths for his source material.

Metropolis (**4–10**) is an elaborate vision of the world of the future and the most expensive movie made in Germany up to that time. Almost universally deplored for the silliness of its story, it was written, as were all his films of this period, by Lang's wife at the time, Thea von Harbou. *Metropolis*'s greatness is in its design, its geometric use of shapes as well as of masses of people. The film's bravura scale and set pieces, such as the creation of the aseptically beautiful robot Maria, are still capable of inspiring awe.

Spies (1928) was a return to the themes of *Dr. Mabuse,* but more artfully done. The super-criminal Haghi, played by the masterful Rudolph Klein-Rogge, submerges his true identity behind alter egos, among them those of a bank president and a circus clown. At the end, surrounded, with no hope of escape, Haghi is on stage in his guise of a clown. He takes out a gun, laughs, and shoots himself in the head. He collapses, the curtain comes down, and the audience, believing this show-stopping stunt to be part of the show, applauds wildly. With its visual scheme of strong diagonals, its sharp camera angles, and its dynamic use of cutting—at least some of which was in response to the film's comparatively modest budget—*Spies* shows that Lang had been watching the films coming out of the U.S.S.R.

Lang's use of melodrama and sensation to deal with moral themes was to be an inspiration to Alfred Hitchcock. Lang's German movies, quite apart from his more realistic films made in America (see Chapter 8), are loaded with symbols and portents. In *Destiny* (1921), Death, personified by a morose, black-clad, ashen-faced man, enters a tavern where flowers wilt and a cat arches his back. In *Siegfried,* the

4–10. *Metropolis* (**Germany, 1926**), *directed by Fritz Lang.*
Lang's genius for geometric architecture utilized studio constructs or masses of people with equal facility. While *Metropolis* made effective use of miniatures and other special effects, most German films tended to rely on full-size reproductions or props, unlike the Americans, who tended to favor special effects.   *(UFA)*

hero and his beloved wife say goodbye before a typically symmetrical bush. As Siegfried leaves, never to return, Lang **double exposes** the innocent shrubbery into a ghastly skull.

Lotte Eisner recognized the essence of Lang's greatness when she wrote: "Nothing in Lang is facade, everything is three dimensional and spatial." Lang's style was to grow sparer with sound, but his evocation of a world where it is always a moral midnight, his camera hovering over the characters like Fate itself, gave even the most superficial of his films the brooding, evocative power of a great moralist.

The world of German films, with their anguished depictions of man's dark struggle, created a sensation around the world, which was more used to the brightly lit cheerfulness of Hollywood. No director was more influential than F. W. MURNAU (1888–1931), a former soldier like Lang, but less of an architect, more of a poet. Murnau's first major success was *Nosferatu* **(4–11),** an adaptation of Bram Stoker's novel, *Dracula*. The film remains notable for the manner in which Murnau integrated the patently unreal—the vampire, brilliantly characterized as a pestilential man-rat on two legs—with realistic settings like the Carpathian woods or the port town of Bremen. This uncanny ability to obliterate the line dividing the real and the unreal was to be a hallmark of Murnau's career.

His most famous movie, *The Last Laugh* **(4–12),** made the world truly take notice, for Murnau and his writer Carl Mayer (1894–1944) dared to make a silent film without titles, except for one at the conclusion of the film. The story is emotionally complex. A doorman for a splendid urban hotel, unutterably proud of the prestige conferred on him by his gaudy uniform, is demoted to the status of a lavatory attendant. The inhabitants of his neighborhood ridicule his fall from grace. His self-image shaken, the old man crumbles.

To bind together this story of differing social spheres and human pride, Murnau adopted a mellifluously moving camera, which tracked, panned, and moved nearly continuously, or so it seemed to audiences used to tripods. The old man is played by Emil Jannings, in a triumphant evocation of the emotional masochism that he specialized in. In one scene he gets drunk; Murnau strapped the camera to

4–11. *Nosferatu* **(Germany, 1922),** *with Max Schreck, directed by F. W. Murnau.*
Murnau's conception of Dracula as a rat in human form was a strikingly original departure from the midnight lover image of the successful stage play, or the sleek, dignified gentleman of the Bram Stoker novel. Murnau's film was strangely compelling, "a chilly draft from doomsday," as one critic put it. Although cruder than his later works, the movie makes good use of what Arthur Lennig called "his ability to create an organic work united by imagery, tone, atmosphere and precise, consistent characterization. He had a superb awareness of . . . theme . . . and subordinates everything to its development." *(Museum of Modern Art)*

4–12. **Production photo from** *The Last Laugh* **(Germany, 1924),** *F. W. Murnau in hat, Karl Freund (cinematographer) obscured behind camera, Emil Jannings at right.*
One light, one camera, and a small crew. The background sets, though elaborately painted, are actually tall versions of stage flats. Although it was to be an enormously influential movie, *The Last Laugh* had a modest budget. *(UFA)*

4–13. *Tartuffe* **(Germany, 1925),** *with Emil Jannings, directed by F. W. Murnau.*
A marginally unsuccessful version of Molière's classic play, *Tartuffe* is rather static and stagy— a movie intimidated by its source. Most of Murnau's films were produced by UFA, which was founded when the German government appropriated 25 million marks to launch the company. It absorbed six smaller companies, bought theaters, and went into distribution as well as production. The crushing financial losses of *Faust* and *Metropolis* forced UFA to turn for help to Dr. Alfred Hugenberg, a financier with fascist leanings. Hugenberg gradually turned the studio into a nationalistically oriented company. Under Hitler's regime, UFA was the most important organization, but although it was put under official state control in 1937, its artistic importance had ceased several years before then. *(UFA)*

the chest of cameraman Karl Freund, who then staggered around. The resulting footage gives a very effective, subjective view of alcoholic excess.

The Last Laugh contains only about 300 shots, a small number for a full-length feature of the period. *Nosferatu,* for instance, a shorter, stylistically more conventional film, contains 540. Instead of cutting, Murnau employed lengthy **takes.** Moving cameras were, in and of themselves, nothing new. But before *The Last Laugh* they had been used sparingly, to emphasize specific moments. Murnau was the first to make camera movement a style sufficient unto itself, the camera expressing emotions and motivations that had previously been the province of the titles, the acting, or expressive lighting.

The Last Laugh was an international hit. Before long, even modestly budgeted Hollywood movies like *Red Raiders* (1926), a Ken Maynard western, became veritable riots of expressive camera movements. After two more German films, including a fascinating but not completely successful *Faust* (1926), Murnau left for Hollywood and his finest achievement (see Chapter 3).

More realistic, plot-oriented stories were the province of G. W. PABST (1887–1967). He specialized in slices of life like *The Joyless Street* (1925), the story of a middle-class family that deteriorates as it falls on hard economic times. On the joyless street, crowds line up for their ration of meat, a scene which is intercut with shots of a symbolic butcher, his forbiddingly large white dog playing favorites in the distribution of the poor-quality meat. The film's gritty truthfulness had critics comparing it to Stroheim's *Greed,* but Pabst's juxtapositions contrasting street-wise profiteers and the destitute middle class, or chi-chi restaurants and impoverished homes, owed more to the journalistic side of Griffith's Biograph films like *A Corner in Wheat.*

Pabst's most famous movie is probably *Pandora's Box* **(4–14),** a relentless parable of the destruction that a sensually insatiable woman brings on herself and all who know her. Its fame rests more on the electric, inscrutable sensuality of its American star, Louise Brooks, than on Pabst's dry, precise direction.

After *Diary of a Lost Girl* (1929), another essay on the subject of Louise Brooks and subliminally glossy nymphomania, Pabst made *The Three-Penny Opera* (1931), from Brecht and Weill's landmark stage-musical fable of corruption and capitalism. It's a good film, but not as good as it should be, given the superlative original material. The slashing ironies and quicksilver wit of the play are weighed down by Pabst's plodding heaviness.

After that came decline, rapid and permanent. Except for the realism of *The Joyless Street,* little in this stolid director's work justified a contemporary reputation that rivaled the more obsessively personal Lang and Murnau. It was they, along with Lubitsch, who constituted the true troika of genius for this most vital of European cinemas.

France

It began with the scandalous premiere of Igor Stravinsky's *Rite of Spring,* at the Paris Opera on May 29, 1913. Suddenly, the arts were awash in experimentation, both in subject and form. The novel, which traditionally had concentrated on storytelling, was suddenly invaded by the radical alterations of James Joyce and Marcel Proust. The world of the visual arts, used to the genteel, sedate impressionists, was invaded by a movement known as dada. **Dadaism** emphasized the illogical or absurd, using

4–14. *Pandora's Box* **(Germany, 1929),** *with Louise Brooks, directed by G. W. Pabst.*
Underappreciated in her day, Brooks had a cool lasciviousness beneath an iconoclastic helmet of hair that put her out of step with the more giddy tastes of the day. By the late 1930s, she was reduced to playing leading ladies in B-westerns. She started writing about films and film people in the 1950s. Her penetrating intelligence and shrewdness are best illustrated by her 1982 memoir, *Lulu in Hollywood*. *(Nero Film)*

buffoonery and other provocative behavior to shock and disrupt a complacent society. Above all else, the dadaists despised **realism,** dismissing it as a superficial style.

Along with theater, art, and literature, filmmakers reacted to the bloodthirsty, disillusioning debacle of World War I with irony, cynicism, and anarchic nihilism. Politics and the rules of society were morally outrageous, authority a joke. All that was possible for an intellectual was sardonic laughter. Nothing mattered, everything was possible—everything but tradition and convention.

Dadaism gave birth to surrealism, a slightly more positive manifestation of the view that life is essentially absurd. Surrealism was an aggressive form of cultural terrorism, out to explode all established forms of expression. The surrealists' aim was to broaden and transform life itself. They attacked the logical, objectivist view of reality, insisting on the superiority of dreams, the instinctive, the subconscious, to produce a reality beyond external reality—a super-reality.

Surrealists like Luis Buñuel, Salvador Dali, and Pablo Picasso were mostly from bourgeois families, but they were in revolt against their staid, middle-class upbringings, attacking their origins with youthful passion and humor of the darkest black. The center for all this inspired madness was Paris, the cutting edge of the art

4–15. *Zero for Conduct* **(France, 1933),** *directed by Jean Vigo.*
This film's famous slow-motion pillow fight scene, dreamlike and surreal, with feathers flying and floating in every direction, is a metaphor for youthful exuberance and absolute freedom. The movie was banned by the censors until 1946, presumably because of its caustic portrayal of French bourgeois institutions and their repressive attitude toward youth.   *(Gaumont)*

world, where the most radical experimentalists congregated, as if answering a tolling bell only they could hear.

The French film industry had been devastated by the war. By 1919, the percentage of French movies on the world's screens was 15 percent, down from more than 50 percent in 1914. French filmmaking in the postwar era was either allied to or in reaction against the tenets of the avant-garde surrealists. JEAN VIGO (1905–1934) belonged to the former category. He used **slow motion** and disjunctive compositions that isolated his characters from any kind of conventional surroundings. During his abruptly curtailed career, Vigo, an anarchist by instinct, regularly characterized authority figures as grotesques. His most famous movie, *Zero for Conduct* **(4–15),** is a story of four boys struggling to maintain their individuality while in boarding school. They pit themselves against a principal, who is, in several senses of the word, a midget—about three feet tall, to be exact, with an absurd, pointed beard. Vigo's antiauthoritarian stance won him no friends among the always power-conscious French. The government banned the movie and it was not shown until after World War II, when it influenced a generation of filmmakers who would become known as the **New Wave.**

Similar in spirit to Vigo, but lighter in tone, was RENÉ CLAIR (1898–1981). Clair began his career by imitating Max Linder and Mack Sennett, in fizzy farces brushed with a thin coating of absurdism or social comment. He ended his career by being inducted into the prestigious—and decidedly Establishment—Academie Française. Clair's movies, like his silent version of the classic farce *The Italian Straw Hat* (1927), are charming, energetic, and effervescent, but they are rarely penetrating in their social criticism. With *Under the Roofs of Paris* (4–16) and *Le Million* (1931), he refined and modulated, maturing as his films became fantasies of French life as the world has always believed it to be.

As critic John Russell Taylor has noted, Clair's films are heavily patterned: An object—a hat, a lottery ticket—is passed from hand to hand, and each person in the chain is defined by what he or she does with the article, how each reacts to it. For example, in *Le Million* (4–17), a poor artist wins a million-franc lottery, only to discover that the ticket is in the pocket of a coat that has been stolen. He pursues the coat through various facets of French society in a comic *la ronde*. In one scene, the artist engages in a tug of war over the coat, while Clair dubs in the sounds of a football match, complete with crowd noises, officials' whistles, and the thud of bodies. *Le Million* ends in celebration: All the participants in the chase join hands and dance.

4–16. *Under the Roofs of Paris* (**France, 1930**), *directed by René Clair.*
Even as early as 1930, the only major competition Hollywood had in terms of excellence in art direction came from France and Germany. Clair preferred shooting within the studio rather than on location, the better to create a self-enclosed universe, which was part musical fantasy, part romance, part social satire. Designers like Lazare Meerson, who created the sets for several of Clair's finest works, demonstrated that the best European artisans were fully the equal of Hollywood's finest. *(Audio-Brandon Films)*

4–17. *Le Million* **(France, 1931),** *directed by René Clair.*
The criminals are picturesque, the jail is clean, the hero is young, befuddled, and sympathetic.
It could only be the Paris of René Clair, whose rhythmic farces made him one of the most successful of French filmmakers in the early 1930s. Even Chaplin adapted one of Clair's scenes
from *À Nous la Liberté* for *Modern Times,* which resulted in Clair's producers suing Chaplin
for plagiarism. Clair wisely interceded and called the suit off, explaining that because he had
borrowed so much from Chaplin, it would have been unseemly and churlish to prosecute the
man who was his inspiration.   *(Audio-Brandon Films)*

After *À Nous la Liberté* (1931), his most widely admired film, Clair went to
England in 1936 and to America during World War II. In the United States he
made some typically light-fingered entertainments, including an underrated vehicle for Marlene Dietrich, *The Flame of New Orleans* (1940). Clair's later career was a
case of diminished energies being greeted with diminishing returns. At his best,
however, Clair was *balletique,* turning life into a constant swirl of motion that was
never without grace, a visual corollary to his wry verbal wit.

If Clair was revered in his time, then ABEL GANCE (1889–1981) was often reviled. His greatest achievement, *Napoleon* (1926), was dismembered by an industry
and forgotten by most audiences. Movies like *La Roué* (1921) and *J'Accuse* (1919),
in which the war dead rise from their graves and march on the living, established
Gance as a prodigious talent given to extremes in both length and style. With

Napoleon, Gance practically reinvented the motion picture. Originally premiered in a version that ran six hours, it was an obviously unwieldy white elephant and, outside of its original engagements, has never been exhibited in its full version.

Gance's extravagance, his nineteenth-century romantic sensibility combined with his wildly expressive avant-garde techniques (hand-held camera, staccato editing), seemed an impossible contradiction for the French, who are usually more coolly reductive than emotionally expansive. The most accurate contemporary criticism of Gance was by Louis Delluc, who wrote that Gance's greatest vice was an inability to be simple; the best later criticism was by Pauline Kael, who called him "an avant-garde De Mille."

But Gance's floridly expressive style transcends period. In *Napoleon,* the emperor-to-be escapes from Corsica and sets sail for the mainland of Europe, using a stolen tricolor for a sail. Intercut with this scene is a tempestuous meeting of the revolutionary convention in Paris. A storm at sea develops, tossing Napoleon and his flimsy boat carelessly from wave to wave. Likewise, the convention, spurred by the fiery oratory of Danton and Robespierre, turns into a riot of political emotionalism. Gance cuts back and forth, the camera floating with Napoleon's boat and at the convention mounted on a pendulumlike device, swinging in a turbulent arc over the enraged mob. Camera movement approximates both natural phenomena and human emotion at the same time. Motion is metaphor for emotion.

Gance's main technical masterstroke involved the invention of what he called "Polyvision," what later generations would know as Cinerama: three cameras mounted, pyramid style, on top of each other, angled to photograph a 160-degree panorama three times as wide as the conventional single camera image **(4–19).** Only one of the movie's three such triptych sequences survives—the picture's climax, as Napoleon begins his march into Italy, into history. The little colonel— played by the fiery Albert Dieudonne—reviews his troops and their encampments,

4–18. Abel Gance meeting D. W. Griffith at Griffith's studio at Mamaroneck, New York (1921).
Above all filmmakers, Gance loved the visionary side of the great American director, his pyrotechnical extravagance and showmanship. It was probably Griffith's experiments with frame size that led Gance to begin development of what he would call Polyvision. *(Universal Pictures)*

a

b

4–19 a & b. Two Polyvision shots from *Napoleon* (France, 1927), *directed by Abel Gance.* Prints of this movie in circulation today show the Polyvision sequences in a heavily masked CinemaScope format that renders the final triptychs with a greatly diminished effect—as if looked at through a mailbox slot. To fully appreciate the grandeur of Gance's conception, it is necessary to know what he had in mind: three projectors shooting three pictures onto three *full-size* screens next to each other. The process creates vistas of such startling clarity that some shots almost achieve a three-dimensional effect. *(Universal Pictures)*

the view spread out as far as the horizon itself. Sometimes Gance uses the triptych for one spectacularly panoramic view, sometimes he sets off the center panel with different images on either side, in a contrapuntal effect that extends the psychological and emotional range of conventional editing geometrically.

Fire, water, a spinning globe. The left panel turns red, the right panel blue—Gance has turned the film itself into the French flag. And then, spread over the vast expanse of the screen, the eagle that has followed Napoleon throughout the film unfurls his wings and screams—the viewer forgets that this is a silent film. As *Napoleon* ends on a triumphant crescendo of image, rhythm, and emotional effect, the screen is filled with the signature of the film's creator, Abel Gance.

In this movie, a work like no other by a director who worked almost entirely in images, a man for whom sound was superfluous, there is not a casual or indifferent scene to be found. Even the intimate moments—the wooing and winning of Josephine, Napoleon's visit to his mother in Corsica—are full of a headlong lyricism transposed to a minor key. Gance believed that Polyvision was the wave of the cinema's future, but the necessary technological retooling and financial outlay was rendered impossible, first by *Napoleon's* financial failure, then by the coming of sound.

In giving birth to *Napoleon,* Gance seemed to tear out some portion of his insides. He was shunted to the commercial fringe, where he directed ordinary films to pay the bills. His grandiose plans were thwarted by unsympathetic producers and his own splendid, Homeric impracticality. But he never stopped experimenting with *Napoleon.* He added sound in 1934, tried it with stereo in the 1950s, and finally reedited it into something approximating a documentary in 1971. *Napoleon* was Abel Gance's *Leaves of Grass,* and he was the cinema's Walt Whitman, an unorthodox lyrical poet.

LUIS BUÑUEL (1900–1983) is widely regarded as the greatest of all the surrealist artists. Like Gance, he had to wait until the world caught up with his very individual sensibility before he could garner the acclaim he deserved. Buñuel was a dashing young Spaniard, lured into film by the work of Fritz Lang, whose uncompromising movies clarified Buñuel's vision of a harsh, corrupt world. Buñuel became embroiled in the Parisian avant-garde, a small group of insolent intellectuals who nonetheless managed to expand the world's artistic horizons. What gave Buñuel's work its originality and made it stand apart from the work of other periods, other filmmakers, was a rigorous psychological harshness common to Spanish artists, fueled by the frustrations of a renegade Catholic and combined with an interest in ideas and a fascination with the sensual common to the French.

Teaming up with his friend and fellow Spaniard Salvador Dali, Buñuel made *Un Chien Andalou* ("An Andalusian Dog," 1928), an amalgamation of dreams and images whose only ruling precept was that there be no rational explanation for any moment in the movie. Strongly influenced by the ideas of Freud, the film is a succession of astonishing, irrational images, mostly startling—a man slits a woman's eyeball with a straight razor, for example **(4–20).** The movie is also cumulatively funny, as only truly accomplished *non sequiturs* can be. *Un Chien Andalou* was a success and a scandal at the same time.

Buñuel and Dali collaborated again, with *L'Age d'Or* ("The Age of Gold," 1930). The film is a short feature made up of mutually exclusive sequences: a semi-scientific documentary on scorpions and, predominantly, a tormented affair between a man and his mistress who are interrupted and separated by his arrest. A minister of the interior phones the man and says, over newsreel shots of catastrophes, "You are the only one to blame for what has happened, murderer." In the end, the survivors of a "brutal orgy" leave a chateau, the procession led by none other than Jesus Christ. This furiously anti-Catholic, anti-everything-but-anarchy movie set off riots in Paris and was more or less impossible to see, except at private screenings, for fifty years. Buñuel and Dali parted acrimoniously during the making of the film, which was executed primarily by Buñuel.

Buñuel next directed *Land Without Bread* (1932), a scabrous documentary on life in the most poverty-stricken corner of Spain. He made the film with all his ironic impassivity and black humor—a stark view of a dirt-walled hovel with a calendar haphazardly tacked to the wall impels the narrator to say that the inhabitants "show a certain flair for interior decoration." Buñuel's apparent cruelty actually concealed a fierce integrity and honesty that formed the foundation of his artistic morality. *Land Without Bread* rendered Buñuel *persona non grata* in Franco's Fascist Spain, and the filmmaker was unable to gather the necessary momentum to resume his career until twenty years later, in Mexico.

For the next quarter of a century, in Mexico and France, this savage old grandee continued his war of dreams in films that never made the least

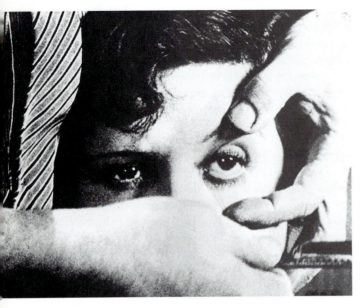

4–20. *Un Chien Andalou* **(France, 1928),** *directed by Luis Buñuel and Salvador Dali.*
The surrealists delighted in assaulting the viewer with aggressive, shocking images, often emphasizing sex or violence. In this scene, for example, Buñuel himself wields a straight razor, which he uses to slash the woman's eyeball in two. Symbolically, the scene is also a kind of assault on us—the "viewing audience." But the surrealists rejected logical and symbolic interpretations of their works. "Nothing in this film symbolizes anything," Buñuel and Dali perversely explained of their movie, which of course doesn't contain any dog, "Andalusian" or otherwise. *(Raymond Rohauer)*

accommodation to fashion. Visually unadorned, with a technique that never extended much beyond the functional, Buñuel's movies resonate with thematic daring, outrageous attacks on conventional morality and matter-of-fact exposés of hypocrisy and self-deception.

The vicious satirist of the 1920s grew old but not bitter, serene but never sentimental. At the end of his life, in his autobiography, *My Last Sigh,* Buñuel said he hated to leave, that he'd like to come back from the grave and pick up a newspaper every decade or so. "Ghostly pale, sliding silently along the walls, my papers under my arm, I'd return to the cemetery and read about all the disasters in the world before falling back to sleep, safe and secure in my tomb."

It is a wonderful image for a movie by Buñuel, who clearly saw and portrayed the extraordinary absurdity that permeates even the most ordinary lives.

FURTHER READING

ABEL, RICHARD. *French Cinema: The First Wave, 1915–1929*. Princeton, N.J.: Princeton University Press, 1984. A scholarly account of early French movies.

ARANDA, FRANCISCO. *Luis Buñuel*. New York: Da Capo, 1976. A critical biography, copiously illustrated, with filmography and bibliography.

BORDWELL, DAVID. *The Cinema of Eisenstein*. Cambridge, Mass.: Harvard University Press, 1993. A well-illustrated critical study.

EISNER, LOTTE. *Fritz Lang*. New York: Oxford University Press, 1977. A film-by-film run-through by one of the most enthusiastic and informed of the early generation of film critics.

———. *The Haunted Screen*. Berkeley: University of California Press, 1973. Expressionism in the German cinema and the influence of Max Reinhardt. Copiously illustrated.

EYMAN, SCOTT. *Ernst Lubitsch: Laughter in Paradise.* New York: Simon & Schuster, 1993. Biography and critical study, with filmography.

KRACAUER, SIEGFRIED. *From Caligari to Hitler: A Psychological History of German Film.* Princeton, N.J.: Princeton University Press, 1947. A controversial assessment whose thesis is that the post–World War I German cinema reflected the mentality that led to the rise of Hitler and Naziism.

LEYDA, JAY. *Kino.* New York: Collier Books, 1973. A dryly written, solidly reported history of the Russian and Soviet cinema by one of Eisenstein's pupils.

NIZHNY, VLADIMIR. *Lessons with Eisenstein.* New York: Hill and Wang, 1962. Transposed classroom notes by one of Eisenstein's students, especially informative on his theories of mise en scène and editing.

OTT, FREDERICK W. *The Films of Fritz Lang.* Secaucus, N.J.: The Citadel Press, 1979. Invaluable account of Lang, his films, his times, and his peers. Copiously illustrated.

5

The Hollywood Studio System

*Studios had faces then. They had their own style. They could bring you
blindfolded into a movie house and you opened it and looked up and
you knew. "Hey, this is an RKO picture. This is a Paramount Picture. This
is an MGM picture." They had a certain handwriting.*
—BILLY WILDER

RKO

Timeline: 1912–1960

1912–1920
The following film companies establish production facilities in the Hollywood area: Fox Film Corporation, Paramount Pictures, Universal Pictures, United Artists, and others

1919
Population of Hollywood: 35,000; by 1925: 130,000

1921–1928
The following film companies establish studios in the Hollywood area: Columbia Pictures, Metro-Goldwyn-Mayer (MGM), Warner Brothers, RKO (Radio-Keith-Orpheum)

1925–1960
Number of films released by the Hollywood studios: 1925: 579; 1930: 509; 1935: 525; 1940: 477; 1945: 350; 1950: 383; 1955: 254; 1960: 154

1929
U.S. box office receipts (in millions) $720; in 1935: $556; in 1940: $735; in 1945: $1,450; in 1950: $1,376; in 1955: $1,326; in 1960: $956

1930
Total studio profits (in millions) $54.5; in 1935: $15.5; in 1940: $19.1; in 1945: $63.3; in 1950: $30.8
Average cost of studio film (in thousands): $375; in 1940: $400; in 1946: $900; in 1955: $1.5 million; in 1960: $2 million
Weekly attendance of American movie theaters: 80 million; in 1945: 82 million; in 1960: 30 million

1930–1939
Most popular genres: comedies, gangster films, dramas, musicals

1935
Top ten stars—Shirley Temple, Will Rogers, Clark Gable, Astaire/Rogers, Joan Crawford, Claudette Colbert, Dick Powell, Wallace Beery, Joe E. Brown, James Cagney

1939–1943
Typical Hollywood star salaries (in thousands): Spencer Tracy, $225; Joan Crawford, $195; Katharine Hepburn, $190; Bette Davis, $252; James Cagney, $360; Errol Flynn, $240

1940–1949
Most popular genres: war movies, action/adventure films, crime movies, westerns, women's pictures

1945
Top ten stars: Bing Crosby, Van Johnson, Greer Garson, Betty Grable, Spencer Tracy, Humphrey Bogart, Gary Cooper, Bob Hope, Judy Garland, Margaret O'Brien

1955
Top ten stars: James Stewart, Grace Kelly, John Wayne, William Holden, Gary Cooper, Marlon Brando, Martin and Lewis, Humphrey Bogart, June Allison, Clark Gable

Box office values: the public is always right. The factory system of production. The rise of the great studios. The majors and the minors. Studio structures. The Front Office. Producer-directors: Hollywood's auteurs. The star system. Star power. Type casting. The system of genres. Genres and society. The classical paradigm. Story construction. The role of writers in Hollywood. The appeal to the subconscious.

A HISTORY OF FILM AS ART must be accompanied by a history of film as industry, for the two are symbiotically intertwined. Cinema is the most expensive artistic medium in history, and its development has been largely determined by the people who paid the bills. Fiction filmmakers need cameras, actors, film stock, sound and **editing** equipment, costumes, lights, and so on. Like all artists, they've got to earn a living, and they do so by providing a product that has a cash value to its consumers. In most European countries, the cinema in its early stages of development fell into the hands of artists who shared most of the values and tastes of the educated elite. European movie houses before World War I were usually located in fashionable districts and catered to the cultivated classes—the same patrons who attended the legitimate theater and the opera. In the Soviet Union and other communist countries, film production was carefully regulated by the government, and the movies produced in these countries reflected most of the values of the political elite.

The Box Office

In the United States, motion pictures developed as a popular art within a capitalistic system of production. In its earliest years, the industry catered primarily to patrons of the lower social echelons, who likewise wanted to see their values, tastes, and aspirations sympathetically portrayed. Movies were a boom industry primarily because audiences were getting what they really wanted. The American cinema was the most democratic art in history, reflecting most of the strengths and failings of the society that nurtured it. To guarantee their continued employment in this expensive medium, fiction filmmakers had to be sensitive to the demands of the box office, to the tastes of those anonymous millions who cared little for "culture," "edification," and other lofty abstractions. Above all, audiences wanted to be entertained, and only at their own peril could Hollywood film artists ignore this fundamental commandment of the box office. The best as well as the worst American movies have been produced within this commercial framework of a mass audience and a competitive marketplace.

Particularly before World War II, many American intellectuals lamented the state of the Hollywood cinema. Movies were routinely dismissed as "cheap shows for cheap people" and "the flimsy amusement of the mob." The reasons for this

5–1. *Marie Antoinette* **(U.S.A., 1937),** *directed by W. S. Van Dyke.*

Lavish spectacle pictures were an MGM specialty, for it was the richest, most profitable studio of the 1930s. "More Stars than there are in Heaven" was its motto, and while that might strike us as a trifle immodest, it did have more top stars than any other studio. MGM boasted 23 sound stages and 117 acres of backlot standing sets, representing various periods and exotic locales. Metro's pictures were usually lit in glossy **high key,** the better to admire the opulent **production values.** The studio "look" was largely the creation of art director Cedric Gibbons, who remained with MGM from 1924 to 1956. Gowns by Adrian. *(Metro-Goldwyn-Mayer)*

hostility are understandable, for out of the five hundred or so pictures produced yearly during Hollywood's golden age—roughly the years between the two world wars—only a small percentage were of enduring aesthetic value. Because of this sheer volume, the best movies were often overshadowed by the worst, or at least by the merely routine. Conversely, only the most prestigious foreign movies were exported to the United States, amounting roughly to 2 percent of the pictures exhibited in this country. For the most part, these dealt with subjects that rarely attracted American filmmakers, particularly that virtually taboo theme—honest failure. Popular audiences regarded foreign movies as arty, downbeat, and very slow—at least when contrasted with American pictures, which were usually unpretentious, optimistic, and fast-moving. Only box office hits were widely imitated in Hollywood, and since foreign films seldom attracted large audiences, American producers were content to leave "highbrow" subjects to European filmmakers.

These cinematic differences were based on totally different social conditions. After World War I, the major film-producing nations of Europe were spiritually exhausted, their economies in shambles. Disillusionment and pessimism were in the air, traditional standards of morality were collapsing, and absolute values were viewed as naive (see Chapter 4). While Europe was plunged in chaos and despair, the United States was thriving, immersed in the "gaudiest spree" of its history, to use F. Scott Fitzgerald's famous phrase. What American audiences wanted to see above all were success stories. It wasn't for nothing that the film industry was sometimes called the Hollywood Dream Factory.

Because the best European movies during this era generally dealt with pessimistic themes, they were regarded by naive intellectuals as innately more "artistic"

5–2. *The Grapes of Wrath* **(U.S.A., 1940),** *with Henry Fonda, directed by John Ford.*
Unlike the other studios, Twentieth Century–Fox was not adept at producing routine entertainments, which were often garish and perfunctorily produced at Fox, if usually profitable.
Darryl F. Zanuck, the studio's production chief, was more interested in quality productions—
so long as they turned a profit. His instincts were often shrewd, and he took risks—like pur-
chasing the rights to John Steinbeck's classic novel, a harsh and moving account of the Great
Depression. Fox's top director, John Ford, created many of his greatest works at the studio,
most notably *The Grapes of Wrath,* one of the crowning achievements of the American cinema.
(Twentieth Century–Fox)

than American pictures. Only after the late 1960s did such themes become popular
in the United States, thanks to America's tragic Vietnam adventure and the jarring
Watergate revelations of the early 1970s. Furthermore, unlike the foremost European filmmakers, who considered themselves serious artists, almost all Hollywood
artists preferred to think of themselves as professional entertainers, though in fact
a good number of them were well-educated and cultivated people.

Nonetheless, the stereotype persisted. "The people who make films don't do
it to ennoble man," wrote the French novelist André Malraux, "they are there to
make money. Consequently, inevitably, they work upon man's lower instincts." Perhaps what was most galling—though it was seldom openly acknowledged—was that
the best American movies often did both: They made money *and* ennobled man.
This hostility, then, was economically as well as aesthetically motivated. Between
the two world wars, American movies dominated more than 80 percent of the
world's screens and were more popular with foreign mass audiences than all but a
few natively produced movies. As much as 40 percent of the grosses of American
pictures was earned abroad, especially in Great Britain, which accounted for nearly
half the total foreign revenue of American films.

Thus, foreign producers and directors complained bitterly that they were being closed out of their own markets, that they were being oppressed by a form of "cultural colonization." Various theories were offered concerning the "mystery" of American movies, but as film historian Benjamin Hampton pointed out, the explanation was perfectly obvious: "The mystery is nothing but a willingness to give the public what it is willing to pay for instead of a desire to 'educate' the public against its will."

The American film industry was able to maintain this preeminence by minimizing the element of risk and maximizing the element of predictability in its movies. Guided by audience tastes—which could shift dramatically even within a brief time span—film producers devised three key concepts to ensure box office profits: (1) the studio system, designed to mass-produce films on an assembly-line basis; (2) the **star system,** the surest guarantee that the principal performers of a film would appeal to a wide audience; and (3) a system of **genres,** popular story types, which provided audiences with a general idea of the subject matter of any given movie.

The Studio System

The studio system was originally devised by Thomas Ince (see Chapter 2). Prior to his time, the production of movies in the United States was chaotic and uncoordinated. Almost from their inception, motion pictures were so popular with the public that there weren't enough of them to satisfy audience demand. New production and distribution companies sprouted like mushrooms, until by 1915 there were over two hundred of them in the United States. As the industry and the art grew more complex, the production of movies became more specialized. The earliest filmmakers were former actors, mechanics, and cameramen who improvised as they went along. The most successful of these eventually became directors, supervising the actual making of a movie from the creation of the story line to the coaching of the actors to the placement of the camera to the final assembly of shots into a coherent continuity.

Ince and others developed a factory system of production that was faster, more prolific, and—most importantly—dominated by financial backers rather than creative personnel, though the two weren't necessarily in conflict. With the rise of the star system in the teens, movies soon revolved around a popular player, with stories specially tailored by studio writers to enhance a star's box office appeal. Set designers, cinematographers, and specialized technicians relieved directors of many of their former responsibilities, allowing them to concentrate on the players and the placement of the camera. With the exception of the most prestigious directors and stars, who insisted upon greater artistic autonomy or simply went into independent production, movies by committee became the general rule.

Under the factory system, the key figure was usually the producer. By controlling the financing of a film, he also exercised significant control over how it would be made. However, the director generally still commanded the camera, and hence the **mise en scène** (i.e., the photographed images). By the mid-1920s, movies were big business, with a total capital investment of over $2 billion and an annual commerce of about $1.25 billion. The film industry was one of the top ten in America, a prominence it maintained for twenty-five years, the so-called golden age of the studio system.

In the earliest years of the film industry, its three main branches—production, distribution, and exhibition—were controlled by different interests. Producers sold their movies by the linear foot, irrespective of quality. The original distributors, called exchanges, were set up in key cities where, for a fee, exhibitors

5–3. *Trouble in Paradise* **(U.S.A., 1932),** *with Miriam Hopkins and Herbert Marshall (seated), directed by Ernst Lubitsch.*
Paramount was regarded as the most sophisticated studio in Hollywood. It was also the most "European," thanks in part to such emigré directors as Lubitsch, who did his finest work there. The studio's films were usually polished and elegantly mounted, the gowns (by Travis Banton) chic and sexy. Like many Paramount regulars, its gifted art director, Hans Dreier, received his early training at Germany's famous UFA, Paramount's sister studio.   *(Paramount Pictures)*

could swap their used prints for those of other theater owners. This system eventually proved too crude for the burgeoning industry. By the late teens, the most aggressive exhibitors and producers had begun to integrate all three phases of the business under one directorship—a method of consolidation known as **vertical integration.** This movement was spearheaded by such cunning businessmen as Adolph Zukor of Paramount Pictures, William Fox of the Fox Film Corporation, and Marcus Loew of Loew's Inc., the parent firm of what eventually became Metro-Goldwyn-Mayer.

Under Zukor's shrewd leadership, Paramount became the leading film company of the teens and twenties, with most of the biggest stars of the period under contract. As early as 1921, the company owned over four hundred theaters, most of them **first-run** city houses, which commanded the highest ticket prices and the largest audiences. Zukor also refined such concepts as **blind** and **block booking,** whereby even independent exhibitors were required to rent Paramount films—sight unseen—as a package rather than individually. The studio thus reduced its risk on any single production and also guaranteed a constant supply of product for exhibitors. (It wasn't until the late 1940s that the U.S. Supreme Court declared this system a monopoly and in restraint of trade. The Court ordered the studios to divest themselves of their theater chains and to cease the practices of blind and block booking.)

Other producers and exhibitors followed Zukor's example by merging their considerable resources. By 1929 only five companies, known in the trade as the Big Five or the **majors,** had a virtual monopoly on the industry, producing more than 90 percent of the fiction films in America. Paramount was responsible for about 25 percent of this output, a percentage matched by Warner Brothers, which had forged into prominence in 1927 with the introduction of talkies. Fox and MGM produced about 40 percent of the movies of that year. Radio-Keith-Orpheum, commonly known as RKO, was established in 1928 as a subsidiary of RCA, but despite this late start, it was capitalized at $80 million, boasted four production facilities, and like the other majors was fully integrated, with a chain of more than three hundred theaters. These five companies controlled more than 50 percent of the seating capacity in America, mostly in urban first-run houses, where the big money was earned. Of the remaining 10 percent of the movies made in 1929, most were produced by the so-called Little Three: Universal, Columbia, and United Artists.

5–4. *The Palm Beach Story* (**U.S.A., 1942**), *with Claudette Colbert, written and directed by Preston Sturges.*
Paramount was especially receptive to comedy. In addition to the screwball comedies of Sturges, it also produced the Jazz Age sex comedies of De Mille, the comedies of manners of Lubitsch, the movies of Mae West, much of W. C. Fields, the early (and best) Marx Brothers, the screwball comedies of Mitchell Leisen, the popular Bing Crosby–Bob Hope vehicles, and the early works of Billy Wilder. *(Paramount Pictures)*

The Hollywood studio system was modeled along the lines of "the American system of manufacture," introduced by Eli Whitney in the mass production of rifles. Henry Ford's concept of the assembly line in the manufacturing of autos was clearly derived from Whitney's ideas, and today, of course, these techniques are commonplace in virtually all forms of industrial mass production. The main features of this system are as follows: A product can be manufactured with greater efficiency and in far greater numbers if it's broken down into standardized interchangeable parts. These parts are assembled not by a single skilled artisan, but by ordinary workers who are responsible only for adding a simple component to the product, which is then passed along for ultimate completion by other workers on the assembly line. Except for an overseer of some sort, no one handles the product from beginning to end.

As several commentators have pointed out, this system works admirably in the production of rifles and autos, where uniformity and predictability are desirable. In the production of movies, however, standardization is inimical to artistic excellence, and often even to commercial success. Assembly-line methods worked most efficiently in the production of the so-called **program films.** Over half the movies

5–5. *The Public Enemy* (U.S.A., 1931), *with James Cagney and Edward Woods, directed by William Wellman.*
The ruling sensibility at Warner Brothers was masculine, tough, and proletarian. Their movies were usually fast-moving and stark. The decor was stripped to basics, the lighting in shadowy **low key.** Their films were also the most violent, especially their gangster movies, which provoked outcries from moralists and reformists. Over two hundred gangster films were made between 1930 and 1932, many of them by Warners, which came to be known as "the Depression studio" because its films picked up on the crisis of confidence of this era.   *(Warner Brothers)*

of the majors consisted of these routine formula pictures, which were also known as **B-movies** and programmers. Program films were seldom box office hits, but they were considered safe investments by the studios. From the early 1930s to the decline of the studio system in the 1950s, B-movies were commonly shown on the second half of double bills and were especially popular in provincial markets. "Poverty Row" studios like Monogram and Republic concentrated almost exclusively on the production of these cheapies, but the majors used them as testing grounds for the raw talent under contract. For the most part, these pictures featured lurid and infantile titles, were made on minuscule budgets, included lots of stock footage, and rarely featured important stars. Most of them took the form of staple genres, like westerns, thrillers, science-fiction, and horror movies. A handful of interesting films were produced in this form, but in general they were regarded even by the industry as a filler product.

Though all the studios attempted to standardize production as much as possible even for their important **A-films,** intelligent producers realized that the key ingredients of box office hits were usually style, boldness, and originality—hardly the qualities encouraged by the assembly-line method of production. In general, studio executives tried to steer a middle course, allowing their most prestigious (i.e.,

5–6. *Forty-Second Street* (**U.S.A., 1933**), *with Dick Powell, Bebe Daniels, and Warner Baxter, directed by Lloyd Bacon.*

"Torn from Today's headlines!" was Warners' motto during this era. It prided itself on reflecting today's concerns, not those of yesteryear. Even the musicals at this studio usually featured what James Cagney wistfully recalled as "a touch of the gutter." This backstage musical incorporated many contemporary anxieties concerning the economic hardships of the Depression. The musical numbers, choreographed and staged by Busby Berkeley, are whimsical and bizarre and, in their social relevance, definitively Warners. *(Warner Brothers)*

commercially successful) employees greater artistic autonomy, while their less accomplished colleagues were expected to do what they were told.

Each of the majors during the era of studio dominance was a virtual city-state, with vast holdings in land and buildings, standing **back lots,** and sound stages. Technical staffs and creative personnel were under long-term contract, and in such tightly organized studios as Warners and Columbia employees often ran rather than walked to their next assignments, so "efficiently" were they scheduled. Each studio had an array of specialized departments, such as publicity, costumes, editing, art design, story departments, and so on.

Most of the decision-making power rested with the "Front Office," which consisted of the studio head, the production chief, the producers, and their assistants. The temper of each studio was determined in part by the personality of the colorful moguls who ran their organizations autocratically. Virtually all of them were immigrants from Eastern Europe, or the sons of immigrants. Most of them were born in poverty and became self-made men whose tastes didn't differ radically from those of the masses who flocked to their movies. All of the moguls were shrewd businessmen, even though some, like William Fox, were barely literate. Others, like MGM's Louis B. Mayer, were incredibly philistine in their taste in movies. A few— like Hunt Stromberg of MGM, RKO's Pandro S. Berman, Hal B. Wallis of Warners and later Paramount—were men of considerable intelligence and taste. Such independent producers as David O. Selznick and Samuel Goldwyn were also admired for the quality of their films.

The production chief was the Front-Office executive who made most of the important decisions concerning what movies to make and how. He was sometimes given the title of vice-president in charge of production. Generally he supervised as many as fifty films per year and was responsible for all the main assignments, budget allocations, and the selection of key personnel for each project. He also made the important decisions concerning potential properties (i.e., novels, plays, and stories that might serve as sources for movies) and the principal emphasis of scripts. Furthermore, he had the final say about how a movie ought to be reshot, edited, scored, and publicized. All of these decisions were based on such considerations as the types of stars and directors under studio contract, the genres that were enjoying the greatest popularity during any given period, and the production chief's gut instincts about the box office.

The title of producer was one of the most ambiguous of the studio era. It could refer to a prestigious mogul or a glorified errand boy, depending on the individual. As a class, however, producers enjoyed more power within the industry than any other group. They were also among the highest paid, accounting for nearly 19 percent of the net profits of a studio. Virtually all of them were male. The rise to power of producers coincided with the rise of the studio system. In the mid-1920s, for example, there were only about 34 major producers in the industry. Ten years later, when the studio system was firmly entrenched, there were 220 of them, even though the studios produced 40 percent fewer pictures. Nepotism was common in the Front Offices of many studios, and a good number of associate and assistant producers were freeloading relatives of the company top brass.

Depending on the complexity of the studio, each Front Office had several producers, most of them specialists in a particular type of work: star vehicles, musicals, B-films, short subjects, **serials,** newsreels, and so on. These producers usually shaped the writing and rewriting of the script, had a major say in the casting, and often selected the cameraman, composer, and art designers. The producer and his assistants oversaw the director's day-to-day problems of filming, smoothing out difficulties if they were good at their jobs, creating more if they weren't. Producers superseded directors in the final cut of a film. If a director was sufficiently prestigious, he was at least consulted on many of these decisions; if he wasn't, he was informed of them.

There were two other types of Hollywood producers, and though they were few in number, they accounted for the majority of the best work in the industry. The so-called **creative producer** was usually a powerful mogul who supervised the production of a film in such exacting detail that he was virtually its artistic creator. Walt Disney and David O. Selznick were among the most famous of these. Selznick's *Gone With the Wind* was the top-grossing movie in history, a supremacy that remained unchallenged for years.

The top-echelon **producer-directors** created most of the artistically significant works of the studio era. By controlling the financing of their movies, they controlled virtually every aspect of their work, without making crippling concessions and compromises. Throughout the studio era, there were about thirty producer-directors, most of them working independently in the majors. They were among

5–7. *The Little Foxes* **(U.S.A., 1941),** *with Bette Davis, directed by William Wyler.*
To such rebellious artists as Warner Brothers' Bette Davis, the Front Office symbolized cautious mediocrity, for she had to fight to make most of her best films, often on loan-out to more adventurous producers, like Samuel Goldwyn, who produced this movie. She was frequently put on suspension by the equally intransigent Jack Warner for refusing to act in routine studio projects. Ironically, the movies she fought for usually made more money than the garbage fare favored by the Front Office. At this time most film stars were under exclusive seven-year contracts, which the studios—but not the stars—could cancel after six months' notice. Suspended employees were legally barred from working for others, and their suspension time was cruelly added to their seven-year terms. Davis claimed—with some justice—that she was trapped in perpetual servitude. *(RKO)*

5–8. *Top Hat* (U.S.A., 1935), *with Ginger Rogers and Fred Astaire, directed by Mark Sandrich.*
RKO was the smallest of the majors and one of the most financially unstable, primarily because it lacked continuity in its leadership. Its last owner, the frivolous playboy Howard Hughes, delivered the death blow in 1953. Americans weary of the Great Depression responded enthusiastically to RKO's nine Astaire–Rogers musicals, which were among the top-grossing films of the 1930s and helped keep the studio afloat during troubled times. The company's two best contract directors, George Stevens and Mark Sandrich, were among the most gifted in the industry. Many independent filmmakers and producers also worked through RKO, for it was traditionally the most hospitable of the majors to the producer-director system of production. RKO also boasted the finest **special effects** unit in the industry. Its brilliant art director, Van Nest Polglase, was strongly influenced by UFA's style, especially in his fondness for massive sets, unusual sources of light, and art deco geometrical designs.   *(RKO)*

the most admired artists in the industry—and also the most successful commercially, or they wouldn't have remained independent for long. In addition to controlling the staging and the placement of the camera (which was true even of most studio-employed directors), producer-directors had the final say about scripts, which they themselves often wrote, or at least closely supervised. In addition, they controlled the casting, scoring, and editing of their movies. Such autonomy was rare, as producer-director Frank Capra pointed out in 1939 in *The New York Times:* "I would say that 80% of the directors today shoot scenes exactly as they are told to shoot them without any changes whatsoever, and that 90% of them have no voice in the story or in the editing."

The studio system began its slow decline in the late 1940s, after the Supreme Court ordered the majors to divest themselves of their theater chains. Deprived of a guaranteed outlet for their product, the majors gradually were supplanted by more aggressive producers, most of them independents. One by one the stars left the studios, some to drift into obscurity, others to freelance successfully, a few to produce independently. In the early 1950s, television supplanted movies as the country's leading mass medium, siphoning off most of the so-called family audience, which had been the mainstay of the industry during the studio era.

The Star System

The star system isn't unique to movies. Virtually all the performing arts—live theater, television, opera, dance, concert music—have exploited the box office popularity of a charismatic or strikingly beautiful performer. In America, the star system has been the backbone of the film industry since the mid-teens. Stars are the creations of the public, its reigning favorites. Their influence in the fields of fashion, values, and public behavior has been enormous. "The social history of a nation can be written in terms of its film stars," Raymond Durgnat has observed. Stars confer instant consequence to any movie they appear in. Their fees have staggered the public. Stars like Tom Cruise and Julia Roberts command salaries of many millions per film, so popular are these box office giants. Like the ancient gods and goddesses, stars have been adored, envied, and venerated as mythic icons.

The majors viewed their stars as valuable investments, as "properties." Promising neophytes served an apprenticeship as "starlets," a term reserved for females, though male newcomers were subjected to the same treatment. They were often assigned a new name, were given a characteristic "look" (usually in imitation of a reigning favorite), and were taught how to talk, walk, and wear costumes. Frequently they had their social schedules arranged by the publicity department to insure maximum press exposure. Suitable "romances" were arranged to fuel the columns of the four hundred and more reporters who covered the Hollywood beat during the studio era.

Top stars attracted the loyalty of both men and women, though as sociologist Leo Handel pointed out, 65 percent of the fans preferred stars of their own sex. The studios received up to 32 million fan letters per week, 85 percent of them from young females. Major stars received about three thousand letters per week, and the volume of their mail was regarded as an accurate gauge of their popularity. The studios spent as much as $2 million a year processing these letters, most of which asked for autographed photos. Box office appeal was also determined by the number of fan clubs devoted to a star. During the early thirties, the stars with the greatest number of fan clubs were Clark Gable, Jean Harlow, and Joan Crawford. All of them were under contract to MGM, "The Home of the Stars." Gable alone had seventy clubs, which partly accounted for his supremacy as the top male star of the 1930s.

As a player's box office power increased, so did his or her demands. Top stars often had script approval stipulated in their contracts, as well as director, producer, and costar approval. Glamorous stars insisted on their own cameramen, who knew how to conceal physical defects and enhance virtues. Many insisted on their own clothes designers, hair stylists, and lavish dressing rooms. The biggest stars had movies especially tailored for them—the so-called star vehicle—thus guaranteeing maximum camera time. And of course they were paid enormous sums of money. In 1938, for example, there were over fifty stars who earned more than $100,000 a year. But the studios got much more. Shirley Temple made over $20 million for Twentieth Century–Fox in the late 1930s.

During the big studio era, most of the majors had a characteristic style, determined in part by the stars under contract. During the 1930s, sophisticated Paramount could boast such polished players as Claudette Colbert, Marlene Dietrich, Carole Lombard, Fredric March, and Cary Grant. Warners was a male-dominated studio, with an emphasis on fast-moving urban melodramas. Many of the stars here were the famous tough guys: Edward G. Robinson, James Cagney, Paul Muni, and

5–9. *Morocco* (U.S.A., 1930), *with Marlene Dietrich and Gary Cooper, directed by Josef von Sternberg.*
Good looks and sex appeal have always been the conspicuous traits of most film stars, and their vehicles are tailored to enhance their particular style of eroticism. Dietrich and von Sternberg were amused by the Trilby–Svengali publicity put out by Paramount Pictures, where they made six movies together in the 1930s. The publicity had some basis in fact, for the director used her as a virtual medium, like a musician and his instrument. No matter how preposterously she was costumed, he usually preserved her shimmering, ethereal beauty and provided at least one occasion for revealing the famous Dietrich gams. *(Paramount Pictures)*

Humphrey Bogart. Even the women at Warners had true grit: Bette Davis, Barbara Stanwyck, Ida Lupino, and Lauren Bacall. At MGM, both Mayer and Thalberg preferred glamorous female stars, Mayer because he could bully most of them, Thalberg because he had a romantic sensibility. Included among the many stars at Metro were Greta Garbo, Joan Crawford, Jean Harlow, Norma Shearer, the Barrymores, Clark Gable, Judy Garland, Mickey Rooney, Katharine Hepburn, Spencer Tracy, William Powell, and James Stewart.

From the beginning, stars were commonly classified into character types. Over the years, a vast repertory of types evolved: the Latin lover, the he-man, the heiress, the good bad girl, the cynical reporter, the career girl, and many others. Of course, all great stars are unique, even though they might fall under a well-known category. For example, the cheap blonde has long been one of America's favorite types, but such important stars as Mae West, Jean Harlow, and Marilyn Monroe are highly distinctive as individuals. A successful type was always imitated.

5–10. *Gone With the Wind* (U.S.A., 1939), *with Vivien Leigh and Hattie McDaniel, directed by Victor Fleming, produced by David O. Selznick.*
Black actors were invariably typecast during the studio era, usually as domestics and menials. In fact, film historian Donald Bogle has argued that all black performers played variations of only five basic types: Toms, coons, mulattoes, mammies, and bucks—the title of Bogle's book on the history of blacks in American movies. McDaniel was usually cast as a maid or a mammy, but within this narrow range she was outstanding. She won an Academy Award for her performance in *Gone With the Wind*—the first African-American player ever to win an Oscar. *(Metro-Goldwyn-Mayer)*

In the mid-1920s, for example, Greta Garbo supplanted such passé vamps as Theda Bara and Pola Negri in favor of a more sophisticated and complex type, the femme fatale. Garbo inspired many imitations, including such important stars as Dietrich and Lombard, who were first touted as "Garbo types," only with a sense of humor.

Stars commonly refused all parts that went against their type, especially if they were leading men or leading ladies. Performers like Gary Cooper would never have played cruel or psychopathic roles, for example, because such parts would have conflicted with his sympathetic image. If a star was locked into his or her type, any significant departure could result in box office disaster.

Many top stars stayed on top by being themselves, by not trying to impersonate anyone. Gable insisted that all he did in front of the camera was to "act natural"—which of course isn't easy at all. Similarly, Gary Cooper's sincerity and homespun decency attracted audiences for over three decades, and the **persona** he projected on the screen was virtually identical with his actual personality. Critics sometimes refer to this type of player as a **personality star (5–11).**

On the other hand, there were—and still are—many stars who refused to be typed and deliberately attempted the widest array of roles possible. Such **actor-stars** as Bette Davis, Katharine Hepburn, John Barrymore, and Edward G. Robinson sometimes played off-beat character roles rather than conventional leading parts in order to expand their range, for variety and breadth have traditionally been the yardsticks by which great acting is measured.

The distinction between a professional actor and a star is not based on technical skill, but on mass popularity. By definition, a star must have enormous personal magnetism, a riveting quality that commands our attention. Few public personalities have inspired such deep and widespread affection as the great movie stars. Some have been loved because they embodied such traditional American values as plain speaking, integrity, and idealism: Jimmy Stewart and Henry Fonda are examples of this type. Others have been identified with antiestablishment images, including such celebrated loners as Humphrey Bogart and John Garfield. Players like Cary Grant and Carole Lombard are so captivating in their charm that they're fun to watch in almost anything. And of course many of them are spectacularly good looking: Names like Garbo and Gable are virtually synonymous with godlike beauty.

Perhaps the ultimate glory for a star is to become an icon in American popular mythology. Like the gods and goddesses of ancient times, some stars are so uni-

5–11. *Red River* (**U.S.A., 1948**), *with John Wayne, directed by Howard Hawks.*

The top box office attractions tend to be personality stars, playing variations of the same character type. Wayne was the most popular star in film history. From 1949 to 1976, he was absent from the top ten only three times. "I play John Wayne in every part regardless of the character, and I've been doing okay, haven't I?" he once asked. In the public mind, he is the archetypal Westerner, a man of action—and violence—rather than words. His iconography is steeped in a distrust of sophistication and intellectuality. Confident of his identity, the Wayne character is chary of his honor and can intimidate by sheer massive presence. Beneath his brusqueness, however, is a sense of loneliness and isolation. His name is virtually synonymous with masculinity—though his persona suggests more of the warrior than the lover. As he grew older, he played more paternalistic figures, chivalrous to the ladies, though generally ill at ease in their presence. He also grew more human, developing his considerable talents as a comedian by mocking his own macho image. Wayne was fully aware of the enormous influence a star can wield in transmitting values, and in many of his films he embodied a right-wing ideology that made him a hero to conservative Americans. He was strongly pro-military in his sympathies and publicly applauded nationalism, guts, and self-sacrifice. *(United Artists)*

versally known that merely one name is enough to evoke an entire complex of symbolic associations—like *Marilyn* (5–12). Unlike the conventional actor (however talented), the star automatically suggests ideas and emotions that are deeply embedded in his or her persona. These undertones are determined not only by the star's previous roles, but often by his or her actual personality as well. Naturally, over the course of many years this symbolic information can begin to drain from public consciousness, but the **iconography** of a great star like Gary Cooper becomes part of a shared experience. As the French critic Edgar Morin pointed out, when Cooper played a character, he automatically "garycooperized" it, infusing himself into the role and the role into himself. Since audiences felt a deep sense of identification with Cooper and the values he symbolized, in a sense they were celebrating themselves—or at least their spiritual selves. The great originals are cultural **archetypes,** and their box office popularity is an index of their success in synthesizing the aspirations and anxieties of an era. As a number of cultural studies have shown, the iconography of a star can involve communal myths and symbols of considerable complexity and emotional richness.

5–12. *Gentlemen Prefer Blondes* **(U.S.A., 1953),** *with Marilyn Monroe, directed by Howard Hawks.*
After the 1950s, stars could no longer count on the studios to mold their careers. Twentieth Century–Fox's Marilyn Monroe was perhaps the last to benefit from—or endure—the buildup techniques developed by the majors. Unfortunately, the studio didn't know what to do with her. She appeared in a series of third-rate studio projects, but despite their mediocrity the public clamored for more Marilyn. She rightly blamed Fox for mismanaging her career. "Only the public can make a star. It's the studios who try to make a system out of it," she bitterly complained. She did her best work with strong directors, who knew how to exploit her considerable talents as a poignant comedienne.   *(Twentieth Century–Fox)*

The System of Genres

The system of genres, like the star system, isn't unique to movies. Most of the other arts are also classified generically. In the plastic arts, for example, there are figure studies, portraits, still-life drawings, landscapes, historical and mythological paintings, abstract expressionist canvases, and so on. Genres help to organize and focus the story materials and are distinguished by a characteristic set of conventions in style, values, and subject matter. Virtually all westerns, for example, deal with a specific era of American history—the western frontier of the late nineteenth century. Within any given genre, however, there can be different emphases and many variations. For example, *Stagecoach, High Noon,* and *Once Upon a Time in the West* are all westerns, but their differences outweigh their similarities. A genre is a loose set of expectations, then, not a divine injunction. That is, each example of a given story type is related to its predecessors, but not in iron-clad bondage. The great French critic André Bazin once referred to the western as "a form in search of a content." The same could be said of other genres.

Three genres were especially popular in the silent era—slapstick comedies, westerns, and melodramas. Wish-fulfillment played an important role in these movies, for the happy ending was almost invariable. Many of them centered on such rags-to-riches myths as the Horatio Alger story and its feminine counterpart, the Cinderella story. Many of these films were violent, grossly sentimental, and aesthetically crude.

Eventually more gifted artists filtered into the industry, and by the mid-teens, the range of dramatic materials was radically expanded, thanks largely to D. W. Griffith. Filmmakers learned to sharpen the narrative thrust of their movies by focusing almost exclusively on goal-oriented characters in a hurry to succeed. Griffith and his contemporaries devised a storytelling formula that could be applied to virtually any genre. Derived primarily from the live theater, this narrative formula is referred to by critics and scholars as the classical paradigm, or simply **classical cinema.**

The conventions of classical cinema are based on dramaturgical techniques that can be traced back to the theater of ancient Greece. Like most aesthetic conventions, they are general tendencies, not high commandments. Classical cinema is rigorously story oriented, posited on a heightened conflict between a protagonist who initiates the action and an antagonist who resists it. Classical narrative structures begin with an implied dramatic question: We want to know how the protagonist will get what he or she wants in the face of considerable opposition. The subsequent scenes intensify this conflict in a rising pattern of action. This escalation is treated in terms of cause and effect, with each scene implying a link to the next. Dramatic details that don't intensify the central conflict are suppressed or subordinated to an incidental function. The conflict builds to its maximum tension in the climax, at which point the protagonist and antagonist clash overtly. After their confrontation, the dramatic intensity subsides in the resolution. The story ends with some kind of formal closure—traditionally, a death in tragedies; a return to normalcy in domestic dramas; and a kiss, a dance, or a wedding in comedies. The final **shot**—because of its privileged position—is often meant to be an overview of some kind, a summing up of the significance of the previous materials.

Classical cinema emphasizes unity, plausibility, and coherence of its constituent parts. Each shot is seamlessly elided to the next in an effort to produce a smooth flow of action, and often a sense of inevitability. To add urgency to the situation, filmmakers sometimes include some kind of deadline that intensifies the emotion. Narrative structures are linear and often take the form of a journey, a chase, or a search. This formula is remarkably flexible and can be equally effective in a gangster film, a screwball comedy, or a musical.

In the earliest years of the silent cinema, filmmakers seldom worked from scripts, preferring to improvise around a sketchy generic outline, which they often carried in their heads. With the introduction of the studio system, the producer usually insisted that stories be outlined in greater detail, for in this way he could guarantee the box office appeal of the generic elements before the director began the actual filming. Genre was second only to stars in box office appeal. Eventually, the construction of the script was taken over by the producer and his hired scenarists, while the director was relegated to matters of execution. Even in the silent period, multiple authorship of scenarios was common. Under the studio system, it was almost invariable. Scripts were assembled rather than written, the collaboration of producers, directors, stars, and writers. Specialists were called in to doctor specific story problems. Some of these writers were idea people, others genre experts, dialogue writers, plot carpenters, comic relief specialists, and so on.

This type of multiple authorship was similar to how myths evolved in ancient times. Most movie genres explore recurring story patterns and myths that are typical of a given culture or period (5–13). The French anthropologist Claude Lévi-Strauss noted that myths have no author, no origin, no core axis—they allow "free play" in a variety of artistic forms. The American critic Parker Tyler defined a myth as "a free, unharnessed fiction, a basic, prototypic pattern capable of many variations and distortions, many betrayals and disguises, even though it remains *imaginative* truth." The stylized conventions and archetypal story patterns of genre films encourage us to participate ritualistically in the basic beliefs, fears, and anxieties of our culture and era.

5–13. *Scarlet Street* **(U.S.A., 1945),** *with Joan Bennett and Edward G. Robinson, directed by Fritz Lang.*
Some genres are relatively short-lived and seem to arise in response to a general social anxiety, then disappear when the anxiety subsides. The so-called deadly female picture was popular during World War II and shortly afterward. The rise of the genre correlated with the skyrocketing divorce rate during the war years and the postwar era. This type of picture deals with the ensnarement of a hapless male by a conniving seductress. Some of the best works of the American cinema are in this form, most notably *The Maltese Falcon, The Letter, The Lady from Shanghai, The Postman Always Rings Twice, Double Indemnity, The Woman in the Window, Gun Crazy, Human Desire,* and *Scarlet Street.* (*Universal Studios*)

During the big studio era, each of the majors had a story editor who headed the story department. His or her job was to scout potential properties for movies—mostly novels, plays, short stories, and magazine articles. During this period, literary properties were generally more prestigious than original screenplays. A novel or a stage drama was thought to have a presold audience. The most popular stories by far dealt with American life. For example, 481 of the 574 features produced in 1938–1939 were set in the United States. Literary sources were generally loosely adapted and made to conform to box office realities and the talent available to the producer.

The assembly-line method was employed with a vengeance in the construction of studio screenplays. During the script conference, the producer (and sometimes the director and stars, depending on their power) outlined what the principal emphasis of the story should be. A studio scribe then worked out a first draft. This was duly criticized and sent back for revision, often to another writer, and then to another, and so on. Action and plot generally took precedence over all, even at the expense of character consistency and probability. After the rough draft was completed, additional writers were instructed to sharpen the dialogue,

5–14. *Frankenstein* **(U.S.A., 1931),** *with Boris Karloff, directed by James Whale.*
Throughout the silent era, Universal Studios specialized in B-genre films, especially westerns. During the talkie era, they upgraded their production values and concentrated on horror movies, which usually dealt with the dangers of science and technology when not kept in check by humanistic values. *(Universal Studios)*

speed up the story, add comic relief, and render a host of other finishing touches.

Little wonder that studio writers enjoyed scant fame in the world of belles let-tres. Many thought of themselves as whores, hired hacks who wrote to order. Writers were the least powerful and least respected group in Hollywood during the studio era. They were also the best educated: Over 80 percent of them had college degrees. Torn by conflicting desires of greed and literary ambition, writers took masochistic delight in mocking themselves. A famous writer's lament has been attributed to a number of Hollywood wits: "They ruin your stories. They massacre your ideas. They prostitute your art. They trample on your pride. And what do you get for it? A fortune." Within the industry, writers were widely regarded as high-brows, with little or no sensitivity to the demands of the box office. They in turn complained that their scripts were vulgarized by clichéd formulas. Studio scribes usually weren't even allowed on the set while the director was filming.

Some of the best Hollywood writers eventually became directors to protect their scripts, especially after the success of writer-director Preston Sturges **(5–4).** Other important scenarists produced much of their finest work collaborating with producer-directors, who were usually more receptive to fresh story ideas. They were also more likely to prefer the writer to remain on the set in case of last-minute adjustments in the script. A number of scenarists frequently teamed with presti-gious directors: Robert Riskin with Capra **(5–15),** Ben Hecht with Hawks and Hitchcock, Dudley Nichols and Frank Nugent with Ford—all of them genre direc-tors.

The main problem with genre pictures of course is that they're easy to imitate and have been debased by stale mechanical repetition. Genre conventions are mere clichés unless they're united with significant innovations in style or content. But this is true of all the arts, not just movies. As Aristotle notes in *The Poetics,* gen-res are qualitatively neutral: The conventions of classical tragedy are basically the same whether they're employed by a genius or a forgotten hack. Certain genres enjoy more cultural prestige because they've attracted the most gifted artists. Gen-res that haven't are widely regarded as crude, but in many cases their déclassé sta-tus is due to neglect rather than to an innate inferiority. For example, the earliest film critics considered slapstick comedy an infantile genre—until such important comic artists as Chaplin and Keaton entered the field. Today, no critic would ma-lign the genre, for it boasts a considerable number of masterpieces.

The most critically admired genre films strike a balance between the form's preestablished conventions and the artist's unique contributions. The artists of an-cient Greece drew upon a common body of mythology, and no one thought it strange when dramatists and poets returned to these tales again and again. Incom-petent artists merely repeat. Serious artists reinterpret. By exploiting the broad outlines of a well-known tale or story type, the storyteller can play off its main fea-tures, creating provocative tensions between the genre's conventions and the artist's inventions, between the familiar and the original, the general and the par-ticular. Myths embody the common ideals and aspirations of a civilization, and by returning to these communal tales, the artist becomes, in a sense, a psychic ex-plorer, bridging the chasm between the known and the unknown.

Filmmakers are attracted to genres for the same reason they're attracted to stars: They automatically synthesize a vast amount of iconographical information, freeing the director to explore more personal concerns. A nongeneric movie must be more self-contained. The artist is forced to communicate virtually all the major

5–15. *It Happened One Night* (**U.S.A., 1934**), *with Clark Gable and Claudette Colbert, directed by Frank Capra.*

Genres can be classified according to subject matter, style, period, national origin, and a variety of other criteria. With this film, Capra inaugurated the era of screwball comedy. Its heyday was roughly from 1934 to 1945. Essentially love stories, these films featured zany but glamorous lovers, often from different social classes. More realistic than the slapstick of the silent era, screwball comedy is also more collaborative, requiring the sophisticated blending of talents of writers, actors, and directors. (This movie was scripted by Capra and Robert Riskin.) The snappy dialogue crackles with wit and speed. Sappy, sentimental speeches are often meant to deceive. The narrative premises are absurdly improbable, and the plots, which are intricate and filled with preposterous twists and turns, tend to snowball out of control. The movies center on a comic/romantic couple rather than a solitary protagonist. Often they are initially antagonistic, with one trying to outwit or outmaneuver the other. Much of the comedy results from the utter seriousness of the characters, who are usually unaware that they're funny. Sometimes one of them is engaged to a sexless prude or a humorless bore. This lends an urgency to the attraction between the coprotagonists, who are clearly made for each other. The genre usually includes a menagerie of secondary characters who are as wacky as the lovers. *(Columbia Pictures)*

ideas and emotions within the work itself—a task that preempts much of his screen time. On the other hand, genre artists never start from scratch. They can build upon the accomplishments of their predecessors, enriching their ideas or calling them into question. The most enduring genres tend to adapt to changing social conditions and can be classified by cycle phases: the primitive, the classical, the **revisionist,** and the parodic.

Some of the most suggestive critical studies have explored the relationship of a genre to the society and period that nurtured it. This sociopsychic approach was pioneered by the French literary critic Hippolyte Taine in the nineteenth century. Taine claimed that the social and intellectual preoccupations of a given era and nation will find expression in its art. The implicit function of an artist is to harmonize and reconcile cultural clashes of value. He believed that art must be analyzed for both its overt and covert meaning: Beneath its explicit content there exists a vast reservoir of latent social and psychic information. In the area of film, for example, genre critics have pointed out how gangster movies are often vehicles for exploring rebellion myths and are especially popular during periods of social breakdown **(5–16).**

The ideas of Sigmund Freud and Carl Jung have also influenced genre theorists. Like Taine, both psychiatrists believed that art is a reflection of underlying structures of meaning, that it satisfies certain subconscious needs in both the artist

5–16. *Scarface, Shame of a Nation* **(U.S.A., 1932),** *with Paul Muni, directed by Howard Hawks.*
Popular genres usually reflect the shared values and fears of the public. As social conditions change, genres often change with them, challenging some traditional customs and beliefs, reaffirming others. Gangster movies, for example, are often covert

critiques of American capitalism. The protagonists—usually played by small men—are likened to ruthless businessmen, their climb to power a sardonic parody of the Horatio Alger myth. During the Jazz Age, gangster films like *Underworld* (1927) dealt with the violence and glamour of the Prohibition era in an essentially apolitical manner. During the harshest years of the Depression, in the early 1930s, the genre became subversively ideological. Movies like *Scarface* reflected the country's shaken confidence in authority and traditional social institutions. In the final years of the Depression, gangster films like *Dead End* (1937) were pleas for liberal reform, arguing that crime was the result of broken homes, lack of opportunity, and slum living. Gangsters of all periods tend to suffer from an inability to relate to women, but during the 1940s, movies like *White Heat* (1949) featured protagonists who were outright sexual neurotics. In the 1950s, partly as a result of the highly publicized Kefauver Senate Crime Investigations, gangster movies like *The Phenix City Story* (1955) took the form of "confidential exposés" of syndicate crime. *The Godfather* (1972) and *The Godfather Part II* (1974) are a virtual recapitulation of the history of the genre and reflect the wary cynicism of a nation still numbed by the impact of the hypocritical hoax of Vietnam and the Watergate conspiracy. *Once Upon a Time in America* (1984) is a mythic treatment of the genre, as is *The Untouchables* (1987). *(United Artists)*

and the audience. For Freud, art was a form of daydreaming and wish fulfillment, the vicarious resolving of urgent impulses and desires that can't be satisfied in reality. Pornographic films are perhaps the most obvious example of how anxieties can be assuaged in this surrogate manner, and in fact Freud believed that most neuroses are sexually based. He thought that art is a by-product of neurosis, though essentially a socially beneficial one. Like neurosis, art is characterized by a repetition compulsion, the need to go over the same stories and rituals in order to reenact and temporarily resolve certain psychic conflicts, which are rooted in childhood traumas.

Jung began his career as a disciple of Freud, but eventually he broke away, believing that Freud's theories lacked a communal dimension. Jung was fascinated by myths, fairy tales, and folklore, which he believed contained symbols and story patterns that were universal to all individuals in all cultures and periods. According to Jung, unconscious complexes consist of archetypal symbols that are as deeply rooted and as inexplicable as instincts. He called this submerged reservoir of symbols the collective unconscious, which he thought had a primordial foundation, traceable to primitive times. Many of these archetypal patterns are bipolar and embody the basic concepts of religion, art, and society: God–Devil, light–dark, active–passive, male–female, static–dynamic, and so on. Jung believed that the artist consciously or unconsciously draws on these archetypes as raw materials, which must then be rendered into the generic forms favored by a given culture. He also believed that popular art offers the most unobstructed view of archetypes and myths, while elite art tends to submerge them beneath a complex surface detail. For Jung, every work of art is an infinitesimal exploration of a universal psychic experience—an instinctive groping toward an ancient wisdom.

FURTHER READING

BORDWELL, DAVID, KRISTIN THOMPSON, and JANET STAIGER. *The Classical Hollywood Cinema: Film Style and Mode of Production to 1960*. New York: Columbia University Press, 1985. A superb study of the big studio era.

DYER, RICHARD. *Heavenly Bodies: Film Stars and Society*. New York: St. Martin's Press, 1986; and *Stars*. London: British Film Institute, 1979. Two scholarly studies of the American star system.

GABLER, NEAL. *An Empire of Their Own*. New York: Crown Publishers, 1988. Subtitled *How the Jews Invented Hollywood*, this book deals with the moguls and how they created an idealistic image of America, its myths, values, and archetypes.

GOMERY, DOUGLAS. *The Hollywood Studio System*. New York: St. Martin's Press, 1986. A scholarly study of the major studios during its golden age, 1930–1949.

GRANT, BARRY K., ed. *Film Genre: Theory and Criticism*. Metuchen, N.J.: Scarecrow Press, 1977. A collection of scholarly essays, with bibliography.

IZOD, JOHN. *Hollywood and the Box Office, 1895–1986*. New York: Columbia University Press, 1988. The ways that money shaped the content of American movies.

JOWETT, GARTH. *Film: The Democratic Art*. Boston: Little, Brown and Company, 1976. A scholarly history of American film and its relation to the mass audience.

MORDDEN, ETHAN. *The Hollywood Studios*. New York: Alfred A. Knopf, 1988. House styles of the majors (and a few of the minors) during the golden age. Very well written.

ROSTEN, LEO. *Hollywood: The Movie Colony, the Movie Makers.* New York: Harcourt Brace, 1941. A sociological study of the studio system, crammed with facts and statistics.

SCHATZ, THOMAS. *The Genius of the System.* New York: Pantheon Books, 1989; and *Hollywood Genres: Formulas, Filmmaking, and the Studio System.* Philadelphia: Temple University Press, 1981. Include chapters on the western, the gangster film, detective thrillers, screwball comedies, the musical, and domestic melodramas.

6

American Cinema in the 1930s

The American cinema is essentially working class.
—PIERRE RENOIR

RKO

Timeline: 1930–1939

1930

Herbert Hoover (Republican) U.S. President (1929–1933)

U.S. population: 122 million

Robert Frost's *Collected Poems* (Pulitzer Prize)

American novelist Sinclair Lewis *(Babbitt)* wins Nobel Prize in Literature

1931

Empire State Building completed, New York City

1932

Democrat Franklin D. Roosevelt defeats President Hoover in a landslide: 472 electoral votes to 59;

Roosevelt (1933–1945) promises the country a "New Deal" to overcome the Depression

Popular song: "Brother, Can You Spare a Dime?"

1932–1933

The most severe depths of the Depression; U.S. unemployment: 13.7 million workers

1933

Repeal of Prohibition—"Happy Days Are Here Again" is the theme song of the Democrats

1935

Social Security Act—one of many New Deal legislative acts

George Gershwin's opera, *Porgy and Bess*

1936

Nobel Prize in Literature awarded to Eugene O'Neill

1937

Thornton Wilder's bittersweet play, *Our Town* (Pulitzer Prize)

1938

Orson Welles's radio show, "The War of the Worlds," panics many Americans, who believe the United States is being invaded by Martians

1939

Partly due to massive arms sales to Europe, the American economy gradually recovers from the Depression; Roosevelt declares U.S. neutrality in the European World War

Time of crisis: The Great Depression. More crises: the technology of sound conversion. Censorship institutionalized—the Production Code. Talkie genres: gangster movies, musicals, and screwball comedies. Fred Astaire. Naughty Mae West. Ace screenwriter Ben Hecht, the Bad Boy of Hollywood. Major filmmakers: Frank Capra, mythmaker. The Sophisticates: the sparkling wit of Ernst Lubitsch and the cool elegance of William Wyler. Howard Hawks, master of entertainment. American titan: the poetics of John Ford.

N INETEEN TWENTY-NINE WAS NOT THE BEST YEAR to be a movie mogul. By the end of the year, 8,700 theaters had been wired for sound, at great expense. Performers, technique, and technicians were all called into question by the advent of talkies. The people who ran the studios also had to worry about the effects of the stock market crash and the rising tide of demands for censorship.

The Talkie Era

The moguls dealt with the talkie problem by throwing money at several dozen Broadway stars and several dozen of the writers who wrote for them. The theory was that only men and women who had written and acted for the stage could successfully write and act for talkies. This conveniently overlooked the fact that few of the silent **stars** were vocal neophytes, and some of them had been stars in the live theater.

But the studio heads were not fools. They correctly sensed that they were now playing a completely different game. Many silent stars made the transition to sound; some didn't. But the *new* stars, the ones who were created by talkies, would never have been so successful in silent films as they were in sound. Actors like James Cagney, Clark Gable, or Spencer Tracy, actresses like Bette Davis, Carole Lombard, or Jean Harlow were of the people and by the people. No more could stars be worshipped as semideities because of their ethereal removal from everyday life. Dialogue made actors *real*, and the kind of dialogue that audiences fell in love with was tough, slangy, and above all, colloquial. For the first time, the life depicted on the screen was as feisty as American movie audiences always had been. Sound made the movies democratic.

And yet it was the vibrant street slang and the behavior that accompanied it that most alarmed censorship boards. The Hays Office had been formed in 1922 in response to three scandals that had rocked the small factory town that was Hollywood: the still-unsolved murder of director William Desmond Taylor, the trial of Roscoe "Fatty" Arbuckle for manslaughter, and the death by drugs of leading man Wallace Reid.

Will Hays, a politician from the Harding Administration, had been hired by the twelve film companies for his political connections rather than his relationship to the film world, which was nonexistent. Under Hays, self-regulation was the order of the day. His organization drew up a list of books and plays considered too touchy for screen adaptation and vowed "to prevent misleading, salacious or dishonest advertising."

Nothing much changed. The studios continued churning out **programmers** that exploited current themes like flaming youth drinking bootlegged gin in speakeasies. The industry pretended the rampant hypocrisy didn't exist. Even though the Hays Office maintained strictures against "pointed profanity—either by title or lips"—silent films like *Wings* and *What Price Glory?* were and are hilariously vulgar to anyone with the least skill at lip reading.

The Depression didn't really hit Hollywood until 1932. Company profits plummeted. Warner Brothers lost $14 million, compared to a 1929 profit of $17.2 million. Paramount lost nearly $16 million and went into bankruptcy the following year. This economic crisis forced the producers into a corner. They were also being pressured by the arrival on the scene of a diminutive, busty woman of middle years and unquenchable verbal lust—Mae West.

6–1. *Freaks* **(U.S.A., 1932),** *with Olga Baclanova (left), directed by Tod Browning.*
Browing was the screen's resident master of the grotesque throughout the 1920s and early 1930s. His movies with Lon Chaney were consistent winners with critics and public alike. When Browning's *Dracula* (1931) turned out to be an enormous hit for Universal, Irving Thalberg, production chief at MGM, determined to give Browning carte blanche. The result was *Freaks*—the story of the humanity of circus freaks and the selfish cruelty of "normal" people. It was and is a compassionate work, but the fact that Browning cast the film with authentic circus freaks was too much for audiences. The movie was critically reviled and a financial disaster. An embarrassed Metro sold the film to subdistributors, who packaged it as an exploitation picture. Browning's career was irreparably damaged, but *Freaks* remains a startling, disturbing moral tale.   *(Metro-Goldwyn-Mayer)*

6–2. *King Kong* (**U.S.A., 1933**), *directed by Ernest Schoedsack and Merian C. Cooper.*
Depression audiences were starved for fantasy—like a movie about a fifty-foot-tall ape on the
loose in New York City. But it was the expert stop-motion animation of Willis O'Brien that
gave the fanciful story believability and Kong himself personality. As Kong is torn to pieces by
dive-bombing biplanes and bids a gentle farewell to the toy-sized woman he loves, the movie
achieves a poignant sense of loss.   *(RKO)*

Caught between the rock of luring back their apparently vanishing audience
and the hard place of appeasing the Catholic church and censorious pressure
groups that were threatening boycotts in 1930, the producers created the
Production Code. It was administered by Joseph I. Breen, who worked hand in
hand with the slightly deemphasized Will Hays. The major companies agreed that
they would bar from their theaters any film that had not been passed by the Code
administration.

The tenets of the Code were many and varied. The excessive depiction of violence was out. So was sex: Even married couples had twin beds. Words like "sex,"
"hell," and "damn" were strictly forbidden, along with dozens of others. "Adultery
and illicit sex must not be explicitly treated or justified," the Production Code insisted. "Passion should be treated . . . so as not to stimulate the lower emotions."
With minor exceptions, like the films of Ernst Lubitsch, whose comedies of sexual
manners relied on the hint of a raised eyebrow rather than the specificity of dialogue, the Production Code became a demonstrable hurdle in the path of serious
adult filmmaking. Mostly, the street-wise gusto that had been the prime attribute of
the earliest talkies—and a major compensation for the loss of silent films—had to

be diverted into more stylized genres that were less threatening than, say, the gangster and his gun.

New Genres: Gangster Pictures, Musicals, Screwball Comedy

Gangster films hadn't been invented specifically for the talkies—von Sternberg's *Underworld* (1927) and Lewis Milestone's *The Racket* (1928) were both silent pictures. But the audible rat-tat-tat of machine guns and the stylized argot of tough-guy talk were an electrifying combination. In addition, the gangster's sneering disregard for society's conventions seemed entirely appropriate to a population whose faith in institutions like banks had been severely shaken.

The gangster cycle was begun by *Little Caesar* (1930), an archetypal story enlivened by the rat-terrier ferocity of Edward G. Robinson in the title role of a sociopath named Caesar Enrico Bandello. Beginning as a hired thug, Bandello works his way up the chain of command, murders his boss, enjoys a brief period when he boorishly savors his lofty position, then is destroyed by his own hubris and the tender ministrations of the law. Little Caesar, as his name implies, does what he does not for money but for status. "Money's all right, but it ain't everything," he snarls. "No, be somebody, know that a bunch of guys will do everything you tell 'em, have your own way or nothing."

In the end, Caesar is a walking dead man, riddled with bullets as he stumbles through the rain to die in the gutter, his final words, "Mother of Mercy, is this the end of Rico?" The stunned moment of truth, the look of dumb amazement in the eyes of an animal killed by a silent bullet, gives resonance to a simple rise-and-fall story that, with minor variations, was to be repeated in *Scarface* (1932) and *Public Enemy* (1931), the other jewels of the gangster Triple Crown.

Scarface was largely written by Ben Hecht, a newspaperman, novelist, and playwright whose command of vernacular was as absolute as his knack for breezy narrative. Hecht's dynamic, no-nonsense writing helped define both comic and dramatic genres for the decade and made him one of the prime artistic forces of the period. For instance, to the plot of *Scarface,* which was in bold outline the same as *Little Caesar,* Hecht added grotesque deadpan humor. Tony Camonte, known as Scarface, is a hilarious *gaffone*—Italian slang for a stupid lout. Hecht also added undertones of Camonte's incestuous desire for his sister. Briskly directed by Howard Hawks in a more stylish manner than the normally laconic Hawks brought to melodramas, *Scarface* made audiences watch with a kind of amused fascination.

Public Enemy grabbed audiences by the lapels and never let them go. Not because of the script—the same old story—but because of the entirely fluid and forceful direction of William A. Wellman and the bravura performance of James Cagney.

These three movies defined the parameters of the genre. Guns and cars are everywhere. Sexual relationships are abnormal, or else women are used as little more than receptacles for either passion or rage. Plotlines detail the rise and fall of Catholic immigrants, garrulously rolling over all obstacles to make a grab for that brass ring that was otherwise impossible to reach. A line Ben Hecht wrote for Tony Camonte sums up the 1930s gangster ethic: "Do it first, do it yourself and keep on doin' it."

Little Caesar, Scarface, and *The Public Enemy* were ironic variations on the American success story and a sign of the desperation of the times. There were scores of other gangster films made in little more than three years. However, with the public surfeited and newly strengthened censors making loud, threatening noises about the genre's violence, the gangster film became more explicitly moralistic, devoting less time to the glamorous nihilism of the Tony Camontes and more on how they got that way and what to do about it.

The genre began branching out, introducing a more liberal social perspective that saw environmental causes for the sociopath. Policemen became the new heroes, whereas before they had been either stooges or thugs who were little better than the men they were battling. Socially crusading films like *I Am a Fugitive from a Chain Gang* (1933) or Wellman's *Wild Boys of the Road* (1933) showed other aspects of the suffering proletariat. There would still be a few great gangster films—*Angels with Dirty Faces* (**6–3**) and *The Roaring Twenties* (1939)—but they were personal triumphs for James Cagney, who with his energy, spunk, and sense of furious rage was the quintessential star of a disenchanted decade.

In his essay "The Gangster as Tragic Hero," Robert Warshow deftly hit on why the gangster struck such a responsive chord in audiences and why he has, with time out for passing diversions, held our imagination ever since: "The gangster is the man of the city, with the city's language and knowledge, with its queer and dishonest skills and its terrible daring, carrying his life in his hands like a placard, like a club. . . . It is not the real city, but that dangerous and sad city of the imagination which is so much more important, which is the modern world."

The first musicals were literal transcriptions of Broadway shows and revues. Because *The Jazz Singer* had been the first successful part-talkie, the follow-ups, whether by Warners or others, tended to follow in the same pattern: declamatory, bombastic personalities in thin, colorful vehicles whose success depended on the quality or palatability of the performer. Nobody quite knew what else to do.

6–3. *Angels with Dirty Faces* (**U.S.A., 1938**), *with James Cagney and Pat O'Brien, directed by Michael Curtiz.*
More than any other actor, Cagney *was* the 1930s—bruised, without illusions, feisty, combative. Warners was the perfect studio for him. The lean meanness of the Warner gangster pictures was an extension of the studio's economic life. While plush MGM was earning profits of $7.6 million in 1935, Warners made do with $700,000. In 1937, a banner year, Warners made $5.9 million, but Metro tallied $14.4 million. The battles for money and power that stars like Cagney and Bette Davis launched against Warners were made all the more difficult because of the studio's thin profit margin—around $10,000 per picture in 1935. With just a slight difference in equilibrium, the studio could have come tumbling down. *(Warner Brothers)*

6–4. *The Merry Widow* (U.S.A., 1934), *with Maurice Chevalier, directed by Ernst Lubitsch.* Lubitsch's musicals rarely have big, splashy production numbers. The characters simply sing as a natural extension of speech, just as they fall in love as a natural extension of sex. Lubitsch agreed with Oscar Wilde, who observed that the chains of matrimony are so heavy it takes two to carry them—sometimes three. *(Paramount Pictures)*

Enter Paramount and ERNST LUBITSCH, as well as his lesser imitator Rouben Mamoulian. In *The Love Parade* (1929), Lubitsch created the first musical to be conceived in film terms. Basically, he brought the audience in on the joke and emphasized the essential unreality of what he was doing by having Maurice Chevalier comment on scenes as they progressed. In *Monte Carlo* (1930), when Jeanette MacDonald boards a train in an escape from an arranged marriage, Lubitsch creates an exhilarating sequence: The pulsing movement of the train turns into a rhythmical accompaniment for MacDonald as she sings "Beyond the Blue Horizon" at her open window, entrancing even the peasants working the fields who joyously wave at her.

Lubitsch's musicals, including his last, *The Merry Widow* **(6–4),** are dreams of perfection, "fairy tales without sorcery," as Ethan Mordden says. Like any good magician, Lubitsch announces that he is going to do something patently impossible and then smoothly does it, reducing every situation to its core, always leaving room for airy silliness. In *One Hour with You* (1932), Charlie Ruggles dresses up as Romeo for a perfectly normal dinner party because he was misinformed by his butler. "Why?" Ruggles asks. "Oh sir," says the butler, "I did *so* want to see you in tights."

But Paramount's musicals were continental, airy pastries in a frankly meat-and-potatoes environment. In any case, their racy innuendo was rendered impossible after the new Production Code was installed. The two great innovative stylists of the movie musical were Busby Berkeley and Fred Astaire, the first a choreographer, the second a dancer—*the* dancer.

BERKELEY (1895–1976) was initially hired away from Broadway by Sam Goldwyn to stage the musical sequences of *Whoopee* (1930). Berkeley first established his style in *42nd Street* (1933) and achieved apotheosis in the musical numbers of *Gold Diggers of 1935* **(6–5).** His style was made up of an alternating of the personal and the impersonal. His dancers were often brought into **closeup** in a kind of showgirl parade, but the dancer was rarely the defining agent of a Berkeley number: The camera was the star, soaring through space as Berkeley arranged his figures in lavishly kaleidoscopic, often geometric displays, using people as objects, objects as people. Either way, the camera did most of the dancing.

Berkeley's trademark was, in the words of Arlene Croce, "a visual orchestration of motifs inspirited by the lyrics of a song rather than the mechanics of the plot." In "The Shadow Waltz" of *Gold Diggers of 1935,* Berkeley had a hundred chorus girls playing a hundred neon violins, which climactically merge into one enormous neon violin, complete with bow. The film's finale, "Remember My Forgotten Man," is a sweeping, impressionistic montage of the plight of many veterans of World War I. Hundreds of doughboys are cast aside and ignored, reduced to cadging cigarettes on street corners, marching from battle into bread lines. Arranged in a sunburst series of ramps as Berkeley's camera **cranes** up and away, the soldiers and Joan Blondell, their advocate, raise their arms in supplication.

Stylistic abstraction and sociological content were brilliantly fused in the "Lullaby of Broadway" number of *Gold Diggers of 1935,* where the frenetically pursued night world of Manhattan leads to a fatal fall from a skyscraper. Berkeley at his best was a musical Eisenstein, working in terms that owed nothing to anything that had gone before, creating pure film out of pure imagination.

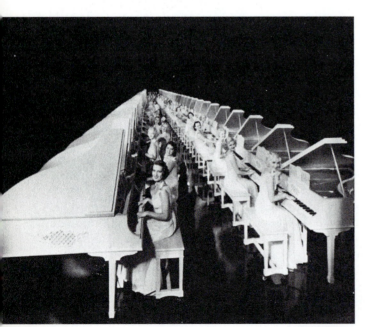

6–5. *The Gold Diggers of 1935* (**U.S.A., 1935),** *dances directed by Busby Berkeley.*
The pianos will shortly begin moving around the polished black floor, forming a dozen or so decorative patterns. Although Berkeley often went to extravagant lengths to achieve his visual ends, moving pianos into patterns was fairly simple. The instruments were dummies made out of plywood. Under each was a small man draped in black velvet moving his piano along predetermined patterns. Lots of rehearsals and presto! Musical magic.   *(Warner Brothers)*

FRED ASTAIRE (1899–1987) was the opposite of Berkeley. For Astaire, nothing was to interfere with the integrity of the performer. It was he who invented the dance musical. A successful Broadway performer, Astaire laid down one basic dictum: "Either the camera will dance or I will. But both of us at the same time—that won't work." In his earliest years at least, he insisted that the camera should be a recording agent, photographing a dance in no more than two or three smoothly flowing **shots.** His dances, amalgams of tap, ballroom, and swing, were unified by his own unerring sense of taste and elegance.

Astaire and Ginger Rogers, his most frequent partner in the decade, made nine films for RKO that served as the standard by which dance musicals are judged **(6–6).** Astaire was concerned with style, both in the manner of presenting the dance musical, its essentially theatrical nature as an uninterrupted lyrical line, and in his use of dance as *the* expressive element of a musical—a metaphor for character, courtship, love, and sex.

6–6. *Follow the Fleet* (**U.S.A., 1936**), *with Fred Astaire and Ginger Rogers, directed by Mark Sandrich.*
Moments from the dance number, "Let's Face the Music and Dance," to which Steve Martin and Bernadette Peters paid generous tribute in the underrated *Pennies from Heaven.* This is one of the simplest, gravest of Astaire's dances. Typically he does not mimic the music or illustrate the lyrics, but works *alongside* them in phrase patterns or occasionally in counterpoint. The distinguished dance critic Arlene Croce said: "Above everything else, he was a master dramatist. . . . At the core of their professionalism was a concentration on dance as dance, not as acrobatics or sexy poses or self-expression. Their absorption gave plausible life and seriousness to . . . lyric fantasy." For Astaire, dance was a means of communicating emotion between men and women.   *(RKO)*

Once the style of the dance musical was established, Astaire continued his innovations, always pushing against the boundaries of what the genre could do. In *Swing Time* (1936), arguably his finest film of the period, Astaire multiplies his image in a remarkable tribute to black dancer Bill Robinson, "Bojangles of Harlem." In 1938, Astaire introduced **slow motion** into dance musicals. What distinguished him in the decade of the 1930s and remains his true claim to greatness is the depth of romantic and erotic emotion Astaire could express through dance.

Enhanced by the art deco set designs in which Astaire and Rogers play out their stylized mating game, the dances and Astaire's solos are *true*, the happy endings seem earned, and their dramatic and romantic validity are the reasons the films were greeted with such joy when they were first released and why they can be viewed today with that emotion entirely undiminished.

Sound comedy differed in an elemental way from silent, if for no other reason than that the sight gag was replaced by the wisecrack. Comedy of the 1930s very much followed the environment created by gangster films and the backstage seediness of musicals like *42nd Street:* snarl, cynicism, and a lack of hypocrisy about the battle of the sexes. It was comedy made to explode in your face. Leading the way were the Marx Brothers and Mae West, dissimilar in that one thrived on chaos, the other on coolly timed *bon mots*, similar in that they both embodied a strong statement against hypocrisy.

MAE WEST (1892–1979) was a truly startling apparition, a woman who enjoyed sex and wasn't shy about letting the world know it **(6–7).** She was Theda Bara with a sense of humor, a Clara Bow who didn't lose her nerve by turning into the girl-next-door in the final reel. "Haven't you ever met a man who could make you happy?" Mae was asked. "Sure, lots of times," she said en route to singing songs like "I Wonder Where My Easy Rider's Gone" or "I Like a Man That Takes His Time."

West was one of the last actor-managers on Broadway and was used to controlling her own career. She was not about to change her ways for the movies. Her character always slavishly fascinated her leading men, which was part of the joke: She was short, not exactly slim, and far from beautiful. But *she* clearly thought she was devastating, and so—for the sake of ego and dramatic unity—did everyone else in her movies. Forty years later, the essential joke would be repeated with the Muppets character, Miss Piggy.

West wrote most of her films, which are basically devoted to showcasing Mae West. Beginning in 1934, strict enforcement of the Production Code dulled her outrageous iconoclasm, and by 1938 she was a hefty shadow of her pre-Code self. The industry and public alike seemed more comfortable with the conventional role of woman as suffering masochist, enacted by industry stalwarts like Joan Crawford and Norma Shearer.

But there were exceptions. Carole Lombard (1908–1942), a former Sennett bathing beauty, earned the lasting affection of her audience for her frank, natural sexuality and high spirits. She had a gift for delicate satire in what would come to be known as screwball comedies, logical outgrowths of the iconoclasm of the gangster films.

The conventions of screwball comedies were a variation on the theme of a world gone mad. Heiresses didn't want their inheritance, pet leopards carried names like "Baby," and women were more than a match for men. Two of the best screwball comedies were *Twentieth Century* (1934) and *Nothing Sacred* (1937), both written by the redoubtable Ben Hecht. *Twentieth Century* is structured as a series of

6–7. *She Done Him Wrong* (U.S.A., 1933), *with Mae West and Cary Grant, directed by Lowell Sherman.*
The cool, lecherous, and cynical Mae West was the battering ram used by the Catholic Legion of Decency to impel the industry to enforce the Production Code. So widespread was the alarm over Mae's lasciviousness that Mary Pickford went on record as saying that under no circumstances would she permit her teenage niece to see one of West's pictures. The joke kept turning in on itself. Personally, West was almost as highly sexed as her characters, and she lived in something of a fantasy world with herself at the center. Cary Grant said of her that "she was totally a creature of artifice." Aside from raucous laugh lines, West may simply have been writing reportage about Mae West.   *(Paramount Pictures)*

mutual humiliations inflicted by two glorious, certifiable crazies, the basis of whose madness is their employment in the theater **(6–8).** Their love, their hate, their jealousies are all phony, pretexts for the contemplation of their own faces simulating various emotions. The script is basically a rewrite of Hecht's earlier hit, *The Front Page,* and derives its strength from the playing of Lombard and John Barrymore.

Nothing Sacred is something a little more personal, a little different. Its protagonist is a reporter (Fredric March) recently exiled to obituaries because he wrote a phony story about an oriental potentate who was really a shoeshine boy ("Best Shine in Town" exults a racist headline next to an enormous picture of a black face). Desperate to get back to the big stories he needs to justify his ego, he seizes on Hazel Flagg (Lombard again). Because of a botched diagnosis by a drunken doctor, Hazel believes herself to be dying of radiation poisoning and wants to see New York once before she dies.

Hecht's dialogue rolls like a calliope. March's editor rages to him that "the hand of God, reaching down into the mire, couldn't elevate you to the depths of degradation." A night club, whose marquee announces "Tootsies of All Nations," presents a salute to Hazel's pluck in the face of her (supposed) cancer: a procession of burlesque beauties in outlandishly garish costumes—Lady Godiva, Pocahontas, Catherine the Great, and Katinka of Holland. Katinka of Holland? Sure. She saved her country from flooding by sticking her finger in a dike. When asked

6–8. *Twentieth Century* (U.S.A., 1934), *with John Barrymore and Carole Lombard, directed by Howard Hawks.*
John Barrymore (1882–1942) was one of those actors who comes along once in a generation. Superlatively equipped by nature to be an actor, he was able to play *Hamlet* or broad farce with equal conviction. The ease with which Barrymore accomplished what took others years to achieve rendered him incapable of respecting his own accomplishments. But his lack of respect for himself had one favorable by-product with his portrayal of Oscar Jaffe in *Twentieth Century*. A frenzied, antic manipulator, a capering creature of the live theater for whom art and artifice are indistinguishable, Jaffe is a whirlwind comic performance of great virtuosity and something of a self-caricature. Barrymore's health began fading soon after the movie was completed. Bedevilled by alcoholism, debts, and a fading memory, the man who was widely regarded as the greatest actor of his time gallantly, cockily played out his string to the end. *(Columbia Pictures)*

by the emcee to show the audience the famous finger, Katinka raises the middle finger of her right hand and, with a magnificent deadpan, does indeed show her audience the finger.

In time, the lack of moralizing or sentimentality became reverse conventions. *It Happened One Night* (1934) reveals the roots of the genre's subsequent dilution, with its homely American types and celebration of down-home values and eccentricities. In 1933, Leo McCarey directed the Marx Brothers in *Duck Soup,* their most overtly **surrealistic** assault on order and reason; by the time McCarey directed *The Awful Truth* (1937), he was operating on lower octane. The tenets of screwball comedy had been reduced to a few flourishes in a frothy domestic comedy of loyalty and love surviving divorce.

Where *Twentieth Century* and *Nothing Sacred* treated everyone with even-handed contempt, the comedy of *The Awful Truth* has gone soft at its center. It neatly divides those characters whose feelings are to be taken seriously (Cary Grant and Irene Dunne) from those who are butts (Ralph Bellamy). This was comedy made to reconcile, not threaten. As critic Andrew Bergman wrote, "these comedies became a means of unifying what had been splintered and divided. Their wackiness cemented social classes and broken marriages." The heartlessness that had been lavished on America by the laws of economics was reflected in the best of its

6–9. *A Night at the Opera* (U.S.A., 1935), *with (right to left) Groucho, Chico, and Harpo Marx, directed by Sam Wood.*
"The Marx Brothers were the legitimate descendants of the American iconoclastic tradition," wrote one critic, which is a nice way of saying that they tore apart whatever they happened upon. For the Marxes to succeed, they had to be placed in opposition to formalized environments that they could disrupt and destroy. The flagrantly disreputable Groucho got most of the laughs, and apart from his bent, gliding walk, his wit was almost entirely verbal. The Marx Brothers were more dependent on their writers than quieter, more behavioral comics like Laurel and Hardy. When the writing is good, as in *Monkey Business* (1931) or *A Night at the Opera,* the Marxes are good. When their writing is bad—almost everything after *At the Circus* (1937)—the Marx Brothers can make you realize how irritating and shallow pseudoabsurdism can be. Nomination for the funniest Groucho line: Margaret Dumont says to a Groucho loaded down with suitcases, "Have you got everything?" Groucho replies, "Well, I haven't had any complaints yet." *(Metro-Goldwyn-Mayer)*

popular art. As the Depression waned, this harshness was being replaced by something more hopeful, something that would be necessary for the taxing years of World War II.

Major Filmmakers

When sound was introduced, the studio moguls presumed that the people who had directed actors on stage should also direct them in talking pictures. For the next twelve to eighteen months, experienced silent film directors were forced into unemployment or had to endure the ignominy of having a codirector for the dialogue sequences. What killed this experiment in cross-pollination was, appropriately, its results. Logy, static, with entire **scenes** played out with one camera **setup,** the earliest sound pictures were a return to the *Film d'Art*. Much has been made about the technical problems imposed by the early microphones, of how it was thought necessary to keep the mikes still and group the actors around them, forcing the camera to sit still and endlessly record. But if 1928 was the year of mass changeover to sound, the movies like *The Bat Whispers* (1929), one of the most impressively fluid of early talkies, showed that the problem was at least as much a paralysis of the imagination as a crisis of technique. In any case, with a few exceptions like John Cromwell and George Cukor, the American film of the 1930s, as both art and industry, was guided by artists who had already achieved notice in silent films **(6–10).**

FRANK CAPRA (1897–1992) came to America from Sicily at the age of six. He grew to love his adopted land with that passion peculiar to immigrants, who see only the virtues and few of the vices of their new homeland. After World War I, Capra roamed the country, seeing "the deserts, the mountains. . . . the people who were working and not complaining. I met a lot of Gary Coopers," he remembered.

Working as a gag man for Mack Sennett led him to collaborating with Harry Langdon. When Langdon left Sennett to make independent features in 1926, Capra went with him, first as a writer, then as a director. Capra's silent pictures like *The Strong Man* (1926) and *That Certain Thing* (1928) already show his characteristic zest and skill with actors, but Capra's was a talent that needed sound to express fully his vision of the hurly-burly aspirations of the human circus.

Capra's films of the decade, like *It Happened One Night* (1934), *Mr. Deeds Goes to Town* (1936), and *Mr. Smith Goes to Washington* **(6–12)** marked him as the American cinema's Brueghel, painting the story of the trials of the downtrodden in colorful, broad strokes. The movies are energetic, irreverent poems to a civics-lesson America. Evil is usually represented by one nasty banker or politician; once he is vanquished, the way is clear for the triumph of decency. Capra's world is a middle-

6–10. *It's a Gift* (U.S.A., 1934), *with W. C. Fields (left), directed by Norman McLeod.*

Fields was evenhanded in the manner in which he assaulted minority groups, wives, girlfriends, morons, children, bankers, lawyers, short people, and, especially, himself. Originally a juggler in vaudeville, Fields devised a screen character of a perennially put-upon, middle-aged wastrel who, more than anything, wanted to be left alone to booze. Mildly successful in silent films, he carved out a tidy niche for himself in talkies, writing the stories for his modestly budgeted pictures himself. Because his movies weren't very expensive and thus occupied a peripheral place in the film-making firmament, the writer/actor was allowed to exercise his alternatively passive and snarling iconoclasm in comparative freedom. In his quiet way, Fields was the *sotto voce* flip side of the sleazy bravado of Groucho Marx. Both comics punched holes in America's most beloved traditions. At their best, both were also very funny. *(Universal Pictures)*

6–11. *For Whom the Bell Tolls* (U.S.A., 1943), *with Gary Cooper, directed by Sam Wood.*

Although Cooper achieved stardom in silent pictures, his deep, grave voice cemented his status as one of America's most beloved male stars. Strong yet capable of expressing doubt, heroic but not in an ostentatious way, Cooper had an appeal that was similar to John Wayne's, except Cooper was less truculent, more quietly noble. He played archetypal heroes like Lou Gehrig, or Hemingway's Robert Jordan in *For Whom the Bell Tolls*. Age gave Cooper an attractive vulnerability, as in *High Noon* (1952). His death in 1961 signaled the beginning of the end for the age of screen heroes. *(Paramount Pictures)*

class one of marriage, family, the neighborhood—all very much springing from nineteenth-century **archetypes.**

As Stephen Handzo points out, although thematically Capra is a fabulist dealing with mythic materials, stylistically he is quite realistic. Roadside taverns look like roadside taverns; bums are authentically whiskered and bedraggled; and for *Mr. Smith Goes to Washington,* Capra built a perfect replica of the Senate chambers whose veracity is still startling.

Despite the fairy-tale sugarcoating of most of Capra's films, there are darker overtones, especially in movies featuring James Stewart, whose qualities of edgy, impassioned desperation gave films like *Mr. Smith* and the later *It's a Wonderful Life* **(6–13)** a neurotic quality that a more passive leading man like Gary Cooper would have been unable to provide.

Capra's pictures were popular with audiences but divided critics then and now. Otis Ferguson, one of the best critics of his day, singled out Capra's timing, his accent, "the instinct for the swing of the words . . . that makes everything so natural and irresistible." James Agee countered by grumbling about Capra's "Christian semi-socialism [whose] chief mistake—is its refusal to face the fact that evil is intrinsic in each individual."

An unhappy ending was both a moral and practical impossibility for an optimist like Capra. His vision—his morality plays of loss followed by reclamation—particularly suited the Depression era, with its legions of dispossessed trying to understand what had gone wrong, trying to explain themselves to themselves. Capra's message to them was "stand up, stick your chest out, fight for what you know is right." Hardly advice calculated to plumb the psychological or philosophical

6–12. *Mr. Smith Goes to Washington* (**U.S.A., 1939**), *with James Stewart (standing center), directed by Frank Capra.*
Stewart's Mr. Smith is stalwart and loyal, but with a quota of idealism and a capacity for rage that borders on the obsessional. The actor had a gift for enacting passion that never lessened with the years. Jefferson Smith is a romantic, a dreamer; he tries to live by "one plain, simple rule: Love Thy Neighbor." Capra's attitude toward his heroes was by no means a mindless endorsement. He believed they lack a pragmatic sense of reality, but such idealists are necessary in the dialectical search for the truth: "Between the idealist and the pragmatist—somewhere in between—lies the truth, and they are often rubbing against each other."   *(Columbia Pictures)*

depths, but his messianic belief in that message and in the country that made it possible for him to promulgate it placed him among the most popular filmmakers in the world.

World War II, and what it revealed, seemed to shake Capra's faith in an elemental way. In *It's a Wonderful Life,* he wrestled with the theme of the worth and courage of an obedient, decent life and did it with remarkable psychological acuity and depth of feeling. The final affirmative verdict the film reaches seemed to have exhausted the director. The rest of his movies are negligible. "Sometimes," said actor-director John Cassavetes, "I'm not sure that there's ever been an America. Sometimes I just think it's all been Frank Capra movies."

Aside from the scintillating musicals that have already been noted, Lubitsch made several of his superior exercises in champagne cinema in this period—witty, attractive people coupling and uncoupling with quizzical grace. At one point, he even took over as production chief at Paramount for a year, the only director to

6–13. *It's a Wonderful Life* (**U.S.A., 1946**), *with James Stewart and Donna Reed, directed by Frank Capra.*
One of the joys of the old Hollywood was the excellence of its character actors. In this scene from Capra's favorite film (and Stewart's as well) can be seen veterans of hundreds of movies—Ward Bond (the cop), H. B. Warner (holding fishbowl), Beulah Bondi (next to Warner), Thomas Mitchell (next to Bondi), and Frank Faylen (between Bondi and Mitchell). They were all expert actors, fully capable of playing high drama or low comedy. The sight of any of them was reassuring and provided a continuity beyond story or stars, making the movies a kind of second neighborhood for millions. *(RKO)*

function as an executive in this era, and one of the few in film history. Lubitsch's influence spawned a tradition of gossamer comedy at Paramount, which would not be dispelled until the arrival of Preston Sturges in 1940.

Despite its stylization, Lubitsch's comedy is never cold or brittle. His 1940 film, *The Shop Around the Corner,* a bittersweet tale of the lives and hopes of the employees of a Budapest luggage store, perfectly captures the precarious social and financial status of the European petit-bourgeoisie in a way that many more overtly theme-oriented films from postwar Europe did not. Lubitsch's most popular film of the period was *Ninotchka* (1939), famous as the movie in which Garbo laughed for the first time on the screen. The picture is just as notable for the humanity of its supporting cast.

A more personal project was *To Be or Not To Be* (1942), the last film of Carole Lombard and the best of Jack Benny. Basically, the film is a loving tribute to the live theater and its inhabitants—actors afflicted with the incomparable tunnel vision of egomania, caught up amidst the humorless brutality of Nazi-occupied Poland. The film was slammed on its release for the "bad taste" of its dialogue, like the retort of

6–14. *Frank Capra (wearing trenchcoat), Max Steiner (pointing), and Dimitri Tiomkin (next to Steiner) at the music scoring session for Lost Horizon* (1937).
The concept of musical underscoring for film took several years after the introduction of sound to establish itself, but by the mid-1930s, underscoring was an accepted convention. Master film composers like Steiner, Tiomkin, and Erich Wolfgang Korngold specialized in thickly orchestrated, Wagnerian thematics that could make even bad films watchable and, because of the music's considerable emotional power, good films great. Composers like Franz Waxman and Bernard Herrmann adopted less emotional but nonetheless evocative techniques. In the 1950s and 1960s, tastes changed: Full orchestral scores went out of fashion and were replaced by song scores or more tinkly, less bombastic confections. Jazz also had a brief vogue. But the orchestral score made a comeback in the 1970s and 1980s, led by composers like the superb, inventive Jerry Goldsmith and John Williams, who appropriated many orchestration techniques from composers like Korngold and Steiner.   *(Columbia Pictures)*

a Nazi who recalls the performance of a preening ham actor (Benny) by saying, "What he did to Shakespeare, we are doing to Poland." Lubitsch was committing the grievous sin of being ahead of his time, using black humor before it had been invented. Worse, he had refused to make a simple propaganda picture of the sort that were flooding America's screens—pictures long forgotten except as sociological artifacts. *To Be or Not To Be* is a finer work of comic satire than practically anything of its—or our—time, including Chaplin's own brave attempt at ridiculing the Nazis, *The Great Dictator* (1940).

Lubitsch made several more movies before his premature death from a heart attack, including the sweet, underrated *Cluny Brown* (1946) and *Heaven Can Wait* (1943), a loving treatise on the gentle benefits of roguish irresponsibility. But Lubitsch's respect and affection for humanity, no matter how self-absorbed or foolish, never glowed brighter than in *To Be or Not To Be.*

The critic Richard Roud has referred to WILLIAM WYLER (1902–1981) as "a ten year man," and the ten years he was referring to were 1936–1946, a decade of achievement that had been preceded by **program pictures.** Wyler came to international prominence with an unusually sober, low-key film, *Dodsworth* (1936), unusual in that it's the story of a good man going through what today would be called male menopause. There is no particular "hook" to the movie, either in terms of narrative or character, just decent human beings trying to understand why they're not happy, a dilemma illuminated by superior performances, especially by Walter Huston.

With time out for the melodrama of *Dead End* (1937), Wyler then made *Jezebel* (1938), *Wuthering Heights* (1939), *The Letter* (1940), and *The Little Foxes* **(6–15).** After the propaganda picture *Mrs. Miniver* (1942) and two war documentaries, Wyler made *The Best Years of Our Lives* (1946), his masterpiece and perhaps the only **epic** film about the American middle class.

With two exceptions, these movies were made in collaboration with producer Sam Goldwyn and cameraman Gregg Toland. In these works, Wyler evolved an austere style involving the use of **lengthy takes, deep-focus** photography, and few **closeups.** This stylistic economy reduced the number of cuts in a given film, creating an effect of seamless unity. Wyler emphasized the mingling of characters rather than the highlighting of stars, an organic dramatic ebb and flow rather than the conventional rising action moving toward a single climax. This style made serious demands on Wyler's actors, and the director soon became an object of much exhausted disgruntlement for the many **takes** he regularly demanded to achieve the unified level of performance his rigorous style required.

Wyler's style was hailed by European theorists as *the* alternative to conventional editing and was especially championed by the French critic André Bazin. As important as Wyler's style was his sense of the single detail that makes a scene come alive. Emotional authenticity and mood were all-important to him. In *The Letter,* the story of an unfaithful wife's murder of her lover, Wyler spends the first few moments of the film creating the stifling, hothouse atmosphere of Malaysia. The natives sway gently in their hammocks, rubber drips slowly down a tree, while the moon, full and indecently bright, illuminates the somnolent scene, which is suddenly transformed by gunshots. Wyler reined in the normally flamboyant Bette Davis, forcing her into defining a clinical exercise in repression. Her character's erotic nature is hidden behind a prim, fastidious demeanor, her fingers stitching a lace bedspread, "each tiny oval . . . a symbol of her will power, ability to build a pattern of deceit and method of steadying her nerves," as critic Charles Higham pointed out.

Wyler's favorite material—rather literary, psychologically oriented character studies—executed with the directorial equivalent of *le mot juste,* the precisely correct camera angle or acutely observed behavioral detail, appeared slightly old-fashioned after World War II. Younger directors like Elia Kazan and Robert Aldrich often had similar thematic concerns but expressed them in more kinetic terms and acting styles. By the time of the late 1950s and such bloated commercial pictures as *Ben-Hur* (1959), Wyler had been relegated to the ranks of stodgy traditionalists, at least by American critics.

6–15. *The Little Foxes* (**U.S.A., 1941**), *with Bette Davis, directed by William Wyler.*
Although Davis prided herself on the diversity of her roles, she was most famous for playing
women who refuse to allow their wills to be thwarted. Her bravura style was intensely physical, punctuated with abrupt, restless movements. Her gestures were almost always decisive,
razor-sharp. For example, she didn't just smoke a cigarette, she attacked it, inhaling deeply
while her nervous darting eyes sized up her opponent. Even when she was still, her hands
often clenched and unclenched at the sides of her tense body. Her speech was fast, brittle, the
words spewed out in a precise, clipped, diction. She was one of the few stars of her era who
enjoyed playing villainess roles. The character of Regina Giddens in *The Little Foxes* is essentially in this same mold, but the setting of the story—the American South in 1900—precluded
the possibility of her using such mannerisms. Regina's fury had to be internalized. Her exterior conforms to the bourgeois ideal of womanhood in the Gibson era, but it conceals a spirit
smoldering in resentment. Her body is imprisoned in tightly corseted gowns, restricting her
freedom. Her face is powdered to a ghostly pallor, her mouth a mean slash of red. It is a mask-
like face, with only the hooded eyes betraying her contempt for weakness, especially in men.
In this shot, Wyler's dramatic scene proceeds in a direct line from the conflicts set up by his
composition. The monstrous Regina takes her ease while coolly pulling the strings of her
brothers and nephew. *(RKO)*

6–16. *The Heiress* (**U.S.A., 1949**), *with Ralph Richardson (seated), directed by William Wyler.*
Wyler's preference for deep-focus photography allowed him to present his scenes more objectively, without the value judgments implicit in a fragmented sequence of close shots. In this scene, for example, an edited sequence would probably focus on the faces of the two characters at the exclusion of the rather undramatic physical context. But Wyler deliberately included the empty tables and chairs as well as the waiting carriage in this shot, thus encouraging the viewer to conclude that there's a subtle interrelationship between them and the heroine's arrogant but lonely father (Richardson).   *(Paramount Pictures)*

His international reputation remained constant. In his prime, with pictures like *Dodsworth, The Best Years of Our Lives,* and *The Heiress* **(6–16),** Wyler had something approaching genius in creating precise ensemble acting and at evoking the consternation in the heart of characters saddened by the fact that, in some elemental way, their homes will never truly be their homes again.

For most of his career, HOWARD HAWKS (1896–1977) worked as an independent **producer-director** with a good amount of financial success and with a critical and industry reputation as a skilled craftsman. By the time of his death, Hawks had been recognized as a major talent by critics at home and virtually canonized by those in Europe, especially France and Great Britain. European critics interpreted his recurring story structures, slightly sadistic sense of humor, and fondness for dealing with male group friendships as quintessentially American and archetypal. Hawks himself was nonplussed by all the adulation. "I try to tell a story as simply as possible, with the camera at eye level," he insisted. "I think a director's a story-

6–17. *Scarface* (U.S.A., 1932), *with Paul Muni and Ann Dvorak, directed by Howard Hawks.*
Begun in 1930, Hawks's movie was tied up for over a year by censorship difficulties. Here, the delicate lace curtains contrast with the raging desires of the rapidly unhinging Tony Camonte, whose paranoia has cost him his criminal empire and whose incestuous feelings for his sister cost him the life of his best friend. *(United Artists)*

teller, and if he tells a story that people can't understand, then he shouldn't be a director."

Hawks actually started out to be an engineer, and that logical, methodical mindset carried over into his movie career. A flyer, an auto racer, an outdoorsman, he made films that were about the kind of men he himself was: competent, self-possessed, not given to ostentatious display.

Indifferently successful in silent films, Hawks first achieved notice with *The Dawn Patrol* (1930), a detailed story of the disintegration brought on by the remorseless responsibilities of military command during wartime. He really came into his own with *Scarface* (6–17), Hawks's own favorite of his movies, an explosively violent, cynical, and sharply characterized film, which is as much black comedy as gangster melodrama. With the exception of an uncharacteristic long-take opening shot that is indebted to German **expressionism,** *Scarface* captures Hawks at his best.

Hawks's terseness and quietly heroic men and women caused some critics to compare him to Hemingway, a friend whose indifferent novel *To Have and Have Not* was adapted by Hawks. But the analogy is too thin. Hawks's films are usually about grace under pressure, Hemingway's definition of courage. But the films never venture into the metaphor or myth that gave the novelist—or a truly Hemingwayesque filmmaker like John Huston—a philosophical resonance that transcends style or story. Hawks's movies are about what they're about, and that's all. He liked it that way.

The 1930s were a period when the director made some of the finest screwball comedies with movies like *Twentieth Century* and *Bringing Up Baby* (1938), stories of desperate pursuers and the frantic pursued, with the laughter coming from the disparity between ardor and inertia. "I don't write funny lines," Hawks said. "It's much easier to get comedy if you don't start out trying to be funny. . . . I think that's committing suicide." Hawks called this style "three-cushion," after a technique in pool, meaning that emotions and ambitions are obliquely expressed. Comedy or drama, Hawks treated it all with equal gravity; he just played comedy faster.

Hawks's women exhibit independence as well as other traditionally "masculine" traits, at least partially because of the director's total lack of interest in conventional domestic life. Hawks's women are as gutsy and tough-minded as his men. As critic Jean-Pierre Coursodon put it, "efficiency is substituted for sexuality."

Although he made only five, Hawks's westerns like *Red River* (6–18) and *Rio Bravo* (1959) have sometimes been ranked with those of the master of the genre,

6–18. *Red River* **(U.S.A., 1948),** *with John Wayne, Montgomery Clift, and Walter Brennan, directed by Howard Hawks.*
John Wayne always moved with the lithe grace of a big cat, and Hawks gambled that the diminutive, coiled intensity of the young stage star Montgomery Clift would provide the necessary tension that this film needed. The contrast worked, and *Red River* provided the impetus for Wayne to continue his career as a character actor for the next thirty years. In the 1950s, the career of Clift was derailed by an auto accident that marred his looks and drove the unstable actor to excessive drinking and drug abuse. *(United Artists)*

John Ford. But where Ford's westerns are rolling, loosely structured, almost ballad-like, Hawks's works in this genre exhibit his usual concise sense of plot and verbal and visual economy. Ford's films feature deeply flawed characters who fail as often as they succeed, while Hawks's may be flawed but they invariably emerge triumphant. Hawks himself thought such comparisons with Ford flattering but inaccurate.

In truth, Hawks's was a narrow talent. Early in his career, he discovered what it was he did well, and he rarely deviated from that familiar ground. But on that ground, of dignified, taciturn men struggling to maintain their self-respect in either a dramatic or comic context, he was something of a master. Don Siegel, a later director who himself embodied many of Hawks's qualities, said of him: "He looked like a director, he acted like a director, he talked like a director, and he was a damn good director."

6–19. *The Informer* **(U.S.A., 1935),** *with Victor McLaglen (right), directed by John Ford.*
When Ford worked with subjects involving Irish Catholicism, his lighting style was usually
moody, expressionistic. Throughout this film, he used a thick, drifting fog to symbolize the
confusion and isolation of Gypo Nolan, the informer. Of all his collaborators, Ford was most
sympathetic and generous to his cameramen, a Who's Who of great American cinematographers: Gregg Toland, Joe August, Arthur Miller, Bert Glennon, William Clothier, and Winton
Hoch. Dozens of interviewers attempted to get Ford to discuss his work, but one of the few
comments he made about his artistic talent was short and sweet: He had, he admitted, "an eye
for composition." *(RKO)*

The creative history of American movies is a subtle struggle between pragma-
tism and idealism. No director straddled these usually disparate poles more successfully than JOHN FORD (1895–1973), an irascible Irishman whom writer George
Sadoul called "a titan of the American cinema." In a career that exceeded fifty
years, Ford created a uniquely American **oeuvre**—films of a rough simplicity, with
intimately observed characters who could be as big as the spires of Ford's beloved
Monument Valley or as petulant as children. Ford captured landscapes with a lyricism and compositional beauty rarely matched in cinema. His themes of family,
duty, and stubborn individualism, his barely concealed suspicion of the present
made him the nostalgic poet who most effectively captured a sense of time lost and
time remembered, of the breadth of the American experience.

Ford first attracted attention with *The Iron Horse* (1924), an epic western of
the transcontinental railroad, which, while not as forcefully personal as his later
works, still has the power to grip because of its compelling narrative sweep and
wealth of period detail. The Ford of the silent era was a competent all-rounder who
could direct almost anything. He was initially influenced by Griffith. (Ford rode as
one of the Clansmen in *The Birth of a Nation*.) Ford's early work showed the same
fresh playing, the same originality of gesture and visual detail as the work of his former boss. Later, Ford's *Hangman's House* (1928), a story of the Irish "troubles," very

much reflects the dark, mist-shrouded manner of Murnau, who, like Ford, was working at the Fox studios.

For Ford, the camera was "an information booth. I like to keep it still and have the characters come to it and tell their story." The compositions are painterly and in-depth, often in deep focus. But it was not until the middle of the 1930s that Ford matured and hit his stride in films that effortlessly combined the naturalistic and the poetic. For example, *Judge Priest* (1934) has the leisurely, ambling narrative and bemused, lonely characters that would become typical. In one scene, Will Rogers's Judge Priest is speaking to a picture of his dead wife, telling her some events of the day. He notices his nephew and his nephew's girlfriend courting in the moonlight and grows lonely. The judge picks up a stool and walks out to the country graveyard to continue the conversation and be a little bit closer to his love.

Ford's first enormous critical hit was *The Informer* **(6–19),** a moody, expressionistic studio piece about an unthinking brute of a man who destroys his own life and that of a friend for the sake of a few pieces of silver. *The Informer* was something of a return to the UFA style, and critics, whose memories are only occasionally longer than audiences', hailed it as one of the most original films of all time. The highly mannered style of the movie and its explicitly Catholic nature (sin, guilt, and the possibility of redemption) have not been popular for several generations.

6–20. ***Stagecoach*** (U.S.A., 1939), *with (from left) John Carradine, Andy Devine and George Bancroft (both seated above), Claire Trevor, and John Wayne, directed by John Ford.*
For Ford, the family was the center of all social order. Those Ford movies that are the most savage and anarchic are the films from which the family is largely absent. In this picture, Ford creates a surrogate family, an interdependent group bonding together for the sake of mutual survival. They put aside their personality clashes and differences in social class to deliver a baby and fight off marauding Indians. Mutual respect and love follow.   *(United Artists)*

It is these qualities—implicit in both the material and its treatment—and people's attitudes toward them that have hurt the reputation of this still-powerful picture.

In 1939–1940, Ford directed five superior movies in the space of eighteen months, an extraordinary achievement. *Stagecoach* **(6–20)**, *Young Mr. Lincoln, Drums Along the Mohawk* (all 1939), and *The Grapes of Wrath* and *The Long Voyage Home* (both 1940) provide an embarrassment of riches. *Stagecoach* is a slightly schematic film in which a cross-section of Old West society finds itself on the same stage-coach, bound for a thematic push toward freedom. Ford contrasts claustrophobic interiors with the expanse of Monument Valley. The linear plot, buttressed by superior ensemble acting, provides a strong metaphoric quality as the film moves from the corrupt city through the wilderness to an ending where rebirth is possible.

In *The Grapes of Wrath*, Ford lends dignity and worth to the Joad family, evicted from their land in Oklahoma, struggling to get to the promised land of California before poverty destroys them (see **5–2**). Ford's sympathies are forcefully clear in a scene where Mulie, who has been driven half mad by loss and deprivation, tells Tom Joad, just out of jail, what's happened to his family and others in the area. Ford flashes back and we see the banks foreclose and neighbors, desperate for work to prevent foreclosure on their own farms, help to level the ramshackle dwellings of the evicted farmers. A devastated Mulie kneels in the Oklahoma dirt and sifts it through his fingers. "It's not ownin' it. It's bein' born on it, and livin' on

6–21. *She Wore a Yellow Ribbon* (U.S.A., 1949), *directed by John Ford.*
Ford was a master of the epic extreme long shot—miles of terrain that dwarf the inhabitants of the shot to temporary insignificance. Beginning with *Stagecoach,* Ford shot most of his westerns, at least in part, in Monument Valley, which he considered "the most complete, beautiful, and peaceful place on earth." The blasted magnificence of its buttes and towers became indissolubly linked with the man his coworkers called "Pappy." It was not until ill health forced Ford into retirement that directors like Sergio Leone, as well as many lesser men, dared to use it as a location.   *(RKO)*

it, and dyin' on it," he cries. "That's what makes it your'n." The sequence typifies Ford's ability to make powerful emotions *felt*, not represented.

This feel for the land and for people's place on it, Ford's nostalgic sense of tradition that carried with it an affection for uneasy outsiders like Tom Joad, deepened with time. So did his portrayal of values like brotherhood, loyalty, and the ability to endure. The characters' refusal to acquiesce constitutes what Peter Bogdanovich referred to as Ford's gift for depicting "glory in defeat," that glory being human companionship and solidarity. As Lindsay Anderson observed, it is not defeat that is destructive, but the acceptance of it.

Ford's later predominant preoccupation was with the outsider who is both estranged from society and dependent on it. He would deal with this idea in films as varied as *The Quiet Man* (1952), *The Searchers* (1956), and *The Man Who Shot Liberty Valance* (1962). *The Quiet Man* is a romantic valentine to the Ireland of legend and Ford's imagination. It is also his most successful dramatization of men and women together, a believable love story. The film deals with a boxer who accidentally kills a man in the ring and returns to his ancestral home in search of rebirth, in search of the purity his life in America has burned out of him. Ford's sense of romance, his

6–22. *Camille* (U.S.A., 1936), *with Greta Garbo and Robert Taylor, directed by George Cukor.* The exquisite, doomed Marguerite Gautier is enacted by Garbo in a film that is one of the finest achievements of its director. Its hoary plot and conventional characters—courtesan with a heart of gold, earnest young lover, concerned father—were made believable by careful writing, a luxurious mise en scène, and, most importantly, underplayed acting. Cukor's characteristic delicacy even had a constructive effect on the normally stiff and unresponsive Robert Taylor, while the reserved Garbo responded with one of her greatest performances. As always, she seems more of a goddess than a mortal, briefly visiting the land of the living, whose fumblings fill her with a profound sadness. Cukor vanquished her coolness, made her communicate vulnerability—she is a woman disappointed in love, giving herself fully one last time.   *(Metro-Goldwyn-Mayer)*

sunlit geniality, and his humor and feeling are triumphantly fused in one of the few unequivocal happy endings of his later work.

The Searchers is considered one of Ford's greatest later achievements. It details the obsessive quest by Ethan Edwards, an embittered ex-Confederate soldier, for his niece, kidnapped by the Indian chief Scar. Edwards's hatred for Indians extends to his niece when he learns that she has become Scar's squaw. Enraged, he vows to kill her as well. Years pass, and this towering Ahab of the West, duly accompanied by his Ishmael, here called Martin, finally corners his elusive prey. Scar is killed by Martin, and Edwards's niece, terrified at the implacable hatred in his eyes, runs away from her uncle, only to be caught by him. Violently, he seizes her and holds her over his head. Then he suddenly brings her close, cradling her as he says, "Let's go home, Debbie." Family loyalty has conquered irrational racism. At the end, Edwards reconciles the scattered family, yet is himself left isolated, doomed to wander alone forever. Ethan Edwards is Ford's most alienated hero, one of those men of proud, anguished loneliness that John Wayne played so well. Like Ford, perhaps, Edwards is essentially a born outsider, forever seeking allegiance but too proud to make his yearnings known directly.

Wayne's Tom Doniphon in *The Man Who Shot Liberty Valance* likewise lives on the outskirts of society, which in this case is a dusty cowtown named Shinbone. He

6–23. *Gone With the Wind* **(U.S.A., 1939),** *with Clark Gable and Vivien Leigh, directed by Victor Fleming.*

Gone With the Wind is distinguished on several accounts but especially because its protagonists are a far cry from the straight arrows Hollywood thrived on. Scarlett O'Hara is a manipulative schemer who complicates or destroys the life of every man she involves herself with, including Rhett Butler, the only man as strong and smart as she is. In terms of real dollars, the movie is easily the most popular ever made and a personal triumph for its producer, David O. Selznick, who is widely regarded as the finest producer in Hollywood history. The picture is a vindication of the studio system as practiced by its most skilled adherents. Five directors actually worked on the project, about twice that many writers, and two main cinematographers, but the film works because of Selznick's overall control and the bold design of art director William Cameron Menzies, whose forceful compositional sketches provided a consistent visual tone. *(Metro-Goldwyn-Mayer)*

is the only man capable of standing up to the madman-outlaw Liberty Valance. By choosing to kill him and allow the well-meaning but hopelessly impotent lawyer Ransom Stoddard to take credit for the act, Doniphon ensures that his kind of man will be gradually squeezed out of the coming, gentrified West. By killing Valance, he has in a sense killed himself. He dies alone, off-screen, his coffin adorned only by a lonely cactus rose.

Bogdanovich asked Ford about this increasingly mordant view of humankind and society, and Ford snorted, "Maybe I'm getting older." But it wasn't that simple. *Hangman's House,* made when the director was a young man, likewise ends with the protagonist alone, exiled by his nature to a solitary existence. The possibility of survival that is reflected in *Stagecoach,* the confident idealism of *Young Mr. Lincoln,* had been slowly eroded by Ford's mournful realization of the omnipresence of regret and loss that fills the lives of those who think and feel.

Lindsay Anderson wrote of Ford that it was his "impassioned humanism that won him his golden reputation . . . his sympathy with the humble, the rejected, the dispossessed. His spirit was not revolutionary; it was radical, reformist. His style, rich, simple, eloquent, represented American classicism at its best." But more than that, Ford's work flared with moral imagination and a deep Irish melancholy. His instinctive knowledge that things usually end in defeat made him the poet laureate of honest men's last stands. He was himself a prickly cactus rose, blooming with an astonishing vividness for all who have the eyes to see.

FURTHER READING

ANDERSON, LINDSAY. *About John Ford.* New York: McGraw-Hill, 1981. A remarkable achievement in criticism by the English director, as he articulates Ford's life and career with logic, sympathy, and imagination.

BAXTER, JOHN. *Hollywood in the Thirties.* Cranbury, N.J.: A. S. Barnes, 1968. A survey of the major studios, stars, and directors of the thirties.

BERGMAN, ANDREW. *We're in the Money: Depression America and Its Films.* New York: Harper and Row, 1971. A cultural study, with chapters on gangster films, musicals, screwball comedy, and other genres.

CORLISS, RICHARD. *Talking Pictures.* New York: Penguin Books, 1974. A well-informed survey of the major screenwriters of the period, including Ben Hecht, Jules Furthman, and many others.

DOOLEY, ROGER. *From Scarface to Scarlet: American Films in the 1930s.* New York: Harcourt Brace Jovanovich, 1981. A survey of over fifty genres, copiously illustrated, and written in a lively style.

EYMAN, SCOTT. *Print the Legend.* New York: Simon & Schuster, 1999. The most complete biography of John Ford.

EYMAN, SCOTT. *The Speed of Sound.* New York: Simon & Schuster, 1997. Hollywood and the talkie revolution from 1926 to 1930.

GLATZER, RICHARD, and JOHN RAEBURN, eds. *Frank Capra: The Man and His Films.* Ann Arbor: University of Michigan Press, 1975. A good anthology on the director, with entries dating from the thirties to the seventies.

MORDDEN, ETHAN. *The Hollywood Musical.* New York: St. Martin's Press, 1981. Idiosyncratic but never dull, this generally reliable book on one of the genres Hollywood did best is written by a well-informed enthusiast.

SARRIS, ANDREW. *The American Cinema: Directors and Directions 1929–1968.* New York: E. P. Dutton, 1968. General survey by one of America's most respected critics.

7

European Cinema in the 1930s

In this world, there is one awful thing and that is that everybody has his reasons.
—From Jean Renoir's *The Rules of the Game*

Museum of Modern Art

Timeline: 1930–1939

1930
Weekly film patrons worldwide: 250 million

1931
German unemployment: 5.66 million out of total population of 64 million (in United States: 4.5 million out of total of 122 million)

1932
German elections: Nazis, 230 seats; Socialists, 133; Center, 97; Communists, 89

1932–1933
Widespread famine in U.S.S.R.—millions starve to death

1933
Adolf Hitler appointed German Chancellor, is granted dictatorial powers; first concentration camps erected by Nazis; official boycott of German Jews; books by non-Nazi and Jewish authors burned; modernism in the arts is suppressed; all political parties except the Nazis are banned
Approximately 60,000 artists (filmmakers, actors, writers, painters, musicians) leave Germany

1935
Purges and mass trials begin in U.S.S.R.—Stalin eliminates thousands of enemies (formerly comrades)

1936
Spanish Civil War between the Loyalists (left-wing incumbents) and Royalists (right-wing insurgents); with the aid of fellow Fascists Hitler and Mussolini, Generalissimo Franco and his Royalist forces triumph in 1939
Max Schmeling (Germany) defeats Joe Louis (U.S.) in world heavyweight boxing championship (Louis regains the title in 1937)

1937
Japanese Imperial Army invades and controls much of China

1939
Germany annexes neighboring states of Poland and Czechoslovakia

1939–1945
World War II; Britain and France declare war on Germany

Darkening clouds: the aftermath of World War. Germany: the rise of Adolf Hitler and the Nazi party. The outstreaming of Germany's artistic elite. The elegant dreamworld of Max Ophüls. Great Britain: the tasteful cinema of Alexander Korda. Alfred Hitchcock, the British period. France: the heritage of Surrealism—Cocteau and Buñuel. Pale shadows: Carné and Prévert. The humanist cinema of Jean Renoir.

T HE EUROPEAN CINEMA OF THE 1930s was dominated by the worldwide Great Depression and by the spreading cancer of totalitarianism. If World War I made World War II probable, the stock market crash of October 1929 made it virtually inevitable. The Depression began in America and was eventually alleviated by the booming war economy of the 1940s.

What created the crash? Among other things, a maldistribution of income—a mere 5 percent of the population received about a third of all income. Shaky corporate organizations, a weak banking system, and a feverishly overextended paper economy also contributed to the collapse. In Europe there was a lopsided international balance of trade. During World War I, America had become a large creditor of European countries like France and Great Britain. High American tariffs made reducing the debt through increased exports impossible. The only alternatives were to ship gold or secure loans, mostly on Wall Street. The stock market crash started the dominoes falling, locking the United States and Europe into a dance of disaster.

In America, what had been a society divided between white collar and factory workers was now simply divided between those who had jobs and those who didn't. By 1932, 13 million people—25 percent of the working population—were unemployed. Paradoxically, this dark decade produced some of the finest American films in history, especially rich in comedy. In Europe, however, the cinema shriveled. Reeling from the effects of the Great Depression, Europe was then plunged into war, which dealt a virtual deathblow to its weakened film industries.

Germany

In Germany, the people had long been smarting from their defeat in World War I. The punitive damages the victors had imposed only increased their sense of suppressed rage. By the late 1920s, a standard subgenre of German cinema called the "mountain film" had sprung into being. Ostensibly, these were movies about heroic rescues on mystically beautiful peaks under warhead clouds. Although beautifully mounted, the films fairly reek of passionate nationalism.

The Depression made the stopgap regime headed by the ancient Paul Hindenburg even more untenable. The reasonable alternative was the Nazi party of

7–1. *The Triumph of the Will* (**Germany, 1935**), *directed by Leni Riefenstahl.*
Hitler himself commissioned Riefenstahl to direct this three-hour-long documentary celebrating the Nazi's first party convention at Nuremberg in 1934. Thirty cinematographers were assigned to photograph the event, which was staged especially for the cameras. Needless to say, Hitler is presented as a virtual deity, the charismatic master of a master race. Riefenstahl's stylistic virtuosity is dazzling, so aesthetically compelling that the Allies banned the film from circulation for several years after the Nazi defeat. Her other major work, *Olympiad* (1938), is less political. Over three hours long, it deals with the 1936 Olympic Games in Berlin and emphasizes the lyrical beauty of the human form. After the war, Riefenstahl served four years in prison for her participation in the Nazi propaganda machine. *(Museum of Modern Art)*

Adolf Hitler. In 1925, Hitler was a political agitator recently released from prison; by 1933 he was the head of the National Socialist party. With the backing of bankers and industrialists like Alfred Hugenberg, chairman of Krupp munitions as well as head of UFA studio, Hitler promoted and put into action policies of extreme nationalism. As a scapegoat for Germany's political, military, and economic troubles of the previous fifteen years, Hitler targeted Jews; as a means of promoting and focusing his policies, he took a page from Lenin's notebook and targeted motion pictures.

Hitler's policies were overt and unhidden. After May, 1933, when he became chancellor, prescient Jewish Germans began packing their bags, for under the Nazis no Jew could be employed in any branch of the film industry. Still, talent was talent, and although he was half Jewish, Fritz Lang was the man who had made the two-part *Nibelungen Saga* and *Metropolis,* three of Hitler's favorite movies. Lang was summoned to a meeting with Hitler's propaganda minister, Joseph Goebbels. Goebbels offered Lang the top position in the German film industry, saying, "You are the man who will make *the* German film." Sweating profusely, Lang promised to think about it. That night, leaving behind his art collection, his fortune—except for five hundred gold marks—and his wife, an ardent Nazi, Lang boarded a train for Paris. He was not to return to Germany for over a quarter of a century.

Lang was the most prestigious of the film industry fugitives, but he was only one among many. Producers like Erich Pommer, directors like E. A. Dupont, Robert Wiene, Robert Siodmak, Douglas Sirk, Billy Wilder, and Fred Zinnemann, and writers by the dozen also left. Indeed, Leni Riefenstahl, a former actress turned director, was the only world-class filmmaker who remained in Nazi Germany.

Foremost among the directors whose exodus left behind a film industry that was a crumbling shell of what it had been only five years before was the Viennese MAX OPHÜLS (1902–1957). In his selection of material—elegant love stories and tales

7–2. *M* **(Germany, 1931),** *with Peter Lorre, directed by Fritz Lang.*

Lang's first talkie used sound naturally and fluently. For him, sound was an accompaniment to his deterministic images rather than an entity unto itself. *M* is the story of a child-murderer, brilliantly characterized by Lorre as a plump, babyish slug who can't help himself. Because of the public and police paranoia brought on by the unsolved murders, the underworld itself joins in the hunt for the killer. Aside from their disgust at the murderer's acts, the crooks realize that the sooner he is caught, the sooner crime can return to normal. Pursued by both sides, Franz Becker becomes a pitiful victim of his compulsions and fears. He is finally cornered by the police, by "ordinary" criminals, and by his own aberrant self. *(Museum of Modern Art)*

of class barriers in the Empire of Franz Joseph—Ophüls was reminiscent of von Stroheim. In his style—sinuously graceful **tracking shots** that encircle the characters and audience alike in a web of complicitous beauty—Ophüls owed a debt to Murnau, but Ophüls's films are less folkloric, more specific. Like Buñuel and Roman Polanski, Ophüls was destined to become an international filmmaker, tied to no particular country. He made movies in Germany, Italy, France, and the United States.

Ophüls's first masterpiece was *Liebelei* (1933), a story of a cavalry lieutenant who falls in love with a young woman also loved by a dissolute baron. The two men fight a duel, the lieutenant dies, and his lover commits suicide. Out of this throbbing melodrama, Ophüls created a romantic vision of sleigh rides in the snow, where lovers commit themselves to each other irrevocably, even as their love is doomed by social circumstance and the cruelty that lay beneath the glittering romance of the Hapsburg Empire.

It was a theme and a time Ophüls would turn to again in films made in France and the United States. For the most part, he set his stories in the past. As one of the characters says in *La Ronde* **(7–4),** "The past is more restful than the present—and more sure than the future." Characters in films as diverse as *Liebelei, La Ronde,* and *The Exile* (U.S.A., 1947) are imprisoned in the rituals of the society they inhabit. They are often destroyed, or at least condemned to a life without their loved ones—as far as Ophüls is concerned, the same thing as destruction—by their attempts to break out of their rigidly structured societies. No director managed to combine both erotic and emotional love in quite so worldly a way. Ophüls was an odd combination of a romantic artist and an understated social critic.

Ophüls frequently used circular narrative structures in his movies. *The Earrings of Madame de . . . ,* his penultimate film, is typical. The profligate Monsieur buys diamond earrings for his wife, who has to sell them to pay her debts. Her hus-

7–3. *The Blue Angel* **(Germany, 1930),** *with Marlene Dietrich, directed by Josef von Sternberg.*

This is the sad tale of how a proper high school teacher is destroyed by Lola-Lola (Dietrich), a sleazy temptress with delicious thighs. Dietrich and von Sternberg created the definitive image of woman as devourer, using men for the pleasure they bring her, not because she's immoral but because she's amoral. Almost bored, Lola sings, "Falling in love again/ Never wanted to/ What am I to do?/ Can't help it." This profound sense of fatalism is especially characteristic of German culture in the last days of the Weimar Republic, just before the advent of the Nazi era. The portrait of casual decadence became the inspiration for the play and film *Cabaret* (see **14–1).** Astonishingly, Dietrich's career and her character—a worldly, weary femme fatale with a sense of humor—continued, with only a few missteps, for nearly fifty years. *(Paramount Pictures)*

band finds out, buys them back, and sardonically gives them to his mistress, who in turn sells them. They are bought by a diplomat, who falls deeply in love with Madame and gives her the earrings.

The sense of inexorable fate produced by these circular narratives acts as an ironic foil to the romantic characters. In the ball scene of *Earrings,* all mirrors and waltzing couples, Ophüls's camera seamlessly slides and follows the characters as they swirl toward their destiny amid sumptuous decadence. "I detest the world!" Madame declares. "I only want to be looked at by you." But her husband discovers her infidelity and confronts her lover, who leaves her. Heartbroken, she dies. Ophüls took the heartless vanity and brittleness of the characters and, by introducing elements of irony, betrayal, and bittersweet nostalgia, he created an ineffable vision of the exaltation that love can bestow and of the heavy toll it exacts. He added a further element of poignance by casting Charles Boyer, Vittorio De Sica, and

7–4. La Ronde **(France, 1950),** *with Danielle Darrieux, directed by Max Ophüls.*
A prostitute meets and spends the night with a soldier, who meets and falls for a chambermaid, who in turn. . . . The play by Arthur Schnitzler was perfect material for Ophüls, whose moving camera replicates the endless circle of love that the film portrays. It is one of the most romantic, gently resigned explorations of the transitory nature of love relationships and of the capacity for self-delusion that most people have when it comes to the opposite sex.   *(Janus Films)*

Danielle Darrieux, all great romantic stars, all no longer youthful. For Madame (Darrieux) and her lover (De Sica), this was the last chance.

By itself, Ophüls's exile, first to France, then to America, would have been a considerable loss to the German cinema. In context with the mass exodus of equally or potentially gifted fellow artists, his departure left the German film industry without the vision that a handful of ambitious artists had traditionally given it. The Nazi experience inflicted a devastating toll on the German cinema. Decades passed before it was able to overcome the trauma of Hitler's Holocaust.

Great Britain

Except for isolated pioneers like the early entrepreneur Charles Urban or producer Michael Balcon, British cinema was traditionally hampered by the defection of native artists like Chaplin, by the country's lack of a strong financial base sufficient to support a broad-based film industry, and by a drearily conservative, unimaginative financial outlook. Also contributing to the lack of vitality in the British cinema was the snobbish, theater-oriented tradition in England, an attitude that contrasted sharply with the French and German art communities, where the best and brightest painters, musicians, and writers were eager to contribute to the cinema.

The movement that was to bring England its first distinctive filmmaking was, in part, a reaction against the artificiality of stage-oriented cinema. The British documentary movement of the 1930s was to take film back to the days of the Lumières, who observed reality and satisfied themselves with reproducing it. John Grierson (1898–1972) was a young sociologist and critic who, after spending a year in Hollywood on a fellowship, became convinced that film was being misused. He believed that film should be used as a medium of social change, especially during the troubled times of the Depression. Film could provide "a service of information on the immediate needs and services of the state . . . a living sense of what is going on."

Grierson's idea of film as a tool for social reform differed from the Soviet ideal in that he saw movies as inspirational, as a teaching device that would involve the population in the democratic process, as a part of the reciprocal relationship between the government and the governed. To support these educational documentaries—which meant they were films few people would willingly pay to see—Grierson was forced to get his financing from the state. From 1927 until World War II, he built up a strong documentary unit that employed filmmakers as varied as Basil Wright, Paul Rotha, and Harry Watt.

The movies and the concerns that Grierson was rebelling against were epitomized by the work of ALEXANDER KORDA (1893–1956), for Korda's studios at Denham were based on the Hollywood system. Korda, a Hungarian emigré, had a stop-and-start career in his native country, Germany, France, and Hollywood. He finally struck gold with *The Private Life of Henry VIII* **(7–5),** an irreverent, raffish fantasia on the lusty English monarch, with a star performance of roistering panache by Charles Laughton. The film was basically an extension of the "humanized history" that Lubitsch had been practicing in Germany ten years before, but sound seemed to add another dimension.

The Private Life of Henry VIII was the first worldwide hit to come out of England, and it had a pronounced ripple effect. Investors and audiences alike discovered British filmmaking, and production steadily increased. By 1937, there were 225 movies made in England, compared to 128 ten years earlier. British film production had risen until it was second only to Hollywood.

7–5. *The Private Life of Henry VIII* **(Great Britain, 1933),** *with Charles Laughton, directed by Alexander Korda.* Laughton was a character actor of prodigious skill. He attained stardom with this picture and maintained it with a series of villainous roles enacted with lip-smacking relish. Perhaps his finest performance is in *The Hunchback of Notre Dame,* where he enacts the tortured hunchback Quasimodo with empathy born of his own hatred for his lumpy, unprepossessing looks. Laughton's rich, oratorical style went out of fashion after World War II, but he came back strong toward the end of his life, directing the brilliant allegorical fairy tale *The Night of the Hunter* (1955) and contributing tour-de-force performances in *Witness for the Prosecution* (1958) and *Spartacus* (1960). *(United Artists)*

Korda, in concert with his talented brothers Zoltan, a director, and Vincent, an art director, was at the forefront of the expansion, embarking on a major production program with himself as beneficent producer presiding over the international artists who flocked to partake of the Korda magic. But Korda never really had another success on a scale big enough to justify the extravagant manner in which he lived and worked.

In a sense, Korda was too sophisticated to be a producer. Unlike his Hollywood counterparts, he was a man of considerable cultural and intellectual achievement. Where the films of, say, Jack Warner were straight lines of dramatic flight that could appeal to the most unlettered audience, Korda's movies tended to lack a strong narrative thrust. Furthermore, many of them had screenplays that were written by members of the British literary elite, like H. G. Wells and R. C. Sheriff. Except for the flamboyant Michael Powell (1905–1990), Korda favored importing filmmakers from the continent or America, directors like René Clair, Jacques Feyder, William Cameron Menzies, and, abortively, Josef von Sternberg. The result of all this conglomerated talent, of artists whose gifts often ran in mutually exclusive directions, was a somewhat ostentatious, overstuffed quality.

Luckily, unlike Warner or Samuel Goldwyn, Korda was a director as well as a producer. Movies that he directed, like *Marius* (1931) and, supremely, *Rembrandt* **(7–6),** reveal him to have been a visually sophisticated filmmaker with a sure touch

7–6. *Rembrandt* (Great Britain, 1936), *directed by Alexander Korda.*
This movie is Korda's high point as a director, an episodic screenplay unified by art direction of delicacy and authenticity, and one of star Charles Laughton's most controlled, quietly anguished performances. Korda served as a kind of divining rod that attracted some of the film world's finest artists. Although his taste, as exemplified by *Rembrandt* and *Things to Come* (1936), was somewhat too rarefied for the worldwide financial successes he needed if his expensive films were to return a profit, their general excellence serves as a testament to his talent and intelligence.   *(United Artists)*

with actors. He was particularly adept at evoking the deepest romantic emotions with a directness and honesty few sophisticates feel comfortable with—to their loss.

Korda's most consistent success came during World War II, after he moved his operation to Hollywood. Stripped of the genteel English traditions he tended to hide behind, Korda's sense of showmanship was set loose. Films like *The Thief of Bagdad* (1940, directed by Ludwig Berger, Tim Whelan, and Michael Powell) and *The Jungle Book* (1942, directed by Zoltan Korda) are storybooks come to life, children's fantasies realized with a sense of wonder as well as a genuine sense of evil—without which any fantasy tends to degenerate into bland make-believe.

After the war, Korda returned to England, where his output and influence both waned. He financed two superb and typically literary scripts by British novelist Graham Greene: *The Fallen Idol* (1948) and *The Third Man* (1949), both directed by Carol Reed. Korda also produced Laurence Olivier's movie version of *Richard III* (1955). As always, Korda's taste was never that of the mass audience. When he died, he left the small estate—for a movie mogul—of approximately five hundred thousand dollars. Documentarist Basil Wright said of Korda that he had "the princely quality of the Renaissance; he made lots of mistakes—but left us with . . . some good films, don't forget that."

It is a mark of the creative poverty of the early English cinema that, in all the decade of the 1930s, it produced only one indisputably world-class director—ALFRED HITCHCOCK (1899–1981). The son of a grocer, Hitchcock began in movies as an art director, working his way up the pecking order until, at the age of twenty-six, he directed his first film, *The Pleasure Garden* (1925).

A stay in Germany during the early 1920s put Hitchcock very much under the influence of **expressionism,** which became especially evident in his movies of the late 1920s and early 1930s. Even before the advent of sound, Hitchcock had devised a thoroughly unique visual style. In *The Lodger* (1926), a version of the Jack the Ripper legend, the man whom the film had led us to believe is the murderer is pacing in his rented room. Rather than show us a prosaic shot of the man walking back and forth, Hitchcock shoots upward at the ceiling, where we see a chandelier gently swaying. Hitchcock **dissolves** the ceiling, which is replaced by a pane of glass, through which we see the lodger nervously striding up and down—a cinematic equivalent of the stage technique of a transparent scrim curtain.

Hitchcock was also an innovator in sound. In *Blackmail* (1929), begun as a silent film but restructured to be Britain's first talkie, he used sound with the same assurance that he had applied to his images. In self-defense, the heroine has killed a man with a knife. In a later scene at a dinner table, the conversation fades into incomprehensibility with only the word "knife" boldly intelligible to the distraught woman.

Hitchcock's early movies were a sometimes thing, very far from an unbroken succession of masterpieces. Rather, he was feeling his way, with tentative adaptations of stage plays alternating with very uneasy musicals and bizarre women's romances. He gradually found his métier in the thrillers that were to bring him a public identity unparalleled in cinema and made him, as far as the public was concerned, the most notable directorial superstar of his era.

Basically, movies like *Number 17* (1932) and an amusing send-up of **serials,** *Secret Agent* (1936), *Sabotage* (1936), and *Young and Innocent* (1937), were very similar in technique. In all of them, Hitchcock was able to create suspense through the skillful application of the **editing** theories of Kuleshov and Pudovkin. Hitchcock grafted to these associational montage techniques a sardonic, deadpan perversity.

As a result, the sinister possibilities of the most ordinary people and places could be mined.

The 39 Steps (**7–7**) is the clearest precursor to the Hitchcock that audiences thought they loved. Its breathless chase across picturesque locations with sympathetic leads was to be later apotheosized in *North by Northwest* (U.S.A., 1959). Perhaps *The Lady Vanishes* (1938) most clearly sums up the virtues of Hitchcock's British period. The passengers on a snow-bound train are introduced while waiting for the tracks to be cleared. After a night in a Balkan hotel, Miss Froy, an elderly spinster, disappears. The only person to have noticed her proclaims foul play. Aided by a young academic whose specialty is the folk dance, the heroine discovers that Miss Froy was an English secret agent kidnapped by the opposing side. After suitable adventures, all the good guys, including Miss Froy, meet safely in London. No mere synopsis can give the flavor of this quirky, delightful piece of work. There are none of the bravura effects that Hitchcock later relied upon, nor is there any of the sexual sadism that underlay much of his later work. *The Lady Vanishes* is a good-humored story told well and with relish by an unpretentious craftsman at the top of his form.

7–7. *The 39 Steps* (**Great Britain, 1935**), *with Robert Donat and Madeleine Carroll, directed by Alfred Hitchcock.*
An innocent man on the run, attached (in this case literally) to a beautiful woman who doesn't believe his patently ridiculous but nonetheless true story—this narrative motif was a Hitchcock staple. He would rework it in films like *Saboteur, North by Northwest* (**10–19**), and *To Catch a Thief.* This photo demonstrates the influence of German expressionism and its moody lighting style on Hitchcock's British works.   *(Gaumont-British)*

7–8. *Sabotage* **(Great Britain, 1936),** *with Sylvia Sidney and Oscar Homolka (back to camera), directed by Alfred Hitchcock.*
By 1936, Hitchcock's films were beginning to outgrow the strictly home-grown English casts that had populated his films since the beginning of his career. Second-string American stars like Robert Young, Sylvia Sidney, and Richard Dix were imported to make some of the more ambitious British products palatable to American audiences. Because Hitchcock's movies had little to do with objective reality, and a great deal to do with the director's humorously paranoid view of the universe, the cross-pollination of actors and accents worked well for him and not so well for other, less gifted English directors. *(Gaumont-British)*

Both in England and later in America, Hitchcock's movies tended toward the formulaic. Even an enthusiastic admirer like Gerald Mast admitted, "Beneath almost every . . . film is the structure of the Sennett chase, the breathtaking, accelerating rush towards a climactic solution." Along the way, Hitchcock manipulated the audience, yanking their strings as surely as he manipulated the little pieces of celluloid with which he constructed his story. But he was smart enough to personalize the wildly improbable chases by making each of the characters—even the villains—often comical, sometimes even vulnerable.

Hitchcock's twenty-four English films served as both technical and psychological run-throughs for his thematically richer American period (see Chapter 10). Technical tour-de-force shots in his American movies often had critics swooning in the aisles, but many of these audacious effects were actually encores of similar **shots** from his British works. The difference between the Hitchcock of 1935 and the later model was that the older man felt freer to project his fascinatingly deviant, obsessive-compulsive nature onto his characters, whereas the earlier protagonists are invariably cheerful, breezy variations on tally-ho English pluck. Put simply, Hitchcock's British work lacks passion—one of the main elements that would later make this most expert of film technicians an artist as well as a stylist.

France

For JEAN COCTEAU (1889–1963), work in film was no less, as well as no more, important than his work in literature, theater, poetry, painting, or, above all, his daily life. He was something of a Renaissance man, given to intense, exhibitionistic self-dramatization. His first film, *The Blood of a Poet* **(7–9),** was financed by the same nobleman who put up the money for Buñuel's *L'Age d'Or.* By this time, Cocteau was already firmly established as a leading member of the French intellectual world.

Although he was too much of a narcissist to ally himself with any movement, *The Blood of a Poet* is clearly **surrealist,** with its dreamy continuum of scenes that re-create the effect of free association. The central character draws a face whose

7–9. *The Blood of a Poet* **(France, 1930),** *with Lee Miller, directed by Jean Cocteau.*
Surrounded by books and a photograph of a Greco-Roman statue, the tormented poet falls
asleep and dreams the dream that is *The Blood of a Poet.* Cocteau's genius was for imagery that
is at once startlingly original and fruitily funny. Not even Buñuel would have thought of using
disembodied human arms for candelabra, as in *Beauty and the Beast* **(9–3),** or motorcyclists in
black leather as angels of death, as in *Orpheus.*   *(Museum of Modern Art)*

mouth comes to life. He tries to rub it out, but the mouth transfers itself to his
hand. In turn, the mouth moves to the face of a statue that urges the artist to pass
through a mirror. In the film's most startling and immediate illusion, the artist
fearfully plunges through the mirror, entering another world, the world of artistic
creation.

After other equally singular visions, the poet is given a gun and told to shoot
himself, but his blood becomes a robe and his head is adorned by a laurel wreath.
At the very end of the film, the fall of a factory chimney—a shot begun in the first
few moments of the movie—is completed. The entire film has taken place in the
few seconds that it took the chimney to collapse.

In its mysterious symbolism, the film is pure Cocteau: The mouth is the
artist's creativity, which compels him to do things he cannot explain. The poet suffers and dies, finally achieving an ironic immortality. The film takes place in no
specific time or place because everything is really happening in the artist's mind.
Even the masochistic flourish of the title is typically Cocteau.

The movie is not, in and of itself, completely successful. It presumes a fascination with its creator, which an objective audience, whether of the 1930s or today,
can hardly be expected to share. The film had—and continues to have—a consid-

7–10. *L'Age D'Or* (**France, 1930**), *directed by Luis Buñuel.*

The French surrealists adored American slapstick comedy, especially the works of Buster Keaton and Laurel and Hardy. Parisian intellectuals like Buñuel regarded their American cousins as the first wave in the battle against logical reality, and these Europeans occasionally paid wry tribute to the American masters, as can be seen in these photos. *(Museum of Modern Art)*

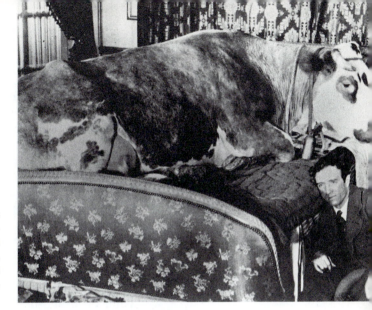

7–11. *Wrong Again* (**U.S.A., 1929**), *with Stan Laurel and Oliver Hardy, directed by Leo McCarey.* *(Metro-Goldwyn-Mayer)*

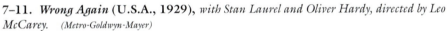

erable influence on the very private esoterica that has always characterized the avant-garde cinema, both in Europe and in America. For the French, Cocteau became a paragon of what would come to be known as the **New Wave.** What the New Wave critics admired most in his movies was his insistence on the purely *personal,* that a film is no different from a novel, a painting, or a play.

Once he made *The Blood of a Poet,* Cocteau turned his back on directing for over fifteen years, although he did write a few scripts. When he returned to the medium, with *Beauty and the Beast* (see **9–3**) and *Orpheus* (1950), the two works that would constitute his claim to filmmaking greatness, the personal obsessions were still there, but the jarring **avant-garde** style was more restrained. The smoothly flowing **mise en scène** of these films conveyed the rarefied rhythm of a sorrowful prince's pavane.

While Cocteau had no particular pretensions toward commercial success, there were directors who combined critical respectability with popular appeal. Foremost among them was MARCEL CARNÉ (b. 1909), a master director whose films, especially those written by Jacques Prévert (1900–1977), are among the finest works of the French cinema before World War II. Carné and Prévert are usually lumped together under the heading of "poetic realism"—a style emphasizing ordinary working-class life and somewhat literary themes and treated in a brooding, romantic manner.

Beginning his career as a journalist and critic who professed admiration for the works of von Sternberg and Murnau, Carné apprenticed as an assistant to René Clair. As a critic, Carné had called for movies that dealt with life as it was lived in the streets of Paris, which would reflect the small triumphs and tragic ironies of the working class.

Carné and Prévert made two movies in the 1930s and one in the 1940s—their masterpiece, *The Children of Paradise* (**9–2**)—that encapsulated their fatalistic view of life and love. *Port of Shadows* (**7–12**) has the impassive presence of Jean Gabin as a deserter who becomes involved with an orphan girl and her avaricious guardian. The deserter kills the guardian but is himself slain by waterfront thugs before he can board a ship for freedom.

In *Le Jour se Lève* ("Daybreak," 1939), poor doomed Gabin murders a man and locks himself in his attic room. The police lay siege but wait for dawn to begin their assault. Waiting to die, the worker remembers his love affairs and his quarrel with the seducer of an innocent girl, the man he killed. At dawn, before the police can launch their assault, he commits suicide.

Carné's films prefigure both existentialism and what would come to be known as **film noir,** an American genre of the 1940s and early 1950s in which the characters' ends seem predestined by a sadistic fate, where the scene is often night and the streets gleam wetly from the reflections of street lamps. In their portrait of helpless, alienated protagonists buffeted by a hostile universe and responding with passive acquiescence, Carné's films are melancholy odes to defeatist stoicism. They also offer a painfully revealing portrait of why the Nazi army paused only briefly at the presumably impregnable Maginot line—then proceeded to invade and occupy a largely unresisting France for the balance of World War II. *Le Jour se Lève* and its premature despair were banned as "demoralizing" by the French censor in September of 1939. Carné angrily responded by saying that an artist is a barometer of his period and a barometer can't be blamed for the storm it forecasts.

Although Carné directed at least three major films between 1938 and 1945, his subsequent movies were disappointing, more the work of a skillful producer

7–12. *Port of Shadows* **(France, 1938),** *with Jean Gabin and Michelle Morgan, directed by Marcel Carné.*
Moody, stark, and fatalistic, Carné's films of this period turned to the beefy, earthy charm of Gabin to help audiences relate to the otherwise abstract characters. The major French leading man of his generation, Gabin was often compared to Spencer Tracy. Both actors shared a rumpled unpretentiousness, and they both made acting look very easy. They rarely raised their voices, were coolly relaxed, and refused to make a big deal of their throw-away gestures.
(Museum of Modern Art)

than a director. He seems to have been essentially an assembler of talent, guiding collaborators like Prévert, art director Alexandre Trauner, and actors Gabin, Arletty, and Jean-Louis Barrault to their finest work. Carné has been called the William Wyler of France, but a Wyler with a taste for the moody and a gift for the poetic.

JEAN RENOIR (1894–1979) is a filmmaker whose works lend themselves equally well to complex analyses or simple emotional responses. His is a cinema of ease—when he is at his best, Renoir's effort never shows. The film flows by, not like a movie, but like life itself. Penelope Gilliatt compared him to Mozart, two artists working with a clear vision that was capable of encompassing biting social satire and a blithe, humane acceptance. Renoir is among the most serene of the world's great filmmakers.

The son of Pierre Auguste Renoir, impressionist painter supreme, the younger Renoir grew up in an atmosphere of love and insight. His attitude toward his art was also similar to his father's. Auguste "didn't care for *tours de force,*" Jean recalled. "To his way of thinking, the beauty of, say, a weightlifter, was at its greatest when he was lifting something light." This unconventional—and in its civilized paradox, quintessentially French—sensibility was imparted to young Jean and never left him.

His service as a pilot during World War I left Renoir with a permanent limp. After the war, with the legacy of much of his father's artwork, the young man embarked on the profession of pottery until the films of Chaplin and von Stroheim seduced him into cinema. Financing his early movies himself—the sale of one of his father's paintings just about equaled the budget of one film—he made a series of silent pictures uneasily divided between the fashionable surrealism of René Clair

173

7–13. *The Passion of Joan of Arc* **(France, 1928),** *directed by Carl Theodore Dreyer.*
Dreyer's classic work has been called one of the "ten most beautiful films in the world." He
was a journalist and editor and in his long life (1889–1968) completed only a handful of
movies (see **9–1**). A precise, intense filmmaker, Dreyer favored the use of exacting closeups to
capture the inner psychology of his characters. He also had a taste for cool, medieval abstractions and spiritual themes and symbols, not to mention imposingly severe compositions such
as this. *(Museum of Modern Art)*

and adaptation of realistic literature. Renoir's 1926 version of Zola's *Nana* has
touches of cruelty worthy of von Stroheim himself. But the mix was not quite right.
The **archetypal,** fantastic nature of silent movies made Renoir a singer working
with music not really suited for his voice.

Because his sensibility was essentially contemplative and **realistic,** sound
suited Renoir much better than silence. In his talkies, he tended to bind his scenes
together unobtrusively, using the fewest possible shots. *The Lower Depths* (1936) tells
a complicated story with nearly a half dozen characters in only 236 shots. Talkies
enabled Renoir to pause, to drink in atmosphere, and to absorb all the natural
sounds he loved so well. Such languorous lyricism would have seemed too static in
a silent movie.

His first talkie, *La Chienne* ("The Bitch," **7–14),** displays this approach. The
film is also a good example of the warm humanism for which Renoir is so famous.

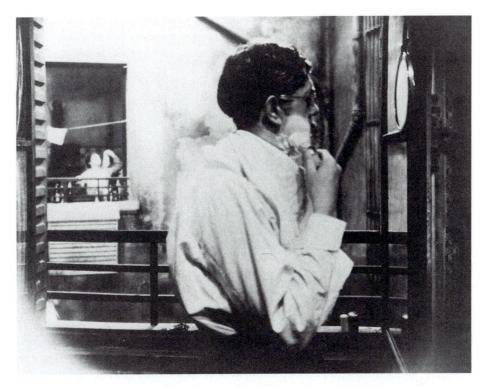

7–14. *La Chienne* **(France, 1931),** *with Michel Simon, directed by Jean Renoir.*
La Chienne is the story of a conventional, well-meaning bourgeois who is fatally undone by his obsession with a compelling slut. The film was less beneficent in tone and subject matter than most of the director's work, but then Renoir was more variable and adaptable than he was generally given credit for. *La Chienne* was shot in the on-the-streets manner that the Italian **neorealists** would popularize nearly fifteen years later. In 1945, the movie would be remade by Fritz Lang as *Scarlet Street* **(5–13).** Lang gave the story a fatalistic resonance that Renoir's original lacked.   *(Europa-Films)*

He begins the movie on the stage of a puppet theater. "The world we show you is neither a drama or comedy," announces a puppet. "It has no moral intentions and will prove nothing at all. The characters are neither heroes nor villains. They are just poor humans like you and me." Throughout many of his films, Renoir contrasted the beguiling artificiality of the stage and of culture in general with the unfettered spontaneity of nature.

The change in form as well as content is observed rather than announced in *Boudu Saved from Drowning* (1932). This charming comedy is a satiric fable of social dysfunction and the joyous possibilities of anarchy. Boudu is a crusty, disreputable tramp who attempts suicide but is fished out of the river by a bookseller, who takes him home to educate him in the niceties of bourgeois life. The bookseller will, he trusts, provide meaning to an otherwise meaningless life.

Unfortunately, Boudu wants none of it. He refuses to sleep anywhere but the floor. He spits on a first edition of the bookseller's beloved Balzac. He smokes cheap stogies, smelling up the apartment. And he seduces the bookseller's wife. Worse, he addresses her by her first name. At the end, Boudu escapes from the trap of marriage with the maid by throwing himself back into the river, floating downstream until he hauls himself up on a bank, where he embraces a scarecrow who likewise enjoys his independence, cadges some food from picnickers, shares it with a goat, and, finally, wanders off to pursue his solitary destiny. The camera turns in full circle and sees a wide world blessedly free of cities, people, or civilization. "Free at last" is the message of this pantheistic, pagan film. *Boudu* is a one-joke trifle, really, but it is also one of the first of Renoir's works to measure out sweetness, congeniality, and tart irony in the mixture that was to become typical of the director.

Until 1937, Renoir was a director best known in France; after 1937, he was known wherever films were shown, for that was the year he made *Grand Illusion*, one of the first European movies to portray events, characters, and social orders with the dexterity of a great novel **(7–15)**. *Grand Illusion* is a microcosmic story of French soldiers in a German prisoner-of-war camp during World War I. Eventually two Frenchmen escape, as their commanding officer sacrifices his life as a diversion. But the film is about many other things as well: caste, the gulf between the working-class soldiers and their upper-class commandants, the subdivisions between Jew and Gentile, and the bond between the French and German officers, united by their aristocratic heritage, their shared knowledge that the world they savored is dying.

Renoir tried to stay open to new possibilities, and his best movies display a lack of processed emotion or stale conventions. When the producers of *Grand Illusion* offered a starring role to Erich von Stroheim, returning to Europe to pick up acting work because his American directorial career had bottomed out, Renoir was thunderstruck. There was no part for von Stroheim, for the film was already in production. But Renoir eagerly allowed von Stroheim to throw out ideas. He suggested that the German commandant—the part he was going to play—be rigidly encased in an orthopedic device that paradoxically concealed an intelligent man of culture and feeling. He thus gave the film an added dimension, for the script had concentrated on the relationships between the French prisoners, between the

7–15. *Grand Illusion* **(France, 1937),** *with Erich von Stroheim, Pierre Fresnay, and Jean Gabin, directed by Jean Renoir.*

In a career that spanned forty years and thirty-five movies, Renoir's overpowering message was that humanity transcended country, gender, or class. Here, two military aristocrats—von Stroheim and Fresnay—find they have much in common (including an old girlfriend), despite their different nationalities, despite the fact that they are on opposite sides of World War I. The working-class Gabin can only watch and wonder. But in time, he too comes to a greater understanding of the mysterious ways of the human species—as do all who enter the world of Renoir. *(Janus Films)*

proletarians and the aristocrat. With von Stroheim's additions, as Alexander Sesonske observed, "a much more complex . . . and . . . profound exploration of the theme of human union and separation" was possible. By remaining open to one of the "happy accidents" that Renoir believed in, he allowed his movie to be immeasurably enriched.

Renoir's next masterpiece, *The Rules of the Game* (7–16), is more formal, more consciously ordered, but it deals with the same theme of social disintegration. A disparate group gathers for a weekend in the country. Masters and servants, bourgeois and working-class alike engage in an elaborate comedy that involves mores more than it does manners. Some of the characters are the descendants of the puzzled philosophical aristocrats of *Grand Illusion,* but grown idle, subtly decadent, and morally flabby. They have few strengthening traditions of honor to govern themselves. As Sesonske notes, their lives "are more performed than lived." In an environment permeated by hypocrisy, conventional social rituals can be destructive. Even the pursuit of love becomes frivolous. In a bitter stroke of Renoirian irony, the one character of honesty and sincerity precipitates the accidental but preordained tragedy of the film's conclusion.

7–16. *The Rules of the Game* (France, 1939), *directed by Jean Renoir.*
Renoir's cinema is one of naturalness and realism—actors don't seem to be acting, exteriors are rarely self-consciously composed. In this famous rabbit hunt, for example, a filmmaker more concerned with the visual beauty of his mise en scène would have shot the scene with the camera lower and the characters dramatically strung out along the horizon, their dark figures contrasting with the white sky behind them. But like most realists, Renoir's concern was to place people in a landscape, a specific context, so that the audience can see how they function within their environment—what they do to it as well as in it, what it does to them.
(Gaumont)

"If France were destroyed tomorrow," wrote critic Richard Roud, "and nothing remained but this film, the whole country and its civilization could be constructed from it." The movie culminates in a complicated sequence involving a dinner and its aftermath. The sequence lurches from low comedy to high drama in the space of only fifty shots. Made in the early part of 1939, *The Rules of the Game* was clearly inspired by the society that Renoir observed around him. "I knew the evils that were gnawing at my contemporaries," he wrote. "The very knowledge that the situation existed gave me my basic situations." Not surprisingly, Renoir's audience didn't appreciate this incipiently unflattering picture of French society. The film's premiere was a disaster. The rightists viewed it as a sneer at the aristocracy; centrists considered it decadent and confusing; and leftists thought it was a comprehensive metaphor for the corruption of France.

They were all right. They were all wrong. Renoir's view of humanity is so complex and full of ambiguity that it holds no one central truth but a multitude of truths. No one thing or person is ever to blame for anything. The decadence and human weakness that lead to stupidity and evil are partially the result of human nature, partially the result of a society that had accustomed itself to asking more of people than they could ever be capable of giving, and partly just the bad luck of the draw of circumstance. In Renoir's world, all of humanity is celebrated, but all of humanity is implicated as well.

The Rules of the Game is a living, breathing portrait, as fully realized and evocative as any canvas by the director's father. But the portrait was not of one person, or even a group of people, but of an entire society, dissolving and sadly shrugging in the face of an evil brought on by their own lassitude, to which one man of moral vision and decency bore witness. Renoir, never an ivory-tower type, tried to salvage the film, shortening it to make it more comprehensible and direct. He finally edited his original 113-minute version down to only 85. It didn't help. In the latter part of 1939, several months before the Nazis goose-stepped into an undefended Paris, the movie was banned by military censors as "demoralizing."

Renoir, like so many of his peers, ended up in Hollywood during the war, where he made several finely wrought, quietly impassioned films—including *This Land Is Mine* (U.S.A., 1943) and *The Southerner* (U.S.A., 1945), which features an uncredited screenplay by William Faulkner. After the war, Renoir returned to France, where he made a few more films, most notably *The Golden Coach* (1953), but he was never to make anything as sublimely perfect as his two masterpieces, *Grand Illusion* and *The Rules of the Game*. In the 1960s, Renoir retired to America. At the time of his death in 1979, he was among the most loved and respected filmmakers in the world.

Further Reading

Eisner, Lotte H. *Fritz Lang.* New York: Oxford University Press, 1977. Includes discussions of all his films, with bibliography and filmography.

Gilliatt, Penelope. *Jean Renoir: Essays, Conversation, Reviews.* New York: McGraw-Hill, 1975. Erudite jog through the director's view of life and art by a good critic.

Gilson, René. *Jean Cocteau: An Investigation into His Films and Philosophy.* New York: Crown Publishers, 1969. Critical articles and excerpts from screenplays originally published in *Cinéma d' Aujourd'hui.*

HARDY, FORSYTH, ed. *Grierson on Documentary*. New York: Praeger Publishers, 1971. Collection of essays written by Grierson, covering both theory and practice.

JENSEN, PAUL M. *The Cinema of Fritz Lang*. Cranbury, N.J.: A. S. Barnes, 1969. Critical analysis, including both the German and American films. Bibliography and filmography.

KULIK, KAROL. *Alexander Korda, The Man Who Could Work Miracles*. New Rochelle, N.Y.: Arlington House, 1980. Exacting, scholarly history-biography of the producer and the stylish manner in which he bankrupted his financiers, entertained his friends, and produced or directed sixty or so movies.

Masterworks of the French Cinema. Introduction by John Weightman. New York: Harper and Row, 1974. Includes texts to Clair's *The Italian Straw Hat,* Renoir's *Grand Illusion,* and Ophüls's *La Ronde.*

ROHMER, ERIC, and CLAUDE CHABROL. *Hitchcock, The First Forty-Four Films*. New York: Frederick Unger Publishing Co., 1979. Includes an analysis of Hitchcock's British **oeuvre,** as well as his American movies to 1957.

SESONSKE, ALEXANDER. *Jean Renoir: The French Films 1924–1939*. Cambridge, Mass.: Harvard University Press, 1980. Exhaustive analysis that breaks down each film into sections for production, narrative and treatment, characterization, and style and form.

WELLMAN, PAUL, ed. *Max Ophüls*. London: British Film Institute, 1978. A compendium of interviews, articles by and about the underappreciated director.

8

American Cinema in the 1940s

*You have to know how not to be timid with the camera, how to do it violence, drive it
to its ultimate limits, for it is a base mechanism. Poetry is what counts.*

—Orson Welles

Warner Brothers

Timeline: 1940–1949

1940
United States begins to mobilize military; U.S. population: 132 million
Franklin D. Roosevelt reelected for unprecedented third term; reelected again in 1944; dies in office in 1945

1941
On December 7, Japanese air force bombs Pearl Harbor, destroying much of U.S. naval fleet; shortly afterward, United States declares war on Japan, Germany, and Italy
"Manhattan Project"—intensive atomic research begins; Enrico Fermi (U.S.A.) splits the atom in the following year

1942
U.S. government forcibly evacuates 100,000 Japanese Americans from their homes on the west coast to inland camps—but they are not called concentration camps
Thornton Wilder's stage masterpiece, *The Skin of Our Teeth,* about the survival of the species

1943
Rationing introduced: meat, shoes, cheese, canned goods, gasoline, and other necessities limited
Race riots in several big cities—Zoot Suit era in African-American ghettos

1944
D-Day: Allied landings on the beaches of Normandy, France; massive Allied bombardments of German and Japanese cities
The tide turns: Fascist alliance on the defensive
Cost of living rises almost 30 percent due to wartime inflation

1945
Vice-President Harry S. Truman (Democrat) becomes President (1945–1953)
United States drops atom bombs on Hiroshima and Nagasaki; Japan surrenders on August 4— "V-J Day"—three months after end of European war

1947
Marshall Plan announced—massive U.S. assistance to help shattered European economies back on their feet
Tennessee Williams's *A Streetcar Named Desire* (Pulitzer Prize)
Over one million war veterans enroll in colleges under the G.I. Bill of Rights

1949
Arthur Miller's *Death of a Salesman* (Pulitzer Prize)

Wartime boom in the Hollywood studios. Postwar decline of the factory system of production. The defining event of the decade: World War II. The bitter truths of John Huston. The Disney version. The writer-directors: Preston Sturges, Billy Wilder, Orson Welles. The colossal *Citizen Kane* and its aftermath. New styles for a new era: **film noir** and social realism. End of another golden age.

T HE AGONY OF WORLD WAR II and the torturous reassembling of the world that followed played hell with politics, economics, and social and political alliances, but the rule of thumb about hard times being good times for the entertainment industry proved true. From 1940 to 1947, it was almost impossible to make a studio film that lost money. By 1944, the five major studios were valued at $750,000,000, as against $605,000,000 only the year before. In 1946, the industry's watershed year, the total industry gross was $1,700,000,000.

Paramount grossed $21,792,000 in the first six months of 1946—four million more than it made in all of 1945. As opposed to the stable management of studios like MGM or Columbia, RKO was torn by eight separate studio regimes between 1929 and 1955. Even so, RKO did quite well in the war period, averaging between five and seven million dollars in profits for each of the war years.

8–1. *Casablanca* **(U.S.A., 1943),** *with Humphrey Bogart and Ingrid Bergman, directed by Michael Curtiz.*
Casablanca, like *The Wizard of Oz,* is one of the happiest accidents of the studio system, one of those films made in an atmosphere of uncertainty and confusion that nevertheless meshed perfectly. For Bogart, his performance synthesized the associations of his earlier, most successful roles—a heroic tenderness and stoicism beneath a tough, unyielding exterior. *Casablanca* was released during the darkest days of World War II, and Bogart's ultimate romantic gesture—giving up the woman he loves and always will for the greater good—struck a responsive chord among Americans, who were also being called upon to make personal sacrifices for the war effort. *(Warner Brothers)*

These figures may appear modest in light of modern mega-hits grossing hundreds of millions of dollars, but keep in mind that the average admission price was thirty-five cents. In fact, more people were going to the movies during this period than have ever gone since. Approximately ninety million people, two thirds of the population of America, went to the movies *every week*. In part, this was because there weren't many competing forms of entertainment. The American love affair with the movies, begun in the teens and nurtured in the 1920s and 1930s, continued throughout most of the 1940s. But this golden financial age didn't last.

Decline of the Studio System

In 1948, the federal government successfully concluded an antitrust action that divested the five major companies (MGM, Warners, Fox, RKO, and Paramount) of their theater chains. Prior to this, the film companies had enjoyed guaranteed distribution of their product. Paramount theaters played Paramount pictures, Warners played Warners pictures, and so on. Since each company knew how many theaters it controlled and what each theater's average gross was, it could calculate, with a fair degree of accuracy, the amount of money a picture with given **stars** could make. (Big hits and big flops were basically unplannable and canceled each other out.)

8–2. *Woman of the Year* **(U.S.A., 1942),** *with Katharine Hepburn, directed by George Stevens.*
Proud, feisty, angular Kate Hepburn (1907–2004), with her breathy Bryn Mawr accent and upper-crust manner, was a star from the moment of her debut in *A Bill of Divorcement* (1932). Her tremulous mannerisms turned many critics against her, and *Woman of the Year* was widely regarded as her comeback picture. Her combative spirit was tempered by Spencer Tracy's phlegmatic calm in their joint vehicles, such as *Pat and Mike* (1953), while her strength supported Henry Fonda against the panic of old age and encroaching senility in *On Golden Pond* (1981). Perhaps her most moving performances, however, are her ardent spinsters fighting insecurity, such as the heroines of *Alice Adams* (1935) and *Summertime* (1955), in which she emerges a better woman for her gutsy determination. *(Metro-Goldwyn-Mayer)*

It took five years for the companies to sell off their theaters. By the time they did, it had become increasingly obvious that, while reliable money was made in production and distribution, the profits were in exhibition.

In 1947, the House Un-American Activities Committee (HUAC) began hearings to investigate Communists and Communist influence in Hollywood. Some actors, writers, producers, and directors informed; some denied the allegations; some refused to either confirm or deny; and some went to jail (see Chapter 10). But all the members of the Hollywood community were affected, if only by the irrevocable loss of the cozy community feel that the town had enjoyed since the moviemakers founded it forty years before.

Bad news kept coming. Britain announced a 75 percent tax on foreign film earnings. Other European countries enacted similar laws. Foreign revenues were sliced by more than half. As if the loss of all that guaranteed revenue wasn't bad enough, television erupted onto the American scene. For the next twenty years, bedeviled by the onslaught of the plug-in drug, the Hollywood studios retrenched. Within the next twenty years, 80 percent of the domestic film audience disappeared.

But before all that happened, America's movies reached standards of fluency and confident expertise comparable to the last days of silent films. Pictures of enduring artistic merit were made, and even the standard assembly-line product had a sheen, a slick command of narrative and character. It was an era when movies communicated.

World War II

Hollywood did itself proud during World War II. Many top stars—James Stewart, Tyrone Power, Douglas Fairbanks, Jr., Robert Montgomery, Clark Gable—entered the service and proved themselves valorous soldiers. Those who didn't take up arms took cameras and did battle in their own way. Frank Capra, along with a crew of Hollywood artisans that included composer Dimitri Tiomkin and editor William Hornbeck, made a series of propaganda films under the umbrella title *Why We Fight*. Proud, noisy, full of saber-rattling and an impressive use of stock footage, sound effects, **animation,** and stentorian narration, the *Why We Fight* films marshal all the tools of film effectively.

Most fiction movies of the Hollywood war effort were in the same vein: With few exceptions, their propaganda content got in the way of their artistic and entertainment value, at least for posterity. Except for *The Story of G.I. Joe* (1945) or *They Were Expendable* (1945), films that concentrated on the interaction of a small group of soldiers and eschewed preachy oratory, the most valuable movies dealing directly with the war were documentaries like William Wyler's *The Memphis Belle* (1944), John Ford's *The Battle of Midway* (1942), and, supremely, John Huston's *The Battle of San Pietro* **(8–3).**

Like the Wyler and Ford documentaries, *San Pietro* was shot on 16 mm, to a great extent by the director himself. Huston's film documents the Allied effort to take an area near Monte Cassino in Italy. The camera lingers on the young faces that always fight wars, while Huston's restrained narration identifies them without condescension or patriotic rhetoric. Later, we see a few of them frozen in death. Huston lets the heartbreaking contrast between the vivacity of life and the grievous stillness of death speak for itself.

8–3. *The Battle of San Pietro* (**U.S.A., 1945**), *directed by John Huston.*
The refuse of war: dead men in body bags. Huston's hand-held 16-mm camera caught all the muddy, matter-of-fact brutality of war, so much so that the War Department, under whose auspices the film was made, cut the film from five reels to an abrupt three. Huston was incapable of the simple, jingoistic propaganda that was apparently expected of him, which may be why this war documentary is so unsettling. Its harsh portrayal of exhausted soldiers, slogging forward, always forward, in the face of ferocious opposition from the entrenched Nazis is genuinely heroic, tragic. *(Museum of Modern Art)*

The film's battle scenes, fragments of troop advances with the hand-held camera nervously peeking over foxholes or around trees, occasionally wobbling as a shell goes off nearby, carry the terror of battle and the stink of death. Impressive today, even after years of videotaped footage shot under fire, the scenes were doubly startling in 1945.

Perhaps too startling. Huston's successor to *San Pietro, Let There Be Light* (1945), was banned by the War Department for nearly forty years because it dared to show veterans of battle suffering from shell shock and other combat-related psychological disorders. When finally released in 1982, *Let There Be Light* proved a typically Hustonian, compassionate view of life's walking wounded.

Major Filmmakers

JOHN HUSTON (1906–1987) had made a spectacular fiction debut only a few years earlier with *The Maltese Falcon* (**8–4**), a lean, mean adaptation of a Dashiell Hammett novel. As a former screenwriter—and a good one—Huston was one of a new

8–4. *The Maltese Falcon* **(U.S.A., 1941),** *with Mary Astor and Humphrey Bogart, directed by John Huston.*

Is she telling the truth or is she lying? Is she a killer or a victim? Woman as instrument of evil is a staple of film noir and detective genres—not because of a latent misogyny in American culture, but because of noir's essentially subversive nature, its tendency to explore deceptive surfaces. What could be more shocking than for the female—traditionally a vessel of purity, the rock upon which the nuclear family is built, an object of idealization since the days of Griffith—to be revealed as a manipulative bitch, a spider, spinning silken strands, luring men to their destruction? *(Warner Brothers)*

generation of filmmakers who were rising from the writing ranks and would exert a markedly constructive influence. The son of actor Walter Huston, John was consistently drawn to works of serious literary merit by writers as diverse as B. Traven, Herman Melville, Tennessee Williams, Carson McCullers, Flannery O'Connor, Rudyard Kipling, and Malcolm Lowry. His sensitivity to writers often led him to put himself at the service of his material.

Huston took his tone from the book or story he was adapting, not seeking to replicate every scene but to synthesize the writer's moral or aesthetic essence. His visual style is simple, unadorned, cleanly functional but always expressive as well as occasionally impressive. An accomplished actor himself, he was very good with actors.

One of Huston's finest early works is *The Treasure of the Sierra Madre* (1947), an uncompromisingly graphic depiction of the psychological deterioration wrought by greed and the lust for gold. The movie traces the decline of one Fred C. Dobbs, a violent paranoid, crafty rather than bright, played by Humphrey Bogart in one of his most expert performances.

Even this early in his career, Huston's gift for filmmaking on more than one level was in evidence. *Sierra Madre's* three prospectors have been unsuccessful in their search for the treasure they believe lies in the mountains. The two who are the least experienced (Bogart and Tim Holt) mistake iron pyrite—fool's gold—for the real thing. At the foot of a great mountain, they find more of what they believe to be useless fool's gold. The old man that makes up the third leg of this uneasy troika (Walter Huston) suddenly breaks into a frenzied, exuberant jig, as he bellows abuse mingled with happiness at his companions. The gold is real, the treasure has been found! The moment is simultaneously joyful, unsettling, and **epic** as the camera **pans** up to the brooding mountains hanging over the site of the treasure. As Dobbs lurches from suspicion to paranoia to murderous madness in the mountains of Mexico, *Sierra Madre* achieves a mad grandeur; it ranks with the early realism of von Stroheim's *Greed* as one of the American screen's most persuasive treatments of human frailty.

It is a subject Huston would delve into more and more frequently in the coming years, often to the discomfort of moralistic critics. From cowardice (*The Red Badge of Courage*, 1951) through obsession (*Moby Dick*, 1956) to fatal hubris (*The Man Who Would Be King*, 1975), Huston charted the down side of humanity, the men and women who try and fail, either through flaws in themselves or because they attempt to circumvent the natural order of a hostile universe. Fate is accepted stoically. Huston's characters know that for them it is too late to change. There is a minimum of self-pity, just a laconic sense of reality, of the way life, stripped of its conventional social niceties, really is.

Huston went into something of a trough in the 1960s. But those who had written him off learned never to count a champion out when the old fox came

8–5. *The Asphalt Jungle* (**U.S.A., 1950**), *with Sterling Hayden (arms crossed) and James Whitmore (standing), directed by John Huston.*
A seedy back room, a bottle of cheap booze, a glaring overhead light, unshaven men dressed in rumpled suits, the smoke-laden aura of three in the morning somewhere in the vast urban underbelly—we are in a netherworld, a world of shadows, the world of film noir. *(Metro-Goldwyn-Mayer)*

back strong in his mid-sixties, with films like the picaresque fable *The Life and Times of Judge Roy Bean* (1972), *The Man Who Would Be King,* the humorous and scary religious mania of *Wise Blood* (1980), *Prizzi's Honor* (1985), and his last masterpiece, *The Dead* (1987), films that firmly placed Huston back among the world's filmmaking giants.

Of all the films of this late reflowering, probably the bravest was *Fat City* **(8–6),** a painfully **realistic** slice of life among the fringe characters of the fight game in Stockton, California. The main character is Billy Tully (Stacey Keach), a club fighter of modest talent, small ambitions, and no luck gone to seed. Pulling himself together, he fights a few fights, getting his brains scrambled for two-hundred-dollar purses and drinking up his share long before the next bout.

At the end of the movie, Tully, an old pug who never was, sits at an all-night cafeteria with a young pug who never will be. They make bleary remarks about nothing in particular; then the conversation lags. Billy looks around and suddenly Huston **fades** the sound out and **freezes** the action. Tully looks on, thunderstruck at the tired old men playing cards, at the cook who can barely stand up, two-legged shells frozen in futility. This is Tully's future, the only possible one. The sound comes back up and Tully, stunned by his epiphany, this sudden presentiment, desperately asks his acquaintance not to go, to stay a while. As the film ends, they sit there not speaking, keeping each other small company against the encroaching darkness.

The antithesis of optimists like Frank Capra, Huston worked in full knowledge that the ultimate end is always death. There is never a sense of defeat or depression in a Huston film, but rather warmth and humor at what Jean-Pierre Coursodon called his "range of human experience" and "youthfulness of spirit." The essence of Huston is in a ribald laugh, a jig in front of a mountaintop, the defiant refusal to cower when confronted by the inevitable. To echo William Faulkner, Huston's characters are often destroyed, never defeated.

8–6. *Fat City* **(U.S.A., 1972),** *with Jeff Bridges (in white), directed by John Huston.*
Huston is as realistic as a right jab to the jaw. *Fat City* is not really about boxing so much as about boxing's day laborers. Championships are irrelevant for the denizens of this squalid milieu, as are women. Sometimes they wait for their men; more often, they just drift away.   *(Columbia Pictures)*

8–7. *High Sierra* (U.S.A., 1940), *with Humphrey Bogart, directed by Raoul Walsh.*
Bogart (1899–1957) began his career at Warners as a gangster—tough, cynical, antisocial. *High Sierra,* written by John Huston, gave Bogart a touch of the existential loner. Mad Dog Earle is destroyed only when he becomes vulnerable because of his love for a crippled girl. The sentimental self-pity inherent in the story was redeemed by Bogart's sardonic rage. This movie, along with *The Maltese Falcon* and *Casablanca,* made him a star, and he remained one until his death. Although his range was not wide, within it he was very good, working hard at variations on a theme. His main quality as an actor was an inability to fit in, and this was interpreted and reinterpreted as, variously, a pathetically paranoid ship's captain in *The Caine Mutiny* (1954) or the outright nonconformism of a hopeless drunk in *The African Queen* (1952). *(Warner Brothers)*

There has always been debate about the quality of Walt Disney's art. Some called his work kitsch; others claimed that along with Chaplin and a few others he was one of the rare authentic geniuses of the cinema. But all agree that without Disney, animation as an art form would never have happened as it did. In a way, WALT DISNEY (1901–1966) was a repetition of the earliest, canniest movie pioneers, persevering in his belief that a children's amusement was an endlessly adaptable form that was fully capable of encompassing whatever the human mind could imagine.

Disney began animating in his native Kansas City, producing out of his garage commercial films as well as "Alice" comedies that mixed live action with cartoons, a long-standing ambition of Disney's that would not be perfected until *Song of the South* (1946). Moving to Hollywood in the early 1920s, Disney began making cartoon shorts for various distributors, always hampered by their indifference to the very idea of animation. Sound changed all that, added the requisite touch of realistic absurdity to the two-dimensional animal caperings that have always been the mainstay of animation. Disney's main character of Mickey Mouse became as much an icon of the 1930s as Chaplin had been during the teens and twenties.

Disney began planning the first feature-length cartoon, diverting all available funds to that end and going deep into debt. It was a pattern that would be repeated until television gave Disney the financial base that the always-risky animation business never could. *Snow White and the Seven Dwarfs* (1937), the first animated feature, was an enormous hit, prompting the ambitious producer to embark on an upgrading of his facilities so they could produce one cartoon feature a year.

The next several years produced *Pinocchio* (1940), *Fantasia* (1940), *Dumbo* **(8–8),** and *Bambi* (1943), the films that constitute Disney's most lasting legacy of quality and films that, because of their producer's own insistent demands for perfection, cost too much money and were financial disappointments.

8–8. *Dumbo* (U.S.A., 1941), *produced by Walt Disney.*
Dumbo, the outcast baby elephant with the big ears, is comforted by his loving mother. Disney's best works usually exploit the **archetypal** childhood fears that reside in all of us—fears of separation, rejection, abandonment. *(RKO)*

The best of Disney's movies, which includes films as late as *The Lady and the Tramp* (1956), work as well as they do because of their emotional directness and their cunning metaphorical underpinnings. In *Bambi,* the baby deer's mother is shot by hunters, leaving him homeless. In *Dumbo,* an elephant with overgrown ears is ostracized by his peers because he doesn't fit in; and his mother is taken away from him as well. The analogies are self-evident, but the emotional pull is not lessened for being obvious.

Disney's films are moving because he made creatures of paint and ink come alive by superimposing universal human fears of alienation, abandonment, and loss. Disney's films are beautiful because of the extraordinary technical expertise of his staff, who, spurred on by the boss, sought to reproduce naturalistic environments with a painstaking verisimilitude. In time, this would produce a slightly antiseptic quality that tentative moves toward stylization did not solve.

Disney is actually analogous to a producer like David O. Selznick more than he is to other cartoon moguls like Max Fleischer. As with Selznick, the overriding sensibility at work on a Disney picture was basically that of the producer, Disney. He led writers, animators, and directors carefully through story conferences and thousands of sketches, using those ideas that jibed with his overall conception of a given film, discarding those that didn't. Disney collaborators came and went, but until his expanding interests began occupying an increasing amount of his time in the 1950s, Disney's style and quality remained remarkably consistent.

Coexisting alongside Disney through his years of greatest success, and gradually growing in esteem through the intervening years, were the animated shorts made by great Warner Brothers animators like Chuck Jones, Friz Freleng, and Tex Avery. Creations like Bugs Bunny, Daffy Duck, and the immortal Wile E. Coyote and his nemesis, the Road Runner, stood in direct contrast to the Disney ethos. Where Disney was sentimental, Warners was anarchic; where Disney was sugary, Warners was astringent; where Disney posited a world in which stability and family are eventually restored, Warners gloried in a world where stability and family didn't exist.

PRESTON STURGES (1898–1959) swept across Hollywood like a thunderstorm of literacy and iconoclasm. Like a thunderstorm, when his energy was spent after little more than five years, nothing much was left except a series of ferociously energetic satires on *Genus Americanus* and the deceptions to which they are native. A moderately successful dramatist and screenwriter, Sturges wrote scripts like *Easy Living* (1937), which gradually won him increasing leverage at Paramount. Sensing

8–9. *The Philadelphia Story* (**U.S.A., 1940**), *with Cary Grant, Katharine Hepburn, and James Stewart, directed by George Cukor.*
For thirty-five years, Grant was the finest light comedian in movies, innately urbane and self-possessed. He could be particularly hilarious when his smooth masculinity was traduced by continuing hysteria, as in *Arsenic and Old Lace* (1944) or by being forced to wear women's clothes, as he was for half the duration of *I Was a Male War Bride* (1949). He also earned respect for dramatic efforts like *Notorious* (1946) and *None But the Lonely Heart* (1944). *(Metro-Goldwyn-Mayer)*

a weakening in the traditional studio prejudice against writers maintaining control over their screenplays, Sturges sold the studio a script called *The Great McGinty* (1941) for one dollar—with the proviso that he direct. The ploy worked.

Sturges movies like *Hail the Conquering Hero* (1944), *The Lady Eve* (1941), and *The Palm Beach Story* (1942) are raucous crosses between Mack Sennett and screwball comedy. The men are usually passive, always naive, the women wily and manipulative. Sturges's pacing was as hectic as Capra's, but his work avoids the sentimentality of the older director. Sturges's *Sullivan's Travels* **(8–10),** a schizoid film, is a possible exception, for it becomes a suspiciously warmed-over tribute to the necessity for laughter and the resilience of the common person.

In general, Sturges was not a celebrator. He was a satirist with a solid line in burlesque broadness that he brought to bear on dopey all-American types, as in *The Miracle of Morgan's Creek* (1943), which tells the story of Trudy Kockenlocker, a typically boy-crazy, small-town girl in a typical Sturges small town, full of rapacious, insular people with small minds and small horizons.

Trudy has been adored from afar by Norval Jones, with whom she cannot be bothered. Disappearing one night with a group of soldiers on leave, Trudy awakens

8–10. Publicity photo of Joel McCrea, Veronica Lake, and Preston Sturges on the set of *Sullivan's Travels* (U.S.A., 1941), *directed by Sturges.*
Sturges was not a director afraid of going too far. In fact, in his prime, he spent a great deal of time and effort finding out where too far was located. Casual, informal, disorganized, Sturges was liked by his actors and crews and distrusted by production executives. Not entirely without reason: He tended to take longer and longer and to spend more and more money as his career progressed. His reputation as an expensive director, coupled with several indulgent, catastrophic failures, helped end his career. *(Paramount Pictures)*

the next morning a hungover mother-to-be. All she can remember is that the soldier who impregnated her (and who, in a throwaway sop to the censors, married her) had a name that is "something like Ratskywatzky." Norval, a born dupe, makes an honest woman of poor pregnant Trudy and loses everything by doing so until Trudy, with the unknowing help of the soldier whose name was something like Ratskywatzky, saves the day by giving birth to sextuplets. Fame, fortune, and success follow. All is forgiven.

Sturges's main point—that success and happiness are as much a matter of dumb luck as talent or skill—could hardly have been less conventional, and his dialogue, rich and oratorical, is as bold as his ideas. "Chivalry is not only dead, it is decomposed," announces Rudy Vallee in *The Palm Beach Story*. Later, he observes, "One of the tragedies of life is that the men who are most in need of a beating are always enormous."

In 1945, Sturges left Paramount and formed a partnership with sometime producer, full-time eccentric, Howard Hughes. His first picture for Hughes was the awkwardly titled *The Sin of Harold Diddlebock* (1946), the last film of Harold Lloyd. Badly recut, but effectively retitled *Mad Wednesday* by Hughes, the movie was a living, effective tribute to silent comedy in general and Lloyd's gentle, indomitable comic character in particular.

After that, Sturges stumbled, began losing his rhythm. *Unfaithfully Yours* (1948), a satire about an orchestra conductor who fantasizes about murdering his wife, sounds better than it plays. His next movie, *The Beautiful Blonde from Bashful Bend* (1949), was a grotesque disaster. Self-destructing rapidly, Sturges made indulgent investments in a restaurant-theater complex that threw him deeply into debt.

8–11. *The Lady Eve* (U.S.A., 1941), *with Henry Fonda and Barbara Stanwyck, directed by Preston Sturges.*
Sturges habitually took the natural qualities of his actors and then forced them to go to extremes with those qualities. In this movie, the normally passive, quiet, rather unworldly Fonda is amplified into a totally reclusive dope, a naive scholar dedicated to the study of the reptilian realm. "Snakes are my life," he earnestly informs con woman Stanwyck. "What a life," she says, profoundly unimpressed.
(Paramount Pictures)

8–12. *Letter from an Unknown Woman* **(U.S.A., 1948),** *with Louis Jourdan and Joan Fontaine, directed by Max Ophüls.*
A horsedrawn carriage, a gaslight, trees in the park covered with fresh snow—the Hollywood artisans of the 1940s, in movies like this, *Magnificent Ambersons,* and *King's Row* (1942), created visions of natural perfection in the sealed-off environment of the studio. Real streets and woods seemed almost vulgar in comparison. The lush romanticism of Ophüls's film, with its superb evocation of pre–World War I Europe, might have been a popular success if it had been made before World War II. But by 1948, audiences had different ideas about the world they wanted to see reflected on the screen. The romantic past was past.   *(Universal Pictures)*

He spent most of the rest of his life in Europe, trying for a comeback that never materialized.

There is a moment in *Unfaithfully Yours* that encapsulates Sturges. One of the musicians questions conductor Rex Harrison about his use of the cymbals. He is afraid, the musician explains, of being vulgar. Harrison smiles and says, "Be vulgar by all means, but let me hear that brazen laugh." If he was not a long-distance runner, the rebellious Sturges at least showed the cozy clichés of the period for the thin homilies they truly were and inspired much brazen laughter along the way.

BILLY WILDER (1906–2002) was, along with Ben Hecht, the prime example of the journalist as filmmaker: fast, scabrous, with a faultless instinct for detecting the hypocrisies of others. As rigorously unsentimental as only a disappointed romantic can be, Wilder made movies that combine the lip-smacking relish for moral grotesqueries of von Stroheim with Lubitsch's taste for precise wit.

Austrian by birth, Wilder worked as a reporter and scriptwriter before coming to Hollywood in 1934. He had a difficult time establishing himself, for his knowledge of English was limited. He was plucked from obscurity by Lubitsch, for whom he worked on several films, most notably *Ninotchka.* The success of that film made Wilder a "hot" writer. He was signed to a Paramount contract, for which several of his screenplays were directed by Mitchell Leisen, whom Wilder loathed because he "ruined my scripts." With the examples of Preston Sturges and John Huston to guide him, Wilder began pressing to be allowed to direct his own scripts.

Finally he got his chance, and he wrote and directed *The Major and the Minor* (1942), a chirpy comedy centering on role reversal which was a large success. With firm footing underneath him, Wilder embarked on a distinguished series of films that included *Double Indemnity* **(8–13),** a definitive example of what would come to be known as film noir, "a pitiless study of human greed, sex and sadism" according to Georges Sadoul, with a superior screenplay by the novelist Raymond Chandler in collaboration with Wilder.

Succeeding efforts, like *The Lost Weekend* (1945) and *Sunset Boulevard* (1950), Wilder's masterpiece, revealed the director's roots in Germany and his **expressionist** leanings. Settings are dark, characterizations are darker. The prevailing mood is sardonic and fatalistic. Charles Higham synopsizes Wilder's world as "ugly and vicious, selfishness and cruelty are dominant in men's lives; greed is the central impetus of the main characters." This overlooks how morbidly intense and funny Wilder's depiction of humanity is.

Sunset Boulevard is the story of Norma Desmond (Gloria Swanson), a faded, forgotten queen of silent pictures. Into her gloomy mansion stumbles Joe Gillis (William Holden), a desperate hack screenwriter on the run from men trying to re-

8–13. *Double Indemnity* (U.S.A., 1944), *with Fred MacMurray and Barbara Stanwyck, directed by Billy Wilder.*

Writers began having more influence in the Hollywood of the 1940s. For this tale of two sleazy people uniting to kill a third sleazy person—her husband—Wilder called on the novelist Raymond Chandler. Chandler's detective stories could make readers almost smell the sweet, cloying gardenias that enveloped southern California like corruption itself. It was an inspired choice of a collaborator. Chandler's dialogue came through unscathed, and the script was nominated for an Academy Award. Despite this acclaim, Chandler, used to working alone, felt uncomfortable in Hollywood, for the collaborative process that is filmmaking is far removed the novelist's art, if not his or her craft. *(Paramount Pictures)*

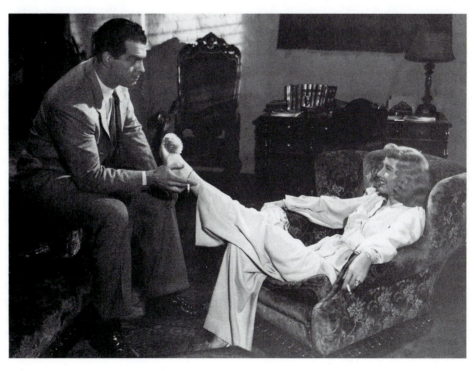

possess his car. "You're Norma Desmond," Holden says. "You were in pictures. You used to be big." Swanson stiffens her spine. "I *am* big," she says defiantly. "It's the pictures that got small."

Gradually, the two outcasts form an unspoken bargain of convenience. Gillis hides out with Desmond and attempts to edit a script she's written for herself. Ultimately he comes to share her bed. There they are, two refugees, one whom Hollywood has forgotten, one it simply ignores.

Norma, desperate to keep her young man amused, does Chaplin imitations and shows him her old movies. As we see a **closeup** of Gloria Swanson vintage 1928, Wilder cuts to a closeup of Swanson vintage 1950, intoxicated by her own image. She leaps up, her face outlined in the harsh beam of the projector's arc light. "We didn't need voices," she proclaims, "we had faces then."

The movie gains an incantatory strength as it goes along. Gillis realizes that he has to be his own man if he is to retain any shred of self-respect. Desmond, abandoned by the industry, abandoned by the public that once adored her, cannot face the possibility of one more abandonment. She shoots Gillis, and, at the end, insane, she believes the newsreel cameras and reporters are there to record her comeback performance in the script she has written. Norma descends the stairs, eyes glazed with an unnatural light, her face moving into the camera lens as the film **fades out.**

Ironic, funny, beautifully acted, with an element of pity that is often missing in Wilder's other works, *Sunset Boulevard* is a fable and meditation on the nature of Hollywood that turns into authentic tragedy. Norma Desmond has a grandeur that the seedy, scrabbling representatives of 1950 Hollywood completely lack. It is the film industry's finest and most meaningful comment on itself.

Wilder maintained his career on a high plane throughout the 1950s. Among other works, he made one of the most savagely disenchanted movies ever made in Hollywood, *Ace in the Hole* (1951). He also directed a historical tribute to Charles Lindbergh, *The Spirit of St. Louis* (1957), a superior courtroom drama, *Witness for the Prosecution* (1958), and a winning romantic comedy in the Lubitsch manner, *Love in the Afternoon* (1957).

It was with two back-to-back comedies, *Some Like It Hot* (1959) and *The Apartment* (1960), that Wilder became Hollywood's most successful and critically honored filmmaker. The succeeding years yanked Wilder back a few steps, as he embarked on films, often in a gently romantic key, that were usually financial failures and occasionally marred by coarseness and overemphasis. Nonetheless, movies like *The Private Life of Sherlock Holmes* (1970), *Avanti!* (1972), and *Fedora* (1978) more than justified his continuing activity.

Critic Stephen Farber wrote that Wilder's chief gift to American films was intelligence, the verbal equivalent of the sharp, knowing world view redolent of Old Europe that filmmakers like Lubitsch **(8–15)** portrayed more gracefully and Lang expressed in more visual, dramatic terms. It was a special kind of intelligence, that of an articulate cynic in search of redemption, one who can't help believing in love.

ORSON WELLES (1915–1985) was famous long before he ever made a movie. Welles was a child prodigy who read at three and was giving performances of *King Lear* at seven. By 1934, his voice already the breathy bass that would be famous the world over, Welles was touring with stage star Katherine Cornell and making a good living in radio.

8–14. *Sunset Boulevard* **(U.S.A., 1950),** *with Gloria Swanson and William Holden, directed by Billy Wilder.*
The scene: A gala party to which former silent movie diva Norma Desmond invites her ghost-writer and soon-to-be-lover in an attempt to sweep him off his feet. They are accompanied only by a discreet orchestra and the paintings and photos of herself from twenty-five years before. The reversal of sex roles is used here for dramatic purposes, but Wilder generally used it for comedy, as in *The Major and the Minor* and *Some Like It Hot*. The role of Norma Desmond was first offered to Mary Pickford, who considered it but finally turned it down. Then it was proffered to Pola Negri, who also refused. Swanson took the part and created a magnificent tour de force, a grotesque, panic-stricken gargoyle. Silent screen star Mae Murray thought the movie was overdone. "None of us floozies were *that* nuts," she said. In fact, some of them were. Mae Murray herself was Exhibit A. *(Paramount Pictures)*

Finally in 1937 at the ripe old age of twenty-one, Welles, in association with John Houseman, formed the Mercury Theater, a classical repertory company. Their first production was Shakespeare's *Julius Caesar*, done as a fascist parable, complete with blackshirted henchmen. After that came a Negro *Macbeth*, then a labor opera. The Mercury Theater was one of the most celebrated repertory companies in the history of the New York Stage, and it was Welles who made it work, who covered the company's losses with the large salary he was able to earn as the hero of the popular radio show, *The Shadow*.

In between plays, Welles produced a radio broadcast that panicked America, his adaptation of H. G. Welles's *The War of the Worlds*, done in the form of news bulletins interrupting regular radio programming. Even though the fact that it was only a dramatization of an invasion of earth by Martians was clearly announced several times during the show itself, panic spread over much of the eastern seaboard in a classic case of mass hysteria.

8–15. *To Be or Not To Be* (**U.S.A., 1942**), *with Jack Benny (sitting on table), directed by Ernst Lubitsch.*
Lubitsch's film deals with a troupe of preening ham actors fighting Hitler and, in the process, gaining the nobility that their profession and lack of talent have previously denied them. It was a critical failure, which stung Lubitsch deeply. Time proved him right and the prissy critics who charged him with bad taste dead wrong. It is among the most delicious and audacious of American comedies.   *(United Artists)*

So it was that in 1939, largely on the basis of the notoriety of *The War of the Worlds,* the struggling RKO studio lured Welles and his company to Hollywood. Welles's contract gave him carte blanche: Once a project was approved by the studio, it was entirely in his hands. He didn't even have to show **rushes** to the executives.

Citizen Kane (**8–16**) was Welles's first approved project, and he gathered around him the crème of the Mercury Theater—most notably actors Joseph Cotten and Agnes Moorehead and composer Bernard Herrmann. Welles added expert film veterans such as screenwriter Herman Mankiewicz and cameraman Gregg Toland, fresh from shooting *The Grapes of Wrath* for John Ford. With a budget of $650,000—not cheap, but far from lavish—*Citizen Kane* was efficiently made in an atmosphere of secrecy, the reasons for which became obvious as rumors of the film's subject matter began leaking out.

Kane bore a more than teasing relationship to the life and career of William Randolph Hearst, the most powerful newspaper publisher in the world, who was still alive. As the movie neared release, Hollywood, in thrall to the Hearst press, began to get nervous. Some people actively panicked. Louis B. Mayer offered the president of RKO the cost of the picture plus a profit if he would simply burn the negative. The offer was refused.

Citizen Kane opened on May 1, 1941. Nobody had ever seen a film quite like it. Filmmakers had experimented with overlapping dialogue, **deep-focus** cine-

8–16. *Citizen Kane* (U.S.A., 1941), *with Orson Welles, directed by Welles.*

Welles's style is an assertive mixture of looming figures, formal compositions, and theatrical lighting often derived from his previous experiments in the live theater—a visual mixture of John Ford and Sergei Eisenstein, with a sense of daring that lessens the formal stateliness of the technique. His least successful works—*Macbeth* (1948) or *Mr. Arkadin* (1955)—are movies in which the director concentrated on visual virtuosity and gave such short shrift to the narrative mechanics that the films are almost incomprehensible. But at his best—*Kane, The Magnificent Ambersons* (1942), *Chimes at Midnight* (1966)—Welles fused style and content into a seamless unit. *(RKO)*

matography, **chiaroscuro lighting,** exotic camera **angles,** oblique narratives from various points of view—but not all in the same movie. Its technical bravado aside, what distinguished *Kane* at the time, and what continues to distinguish it, is its energy, its air of command combined with youthful vivacity. The film is structured as a series of interlocking **flashbacks,** with the same man described by different people who knew him. It's a sophisticated style that paralleled the fragmented manner of much modern fiction. Style, in this case highly expressionistic, is actually just as important as content.

The movie traces the life of Charles Foster Kane, inheritor of a mining fortune who grows up to be a flamboyant newspaper tycoon. He is gradually alienated from romance, from love, from life itself by the ossifying blanket of his money and the will to power that it breeds. He becomes an artifact of his own fame, an increasingly remote speck of humanity adrift in the vast halls of his palatial home, Xanadu. The film is also the story of a faceless reporter out to tell the story of Kane's life and its meaning, as revealed in his enigmatic last word, "Rosebud." At its core it is a story of ideals betrayed, of disillusionment and the petrifying nature of power, but it is also a film on fire with itself and the possibilities of film.

Citizen Kane is a series of sharply pointed, acutely observed scenes. The protagonist grows up in a series of scenes somewhat Dickensian in tone. He achieves a raffish young adulthood and determines to use his newspapers for the good of the common people. Then, little by little, Kane becomes rigid with age, betrays his ideals and friends. In a classic vignette, Welles creates a **montage** of Kane and his wife at the breakfast table over the years. Welles takes them from loving newlyweds to middle-aged hostility in less than two minutes. At the end of the scene, Kane is at one end of the table reading his paper; his wife is at the other end reading the opposition paper. They glare at each other and do not speak. Welles is not just showing off—though there is an element of that in much of his work—but creating new ways of stating old themes or plot points, like a great jazz musician.

With all the flashiness of the film's style, what the movie leaves behind is a solitary silence. One old man dismisses the inquiring reporter and, noting his age, says philosophically, "Old age is the only disease that you don't look forward to being cured of." Another old man sits in a hospital, unsuccessfully trying to cadge

8–17. *Citizen Kane* (U.S.A., 1941), *with George Couloris, Orson Welles, and Everett Sloane, directed by Welles.*
Gregg Toland's deep-focus photography gives *Kane* a sense of size and grandeur. Here, artful composition and deep focus combine to create a vast, imposing banker's office, though in fact the set is really just two walls, cleverly lighted. Much of *Kane* depends on such deceptions, as well as many unobtrusive **matte shots** and **double exposures.** *(RKO)*

cigars from visitors, and remembers Charlie Kane: "I guess I was what you would nowadays call a stooge. . . . He never believed in anything except Charlie Kane. He never had a conviction . . . in his life. I suppose he died without one. . . . Of course, a lot of us check out without any special convictions . . . but we know what we're leaving, we do believe in *something.*"

The movie is also, but not primarily, a peculiarly American story of how the goals of success, money, and power pursued without defining reasons can turn rancid and can destroy love. In its drive, energy, and opulent ambition, *Kane* is a very American film. Penelope Houston made an analogy between *Kane* and F. Scott Fitzgerald's novel *The Great Gatsby.* "In both cases, the works are powered by a strong romantic appetite, an American baroque style, a feeling not so much for the shattered reality as for the promise of the receding dream." Thus, Kane's castle is a tomb just as surely as the grave itself—a tomb for the dreams of an American who metaphorically stands for a great many of his compatriots whose values were lost, strayed, stolen, or nonexistent.

Citizen Kane was critically hailed, but it turned out to be a financial disappointment. More than nice reviews, RKO was hoping for a bonanza. The notoriety and general bad vibes that Welles had created were more trouble than a *succès d'estime* was worth. Already at work on his next film, *The Magnificent Ambersons,* by the time *Kane* was released, Welles got caught in the middle of a change in studio regimes.

The Magnificent Ambersons (**8–18**) was cut by a third to fit into a second feature time slot. Even hacked to only eighty-eight minutes, *Ambersons* is preferred to *Kane* by some, including Joseph Cotten, who played major roles in both movies: "*Kane* is a kind of trick film," he remembered. "It's just a story but it was beautifully told. *Ambersons* has a better story; it has something to say. It's about the passage of a way of life."

The Magnificent Ambersons is about the process of decay that destroys a proud old midwestern family. Most of its members regard Eugene Morgan (Cotten), an

8–18. *The Magnificent Ambersons* (U.S.A., 1942), *with Agnes Moorehead and Tim Holt, directed by Orson Welles.*
The mood of *Ambersons* is 90 degrees away from *Kane.* The theme is the same one of loss and the end of innocence, but the movie is about passive people rather than the aggressive Charles Foster Kane. Welles adopts a measured, contemplative tone, and his narration is weighted with a nostalgic sadness leavened only slightly with irony. The great cameraman Stanley Cortez provided photography of lacelike delicacy. With images of silhouettes against leaded glass windows, the frozen breath of a happy family on a sleigh ride, the vanished custom of the serenade, Welles created a sad valentine to an America that had vanished before he was born, to what was obviously his deep regret.   *(RKO)*

inventor who comes up with a newfangled contraption called an automobile, as a hopelessly deluded dreamer. *Ambersons* is a reflective lament for a gentler, more graceful time. By comparison, *Kane* is a rowdy three-ring circus. Despite a non-Wellesian ending that is taken from the very fine Booth Tarkington novel, the prevailing mood is one of regret, of despair tempered by romance. (It was not for nothing that Welles studied the work of Ford before he began work on *Kane* or that, when asked to name the old masters of film, he replied, "John Ford, John Ford, and John Ford.")

Welles's contract at RKO was canceled, which caused a rupture in his career that would never be repaired. He would do fine work again—*The Stranger* (1946) and *Touch of Evil* (1958) need no apologies—but the truly irreparable loss was Welles's estrangement from the American scene, from which his work had derived both its subject matter and its idiosyncratic strength.

In a European exile that stretched on for nearly thirty years, Welles became a peripatetic international figure, acting in other men's mostly inferior movies. He assembled his own films a scene at a time, piecemeal fashion, with some productions taking four and five years to complete. Making technical demands that less sophisticated European technicians couldn't satisfy, Welles turned increasingly toward Shakespeare, whom he had adored since childhood.

Welles's Shakespeare is not the euphonious, graceful poet of *Romeo and Juliet* or the Olivier films but the dark, tortured barbaric tragedian of plays like *Macbeth* and *Othello,* adapted by Welles in 1948 and 1952. But it was in Welles's amalgam of Shakespeare's Falstaff plays, *Chimes at Midnight,* also known as *Falstaff,* that the director's later work is most fully realized. Cobbling together fragments of *Richard II, Henry IV, Parts I and II, Henry V,* and *The Merry Wives of Windsor,* shooting in and against the medieval castles of Spain, Welles seamlessly created an environment of cold, dank castles inhabited by dirty, Rabelaisian peasants.

Most memorably, Welles plays Falstaff, the role that he was designed by nature and his own appetites to inhabit. According to critic Peter Moriss, "The film moves inexorably from the jolly worlds of taverns and wenches towards a sense of darkness and decay where all around is talk of death." Falstaff and Prince Hal are roistering pals when the prince is elevated to the throne. The newly crowned monarch must leave his tavern days and disreputable friends behind. The rejection of the giant, good-hearted Falstaff—his face crumbling as Hal cruelly indicts him by saying, "How ill doth white hairs become a fool and knave"—constitutes some of Welles's finest screen acting. His direction in this film is an intelligent balance between spectacle and emotion.

Welles was long the object of condescension for the apparent anticlimax that followed his stunning film debut at the age of twenty-five. But even presuming that it is not enough for a man to make two undisputed masterpieces of world cinema, the old dictum "fast start, fast finish" does not really apply if Welles's films are examined dispassionately. Because of fate, his own intransigence, and the basic industrial nature of studio production that left little room for a talent like Welles's, quite without careerist guile or the money-making ability that could take guile's place, Welles was simply left without the nurturing soil he needed if he was to continue to grow and thrive as an artist. But *Chimes at Midnight,* at least, is proof that if Welles's opportunities lessened, his talent didn't.

Film Noir and Postwar Realism

The year after World War II ended, the Hollywood studios released 405 movies and earned their greatest profits in history. But the changing social conditions and the vanishing of a world full of simple pleasures like going to the movies was foretold in a series of films that the French collectively referred to as **film noir,** literally "black films," so called because of their prevailing mood, generally pessimistic or, in moments of extreme jubilation, ambiguous. Films like *The Maltese Falcon* and *Murder My Sweet* (1944) presaged the prime achievements of the movement, including Fritz Lang's *Scarlet Street* (1945), Robert Siodmak's *The Killers* **(8–19),** Jacques Tourneur's *Out of the Past* (1947), and Henry Hathaway's *Kiss of Death* (1947).

Film noir is mood, images, men fatalistically entrapped by deceitful women, city streets at three in the morning, streetlights reflected in puddles left from a drizzling rain, dingy hotel rooms containing characters for whom there is no escape. As a **genre,** noir owned much to the UFA tradition of German expressionism. The style was introduced to America by expatriot directors like Lang in films like *You Only Live Once* (1937) or men like Siodmak and Wilder, who provided a continental sophistication that was entirely absent from the homely optimism endemic to mainstream American directors like Capra and Hawks. For these expatriots, who were mostly Jewish, Hitler was only the most obvious example of the evil that spreads beneath the surface of everyday life like water under a thin crust of ice.

The netherworld aspects of noir naturally appealed to John Huston, whose *The Asphalt Jungle* (1950) encapsulates some prime aspects of the genre. The police barely exist. Screen time and audience sympathy are directed toward the criminals, much like the earliest gangster films, but this time with strong elements of existential futility. Noir is darkly fatalistic, running counter to the long-standing American tradition of optimism.

Film noir, World War II, the Holocaust and its aftermath, the popular dissemination of Freudian psychology—all combined to persuade filmmakers and audiences alike that, just maybe, there was more to life than Hollywood had heretofore suggested.

8–19. *The Killers* (**U.S.A., 1946**), *with Burt Lancaster (center), directed by Robert Siodmak.* Lancaster (1913–1994) was originally a circus acrobat, and his early movies made use of little else but his beefy physicality and star presence. He came to prominence through a series of dashing swashbucklers in which he did most of his own stunts. He became his own producer in the early 1950s, and his serious ambition began to assert itself in films like *The Rose Tattoo* (1955) and *Sweet Smell of Success* (1957). By the 1960s, with movies like *Elmer Gantry* (1960) and *Birdman of Alcatraz* (1962), Lancaster's natural gusto had relaxed, allowing for a watchful contemplative intensity. His reach had finally equaled his grasp. After then, he became one of world cinema's leading character actors, working with distinction for directors as varied and excellent as Visconti, Bertolucci, Louis Malle, and Bill Forsyth. Lancaster was not the first— nor will he be the last—to exploit his sex appeal to fulfill his artistic ambitions.   *(Universal Pictures)*

Social realism, a movement concurrent with film noir, was also the result of European influences. The Italian **neorealists** led the way in trying to portray factually the rubble and despair of postwar Europe (see Chapter 9). Within five years, Hollywood production techniques, which had long concentrated on purest artifice, began to adapt to these European influences. The heyday of social realism in the American cinema was the 1950s, but the movement had its roots in the immediate postwar period **(8–20).**

A prime mover in this movement was the producer-director team of Darryl Zanuck and Henry Hathaway. Zanuck had established a tradition of films drawn from current events when he had been production chief at Warner Brothers in the early 1930s. Now, with the national mood one of similar disenchantment, he turned to it again. This time, he sent the brusque, all-purpose contract director Hathaway out to actual locations to shoot films like *13 Rue Madeleine* (1946), *Kiss of Death*—noir with location verisimilitude—and, best of all, *Call Northside 777* (1948), a true story with James Stewart as a dogged reporter out to free a man unjustly imprisoned for murder. The film was shot in the places in Chicago where the story really took place—reality twice over.

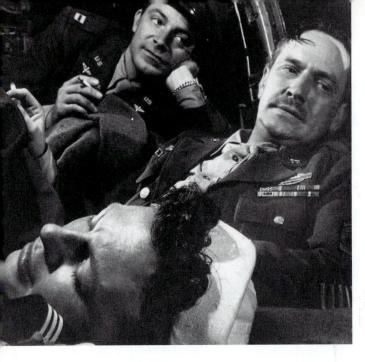

8–20. *The Best Years of Our Lives* (U.S.A., 1946), *with Dana Andrews (top center), Fredric March (right), and Harold Russell, directed by William Wyler.*
This was the mood and the film that captured the postwar era—austere, deglamourized, emotionally ambivalent. The characters' confusions and ambiguities are reflected in their expressions as well as their placement in the constricted mise en scène. Wyler believed that the camera, the staging, the externals of a scene are "important only as they help the audience understand what the characters are thinking, feeling or doing." *(RKO)*

Film noir was psychologically morbid and largely studio made; the social realism of Zanuck, Hathaway, and others like Elia Kazan, Fred Zinnemann, and Stanley Kramer was psychologically realistic and made on location. These twin thrusts at conventional Hollywood production signaled the beginning of a change in style and content that would be as radical as the economic and social dislocations of the changeover to sound. By February, 1949, only twenty-two films were in production, about half of the usual number. Retrenchment was the order of the day, and in more ways than one. The days when Hollywood had a guaranteed audience with whom it had a reciprocal relationship were fast drawing to a close. From now on, Hollywood would follow, not lead. As the founding generation of moguls died out in the 1950s, they would be replaced by businessmen and agents, people with more of an understanding of marketing than of entertainment, audiences, or art. It showed.

No film demonstrated the change in attitude quite as succinctly as Robert Rossen's *Body and Soul* (1947). The screenplay by Abraham Polonsky overtly points up the economic and class differences between boxing champion Charlie Davis (John Garfield) and the socialite women and the lure of their world. Charlie's mother is against his choice of profession. "Better you should buy a gun and shoot yourself," she suggests. "You need money to buy a gun," Charlie retorts.

Charlie fights his way to the top, but at terrible moral cost. His black trainer, a former champion deposed by Charlie, dies because Charlie has compromised his integrity by selling out to the mob. In the end, Charlie reclaims his soul by winning a fight he had been ordered to throw. He leaves the ring and is met by an ominous threat. He faces down the thugs. "What are you going to do, kill me?" he says. "Everybody dies." He walks away, freed, not frightened, by the knowledge of his own mortality.

A cross between a pre-Code social-problem picture and a Marxist tract, *Body and Soul's* fatalistic last line served notice that the days of the rosy dream merchants were over. A new era of films had arrived.

FURTHER READING

FINCH, CHRISTOPHER. *The Art of Walt Disney*. New York: Harry N. Abrams, 1973. Beautifully illustrated in color.

GOTTESMAN, RONALD, ed. *Focus on Orson Welles*. Englewood Cliffs, N.J.: Prentice-Hall, 1976. A collection of scholarly essays about Welles and his movies.

————, and JOEL GREENBERG. *Hollywood in the Forties*. New York: A. S. Barnes, 1968. Survey of the decade, by genre.

HIRSCH, FOSTER. *Film Noir: The Dark Side of the Screen*. New York: Da Capo Press, 1981. Critical analysis, well illustrated.

HUSTON, JOHN. *An Open Book*. New York: Alfred A. Knopf, 1980. Huston's autobiography—a lively yarn by a master storyteller.

KOPPES, CLAYTON R., and GREGORY D. BLACK. *Hollywood Goes to War*. Berkeley: University of California Press, 1987. Propaganda and morale pictures during World War II.

NEVE, BRIAN. *Film and Politics in America: A Social Tradition*. New York: Routledge, 1992. Politics of the 1930s and 1940s, in theater and film.

POLAN, DANA. *Power and Paranoia*. New York: Columbia University Press, 1986. Narrative in American movies of the 1940s.

SCHATZ, THOMAS. *Boom and Bust: American Cinema in the 1940s*. Berkely: University of California Press, 1999. Survey of the decade.

ZOLOTOW, MAURICE. *Billy Wilder in Hollywood*. New York: Putnam, 1977. Biography, with emphasis on Wilder's personality rather than his works.

9

European Cinema in the 1940s

This is the way things are.
—ROBERTO ROSSELLINI on the premiere of his Resistance masterpiece, *Open City*

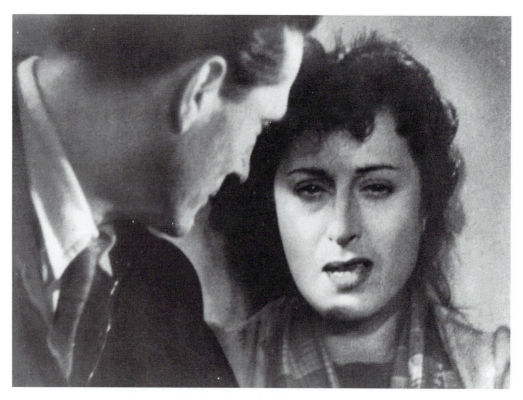

Timeline: 1940–1949

1940–1945

World War II; Japan, Italy, and Germany form a military and economic alliance; massive Nazi bombardments of many British cities

1941

Nazi Germany dominates most of western Europe and much of the U.S.S.R.

1942

Japanese Imperial Army spreads over many of the South Pacific islands

Murder of millions of Jews, homosexuals, and political dissenters in Nazi gas chambers—continues until the end of the war

1943

Hitler orders a "scorched earth" policy in the U.S.S.R.; massacre in Warsaw Jewish ghetto

Political revolution in Italy: Mussolini deposed; new Italian government switches sides and declares war on Germany; American military forces invade southern Italy and march northward, meeting fierce Fascist resistance

Teheran Conference: Roosevelt, Churchill, and Stalin meet

1944

Jean-Paul Sartre's existential play, *No Exit*

1945

Fascists in retreat; Mussolini killed by Italian Partisans; Hitler commits suicide; "V-E Day" (Victory in Europe) May 7; War ends in Europe

Allied occupation of Germany and Japan; Nuremberg trials of Nazi war criminals begin; black markets for consumer goods spring up all over Europe

1947

Berlin airlift begins—penetrates Stalin's "Iron Curtain"

1949

Civil war in China—Communist People's Republic proclaimed under strongman Mao Zedong

U.S.S.R. tests first atom bomb; "Cold War" intensifies between capitalist and Communist worlds

A civilization in ruins: wartime and reconstruction. Germany and the Occupation—a cinema in eclipse. France: poetic realism and the escapist allure of the past. The Soviet Union: propaganda and its discontents in the age of Stalin. Great Britain: glory amidst the ashes. John Grierson and the documentary tradition. Laurence Olivier. Eternal Shakespeare. The literary tradition of David Lean and Carol Reed. Italy: the Neorealist movement. *Open City* and other cries of pain. Rossellini, De Sica, Zavattini, and Visconti. The waning of neorealism.

T HE EUROPEAN CINEMA OF THE 1940s was dominated by World War II and the postwar reconstruction. The major film-producing countries were also the principal combatants, and to varying degrees their production facilities were devoted to the war effort. For the most part, however, overt propaganda was restricted primarily to government-sponsored documentaries and newsreels, while fiction films were devoted pretty much to escapist fare or sentimental home-front movies, which were made to boost public morale. The production of fiction movies declined sharply during the war years—1939 to 1945—for production matériel was scarce and was usually diverted to the war effort. Similarly, most of the experienced film artists and technicians turned their energies toward the war, either in the production of documentaries or as actual combatants.

Those who returned from battle often came back to bombed-out ruins. During the postwar era, the film industries of all the combatant countries except the United States were severely crippled by the devastations of the war. The awesome toll of human misery inflicted by World War II makes even the barbarism of ancient times seem parochial in comparison. No one has been able to determine the number of people killed, but estimates vary from a conservative 35 million lives lost to a high figure of 60 million. In the U.S.S.R. alone, 7.5 million combatants were killed, not including 2.5 million innocent civilians. Poland lost a quarter of its population, most of them Jewish civilians who were systematically murdered in the Nazi death camps. Germany lost over 4 million people, including 780,000 civilians.

Indeed, historians have pointed out that the civilian population of the warring nations suffered worse casualties than the military. Over 20 million people died from bombings, starvation, epidemics, and massacres. Cities like Dresden were reduced to pulverized rubble. Those who survived endured the cruelest hardships. In western Europe alone, over 35 percent of the housing was destroyed, leaving more than 20 million people homeless. It was a dark time, unprecedented even in the grimmest annals of human history.

Little wonder that these countries produced very few movies in the immediate postwar era. Nearly 60 percent of the film production facilities in Germany were destroyed by the massive Allied bombardments, and even Great Britain lost more than 25 percent of its movie theaters. Miraculously, three great national cinemas endured amidst this rubble and despair—those of Great Britain, Italy, and Japan. (The Japanese cinema is discussed in Chapter 11.) In England, such important film-makers as Laurence Olivier, David Lean, and Carol Reed directed their finest movies during this era. In Italy, too, a startling outburst of creativity ushered in a famous humanistic film movement, **neorealism.** It was spearheaded by such gifted artists as Roberto Rossellini, Vittorio De Sica, and Luchino Visconti.

Other countries were less fortunate. Worst hit of all was Germany. Most of its film artists had fled the country during the 1930s, when Hitler's Holocaust was still in the planning stages. During the war years, nothing of artistic significance was produced. Nothing emerged during the postwar era. In fact, so traumatized was Germany by the war that its cinema did not reemerge on the international scene until the 1960s, and then only in a modest way. The celebrated *Das Neue Kino,* or New German Cinema, had to wait until the 1970s to be born. In France, a few masterpieces were produced, but they were sporadic, the works of a handful of independents rather than the products of a coherent national industry. In the Soviet Union, the major achievements were in documentary rather than fiction movies. The rest of Europe went dark.

Germany

It all began in Germany. When Hitler became chancellor in 1933, he appointed his campaign manager, Dr. Joseph Goebbels, as his minister of propaganda and culture. Within a short time, all the media—music, film, radio, theater, literature, art, and the press—were under the domination of the Nazi party and its authoritarian dogma. As in the United States, Jews were prominent in the German film industry and in the arts in general. When these Jewish artists and businesspeople were forbidden employment in motion pictures (and the other media), Germany was depleted of much of its finest talent. Soon any form of dissidence was forbidden by law, and the exodus was nearly complete. Leni Riefenstahl was the only world-class filmmaker who remained in Nazi Germany, and her best work was completed before the war (see **7–1**).

As early as 1934, by law all film scripts had to be submitted to Nazi censors in advance. Nothing "subversive" escaped their scrutiny. Tax breaks were given to producers of "works of distinction," especially those that were pro-Nazi. However, very few fiction films dealt overtly with politics. For the most part, German movies during the Nazi era were harmless **genre** pictures like operettas, nationalistic sagas, romantic dramas, and historical spectacles—the cinematic opiate of the masses. Goebbels issued an edict that critical reviews of these movies had to be "positive."

Goebbels's plan was shrewd and simple, a variation on the old sugar-coated pill theory. Knowing that the public loved this escapist fodder, he lured them into the theaters by featuring such fiction movies as main attractions. Every theater was required by law to show government-produced newsreels and documentaries as second features, and it was in these "nonfiction" films, with their illusion of presenting factual information, that the Nazis promulgated their propaganda. These documentaries were highly manipulative, filled with distortions, half-truths, and often outright lies. The worst of them were anti-Semitic and were steeped in hypocrisy.

For example, in *The Eternal Jew* (1940, directed by Franz Hippler), the squalor of the infamous Warsaw ghetto is portrayed as the "natural state" of Polish Jews, their preferred style of living—rather than the way they were forced to live by their Nazi captors. There is no mention of the death camps and Hitler's "final solution"

9–1. *Day of Wrath* **(Denmark, 1943),** *directed by Carl Theodor Dreyer.*

The Nazi occupation had a chilling effect on Denmark's small film industry. Even Dreyer (1889–1968), who was not interested in political subjects, departed for neutral Sweden after making *Day of Wrath,* which contains a veiled allusion about the tyranny of foreign occupation. Dreyer is Denmark's greatest filmmaker. Although he directed only about a dozen features, his career spanned six decades, beginning in the teens and concluding in the 1960s. He made movies in France, Germany, and Norway as well as his native Denmark. Though few of his films were commercially successful, they are admired by critics for their thematic complexity and the beauty of their images. Dreyer was interested in exploring psychological and religious themes. He grew up in a strict Lutheran household, and the austere Puritanism of his youth found expression in many of his movies. His characters are often trapped in a constricting social environment that prevents them from expressing their emotions openly. Dreyer was fascinated with the idea of spiritual transcendence—how a person's soul can rise above the constraints of the physical world. His most admired works include *The Passion of Joan of Arc* (France, 1928, see **7–13**), *Vampyr* (France, 1932), *Day of Wrath, Ordet* (1954), and *Gertrud* (1964). *(Museum of Modern Art)*

of genocide, but the narrator emphasizes the need to "cleanse" Europe of these "parasites." Phony statistics are offered as proof of Jewish degeneracy—for instance, "98 percent of the white slave traffic is Jewish." Jewish artists, intellectuals, and entrepreneurs are presented as members of a worldwide conspiracy devoted to seizing power in their host countries. The documentary ends with romanticized images of "Aryan" youths on the march, Nazi banners and processions, and the concluding warning: "Keep our race pure. Racial purity forever."

After the crushing defeat of the Nazis, the country was partitioned into four sectors, presided over by the victorious Allies: in the West by the United States, Great Britain, and France; in the East by the U.S.S.R. East Germany was the first to reestablish its film industry. It was carefully regulated by the central government—not so radical a departure from the Nazi system, though of course the propaganda was now Communist rather than Fascist. In the West, the film industry was more chaotic and uncoordinated. A few enterprising producers came forth, but there was a serious shortage of capital, and only about 20 percent of the movie theaters were still standing.

The first movies to emerge during the postwar period were the so-called rubble films, which were photographed in the actual bombed-out ruins of Germany's cities. Most of these films were didactic and attempted to correct the lies of the Nazi regime. Within a short time, however, overtly political movies became rare in the West. They were replaced by such popular genres as romances, operettas, third-rate comedies, and period pictures. Few of these films were exhibited outside Germany's borders, and today they are largely forgotten. For the next two decades, German movies were cautious, bland, and for the most part gutless. In the words of film historian Roger Manvell, they suffered from "a paralysis of the imagination." The German people had had enough excitement, cinematic or otherwise. They wanted to forget.

France

France was one of the first countries to capitulate to the Nazi war machine. From 1940 to 1945, the country was occupied by the triumphant German forces. The occupation had a devastating effect on the film industry, which was cut off from its foreign markets. Prior to the occupation, some of France's greatest filmmakers—including René Clair and Jean Renoir—had fled to the United States, where they managed to find work in Hollywood. Those filmmakers who remained in occupied France concentrated on period and fantasy films, far removed from the grim realities of contemporary life.

Perhaps the finest film of the occupation is *The Children of Paradise* **(9–2),** which was made in the final two years of the war, mostly in bits and pieces. The enormous cast boasted some of France's best actors, including Arletty, Jean-Louis Barrault, Pierre Brasseur, Pierre Renoir, and Maria Casares. The vast, studio-created sets (by Alexandre Trauner) are faintly stylized to produce an air of remote familiarity—like faded etchings of a bygone era. Romantic and richly textured, the movie is by turns robust, symbolic, and poetic. Though Carné continued to work in the postwar era, *The Children of Paradise* is widely regarded as his last major work.

In the postwar period, the French film industry reverted to its customary state of semianarchy. Plagued by a lack of capital, limited studio space, and scarce or outmoded equipment, even the best French directors, like Clair, Renoir, and Jacques Feyder, were hard pressed to find employment. The government hardly helped matters by imposing a stiff 60 percent tax on the gross receipts of French

9–2. *The Children of Paradise* **(France, 1945),** *directed by Marcel Carné.*
Inspired by the sprawling nineteenth-century romantic novels of Dumas and Balzac, this movie was written by Carné's frequent collaborator Jacques Prévert, a poet and novelist. Like their famous prewar collaborations, *The Children of Paradise* is imbued with a sense of loss and a melancholy atmosphere of fatalism. The dialogue is deliberately artificial—crystalline, elegant, literary. The film features several plot strands and a network of philosophical themes exploring the central metaphor of life as theater. The "children" of the title refers not only to the naively hopeful central characters, but also to the lower-class patrons of the theater, who can afford to sit only in "paradise"—the rear balconies.   *(Museum of Modern Art)*

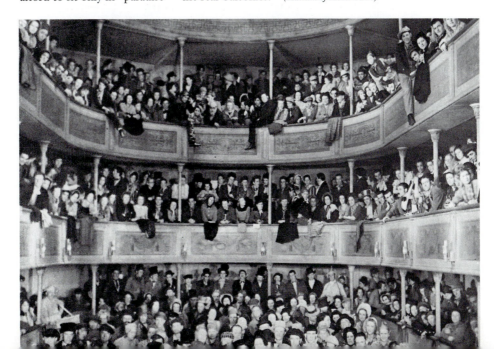

9–3. *Beauty and the Beast* (France, 1946), *with Josette Day, directed by Jean Cocteau.*
Like Cocteau's earlier avant-garde movies, this elegantly wrought fairy tale stresses "the realism of the unreal." Dreamlike scenes of the most exquisite artificiality—like real arms and hands serving as candelabra sconces—are presented with matter-of-fact precision. Despite its literary dialogue and knowing sophistication, the movie conveys a sense of childlike innocence and wonder. *(Janus Films)*

movies. A few interesting works were produced in the second half of the decade, most notably Cocteau's *Beauty and the Beast* **(9–3),** but for the most part these were created by mavericks who worked outside the established industry. American movies, suppressed during the Nazi occupation, flooded the market after the Liberation. They virtually annihilated the French film industry, which had to content itself with crumbs. Many years would pass before the French cinema regained its prominence on the international scene.

Soviet Union

In the Soviet Union, the film industry was subject to the whims and vicissitudes of the party line. Josef Stalin, a dictator as ruthless and depraved as Hitler, took a personal interest in film. (Interestingly, his favorite movies were American westerns.) Despite the international prestige garnered by Soviet filmmakers in the 1920s, he disliked the movies of Eisenstein, Pudovkin, Vertov, and Dovzhenko—the preeminent film artists of the U.S.S.R.'s golden age. Accordingly, after Stalin's take over in the early 1930s, all these artists and others were denounced for "formalism." They were condemned for their "barren intellectualism," for creating movies that appealed only to foreigners, aesthetes, and intellectuals rather than ordinary Soviet citizens. Reduced to serving as "artistic advisors," Eisenstein and his like-minded colleagues were not permitted to direct their own movies during this period except on a sporadic basis. Most Soviet films of the 1930s were boy-loves-tractor movies and dull costume dramas filled with edifying patriotic speeches. They were well crafted, impersonal, and, above all, safe. Many of the drudges who churned out these films were cited as "Honored Artists of the Republic."

As World War II drew closer, the Soviet cinema twisted and coiled with each new development. When a Nazi invasion seemed imminent, Stalin ordered the film studios to stress Russian nationalism and unity by producing movies that dealt with historic prerevolutionary figures—"heroes of Mother Russia." The best of these was Eisenstein's *Alexander Nevsky* (1938), a story set in medieval times when a German invasion was crushed by a newly unified Russian army under the inspired leadership of a paternal aristocrat. When Hitler and Stalin signed their nonaggression pact in 1939, such films were immediately withdrawn from circulation.

In the following year, the Nazis invaded the U.S.S.R. Immediately such films as *Alexander Nevsky* were put back into circulation, and the studios were ordered to produce more of the same. Eisenstein's *Ivan the Terrible* (9–4) is the most famous of these.

During the harsh years of the war, the film studios were moved to Soviet central Asia, where they were safe from Nazi encroachments. The production of fiction movies was cut back to less than half the prewar level, and the films were crudely propagandistic. The Nazis were portrayed as "devils," and the U.S.S.R., the United States, and Great Britain as "glorious defenders" of the Allied cause. Newsreels and documentaries received top priority. The overwhelming majority of technicians and artists devoted themselves to capturing the extraordinary heroism of the Soviet people under siege. Many brave cameramen were killed on the front lines while attempting to photograph the carnage of warfare.

In the postwar period, the party line made another about-face. Movies about prerevolutionary "folk heroes" abruptly disappeared. Boy-loves-tractor stories and

9–4. *Ivan the Terrible, Part I* (U.S.S.R., 1944), *with Nikolai Cherkasov, directed by Sergei Eisenstein.*
This was one of many period films made during the war that dealt with prerevolutionary "heroes of the people." It was a genre strongly encouraged by Stalin to foster a favorable comparison with his own leadership during troubled times. In *Ivan the Terrible, Part II,* Eisenstein encountered many obstacles, mostly from Stalin and his cultural stooges, who objected to the director's ambivalent portrait of Ivan, who had become intoxicated with power. A number of critics interpreted the movie as a veiled portrait of Stalin. The film was not released until 1948, after Eisenstein was forced to make it conform to the current party line. A projected Part III was never completed, for Eisenstein died of a heart attack at the age of fifty in 1948. *(Janus Films)*

their ilk made a comeback. Fictionalized accounts of the war years and the reconstruction emphasized the need for individuals to make sacrifices for a higher social cause. As the Cold War became more intense, the former "glorious defenders" became the new "devils." (The same phenomenon took place in the United States, when the Hollywood studios produced a spate of anti-Communist movies, most of them as shrill as their Soviet counterparts.) The majority of Russian movies during this period were plodding biographies of Soviet public figures and films dealing with the advances in science and culture in the U.S.S.R. Another common genre was the prestige picture—recordings of famous opera, ballet, and theater productions. Few of these films were exhibited outside the Soviet sphere of influence. As the examples of Hitler and Stalin demonstrate, film art rarely flourishes under totalitarian regimes. It was not until after 1953, the year of Stalin's death, that the Soviet cinema began its slow—and very cautious—ascent on the international scene.

Great Britain

In the early phases of the war, Great Britain was the only country with the determination and force to stand up to the Nazi war machine. In an attempt to bring the country to its knees, Hitler initiated the blitzkrieg—barrages of bombs dropped on Britain's major civilian population centers, especially London. Britain responded with more determination and more force, doggedly refusing to capitulate.

To shore up public morale, the government commissioned a series of documentaries, produced under the leadership of John Grierson. Throughout the 1930s, Grierson had been the most influential spokesman of the documentary movement, championing the genre as an essential component of public education. As a result of his efforts, Great Britain boasted the most prestigious school of documentary in the world. When hostilities broke out, virtually all the country's documentarists turned their energies toward the war effort.

In the area of fiction, the British film industry produced a few movies dealing with the war, most notably by producer Michael Balcon, who was the chief executive of Ealing Studios. For the most part, however, English fiction films steered clear of the war in favor of home-front movies and those traditional strongholds of the British cinema—literary and theatrical adaptations.

The most famous of these was *Henry V* (1944), starring and directed by LAURENCE OLIVIER (1907–1989). The movie is based on one of Shakespeare's most nationalistic plays and was produced to bolster public morale. Olivier had acted in a number of movies throughout the 1930s, both in Britain and the United States. In England he had played Orlando in Paul Czinner's Shakespearean adaptation, *As You Like It* (1936). Olivier's most famous roles in American films were the leads in William Wyler's *Wuthering Heights* (1939) and Hitchcock's *Rebecca* (1940). Shortly after the war broke out, Olivier returned to his native country and to his first love—the live theater.

He chose to make his film directing debut with *Henry V* because the story was roughly parallel to the contemporary situation in England: a British army poised for an invasion of German-occupied France. The rich pageantry of the movie, with its bold colors and a stirring score by William Walton, lifted the spirits of war-weary Britons. Critics strongly praised the actors, especially for their skill in making the English language soar with majestic lyricism. James Agee, America's best film critic of this period, wrote: "The one great glory of the film is the language. Olivier does many beautiful pieces of reading and playing. There are dozens of large and hundreds of small excellences which Sir Laurence and his associates have developed to sustain Shakespeare's poem."

Hamlet (1948) was an even greater success, especially in America and on the Continent, where it enjoyed considerable popularity and prestige **(9–5).** Photographed in black and white, the film is technically more sophisticated than its predecessor, filled with strikingly composed images, gliding **crane** and **dolly shots,** and startling camera **angles.** Olivier minimized **editing,** preferring to use **deep-focus** photography, **lengthy takes,** and subtle regroupings in the **mise en scène**—techniques he derived from his American mentor Wyler. Some of the soliloquies are "thought" rather than spoken aloud, and others combine speech with **voice-over** interior monologues, producing a more cinematic effect and giving these familiar soliloquies more interesting, off-beat interpretations.

In the last of his Shakespearean trilogy, *Richard III* (1955), Richard (played by Olivier) delivers many of his soliloquies directly at the camera—at us—thus establishing an intimate if uneasy rapport between this brazen villain and ourselves. Olivier's other two directorial efforts are less impressive. *The Prince and the Showgirl* (1957) featured Marilyn Monroe as his costar, and though the film contains some

9–5. *Hamlet* (**Great Britain, 1948**), *with Laurence Olivier and Eileen Herlie, directed by Olivier.*
Widely regarded as the best of the five movies directed by Olivier, *Hamlet* was successful in the United States as well as Great Britain. Unusual for a foreign film, it won five American Academy Awards, including the Best Picture Oscar and the Best Actor award for Olivier. *(J. Arthur Rank–Two Cities)*

charming comic scenes, it is a lightweight work, unworthy of their talents. *The Three Sisters* (1970) was a rather literal transcription of Chekhov's great play, which Olivier had originally staged for the live theater.

Olivier was one of Great Britain's major national resources. After the war he took over the country's National Theatre and transformed it into the most prestigious repertory theater of the English-speaking world. He was regarded as the dean of British actors, and that scepter'd isle is widely conceded to have the finest actors in the world. His range was extraordinary, encompassing most of the Shakespearean repertory as well as many roles of the classical continental drama. He played principals, character roles, and cameo parts. He moved freely from movies to television to live theater, both as an actor and director, in America as well as England. Lord Olivier was the only actor in British history to have been elevated to the House of Lords on the basis of his art.

Many other British actors became film stars during the war years and the immediate postwar era, including Rex Harrison, Vivien Leigh, Richard Attenborough, Deborah Kerr, Trevor Howard, Alec Guinness, Michael Redgrave, James Mason, Jean Simmons, David Niven, Robert Donat, Jack Hawkins, Dirk Bogarde, Richard Burton, Peter Finch, and Margaret Leighton, to mention only some of the most prominent. Most of these performers also distinguished themselves in the American cinema. British acting tends to favor a mastery of externals, based on close observation. Virtually all players are trained in diction, movement, makeup, dialects, fencing, dancing, body control, and ensemble playing. Above all, British actors have perfected the art of reciting highly stylized dialogue—the language of Shakespeare, Shaw, and Wilde—without violating the believability of their characters.

A long-cherished goal of British film producers was to crash the enormous American market, and in the 1940s they gained a foothold by producing a series of prestige pictures based on famous novels and plays. Two of George Bernard Shaw's dramas were made into movies, both directed by Gabriel Pascal: *Major Barbara* (1941) and *Caesar and Cleopatra* (1945). Thorald Dickinson directed *The Queen of Spades* (1948), based on a story by Pushkin, with the brilliant Edith Evans in the leading role. *The Red Shoes* (1948), a lavishly produced ballet film directed by Michael Powell and Emeric Pressburger, was surprisingly popular in the United States and was nominated for a Best Picture Academy Award. The most successful prestige pictures were directed by two of the top British filmmakers of this period, David Lean and Carol Reed.

DAVID LEAN (1908–1992) began his film career as a lowly **go-fer** and eventually rose to become an editor in 1934. He got his first chance to direct when he executed the action sequences of *In Which We Serve* (1942), a powerful wartime drama that takes place on a British fighting ship. Noel Coward starred in the film in addition to scripting, scoring, and codirecting it. Lean went on to direct three other Coward projects: *This Happy Breed* (1944), *Blithe Spirit* (1945), and *Brief Encounter* (1945).

Brief Encounter deals with an improbable love affair between a dedicated physician (Trevor Howard) and a middle-class housewife (Celia Johnson). Both are married to other people by whom they have children. Neither intended to fall in love: Their affair develops out of friendship, respect, and admiration. The movie is unusual in that the lovers are not stereotypically portrayed as glamorous victims of their raging passions. In fact, they are ordinary almost to the point of drabness.

Love takes them by surprise. Prior to their meeting, they had resigned themselves to a life of prim middle-aged respectability. She is married to a dull but decent man who is totally insensitive to her romantic nature. Out of a sincere sense of duty and principle, the lovers decide to remain with their spouses. Their self-sacrifice causes them anguish, but Lean conveys their suffering not through the acting, which is understated, but through the music that accompanies her voice-over narration, Rachmaninov's dramatic Second Piano Concerto.

Lean followed this film with two adaptations of novels by Dickens: *Great Expectations* **(9–6)** and *Oliver Twist* (1948). In films like these we can see British craftsmanship at its finest. In fact, they are typical not only of the best English movies of this period, but of the British cinema in general. The main characteristics of this tradition are (1) an emphasis on team work and an ensemble effect, rather than the dominance of a single artist; (2) well-written scripts, often based on distinguished literary sources; (3) excellent acting, with an emphasis on the expressiveness of the spoken word; (4) a clean **classical style,** with no conspicuous directorial flourishes; (5) a preference for period genres rather than contemporary stories; (6) high-quality **production values,** especially in the sets and costume design; and (7) a pervasive class consciousness, at least implied and often overtly dramatized.

Subsequent to this period, Lean's films became fewer and less consistent in terms of quality. In the 1950s and after, he often directed international coproductions, usually in association with American producers. *Summertime* (1955, known in Great Britain as *Summer Madness*) was photographed in Venice, with Katharine Hepburn in the leading role of a fortyish spinster who has an affair with an Italian merchant. It is one of her finest performances—funny, brave, and touching.

9–6. *Great Expectations* **(Great Britain, 1946),** *directed by David Lean.*
Like most British literary adaptations, which are usually faithful to their original sources, Lean's film preserves the major materials of Dickens's novel. But the movie is also a movie, embodying Dickens's vision in *cinematic* terms. Many pages of the novel's descriptive detail—like the eerie atmosphere of terror—are transformed into images of great beauty and emotional power. *(Museum of Modern Art)*

The Bridge on the River Kwai (1957) deals with a Japanese prisoner-of-war camp during World War II and features an international cast including Alec Guinness, William Holden, and Sessue Hayakawa. An absorbing psychological study, the film was a worldwide success, winning many awards, including five American Oscars: Best Picture, Best Director, Best Actor (Guinness), and the top writing and editing awards.

Lean's next film, *Lawrence of Arabia* (1962), another Anglo-American production, repeated this international success. Like its predecessor, *Lawrence* is both an **epic film** and a subtle character study. It introduced a young British actor named Peter O'Toole in the title role, garnering him the first of many Academy Award nominations. In all, the movie won six Oscars: Best Picture, Director, Color Cinematography, Art Direction, Editing, and Music.

Doctor Zhivago (1965) was also popular with the public, though critics complained of the movie's mishmash of acting styles, which fail to cohere as effectively as in Lean's previous works. Based on the novel by Boris Pasternak, the film deals with the epic events preceding and following the 1917 Russian Revolution. *Ryan's Daughter* (1970), a period romance, was a box office disappointment and was ravaged by critics for its overblown length, its overwrought style, and its grandiose pretensions. It was Lean's last movie until his triumphant comeback film, the splendid *A Passage to India* (1984), based on the novel by E. M. Forster.

SIR CAROL REED (1906-1976) began his career as an actor in the live theater, but he soon realized that his métier was directing movies. Throughout the 1930s, he directed a series of **program films** that were moderately successful at the box office but failed to excite much critical enthusiasm. His first important movie was *The Stars Look Down* (1939), which deals with the strife between workers and management in a Welsh mining community. The film is somewhat similar to John Ford's *How Green Was My Valley*, only Reed's work is less sentimental, more realistic, and overtly ideological. It is one of the very few British movies of this period to explore a working-class milieu from a sympathetic perspective—or, for that matter, from any perspective.

After the war, Reed produced and directed a string of four small masterpieces that were highly acclaimed by critics and were popular in America as well as Great Britain. Several of them were written by Graham Greene, a former film critic as well as one of England's greatest modern novelists. *Odd Man Out* (**9–7**) deals with the last hours of a fugitive Irish revolutionary. In its taut suspense, the film recalls the thrillers of Hitchcock, though Reed's movie is more complex thematically than most of Hitchcock's films up to this time. *The Fallen Idol* (1948) was based on Greene's story "The Basement Room." It explores a young boy's hero worship of a household servant who—thanks to the boy's inadvertent police testimony—is suspected of murdering his nagging wife. Like many of Reed's works of this period, *The Fallen Idol* explores a process of spiritual degeneration through a series of ritual humiliations.

The Third Man (**9–8**) is Reed's finest achievement. A triumph of mood and ambiance, the film is set in war-scarred Vienna during the Allied occupation. But the bombed-out locale is not used merely as a picturesque backdrop: It serves as a symbolic embodiment of the theme of moral decay. The chilly nighttime settings, the wet empty streets, the rain and impenetrable fog—all combine to produce an atmosphere of mystery, deception, and unspeakable evil. Anton Karra's weirdly un-

9–7. *Odd Man Out* (Great Britain, 1947), *with James Mason and Kathleen Ryan, directed by Carol Reed.*
This superbly crafted political thriller features a brilliant performance by Mason as an Irish rebel leader who is being hunted by the police after an audacious robbery. The script is a characteristic blend of suspense, metaphysics, and complex characterization. *(J. Arthur Rank)*

nerving zither music is at once exotic, brisk, and inexorable. Graham Greene's script features a variety of quirky, unpredictable characters who are sometimes funny as well as vaguely sinister. The story deals with the black market in penicillin and is steeped in moral ambiguities—pitting one kind of loyalty against another, one kind of corruption against another. Everybody loses.

Like David Lean, Reed fell into an artistic decline after the early 1950s. Most of his movies of that decade and after were minor projects, unworthy of his talent. Only two exceptions stand out. *Our Man in Havana* (1960) reunited Reed with scriptwriter Greene, though in a lighter vein. A sophisticated parody of a spy thriller, the movie is witty and wryly ironic. It features Alec Guinness as a sly vacuum cleaner salesman who is recruited to become an espionage agent and concocts reports based on the workings of a vacuum cleaner. *Oliver!* (1968), a vigorous and stylish adaptation of a stage musical based on Dickens's *Oliver Twist*, was a big international success. It won five Academy Awards, including those for Best Picture and Best Director.

9–8. *The Third Man* **(Great Britain, 1949),** *with Orson Welles (standing on ramparts), directed by Carol Reed.*
Thanks in part to Robert Krasker's striking black and white cinematography, *The Third Man* is a magnificent stylistic achievement. The movie features many dramatic **high-contrast** and **low-key** lighting effects, baroque compositions, rich textures, and bizarre **tilt shots** such as these, in which the vertical and horizontal lines of a bombed-out ruin are converted into tense diagonals, suffusing the sinister setting with a sense of visual anxiety.   *(Continental 16)*

Italy

Italian neorealism seemed to have flowered spontaneously from the smoke and debris of the war, but in fact the movement had its roots in the prewar era. When Benito Mussolini and his Fascist thugs seized power in 1922, one of his many promised reforms was to recapture the international prestige that the Italian cinema had enjoyed briefly in the early teens. Unlike most of Mussolini's other promises, this one was carried through—though the anticipated cinematic masterpieces never materialized until after his political overthrow in 1943.

Throughout the early Fascist era, the film industry was in a state of serious decline, its output dwindled to about ten features annually—a mere 6 percent of the movies exhibited in the country. Most of these were mediocre genre films, strictly for local consumption. The Fascist regime, preoccupied with more pressing concerns, paid little attention to the problem. By the early 1930s, however, the film industry was on the verge of extinction, and Mussolini was finally forced to make good his political promise.

In 1935, he established the Centro Sperimentale di Cinematografia, a national film school that was run by Luigi Chiarini, a left-wing intellectual. Unlike the Nazi regime in Germany, the Italian Fascists were somewhat tolerant of political deviance, provided it was discreet. Chiarini was discreet. However, he was no hypocrite, nor was he a flunky for the Fascists. Indeed, he encouraged a considerable number of promising students who, like himself, were **Marxist** in their sympathies, disaffected from the political establishment. Among these students were such future filmmakers as Roberto Rossellini, Luigi Zampa, Pietro Germi, Giuseppi De Santis, and Michelangelo Antonioni. The school also published a prestigious film journal, *Bianco e Nero,* which attracted some of the finest theoreticians of the period. (A rival journal, *Cinema,* was edited by Vittorio Mussolini, the dictator's son. It too was surprisingly permissive and published numerous articles critical of the contemporary Italian cinema.) In 1938, the Mussolini regime constructed the vast Cinecittà studio outside of Rome. It was the most sophisticated production facility in Europe, boasting the most advanced equipment, sixteen sound stages, and many **back-lot** sets.

All of this had its price, of course. After 1935, the Fascists largely controlled the output of the film industry. Top priority in financing went to pro-Fascist films. As in Germany, however, most fiction movies produced in Italy during this era were escapist entertainments. For example, the so-called white telephone films of the 1930s were inferior imitations of Hollywood originals, in which glamorous characters suffered from rarefied passions in swanky apartments that featured white telephones.

The term *neorealism* (i.e., new realism) was originally coined in 1943 by Umberto Barbero, an influential film critic and a professor at the Centro Sperimentale. He attacked the Italian cinema for its mindless triviality, its refusal to deal with pressing social concerns, especially poverty and injustice. He turned to the French cinema of the 1930s for models, lauding the poetic realism in the movies of Carné and Duvivier and the warm socialist humanism in the works of Renoir. Barbero also lamented the phony glamour of Italian movies, insisting that the glossy production values and stylistic flourishes were merely camouflaging a moral sterility. Above all, he called for a cinema of simplicity and humanity.

ROBERTO ROSSELLINI (1906–1977) inaugurated the neorealist movement in 1945 with his stark wartime drama, *Open City* **(9–9).** The movie deals with the collaboration of Catholics and Communists in fighting the Nazi occupation of Rome shortly before the American army liberated the city. Reputedly, Rossellini shot some of the footage while the Nazis were actually evacuating the capital. Technically, the film is rather crude. Since good-quality film stock was impossible to obtain, Rossellini had to use inferior newsreel stock. Nevertheless, the technical flaws and the resultant grainy images convey a sense of journalistic immediacy and authenticity. (Many neorealists began their careers as journalists, and Rossellini himself began as a documentarist.) Virtually all the movie was shot in actual locations, and there are many exterior shots in which no additional lights were used. With the exception of the principals, the actors were nonprofessionals. The structure of the movie is episodic—a series of vignettes showing the reactions of Roman citizens to the German occupation.

Rossellini refused to idealize his characters, focusing not on heroes but ordinary people in heroic moments. His blending of Marxism and Catholicism was historically accurate, for the Partisan movement was largely organized by Italian

9–9. *Open City* (Italy, 1945), *with F. Grand-Jacquet and Anna Magnani, directed by Roberto Rossellini.*

Open City catapulted Magnani to international stardom. A gifted comedienne as well as a powerful dramatic actress, she specialized in playing fiery working-class heroines. She was not conventionally glamorous and wore little or no makeup. Her gestures were spontaneous, abrupt, often contradictory. Even in quiet scenes such as this, she must make an effort to control her volatile feelings. Her hair and clothing, like her movements, fly in every direction, scarcely attended to. She can be brave and forceful, as well as feminine, sexy, and maternal. Magnani was the most admired Italian actress of her generation. Her naturalistic style of playing was so seamlessly artful that it looked more like behaving than performing. She was also popular in the United States and appeared in three American movies. The best of them is *The Rose Tattoo* (1955, directed by Daniel Mann), for which she won the Best Actress Academy Award. The role was written especially for her by dramatist Tennessee Williams.   *(Contemporary Films)*

Communists, and a number of Catholic clergymen also joined the Resistance. Rossellini's compassion for the victims of oppression was not narrowly ideological, however, for he sympathized even with those who betrayed their better instincts. The film is saturated with a sense of unrelenting honesty.

   Open City was an international success, both commercially and critically. It won several awards, including the Grand Prize at the Cannes Film Festival. It was especially popular in the United States, Great Britain, and France. It was also the only neorealist movie that enjoyed wide box office popularity in Italy itself. The film provided a rallying point for an entire generation of Italian filmmakers whose creative talents had been stifled by the repressive Fascist regime. Within the next few years, there followed an astonishing series of movies that swept the Italians into the front ranks of the international cinema: Rossellini's *Paisà* and *Germany: Year Zero;* De Sica's *Shoeshine, Bicycle Thief,* and *Umberto D.;* Visconti's *La Terra Trema;* Luigi Zampa's *To Live in Peace;* Alberto Latuada's *Senza Pietà* ("Without Pity");

Pietro Germi's *In the Name of the Law* and *The Path to Hope;* Giuseppi De Santis's *Bitter Rice;* and others.

There are considerable differences between these directors and even between their early and later works. Furthermore, neorealism implied a style as well as an ideology. Rossellini emphasized the ethical dimension: "For me, Neorealism is above all a moral position from which to look at the world. It then became an aesthetic position, but at the beginning it was moral." De Sica and Visconti also stressed morality as the touchstone of neorealism. The main ideological characteristics of the movement can be summarized as follows: (1) a new democratic spirit, with emphasis on the value of ordinary people like laborers, peasants, and factory workers; (2) a compassionate point of view and a refusal to make facile moral judgments; (3) a preoccupation with Italy's Fascist past and its aftermath of wartime devastation, poverty, unemployment, prostitution, and the black market; (4) a blending of Christian and Marxist humanism; and (5) an emphasis on emotions rather than abstract ideas.

The stylistic features of neorealism include (1) an avoidance of neatly plotted stories in favor of loose, episodic structures that evolve organically from the situations of the characters; (2) a documentary visual style; (3) the use of actual locations—usually exteriors—rather than studio sets; (4) the use of nonprofessional actors, even for principal roles; (5) an avoidance of literary dialogue in favor of conversational speech, including dialects; and (6) an avoidance of artifice in the editing, camerawork, and lighting in favor of a simple "styleless" style.

Rossellini's next two pictures also dealt with the war. *Paisà* (1946) is an anthology of six separate episodes, structured geographically, beginning with the American invasion of Sicily and working northward up the Italian peninsula to the Po Valley. Each episode was shot on authentic locations, and all the actors were nonprofessionals. Much of the movie was improvised by Rossellini and his two writers, Federico Fellini and Sergio Amidei. *Germany: Year Zero* (1947) was shot in the rubble of Berlin and was also acted by nonprofessional players. It is generally regarded as the weakest film of the War Trilogy.

In the following years, Rossellini's career was a series of ups and downs, mostly downs. He made several movies featuring his lover Anna Magnani, the most famous of which is *The Miracle* (1948). Then he directed a series of films with his new wife, Ingrid Bergman: *Stromboli* (1949) and *Voyage to Italy* (1953) are the most critically admired of these. *General Della Rovere* (1959) was a commercial and critical success, starring Vittorio De Sica in one of his finest performances, as a con man who impersonates a famous military hero during World War II. After the late 1950s, Rossellini returned to his first love—documentaries. Most of them were produced for French and Italian television and dealt with historical figures and their times. The most admired of these period reconstructions is *The Rise of Louis XIV* (France, 1966).

VITTORIO DE SICA (1901–1974) began his career as an actor in the live theater, specializing in musical comedy. Throughout the 1930s the handsome actor was a popular leading man in a variety of light entertainment films that exploited his roguish charm and flair for comedy. In 1940 he began directing as well as acting in movies, most of them comedies. After he met Cesare Zavattini, a Marxist and a film theorist as well as a screenwriter, De Sica's movies became deeper, more sensitive, more ambitious. Their first collaboration, *The Children Are Watching Us* (1943), is also De Sica's first important work and established him as a gifted director of juveniles.

The De Sica–Zavattini team became one of the most famous collaborations in film history. Although both artists worked apart from each other, their solo achievements seldom approached the genius of their joint efforts, which include *Shoeshine* (9–10), *Bicycle Thief, Miracle in Milan, Umberto D., Two Women, The Garden of the Finzi-Continis,* and *A Brief Vacation,* not to mention a half dozen lighter films. The dialectical tension between the Catholic De Sica and the Communist Zavattini fused poetry with politics, feeling with fact.

Zavattini became an unofficial spokesman for the neorealist movement, though his strong Marxist leanings and hostility to technical artifice didn't always match up with the beliefs of his colleagues. His compassion for the plight of the underprivileged and his anti-Fascist fervor, however, were shared by all neorealists. More than any single individual, Zavattini defined the ordinary and the everyday as the main business of the cinema. Spectacular events and extraordinary characters should be avoided at all costs, he believed. He claimed that his ideal movie would consist of ninety consecutive minutes from a person's actual life. There should be

9–10. *Shoeshine* **(Italy, 1946),** *with Rinaldo Smordoni and Franco Interlenghi, directed by Vittorio De Sica.*

Of all the neorealists, De Sica is the most accessible and emotionally powerful. But the emotions are artistically earned, not piously extorted. He turned to life, not to cheap theatrics, to explore the feelings of his characters. He is equaled only by François Truffaut as a great director of children and, like Truffaut, he is capable of presenting the innocence of childhood without coyness, without reducing children to adorable tykes. In this movie, the loving bond of friendship between two street urchins is perverted not by stereotypical villains, but by ordinary adults who are too busy, too greedy, or too preoccupied with their own desires to question the morality of their cynical indifference. Such real-life stories were commonplace in postwar Italy. *(Museum of Modern Art)*

no barriers between reality and the spectator, no directorial virtuosity to "deform" the integrity of life as it is. The artistry should be invisible, the materials "found" rather than shaped or manipulated.

Suspicious of conventional plot structures, Zavattini dismissed them as dead formulas. He insisted on the dramatic superiority of life as it is experienced by ordinary people. Filmmakers should be concerned with the "excavation" of reality. Instead of plots, they should emphasize facts and all their "echoes and reverberations." According to Zavattini, filmmaking is not a matter of "inventing fables" that are superimposed over the factual materials of life, but of searching unrelentingly to uncover the dramatic implications of these facts. The purpose of the cinema is to explore the "dailiness" of events, to reveal certain details that had always been there but had never been noticed.

Zavattini's sociological rigor was the perfect foil for De Sica's poetic sensibility and comic poignancy. A good example of their artistic synthesis is found in *Bicycle Thief,* their greatest triumph **(9–11).** The film was acted entirely by nonprofessionals and consists of simple events in the life of a laborer (played by Lamberto Maggiorani, who was an actual factory worker). At the time that the film was made, nearly a quarter of the work force in Italy was unemployed. At the opening of the movie, we are introduced to the protagonist, a family man with a wife and two children to support. He has been out of work for two years. Finally, a billboard-posting job opens up, but to accept it, he must have a bicycle. To get his bike out of hock, he and his wife pawn their sheets and bedding (her wedding dowry). On his first day on the job, the bicycle is stolen. The rest of the movie deals with his attempts to recover the bike. The man's search grows increasingly more frantic as he crisscrosses the city with his idolizing son, Bruno. After a series of false leads, the two finally track down one of the thieves, but the protagonist is outwitted by him and humiliated in front of his boy.

Realizing that he will lose his livelihood without a bike, the desperate man—after sending his son away—sneaks off and attempts to steal one himself. But the boy observes from a distance as his father peddles frantically to escape a pursuing mob. He is caught and again humiliated in front of a crowd—which includes his

9–11. *The Bicycle Thief* **(Italy, 1948),** *with Enzo Staiola and Lamberto Maggiorani, directed by Vittorio De Sica.*
De Sica's idol was Charlie Chaplin, and there is a Chaplinesque blend of pathos and comedy in almost all of the Italian master's works. In this movie, the comedy is found primarily in the character of Bruno, the protagonist's son, who trails after his distracted, anxious father like a little old man, filled with worry and concern.   *(Audio-Brandon Films)*

9–12. *General Della Rovere* **(Italy, 1959),** *with Vittorio De Sica and Hannes Messemer, directed by Roberto Rossellini.*

A matinee idol as a young man, De Sica in middle age delighted in mocking his former persona, precariously straddling the line between comic absurdity and frayed dignity. In this movie, he plays a petty swindler who is forced to spy for the Nazis by impersonating an Italian general. It is a brilliant performance, filled with the contradictions of life. In the early portions of the film, the protagonist is a sleazy roué, his forced air of affability barely concealing the pompous blowhard beneath the grand seigneur affectations. Gradually, almost against his will, he begins to envy the hero he is impersonating. Despite his fears and bouts of hysteria, he grows in moral stature, acting with genuine courage. Paradoxically, his most audacious con job allows him to transcend his former self by discovering his own capacity for heroism: He chooses to be shot along with some Partisans rather than to reveal the secrets he has discovered as a Nazi spy. *(Continental Distributing)*

incredulous son. With the bitterness of betrayed innocence, the youngster suddenly realizes that his dad is not the heroic figure he had formerly thought, but an ordinary man who in desperation yielded to a degrading temptation. Like most neorealist films, *Bicycle Thief* doesn't offer a slick solution. There are no miraculous interventions in the final reel. The concluding scene shows the boy walking alongside his father in an anonymous crowd, both of them choking with shame and weeping silently. Almost imperceptibly, the boy's hand gropes for his father's as they walk homeward, their only comfort a mutual compassion.

De Sica followed this film with other explorations of social indifference, such as *Umberto D.* (1952), which deals with the economic hardships of a crusty old pensioner. *The Roof* (1956) centers on a young working-class couple and their problems in finding a place to live. "My films are a struggle against the absence of human solidarity," De Sica pointed out, "against the indifference of society towards suffering. They are a word in favor of the poor and the unhappy." Not all of his movies explored this theme in the style of neorealism. For example, *Miracle in Milan* (1951) is a charming fable in which the main characters, economically dispossessed and finding no justice on earth, mount their broomsticks and fly up to heaven in the hopes of finding better living conditions.

In the following years, De Sica was often forced to direct light entertainment movies to finance his more serious projects. Other films were compromises, fusing social themes with box office viability. For example, *Gold of Naples* (1954) initiated a series of lusty comedies starring Sophia Loren, one of his favorite performers. Others in this series include *Yesterday, Today and Tomorrow* and *Marriage, Italian Style* (both 1964). Their finest joint venture, *Two Women* (1961), was written by Zavattini and was a return to the tenets of neorealism. The movie deals with an earthy peasant (Loren) and her thirteen-year-old daughter in their efforts to avoid the bombardments of World War II. Loren's powerful performance was a startling revelation even to her admirers, and it won her the Best Actress Academy Award, The New York Film Critics Award, and the top prize at the Cannes Film Festival.

De Sica's final masterpiece, the understated, exquisitely crafted *Garden of the Finzi-Continis* (1970), deals with the exportation of Italian Jews to Nazi Germany. The director drew from personal experience in making the movie, for during the worst period of anti-Semitic persecution, he harbored several Jewish families in his home, saving them from almost certain extermination.

LUCHINO VISCONTI (1906–1976) had the unusual distinction of being both a Marxist and an aristocrat—he was the Duke of Modrone. Of all the neorealists, he was the most overtly political. He was also the movement's preeminent aesthete, departing considerably from the plain, unadorned style favored by most neorealists. A famous opera director as well as a filmmaker, Visconti staged some of the most celebrated productions of Milan's La Scala opera house, most notably those of his protégée, American soprano Maria Callas. Visconti also directed in the live theater and won worldwide recognition for his productions of such plays as *Antigone, No Exit,* and several Shakespearean works.

As a youth, Visconti enjoyed a life of luxury and plenty. His main interests were art and horse breeding and racing. He eventually developed a serious interest in costume and set design and traveled to London and Paris in search of practical outlets for these interests. In France he worked as an assistant to Jean Renoir in the production of *The Lower Depths* and *A Day in the Country* (both 1936). Visconti was deeply altered by the left-wing humanism of the Popular Front, a broad coalition of French artists, intellectuals, and workers who decried the growing menace of totalitarianism that was engulfing Europe.

His first movie, *Ossessione* ("Obsession," 1942) was made in the face of considerable opposition by the Fascist authorities. Loosely based on James M. Cain's American novel, *The Postman Always Rings Twice,* the film is a sordid tale of adultery, greed, and murder—hardly the kind of cinema favored by the Fascist regime. The movie was heavily censored by the authorities, who insisted on many cuts before it was permitted to be shown. *Ossessione* is sometimes said to be a precursor of neorealism because it deals with working-class characters, was photographed in a documentary style on actual locations, and featured intensely realistic performances by unglamourized actors. However, the film lacks the moral dimension of neorealism. Visconti's tone is detached and objective rather than compassionate. The story is essentially a character study and is presented without much ideological context. The movie is tough, gritty, and unsentimental, a minor masterpiece that is uncharacteristic not only of its period but of its creator as well.

Visconti's next film, *La Terra Trema* ("The Earth Trembles," 1948), was the first of a projected trilogy that was to deal with the problems of the mezzogiorno—the traditionally impoverished south of Italy **(9–13)**. Partly financed by the Communist Party, the movie is set in a barren fishing village in Sicily and explores how the fishermen and their families are exploited by a small group of wholesalers, who reap the lion's share of the profits, leaving only crumbs to the workers. One of the fishermen leads a revolt despite opposition from conservative members of his own family and class. In the end he and his comrades suffer a crushing defeat, and they are reduced to even more abject poverty than before.

La Terra Trema has an epic sweep and contains images of great power and emotional force—reminiscent of the works of Eisenstein and Robert Flaherty. The cast was composed entirely of nonprofessionals, who spoke in a peasant dialect so severe that many mainlanders were unable to understand the dialogue. Visconti's staging is formal and complex, the characters' movements elegantly choreographed to suggest the stark grandeur of a Greek tragedy. The film, over three hours long, was a box office failure, and the other two installments of the trilogy were never completed. The combination of his Marxist point of view and refined sensibility prompted several commentators to refer to Visconti as "the Red Duke"—a nickname that rather pleased him.

In the following decades, Visconti's movies became progressively more stylized, like those of most Italian filmmakers. *Bellissima* (1951), a warm, domestic drama starring Anna Magnani, was one of his few attempts at comedy. *Senso* (1954), his first period film, is a meticulously crafted romantic melodrama about the masochistic agony of sexual passion—a frequent theme in Visconti's works. *Rocco and His Brothers* (1960) was a return to realism; it chronicles the disintegration of a family of southern peasants after they emigrate to Milan in search of a better life.

9–13. *La Terra Trema* (Italy, 1948), *directed by Luchino Visconti.*
Because of its nonprofessional cast and authentic locations, this film superficially resembles a documentary. But Visconti's mise en scène is not a haphazard collection of "found objects." The images are carefully composed, with the squalid environment serving as a foil to the dignity of the statuesque figures.   *(Museum of Modern Art)*

The Leopard (1963), one of Visconti's greatest triumphs, is based on a novel by Giuseppe de Lampedusa and stars Burt Lancaster as an aging Sicilian aristocrat in the turbulent final decades of the nineteenth century. The movie is a stunning re-creation of the period, filled with panoramic battle scenes, lavish balls, and the elaborately formal rituals of a dying class **(9–14).** The tone is melancholy and elegiac. Despite his sympathetic treatment of the central character, Visconti's analysis of class antagonism is objective and rigorously Marxist. Like several of the director's later works, The Leopard was released in the United States in a shortened version and dubbed into English, but the original length Italian-language version is infinitely superior.

9–14. ***The Leopard*** **(Italy, 1963),** *with Rina Morelli (center), directed by Luchino Visconti.* Clothing is never mere body covering in a Visconti film, nor is décor a neutral backdrop. The costumes and settings are profoundly ideological, symbolizing psychological and social values within a precisely defined economic milieu. For example, the clutter, texture, and florid patterns of the Victorian furnishings in this movie suggest a stifling, hothouse artificiality, sealed off from nature. The costumes, impeccably accurate to period, are elegant, constricting, and totally without utility. They were meant to be. Idle people of independent income—that is, income derived from the labor of others—rarely concern themselves with utility in clothing. *(Twentieth Century–Fox)*

9–15. *Bitter Rice* **(Italy, 1948),** *with Silvana Mangano,*
directed by Giuseppi De Santis.
Bitter Rice was a box office hit in Italy and enjoyed wide popularity abroad as well. The success of the movie owed more to
Mangano's sultry eroticism than to the tenets of neorealism,
which are only superficially observed. Indeed, many critics
considered the film a sexploitation picture, for instead of ordinary events, the movie concentrates on high-pitched passions,
rape, and violence.   *(Museum of Modern Art)*

In subsequent years, Visconti directed several literary adaptations, including
The Stranger (1967), starring Marcello Mastroianni, based on the French existential
novel by Albert Camus. *Death in Venice* (1970), with Dirk Bogarde, was an adaptation of the famous German novella by Thomas Mann. Visconti also directed two
period films about German culture: *The Damned* (1969), which deals with the Nazi
era, and *Ludwig II* (1972), about a notoriously decadent aristocrat of the nineteenth century. The florid, overripe style of these pictures is deliberately garish, a
visual embodiment of waste, excess, and moral decay. Visconti's final two works
were *Conversation Piece* (1975), once again starring Burt Lancaster, and *The Innocent*
(1976), a wry morality tale about sexual liberation set in the late nineteenth century and starring Giancarlo Giannini and Laura Antonelli. Visconti, a bisexual,
viewed the sex drive as an essentially self-destructive force, whether straight or gay.
He also believed that great wealth and power contain the seeds of their own destruction. In short, in many of his movies he turned against a part of himself—
hence their tortured ambivalence.

According to most film historians, neorealism died in the early 1950s. This is
both true and not true. Certainly neorealism waned during this period, but it never
entirely disappeared. The early works of Fellini and Antonioni are clearly indebted

to the movement, both aesthetically and ideologically. The movies of such later Italian filmmakers as Ermanno Olmi and Paolo and Vittorio Taviani are in the neo-realist vein. Neorealism also exerted a strong international influence, as can be seen in the works of the Indian filmmaker Satyajit Ray, the Czechoslovakian Prague Spring movement, the British "Kitchen Sink" school of realism of the 1950s, and the films of Ousmane Sembene from Senegal, to mention only a few.

The waning of neorealism can be traced to the late 1940s, when the left-center parties that dominated the Italian parliament in the postwar years lost their majority. In 1949, the right-center ruling coalition passed the Andreoti Law, which allowed government censors to ban from export any film that presented the country in a "negative" manner. Most neorealist movies were not popular with Italian audiences and had to earn back their costs through foreign export, especially to the United States, France, and Great Britain. Cut off from their audiences, Italian neorealists turned to other subjects to survive. Sex was especially popular **(9–15).**

But the times were changing anyway. The "economic miracle" of the 1950s increasingly made neorealism seem obsolete, and even a Marxist artist like Antonioni admitted that movies about stolen bicycles were not very relevant to the more prosperous decades following the 1940s. "The Italian cinema produces masterpieces because it has few resources," said the prophetic René Clair about neorealism. "But that will soon end, because the Italian cinema will soon be rich."

FURTHER READING

ARMES, ROY. *Patterns of Realism: A Study of Italian Neo-Realist Cinema.* Cranbury, N.J.: A. S. Barnes, 1971. A scholarly exploration of the origins and achievements of neorealism up to 1952.

BAZIN, ANDRÉ. *French Cinema of the Occupation and Resistance.* New York: Frederick Unger, 1981. A brief survey by France's greatest film critic.

BONDANELLA, PETER. *Italian Cinema: From Neorealism to the Present.* New York: Ungar, 1983. A comprehensive history, especially strong on the political and social context of Italian movies.

CRISP, COLIN. *The Classic French Cinema, 1930–1960.* London: British Film Institute, 1993. Good coverage of technology and mode of production.

HALL, DAVID. *Films of the Third Reich.* Berkeley: University of California Press, 1969. Nazi cinema.

INSDORF, ANNETTE. *Indelible Shadows: Film and the Holocaust.* New York: Vintage, 1983. International coverage, including both documentaries and fiction, from the 1930s to 1983.

MANVELL, ROGER. *Films of the Second World War.* New York: Delta, 1976. International coverage, including fiction and documentaries, spanning the prewar era to the 1970s.

OVERBEY, DAVID, ed. *Springtime in Italy: A Reader on Neo-Realism.* Hamden, Conn.: Archon Books, 1978. A collection of essays by Zavattini, Antonioni, De Sica, Rossellini, Chiarini, and others.

RENTSCHLER, ERIC. *The Ministry of Illusion.* Cambridge: Harvard University Press, 1996. Nazi cinema and its afterlife.

WELCH, DAVID. *Propaganda and the German Cinema, 1933–1945.* New York: Oxford University Press, 1983. A fascinating study.

10

American Cinema in the 1950s

Why, the times are almost ripe for a movie about a
young man who has a passionate love affair with his
mother. At the end he learns that she is not his mother
and he commits suicide.
—BILLY WILDER, after seeing the "scandalous" *Baby Doll*

Timeline: 1950–1959

1950
U.S. population: approximately 151 million; approximate number of TV sets in America: 15 million; by 1954: 29 million
Senator Joseph McCarthy begins Communist-baiting agitation in U.S. Senate; continues until 1954
Cool Jazz evolves from bebop

1951
J. D. Salinger's novel, *The Catcher in the Rye*

1952
Dwight D. Eisenhower (Republican) U.S. President (1952–1961), a popular and beloved leader

1953
A rocket-powered U.S. plane flies at more than 1,600 mph

1954
U.S. Supreme Court rules that racial segregation in public schools must end
Dr. Jonas Salk develops antipolio vaccine

1954–1959
Years of prosperity: United States contains 6 percent of world's population but 60 percent of all cars, 58 percent of telephones, 45 percent of radios, 34 percent of all railroads

1955
Black boycott of Birmingham Alabama's segregated bus lines

1956
Spurred by the immense popularity of singer Elvis Presley, rock 'n' roll enters the mainstream of American pop music
Emergence of Reverend Martin Luther King, Jr., as leader of desegregation drive in the South
My Fair Lady, Broadway musical by Alan Jay Lerner and Frederick Loewe

1957
West Side Story, Broadway musical by Leonard Bernstein

1958
John Kenneth Galbraith's *The Affluent Society*
California "beatnik" movement gains popularity and spreads to major U.S. cities

1959
Total U.S. auto accident death toll: 1.25 million—more than have died in all U.S. wars combined

The rise of television and the decline of the Hollywood studio system. Desperate remedies: Cinerama, 3-D, and CinemaScope. The Cold War and the anti-Communist hysteria—the HUAC hearings. The Hollywood Ten. Modifications in the Production Code. Social realism and the cinema of social consciousness: Stanley Kramer and Fred Zinnemann. Method acting and a new generation of stars: Marlon Brando and other rebels. Revisionist genres. Elia Kazan, "two-coast genius." Alfred Hitchcock, light and dark. Lost innocence.

F OR THE COUNTRY AT LARGE, THE 1950s was a decade of "Peace, Progress, and Prosperity," to use the slogan of President Dwight D. Eisenhower, whose staid tenure set the tone of much of the period. The Cold War hysteria produced an ugly Red Scare in the early 1950s, but a kind of bland optimism took over by the end of the decade. Hollywood was often described as an island of depression in a sea of prosperity. The studios continued to decline because public attendance continued to decline. The main culprit: television. TV siphoned off most of the so-called family audience, leaving behind only specialized groups, the largest of which was the youth audience. By the end of the 1950s, more than 85 percent of all U.S. homes had a television set. Most of these people got out of the habit of going to the movies and went only on special occasions.

What would draw them back to the theaters? The moguls tried almost everything. Wider screens? Three-dimensional images? More sex and violence? More youth **genres,** like biker films, beach party movies, and so on? Since the Supreme Court divorce decree, the studios no longer owned their own theaters and hence were required to compete, for the most part unsuccessfully, with independent producers, who were usually more daring, more willing to try new ideas.

Historians have noted other reasons for the waning of the studios. After World War II, American audiences began to develop more mature tastes in themes, but studio regulars were inclined to favor the romantic, sentimental, and escapist themes of the prewar cinema. MGM, the most prosperous studio since the early 1930s, began to lose touch with audience tastes, and except for its excellent musicals of the 1950s **(10–1 and 10–2),** the studio never regained its former eminence. Another factor contributing to the deterioration of the studios was the increasing tendency of filmmakers to shoot on location rather than in Hollywood. The huge **back lots** and sound stages thus became too expensive for the studios to maintain, especially during a period of rapidly escalating production costs. Eventually these facilities were sold or rented out, mostly to television production companies.

By the mid-1950s, most of the old moguls had been replaced by younger men, but it became increasingly apparent that the new era belonged to the independents. They were producing not only the best movies but the lion's share of the box office hits as well. Of course the two are by no means incompatible and never

10–1. *The Band Wagon* (**U.S.A., 1953**), *with Cyd Charisse and Fred Astaire; dances and musical numbers staged by Michael Kidd, directed by Vincente Minnelli.*
MGM enjoyed a golden age of musicals in the 1950s. Virtually every important singer, dancer, and choreographer was employed at the studio, not to speak of the top directors in the genre: Kelly, Donen, and Minnelli. The writing team of Betty Comden and Adolph Green wrote not only this nifty musical, but also *On the Town, Singin' in the Rain, It's Always Fair Weather,* and *Bells Are Ringing.* Comden and Green enjoyed incorporating literary jokes into their scripts, like this spoof on the "hard-boiled" fiction of Mickey Spillane. Among MGM's most valuable assets was Cyd Charisse, she of the sensational killer gams, who could rivet a partner with a sizzling stare or torment him with an insolently lifted thigh. You just know she's bad.   *(Metro-Goldwyn-Mayer)*

have been: Some of the greatest films of the American cinema are also its box-office champions.

European movies were beginning to make sizable inroads into the American market. The so-called art house theaters, located primarily in large cities and university towns, catered primarily to these more sophisticated audiences. There were only about fifty of these theaters in 1945, but by 1950 there were already more than five hundred of them, and they continued to grow throughout the decade.

10–2. *Singin' in the Rain* (U.S.A., 1952), *with Gene Kelly, choreography by Kelly, directed by Kelly and Stanley Donen.*
Kelly was the outstanding musical personality of this era. Like his friend Fred Astaire, he worked in a broad range of dancing styles. He is a vigorous hoofer, earthy rather than airborne like Astaire. Kelly's tap dancing is muscular, gymnastic, and virile rather than light or nonchalant. He was fond of incorporating lengthy ballet sequences in his films. Above all, Kelly's dancing is sexy, with an emphasis on pelvic movements, tensed loins, twisting torsos, and erotic, close-to-the-floor gyrations. He usually wore close-fitting costumes to emphasize his well-muscled body. He also allowed his personality to shine through, breaking the formality of the choreography with a cocky grin or an ecstatic smile that's as hammy as it is irresistible. *(Metro-Goldwyn-Mayer)*

New Screens

Early on, movies found their shape. By 1910, it was basically that of a classic rectangle, slightly wider than it was high. The width of the film itself was 35 mm, and the dimensions of the projected picture were in a ratio of 4 to 3—that is, a screen twenty feet wide would be fifteen feet high. But there was experimentation going on. In the earliest days, Lumière devised a giant screen, seventy by fifty-three feet, and we have seen how Abel Gance's experiments with widening the proportions of the screen by using three synchronized projectors proved too complicated for the industry of 1926. Gance was only one of many. In 1922, Henri Chretien patented a lens that had originally been devised for use in periscopes. The anamorphic lens "squeezed" nearly 180 degrees of sight and compressed it by 50 percent. For motion picture purposes, Chretien devised a lens that would unsqueeze film photographed with the special lens, thus producing a picture nearly two and a half times as wide as it was high.

And then came television. As Kenneth McGowan put it, "economic pressure at last forced a change in production and exhibition and Hollywood fell back on processes it had long ignored." With receipts plummeting and increasing numbers of people staying home to watch the novelty in their living rooms, Hollywood decided that it had to offer a bigger and better novelty to lure back the 30 percent of the audience that had defected in five years' time. The initial tactics involved three processes: (1) 3-D; (2) Cinerama, which was basically a modified version of Gance's Polyvision under another name; and (3) Chretien's **widescreen** lens, christened CinemaScope by the patent holder, Twentieth Century–Fox, and offered as a low-cost alternative to the expensive Cinerama process.

10–3. *Ben-Hur* (U.S.A., 1959), *directed by William Wyler.*
The 4-by-3 **aspect ratio** of the traditional movie screen was roughly the same as that of the dreaded competition, television. The Hollywood studios reasoned that they ought to be providing what the small screen couldn't: color, stereophonic sound, and a wider screen. Widescreen—whether it was called CinemaScope, Cinerama, Todd-AO, VistaVision, or whatever—boasted an aspect ratio of roughly 2.5 by 1, a virtual epic mural. The new screen size was especially effective in capturing panoramic vistas and huge-scale events, like this Roman chariot race sequence, the high point of the film. A remake of Metro's 1926 hit, *Ben-Hur* grossed an astonishing $80 million, rescuing MGM from financial difficulties. *(Metro-Goldwyn-Mayer)*

The 3-D concept went back a long way—there are three-dimensional drawings that date from 1600. All three-dimensional effects are based on the same principle—that each eye sees a slightly different picture. A 3-D camera likewise has two lenses, each lens standing in for an eye. To get the 3-D effect, a viewer has to wear cumbersome cardboard glasses that direct the left-hand image to the left eye, the right-hand image to the right eye. Early 3-D movies like *Bwana Devil* (1952) used two projectors in addition to the cardboard glasses, but the problem of keeping the projectors in perfect synchronization defeated the system. The twin images were then optically printed on the same piece of film, with the glasses remaining in place. In 1953–1954, some thirty-eight 3-D films were released, most of them terrible. The possibility of creating the illusion of objects reaching out of the screen toward the audience proved too great a temptation for unimaginative filmmakers. In short order, arrows, hatchets, bosoms, anything that could be thrown or thrust at the camera, was.

Cinerama, like Polyvision, used three separate 35-mm films shown on three projectors. Unlike Polyvision, the Cinerama projectors were located in three different booths on the main floor of the auditorium and projected onto a deeply curved screen that wrapped around much of the audience. At its best, Cinerama offered an extraordinary illusion of involvement, largely because the screen occupied all of a viewer's range of vision, even peripheral view. But the process was expensive—about $75,000 to install per theater—and invariably a good number of seats were lost because of the size of the screen and the projection booths. The process was also ungainly in terms of storytelling. The early Cinerama films amounted to optically elaborate travelogues, whose novelty soon wore thin.

CinemaScope, which required only that the theater buy a new screen and a pair of lenses, was considerably cheaper and provided a watered-down version of the Cinerama effect. By February, 1953, Fox announced that all future productions would be in CinemaScope. Even though the process was accepted by audiences, it carried its share of problems. The lenses were imperfect and had a very narrow depth of field. **Deep focus** was impossible. Because of the long, thin shape of the CinemaScope screen, **closeups** were difficult, and when they were used, they chopped foreheads and chins off the actors. Because of these difficulties, the early CinemaScope movies tended to be a photographically prosaic succession of **medium shots,** which led Sam Goldwyn to say: "A widescreen makes a bad film twice as bad."

Still, public acceptance of widescreen sent the other studios scrambling for reasonable facsimiles. Many of the results, like Todd-AO and Technirama, involved larger negatives and prints than conventional 35-mm to produce the desired effects and for that reason were short-lived. Of all the alternatives to CinemaScope, the best was undoubtedly Paramount's VistaVision, which used 35-mm film moving horizontally through a special camera. The image was about twice the size of a normal 35-mm frame, and when reduced for positive printing for projection in the normal manner, it severely reduced grain, thus enhancing sharpness and resolution. Even 16-mm prints of films photographed in VistaVision are notable for their clarity and brilliant images.

10–4. *East of Eden* (U.S.A., 1955), *with James Dean and Jo Van Fleet, directed by Elia Kazan.*

Widescreen was fine for spectaculars and epic genres, many serious filmmakers complained, but it was not suited to small, intimate subjects or psychological nuances. Fritz Lang claimed it was suitable only for photographing funeral processions and snakes. But before long, sensitive filmmakers like Kazan began using the widescreen to communicate subtleties through the mise en scène. For example, in this scene, an anguished youth tries to establish contact with the mother he has never known—the madam of a notorious bordello. By exploiting the "empty space" between the suspicious woman and her tentative son, Kazan is able to communicate their estrangement visually, without the need for verbal comment. We are thus able to see their interreactions simultaneously. With a conventional 4-by-3 aspect ratio, the two characters would be too intimate if crowded into a **medium two-shot.** A director would be forced to cut from one character to the other, thus denying us the privilege of seeing them in the same space at the same time.   *(Warner Brothers)*

As a compromise between the extreme variations between widescreen ratio—about 2.5 times as wide as it is high—and the old-style classic rectangle, a new standard ratio of 1.85 to 1 gradually evolved, which is now the standard ratio for films not photographed in an anamorphic process.

The Red Scare

The Red Scare constituted one of the most bizarre chapters in American history. In Hollywood, the anti-Communist hysteria began in 1947, and its effects could still be felt until the late 1950s. It was inflamed by Stalin's takeover of eastern Europe and by the Korean War (1950–1953), in which fifty thousand Americans were killed. The Congressional House Un-American Activities Committee (HUAC) set out to investigate Communist propaganda in American movies. A handful of pro-Soviet films had been produced during World War II, ironically at the request of the U.S. government, to bolster the image of our wartime ally. Most of these pictures failed at the box office.

HUAC was chaired by J. Parnell Thomas, a notorious Red-baiter who had considered Roosevelt's New Deal to be Communist inspired and who opposed the Congressional antilynching bill as well as fair-employment legislation. Other HUAC members included John E. Rankin, an admitted racist and anti-Semite, and young Richard M. Nixon, who learned a great deal during the proceedings.

Many careers were launched as a result of HUAC hearings. Many more were destroyed. "Friendly" witnesses were allowed to make opening statements and were granted immunity from prosecution for libel. There followed an orgy of character assassination, almost all of it based on hearsay and malice. Many of the fingered victims were writers, many of them Jewish, with roots in the New York Theater of the 1930s, a period of intense political ferment, mostly **left-wing.** Friendly witness Ayn Rand went so far as to brand Louis B. Mayer as "not much better than an agent of Communism," because MGM (the least political of the **majors**) had produced *Song of Russia* (1944), which actually showed Russian peasants smiling.

"Unfriendly" witnesses, who were mostly liberals and not Communists, were not allowed to make opening statements or to cross-examine their accusers. Unfriendly witnesses were widely branded as Communists. Witnesses were coerced into revealing not only their own political pasts, but those of their associates as well. Actor Larry Parks was reduced to tears when he was forced to inform on his friends, most of whom had long abandoned their interest in politics. (Being left had been chic in the 1930s.) Their careers were ruined.

Under this kind of pressure, even decent men and women behaved badly. Most witnesses were "friendly." A few brave souls defied the committee and damned their torpedoes. Ten witnesses, mostly screenwriters, refused to cooperate entirely, and they served prison sentences for contempt of Congress. The famous Hollywood Ten were Alvah Bessie, Herbert Biberman, Lester Cole, Edward Dmytryk, Ring Lardner, Jr., John Howard Lawson, Albert Maltz, Samuel Ornitz, Adrian Scott, and Dalton Trumbo. When they were released from jail, they found themselves **blacklisted** by the industry, along with an estimated four hundred others. Senator Joseph McCarthy joined in the hunt and upped the stakes. He produced a list of 324 "known Communists" within the industry. The American Legion provided 356 more names. None of the accusations was substantiated, nor did HUAC even deign to offer the title of a single movie that was Communist inspired.

10–5. *Invasion of the Body Snatchers* **(U.S.A., 1956),** *directed by Don Siegel.*
A number of cultural commentators have remarked on the "paranoid style" of many movies of
the Cold War era, especially sci-fi films, a popular genre during the 1950s, though not a prestigious one. Siegel's low-budget classic deals with how some alien pod-people insidiously invade human bodies, reducing their owners to anonymous zombies, incapable of feelings. The
film was produced during an era when many Americans were seriously discussing the possibility of building bombshelters to "protect" themselves from an expected nuclear attack by the
U.S.S.R. *(Allied Artists)*

The industry was paralyzed with fear, for the Hearst press and others had
been calling for stringent federal censorship of films. To show their good faith, the
studios produced a spate of blatantly anti-Communist movies, most of which were
awful and failed at the box office. Such industry liberals as William Wyler, John
Huston, Humphrey Bogart, and Lauren Bacall helped form the Committee for the
First Amendment, which publicized the Constitutional violations of HUAC and
McCarthy. The Writers Guild strongly opposed the blacklist, which was condemned
by a vote of four hundred to eight. Eventually even industry conservatives like John
Ford spoke out against the witch hunts.

In 1954, the televised Army–McCarthy hearings revealed the senator for what
he was—a cynical opportunist. Public sentiment veered sharply against him. Later
he was censured by the Senate. The hysteria began to subside—very slowly, like the
Cold War itself. By the end of the decade, such producer-directors as Otto Preminger and Stanley Kramer openly defied the blacklist and gave public credit for
honest work, no matter what the political beliefs of the artists.

10–6. *Anatomy of a Murder* (U.S.A., 1959), *with George C. Scott, James Stewart, and Eve Arden, directed by Otto Preminger.*

Preminger, a **producer-director** who took his civil liberties seriously, was the gadfly of the **Production Code** during this era. When he filmed a slick Broadway comedy, *The Moon Is Blue* (1953), he refused to delete such words as "virgin" and "seduction." It was a matter of political principle, not aesthetic importance. Preminger believed that the screen should be covered by the same freedom of expression guaranteed to the other media by the First Amendment. The movie was denied the Seal of Approval. It turned out to be a huge hit, in part because of the publicity. In *The Man With the Golden Arm* (1955), he undertook another taboo theme, drug addiction. Once again the Seal was denied; once again the film was a hit. The times were changing. In 1956, the Code was revised, allowing the treatment of drugs, prostitution, abortion, and kidnapping, but not sexual deviance or venereal disease. Nudity was still a no-no, and there were still strong restrictions against language. For example, the word "panties" in *Anatomy of a Murder* provoked considerable controversy. The Production Code people let it pass—they were tired of fighting with Preminger. What the director and many others wanted was a rating system that would allow mature subjects to be seen by adults. The rating system went into effect in 1968. *(Columbia Pictures)*

Social Realism

If the major achievements of the pre–World War II American cinema were in comedy and stylized genre films, the postwar era excelled at realism. Young filmmakers like Fred Zinnemann, Elia Kazan, and Stanley Kramer **(10–7)** were especially influenced by the Italian **neorealist** cinema. They wanted to use movies to arouse the social conscience of the audience. They wanted to make movies that dealt with serious social themes and stories revolving around contemporary problems, but without a sacrifice in drama, suspense, or excitement. They also tended to avoid glossiness and a slick look in favor of authenticity and a sense of discovery.

Actually, **social realism** is neither a style nor a movement in the usual sense of those terms. Perhaps it would be more accurate to describe it as a set of values, both social and aesthetic, that cuts across national boundaries and historical periods. For many years it was the most prestigious branch of the cinema, enjoying wide support among the liberally educated classes of most filmgoing nations. One of the broadest of film classifications, social realism encompasses many movements and styles, including the neorealists of postwar Italy, the films of socialist realism in the Communist bloc countries, the so-called kitchen-sink realism of the British cinema in the late 1950s and early 1960s, and the films of many individual moviemakers who are concerned with themes of social anxiety and change: Sergei Eisenstein, Satyajit Ray, and Yasujiro Ozu, to name only a few.

10–7. *The Defiant Ones* **(U.S.A., 1958),** *with Sidney Poitier and Tony Curtis, directed by Stanley Kramer.*
Kramer (1913–2001) was a major contributor to the revival of social realism in the postwar era. Most of his productions were not commercially successful, but he had enough hits to offset the losses. His films frequently revolved around serious social issues, like *The Defiant Ones,* perhaps his most respected movie. He also directed *On the Beach* (1959), *Inherit the Wind* (1960), *Judgment at Nuremberg* (1961), *Ship of Fools* (1965), *Guess Who's Coming to Dinner?* (1967), and *Bless the Beasts and the Children* (1971), among others.   *(United Artists)*

In America, some of the most respected directors have made major contributions in this area: Griffith, von Stroheim, King Vidor, John Ford, Elia Kazan, Fred Zinnemann, Sidney Lumet, Martin Ritt, Delbert Mann **(10–8,)** Hal Ashby, and many others. Social realism tends to emphasize the documentary aspects of the medium, its ability to photograph authentic people, details, and places. Movies in this form are usually shot on location, seldom in the studio. Sometimes these films use nonprofessional performers rather than trained actors or **stars.** Though occasionally stiff, nonprofessionals seldom seem slick, glamorous, or hammy—qualities that are especially incongruous for working-class characters. Social realism is a view from the left: Filmmakers assume a reformist or revolutionary perspective on the narrative materials and explore, at least implicitly, the ways in which people near the bottom of the social heap are shafted.

A few social realists—most notably Eisenstein—are relatively unconcerned with the subtleties of character and concentrate more on style, sociology, or a didactic theme. This lack of concern for characterization is rather unusual, however. In the 1950s especially, filmmakers showed a strong interest in the complexities of character within the context of social realism. Characters were portrayed in all their contradictions, without the idealization that usually took place in earlier years.

10–8. *Marty* **(U.S.A., 1955),** *with Ernest Borgnine, directed by Delbert Mann.*
By the mid-decade, Hollywood could no longer ignore the reality of television or sneer at it as a déclassé medium. *Marty* had been written originally by Paddy Chayefsky for the small screen. Hecht-Lancaster bought the script and produced it as a movie for a modest $500,000, using all television talent. The producers expected the film to be a tax write-off. To everyone's astonishment, it won the Grand Prize at Cannes and became a sleeper hit in the United States, where eventually the movie won the Best Picture Oscar, along with Mann's Best Director, Borgnine's Best Actor, and Chayefsky's Best Screenplay Oscars. Television scripts suddenly became more viable properties for film producers. Indeed, the 1950s came to be known as TV's golden age, and many artists who began in TV during this era ended up working in the film industry. *(United Artists)*

Because the subject matter of the social realist cinema is innately important, some naive viewers feel coerced into accepting all movies of this type as likewise important—as though it were the subject itself and not its sensitive treatment that determines artistic excellence. In fact, there are as many mediocre directors working within the tradition of social realism as there are in any other genre, style, or movement. A movie can be accurate sociology, edifying in its high-mindedness, and still be clumsy as art, boring as entertainment. Some social realist movies are self-congratulatory, psychologically dishonest, and patronizing in their attitude toward the Little People and their dull, drab lives. Films of this sort are sometimes called "message movies" because their preachments take precedence over most aesthetic and psychological considerations.

Method Acting

The 1950s gave rise to a new style of acting in American movies—the **Method.** It was popularly associated with Elia Kazan, who was often said to have "invented" it, but he repeatedly pointed out that Method acting was neither new nor his. It was an offshoot of Constantin Stanislavsky's system of training actors and rehearsing, which the Russian director had developed at the Moscow Art Theatre. During the 1930s many of Stanislavsky's ideas were adopted by Lee Strasberg and Harold Clurman at the famous Group Theatre in New York. Kazan had been an actor, writer, and director at the Group Theatre, which folded in 1941.

In 1947, Kazan and his associates Cheryl Crawford and Robert Lewis founded the Actors Studio, which received much publicity during the 1950s because it had developed such well-known actors as Marlon Brando, Marilyn Monroe (10–9), James Dean, Julie Harris, Karl Malden, Paul Newman, Geraldine Page, Rod Steiger, and many others, including Montgomery Clift (10–10), who was often associated with Method acting, even though he did not study at the Actors Studio. "The Actors Studio was my artistic home," Kazan said. He continued there as a teacher until 1954, when he asked his old mentor, Strasberg, to take over the organization. Within a short period, Strasberg became the most celebrated acting teacher in America, and his former students were—and still are—among the most famous performers in the world.

The central credo of Stanislavsky's system was "You must live the part every moment you are playing it." He rejected the tradition of acting that emphasized only externals—declamatory vocal techniques, stylizations, "correct" body positions, and so on. He believed that truth in acting can only be achieved by exploring

10–9. Publicity photo of Marilyn Monroe in *Some Like It Hot* **(U.S.A., 1959),** *directed by Billy Wilder.*
Marilyn Monroe (1926–1962) was one of the top female stars of the 1950s and has been a legendary personality ever since. Her story is in the classic rags-to-riches mold—but without the happy ending. She was born illegitimate, to a mother who was mentally unstable and spent most of her adult life in institutions. For Norma Jean Baker, childhood was a series of humiliating foster homes. Disconnected life: insecure, lonely. Raped at eight. Married at sixteen. Suicide attempt. Divorced. Pinup photos, modeling. Movie starlet at Twentieth Century–Fox. A new name for a new life: Marilyn Monroe. She plays a series of forgettable roles. The only two worth anything are bit parts as dumb blondes in *The Asphalt Jungle* and *All About Eve,* both in 1950. (Her coactor George Sanders claimed he knew Marilyn would one day become a star "because she desperately needed to be one.") By 1954 she was Fox's top star and married to baseball idol Joe DiMaggio. Miscarriage. Nervous breakdown. Drugs, alcohol. Divorce. She leaves Hollywood in disgust to study in New York at the Actors Studio. She becomes more introspective, associates with an arty New York group of intellectuals, including playwright Arthur Miller, whom she marries. When she returns to Hollywood, she demands more money and better roles and gets both. Many critics remark on the much-improved actress in such movies as *Bus Stop* (1956), *Some Like It Hot,* and her last film, *The Misfits* (1961). Throughout this period of artistic triumph, her personal life was in shambles. Depression. Sleeping pills. Miscarriage. Divorce. Collapse. She was found dead in 1962, of a lethal combination of drugs and alcohol. She was at the height of her beauty. *(United Artists)*

10–10. *A Place in the Sun* **(U.S.A., 1951),** *with Elizabeth Taylor and Montgomery Clift, directed by George Stevens.*
Stevens (1904–1975) enjoyed a long and distinguished career in filmmaking. In 1927 he joined producer Hal Roach as a cinematographer, photographing many of the short films of Laurel and Hardy. Eventually Stevens moved into directing. His first important feature was *Alice Adams* (1935), a superb piece of comic Americana. He also directed *Swing Time* (1936), one of the best of the Astaire–Rogers RKO musicals. A versatile director, Stevens went on to make the male-adventure film *Gunga Din* (1939) and movies in various other genres as well. During World War II, he was in charge of the film unit of the Army Signal Corps and photographed the appalling horrors of the Nazi concentration camp in Dachau. This experience profoundly influenced him as a man and as an artist, for his work took on a darker tone in the postwar period. His prestige reached its peak in the 1950s with such movies as *A Place in the Sun,* a loose adaptation of Theodore Dreiser's famous novel *An American Tragedy.* Stevens won a Best Director Oscar for his work. His pictures got more **epic** during this period and included the pastoral western *Shane* (1953) and the sprawling Texas saga *Giant* (1956).   *(Paramount Pictures)*

a character's inner spirit, which must be fused with the actor's own emotions. One of the most important techniques he developed is emotional recall, in which an actor delves into his or her own past to discover feelings that are analogous to those of the character. "In every part you do," Julie Harris explained, "there is some connection you can make with your own background or with some feeling you've had at one time or another." Stanislavsky's techniques are strongly psychoanalytical: By exploring their own subconscious, actors are able to trigger off real emotions, which are recalled in every performance and transferred to the characters they are playing. He also devised techniques for helping actors to focus their concentration on the "world" of the play—its concrete details and textures.

10–11. *Julius Caesar* (**U.S.A., 1953**), *with Marlon Brando, directed by Joseph L. Mankiewicz.*
Brando is the actor most frequently associated with the Method style of acting. Throughout the decade, he varied his roles considerably, refusing to be typecast. A common complaint about the Method was that it was suited only to realism and didn't apply well to stylized works like the plays of Shakespeare. Brando's Marc Antony demonstrated that emotional intensity and Shakespearean verse are not necessarily at odds. British critics were especially lavish in their praise of Brando's artistry. In America, he was idolized as a symbol of rebellion and nonconformity. The actor fell on hard times in the 1960s, trying without much success to reconcile his liberal political views with his aesthetic judgments in scripts. In the early 1970s, he returned to favor with two brilliant performances, in *The Godfather* and *Last Tango in Paris.* *(Twentieth Century–Fox)*

In some form or another, these techniques are as old as the acting profession itself, but Stanislavsky was the first to systematize them with exercises and methods of analysis; hence the terms *the system* and *the method*. Stanislavsky did not claim that inner truth and emotional sincerity are sufficient unto themselves. He insisted that actors must master all the externals as well, particularly for classic roles, which require a somewhat stylized manner of speaking, moving, and wearing costumes. He was famous for his lengthy rehearsals, in which performers were encouraged to improvise with their roles to discover the resonances of the text—the subtext, which is analogous to Freud's concept of the subconscious.

In Method acting, the text is just the 10 percent of the iceberg that shows. The rest is **subtext.** As Kazan explained,

The film director knows that beneath the surface of his screenplay there is a subtext, a calendar of intentions and feelings and inner events. What appears to be happening, he soon learns, is rarely what is happening. The subtext is one of the film director's most valuable tools. It is what he directs. You will rarely see a veteran director holding a script as he works—or even looking at it.

10–12. *A Streetcar Named Desire* (U.S.A., 1951), *with Marlon Brando and Vivien Leigh, directed by Elia Kazan.*

The New York theater enjoyed a golden age in the 1950s, with premier productions of major plays by Eugene O'Neill, Arthur Miller, William Inge, and above all, Tennessee Williams. Many of Williams's plays were directed by Kazan, who also created the finest of the movie adaptations, *Streetcar*. Though the Production Code required some laundering of the story and dialogue, the film version is true to the spirit of the original. Williams also wrote an original screenplay for Kazan's controversial *Baby Doll* (1956). Other Tennessee Williams adaptations during the decade were *The Glass Menagerie* (1950, directed by Irving Rapper), *The Rose Tattoo* (1955, Daniel Mann), *Cat on a Hot Tin Roof* (1958, Richard Brooks), and *Suddenly Last Summer* (1959, Joseph L. Mankiewicz). *(Twentieth Century–Fox)*

The subtext involves what's beneath the language of the script: not what people say, but what they really want but are afraid to ask for. Spoken dialogue is always secondary to Method actors. Their concern is with an inner dialogue, and to capture this, they sometimes throw away their lines, choke on them, or even mumble. Throughout the 1950s, Method actors like Brando and Dean were ridiculed by some critics and industry regulars for mumbling their lines.

Stanislavsky condemned individual virtuosity and the star system. He insisted on ensemble playing, with genuine interactions among the actor-characters. Players are encouraged to analyze all the specifics of a scene: What does the character really *want?* What has happened before the immediate moment? What time of day is it? And so on. When presented with a role utterly foreign to their experience, actors are urged to research the part so that it will be understood in their guts as well as their minds. For example, to play a prison inmate, an actor might actually ask to spend some time in a prison cell, studying its smells, sounds, and textures.

Method acting is especially strong in bringing out the emotional intensity of a character, especially working-class characters or people who are not very verbal.

10–13. *All About Eve* **(U.S.A., 1950),** *with Bette Davis, Marilyn Monroe, and George Sanders, written and directed by Joseph L. Mankiewicz.*
Mankiewicz (1909–1993) was one of the most literate of postwar filmmakers, a *writer*-director who valued words above all else. His best movies are mostly literary and theatrical adaptations, though his greatest film, *All About Eve*, is an original screenplay. It explores the milieu of the New York theater with characteristically bitchy dialogue and witty repartee. Other major works by Mankiewicz include *The Late George Apley* (1947), *The Ghost and Mrs. Muir* (1947), *A Letter to Three Wives* (1949), *Julius Caesar* (1953), *Guys and Dolls* (1955), *Suddenly Last Summer* (1959), and *Sleuth* (1972). *(Twentieth Century-Fox)*

Emotions are frequently expressed with gestures rather than words. Directors who favor the Method believe that an actor must have the character's experience within him or her. The actor's job is to reach into his or her subconscious to dredge up these experiences and transfer them to the character—this is the *art* of acting. The rest is just mechanics. Since the 1950s, the Method has been the dominant American tradition of acting in movies, television, and the live theater. It was—and is—by no means universal, however. For example, old-style performers like Bette Davis **(10–13)** thought that Method acting was too intellectualized. Similarly, Alfred Hitchcock hated working with Method actors because they were constantly hounding him about their characters' motivations.

Major Filmmakers

FRED ZINNEMANN (1907–1997) was one of the most successful and respected of the postwar American **realists.** Though often praised in retrospect, he had to fight to make most of his movies, which were almost routinely dismissed by studio sages as too uncommercial, too depressing, or too highbrow for the mass audience. Even his popular hits, like *From Here to Eternity* (1953), *The Nun's Story* (1958), and *A Man for All Seasons* (1966), were regarded as off-beat, freakish successes.

Like most European-Jewish immigrants of his generation, Zinnemann wanted to be a serious film artist, but within the commercial industry. A documentarist by training, he brought to the American fiction feature a rigorous authenticity and maturity of subject matter. Even his genre films, like the western *High Noon* **(10–14)** and the thriller *The Day of the Jackal* (1973), are characterized by an unconventional astringency, a documentary visual style, and an objective tone.

After an apprenticeship as a documentarist at MGM's short subjects department, Zinnemann signed a three-picture agreement with producer Stanley Kramer in 1949. Both men were political liberals. Both wanted to make movies dealing with serious themes and social issues, yet without sacrificing drama, suspense, or excitement. Three of Zinnemann's finest movies were produced by Kramer's company: *The Men* (1950), *High Noon*, which was a huge hit, and *The Member of the Wedding* (1953), based on the play by Carson McCullers.

10–14. *High Noon* **(U.S.A., 1952),** *with Gary Cooper and Lloyd Bridges, directed by Fred Zinnemann.*
High Noon started a trend in the evolution of the western, away from the romantic heroism of the past toward a more realistic, deglamourized image of the West. These so-called adult westerns emphasized the psychology of the characters rather than their mythic dimensions, as in the classical westerns of the past. This **revisionist** tendency has been called the "demythologizing of genres," a pronounced characteristic of the 1950s, as Andrew Dowdy has pointed out: "Like the detective story, the gangster film, and the thriller, the Western retained its durability in the fifties by shedding its more innocent past, and then turning . . . to comment on it." *(United Artists)*

10–15. *From Here to Eternity* (U.S.A., 1953), *with Deborah Kerr and Burt Lancaster, directed by Fred Zinnemann.*
Throughout the 1950s, there was a mania for film adaptations, especially of famous plays and novels. Though these original properties became expensive as the decade wore on, best-selling novels or long-running plays were thought to have a presold audience. Both literature and the live theater were freer of censorship than the movies, so adapters often confronted serious problems. In this film, much of the coarse language and steamy sexuality of James Jones's original novel had to be sacrificed in the movie version, which was written by Daniel Taradash. Instead, the sexuality is romanticized aesthetically. In this scene the lovers are photographed in part with a sensuous **crane shot** that floats in from a high **angle** to a closer view of the two lovers kissing passionately on a deserted beach at dusk. An ocean wave sweeps over their bodies as they continue to cling to each other. The rhythmical pounding of the waves, the slowly penetrating camera, and her exclamation, "Oh, I never knew it could be like this," combine to produce one of the most erotic love scenes ever filmed up to that time.   *(Columbia Pictures)*

Virtually all of Zinnemann's mature films might be entitled *No Exit*. Most of his protagonists are trapped in a social crisis that forces them to confront their own sense of identity. Identity was a pervasive theme in the American cinema of the 1950s, as was the conflict between the individual and society. Zinnemann often quoted the words of Hillel as his major theme: "If I am not for myself, who will be for me? And if I am only for myself, what am I? And if not now, when?" Zinnemann's movies often deal with a conflict of conscience, in which an individual strives to preserve his or her integrity in the face of increasing pressures. The conflict can be social, psychological, or both.

The individual clashing with society can be seen in such works as *High Noon* and *From Here to Eternity*. An example of an interior clash is *The Nun's Story*. Sir Thomas More in *A Man for All Seasons* and the title character of *Julia* (1977) are perhaps the ultimate examples, for both of them lose their lives for their beliefs. Most of Zinnemann's protagonists are reluctant loners, men and women who long to be part of a larger social unit, yet are unable in the end to pay the price—a yielding of personal identity.

Zinnemann contributed substantially to a decade of good acting in American movies. His performers were almost routinely nominated for Academy Awards, and many won. Actors frequently praised his patience, understanding, and intelligence as a director. Although Elia Kazan was generally associated with Method acting, it was Zinnemann who introduced the most famous Method actors: Montgomery Clift, Julie Harris, and Marlon Brando, to mention the most obvious.

ELIA KAZAN (1909–2003) was more radical politically than Zinnemann, at least as a young man. Kazan's Greek immigrant parents kept him virtually isolated from his American environment until he went away to college, where he was introduced to the ideas of Freud and Marx, among others. In the 1930s, Kazan became a dedicated Communist and joined forces with the famed Group Theatre as an actor, writer, and director. He idealized the U.S.S.R. and such Soviet artists as Meyerhold, Vakhtangov, and Stanislavsky. Kazan eventually repudiated Communism and the Soviet Union, especially after the Hitler-Stalin pact was signed in 1939. Although still a **leftist,** Kazan opposed the totalitarian form of Marxism that came to be known as Stalinism.

Kazan came to prominence in the New York theater during the 1940s, after he directed the premier production of Thornton Wilder's *The Skin of Our Teeth* (1942). Throughout the following two decades, Kazan was called a "two-coast genius" and continued to work in both movies and the live theater. He mounted the premieres of such classic plays as Arthur Miller's *All My Sons* (1947), Tennessee Williams's *A Streetcar Named Desire* (1947), Miller's *Death of a Salesman* (1949), Williams's *Camino Real* (1953) and *Cat on a Hot Tin Roof* (1955), William Inge's *The Dark at the Top of the Stairs* (1957), Archibald MacLeish's *J.B.* (1958), Williams's *Sweet Bird of Youth* (1959), and Miller's *After the Fall* (1964).

Kazan eventually signed a contract with Twentieth Century–Fox, which was headed by the cocky and diminutive Darryl F. Zanuck. Most of the moguls were politically conservative, but Zanuck was relatively liberal—in theory if not always in practice. Although the studio's pictures were diversified, he tended to favor topical and controversial subjects, with an emphasis on **story values** rather than stars. In the postwar era, Zanuck was one of the first to sense that American audiences had matured as a result of the war. Fox became the leading producer of films of social commentary. "Zanuck was always a man of the people," Kazan said. "If something was being felt, he felt it."

Kazan's movies at Twentieth Century–Fox were in this reformist-liberal tradition. *Gentlemen's Agreement* (1948) dealt with anti-Semitism, still virtually a taboo theme in Hollywood. The film won the Oscar for Best Picture, as well as one for Kazan's direction. He went on to direct another social exposé, *Pinky* (1949), which turned out to be Fox's top grosser of the year. As a result of these movies, Kazan was admitted to the forefront of American directors. He initiated most of his subsequent projects and usually enjoyed total artistic independence.

Kazan frequently portrays the family as a repressive institution in his movies. Beginning in the early 1950s, American film audiences no longer consisted of the monolithic family trade of the prewar era but of smaller, more specialized audiences. By far the largest of these was the so-called youth audience, which responded enthusiastically to films that pleaded the cause of adolescents **(10–16).**

10–16. *Rebel Without a Cause* (**U.S.A., 1955),** *with James Dean, directed by Nicholas Ray.*
With the advent of television, family pictures became a thing of the past. Mom and Dad were home watching TV, which catered primarily to the family. By the end of the 1950s, over 75 percent of the film audience was under thirty years old. Movie theaters became palaces of subtle subversion. Films like *Rebel Without a Cause, The Wild One* (1954), and *The Blackboard Jungle* (1955) portrayed young people as disaffected outsiders, contemptuous of the System and its dull, hypocritical morality. Three of the most popular new stars—Brando, Clift, and Dean—were commonly perceived as rebels. Dean especially was a popular symbol of misunderstood youth, struggling to define his identity in an adult world dominated by shallow, materialistic values. Dean (1931–1955) became a huge overnight star as a result of only two movies, *Rebel* and *East of Eden*. (His only other film, *Giant*, was released after his death.) A cult developed around the young star after he was killed in an auto crash at the age of twenty-four. Many fans refused to believe their idol was dead. A year after his death, Warner Brothers was still receiving nearly seven thousand letters a month, asking for photos.   *(Warner Brothers)*

Two of Kazan's biggest hits dealt with the problems of young people with their parents: *East of Eden* (1955) and *Splendor in the Grass* (1961). Tortured relationships within families are common in his films. Some of these conflicts are between brothers; some are between generations. Most often the conflict is Oedipal, usually between sons and fathers, or father figures: *Viva Zapata* (1952), *On the Waterfront* **(10–17),** *East of Eden, Splendor in the Grass, America, America* (1963), *The Arrangement* (1969), *The Visitors* (1971), and *The Last Tycoon* (1976).

Critic Jim Kitses has pointed out that "Kazan's career can be seen as a set of variations on the basic theme of the individual as victim of social pressures that demand a caricature of the self and betrayal of the past." Most of Kazan's movies deal with a conflict of loyalties, in which the protagonist (usually male) struggles inarticulately to find his essential nature. His struggle is usually dialectical, cutting across cultural boundaries, impelling him to adapt to an alien world whose values are both alluring and repugnant. To fit in, he initially believes that he must repudiate his family, his past, and his cultural origins. He becomes, in effect, a spiritual exile, devoured by guilt and feelings of ambivalence.

Kazan's main fault as a filmmaker was his tendency to overheat the materials, to hype up the action with explosive effects. "My problem is that I can always make things forceful," he admitted. "I used to make every scene GO GO GO! mounting

10–17. *On the Waterfront* **(U.S.A., 1954),** *with Rod Steiger and Marlon Brando, directed by Elia Kazan.*
"At his best," Kazan said, "Brando was the best actor we've had in this country in my time." Many regard this performance as his very best—emotionally powerful, tender, poetic. It won him his first Academy Award for best actor, as well as the New York Film Critics Award and the British Oscar as best foreign actor—his third year in a row. Kazan was often surprised by his gifted protégé, because he came up with ideas so fresh and arrived at in so underground a fashion that they seemed virtually discovered on the spot. *On the Waterfront* was a huge international hit. It won the Best Picture Academy Award, Kazan won for his direction, and Budd Schulberg won for his screenplay.   *(Columbia Pictures)*

to a climax, and if I had sixty minutes in a picture there were sixty climaxes." In his later works, he relaxed more, allowing the emotional moments in the action to assert themselves without overstatement.

Kazan's career began its slow decline in the mid-1960s when his movies became increasingly personal. He began to devote more time to writing his novels, less to his stage and screen work. His most fervent critical champions have been associated with the French Marxist journal, *Positif.* One of its finest critics, Michel Ciment, regards Kazan as a seminal force in the postwar American cinema. "Few directors of the younger generation would deny Kazan's influence on their work," Ciment pointed out. Among the most conspicuous of Kazan's spiritual heirs are

10–18. *Gigi* **(U.S.A., 1958),** *with Louis Jourdan, Leslie Caron, and Hermione Gingold, music by Frederick Loewe, screenplay and lyrics by Alan Lerner, directed by Vincente Minnelli.* Before the 1950s, the genre was called "musical comedy"; after the 1950s, the "comedy" was often dropped. Like other genres, the musical darkened and matured in the 1950s, exploring ideas that would have been thought too downbeat in earlier years. *Gigi* is based on a story by Colette and deals with the grooming of an exuberant schoolgirl (Caron) into a courtesan for a rich lover—any rich lover who can afford to keep her. The movie won an Oscar as Best Picture, and Minnelli also won for his direction. Musicals rarely won Best Picture Awards prior to the 1950s because the genre was traditionally thought to be lightweight entertainment. *(Metro-Goldwyn-Mayer)*

such filmmakers as Arthur Penn, Sidney Lumet, John Cassavetes, Martin Scorsese, Francis Ford Coppola, Oliver Stone, Spike Lee, and Ice Cube.

When ALFRED HITCHCOCK came to America in 1939, he was already England's most successful fiction filmmaker (see Chapter 7). His first American project, *Rebecca* (1940), was produced by David O. Selznick and was a huge hit, winning the Best Picture Oscar. Hitchcock continued to work for Selznick for most of the 1940s. The decade was a series of ups and downs for the odd Englishman, mostly downs. However, he directed two of his finest works during this period: *Shadow of a Doubt* (1943), which many critics regard as his first masterpiece, and *Notorious* (1946), a romantic spy thriller, with Ingrid Bergman and Cary Grant, two of Hitchcock's favorite players.

His slump came to an end at the beginning of the next decade, with the dazzling *Strangers on a Train* (1951). The 1950s was to be his greatest period, both commercially and artistically. The movies of this decade are varied and include such elegant entertainments as *To Catch a Thief* (1955), a superior remake of his earlier *The Man Who Knew Too Much* (1956), and the stylistic tour de force *North by Northwest* **(10–19).** He also attempted more thematically ambitious movies, like *Rear Win-*

10–19. *North by Northwest* **(U.S.A., 1959),** *with Cary Grant, directed by Alfred Hitchcock.* Would you believe this man to be innocent? The murder victim lies motionless at Grant's feet. The bloodied knife is clearly in his hand. The scene is photographed in the United Nations Lounge. The photo is plastered across the front pages of America's newspapers. Incredibly, absurdly—Grant *is* innocent. The Wrong Man theme is found in virtually all Hitchcock's movies, never so audaciously as in *North by Northwest,* a chase film in which each episode is a stylistic tour de force synthesizing irony, wit, and terror with exhilarating mastery. *(Metro-Goldwyn-Mayer)*

dow (1954), *The Wrong Man* (1957), and *Vertigo* (1958). This period culminated with *Psycho* **(10–20),** which is widely regarded as his finest achievement and his most complex work. It was also his biggest hit, costing $800,000 and grossing over $15 million in its **first run.** Hitchcock went into another decline in the 1960s, but in 1972 he came back strong with *Frenzy.* His final work was the impish self-parody *Family Plot* (1976), which he directed when he was seventy-seven years old.

Early in his American career, Hitchcock became a savvy self-publicist. Beginning with *Saboteur* (1942), he had his name prominently displayed above the title. After his popular television series, he was as well known to the general public as any top star. Almost from the beginning, he was in control of his own career. He never regarded movies primarily—and certainly not solely—as a commercial enterprise, but he believed that if a filmmaker is not realistic about his public, he will eventually be out of work. He was one of the shrewdest analyzers of audience

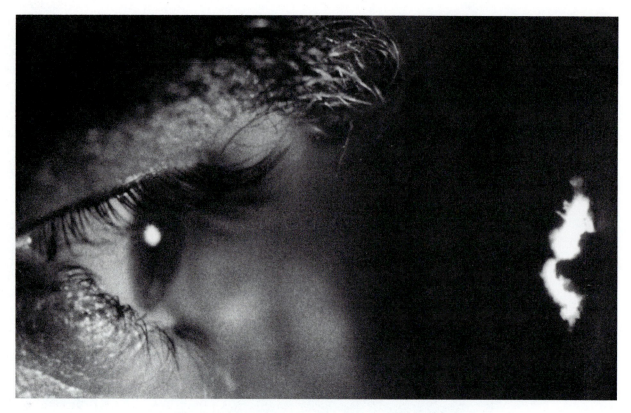

10–20. *Psycho* (**U.S.A., 1960**), *with Anthony Perkins, directed by Alfred Hitchcock.*
Voyeurism is at the heart of Hitchcock's art. Indeed, he regarded cinema as the ultimate voyeuristic art, stealing furtive glances at the hidden, the secret, the forbidden. Movies are watched in darkness, a medium of guilt and complicity, a medium of sin.   *(Paramount Pictures)*

psychology and prided himself on being an international artist whose movies were popular all over the world. "You have to design your film just as Shakespeare did his plays," Hitchcock explained, "for an audience."

He was so successful as a commercial entertainer that for many years that's all he was regarded as. But the French changed all that. As early as 1954, *Cahiers du Cinéma* devoted an entire issue to Hitchcock's works. Such critics as Truffaut, Godard, Chabrol, and Rohmer idolized Hitchcock, not only as a superlative stylist but as a moralist, and a bleak one at that. Many other reappraisals followed, first in France, then in England and America.

Hitchcock resisted symbolic interpretations of his work, in part because highbrow labels can be the kiss of death at the box office. Throughout his American career, he promoted himself as The Master of Suspense—no doubt because it sold more tickets. Like many of his characters, however, he was something of a split personality. He *was* the master of suspense, but his movies are also *about* ideas and feelings. As Truffaut noted in his famous book-length interview, to reproach Hitchcock for specializing in suspense is to accuse him of being the least boring of great filmmakers. Truffaut also suggested that Hitchcock's deadpan drollery concealed a profound pessimism. The American critic Richard Schickel pointed out that the director's **persona**—the jolly fat man with a macabre, punning sense of humor—was almost entirely fictional.

"The man who excels at filming fear is himself a very fearful person," François Truffaut observed. "Under the invariably self-possessed and often cynical surface is a deeply vulnerable, sensitive, and emotional man who feels with particular intensity the sensations he communicates to his audience." Fears and anxieties dominated Hitchcock's life as well as his art. His mania for order was legendary. He detested surprises and conflicts and tried to regularize his life as much as possible. "I like everything around me to be clear as crystal and completely calm. I don't want clouds overhead," he said. "When I take a bath, I put everything neatly back in place. You wouldn't even know I'd been to the bathroom."

Hitchcock's artistic vision was ironic, rooted in a sense of the absurdity of life. He was seldom attracted to mystery, claiming it keeps the audience in the dark as much as the characters. Suspense, on the other hand, lets the spectator in on the dramatic variables. "I believe in giving the audience all the facts as early as possible," he pointed out. We are encouraged to identify strongly with the characters, and in this way, he was able "to put the audience through it"—his stated aim—and thereby jolt us out of our smug sense of security.

Hitchcock encourages us to identify with his characters through a variety of techniques. He frequently cast attractive stars, and even though the characters they play are sometimes morally dubious, the good will they generate as cultural icons tends to smother our moral objections. For example, in *Rear Window,* the protagonist is literally a voyeur, snooping on the lives of his neighbors. But because he's played by Jimmy Stewart, the all-American boy, we make generous allowances for his unsavory compulsions. Seldom does Hitchcock attempt to persuade us of the value of what the characters are seeking. He referred to such arbitrary gimmicks as microfilm, government documents, and so on as a MacGuffin—"something the characters in the film care a lot about, but the audience doesn't worry about it too much."

Since the thriller is one of the most popular of genres and Hitchcock was regularly imitated, his greatest worry was avoiding clichés. Like all genre artists, he was constantly trying to "find new ways to do the same thing." One way of avoiding repetition is to vary the tone. Some of his films are romantic and dreamlike, such as *Vertigo*. Others, like *Frenzy,* are unremittingly nasty and filled with outbursts of cruelty. Hitchcock liked to shift moods in midscene as well. In *Strangers on a Train,* the tone volleys like a tennis ball in play. At his most perverse, he fuses contradictory emotions to produce a bizarre paradox. His most outrageous sequences—like the famous crop-dusting episode in *North by Northwest*—are simultaneously terrifying and funny.

"I am interested not so much in the stories I tell as in the means of telling them," Hitchcock stated. He described himself as a formalist, and he enjoyed the technical play involved in charging the materials with emotion. Strongly attracted to abstraction in the cinema, he frequently compared movies with music and painting. "When I say I'm not interested in content, it's the same as a painter not worrying about the apples that he's painting—whether they're sweet or sour. Who cares? It's his style, his manner of painting them—that's where the emotion comes from."

Hitchcock's precut scripts were legendary. No other director worked from such precisely detailed plans. He often provided frame drawings of his shots (a technique called **storyboarding**), especially for those sequences involving complex **editing.** Some of his scripts contained as many as six hundred **setup** sketches. Every shot was calculated for a precise effect. Nothing was superfluous, nothing left to chance. By the time the script was finished (usually in collaboration with another writer), Hitchcock knew every detail by heart and rarely consulted the screenplay during production. He compared himself to a conductor directing an orchestra without a score.

Hitchcock liked to blur moral distinctions between his characters. "All villains are not black and all heroes are not white. There are grays everywhere." His heroes are generally superficially ordinary but with curious—and sometimes kinky—psychological quirks. The heroines tend to be more appealing—instinctive, more emotional, and often victimized by the hero. The villains are almost invariably charming and polite, like the love-smitten Claude Rains in *Notorious* or the diabolically witty Robert Walker in *Strangers on a Train*. The distinction between the hero and the villain can be entirely academic, as in *Psycho* and *Frenzy*, two of his most misanthropic works. Hitchcock's mother figures constitute a grim gallery of ogres. Mother–son relationships in his movies are generally neurotic, with sadomasochistic undertones. Family life is seldom a comfort in Hitchcock's **oeuvre.**

The Hitchcock universe at its bleakest is like a perverse machine—inscrutable, implacable, absurd in its whimsy. There is a sense of predestination at work. It's a world where "happy endings" are conspicuously arbitrary, a cynical mockery of justice rather than a sentimental affirmation. The police and other agents of security are almost invariably on the wrong track. They turn up too late to be of much help, and they never inspire confidence. Governments and other social institutions are portrayed as impersonal and repressive, indifferent if not outright hostile to the fate of their charges.

After talking with Hitchcock at some length, the French critic André Bazin concluded that the director's obsessions as an artist were intuitive rather than consciously worked out. For example, until Bazin pointed it out, Hitchcock was totally unaware of the transfer-of-guilt **motif** found in virtually all his movies: An innocent weak character yields to a stronger evil figure by sharing his guilt. Numerous French critics insist that this idea is the dramatization in psychological and philosophical terms of the Catholic doctrine of original sin. Richard Schickel shares this view, pointing out that though Hitchcock rarely commented directly on these matters, he seemed to believe that he was as guilty as the next person of some vague imperfection for which he deserved punishment. Like the French, Schickel insisted that Hitchcock was not only a supreme technician but also—at least in his thematically ambitious works—a sardonic moralist who offered little hope of spiritual salvation.

Cultural historians fondly recall the 1950s as the last decade of American innocence—the era of the Hula-Hoops, *I Love Lucy,* and drive-in theaters. American power and prestige seemed to have no limits. "Made in the U.S.A." was a guarantee of the highest quality and craftsmanship. In the next decade, all of this would change. So did the movies. Though no one could have guessed it at the time, Hollywood's golden age was winding to a close. Soon the powerful studio system would be history.

FURTHER READING

BELTON, JOHN. *Widescreen Cinema*. Cambridge, Mass.: Harvard University Press, 1992. Covers technical, social, economic, and aesthetic aspects of widescreen films.

DOWDY, ANDREW. *The Films of the Fifties*. New York: William Morrow, 1973. Survey of the decade, with emphasis on genres, trends, and cycles, written in a lively style.

FORDIN, HUGH. *The World of Entertainment*. New York: Avon Books, 1976. A study of the Freed unit at MGM.

GIANNETTI, LOUIS. *Masters of the American Cinema*. Englewood Cliffs, N.J.: Prentice-Hall, 1981. Contains chapters on Zinnemann, Kazan, Hitchcock, Wilder, and other directors of the 1950s.

GOW, GORDON. *Hollywood in the Fifties*. Cranbury, N.J.: A. S. Barnes, 1971. Survey of the decade, emphasis on major works.

NAVASKY, VICTOR S. *Naming Names*. New York: Viking, 1980. A study of the Red Scare.

NOLLETTI, ARTHUR, JR., ed. *The Films of Fred Zinnemann*. Albany: SUNY Press, 1999. A collection of scholarly essays covering all his major films and some minor works.

PAULY, THOMAS H. *An American Odyssey: Elia Kazan and American Culture*. Philadelphia: Temple University Press, 1983. Cultural study.

TRUFFAUT, FRANÇOIS, with the collaboration of HELEN G. SCOTT. *Hitchcock*. New York: Simon and Schuster, 1967. Copiously illustrated book-length interview, with fascinating insights.

WHITE, DAVID MANNING, and RICHARD AVERSON. *The Celluloid Weapon*. Boston: Beacon Press, 1972. Social comment in the American film.

11

International Cinema in the 1950s

To be an artist means never to avert one's eyes.
—AKIRA KUROSAWA

Museum of Modern Art

Timeline: 1950–1959

1950
Communist North Korea invades South Korea; beginning of Korean War (1950–1954); U.N. forces, led by United States, attempt to repel invasion, unsuccessfully; stalemate and final resolution (Americans killed: 54,000; over one and a half million Chinese and North Koreans killed)

1952
Samuel Beckett's play, *Waiting for Godot,* Paris

1953
Death of Josef Stalin; slow thaw in Cold War; U.S.S.R. explodes hydrogen bomb
Simone de Beauvoir's *The Second Sex* ignites the French feminist movement

1954
French defeat in Vietnam—Indochinese war: 1946–1954

1955
Formation of the Warsaw Pact: U.S.S.R.-dominated mutual defense alliance of eastern European satellite nations

1956
Marriage of Monaco's Prince Rainier of Monaco to American actress Grace Kelly
U.S.S.R. party chief Khruschev denounces Stalin era abuses

1957
International Atomic Energy Agency established, Vienna
U.S.S.R. launches *Sputnik I,* space satellite; intensification of science and technology rivalry with United States

1958
European Common Market comes into being—"Economic Miracle" produces boom years in western Europe

1959
Fidel Castro and his guerrilla rebels oust dictator Batista from Cuba, replacing his regime with a Communist government
Pope John XXIII announces first Ecumenical Council, an attempt to establish ties with other world religions

The emergence of a Third Cinema—India's Satyajit Ray. The Japanese studio system and system of genres. The conflict between traditional and modern values in Japan. Three great Japanese masters: Kurosawa, Mizoguchi, and Ozu. Colossus of the North: Sweden's Ingmar Bergman. Colossus of the South: Italy's Federico Fellini. Early ripples in a French New Wave: The *Cahiers du Cinéma* critics. Mavericks: France's Bresson, Clement, and Tati.

THE 1950s WAS A DECADE OF GREAT individual filmmakers rather than film movements. True, the Japanese cinema emerged as a major international force during this period, but this was an accident of history. Akira Kurosawa, who triggered Western interest in Japanese movies, had begun his career during the World War II era, and Kenji Mizoguchi and Yasujiro Ozu had been working steadily since the 1920s. They were new only to the West. India's Satyajit Ray, the dean of Third World filmmakers, made his spectacular debut during this period **(11–1)**. The British cinema fell into a decline, though the charming Alec Guinness comedies produced by Ealing Studios were bright spots **(11–2)**. On the Continent, two towering figures emerged: Sweden's Ingmar Bergman and Italy's Federico Fellini. In France, the major filmmakers of the decade were Robert Bresson and the comic artist Jacques Tati.

Japan

The West "discovered" the Japanese cinema when Kurosawa's *Rashomon* **(11–4)** won the Grand Prize at the Venice Film Festival of 1951. Throughout the decade and up until the mid-1960s, the Japanese cinema enjoyed a golden age, winning over four hundred prizes at various international festivals. Japan's three greatest filmmakers—Kurosawa, Mizoguchi, and Ozu—created their finest works during this period, not to speak of a half dozen other major filmmakers whose movies are still relatively unknown in the West. Thanks in large measure to the pioneering studies of the American film critic Donald Richie, today Japanese movies are better understood, though even now only a handful of them have been widely exhibited here.

The Japanese film industry has always been one of the largest in the world, rivaling those of India and the United States in terms of output. In fact, the Japanese modeled their industry on the American studio system. For most of its history, the Japanese industry was dominated by five or six major studios, each of which specialized in a typical **genre** or complex of genres and catered to a given segment of the public.

The Japanese system of genres is even more elaborate than that of the American film industry. The two broadest classifications are period films and stories of contemporary life. Under each of these categories there are literally hundreds of

11–1. *Pather Panchali* **(India, 1955),** *with Kanu Bannerjee, directed by Satyajit Ray.*
India is the largest film-producing nation in the world, averaging about seven hundred movies annually, in sixteen languages and dialects. Most of these pictures are stylized musicals featuring popular Indian stars, songs and dances, mythological characters, and an abundance of miraculous transformations. They cater almost exclusively to the Indian mass market and are rarely exported. Satyajit Ray (1921–1993) is an exception: He was the only Indian filmmaker of international stature. Born into a prosperous and cultured Bengali family, Ray studied art as a young man. Strongly influenced by De Sica's *Bicycle Thief* and encouraged by the French filmmaker Jean Renoir, the young Indian artist decided to make *Pather Panchali* ("The Song of the Road"). It created a sensation among critics at the Cannes Film Festival, where the movie won the Jury Prize. Ray followed with *Aparajito* ("The Unvanquished," 1957) and *The World of Apu* (1958). The three pictures comprise *The Apu Trilogy,* the story of a young Bengali boy growing to maturity. Like his idols De Sica and Renoir, Ray was a humanist and a **realist,** concentrating on "small" subjects, ordinary people, and the details of everyday life. His other major works include *Devi* ("The Goddess," 1960), *Two Daughters* (1961), *The Music Room* (1963), *Charulata* ("The Lonely Wife," 1964), *Days and Nights in the Forest* (1970), *Distant Thunder* (1973), *The Chess Players* (1978), and *The Home and The World* (1984). *(Audio-Brandon Films)*

subcategories. The three genres most popular in the West are science-fiction, animation, and samurai films. The Japanese have a highly developed sense of history, and their period genres are generally classified by historical epoch, each of which has a characteristic set of attributes.

Contemporary stories are subclassified by thematic emphasis. For example, home dramas deal with the domestic life of an ordinary Japanese family. These can be broken down even further. For instance, mother films deal with the hardships and rewards of motherhood and are somewhat similar to the American woman's picture **(11–3).** As is the case in other countries, Japanese genre films are merely a set of expectations, a given aesthetic turf. The qualitative worth of a genre film depends on the artistry of the filmmaker, not on the genre per se.

Virtually all Japanese film artists produced their work under the aegis of one of the major studios. Like their American counterparts, the studios' main concern was with the mass production of movies for profit, and consequently the overwhelming bulk of their output was garbage fare, soullessly ground out for a quick yen. The film masterpieces produced under this system were created by strong-willed directors who commanded such prestige that the studios rarely interfered with their work—provided their movies returned a profit. Since most Japanese movies were made on small budgets, most of these films returned at least a modest profit.

Under the Japanese studio system, directors usually enjoyed more creative autonomy than their American counterparts. Generally they were accountable only to the studio chief rather than the film's producer, who was merely an assistant to

11–2. *The Ladykillers* (Great Britain, 1955), *with Alec Guinness, Peter Sellers, Danny Green, Herbert Lom, and Cecil Parker, directed by Alexander Mackendrick.*
Some of the best English movies of this era were the comedies produced by Ealing Studios and often starred Alec Guinness at his funniest. In *Kind Hearts and Coronets* (1949, directed by Robert Hamer), a satirical black comedy, Guinness plays nine different roles, including a female. In *The Lavender Hill Mob* (1951, directed by Charles Crichton), he plays a timid bank clerk with a fiendishly clever scheme for a perfect robbery. In *The Ladykillers,* he is a weird mastermind criminal and the leader of an odd assortment of crooks pretending to be amateur classical musicians. Their plans are accidentally thrown awry by a sweet little old lady who thinks they are splendid gentlemen.   *(Ealing Studios)*

the director. Prestigious directors received top billing, even over the **stars** and the title of the film. Of course, such autonomy was granted only to the most respected filmmakers; newcomers were expected to do as they were told by their wiser elders.

Each of the majors employed an apprentice system. Promising directors, actors, and technicians were hired on exclusive long-term contracts and assigned to experienced personnel who served as teachers or mentors—a paternalistic system based on the ubiquitous family structure that permeates Japanese society. The **majors** produced about four or five hundred films per year, most of them routine **program pictures.** The studios also owned their own chain of theaters, thus guaranteeing an outlet for their product. But even independent exhibitors were coerced into renting studio films because of the widespread practice of **blind** and **block booking.**

During the World War II era, the government took over the film industry and dictated its content. The ten major studios were consolidated into three, which made them easier to control. Except for the movies of their fascist cronies, Germany and Italy, foreign films were banned. The studios were also forced to set up documentary units for the production and distribution of government propaganda newsreels, which were required viewing in all Japanese movie theaters. Fiction

11–3. *Late Chrysanthemums* **(Japan, 1954),** *directed by Mikio Naruse.*

The works of many important Japanese filmmakers are still relatively unknown in the West. For example, Mikio Naruse (1905–1969) had a career that spanned four decades and included eighty-seven movies. He was a specialist in women's films set in contemporary times. His heroines are usually strong and intelligent, but they're also unlucky: They've been stood up by life. "Women alone: widows, geisha, bar hostesses, young women from poor families with poor marriage prospects—all those who are not favored by the traditional family system form the essential material of the Naruse film," critic Audie Bock has noted. "The Naruse heroine can be seen as a symbol for everyone who has ever been caught between ideals and reality." *(East–West Classics)*

films were heavily censored and had to reflect "the spirit of sacrifice for the fatherland." Filmmakers were pressured to make movies glorifying such values as nationalism, militarism, class distinctions, self-sacrifice, submission to authority, and the sanctity of the family unit.

Unlike Germany and Italy, which produced little of value during the fascist era (see Chapter 9), Japan managed to produce a number of excellent movies even during the harshest years of the war. In the first place, Japanese cultural values have always been more conservative than their Western counterparts. The militarists who ran the country during the fascist era were extreme and authoritarian in their right-wing ideology, and there was virtually no countertradition of respect for individual rights or encouragement of cultural diversity. Consensus was—and still is—a highly revered concept in Japan, and social nonconformity is viewed with abhorrence by most of its citizens.

Those filmmakers who opposed the values of the military junta did so discreetly, by retreating into period genres. Mizoguchi created some of his finest works during this era, most of them set in the distant past. Kurosawa made his debut as a director during the war years, and he too favored a period genre, the samurai film. Ozu worked in only one genre, the home drama, usually in a contemporary setting. But he treated his tales of family life from an apolitical perspective, relatively divorced from the pressures of outside ideologies.

Japan was devastated by the war, suffering over 2,000,000 casualties, including nearly 700,000 civilians who died in the massive bombardments that leveled virtually every big city in the country. For the first time in its history, Japan was ruled by a foreign power: The American occupation lasted from 1945 to 1952. The Japanese population responded with surprising eagerness to the American policy of democratization. Parliamentary democracy replaced the semifeudal military dictatorship of the fascist era. A new constitution was drawn up, based on the American model, complete with a Bill of Rights guaranteeing individual liberties—a totally foreign concept. Women were accorded equal rights, including the vote. To the Japanese, it was all very bewildering, but they adapted with that extraordinary ability to assimilate foreign ideas that constitutes a kind of national genius.

Most of Japan's movie houses were destroyed by the bombs. In 1945 there were only 845 theaters still standing. Films were censored by the American authorities and made to conform with democratic principles. Period films were discouraged because they were thought to be "too feudal" in their values. For example, Kurosawa's samurai parody, *The Men Who Tread on the Tiger's Tail* (1945), was banned despite its humanist emphasis. On the other hand, Mizoguchi's *Utamaro and His Five Women* (1946) was approved because it dealt with a progressive theme, female emancipation. Anything "traditional" was suspect; anything "modern" encouraged.

Actually, the conflict between traditional and modern values is characteristic of virtually all Japanese movies, and Japanese society in general. The roots of this conflict extend back to the later nineteenth century, when Japan transformed itself from a feudal country to a modern technological society patterned after the Western industrial states, especially Great Britain and the United States. The Japanese are simultaneously repelled and attracted by both traditional and modern values, which can be schematized by the following sets of polarities:

Traditional	Modern	Traditional	Modern
Japanese	Western	Consensus	Diversity
Feudal	Democratic	Age	Youth
Past	Future	Authority	Autonomy
Society	Individual	Conservative	Liberal
Hierarchy	Equality	Fatalism	Optimism
Nature	Technology	Obedience	Independence
Duty	Inclination	Form	Substance
Self-sacrifice	Self-expression	Security	Anxiety

Almost every Japanese filmmaker can be classified according to his attitudes toward these ideological polarities. For example, Kurosawa is regarded as the "most Western" of filmmakers and accordingly is grouped with the modernists; Ozu, on the other hand, is a champion of traditional values. Mizoguchi falls somewhere between these two poles. However, very few Japanese artists identify with only one set of values. Like the Japanese population in general, filmmakers acknowledge the virtues and vices of both ideologies, and though they might lean toward one or the other, they know that there are trade-offs that must be accepted in a less-than-perfect world.

A key concept in the understanding of Japanese movies and Japanese culture in general is *mono no aware*, a Zen Buddhist formulation roughly analogous to the stoical acceptance of things as they are, as they must be, whether we like it or not. What this concept involves is the traditional Japanese view that wisdom consists of yielding gracefully to what can't be changed. It is a sad acceptance of necessity, whether in the form of human nature, family expectations, the ways of society, natural catastrophes, or such wider spiritual issues as the inevitability of disappointment and death. Japanese movies are filled with characters who sigh, "But that's life" or "Isn't life disappointing?" All that an individual can do in the face of life's transience and inexorable indifference to human suffering is to accept one's fate with dignity and quiet resignation, to do one's duty without complaint or vulgar remonstrance. Unhappy endings are common in Japanese movies, and many of them end on a note of loss.

AKIRA KUROSAWA (1910–1998) was known as "The Emperor" in Japanese film circles, in part because of his preeminence as an artist, in part because of his imperiously uncompromising standards—the cause of considerable grief and lamentation among his thrifty studio bosses. He began his career as a painter, then switched to motion pictures, and he made his directorial debut with *Sanshiro Sugata* (1943), a samurai film. Prior to Kurosawa, this genre tended to emphasize action for its own sake and featured trite, stereotypical characters. Kurosawa infused the samurai film with more depth and thematic complexity. From the beginning of his career, he was regarded as an experimentalist, bending traditional genres to accommodate new ideas and techniques.

He often turned to Western sources for inspiration, especially to literature. Many of his movies are literary adaptations: *The Idiot* (1951) is based on a novel by Dostoyevsky; *Throne of Blood* (1957) is a loose adaptation of Shakespeare's *Macbeth; The Lower Depths* (1957) is a transcription of Gorky's play; *High and Low* (1963) is based on Ed McBain's American novel *King's Ransom;* and *Ran* (1985) is based on *King Lear.*

American movies, especially those of John Ford, also exerted a strong influence on Kurosawa. In this respect, however, he is hardly unique. Except for the fascist era, American movies have always been the most popular foreign fare in Japanese theaters, and many directors have admitted to being influenced by them. The American William Wyler was the favorite director of both Mizoguchi and Ozu, and the works of Chaplin, Lubitsch, and Capra—to name only a few—enjoyed wide admiration among Japanese filmmakers.

11–4. *Rashomon* **(Japan, 1950),** *with Toshiro Mifune and Machiko Kyo, directed by Akira Kurosawa.*
Rashomon established Mifune as the most widely known Japanese star of the postwar era. He appeared in sixteen of Kurosawa's thirty movies, and they became one of the most famous actor-director teams in film history. Bold, virile, and sexy, Mifune specialized in samurai roles, but he was equally proficient in playing quieter, contemporary parts in which his speed and power were reined in, barely suppressed. In period roles, Mifune is a kinetic actor, expressing his emotions through movement, snorting and thrashing like an enraged animal. "I'm a person who is rarely impressed by actors," Kurosawa said, "but in the case of Mifune I was completely overwhelmed." *(Museum of Modern Art)*

Kurosawa was also "Western" in his attitude toward traditional values. In the conflict between society and the individual, his sympathies are usually with individuals, though he doesn't deny the valid claims of social groups. Furthermore, in Kurosawa's movies the protagonists often choose to fight against the odds rather than yield to the fatalistic resignation implied by *mono no aware*. For example, the cancer-stricken old man in *Ikiru* (1952) refuses to die in despair, and in the final months of his life, for the first time in his life, he decides to do something meaningful by facilitating the construction of a children's park in the face of overwhelming bureaucratic apathy. (He is played by the great Takashi Shimura, a Kurosawa regular.) Similarly, the driven physician of *Red Beard* (1965) does his best to heal the sick in a pestilential slum, even though he realizes he's fighting for a lost cause—the cause of the unlucky, the oppressed, the despised outcasts of society.

Kurosawa consistently championed the equality of human emotions, whether they are found in noblemen or beggars. In *Seven Samurai* (1954), the bravest fighter is not from the aristocratic warrior class, but a peasant masquerading as a samurai. In *Kagemusha . . . The Shadow Warrior* (1980), a man's wrenching separation from his surrogate young son is no less moving merely because the military chieftain is actually an impostor of low social origins: His *feelings* are real. Class dis-

11–5. *Seven Samurai* **(Japan, 1954),** *with Toshiro Mifune and Seiji Miyaguchi, directed by Akira Kurosawa.*

Kurosawa was a master of the **epic** form, and his samurai films are the best examples of what one critic described as "the Shakespearean cast of his genius." His battle scenes are among the most brilliant ever filmed, with slashing movements, violent outbursts, and grisly flashes of humor. A samurai, a humanist, Kurosawa was able to convey the epic sweep of battle without losing sight of the human dimension, the significance of the violence to the individuals involved. Critic Donald Richie called *Seven Samurai* the greatest of all Japanese films, and in a 1982 *Sight and Sound* poll of international critics, the movie was voted one of the ten greatest films of all time.   *(Landmark Films)*

tinctions in Kurosawa's movies are arbitrary accidents of birth, preventing people from being fully human: "Why, I ask, is it that human beings cannot get along with each other? Why can't they live with each other with more good will?"

Kurosawa worked on the scripts of all his movies, and he generally knew precisely what he wanted from every scene. During production, he was a paternalistic mentor, socializing with his cast and crew, creating an atmosphere of a communal enterprise. He was known to wait for days for the precise weather conditions for a given sequence. He often had sketches for the costume and set designs, which he insisted had to be executed exactly as rendered. He often used multiple cameras for photographing scenes. This not only allowed him copious amounts of footage at the **editing** bench, it also encouraged more natural performances from his actors, who were thus unable to play to the camera, since they were never sure which camera was photographing the action.

Kurosawa is one of the supreme stylists of the cinema, and his movies are filled with bravura effects. Unlike most Japanese filmmakers, his editing style is often brisk. In his action scenes especially, he bombards the screen with a barrage of split-second shots, hurtling the viewer into a chaotic explosion of shifting perspectives. He is also a master of the **widescreen,** which in his hands is truly an epic

11–6. *Yojimbo* **(Japan, 1961),** *directed by Akira Kurosawa.*
Kurosawa's samurai films are often described as "Eastern westerns." Himself influenced by the westerns of John Ford, the Japanese master has in turn influenced many Western directors—and directors of westerns. John Sturges's *The Magnificent Seven* (U.S.A., 1969) is a western remake of *Seven Samurai*. Sergio Leone's *A Fistful of Dollars* (Italy, 1964), starring Clint Eastwood, is a remake of *Yojimbo* in western form. Many of Eastwood's films are indebted to Kurosawa's works, as are the westerns of Sam Peckinpah, most notably *The Wild Bunch* (U.S.A., 1969). Less obviously, Kurosawa has also influenced the epic works of his two good friends, Francis Ford Coppola *(Apocalypse Now)* and George Lucas *(The Star Wars Films).* *(Janus Films)*

canvas, as can be seen in such brilliantly composed movies as *The Hidden Fortress* (1958), *Yojimbo, Sanjuro* (1962), *Red Beard, Dodes'kaden* (1970), *Dersu Uzala* (1976), and *Kagemusha* (1980).

Few directors were so painstaking in their use of sound. "Cinematic sound is that which does not simply add to, but multiplies, two or three times, the effect of the image," Kurosawa said. For example, in the final battle scene of *Seven Samurai,* which takes place in a torrential downpour **(11–5),** the sounds are orchestrated like a thunderous symphony. We hear the ferocious wind as it tears at the fluttering banners and clothing of the combatants—the rain pelting down from the angry heavens, creating a quagmire of squishy mud that sucks at the feet of the running warriors—the whiz of an arrow and the thud of its penetration—the swift slash of a samurai blade as it fells an opponent—the horses' hooves clacking over rocks—and, barely discernible, the anguished wail of human terror.

After the mid-sixties, Kurosawa's output diminished. Partly as a result of two box office failures (his only two), he was unable to find financing for his films, which tended to be expensive and lengthy—several run over three hours long. He was also considered old-fashioned, passé. *Dersu Uzala* was made in the Soviet Union with Soviet financing. It won the Grand Prix at the Moscow Film Festival of 1976 and an Academy Award in the United States. *Kagemusha* was stalled for years until Kurosawa's friends, Francis Coppola and George Lucas, convinced Twentieth Century–Fox to invest in the picture. Kurosawa got the last laugh. The film won the Grand Prize at the Cannes Film Festival, and it was Japan's highest grossing movie in 1980.

Ran **(17–25),** Kurosawa's long-awaited adaptation of *King Lear,* stunned the film world with its technical brilliance and emotional richness. Released in 1985, it is one of the old master's greatest works—powerful, profound, implacably pessimistic. His last movies, *Akira Kurosawa's Dreams* (1990) and *Rhapsody in August* (1991), contain some dazzling scenes, but they tend to be sprawling and excessively personal.

KENJI MIZOGUCHI (1898–1956) directed eighty-seven movies, yet only a few—mostly those of the postwar era—have been seen in the West. He began his career in 1922 but didn't attract much critical acclaim until *The Water Magician* (1933). Three years later, two of his works, *The Sisters of Gion* and *Osaka Elegy,* placed first and second in the prestigious *Kinema Jumpo* Ten Best list of 1936. He continued to be one of Japan's most respected filmmakers until the end of World War II, when Mizoguchi fell from favor. He was then considered out of touch with modern problems and obsolete in his techniques.

All this changed when Mizoguchi's masterpiece, *Ugetsu* **(11–8),** won the Silver Lion Prize at the Venice Film Festival of 1953. As a result, he became the darling of European critics, especially the French. He was a favorite with the writers of the influential *Cahiers du Cinéma,* which was edited by André Bazin, the most internationally respected film critic of the 1950s. What Bazin and his colleagues admired in Mizoguchi's movies were precisely those qualities that had been dismissed by the Japanese—his use of traditional story materials to create universal truths, the poetic atmosphere of his **mise en scène,** his fluid camera movements, and his elegantly choreographed **lengthy takes.** Largely as a result of the enthusiasm of the French for Mizoguchi's works, today he is regarded as a pillar of the Japanese cinema—even by the Japanese.

11–7. *The Life of Oharu* (Japan, 1952), *with Kinuyo Tanaka (on ground), directed by Kenji Mizoguchi.*
Mizoguchi was famous as a great woman's director. In period films as well as contemporary stories, he chronicles the oppression of women in a rigidly patriarchal society, championing their cause with compassion, restraint, and exquisite delicacy. *The Life of Oharu,* which won the International Prize at the Venice Film Festival, deals with the downfall of a wealthy court lady who is eventually reduced to becoming a common prostitute to survive. *(New Yorker Films)*

Like Naruse, Mizoguchi's main concern was usually with the problems of women in Japanese society. As Donald Richie has pointed out, Mizoguchi's recurrent theme is that man's soul is saved by a woman's love, and without it he is damned. Whatever their class origins, whether aristocratic as in *The Life of Oharu* **(11–7)** and *The Empress Yang Kwei-fei* (1955), middle class as in *Sansho the Bailiff* (1954) and *The Crucified Lovers* (1954), or lower class, like the prostitutes of *Women of the Night* (1948) and his final film, *Street of Shame* (1956), Mizoguchi exposes the cruel injustices of a society that traditionally has treated women as second-class citizens.

There is an old Confucian adage that a female should obey her father when she is a girl, her husband when she is mature, and her son when she is old. This has been the prevailing view in Japan throughout most of its history. Japanese girls are raised much more strictly than boys, who are allowed considerable freedom. Females are brought up to believe that marriage and motherhood are the most rewarding achievements in life; a career and economic independence are poor substitutes. Women constitute only about 20 percent of the university population in Japan, and they are still discriminated against in the job market. Women rarely hold upper management positions. Although 40 percent of the work force is female, women receive less than half the average income of males. In the pre–World War II era, arranged marriages were the rule, and even today they are far from unusual, though young people are seldom forced into marriage against their inclinations.

After marriage, a wife is often treated coldly by her mate. She is expected to endure indifference and insults with dignified meekness. The sexual double standard is common: A husband's philandering is winked at, providing it doesn't endanger the family; a wife's infidelity is harshly censured. Not that she has many chances. Married women rarely go out with their husbands to dinners and parties, and a wife's social life is pretty much confined to her husband, children, close relatives, and perhaps a few girlhood friends. Family life is dominated by the mother, who is expected to devote her life to the upbringing of her children. Fathers are primarily wage earners and have relatively little contact with their offspring.

After raising their children, women often return to the work force, but they are usually relegated to minor positions, receive meager wages, and enjoy none of the privileges of seniority. Until the postwar occupation, divorce was easy for men to obtain, but very difficult for women. The divorce rate in Japan is still only about one eighteenth of that in America, in part because older women find it virtually impossible to make a decent living wage. In present-day Japan, the lot of women is improving, but they are still an exploited group compared to their Western counterparts. Mizoguchi's sympathy for women was not based on sentimentality, then, but on hard social realities.

In his films of contemporary life, Mizoguchi dealt with these issues realistically. The stories are harsh, the milieu objectively presented, the tone pessimistic though compassionate. The images are rarely striking in their beauty: Cold facts

11–8. *Ugetsu* **(Japan, 1953),** *with Masayuki Mori and Machiko Kyo, directed by Kenji Mizoguchi.*
Above all, the Japanese cinema excels in the creation of mood, in presenting characters within a richly textured environment, such as the hauntingly diaphanous dream world of *Ugetsu*. Trained as a painter, Mizoguchi was an unsurpassed master of atmospheric effects, capable of creating images of striking pictorial beauty.   *(Janus Films)*

take precedence over aesthetic allure. In his period films, however, the treatment is more stylized. The stories are often based on legends, mythology, and fables. Fantasy elements such as spirits, dreams, and omens are common (11–8). There is a pronounced emphasis on ritual and symbolism. The mise en scène is often breathtakingly beautiful, with the frequent use of such dreamlike elements as enchanted landscapes, fog, mist, and shadows—suggesting psychological and spiritual states. His images are richly textured, exotic, and mysterious, especially in their eerie stillness. He was expert in his use of the **frame**—as much for what he left out as for what he included within its confines.

Mizoguchi frequently used a single **take** for an entire scene—**dollying, panning,** or **tilting** the camera rather than cutting to separate shots. He generally cut within a continuous take only when there was a sharp psychological shift within the scene. Used sparingly in this way, the cut acquires a greater dramatic impact than can be found in most conventionally edited movies. The Japanese film critic Tadao Sato pointed out that Mizoguchi's lengthy takes are aesthetic equivalents of the Buddhist belief in the eternal flux of the universe. The lovely compositions are fixed for a time, then destroyed, then recomposed, like the successive movements of a dancer: "That which is active is changing at every moment and is difficult to grasp firmly," Sato observed. "One attempts to embed this elusive reality in some form of a single moment, but no sooner does it appear to be fixed than the balance in that form crumbles."

The films of YASUJIRO OZU (1903–1963) were not widely seen in the West until the 1970s. Prior to that time, his movies were regarded as "too Japanese" to be appreciated by foreign audiences, and producers made few efforts to export his works. In addition to being a popular filmmaker in his native country, Ozu was also Japan's most honored director, the winner of six *Kinema Jumpo* Best Picture awards.

Unlike most filmmakers, Ozu's **oeuvre** is remarkably consistent: People who like one of his movies will probably like them all. Working almost exclusively in the genre of the home drama, he often used the same actors, the same character types, the same techniques, and the same story elements in his fifty-six films. Only the details vary. But in the rarefied cinema of Ozu, the details—no matter how small—are everything. Like Chekhov and Vermeer, Ozu concentrated on the commonplace minutiae of everyday life. Paradoxically, from these apparently unpromising materials, he was able to fashion a profoundly philosophical cinema.

If Kurosawa is the artistic spokesman for the anguished individual, and Naruse and Mizoguchi for the exploited female, then Ozu speaks for the conservative majority, especially parents. For the most part, his characters are ordinary middle-class Japanese—conscientious, hard working, and decent. Most of them are devoted to their families, eager to do the right thing by them, though not always certain of what the right thing is. Generally, they fall back on social convention, the accumulated wisdom of consensus: Young people should marry and raise children. Old people should be revered (11–9). Everyone should do his or her duty, regardless of personal feelings. Authority and tradition should be respected. The inevitable should be accepted with dignity and stoical resignation. No other filmmaker embodies the essence of *mono no aware* as profoundly as Ozu.

Ozu detested plots. Like most **realists,** he believed that plots tend to force characters into contrived situations, thus violating their plausibility. Above all, he was interested in exploring character, and he believed that the best way to do this was to portray people in their normal course of activities and to adhere to the

11–9. *Tokyo Story* **(Japan, 1953),** *directed by Yasujiru Ozu.*
In his native land, Ozu was regarded as the "most Japanese" of filmmakers, primarily because he extolled that quintessentially Japanese institution—the family. But his movies are not cheerful endorsements of family life, for Ozu was also an ironist, well aware of the gap between reality and the ideal—the principal source of his irony. In this film, for example, an elderly couple (Chieko Higashiyama and Chishu Ryu, front center) decide to go visit their children and grandchildren in Tokyo. They are disappointed with their reception. Their children are too busy to offer them anything but the most perfunctory attention, and they are utterly incapable of relating to their parents as people. They're just parents. Ironically, the only person who is kind and attentive is not a blood relation but their daughter-in-law (Setsuko Hara, upper left), the widow of their son who was killed during the war. Family life in Ozu's movies, as elsewhere, is not always what it's cracked up to be. *(New Yorker Films)*

rhythms of nature. Hence the slow pace of his movies, even by Japanese standards. His films are usually centered on the basic cycles of family life—births, deaths, illnesses, marriages, visits, separations, and so on. Instead of zeroing in on these events, however, Ozu preferred to explore them in a leisurely manner, through "incidental" detail rather than dramatic confrontation. He never rushed his scenes to score plot points. He was usually concerned with the emotional significance of an event rather than the event for its own sake. His movies are deliberately dedramatized, avoiding even the hint of pushiness or theatricality. Nuance is all.

In his characterization too, Ozu is a master of understatement. Many of his scenes take place in public settings—bars, restaurants, schoolrooms, work places. Even family scenes are somewhat formal and ceremonial, where politeness and social decorum require the stifling of personal disappointment. Fearful of offending or appearing selfish—the ultimate social sin in Japanese society—his characters are generally tactful, oblique in their inquiries. They often remain silent when confronted by unpleasant choices, hopeful of undiscovered alternative options. Ozu frequently instructed his actors not to "act," but to behave realistically, to express their feelings only with their eyes rather than pointed gestures or exaggerated facial expressions. The conflict between individual desires and social necessity is all the more moving precisely because it rarely flares out at us.

Ozu's screenplays, often written in collaboration with his longtime associate Kogo Noda, were painstakingly crafted to include only realistic events and dialogue. They were written with specific actors in mind. "I could no more write, not knowing who the actor was going to be, than an artist could paint, not knowing what color he was using," Ozu explained. Lean and unadorned, these scripts were frequently published and were widely appreciated as realistic literature. The titles of his movies are often concrete images, like *Floating Weeds* (1934, remade in an updated version in 1959), *The Flavor of Green Tea over Rice* (1952), and *Equinox Flower* (1958). Many of his films have seasonal titles, evoking appropriate human analogues: *Late Spring* (1949), *Early Summer* (1951), *Early Spring* (1956), *Late Autumn* (1960), and *The End of Summer* (1961).

Ozu's style embodies the Buddhist ideals of simplicity, restraint, and serenity. Restricting himself to only a few basic techniques, he has been described as a **minimalist,** rejecting all superfluous adornments in favor of the utmost economy of expression. "Less is more" might well serve as his artistic credo. In this respect, Ozu is characteristically Japanese. His films have been compared to *haiku* poems, which consist of only a few lines encapsulating a striking image, or to a *sumi-e* ink drawing, which evokes its subject through a few strokes of the pen or brush. The fragment symbolizes the whole; the microcosm evokes the macrocosm. Similarly, Japanese flower arrangements often consist of a single stem with two or three blossoms floating on its delicate branches. In a like manner, the art of samurai swordsmanship consists of a few elegantly executed strokes, valued as much for their artistic form as for their practical function.

Ozu's camerawork is Spartan in its austerity. Virtually every shot is photographed from the same **angle:** three or four feet off the floor, the position from which a person would view a scene if seated on a tatami mat. Ozu hardly ever used such optical devices as **fades** and **dissolves,** nor did he move the camera during the shot: It remains inexorably fixed in a single position, a detached observer.

His mise en scène is tasteful and pleasing to the eye, while still remaining realistic. The images are composed according to **classical** conventions: The visual elements are harmoniously distributed and attractively arranged, but rarely striking in their virtuosity, as is often the case with Kurosawa and Mizoguchi. Ozu's most beautiful images are usually his still-life compositions, landscapes, and cityscapes that intersperse his dramatic scenes, often as a transition between sequences. But even these images are serenely tranquil rather than boldly dramatic.

His **editing** style is spare. In dialogue scenes involving some tension, he usually employs **medium shots,** cutting from one character to the other as they speak. In moments of harmony, he uses **two-shots,** with both characters sharing the same space. In group scenes, he favors **tightly framed full shots,** excluding all nonessentials. He rarely uses **closeups** and employs **extreme long shots** only for nature scenes and cityscapes. He often begins a scene on an empty set, creating a sense of anticipation in the viewer, while we wait for the characters to enter and confront each other. Sometimes Ozu holds the camera on the set after the characters have left, creating a poignant sense of desolation, of emptiness. Between scenes, he often cuts to the outside landscape, suggesting the sublime indifference of nature. Life goes on, despite the problems of the characters.

Though he was a champion of the Japanese family system, Ozu was no sentimentalist. His movies are usually in the elegiacal mode: Most of them deal with the dissolution of the family, often in the form of a marriage, when children leave their families to start their own, or—less consolingly—when a loved member of the family dies. True, the characters generally have the satisfaction of having performed their duty faithfully. But in so doing, they often must suffer the ironic consequences: solitude and loneliness. Ozu's movies usually conclude on a tender note of bittersweet loss **(11–10)**.

11–10. *An Autumn Afternoon* **(Japan, 1962),** *with Chishu Ryu, directed by Yasujiro Ozu.* In this, Ozu's final movie, the story materials are as simple as ever, consisting entirely of "little things." Precisely because the treatment is understated, the film's emotional impact is poignant. The protagonist (Ryu) is a gentle, aging widower who lives with his unmarried daughter in mutual devotion. His loneliness is assuaged by a few drinking buddies who spend much of their free time at the local bar. After hearing of the marriage of a friend's daughter, the widower decides that it's time for his daughter to move on as well. He arranges a marriage with a decent young man recommended by his friends. At the end of the movie, he muses contentedly on the success of his arrangements. He also realizes that he's getting on in years. And that he is alone.   *(New Yorker Films)*

Ingmar Bergman

INGMAR BERGMAN (b. 1918), Sweden's greatest filmmaker, is a towering figure in the history of world cinema. Religiously dedicated to his art, he consistently addressed himself to exploring ambitious metaphysical themes. A writer-director, he has been compared to Dickens and Shakespeare in the rich diversity of his characters; and to Joyce, Proust, and Faulkner in the complexity of his techniques. Despite his pessimistic vision and the cold, bleak, joyless universe he created in nearly fifty movies, Bergman is one of the few European directors who appealed to a popular audience in the United States. His works were usually well received here, both critically and commercially. They received more Academy Award nominations than those of any other foreign filmmaker.

Bergman was born into a prosperous, middle-class family. His father was a stern Lutheran minister who eventually became court chaplain to the Swedish royal family. As a boy, Bergman spent much of his time at his grandmother's home—the happiest, most secure period of his life. He majored in literature and art at the University of Stockholm, writing his thesis on August Strindberg, Sweden's greatest dramatist and the major artistic influence on Bergman's work. Like many young artists and intellectuals of the 1940s, Bergman was also strongly impressed by the nihilistic fiction of Franz Kafka, whose brooding allegories of guilt, paranoia, and angst exerted a lasting influence on Bergman's sensibility.

Throughout most of his career, Bergman was also Sweden's foremost stage director. He has mounted over one hundred stage productions, including operas and the plays of Strindberg, Chekhov, Ibsen, Molière, Goethe, Pirandello, Brecht, Tennessee Williams, and Edward Albee. During his early years as a stage director, Bergman gathered together a first-rate company of actors, including Max von Sydow, Bibi Andersson, Gunnar Björnstrand, Harriet Andersson, Ingrid Thulin, Gunnel Lindblom, and Eva Dahlback. Erland Josephson and Liv Ullmann joined the Bergman group after the mid-1960s. All of them performed in his films as well as his stage productions. Also included among his regulars were the much-admired cinematographers Gunnar Fischer and Sven Nykvist, who photographed virtually all of Bergman's movies.

Throughout the early 1940s, Bergman was a scriptwriter at Svensk Filmindustri, the state-subsidized company that has produced most of his movies. His first credited screenplay was for Alf Sjöberg's *Torment* (1944), a fitting title for Bergman's oeuvre as well. Between 1945 and 1955, he wrote and directed thirteen movies, most of which were explorations of youthful tensions between generations and between lovers. Generally, Bergman is more sympathetic to his female characters—hence his reputation as a great woman's director. The most critically admired of these early works is *Sawdust and Tinsel* (1953, also known as *The Naked Night)*, a grim tale of humiliation and spiritual degradation involving a group of circus performers.

Bergman burst on the international scene with *Smiles of a Summer Night* (1955), a period comedy of manners and his only successful film in a comic vein. He followed this with two more masterpieces: *The Seventh Seal* (1956) and *Wild Strawberries* (1957). *The Seventh Seal* is a poetic **allegory** about a medieval knight's religious anguish and gnawing doubts about the existence of God—a theme that was to obsess Bergman for years. The film is a stunning re-creation of the Middle Ages, filled with bold, dramatic images that were partly modeled on the works of medieval artists. *Wild Strawberries* is also visually striking. Realistic scenes dealing with the life of an aloof old medical scientist are interspersed with terrifying night-mares and fantasy sequences, revealing his repressed fears and anxieties. Like most of Bergman's movies, it is strongly indebted to Freud's theory of the subconscious. *The Virgin Spring* (11–11), another medieval story dealing with religious themes, was stylistically indebted to the works of Mizoguchi; it won Bergman his first American Academy Award for Best Foreign Language Picture.

By the end of the 1950s, Bergman was regarded as a major figure of the international cinema. In the 1960s, his work became radically experimental. He wrote and directed a trilogy of movies dealing with psychic and religious torments. Made on low budgets with small casts and simple settings, these works are so stark and stripped to essentials that they are referred to as "chamber films." *Through a Glass Darkly* (1961) explores a recurring theme in his work—the shameless immorality of artists, their spiritual cannibalism. A writer watches his own daughter slipping into schizophrenia and keeps a journal to use his observations for a future novel. In *Winter Light* (1963), a village pastor agonizes over his inability to provide comfort to his parishioners because he lacks the gift of faith. At the end of the film he is spiritually drained, praying to God—if He exists—to send him a sign, anything to cling to in his desperate need. *The Silence* (1963) is the severest film of the trilogy. Two sisters, who are also apparently lovers, are stranded in a foreign country. One of them has a young son who accompanies them. Like most of Bergman's children, he is frightened and bewildered by the intensity of the bitterness between the

11–11. *The Virgin Spring* **(Sweden, 1959),** *with Birgitta Valberg and Max von Sydow, directed by Ingmar Bergman.*
Bergman's Christianity is cold, austere, inscrutable. The characters pray and ask for guidance, for answers. But except for those of childlike faith and innocence, God is silent.   *(Janus Films)*

adults, who barely bother to speak anymore. The film is steeped in alienation and despair. God, as usual, is silent.

After completing his trilogy, Bergman rarely concerned himself with religious themes, turning his attention to human suffering in a more secular context, usually with a psychological emphasis. *Persona* (11–12) is his most complex work, dazzling in its technical audacity, thematically rich and profound. It is a movie that explores many ideas simultaneously yet still retains an inner core of mystery, of the unfathomable. *Shame* (1968) is a powerful account of two musicians, married to each other, who are trapped in the cross fire of an unending civil war, which eventually reduces them to a state of savagery and mutual hatred. *The Passion of Anna* (1969) explores the relationships of four characters trying to coexist on a small island. Someone on the island is senselessly slaughtering the livestock in irrational outbursts of fury. Throughout the film, Bergman intersperses brief interviews with the actors commenting on their characters, thus maintaining an ironic double perspective.

11–12. *Persona* (Sweden, 1966), *with Liv Ullmann (rear) and Bibi Andersson, directed by Ingmar Bergman.*

"The great gift of cinema photography is the human face," Bergman has observed. In this and other films, he employs many closeups, exploring the human face as if it were a spiritual landscape. *Persona* is one of the most radically experimental movies ever made, synthesizing most of Bergman's characteristic obsessions: the relationship of the artist to his or her audience, the futility of communication, the need to humiliate and be humiliated, isolation and alienation, the inscrutability of the human psyche, the need for masks and deceptive poses, unconscious sexual desires, and the ultimate "cancer of the soul"—the inability to love.   *(United Artists)*

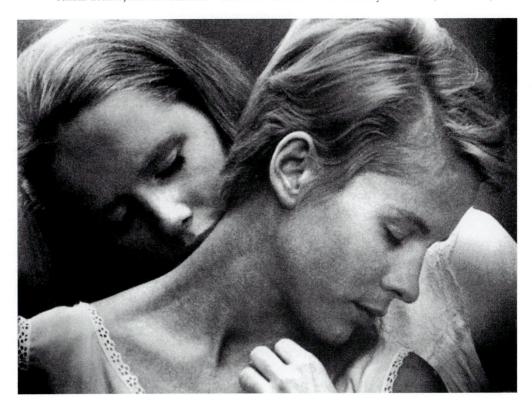

Bergman's best works after 1970 include *Cries and Whispers* (1973), a superbly mounted period film about four women who are confronted with a death in the family. The movie contains many scenes of harrowing emotional intensity. One of the women is so filled with self-loathing because of the hypocrisy of her marriage that she mutilates her vagina with a jagged piece of glass. *Scenes from a Marriage* (1973) chronicles the tensions and gradual disintegration of a middle-class marriage that eventually ends in divorce. *The Magic Flute* (1975) is an anomaly—an enchanting re-creation of Mozart's great opera as it was staged in the eighteenth century, only seen by a modern audience. *Autumn Sonata* (1978) is a return to Bergman country—a rancorous depiction of the love/hatred between a famous pianist and her mousy daughter, who is smoldering in anger and resentment. The principals are played by two great actresses in tour-de-force performances: Ingrid Bergman (no relation) and Liv Ullmann.

Ullmann and Bergman made eighteen movies together. Most of them deal with the war between the sexes, which was also the most frequent theme of August Strindberg, the filmmaker's idol. Bergman has been married five times and has had many love affairs, mostly with artists. He and Ullmann were lovers from 1966 to 1971, a union that resulted in the birth of their daughter. The two artists continued to work together even after they went their separate ways in private life. The great Norwegian actress, usually performing without the aid of makeup, can be radiantly beautiful or drab to the point of invisibility, depending on her role. Oddly, her work outside Scandinavia has been mostly lackluster.

Bergman claimed that *Fanny and Alexander* (1983) would be his last movie. It is a warm, mellow period film, synthesizing many of his recurrent themes. A blending of comedy, tenderness, and intense passions, in fact it does seem to be a kind of summing up, like Shakespeare's *Tempest*. Bergman offers us a philosophical overview on the meaning of human suffering, which is redeemed by the two positive constants in his oeuvre: love and art.

Like most artists, Bergman suffers from the vices of his virtues. Some of his movies are so personal as to be downright obscure: *The Magician* (1958), *The Hour of the Wolf* (1968), and *The Rite* (1969) have provided a bonanza for film critics, no two of whom seem to agree on what these movies are about. In some films, his pessimism verges on shrillness and hysteria, like *From the Lives of the Marionettes* (1980), his most fatalistic work. But these are minor lapses. Very few filmmakers can match Bergman's depth and breadth as an artist, not to speak of his broad stylistic spectrum, which ranges from stark realism to startling technical virtuosity.

Federico Fellini

FEDERICO FELLINI (1920–1993) was Italy's most famous filmmaker and a colossus of the international cinema. His movies were especially admired in America, where they won four Academy Awards for Best Foreign Language Picture. Unlike most Italian filmmakers, he was relatively apolitical, preferring to explore more private obsessions, often with an autobiographical emphasis. Nor was he a particularly intellectual artist: Rather than ideas or analysis, he stressed moods and feelings, conveyed by a voluptuous lyricism. After the early 1960s, he was a master of the grand style—sensuous, baroquely ornate, operatic.

Fellini was born into a middle-class family in the town of Rimini, on the northern Adriatic coast. As a child, he ran away from home to join the circus, and this fascination remained with him throughout his life, constituting a major motif in his movies. "The cinema is very much like a circus," he pointed out. "And in fact, if it didn't exist, I might well have become a circus director." In many of his works, Fellini explores other aspects of show business—vaudeville, comic strips, magic acts, movies, opera. Show business is usually treated as a symbol of life at the fringes of respectability—tawdry, often deceptive, liberatingly vulgar. Paradoxically, show business, a metaphor for art, is also redemptive, transcending the loneliness and boredom of everyday life.

As a young man, Fellini moved to Rome, where he worked for a while as a cartoonist, then as a gag writer in radio. In 1943 he married actress Giulietta Masina, who was to appear in several of his later films. Fellini soon became involved in the **neorealist** movement, serving as a writer (mostly comic) for such filmmakers as Alberto Lattuada and Pietro Germi. His true mentor was Roberto Rossellini. Fellini helped to write the scripts of Rossellini's *Open City, Piasà, The Miracle,* and *St. Francis, Fool of God.* Rossellini's Christian humanism had a lasting effect on Fellini's sensibility, particularly in his fondness for the Holy Fool, an Italian character type loosely based on the revered figure of St. Francis of Assisi. Although a nonbeliever, Fellini was strongly drawn to naive, foolish characters of childlike faith and simplicity. The most poignant of these are the child-women played by Giulietta Masina.

Fellini's earliest movies were clearly indebted to the neorealist movement. Most of them were shot on actual locations and feature loose, episodic narratives, which are often circular rather than linear. The characters are generally from the lower social echelons—misfits, outcasts, con men, prostitutes, vagabonds, and fourth-rate "artistes." Most of these early movies are photographed in an unadorned style and are edited according to classical conventions.

His first film, *Variety Lights* (1950), was codirected by Lattuada and deals with the seriocomic tribulations of a seedy vaudeville troupe touring the provinces. *The White Sheik* (1952) satirizes the world of the *fumetti*—photographed comic strips featuring exotic adventurers in faraway lands. While on her honeymoon, a gullible newlywed from the provinces becomes involved with a blowsy ham actor of lecherous intent. *I Vitelloni* ("The Loafers," 1953), one of Fellini's most critically admired works, is far less comic and deals with the wasted lives of a group of small-town dreamers. Like most of Fellini's works, it contrasts scenes of boisterous public revels with revelations of private anguish and regret.

Fellini's first big international success was *La Strada* ("The Road"), which starred Anthony Quinn as a circus road-show strongman and Giulietta Masina as his simple-minded assistant **(11–13).** Perhaps the finest of these early works is *The Nights of Cabiria* (1956), with Masina playing a tenderhearted prostitute who fancies herself as street-wise and tough. The movie abounds with grotesquely comical characters—a Fellini trademark. *Cabiria* is alternatingly bawdy, sentimental, cynical, noisy, ironic, and moving—in short, a typical Fellini circus.

La Dolce Vita ("The Sweet Life," 1959) was another huge international hit. Though tame by today's standards, the picture created something of a scandal by its depiction of decadence among Rome's privileged class. The movie centers on a dissolute journalist who yearns to create something meaningful with his talent yet is constantly seduced by the lure of life in the fast lane. He is played by Marcello Mastroianni, who was to become the foremost Italian film actor of his generation. *La Dolce Vita* also represents a stylistic shift for Fellini. It is less realistic in its mise en scène, more richly textured and photographically ornate. It is filled with fantas-

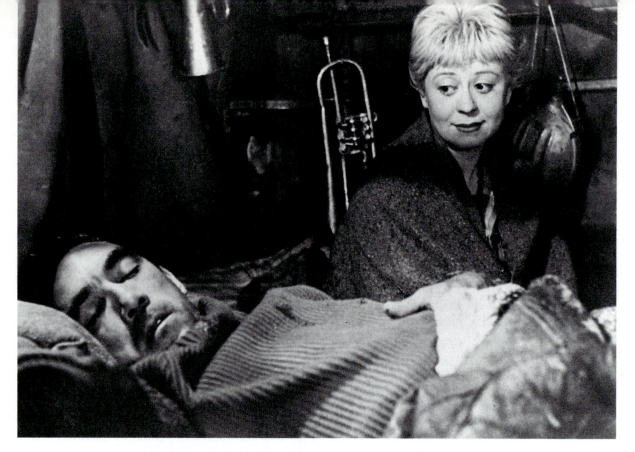

11–13. *La Strada* **(Italy, 1954),** *with Anthony Quinn and Giulietta Masina, directed by Federico Fellini.*
Thanks to Masina's Chaplinesque blending of comedy and pathos, the tone of this film is elusive—brutal, funny, and touching at the same time. It contains a haunting score by Nino Rota, who composed the music for most of Fellini's movies. Its screenwriters, Tullio Pinelli and Ennio Flaiano, were also frequent collaborators during this period. *(Audio-Brandon Films)*

tic processions, weird characters, and quasi-surrealistic settings—characteristic elements of Fellini's later works.

The movie *8½* (1963) was a radical break with the past. Almost plotless, it concentrates rather on a state of mind—the mind of its protagonist, an indecisive film director (Marcello Mastroianni), whose personal life is as complicated as the movie he wants to make but never does. Interspersed between scenes with his wife, his mistress, and his professional colleagues are scenes from his past, his fantasies, and nightmares. At first, we are able to differentiate these various levels of consciousness, but eventually they begin to merge **(11–14).** The movie that Guido fails to make is the one Fellini succeeds in making, the movie we are watching—*8½*. Stunningly photographed by Gianni de Venanzo, the film is a feast for the senses—overflowing with fascinating faces, costumes and settings, lyrical traveling shots, and images of phantasmagorical beauty.

Strongly autobiographical (the title is virtually an opus number), *8½* was originally condemned by critics as "a self-indulgent display of egotism," a charge that was to plague Fellini for the rest of his career. Sometimes critics—and audiences—need a little time to digest a movie as complex and rich as *8½*, for in a 1982 *Sight and Sound* poll of international critics, it was voted one of the ten greatest films of all time. It also placed in the top ten in a 1992 poll.

11–14. *8½* (Italy, 1963), *directed by Federico Fellini.*
This famous concluding episode, which takes place in the protagonist's imagination, combines characters from his past, his present, his dreams, and his fantasies, all of them dressed in purified white, as they stream inexplicably toward a circus ring, where the hero, a film director, urges them to join hands and dance joyously around the ring—a symbolic analogue of the artistic fusion of his various levels of consciousness and an exhilarating affirmation of the unifying power of the human imagination. *(Embassy Pictures)*

Fellini's subsequent works were in this same personal vein and baroque style. *Juliet of the Spirits* (1965), his first feature in color, stars Giulietta Masina as the sorrowful wife of a philandering show-biz entrepreneur. Much of the movie consists of her fantasies and childhood memories, which are presented in a glitzy, stylized manner. *Fellini Satyricon* (1969) is even more garish, if beguiling. Loosely based on Petronius's fragmentary epic of the decadence of ancient Rome, the film is a series of lavishly produced extravaganzas populated by freaks, loonies, and grotesques, who stagger through the disjointed narrative like stoned zombies.

Technically speaking, *The Clowns* (1970) and *Fellini's Roma* (1972) are documentaries, though hardly conventional ones. The first is a personalized exploration of the traditions of circus performers, with several studio-created episodes comparing the director's childhood memories with famous clown acts. *Fellini's Roma* is a tour of the Eternal City, not as an average tourist would see it but as filtered through the filmmaker's unique sensibility. Like most of Fellini's later productions, the film's art director is Danilo Donati and its cinematographer Giuseppe Rotunno—two great artists in their own right.

Amarcord (1974) is a stylized reminiscence of Fellini's boyhood in Rimini during the 1930s. Its title, in the Romagnan dialect, means "I Remember." Eschewing plot, the film is unified by a seasonal structure, beginning and ending with the arrival of spring, a time of rebirth. Robust, bawdy, and poignant, the movie is steeped in tenderness and love. It features a wide assortment of off-beat personalities who are sketched in with a few bold strokes, more like cartoon figures than conventional characters. Most critics consider *Amarcord* Fellini's last great movie.

Fellini's subsequent films were uneven, though all of them contain at least flashes of brilliance. The sumptuously mounted *Casanova* (1976) is perhaps his coldest work, dead beneath the elegantly glacéed veneer—a stylistic embodiment of its central character. *Orchestra Rehearsal* (1979) is a symbolic parable on the potential for anarchy during those politically troubled times in Italy. *And the Ship Sails on . . .* (1984) takes place in the era just before World War I and spoofs the fanaticism of opera cultists and their idols. Several sequences substitute snatches of operatic arias for dialogue, producing a surprisingly enchanting incongruity. *Ginger and Fred* (1986), a satire of Italian television, repeats many of Fellini's earlier themes and combines two of his favorite actors, Masina and Mastroianni, in the title roles. The movie fared badly with both the public and the press, though the final dance sequence recaptures some of the old magic. *Federico Fellini's Intervista* (1987) and *Voices of the Moon* (1990) were his last movies. Neither is regarded as a major work.

France

Until the advent of the *nouvelle vague,* or **New Wave,** at the end of the decade, the French film industry of the 1950s was disorganized and mediocre. Perhaps the best of the mainstream commercial filmmakers was René Clement (1913–1996), who created his two finest works during this period: *Forbidden Games* (1952), which won the Grand Prize at the Venice Film Festival; and *Gervaise* (1956), a powerful adaptation of Zola's naturalistic novel, *L'Assommoir.* The most respected achievements of the French cinema of this era were created by mavericks, most notably Robert Bresson and Jacques Tati.

BRESSON (1907–1999) was an enigmatic figure, reclusive and aloof, working in virtual isolation. In his forty years as a filmmaker, he made only about a dozen movies. His films are admired by intellectuals, artists, and critics, but he was never a popular artist, nor did he court the mass audience. His works are typically French in that they are cerebral, thematically elusive, and rather literary, but in most respects, he stands alone. He began his career as a writer in the 1930s. During World War II he spent a year in a Nazi prison camp, an experience that profoundly influenced him as an artist.

Bresson's literary sensibility was apparent in his first two films: The dialogue of *Les Anges du Péché* (1943) was written by the great dramatist Jean Giraudoux, and Jean Cocteau worked on the screenplay of *Les Dames du Bois de Boulogne* (1945). Bresson himself wrote the script of *Diary of a Country Priest* (1950), a **faithful adaptation** of a novel by Georges Bernanos. After that, Bresson wrote all of his movies, several of which are loose adaptations of the works of Dostoyevsky: *Pickpocket* **(11–15),** *Une Femme Douce* (1969), and *Four Nights of a Dreamer* (1971).

Critics often compare Bresson to Ozu, Mizoguchi, and Carl Dreyer, in that they are all concerned with themes of spiritual transcendence and that they tend to be stylistically austere, keeping their techniques to a bare minimum. As Bresson pointed out, he was concerned "not with beautiful images, but necessary ones." Everything superfluous was ruthlessly eliminated. Though he usually shot on loca-

11–15. *Pickpocket* **(France, 1959),** *with Martin Lasalle, directed by Robert Bresson.*
Most of Bresson's protagonists are trapped in constricting prisons, either literal or symbolic—
sometimes both, as in this film. Bresson's main concern is how the characters transcend their
imprisonment, how their souls may be set free even though their bodies are confined.   *(New
Yorker Films)*

tion, and most of his films are superficially realistic, the details were so rigorously
selected that they constituted a virtual abstraction of reality—reality's essence,
stripped of its clutter.

"I don't work very well without obstacles," Bresson stated, and his obstacles
usually took the form of self-denial. Instead of plots, he often featured static situations. The emphasis is not on actions so much as reactions. His mise en scène is
stark, the tightly framed images limited to a circumscribed area. For example, *A
Man Escaped* (1956) is confined almost completely to the protagonist's jail cell. *The
Trial of Joan of Arc* (1961), like Dreyer's film on the same subject, consists primarily
of close shots, the dialogue a concise précis of the actual court transcript. Movies
like *Balthazar* (1966) and *Mouchette* (1966), among others, contain very little dialogue. Bresson also uses music and sound effects sparingly. His impulse was always
to subtract.

The acting in his movies is matter-of-factly understated. Most of his performers were nonprofessionals who were cast not for their acting skills but for their spiritual qualities. He refused to allow them to interpret their roles, insisting that they
perform their scenes as neutrally as possible. He instructed them to recite their
lines simply, without vocal inflection. "Films can be made only by bypassing the will

of those who appear in them, using not what they do but what they are," Bresson stated. He was not interested in psychology, nor did he try to explain the motivations of his characters. For the most part they are quiet and withdrawn, suffering an inner torment that is seldom overtly expressed.

Bresson's characters hold back on their feelings. We can only infer them from the director's sequence of shots. Like Pudovkin (and Hitchcock), Bresson believed that emotions in movies are created not by the actor's interpretive performance, which is the mode of the live theater, but by the editing: "Film can be a true art because in it the author takes fragments of reality and arranges them in such a way that their juxtaposition transforms them." The emotion, then, is created in our minds, by the director's manipulation of details. For example, in *Une Femme Douce,* the suicide of a despairing woman is conveyed through the linking of a few shots: We see her looking from a high balcony. Cut to a medium shot of a balcony chair tipping over. A shot of the empty balcony. Finally, a shot of her delicate scarf floating in the air beyond the balcony's railing.

The purpose of Bresson's ascetic style is to communicate his themes in an organic manner. His films have been described as "Jansenist," an allusion to the quasi-mystical Catholic sect that flourished in the seventeenth century and continues to exert an influence on French culture even to the present time. Austerity, restraint, and economy are characteristic Jansenist virtues. Somewhat akin to Calvinism (and to the Japanese concept of *mono no aware),* Jansenism emphasizes predestination, cosmic fate, and the futility of human struggle against a Divine Will. Bresson's characters are spiritually redeemed only when they humbly accept what God has ordained, perhaps to test their faith, to measure their worthiness for salvation.

JACQUES TATI (1908–1982) is a more cheerful artist, a comic actor-director, though he too tends toward austerity in his style. He began his career as a pantomimist and music hall performer, turning to motion pictures after World War II. A meticulous craftsman who took years to prepare a production, he completed only five movies after his film debut with *Jour de Fête* ("The Village Fair," 1949).

The film artist Tati most closely resembles is Buster Keaton, though Keaton's surreal, metaphysical comedy would be as foreign to Tati as his wry social satire would be to Keaton. Both comedians are masters of slapstick, emphasizing their bodies rather than their faces, with a preference for lengthy takes and **long shots** rather than closeups, which they seldom use. Both are dry, understated, and rather intellectual in their appeal. Both are fond of using intricate, impeccably timed gags that often incorporate vehicles, mechanical systems, and the infernal machines of modern technology. Both tend to favor passive protagonists to whom funny things happen and who are usually unaware that they're funny.

Tati's most popular films were *Mr. Hulot's Holiday* (1953) and *Mon Oncle* ("My Uncle," 1958), which featured the same likable protagonist, Mr. Hulot. He is a clumsy if earnest bumbler whose eccentric humanity sets him off as something of a middle-aged innocent, gamely traversing the landscape of modern life like a stranger in a strange land. Mr. Hulot is a trajectory of almost constant motion, his disjointed, loping gait propelling him forward—with due allowances for an occasional stumble—as he bumps into obstacles that perversely materialize out of nowhere, his head bobbing and twisting rearward and sideways like a bird's, alertly attending to every random distraction. The films contain virtually no dialogue, or at least none that's important: Talk is used almost like a sound effect, in counterpoint with the musical score and the noises of everyday life. The movies are good-natured and droll, bubbling with deadpan wit and a Gallic lightness of touch.

Tati's next two comedies, *Playtime* (1967) and *Traffic* (1971), are somewhat sharper in their social satire. They are still funny, but the comedy is less cheerful, muted, with undercurrents of pessimism. As in all of his works, Tati contrasts the homely, old-fashioned values of pre-World War II France with the sleek dehumanization of life in the American Age, with its steel and glass skyscrapers and its gleaming mechanization. But humanity always emerges triumphant in Tati's universe. The triumphs might be small ones, but they are enough.

In 1959, the young filmmakers of the *nouvelle vague* catapulted the French into the front ranks of the international cinema, altering the ways that movies were made in America and the Third World as well as Europe. But the revolutionary impact of the New Wave was strongest during the 1960s, and accordingly the movement is discussed in Chapter 13.

FURTHER READING

ANDERSON, JOSEPH L., and DONALD RICHIE. *The Japanese Film.* New York: Grove Press, 1960. The most comprehensive history of the Japanese cinema, both as art and industry. Illustrated.

ARMES, ROY. *French Cinema Since 1946.* Cranbury, N.J.: A. S. Barnes, 1966. Volume II, *The Great Tradition*, of this two-volume study includes sections on Bresson, Tati, Clement, and other filmmakers.

BOCK, AUDIE. *Japanese Film Directors.* New York: Japan Society, 1978. Interviews and brief introductions to a variety of filmmakers, including Kurosawa, Naruse, Mizoguchi, and Ozu.

BONDANNELLA, PETER, ed. *Federico Fellini: Essays in Criticism.* New York: Oxford University Press, 1978. A collection of interviews and essays on Fellini and his work.

KAMINSKY, STUART M., ed. *Ingmar Bergman: Essays in Criticism.* New York: Oxford University Press, 1975. A collection of critical articles.

MELLEN, JOAN. *The Waves at Genji's Door.* New York: Pantheon Books, 1976. A cross-cultural study of Japan through its cinema. Illustrated.

RICHIE, DONALD. *The Films of Akira Kurosawa* and *Ozu* (both Berkeley: University of California Press, 1970, 1974). Indispensable, copiously illustrated critical studies—the best in English.

———. *Japanese Cinema.* Garden City, N.Y.: Doubleday Anchor Books, 1971. A well-illustrated, well-written history and analysis of the Japanese cinema by its best-known English language apologist.

SALACHAS, GILBERT. *Federico Fellini.* New York: Crown Publishers, 1969. A collection of interviews, script excerpts, and analyses from the French film journal, *Cinéma d'Aujourd'hui.*

SIMON, JOHN. *Ingmar Bergman Directs.* New York: Harcourt Brace Jovanovich, 1972. A lengthy interview and in-depth analyses of *Sawdust and Tinsel, Smiles of a Summer Night, Winter Light,* and *Persona,* well illustrated with frame enlargements from the films.

12

American Cinema in the 1960s

*A time creates its own myths and heroes. If the heroes are less than ad-
mirable, that is a clue to the times.*
—ARTHUR PENN

ABC Pictures

Timeline: 1960–1969

1960

U.S. population: 179 million; TV sets: 85 million

1961

John F. Kennedy (Democrat) U.S. President (1961–1963); assassinated in office

"Freedom Rides" by black and white liberals to challenge segregation laws in the South—often met with violence

1962

U.S. spacemen orbit earth

Rachel Carson's *Silent Spring* ushers in the environmental movement

1963

Mass marketing of the birth control pill—the second sexual revolution begins

Pop Art exhibition at Guggenheim Museum, New York City

Vice-President Lyndon B. Johnson (Democrat) becomes President (1963–1969); Kennedy's assassin, Lee Harvey Oswald, is shot and killed on live TV by Jack Ruby

1963–1964

Race riots in many U.S. cities as civil rights campaign intensifies; mass demonstrations in Washington, D.C.

1964

President Johnson escalates American military involvement in Vietnam

1965–1967

U.S. protesters demonstrate in Washington against the widening war in Vietnam; riots and burnings in many black ghettos of U.S. cities

1968

Assassination of Presidential candidate Robert F. Kennedy and Reverend Martin Luther King, Jr.; rise of the Black Power movement

Riots and police brutality at Chicago National Democratic Convention—all is recorded live by TV cameras

1969

Widespread antiwar demonstrations across many U.S. cities and college campuses

Richard M. Nixon (Republican) elected President of U.S. (1969–1974)

U.S. manned lunar module lands on the moon; the *Apollo 11* astronauts are the first humans to walk on the moon

The demise of the Hollywood studio system: conglomerates. Desperate final measures: aesthetic elephantiasis. Whiz kids from television. Sidney Lumet and the sidewalks of New York. John Cassavetes: *cinéma vérité*. Mike Nichols, the actors' director. The protest era. Civil rights, Vietnam, and the swing to the Left. Years of fire and bombast. Arthur Penn's *Bonnie and Clyde:* the lure of violence. Sydney Pollack. Bloody Sam Peckinpah. The gray matter of Stanley Kubrick. End of Woodstock.

T HE 1960S WAS A SCHIZOID DECADE in the American cinema. It began in overstuffed complacency and ended in shrill militancy. Many important films were made during this period, but the overwhelming number of them were produced in the final three years of the decade. The early 1960s was an era of romantic idealism, best typified perhaps by the youthful President John F. Kennedy and his glamorous wife. Hollywood movies also emphasized glamour, but at the expense of practically everything else. Until the final years of the decade, when something of a social revolution galvanized the industry into a totally new direction, the studios thrashed and heaved like fatally wounded dinosaurs gasping for air, with no one to put them out of their misery.

The Bloated Era

Paradoxically, the Hollywood studios were crumbling financially, yet their products, mostly big-budget spectacle pictures, were lavishly produced—the overripe artifacts of an era of artistic decadence. Reeling from the competition of television, the industry cut back on production, averaging only 159 movies per year throughout the decade. The pictures got bigger and more expensive: More of everything seemed to be the only solution the studios could come up with. It didn't help. By 1962, box office receipts in real dollars had shriveled to less than half the industry's peak year, 1946. Hundreds of movie theaters across the country were closing for lack of product—and lack of audiences.

True, a few excellent movies were made during this period, mostly by veteran film artists like Cukor, Zinnemann, and Wilder (12–1). But these were exceptions. In fact, most of the established masters retired or went into a period of artistic decline during this era—Huston, Hitchcock, and Wyler, among others. The British invasion was at its height during the 1960s, and some of the biggest hits were essentially English movies, though financed with American capital: *Lawrence of Arabia, Tom Jones, Dr. Zhivago, A Man for All Seasons, Oliver!,* and *Romeo and Juliet,* among others.

The first half of the decade was afflicted by a case of aesthetic elephantiasis. The blockbuster spectacle film, modeled on the vastly popular *Ben-Hur* (10–3), was the **genre** that producers hoped would bring back the long-departed family audi-

12–1. *The Apartment* (U.S.A., 1960), *with Jack Lemmon, directed by Billy Wilder.*
Lemmon, one of the top stars of the 1960s, appeared in many of Wilder's movies, most notably *Some Like It Hot* (1959) and *The Apartment*. In this film, Lemmon plays the quintessential Wilder protagonist—the weak compromiser who's not as smart as he thinks he is. To further his career, he allows his sleazy superiors at work to use his apartment for their illicit sexual liaisons. Like most of his roles written by Wilder, the Lemmon character is neurotic and fussy, usually sucked into conspiracies that promise easy success but somehow turn rancid. Paralyzed with indecision, he thrashes and frets and sighs and occasionally explodes into paroxysms of self-loathing. His character abounds with contradictions. He's both a schnook and an opportunist, a victim and a victimizer. But in the end, he prefers being a mensch to a swine, and he reforms his pimping ways. He's Wilder's portrait of the loser as a winner, with more class than he realizes. *(United Artists)*

ence. Movies like *Cleopatra* **(12–2),** the most financially disastrous of this cycle, were examples of "films for people who don't go to the pictures," to quote critic John Gillett. The prevailing studio wisdom was that only "big" films would lure audiences away from their TV sets back to the theaters.

Sometimes it worked, sometimes it didn't. Twentieth Century–Fox almost collapsed from the costly weight of the *Cleopatra* debacle, yet *The Sound of Music* (1965) was a huge box office success, providing the studio with some measure of stability until it backed such financially disastrous movies as *Doctor Dolittle* (1967) and *Star!* (1968), which nearly bankrupted the studio. *The Sound of Music* is an apt example of the aesthetic crassness of these pictures. Encrusted in gloss, the film fairly oozes in pious bilge and cheap emotion. Its pseudo-reverent story, punctuated by some of the most sugary music and lyrics of Rodgers and Hammerstein, appealed to the lowest common denominator of the audience. Serious critics were

12–2. *Cleopatra* (U.S.A., 1963), *with Elizabeth Taylor, directed by Joseph L. Mankiewicz.*

Cleopatra was described as the most costly fiasco in the history of movies—a project that was originally budgeted at $1.2 million and eventually ran away at nearly $40 million. A four-hour exercise in overkill, it groans under the weight of its mindless extravagance. The project was stalled for years because of production foul-ups, illness of its star Elizabeth Taylor, various personnel changes (including new leading men), new rewrites for the script, and a new director. (Mankiewicz was more suited to sophisticated drawing-room comedy than to **epic** spectacles, but he did his best with a bad situation.) Taylor was one of the top stars of the 1960s, commanding a salary of $1 million per picture plus a percentage of the profits. During the production of the film, she was engaged in a much-publicized love affair with leading man Richard Burton, who later became her husband—twice. Among the many extravagances of the picture was Taylor's insistence that Twentieth Century–Fox hire hairdresser Sidney Guilaroff at $1700 per week to style her hair. She was so burdened by gaudy headdresses and costumes that her beauty was actually undermined—she looks like a plump gilded pigeon about to topple over from the sheer weight of it all. The same thing happened to the movie. Twentieth Century–Fox almost toppled with it. *(Twentieth Century–Fox)*

appalled by the movie, referring to it as *The Sound of Money*. Pauline Kael correctly predicted that its commercial success would exert a repressive influence on the artistic freedom of more ambitious filmmakers: "The success of a movie like *The Sound of Music* makes it even more difficult for anyone to try to do anything worth doing, anything relevant to the modern world, anything inventive or expressive."

When art becomes decadent, George Bernard Shaw observed, realism always provides the cure. Well, nearly always. During this period, even realism became big, gaudy, and expensive. Stanley Kramer's *Judgement at Nuremberg* (1961) deals with the war-criminal trials of former Nazis, but the major roles are played by big box office **stars** like Spencer Tracy, Judy Garland, Montgomery Clift, Oscar Werner, Marlene Dietrich, and Burt Lancaster—who are provided with spectacular star turns, punctuating the narrative like arias in an opera. In fact, the performances are for the most part quite good, yet the very star power of the cast dwarfs the significance of the subject. This wasn't realism, this was REALISM!

This same inflationary trend afflicted other aspects of film production. Stars were demanding huge salaries, plus a percentage of the profits. Literary and stage properties grew more and more expensive, escalating the cost of movies to unprecedented heights. Genre films were no longer considered safe investments unless they were studded with stars, embalmed in gloss, and weighed down with lavish

production values. International coproductions flourished: American movies were shot in England, Italy, Spain, and what was then Yugoslavia, not because they had to be for authenticity's sake, but because nonunion labor abroad was cheaper. But the savings gained were often squandered away by the expense of moving and housing entire production companies. "Bigger is better" might well have served as the credo of the industry.

The result of this epic folly was the eventual collapse of the studios as independent entities and their gradual takeover by huge commercial conglomerates. Universal was taken over in 1962 by Music Corporation of America. Paramount became part of Gulf and Western Industries in 1966. United Artists was absorbed by Transamerica Corporation in 1967. Warner Brothers in 1969 became one of numerous companies controlled by Kinney Services. Many of these conglomerates had tie-in companies in related industries like publishing, TV production, and the music industry. Hence, a movie could be packaged as a multi-industry product, with publishing rights going to one subsidiary, soundtrack recordings to another, and so on. Colorful moguls like Selznick, Zanuck, and Goldwyn were a thing of the past. The new minimoguls were anonymous businessmen with no real commitment to movies except as profit-returning commodities, like deodorants or

12–3. *West Side Story* (U.S.A., 1961), *directed by Robert Wise and Jerome Robbins.*
Relatively few musicals were produced in Hollywood during the 1960s, compared with previous decades, and almost all of them were adaptations of big, brassy—and expensive—Broadway hits, which were thought to have a presold audience. Original screen musicals were rare. Though hampered by two lackluster leading players, *West Side Story* was one of the most successful adaptations, thanks primarily to the Leonard Bernstein–Stephen Sondheim score and the brilliant choreography of Jerome Robbins. *(United Artists)*

hemorrhoid creams. In short, by the end of the decade, the studio system was finally put out of its misery.

Major Filmmakers

If the 1960s produced few great American filmmakers, the decade did produce a number of good ones, most of them former television directors. They learned the rudiments of their craft in live television, which was New York based in the 1950s. Because of this, they were more inclined to favor small, dialogue-oriented stories—the kind of materials that could be transferred to the live theater. Before long, however, a number of them were able to disprove the theory that TV-trained directors were not very cinematic—filmmakers like John Frankenheimer and Sam Peckinpah were brilliant stylists. New York directors also tended to be regarded by Hollywood regulars as more intellectual, more arty. They were often Jewish and liberal in their values. They were also ambitious: They regarded film as a medium of artistic self-expression as well as popular entertainment, and they were eager to fuse the two.

SIDNEY LUMET (b. 1924) was among the first television directors to turn to filmmaking. His background is paradigmatic: New York upbringing and a Jewish family that was intellectual, artistic, and **left-wing.** During the 1950s, he was one of television's most respected directors, working on many prestigious programs while also directing in the live theater, mostly Off-Broadway. After he turned to filmmaking, he became the most prolific director of his generation, averaging better than a movie per year. Since his debut with *Twelve Angry Men* (1957), a one-set adaptation of a television drama, he has completed over thirty movies.

It's difficult to generalize about Lumet because consistency is not his strong point. Within the industry, he is respected for his ability to make serious movies that also do reasonably well at the box office, sometimes better. He has had to direct relatively few commercial potboilers to survive. He generally works fast, bringing his pictures in on time and within budget, and often before schedule and under budget. On the other hand, because he works so fast, Lumet is often uneven. Critics have lamented the slapdash haste of some of his productions, which look as though they were thrown together at the last minute.

Lumet is good with actors and has worked with some of the best of them, including Henry Fonda, Marlon Brando, Anna Magnani, Katharine Hepburn, Rod Steiger, Vanessa Redgrave, Al Pacino, Paul Newman, and many others. His movies have won thirty-seven Oscar nominations to date, most of them for their acting. Lumet is famous for bringing out the emotional intensity of his actors, who have turned in powerful performances under his guidance. Unfortunately, Lumet's casts are not always compatible in terms of acting styles, particularly when he mixes American, British, and Continental actors in the same movie. Individual performances are fine in their own right, but they sometimes fail to mesh with the others, fail to elide into an ensemble effect. This problem occurs in such movies as *The Fugitive Kind* (1960), *A View from the Bridge* (1962), *The Sea Gull* (1968), *Murder on the Orient Express* (1974), *Network* (1976), and *The Verdict* (1982).

Lumet's works can be divided into three broad categories: (1) literary and theatrical adaptations of prestigious properties; (2) purely commercial projects

12–4. *Long Day's Journey into Night* (U.S.A., 1962), *with Ralph Richardson, Jason Robards, and Katharine Hepburn, directed by Sidney Lumet.*

Lumet has always had strong ties with the live theater, and he has made his home base his native New York City, not Hollywood. His father was an actor in the New York Yiddish theater, and Sidney made his own Broadway debut at age eleven. As a young man, he acted in and directed plays Off-Broadway. Several of his movies are theatrical adaptations, such as this fine film version of Eugene O'Neill's masterpiece. Lumet has also adapted Tennessee Williams's *The Fugitive Kind* (1960), Arthur Miller's *A View from the Bridge* (1962), and Anton Chekhov's *The Sea Gull* (1968), though not with such felicitous results. *(Embassy Pictures)*

made for cash or for the fun of it, like *Orient Express, The Anderson Tapes* (1971), and *The Wiz* (1978); and (3) realistic social dramas, the best of which take place in the streets of Lumet's home town, New York City **(12–5).**

The third group constitutes his most critically admired works. Lumet captures the complexity of urban life with matter-of-fact toughness. He is a street-wise insider and thus, by definition, an ironist. For example, *Prince of the City* (1981) is based on an actual event; it deals with a Serpico-like New York cop (Treat Williams) who testifies against his corrupt comrades on the police force. The film is steeped in ironies. The crooked cops are almost indistinguishable from the criminals they're supposed to police. Virtually unsupervised, the detectives take bribes, traffic in drugs, perjure themselves in court, and carouse with Mafia types and other forms of low life.

On the other hand, whatever else they might be, these cops aren't stupid. They see how the system really works, they recognize its hypocrisy. They know that most of the criminals they apprehend—a small fraction at best—will be on the streets again within hours. They know that some judges are the creatures of

12–5. Publicity photo composite of *Dog Day Afternoon* **(U.S.A., 1975),** *with Al Pacino (center), directed by Sidney Lumet.*
Lumet is generally at his best in his gritty New York City films, like *The Pawnbroker* (1965), *Serpico* (1973), *Dog Day Afternoon, Prince of the City* (1981), and *Q and A* (1990). He is attuned to the pulsating rhythms of the city, its energy and abrasiveness. His movies are tough, noisy, unsentimental. The characters are never generalized but are vividly ethnic: Jews, blacks, Hispanics, Italians, and so on. Colorful, exciting, and slightly scary in its unpredictability, city life in Lumet's films is a life of extremes. "Drama is conflict," he insists, and what better place to find conflict than in the mean streets of the Big Apple?   *(Warner Brothers)*

organized crime, others are incompetent, jaded, or outright hostile toward police officers. These cops perform illegal wiretaps, lie under oath, and steal the drugs and cash of pushers to put them out of business. They reward informers—mostly junkies—with illegally confiscated drugs. They know that even by breaking the law themselves, the best they can hope for is the conviction of a few low-echelon hoods—the reckless, the inept, the desperate. The fat cats remain free. These cops trust only each other. They're intensely loyal to their partners and live by a fraternal code of honor. It is this code of honor that the hero betrays. Lumet's *Q and A* (1990) is filled with many of the same moral complexities.

Perhaps the most powerful of Lumet's New York City dramas is *The Pawnbroker* (1965), a key film of the 1960s, in part because of its radical **editing** style. Lumet uses a kind of subliminal cutting. Some **shots** are held on the screen for only a fraction of a second. Rod Steiger plays a middle-aged Jew who survived a Nazi concentration camp twenty-five years earlier. But all his loved ones were killed there. He tries to repress the memories of these horrible experiences, but they insistently force their way into his consciousness. Lumet suggests this psychological process by

intercutting a few **frames** of the memory shots during a scene that is taking place in the present. A present-tense event detonates the protagonist's memory of something similar from his past. As past contends with present, the flickering memory shots endure longer, until a **flashback** sequence eventually becomes dominant, and the present is momentarily suspended.

JOHN FRANKENHEIMER (1930–2002) also began as a New York television director in the 1950s and, like many of his peers, his first movie, *The Young Stranger* (1957), was a remake of a television drama. Throughout the 1960s, Frankenheimer was one of the most prolific and interesting of American directors, but he pursued no single theme, genre, or style and hence is difficult to classify. His first important movie was *The Young Savages* (1961), with Burt Lancaster. His association with Lancaster continued with four other films: *Birdman of Alcatraz* (1962), *Seven Days in May* (1964), *The Train* (1965), and *The Gypsy Moths* (1969)—all absorbing dramas, well crafted and polished.

All Fall Down (1962) is a characteristically off-beat family drama and love story, filled with shrewd psychological observations. It is well acted, especially by Angela Lansbury, Eva Marie Saint, and Warren Beatty. The political thriller, *The Manchurian Candidate* **(12–6),** was a big hit and Frankenheimer's most critically praised work. Technically dazzling, the movie abounds with energy, dramatic images, shocking editing juxtapositions, and bizarre twists and turns in the plot. This was Frankenheimer the action director at the top of his form.

12–6. *The Manchurian Candidate* **(U.S.A., 1962),** *with Laurence Harvey and Angela Lansbury, directed by John Frankenheimer.*
Teetering between scary paranoia and deadpan solemnity, this political thriller was written by George Axelrod (based on the novel by Richard Condon) and jumbles the clichés of the Cold War with perverse wit. Frankenheimer's direction is brazenly audacious—confident, brisk, flamboyant. *(United Artists)*

But Frankenheimer also had his quiet, introspective side. The underrated sci-fi film *Seconds* (1966) is essentially a character study of a middle-aged man, lonely and alienated, who gets a chance to start his life again as someone else. He screws up his second existence even worse than his first. He is played by Rock Hudson in a surprisingly subtle performance. *The Fixer* (1968) is a big-budget adaptation of the respected novel by Bernard Malamud, with Alan Bates in the leading role. *The Gypsy Moths* is ostensibly about a group of parachutists, but the emphasis is more on the psychological interactions among the characters. In his four-hour-long version of Eugene O'Neill's *The Iceman Cometh* (1973), Frankenheimer is totally self-effacing stylistically, reining in his techniques to heighten the performances and the text. The first-rate cast is headed by Fredric March, Robert Ryan, Lee Marvin, and Jeff Bridges. Similarly, in *The French Connection II* (1975), Frankenheimer concentrated on an in-depth exploration of the neurotic central character, detective Popeye Doyle (Gene Hackman), rather than the technical virtuosity that typified the first movie, which was directed by William Friedkin.

Frankenheimer's artistic vision tended to be pessimistic. As Jean-Pierre Coursodon has pointed out, the director's characters are usually alienated loners. They are often mismatched in their love relationships, which tend to be destructive. Family life is often portrayed as empty, stagnant, even suffocating. The **motif** of imprisonment reappears throughout his **oeuvre,** either literally, as in *Birdman, Manchurian Candidate, The Fixer,* and *French Connection II;* or psychologically, as in

12–7. *Lilies of the Field* (**U.S.A., 1963**), *with Sidney Poitier and Lilia Skala, directed by Ralph Nelson.*
Poitier was the first black performer to crash the top ten box office attractions in America. Furthermore, he rose to the top not as a singer, dancer, or comedian, but as a straight leading man. He won a Best Actor Award for his performance in this sentimental favorite. Poitier's goal was to play the kind of roles traditionally denied to black actors: doctor, teacher, psychiatrist, detective. As the civil rights movement gained momentum, he favored more militant roles that consciously reflected the frustrations and aspirations of black Americans: jazz musician, revolutionary, urban hustler. However, audiences preferred Poitier straight, clean-cut, and wholesome. These later roles, though more challenging to him as an artist, were less popular with the public.   *(United Artists)*

many of his other movies, in which the characters are imprisoned by their own fears, inadequacies, and limited imaginations.

To the majority of moviegoers, JOHN CASSAVETES (1929–1989) was an interesting character actor, especially good in villainous roles, like those in *The Killers, The Dirty Dozen, Rosemary's Baby,* and *The Fury.* To a much smaller audience he was the creator of a handful of off-beat movies—controversial, eccentric, and extremely personal. Born in New York City of Greek immigrant parents, Cassavetes was a popular actor in television during the 1950s, specializing in ethnic juvenile delinquents—usually Italian, Greek, or some other Mediterranean variant.

With his earnings as an actor, Cassavetes directed his first feature film, *Shadows* (1961), which was shot in New York City with lightweight 16 mm equipment. The story of a love affair between a black woman and a white man, the film was virtually improvised and cost a mere forty thousand dollars. It won the Critics Award at the Venice Film Festival and was highly praised by a number of highbrow critics. On the basis of this film, Cassavetes was able to direct two Hollywood projects, *Too Late Blues* (1962) and *A Child Is Waiting* (1963), which are competent but rather ordinary movies. Neither fared well with the public or critics.

Cassavetes returned to a more congenial idiom with *Faces* (1968), which was shot in bits and pieces over a period of four years. Once again, he used 16 mm, but he had the print blown up to the standard 35 mm for theatrical exhibition. Cast with unknowns, it turned out to be surprisingly successful for a low-budget personal film and even received three Oscar nominations. Cassavetes's subsequent movies were in this same vein, though most of them were shot in 35 mm and were scripted in advance by Cassavetes—with the active collaboration of his actors.

12–8. *Husbands* (**U.S.A., 1970**), *with Peter Falk, Ben Gazzara, and John Cassavetes, directed by Cassavetes.*
The three close pals of this film are like overgrown boys—selfish, immature, and immensely likable. Cassavetes is especially strong in evoking the warmth of masculine camaraderie. His characters have Soul. *(Columbia Pictures)*

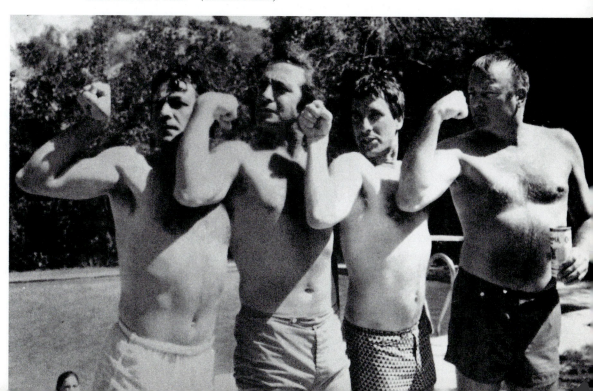

Husbands (12–8) deals with the midlife crisis of three pals. The film is a good instance of Cassavetes's cinema of cronyism, for its three principals were close friends in real life and their affection for one another spills over into the roles they play. His closest crony was Gena Rowlands (Mrs. Cassavetes in private life), for whom he created some of his finest characters: *Minnie and Moscowitz* (1971), *A Woman Under the Influence* (1974), *Opening Night* (1977), *Gloria* (1980), and *Love Streams* (1984). These were virtually home movies, with Cassavetes's family, friends, and in-laws for actors.

Critics either love his films or hate them. Even his partisans concede that Cassavetes's works are uneven, self-indulgent, and rambling. Most of them were shot like documentaries, with hand-held shots of actors in **tightly framed closeups** or **medium shots,** talking endlessly. There is very little in the way of fancy camerawork, **production values,** or flashy cutting. The actors' performances are paramount— the feelings, confusions, and contradictions of the characters. Cassavetes lovingly records it all. He liked to use very long scenes to reveal his characters. The pace is unhurried, filled with hesitations, digressions, sly evasions.

The rambling narrative structures are organically related to his characters, who seldom have well-defined goals and are often confused or engaged in a strenuous effort of self-definition. In short, they are searching for something, and Cassavetes includes their dead ends and detours as well as their occasional steps forward—hence his loose, digressive plotlines, which just barely manage to limp toward aesthetic closure.

But like Truffaut, Cassavetes was interested not so much in his plots as in capturing privileged moments of emotional poignance between the characters—their comic absurdities, their garrulousness, their fears and anxieties. As with such people in real life, a little can go a long way, for they can be exasperating and wearying in their intensity. But despite their kamikaze tendencies, their humanity always comes through—especially their dogged love, which somehow manages to bind them together, however precariously. As critic Myron Meisel has pointed out, "Cassavetes demonstrates that people do try to love the very best they can and that while it may never be enough, it has to go a long way, because it may be all they've got."

MIKE NICHOLS (b. 1931) began his career as an aspiring actor and studied with Lee Strasberg at the Actors Studio. In the 1950s Nichols found his way to Chicago, where he joined the Second City improvisational comedy troupe, which also included Elaine May. Eventually Nichols and May formed an act and took it on tour. They also made several comedy recordings, which were very popular. Their professional relationship culminated with a successful Broadway engagement: *An Evening with Mike Nichols and Elaine May.* In the 1960s, Nichols embarked on a successful career as a Broadway director, and he continues to this day alternating his energies between movies and the stage.

Nichols's first film, *Who's Afraid of Virginia Woolf?* (1966), was an adaptation of a famous Edward Albee drama about a drunken evening with a middle-aged college professor, his shrewish wife, and their two guests, a young academic couple. All four principals were nominated for acting Oscars, and two won—Elizabeth Taylor and Sandy Dennis. A box office success, the film was praised by critics for its fine ensemble acting and its artistic integrity. Because of the literary prestige of Albee's Broadway play, the movie version is surprisingly faithful, including most of its strong language and sexual frankness. Screenwriter Ernest Lehman broke several long-standing **Production Code** taboos with his remarkably professional script, which preserved most of Albee's biting dialogue intact. It was the beginning of the end of the Production Code, which was abolished in 1968. Movies were thereafter rated according to audience age and maturity levels.

Nichols's next movie, *The Graduate* (**12–9**), was a box office champion of the decade. It introduced an obscure Off-Broadway character actor, Dustin Hoffman, who was to become one of the foremost **actor–stars** of his generation. Young audiences identified strongly with the confused protagonist, who doesn't know what he wants to do with his life. He just knows he doesn't want what his parents and their friends have—an overstuffed yet empty existence. The film presents an acid portrait of the sterile materialism of the bourgeoisie.

Nichols's directorial style in *The Graduate* is clever and witty. The editing, sprinkled with deliberate **jump-cuts** and leaps in **continuity,** comically throws us off guard. The scenes are often accompanied by the sad songs of Simon and Gar-

12–9. *The Graduate* (**U.S.A., 1967**), *with Anne Bancroft and Dustin Hoffman, directed by Mike Nichols.*

Nichols was highly praised by critics for the sophistication of his mise en scène, which is indebted to such "difficult" European filmmakers as Antonioni. Yet the movie is also very funny, thanks to Hoffman's winning performance as the confused, scared Benjamin Braddock, college graduate. In this scene, for example, an older woman, a friend of his parents, tries to seduce Ben—he thinks. He's not sure. His feelings of entrapment and imminent violation are conveyed not by his words, which are stammering and embarrassed, but by the mise en scène. Blocked off in front by her seminude body, he is also visually confined at his rear by the window frame—an enclosure within an enclosure within the enclosure of the frame. The scene is comical, sexually threatening, and intellectually provocative, for the ideas are conveyed cinematically, through the editing and the carefully composed images.   *(Avco Embassy Pictures)*

funkel, which comment obliquely on the action. The **widescreen** images are strikingly composed, suggesting a multitude of feelings and ideas through the **mise en scène.** And like most of Nichols's films, the acting is first-rate, filled with freshly observed details, subtle quiet moments, and brilliant touches of deadpan comedy on the part of Hoffman.

Nichols went into a decline in the 1970s. *Catch 22* (1970) contains some effective scenes, but the film lacks unity. Its narrative is disjointed, its tone unfocused. Individual performances are excellent, but there is very little sense of ensemble acting—everyone seems to be in his own orbit. *Carnal Knowledge* (1971) is much stronger, thanks to a bitterly funny script by Jules Feiffer and superior performances by Jack Nicholson and Ann-Margaret. *The Day of the Dolphin* (1974) and *The Fortune* (1975) were Nichols's least successful films. He returned to the New York stage, no longer Hollywood's golden boy.

Nichols's fortunes improved slightly in the 1980s. His movies during this period were generally lighter, less ambitious, but also more successful. The best of them, *Silkwood* (1984), is a political suspense thriller based on actual events, with Meryl Streep in the leading role. The bittersweet *Heartburn* (1986), again with Streep and Jack Nicholson, is about the breakup of a marriage. The charming *Working Girl* (1988) is a graceful if lightweight romantic comedy, with winning performances by Sigourney Weaver, Harrison Ford, and Melanie Griffith. Nichols' most recent work includes the brilliant television mini-series, *Angels in America*, written by Tony Kushner.

12–10. *The Molly Maguires* (**U.S.A., 1969**), *with Sean Connery, directed by Martin Ritt.*
Most of Ritt's works were in the tradition of **social realism,** movies that champion the cause of oppressed minorities, exploring

the tensions between classes, races, and sexes from a liberal-humanist perspective. Ritt (1914–1990) was born in New York, trained as an actor at the famous Group Theatre, and made his Broadway acting debut at the age of seventeen in *Golden Boy*. In the 1950s, he divided his time between directing for television and the stage and taught acting at the celebrated Actors Studio, where his students included Paul Newman, Joanne Woodward, and Rod Steiger. Ritt's first movie was *Edge of the City* (1957), a waterfront drama dealing with racial tensions, adapted from a television play and starring two promising newcomers, John Cassavetes and Sidney Poitier. Ritt's other important movies include *The Long Hot Summer* (1958), *Hud* (1963), *The Spy Who Came in from the Cold* (1965), *Hombre* (1967), *The Molly Maguires, The Great White Hope* (1970), *Sounder* (see **14–3),** *The Front* (1976), *Norma Rae* (1979), and *Cross Creek* (1983). To make movies he felt strongly about, Ritt sometimes worked for a fraction of his salary. "It is possible to survive making films that basically represent who you are and what you're about," he said, "but it ain't easy." *(Paramount Pictures)*

New Directions

In the last few years of the decade, the American cinema shifted into a strident direction, like American society in general. Most film critics are agreed that the escalation of the war in Vietnam was the principal reason for this shift in sensibility—which was angry, militant, and harshly critical of the Establishment. Prior to 1968, Americans were more or less resigned to sending American troops to this faraway land, but in the last years of the decade, majority opinion veered against continued U.S. involvement in what was increasingly perceived as a civil war in which America had no vital interests. To make matters worse, many people believed Americans were fighting for the wrong side—a corrupt puppet regime propped up only by American military might.

There were other reasons for this shift in sensibility. The 1960s was a prosperous decade for the most part, and it was accompanied by an increasing permissiveness, especially among the young. Youth was enjoying the fruits of the sexual revolution brought about by the perfection of reliable and accessible birth control techniques. The widespread use of marijuana as a recreational drug became a symbol of youthful rebellion. The new "hip" movies often showed the characters

12–11. *Medium Cool* **(U.S.A., 1969),** *directed by Haskell Wexler.*
Until this period, overtly political movies had rarely done well at the box office. Americans are said to be essentially apolitical—especially by European commentators dating back to de Tocqueville. *Medium Cool* deals with the notorious 1968 Democratic Convention in Chicago and includes authentic footage of the event interspersed with fictional scenes. The movie is intensely political and examines the role of television in shaping and manipulating values. Like many of the new breed of filmmakers during this era, Wexler (who is primarily a cinematographer, and a highly admired one) is left-wing and humanistic in his perspective. *(Paramount Pictures)*

smoking pot as part of their everyday life style. Eventually even stronger drugs, equally illegal but more dangerous, became popular—LSD, amphetamines, barbiturates, and a multitude of others.

It was an era dominated by youth. Rebellion and revolution were in the air. On college campuses across the country, students protested passionately against the American involvement in Vietnam. "Don't trust anyone over thirty!" was the motto of many leaders of the protest movement. The pioneering innovations of The Beatles and Bob Dylan politicized rock 'n' roll, which often expressed the anger and frustrations of the young. The new movies frequently featured rock music soundtracks, fueling their anti-Establishment sentiments **(12–12).**

By 1968, America was a polarized nation, torn by strife. The civil rights movement began as a nonviolent, Christian-based effort to secure Constitutional rights for black people, but after the assassination of its leader, the Reverend Martin Luther King, Jr., the movement became radicalized. The result was the rise of the Black Power movement, which was militant, antiwhite, and violence prone. In the same year, presidential candidate Robert F. Kennedy was gunned down like his

12–12. *Easy Rider* (U.S.A., 1969), *with Peter Fonda, directed by Dennis Hopper.*
The phenomenal success of *Easy Rider* stunned the industry. It was made for a piddling $375,000. To make matters worse, it was a biker film, a déclassé genre usually associated with redneck audiences and sleazy drive-in theaters. It featured no important stars. The music soundtrack consisted entirely of contemporary rock 'n' roll. But it was clearly more than just a biker film. It was saying something about America—its myths, its hypocrisies, its strengths. The film won an award at the Cannes Film Festival, and its American reviews were grudgingly favorable. It grossed a spectacular $50 million. The success of the movie opened a floodgate of opportunities for other young filmmakers.   *(Columbia Pictures)*

brother before him, ending most hopes for peaceful reconciliation of the two Americas.

The movies reflecting this new sensibility were generally independently produced on low budgets, often without important stars. Many of these films featured youthful protagonists—rebels against the American mainstream. The staid, overstuffed studio productions of the earlier half of the decade gave way to smaller, more personal films, films that were clearly indebted to the movies coming out of Europe, especially those of the French **New Wave.**

An Arab immigrant, Fouad Said, developed the Cinemobile Mark IV in 1967, a virtual movie studio on wheels, which allowed filmmakers to make movies on very small budgets. Said's van was thirty-five feet long and included dressing rooms, a bathroom, space for a crew and actors, plus all the necessary equipment to make a movie on location.

In 1968, the outmoded Production Code was finally scrapped in favor of a rating system, the prototype of the system now in use, thus ushering in an era of unprecedented frankness, particularly in the areas of sex and violence, the two

12–13. *Midnight Cowboy* (U.S.A., 1969), *with Jon Voight and Dustin Hoffman, directed by John Schlesinger.*
Movies of the late 1960s were sexually frank to an unprecedented degree, thanks to the substitution of a rating system in 1968 to replace the old Production Code. *Midnight Cowboy* is the only X-rated movie to win a Best Picture Oscar. However, by present-day standards, the film is relatively mild and would probably be awarded an R rating today. Since the early 1970s, the X rating has been assigned almost exclusively to pornographic films. *(United Artists)*

most popular subjects of the new movies. The upshot of all these innovations was an increased interest in movies, particularly among the young, who constituted over three quarters of the filmgoing population. By 1969, for the first time in twenty years, movie attendance in America rose rather than declined, a pattern that continued throughout the following decades.

Most film historians point to Arthur Penn's *Bonnie and Clyde* (1967) as the turning point from the old sensibility to the new. PENN (b. 1922) was a former television and New York stage director. *Bonnie and Clyde* (**12–14**) triggered a furious controversy among commentators. Of course, violence was hardly something new in the American cinema. (Anthropologist Hortense Powdermaker wryly noted that even in the silent era, South Sea Islanders divided American movies into two genres: Kiss-Kiss and Bang-Bang.) What was new in Penn's film was the visceral intensity of the violence, which "puts the sting back into death," to quote from Pauline Kael's panegyric on the movie. Bosley Crowther of *The New York Times* condemned the movie in the harshest terms and conducted a crusade against the increasing brutality of American movies.

Penn was dismayed that most of the film's detractors had missed the point. He regarded the "tasteful" presentation of violence and killing as an obscene hypocrisy and an evasion of our national heritage:

12–14. *Bonnie and Clyde* (U.S.A., 1967), *with Warren Beatty, directed by Arthur Penn.*
A gangster film set in the Depression thirties, *Bonnie and Clyde* was widely perceived as a statement about 1967. Warner Brothers advertised the movie with an appeal to the Vietnam generation: "They're young! They're in love! And they kill people!" Penn has said of his characters: "The only people who really interest me are the outcasts from society. My sympathies lie with that person who cannot accommodate himself to society and may have to lose his life to change it." Penn's outsiders and misfits rarely analyze their actions. Ideology is a foreign concept to most of them. Their rebellion is instinctive, spontaneous, and usually unfocused. Often they're swept up by the immediacy of the moment, unable to anticipate the apocalyptic destiny that awaits them. *(Warner Brothers)*

It's absurd to suggest that the film is the central issue in violence in a violent society which has been repressing the black race for two hundred years and which has been ridden with prejudice and violence of the most flagrant character through all its history—the West, the 20s and 30s. It's a violent society engaged in a violent and ridiculous war.

Many critics also misinterpreted the function of comedy in *Bonnie and Clyde*, assuming that it was meant only to glamorize crime and ridicule the law. The unpredictable shifts of tone in the film, clearly indebted to the French New Wave, were intended to keep the audience off balance and to make the characters less threatening—'jes folks. One of the bank robbery sequences begins almost like a Keystone comedy. While Bonnie and Clyde are robbing the bank, their accomplice, C. W. Moss, who's as endearing as he is cretinous, waits outside in the getaway car, primed for action. When he observes another car leaving its parking space, C. W. decides to take it over. His partners rush out to the street to make their getaway: They find themselves stranded without transportation! Nearby, C. W. furiously rams and batters the two cars abutting the getaway vehicle. Miraculously, the three gangsters just barely manage to escape. The scene is simultaneously suspenseful, exhilarating, and funny. As the getaway car pulls away from the scene, an elderly bank teller impulsively leaps on the vehicle, clinging to it as it roars through town. Seeing the old man's face in the window, Clyde panics and shoots him point blank. In a shocking close shot of the teller's bloodied face, the screen erupts in red. The transition from comedy to tragedy is swift as a gunblast.

Penn followed his most violent film with his most gentle, *Alice's Restaurant* (1969), which is loosely based on a popular recording by Arlo Guthrie, the son of the folk singer Woody Guthrie, who was the creator of many protest songs in the 1930s. *Alice's Restaurant* affectionately celebrates the values of the hippie movement—its rejection of racism, militarism, materialism, and authoritarianism. The film's tone swings abruptly from slapstick comedy to moments of poignant anguish. It also contains a few brutal sequences, mostly centering on the heroin-addicted motorcyclist, Shelly. Penn wanted to pay tribute to the young men who defied the military draft for reasons of moral conscience. The movie is one of the few of its era to explore the hippie counterculture in an honest manner. Their music, rituals, and clothing are authentic depictions of their laid-back life style and innocent (and sometimes not so innocent) hedonism. But Penn refused to sentimentalize his characters. The Children in the Age of Aquarius—Godard dubbed their French counterpart "The Children of Marx and Coca-Cola"—are sometimes unable to handle the responsibility of their freedom.

The violent films of SAM PECKINPAH (1925–1984) also stirred up a storm of controversy during this period. Peckinpah was something of an anomaly in his cinematic generation. A native Californian, he was descended from frontier stock, settlers of the Old West. He attended the University of Southern California and received his master's degree in drama. In the mid-1950s he served as an assistant to action director Don Siegel, who became Peckinpah's mentor. Throughout the 1950s, Peckinpah wrote scripts for various television series, most of them westerns—*Gunsmoke, The Rifleman, The Westerner,* and others.

He made his theatrical film debut with *The Deadly Companions* (1961), a western, but did not attract much critical attention until *Ride The High Country* (1962), a lyrical, elegiacal lament for the passing of the Old West, a recurrent theme in his work. Most of Peckinpah's important subsequent works were westerns: *Major Dundee*

12–15. *They Shoot Horses, Don't They?*
(U.S.A., 1969), *with Jane Fonda, directed by*
Sydney Pollack.
Until this era, films with downbeat themes
rarely prospered at the box office. This movie
deals with a 1930s marathon dance contest
that is clearly intended as a symbol of life in
general. It is among the most fatalistic and
deeply pessimistic of all American movies.
Human effort is equated with futility: The
dance is rigged. The film is punctuated with
flash-forwards of the death of the heroine
(Fonda), suggesting an air of inexorability.
Pollack (b. 1934) began his career in the mid-
sixties. Most of his best films deal with social
issues: *The Scalphunters* (1968), *Castle Keep*
(1969), *They Shoot Horses, Jeremiah Johnson*
(1972), *The Way We Were* (1973), *Three Days
of the Condor* (1975), *The Electric Horseman*
(1979), *Absence of Malice* (1981), the superb
Tootsie (1982), and *Out of Africa* (1985).
(ABC Pictures)

(1965), *The Wild Bunch* **(12–16),** *The Ballad of Cable Hogue* (1970), *Junior Bonner*
(1972), and *Pat Garrett and Billy the Kid* (1973). *Bring Me the Head of Alfredo Garcia*
(1974) is set in Mexico, but it has a strong western flavor. Of his major works, only
one, the controversial *Straw Dogs* (1971), is a contemporary story not set in the West.

Peckinpah's westerns are **revisionist**—that is, they subvert or call into question many of the values and traditions of the western genre in its **classical** phase.
His stories take place not in the heroic nineteenth century, but in the neurotic
twentieth century, which is portrayed as mechanistic, repressive, and emotionally
sterile. This is the revisionist principle: Unlike the classical western, which usually
pits the good guys against the bad guys, Peckinpah's films pit the bad guys against
the guys who are even worse. There is an old adage that in the country of the
blind, the one-eyed man is king. So too in Peckinpah's spiritual wastelands, the romantic outlaw is cynical, opportunistic, and corrupt in many of his moral values,
but he does abide by a private code of honor that sets him above the Establishment—*any* establishment. Peckinpah was a passionate champion of individualism,
and his hostility toward all forms of authority verged on the implacable.

Peckinpah had a long history of feuding with his producers. Some of his
movies were released with virtually no promotion or publicity. Others, including

12–16. *The Wild Bunch* (U.S.A., 1969), *directed by Sam Peckinpah.*
Despite his essentially anarchistic nature, Peckinpah was also a romantic conservative, looking back on a simpler past with nostalgic yearning. His westerns are not set in the pastoral nineteenth century, but in the opening decades of the heartless twentieth century, with its impersonal machines of war and its cold, ruthless technology—most often symbolized by the automobile. The auto in Peckinpah's westerns is like the rifle in Kurosawa's samurai films—a new technology that will render traditional martial skills and individual courage obsolete. A samurai sword, however gracefully wielded, is no match for bullets, even when fired by a stupid brute. So too, the noble horse is no match for the tireless horseless carriage. *(Warner Brothers)*

his masterpiece, *The Wild Bunch,* were reedited by the studios to make them a more commercially viable length. He was fired on a number of occasions, usually over "creative differences." It's the old von Stroheim syndrome: Peckinpah's movies tended to be personal, lengthy, and loosely structured, with many digressions and lyrical interludes, somewhat in the manner of Kurosawa, one of his idols. Peckinpah's producers complained that he had no practical commercial sense, that he was self-indulgent, treating a simple genre as a form of artistic self-expression rather than popular entertainment.

Peckinpah was also severely criticized for his romantic glorification of violence. *The Wild Bunch* contains what one critic described as "the bloodiest massacre in screen history." In the final shootout, virtually an entire Mexican village is destroyed—heroes, villains, and innocent bystanders—in a stylized, balletic orgy of **slow-motion** violence. Peckinpah was subsequently known in the trade as "Bloody Sam." Like many male-action directors, he treated violence as the ultimate test of manhood, and he was often imitated **(12–18).**

Indeed, his treatment of sex was as controversial as his treatment of violence. They are often combined. Women are almost invariably sex objects in his movies, and his most attractive female characters are usually whores. But Peckinpah believed that we are all whores—himself included—and the professional hooker is

12–17. *Straw Dogs* **(Great Britain/U.S.A., 1971)**, *with Dustin Hoffman, directed by Sam Peckinpah.*

One of Peckinpah's major themes is the flabbiness—both physical and spiritual—of modern life, our alienation from our own natural instincts. *Straw Dogs,* which was described as a "Fascist film" by several critics, dramatizes what happens when a man refuses to acknowledge the hostile forces around him. The bullies of an isolated English village despise the nonviolent college professor (Hoffman) who settles in their community with his sexy young wife. Throughout the film, the resentful villagers close in around the protagonist, who refuses to read their signals. Their attack begins at the periphery of his existence, but they soon invade his immediate environment. Meeting only token resistance (pictured), they eventually move in for the kill. Shattered glass is used as a motif in a number of scenes. The hero's eyeglasses serve as an ironic symbol of his refusal to see what's really happening. When his glasses are broken during a vicious attack, he is forced to rely on his animal instincts to survive, exploding in a paroxysm of fury. *(ABC Pictures)*

simply more honest about her work. Many of his female characters are sexual teases, and several of his films contain rape scenes, the most notorious of which is in *Straw Dogs* **(12–17).** His female characters are rarely central to the action, and usually they are played by relatively unknown actresses who project an air of earthy sensuality—who are, in short, sexy.

Above all, Peckinpah is a superlative stylist, a master of the lyrical grand style, reminiscent of Eisenstein and the "baroque" Italian masters, such as Visconti, Fellini, and Leone. Cinematographer Lucien Ballard, who photographed five of Peckinpah's movies, said of him: "Sam will work until you take the cameras away from him. He is a writer, and he works like a writer with the camera, rewriting as he goes." His stylistic signature is best illustrated by his scenes of violence, which are orgasmic explosions of kinetic energy. The slow motion aestheticizes the gore, converting the mindless bloodletting into a **surrealistic** ballet of color and motion. His style could be compared to the works of the great nineteenth-century English Romantic painter J. M. W. Turner, whose canvases capture the violence of man in nature with an almost abstract beauty—explosions of color streak from a white-hot

12–18. *Butch Cassidy and the Sundance Kid* (**U.S.A., 1969**), *with Robert Redford and Paul Newman, directed by George Roy Hill.*

During the Vietnam era, even commercial entertainments like this popular western often ended with the deaths of their protagonists. Paul Newman was second only to John Wayne (see **5–11**) as the top male box office attraction during the 1960s. An ambitious, risk-taking actor, combining the striking looks of the proverbial Greek god, a flawless physique, a first-class critical intelligence, and enormous personal charm, Newman is one of the most admired film personalities of his generation. In 1968, he made his debut as a director with the sensitive *Rachel, Rachel*, starring Joanne Woodward, his wife of many years. A political activist, public benefactor, professional racecar driver, independent producer, filmmaker, star, husband, and father, Newman likes to keep busy. *(Twentieth Century–Fox)*

center of energy into dramatic trajectories and ecstatic swirls of motion. The mesmerizing lyricism of Peckinpah's brilliantly edited images blinds us to the fact that people are dying in all that terrible, apocalyptic beauty.

The most important American filmmaker to emerge during this decade was STANLEY KUBRICK (1928–1999). He began his career as a still photographer for *Look* magazine. In the 1950s he made a number of low-budget genre films, which he financed independently. None of them created much of a stir. He broke into the big time with *Paths of Glory* (1957), which is based on an actual event that took place during World War I. The film deals with a French infantry attack against an impregnable German hill fortification—the futile scheme of two cynical French generals who cared more about advancing their careers than protecting the lives of their troops. The movie ends grimly, with three French soldiers arbitrarily chosen to be shot by a firing squad for their presumed cowardice under fire. The battle scenes, photographed mostly by Kubrick himself, are stunning in their power and technical brilliance. Though *Paths of Glory* was praised by critics, it failed at the box office, like all of Kubrick's earlier works.

His next movie, *Spartacus* (1960), was a spectacle picture; it inaugurated a reversal of fortunes, for it was a big hit and allowed him to work independently from then on. The movie is considerably superior to most examples of its genre, thanks primarily to Kubrick's action footage, but it was his least favorite work and the only movie he ever made in which he didn't have total artistic control. But *Spartacus* set him free: Ever after, Kubrick worked only for himself.

For financial reasons, he went to England for his next project, and he liked it so much he decided to stay. All his movies after 1961 were officially produced in Great Britain, but he regarded himself as an American artist, and his financing came from the American studios.

Beginning with *Lolita* (1961), Kubrick advanced to the forefront of American directors. Even within the more permissive world of publishing, Vladimir Nabokov's brilliantly written novel of sexual obsession was regarded as too raunchy to handle. It was finally published by the Olympia Press in Paris, which specialized in serious erotic literature. The story revolves around the tragicomic characters of Humbert Humbert (James Mason), a middle-aged college professor who's smitten by a jaded thirteen-year-old nymphet. The censorship restrictions of the period severely limited Kubrick in his handling of the sexual scenes, which needed to be more explicit to be effective, but despite this flaw, *Lolita* was a hit with the public. Nabokov considered it a first-rate film, with magnificent actors, and he called Kubrick "a great director."

Dr. Strangelove, or How I Learned to Stop Worrying and Love the Bomb **(12–19)** was even more popular and received virtually unanimous raves from critics. A satire of the nuclear follies of the United States and the U.S.S.R., the film is a black comedy about a deadly serious subject. The catastrophe is triggered off by a SAC commander, General Jack D. Ripper (Sterling Hayden), a certifiable loon and paranoid, who believes that his "precious bodily fluids" have been contaminated by a Commie conspiracy—the fluoridation of the American water supply. To save the nation, he launches a nuclear attack on the Soviet Union by setting off the red-alert mechanism. The remainder of the movie is a grotesque parody of the domino principle: Hundreds of American B-52s armed with hydrogen warheads streak toward their targets in the U.S.S.R. After a series of spooky twists and turns in the plot, all the planes except one are recalled, but it manages to sneak through every fail-safe mechanism, and in a burst of glory the aircraft releases its deadly load, thus detonating the Soviet Doomsday Machine—an automatic "ultimate weapon," which convulses the globe in nuclear Armageddon.

Kubrick's next film, *2001: A Space Odyssey* **(12–20),** was more than four years in the making, and the originality of its concept created a sensation with the public. Youthful audiences especially were astonished by the movie's **special effects** and its provocative mysticism. Kubrick set out to make a new kind of film—nonverbal, ambiguous, and mythical. He wanted to create a *visual* experience about ideas, an experience that reached the mind through the feelings and penetrated the subconscious with its emotional and philosophical content. To accomplish this, he discarded the concept of plot almost completely—an audacious decision, considering the movie's 141-minute length. *2001* was one of the top-grossing movies of the decade, garnering over $31 million in its first year of release.

A Clockwork Orange (1971), based on a novel by Anthony Burgess, was Kubrick's most violent film to date. Its punk protagonist (Malcolm McDowell) is vicious, cruel, and fascinating. The movie is fablelike in its construction and highly stylized visually. Like most modernist artists, Kubrick had little faith in traditional value systems and was inclined toward a pessimistic view of the human condition.

12–19. *Dr. Strangelove, or How I Learned to Stop Worrying and Love the Bomb* (**Great Britain/U.S.A., 1963**), *with Peter Sellers, directed by Stanley Kubrick.*
Dr. Strangelove was only one of several films of this period to deal with the dangers of militarism and nuclear holocaust. Others include Lumet's *Fail Safe* (1964) and Frankenheimer's *Seven Days in May* (1964), both of them suspense thrillers. *(Columbia Pictures)*

He believed that most people are irrational, weak, and incapable of objectivity where their own interests are involved. Most of his films portray people as corrupt and savage, and each movie contains at least one killing. "I'm interested in the brutal and violent nature of man because it's a true picture of him," he stated.

Kubrick was one of the supreme stylists of the contemporary cinema. Despite his reputation as an intellectual artist, he regarded filmmaking as primarily intuitive and emotional. "What I'm after is a majestic visual experience," he said of his movies. The images of *Barry Lyndon* (1975), a costume picture set in eighteenth-century Europe, are ravishing in their beauty. *The Shining* (1980), a horror film starring Jack Nicholson, is rich in mystery and atmospheric effects. Kubrick was also a master of the moving camera and used traveling shots in most of his films: *2001* is filled with lyrical ballet sequences in which the camera swirls rapturously around the spacecrafts gliding through the vastness of space. His editing style is powerful and jolting, especially in violent scenes like those of *A Clockwork Orange*. His Vietnam War film, *Full Metal Jacket* (1988), is totally unnerving, in part because of its unpredictable editing that constantly keeps us off guard, especially in the battle scenes, which are among the best ever filmed.

Kubrick's final movie, *Eyes Wide Shut* (1999), was literally finished a few days before he died in his sleep at the age of 70. A loose adaptation of a novella by the early twentieth-century Austrian writer Arthur Schnitzler, the film stars husband and wife Tom Cruise and Nicole Kidman as a rich and complacent New York physician and his restless wife. The movie explores the theme of sexual obsession in a somewhat dreamy surrealistic style. Critics were divided in their responses, some

12–20. *2001: A Space Odyssey* (**Great Britain/U.S.A., 1968**), *with Keir Dullea, directed by Stanley Kubrick.*

A golden age of science fiction was inaugurated by *2001*. The special effects in the movie took eighteen months to create, cost $6.5 million (out of a total budget of $10.5 million), and were carefully researched to conform to actual scientific predictions. Kubrick viewed hundreds of other sci-fi movies and consulted with over seventy aerospace specialists and research corporations. His production unit consisted of 106 people, including 35 artists and designers and 20 special-effects technicians to create the **animation shots, miniatures, matte shots,** and front and **rear projections.** A centrifuge, to create a realistic weightless atmosphere, cost $750,000. Over sixteen thousand separate shots had to be taken for the 205 composite special-effects shots in the movie.   *(Metro-Goldwyn-Mayer)*

hailing the film as a mellow masterpiece, while others were disappointed with its cold and decidedly nonerotic treatment. The sex is all in the head.

In the popular imagination, the decade of the 1960s is usually associated with politics, shrill rhetoric, and bloody confrontations. But it wasn't all vitriol. The violence was confined primarily to the final two years of the decade, when the country seemed headed for a nervous breakdown. The worst was yet to come. In the turbulence of the early 1970s, the traumas of Vietnam and racial strife at home were compounded by the disillusioning revelations of the Watergate conspiracy (see Chapter 14).

The early 1960s had been a period of hope in the clean-cut, glamorous Kennedy era. Perhaps the final vestige of this romantic idealism was absorbed by the hippie movement, with its garlanded flower children and naive optimism. For many, this youthful spirit of hope and community was epitomized by the famous concert in Woodstock, New York, at the end of the decade. The movie documentary of the event, *Woodstock* **(12–21),** was released in the first year of the new decade. Vincent Canby, the film critic of *The New York Times,* observed prophetically: "Underlying every moment of the film is the suspicion that what Woodstock came to represent—a spirit of tolerant, sweet togetherness in rain, mud and refuse—has already vanished, passed into history and become obsolete."

12–21. *Woodstock* (U.S.A., 1970), *directed by Michael Wadleigh.*
This rock documentary includes music by Joan Baez, Richie Havens, Jefferson Airplane, Joe Cocker, Sly and the Family Stone, Ten Years After, Santana, Jimi Hendrix, Country Joe and the Fish, John Sebastian, The Who, and Crosby, Stills, and Nash. Just as "Camelot" conjures images of the youthful idealism of the Kennedy era in the early 1960s, so does "Woodstock" evoke an almost Edenic image of youthful liberation and innocence at the end of the decade. Like Camelot, Woodstock didn't last.
(Warner Brothers)

FURTHER READING

BAXTER, JOHN. *Hollywood in the Sixties.* Cranbury, N.J.: A. S. Barnes, 1972. Survey of the decade, mostly by genre.

CIMENT, MICHEL. *Kubrick.* New York: Holt, Rinehart and Winston, 1983. A sophisticated critical study by one of France's best critics.

COURSODON, JEAN-PIERRE, with PIERRE SAUVAGE, et al. *American Directors.* New York: McGraw-Hill, 1983 (in two volumes). A collection of critical essays on more than one hundred filmmakers. The first volume concentrates on pre–World War II directors, while Volume II emphasizes postwar figures. Astute, sane, and well written—a major achievement in film criticism.

FRENCH, PHILIP. *Westerns.* New York: Viking Press, 1974. Studies in the social context of the genre in its postwar development.

KAEL, PAULINE. *I Lost It at the Movies.* Boston: Little, Brown, 1965. A collection of essays, mostly about films of the early 1960s, by one of America's most influential critics.

MALTBY, RICHARD, and IAN CRAVEN. *Hollywood Cinema.* Oxford, U.K. and Cambridge, Mass.: Blackwell, 1995. Two British critics look at Hollywood movies.

MONACO, PAUL. *The Sixties 1960–1969.* Berkeley: University of California Press, 2003. Survey of the decade.

MURRAY, JAMES. *To Find an Image.* Indianapolis, Ind.: Bobbs-Merrill, 1973. An analysis of black films and performers from *Uncle Tom* to *Superfly.*

WALKER, ALEXANDER. *Stanley Kubrick Directs.* New York: Harcourt Brace Jovanovich, 1972. Critical study of major films, copiously illustrated.

WOOD, ROBIN. *Arthur Penn.* New York: Praeger, 1970. A perceptive critical study.

13

International Cinema in the 1960s

Art attracts us only by what it reveals of our most secret self.
—Jean-Luc Godard

Paramount Pictures

Timeline: 1960–1969

1960
U.S.S.R. shoots down U.S. spy plane; Soviet Premier Khruschev scores big propaganda victory

1961
Cuban Bay of Pigs fiasco: Kennedy-backed Cubans repelled by Castro's military
Berlin wall constructed; U.S.S.R. astronauts orbit earth in six-ton satellite

1962
Cuban missile crisis—Kennedy and Khruschev take their countries to the brink of nuclear war

1963
Nuclear test ban signed by U.S.S.R., Great Britain, United States
Widespread labor strikes in Britain

1964
Khruschev replaced by Party Secretary Brezhnev in U.S.S.R.
British pop singing group, The Beatles, become international craze: beginning of "British Invasion" in music

1965
Indira Gandhi, Nehru's daughter, becomes Prime Minister of India

1966
Soviet spaceship makes successful soft landing on moon; shortly afterward, U.S. spacecraft also lands on moon with TV cameras
Miniskirts come into fashion, London; "Swinging England" is the heart of the new "mod" fashions

1967
Six-Day War between Israel and Arab nations—Israel conquers much Arab territory, including Jerusalem
Dr. Christiaan Bernard performs world's first human heart transplant in South Africa

1968
Soviet tanks suppress popular government of Czech Premier Dubcek, who is deposed; Czech government is replaced by a Soviet puppet regime

1969
Violent fighting between Protestants and Catholics in Northern Ireland
Mylai Massacre in Vietnam; U.S. military personnel stand trial on murder charges of Vietnamese civilians

A European golden age. The French *nouvelle vague*—an explosion of talent. The *Cahiers du Cinéma* crowd: Truffaut, Varda, Malle, Resnais, Costa-Gavras, Chabrol, and Godard. Great Britain: Kitchen Sink Realism and Swinging England. Tony Richardson, Lindsay Anderson, Karel Reisz, and Jack Clayton. American expatriates: Joseph Losey and Richard Lester. John Schlesinger and the migration to Hollywood. Italy: Sergio Leone's America. Antonioni and the cinema of angst. The Christian footnotes of Ermanno Olmi. Loners: Zeffirelli, Germi, and Pontecorvo. Eastern Europe: Hungary, Poland, and the U.S.S.R. The Prague Spring in Czechoslovakia: Kadar, Klos, Menzel, Chytilova, Passer, and Milos Forman.

THE 1960s WAS A PERIOD OF EUROPEAN ASCENDANCY in the international cinema. While the American industry floundered, not finding a viable direction until the end of the decade, the Europeans dazzled the film world with their radical experiments in form. It was an era of burgeoning film movements—the French **New Wave,** the revitalized British industry, and the short-lived Prague Spring in Czechoslovakia. It was also a period of important individual filmmakers, like Greece's Michael Cacoyannis (13–1) and Italy's Michelangelo Antonioni, not to speak of the innovative masterpieces of such established figures as Bergman, Fellini, and Buñuel.

France

No one has been able to offer an adequate explanation for the emergence of the *nouvelle vague* (New Wave)—a term coined by a journalist in 1959 to describe the sudden prominence of a group of young filmmakers. Like most labels, *New Wave* is a term of convenience, for the newcomers who constituted the driving wedge of the movement were by no means a homogeneous lot. Perhaps what was most extraordinary was that so *many* filmmakers came forth during a very brief period— over one hundred feature debuts between 1958 and 1963. Most of these neophytes were young—still in their twenties or early thirties. Many of them were hard-core movie addicts, with an impressive command of film history gained largely at the Cinémathèque Française in Paris, a repertory movie house and archive presided over by the eccentric curator, Henri Langlois, who screened thousands of films, both old and new, popular and highbrow, often in comprehensive retrospectives that included all the major works of a given director.

The most famous New Wave filmmakers began their careers as critics, writing for the lively journal *Cahiers du Cinéma*, which was edited by André Bazin (1918–1958), a mentor to such important figures as François Truffaut, Jean-Luc Godard, Eric Rohmer, Claude Chabrol, and others. Both as critics and later as directors, these young men and woman (13–2) favored films of intellectual depth rather than light entertainment—though they didn't consider these traits to be mutually exclusive. Most of them rejected the commercial French cinema of their day—*"le cinéma de Papa,"* to use Truffaut's contemptuous phrase. Most French

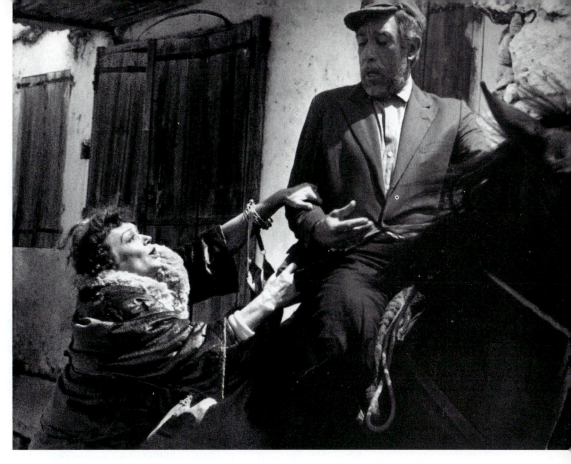

13–1. *Zorba, the Greek* **(Greece/U.S.A., 1964),** *with Anthony Quinn and Lila Kedrova, directed by Michael Cacoyannis.*
Cacoyannis (b. 1922) is the foremost filmmaker of Greece and a noted stage director of classical plays. His most famous movies are adaptations of ancient and modern Greek authors. In addition to this adaptation of the celebrated novel by Nikos Kazantzakis, Cacoyannis has also directed a trilogy of films based on the plays of Euripides: *Electra* (1961), *The Trojan Women* (1971), and *Iphigenia* (1977). *(Twentieth Century–Fox)*

movies were overliterary, visually dull, and impersonal, they claimed, not always correctly.

Almost all of them shared a fanatical love for American movies. The directors they most admired were such **genre** masters as Hitchcock, Ford, and Hawks, in addition to such traditionally respected figures as Griffith and Welles. Bad movies, these young directors insisted, were directed by anonymous hacks, devoid of personal vision, who employed images merely as illustrations of the script instead of exploiting their **mise en scène** as a complex, highly expressive language in its own right.

Truffaut coined the phrase *"la politique des auteurs"* in 1954, and this committed policy of authors became the prevailing ideology with most of the Cahiers critics. It emphasized the director's personality as the main criterion of value in a film, especially a genre film. The idea was to contrast the director's personality—that is, recurring themes, obsessions, and stylistic traits—**dialectically** with the genre's established conventions, thus producing an exciting aesthetic tension.

Around the mid-1950s, the *Cahiers* critics began making independently produced documentaries and short fiction films that incorporated many of their

13–2. *One Sings, the Other Doesn't* (**France, 1977**), *with Valerie Mairesse and Thérèse Liotard, directed by Agnès Varda.*

Varda (b. 1928) began her career as a photojournalist, then made a number of documentaries and short fiction films in the late 1950s. She was the only woman filmmaker of any stature among her New Wave peers. Her first feature was *Cleo from 5 to 7* (1962), about a singer who fears she has cancer. The movie is unusual in that its two-hour playing time is the same as the two hours she must wait to receive word about her biopsy. *Le Bonheur* ("Happiness," 1965) is a ravishingly photographed story about a man who ardently loves two women, told from his point of view. The film is strongly indebted to the lyrical works of Jean Renoir, like many other New Wave pictures. *One Sings, the Other Doesn't* recounts the longtime friendship between two women and the men in their lives. Varda concentrates on the typical rather than the extraordinary. She refuses to reduce her characters to stereotypes: The men as well as the women in the movie are presented as decent but contradictory individuals, trying their best to cope in a world of compromise and failed expectations.   *(Cinema 5)*

critical tenets. Toward the end of the decade, many of them embarked on careers as directors of features. These were made on low budgets and were generally shot outside the studios. Several of them turned out to be surprise box office hits, most notably Truffaut's *The 400 Blows* and Godard's *Breathless*, both released in 1959.

Most of the New Wave directors took advantage of recent advancements in television technology, which allowed them to make their movies quickly, cheaply, and spontaneously: (1) lightweight hand-held cameras, which allowed the operator to roam freely without the use of a **dolly;** (2) portable **synchronous-sound** recorders, which could be handled by a single operator and likewise could move freely while the action was taking place; (3) light-sensitive **"fast" film** stocks, which used available lighting, thus eliminating the need for cumbersome artificial lamps; and (4) **zoom lenses,** which could shift from **closeups** to distant shots (and vice

13–3. *Murmur of the Heart* (**France/Italy/West Germany, 1971**), *with Lea Massari, directed by Louis Malle.*

Malle (1932–1995) was the maverick of the New Wave, never quite fitting in. After attending film school for a brief period, he served his apprenticeship as cameraman and codirector of Jacques Cousteau's *The Silent World* (1956), which won the Grand Prize at Cannes. Malle's first solo success was *The Lovers* (1957), which created something of a scandal in its day because of its frank depiction of sex. An eclectic artist, Malle pursued a variety of themes in an assortment of styles and genres in different countries—hence the inability of critics to pigeonhole him. Among his best works are *Le Voleur* ("The Thief," 1967); a series of documentaries on the Indian subcontinent entitled *Phantom India* (1970); the rite-of-passage social comedy *Murmur of the Heart; Lacombe Lucien* (1973), a low-keyed drama about a peasant youth who becomes a Nazi collaborator; *Au Revoir, les Enfants* ("Goodbye Children," 1987), another semiautobiographical study of Nazi-occupied France; and *May Fools* (1990). Malle also made several off-beat pictures in the United States, including *Pretty Baby* (1977), the superb *Atlantic City* (1981), *My Dinner with André,* (1982) and *Vanya on 42nd Street* (1994). *(The Walter Reade Organization)*

versa) in one continuous movement, thus suggesting a traveling shot without actually moving the camera. The flexibility of this new technology allowed filmmakers to shoot in actual locations, at any time of the day or night, using only two- or three-member crews. It also allowed them to improvise scenes on the spot and to incorporate unscripted details that were discovered in the process of shooting.

The fascination with American genre films that typified the *Cahiers* critics was carried over into their own movies, which were often modeled on them. The New Wave directors were also fond of mixing genres and alternating tones by including incongruous touches of comedy in the middle of serious scenes, lyrical interludes or sudden explosions of violence in the middle of comic scenes, and so on. Drawing from their vast knowledge of films of the past, the New Wave directors were fond of incorporating such self-conscious techniques as **iris shots, freeze frames, wipes,** and **fast** and **slow motion.**

13–4. *The Confession* (**France, 1970**), *with Yves Montand, directed by Costa-Gavras.*
Costa-Gavras (b. 1933) was born and raised in Greece. At the age of eighteen he went to film
school in Paris and remained there to pursue his career. He made his feature debut with the
suspense thriller *The Sleeping Car Murders* (1965). He gained international fame with his electrifying political thriller, *Z* (1969), a harsh indictment of the Fascist military junta then ruling
Greece. He subsequently made a number of other political thrillers, most of them starring his
favorite actor, Yves Montand. *The Confession* is based on a true story of an idealistic Czechoslovakian **Marxist** who was persecuted and tried for treason in the Communist purges of the
early 1950s. *State of Siege* (1972) features Montand as a CIA agent stationed in Uruguay. In
the United States, Costa-Gavras made *Missing* (1982), with Jack Lemmon and Sissy Spacek,
which deals with the repressive Fascist regime in Chile; and *Betrayed* (1988), an FBI undercover thriller, with Debra Winger, followed by *The Music Box* (1989), a drama of an ex-Nazi
who has lived a modest, middle-class life in America for more than forty years.   *(Paramount Pictures)*

Despite their admiration for the tight narrative structures of American
movies, the films of the *nouvelle vague* tended to favor loose, discursive plots that allowed for considerable improvisation and personal digressions. Their films were
often self-reflexive, filled with authorial intrusions and reminders to the audience
that the movie is a movie. Some of them called attention to the fact that a film
image is a manipulated construct of the director, not an objective mirror of reality.
They also liked to sprinkle their works with playful homages to other films and previous masters.

The **editing** in many of these movies—especially those of Truffaut, Godard,
and Resnais—is unconventional. There are abrupt **flashbacks** and leaps in time
and space that are deliberately disorienting. Images often clash violently, in imitation of Eisenstein. Instead of **fading** or **dissolving** between scenes to suggest the
passage of time, they are often connected by a straight cut, which speeds up the ac-

tion. Whimsical "asides" are inserted between shots of a continuous scene as a kind of directorial joke. Sequences are sometimes begun not with an **establishing** shot but with a closeup, thus deliberately confusing the viewer as to the closeup's context. Some scenes are photographed in an uninterrupted **lengthy take**—like Mizoguchi—rather than broken down into a series of closer shots.

Because of their low budgets, the New Wave filmmakers seldom used established **stars.** Several of their young actors went on to become the new stars of the French cinema: Jean-Paul Belmondo, Jeanne Moreau, Catherine Deneuve, and especially Jean-Pierre Léaud.

Until his tragically premature death at the age of fifty-two, FRANÇOIS TRUFFAUT (1932–1984) was regarded as the dean of French filmmakers. He had once been regarded as little more than a street punk. As a child, he was in and out of trouble with the authorities and given up as incorrigible by his parents. Because of a broken love affair, he enlisted in the army and then deserted on the eve of his

13–5. *Shoot the Piano Player* (**France, 1960**), *directed by François Truffaut.*
Like many of Truffaut's works, this movie plays affectionately with the conventions of American genre films, combining elements from gangster pictures, romantic melodramas, screwball comedies, and noir thrillers. Charles Aznavour plays the sad, wistful Charlie Kohler (aka Edouard Saroyan), a man who loves and loses—twice. Most of Truffaut's movies deal with love, its joys and its pains. *(Janus Films)*

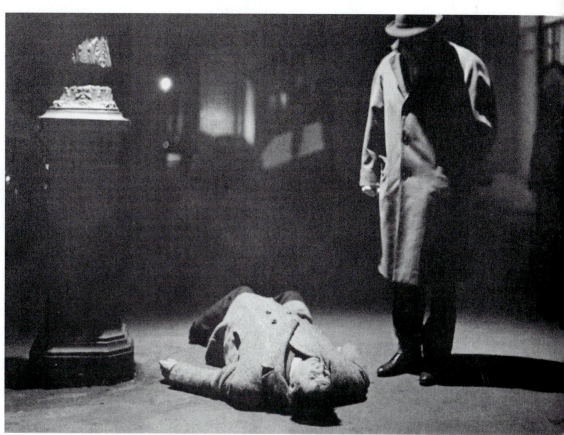

scheduled departure for French Indochina (Vietnam). He served six months in a military prison; then, thanks to the intervention of André Bazin, who took a fatherly interest in the youth, he was discharged from the army for "instability of character." Bazin got him a job as a film critic at *Cahiers du Cinéma,* where Truffaut's articles were so vitriolic that he was banned from the Cannes Film Festival in 1958. Ironically, the next year, his semiautobiographical film *The 400 Blows* won the Grand Prize at Cannes. He was suddenly internationally famous. He also mellowed.

Truffaut followed this movie with two more masterpieces: *Shoot the Piano Player* **(13–5),** "a respectful tribute to the Hollywood B-film," according to Truffaut; and *Jules and Jim* **(13–6),** a lyrical period piece about two friends who love the same perversely unpredictable woman. Both movies demonstrate Truffaut's characteristic virtues as an artist: urbanity and wit, a warm humanism, sudden shifts in tone, an infectious charm and lightness of touch, and a delicate romanticism. Also, like many other of Truffaut's films, these feature shy, vulnerable protagonists who are almost comically inept at expressing their strong emotions. The movies are also technically sophisticated, playful, and utterly poised.

Throughout his career, Truffaut was influenced by the films of two antithetical masters—Jean Renoir and Alfred Hitchcock. The Renoirian influence proved enriching. Both Truffaut and Renoir had relaxed, generous temperaments and

13–6. *Jules and Jim* **(France, 1962),** *with Henri Serre, Oscar Werner, and Jeanne Moreau, directed by François Truffaut.*

Two recurring preoccupations in Truffaut's works are the importance of friendship and the mysterious allure of the female. Often they are combined and set in delicate opposition, as in this movie. The character of Catherine (Moreau) is one of Truffaut's many fascinating females—sexy, independent, clever, willful, silly, charming, bitchy, selfish, destructive, and totally exasperating. In short, an irresistible creature, alas.   *(Janus Films)*

were at their best when they were least insistent, when they allowed their lyrical impulses free sway. Their finest films are almost leisurely in their narrative development. They were rarely interested in strident clashes or grand pronouncements about the human condition. Rather, their preference was for understatement, intimate nuances, for "little things." Truffaut once said: "I enjoy unexpected details, things that prove nothing, things that show how vulnerable people are." The French are generally among the most cerebral of film-makers, but both Renoir and Truffaut stress feelings over ideas. Their themes are explored obliquely, cunningly deflected by the surface charm of their throwaway style.

Truffaut's book-length interview, *Hitchcock*, demonstrates a discerning appreciation for the old master's genius, but his influence on Truffaut's **oeuvre** did not prove salutary. Truffaut was rarely at his best with tightly plotted stories, which he couldn't sustain anyway, nor was he particularly skillful in creating suspense. In fact, Truffaut's most Hitchcockian films are among his least successful; his most successful, both commercially and critically, were his most personal movies.

Jean-Pierre Léaud plays Truffaut's surrogate, Antoine Doinel, in his five semi-autobiographical films: *The 400 Blows* (1959); "Antoine et Colette," an episode from the anthology film, *Love at Twenty* (1962); *Stolen Kisses* (1968); *Bed and Board* (1970); and *Love on the Run* (1979).

The Wild Child (1969), one of Truffaut's finest works, suggests Bazin's steadying influence over the young Truffaut and, later, Truffaut's similar effect on Jean-Pierre Léaud, to whom the film is dedicated. Set in the eighteenth century, the movie is based on fact. It deals with the education of a savage boy who survived the wilderness alone. The role of the doctor who tries to civilize him is played by Truffaut himself. This film, along with *The 400 Blows* and the enchanting *Small Change* (1976), established him as a sensitive director of children. Like De Sica, Truffaut is able to capture the artless innocence and resilience of childhood without condescension or coyness.

Day for Night (1973) is Truffaut's valentine to the cinema, a lyrical movie about the chaotic making of a movie. It is populated with a variety of funny, appealing characters, like most of his best works. The darker *Story of Adele H* (1976) and *The Woman Next Door* (1981) deal with *l'amour fou*—crazy, self-destructive love, a recurring preoccupation with Truffaut and a characteristic theme of many New Wave directors.

Above all, Truffaut is a master of what has been called the "cinema of the privileged moment"—an intimate, poignant revelation of humanity, expressed with tact and economy. In *The Last Metro* (1980), for example, Marion (Catherine Deneuve), a married stage actress, finds herself falling in love with a fellow actor, Bernard (Gérard Depardieu). Devoted to her husband, she tries to resist her feelings, acting aloof whenever Bernard is around. Finally, she resolves to give in to her secret yearning when she agrees to join the members of the company at a nightclub. She saves the seat next to her for Bernard, who has yet to arrive. When he does, he's accompanied by a date. Cut to a shot of Marion's reaction: She lowers her eyes, gazes off in another direction, then gently sips her wine, betraying only the slightest trace of agitation by her trembling fingers. A sleazy lounge lizard asks to be introduced to the party, and when he suggests that they go to a more lively club, Marion quickly departs with him, leaving the others to puzzle over her unpredictability.

JEAN-LUC GODARD (b. 1930) was the most radical innovator of the New Wave filmmakers. He was also the most prolific, averaging nearly two movies per year throughout the 1960s. Except for *Breathless,* his first feature, none of his early movies could be described as a masterpiece, but all of them contain brilliant scenes, audacious techniques, and inventive thematic concepts. He became the darling of intellectuals and highbrow critics, who admired his revolutionary experiments in form and his constant attempts to expand the parameters of film as art.

Early in his career, Godard had to decide whether to make polished films, which would require a great deal of time and preparation, or to "throw the rough draft at the public"—to improvise his movies by exploiting the inspiration of the moment. Godard chose the latter course. Working without scripts, he and his gifted **cinematographer,** Raoul Coutard, would usually begin a picture with only a few scribbled notes. Along with a handful of actors, they would create the movie as they went along. Inevitably, this produced uneven results: Most of his films are seriously flawed by boring sections, clumsily executed scenes, and ideas so private as to be downright obscure.

13–7. *Masculine–Feminine* **(France, 1966),** *with Jean-Pierre Léaud and Catherine-Isabelle Duport, directed by Jean-Luc Godard.*
Godard's scenes are often played before posters or billboards to remind the viewer of the sinister omnipresence of the media in shaping our lives and values. Throughout this film, we are assaulted by advertising slogans, commercial products, sales pitches—the Big Sell. The youthful protagonists—Godard calls them "the children of Marx and Coca-Cola"—are alienated and rootless, with no permanent homes or family ties. In a series of loosely connected, semi-documentary episodes, he investigates such characteristic themes as the battle of the sexes, the dehumanizing effects of capitalism, the difficulty of honest communication, and the loneliness and sterility of contemporary urban life.   *(Royal Films International)*

Godard's earliest films fall into what might be described as his Americanesque phase, roughly from 1959 to 1965. *Breathless* was an homage to Howard Hawks's gangster picture, *Scarface*. Godard described *A Woman Is a Woman* (1961) as a Lubitsch comedy and "a neorealist musical"(!). *My Life to Live* (1962) and *A Married Woman* (1964) are women's pictures, featuring Anna Karina, Godard's wife at the time and a frequent performer in his early works. *Contempt* (1963) is an exposé of the film industry and features one of his culture heroes, Fritz Lang, playing himself. *Les Carabiniers* ("The Riflemen," 1963) is a weird species of war movie; *Band of Outsiders* (1964) is a shaggy-dog caper film. *Alphaville* (1965) is a sci-fi home movie, and *Pierrot le Fou* ("Crazy Pete," 1965) is loosely—very loosely—based on Lang's *You Only Live Once*. Most of these films are replete with visual and verbal homages to Godard's cinematic idols—as well as quotations from his favorite books and anything else that struck him as interesting while he was making the movies.

The films of Godard's second phase—lasting only from 1966 to 1968—are his most critically admired works. Such movies as *Masculine–Feminine* **(13–7)**, *Two or Three Things I Know About Her* (1966), *Made in U.S.A.* (1966), *La Chinoise* (1967), and *Weekend* **(13–8)** are virtually plotless. "The Americans are good at storytelling, the French are not," Godard observed. "I don't really like telling a story. I prefer to use a kind of tapestry, a background on which I can embroider my own ideas." He described his movies of this period as "essays" and compared making a film to keeping a personal diary, an assemblage of observations from everyday life.

13–8. *Weekend* **(France, 1967),** *with Jean Yanne and Mireille Darc, directed by Jean-Luc Godard.*
This apocalyptic vision of contemporary life is strewn with violence, pessimism, and despair. Its technical virtuosity is sometimes breathtaking. Documentary scenes are juxtaposed with stylized tableaux, lengthy takes with shots that splatter the screen with machine-gun rapidity. Godard also includes interview scenes, enigmatic private ruminations, speeches directed at the camera, puns, wordplay and jokes, audacious traveling shots, abrupt **jump-cuts, allegorical** characters, and frequent reminders that the movie is a movie—and a weird one at that. *(An Evergreen Film)*

Godard was the most intellectual of the New Wave filmmakers, and in the movies of this period, ideas take precedence over everything. A political **leftist,** he grew increasingly more radical in his thinking, attacking the vices of capitalism by comparing it to prostitution—a favorite metaphor. Even the cinema is "capitalism in its purest form" he reluctantly concluded. "There is only one solution, and that is to turn one's back on the American cinema." A man of extremes, Godard now attacked American movies as bourgeois, reactionary, and insidiously seductive in their narcotizing effects on the viewer.

Borrowing a concept from the German Marxist dramatist Bertolt Brecht, Godard used a variety of distancing techniques to prevent the audience from identifying emotionally with his characters. (Emotion and characterization were never his strong points, anyway.) The viewer should think rather than feel, analyze the events objectively rather than enter them vicariously. The destruction of plot is only one method of distancing the spectator. Other techniques include political debates, an avoidance of emotionally involving closeups, authorial intrusions in the form of written titles or **voice-over** commentaries, constant reminders that the images of a movie are ideologically weighted, interview scenes, lengthy monologues directed at the camera, and so on.

Godard was totally radicalized by the political events of May, 1968, in which a coalition of college students, intellectuals, and workers was suppressed by the government. Repudiating all his previous movies as "bourgeois," he now entered his Maoist phase, vowing to use film as a tool of Marxist revolution. This period might also be called his kamikaze phase, for it marked a serious decline in the quality of his work. His films during the next ten years were strident, dogmatic, crudely propagandistic, pagandistic, and often obscure to the point of incomprehensibility. A few of them struck intermittent sparks, most notably *Vladimir and Rosa* (1970) and *Tout va Bien* ("Everything's O.K.," 1972), with Jane Fonda and Yves Montand. But the majority of his movies of this period didn't even get distributed in the United States. Gradually, Godard lost most of his audience, which was never large even in the best of times.

Only one of Godard's subsequent films attracted much attention, and for the wrong reasons: *Hail Mary* (1984) is a loose, contemporary retelling of the story of the birth of Jesus. Though far from blasphemous in its treatment, the movie was picketed by outraged Catholics both in France and the United States. Almost everyone else ignored it.

Whatever his future, Godard's place in film history is assured. He was the most influential filmmaker of the 1960s, and an idol to ambitious young artists on several continents. His early disciples included America's Brian De Palma and Quentin Tarantino, Italy's Bernardo Bertolucci, West Germany's R. W. Fassbinder, and Brazil's Glauber Rocha **(13–9).**

ALAIN RESNAIS (pronounced reh-**nay,** b. 1922) was not associated with the *Cahiers* group, and his films in many respects are not typical of the New Wave. He attended film school as a young man and then apprenticed as an editor and assistant director. In the 1950s he made seven short films, mostly documentaries. The most famous of these is *Night and Fog* (1954), which deals with the atrocities of the Nazi concentration camps and their significance today.

Virtually all of Resnais's movies deal with time and memory. His first feature, *Hiroshima, Mon Amour* **(13–10)** explores how the memory of a World War II experience affects the consciousness of people living in the present. It was written by nov-

13–9. *Antonio Das Mortes* (**Brazil, 1969**), *directed by Glauber Rocha.*
Godard's influence extended not only over the cinemas of Europe and the United States, but those of the Third World as well. The works of Glauber Rocha (1938–1981) are a good example. A former film critic, Rocha was a leading figure in Brazil's short-lived Cinema Nuovo. This movie fuses Marxist ideas with native peasant myths in a freewheeling style that combines realism, allegory, satire, generic conventions borrowed from the western and the musical, and a revolutionary consciousness in interpreting Brazil's tortured political past. Through "the aesthetics of violence" (Rocha's term), the audience is politicized by participating in a symbolic ritual of class retribution.   *(Grove Press)*

elist Marguerite Duras. The themes of time and memory are treated most abstractly in *Last Year at Marienbad* (1961), which was written by Alain Robbe-Grillet. The film is a baroque cinematic game, in which the characters—identified only as M, X, and A—cannot agree on whether they ever met before and, if so, where or when. (Resnais later said they had; Robbe-Grillet claimed they hadn't.) Elegantly mounted like a fashion layout from *Vogue,* the movie was praised by some critics as a milestone in **avant-garde** filmmaking and condemned by others as a chilly exercise in style: "He has the skill to say whatever he wants to say on film," said one critic. "Unhappily, he has nothing, or almost nothing, to say."

In *Je t'aime, Je t'aime* ("I Love You, I Love You," 1968), a philosophical sci-fi parable, the despairing protagonist gets trapped in a time machine in which he must constantly relive a traumatic experience. Similarly, *La Guerre est Finie* ("The War Is Over," 1966), deals with the life—past and present—of an anti-Franco revolutionary, played by Yves Montand. This movie contains flash-forwards as well as flashbacks. It was written by the Spanish novelist Jorge Semprun, who also scripted the elegantly glacéed *Stavisky* (1975), about a famous con man of the 1930s.

Unlike most New Wave filmmakers, Resnais always preferred tightly written scripts, and his movies were meticulously planned in advance—hence his relatively small output (fewer than a dozen features in over twenty-five years). He preferred original screenplays, but most of them were written by respected literary figures, like the avant-garde novelists Duras and Robbe-Grillet, who both became occasional filmmakers themselves. Their movies, like those of Resnais, are formal, abstract, and cerebral. Their images are often striking in their beauty, but there is none of the energy and spontaneity of most New Wave movies.

13–10. *Hiroshima, Mon Amour* **(France, 1959),** *with Emmanuèle Riva (left), Bernard Fresson (center rear), and Eiji Okada (right), directed by Alain Resnais.*
The images in Resnais's movies are generally polished and elegant, seldom spontaneous or casually composed. Throughout this film, he uses lingering **dissolves** to overlap events from the past with those of the present. The story deals with an affair between a French actress and a Japanese architect, some years after the atom bombing of Hiroshima. Their relationship is doomed, in part because she is unable to escape the memory of her traumatic love affair with a German soldier during the Nazi occupation of her country. Note how the shadowy German youth of her past seems to come between the lovers of the present.   *(Audio-Brandon Films)*

CLAUDE CHABROL (b. 1930) has worked almost exclusively in one genre, the psychological thriller. In 1957, he and Eric Rohmer (pronounced ro-**mare**) coauthored the first book on the works of Hitchcock, and Chabrol's own movies are heavily indebted to the American master's oeuvre. Both Hitchcock and Chabrol are concerned with the sadomasochistic undertones of human relationships, which usually involve symbolic power struggles for dominance. Both Hitchcock and Chabrol reveal the festering abnormalities beneath the surface details of "normal" bourgeois life. Their films are filled with sudden outbursts of violence by characters who are stifling from suppressed rage and subconscious fears and desires.

But there are also important differences. Chabrol's movies are more **realistic** and slower paced. There is none of Hitchcock's mischievous sense of fun or bravura editing style. Chabrol's tone is more bitter, cynical, and overtly pessimistic. Hitchcock invites our complicity, forces us to identify with his sympathetically drawn characters. Chabrol is cold, aloof, almost clinical. Such early films as *Le Beau Serge* ("Handsome Serge," 1958), *Les Cousins* ("The Cousins," 1959), and the grimly fatalistic *Les Bonnes Femmes* ("The Good Ladies," 1960) are almost like laboratory experiments in which the human specimens are coolly observed from a distance.

Chabrol's films are radically inconsistent in terms of quality. Many of his movies are commercial potboilers, as impersonal and mechanical as the films he condemned in his early years as a critic at *Cahiers du Cinéma*. Interspersed among the hack entertainments are works of genuine worth, like *Les Biches* ("The Does," 1968), *La Femme Infidèle* ("The Unfaithful Wife," 1968), *Le Boucher* ("The Butcher," 1969), *La Rupture* ("The Break-Up," 1970), *A Piece of Pleasure* (1974), *Story of Women* (1989), and *Madame Bovary* (1992), a rather chilly adaptation of Flaubert's famous novel. Many of these movies and others were photographed by Jean Rabier, written by Paul Gégauff, and acted by Chabrol's one-time wife, Stéphane Audran.

Some of the films of the New Wave have already been forgotten or relegated to footnotes in academic tomes. But the legacy of the movement has endured. The film-makers of the *nouvelle vague* proved indisputably that a great movie is the product of an artist's personal vision. They demonstrated that good films can be made cheaply, with small crews and modest resources. They showed that narrative is only one way of structuring a movie, and not necessarily the best way. They also proved that stylistic virtuosity can be a value for its own sake. Above all, they served as an inspiration to other ambitious filmmakers, encouraging them to explore fresh ideas, to risk failure rather than to clutter up the cinematic landscape with safe, predictable movies.

Great Britain

The British cinema enjoyed a golden age in the 1960s, not only at home but abroad. Three English movies and their directors swept the Best Picture and Best Director Oscars in the United States during this decade: David Lean's *Lawrence of Arabia* (1962), Tony Richardson's *Tom Jones* (1963), and Carol Reed's *Oliver!* (1968). Other Best Picture winners were heavy with English talent, like George Cukor's *My Fair Lady* (1964) and Fred Zinnemann's *A Man for All Seasons* (1966). The popular *James Bond* **(13–11)** series was begun during this era; these movies were among the top box office champions of the British cinema.

British movies of this era can be divided into two phases: the so-called Angry Young Man movement, which was also described as the period of "Kitchen Sink" realism, lasting roughly from 1958 to 1963; and the "Swinging England" period, lasting from 1963 to the end of the decade. Movies of the earlier phase were generally stark, socially committed, photographed in black and white; they often dealt with the gritty realities of working-class life. Films of the second phase were more upbeat, reflecting the prosperity and trendy stylishness of the era. They were photographed in color and were indebted to the French New Wave for their free-wheeling techniques.

The origins of this creative outburst were similar to those of the *nouvelle vague*. While still undergraduates at Oxford, Lindsay Anderson and Karel Reisz edited and wrote for the film journal *Sequence*. They harshly criticized the British cinema for its lack of social relevance and its class-bound "tradition of quality." Like the *Cahiers* critics, these young Englishmen admired the American cinema, especially for its stylistic verve and its democratic spirit.

13–11. *From Russia with Love* (**Great Britain, 1963**), *with Sean Connery and Lotte Lenya, directed by Terence Young.*
The immensely popular James Bond films, loosely based on the espionage thriller novels of Ian Fleming, were—and still are—among the most commercially successful British productions in history. The earlier and better movies of the series featured Sean Connery as the dashing, suave, and sexy Agent 007. Produced by Harry Saltzman and Albert R. Broccoli, with set designs and **special effects** (which became progressively more elaborate) by the gifted Ken Adam, the series is strictly mindless entertainment, but in its earliest years at least it was entertainment with panache and style. *(United Artists)*

   In the mid-1950s, Anderson, Reisz, and their friend Tony Richardson organized the Free Cinema movement, which implemented many of their critical beliefs. They made and exhibited a series of strongly personal documentaries that dealt with various aspects of British working-class life. Free Cinema emphasized democratic values, the significance of the everyday, and a respect for individuals, somewhat like the Italian **neorealist** movement.

   The phrase "Angry Young Man" was inspired by John Osborne's stage play *Look Back in Anger*, which Richardson directed in the live theater in 1956. Osborne's play triggered a revolution that eventually filtered into the other arts as well, especially literature and cinema. Indeed, the three were often combined: Many of the best English movies of this period were adaptations of plays and novels written by a new breed, most of them from Britain's blue-collar class. Such novelists and playwrights as Alan Sillitoe, David Storey, Harold Pinter, John Braine, Alun Owen, and Shelagh Delaney concerned themselves primarily with life at the lower social echelons.

   The Angry Young Man movement began in the cinema in 1958, with the release of Jack Clayton's *Room at the Top* and Richardson's movie version of *Look Back in Anger* (**13–12**). In the following years, many of the best English films were in the vein of Kitchen Sink realism—thus called because a reviewer complained that these movies presented a dismal picture of working-class life in all its grubby details, including the kitchen sink. The following generalizations are characteristics of most of the films of the 1958–1963 period:

13–12. *Look Back in Anger* **(Great Britain, 1958),** *with Claire Bloom, Richard Burton, and Gary Raymond, directed by Tony Richardson.*
The movie version of John Osborne's famous play retained much of its corrosive, slashing dialogue, as well as its anti-Establishment sentiments. It was during this period that the term Establishment gained currency. It referred to Britain's exclusive, interlocking power structure, including the "established" Church of England, such institutions as the elite "public school" system (actually private, expensive, and decidedly upper-crust), the top echelons of the media, the major banks and corporations, and the royal family (which Osborne referred to as "the gold filling in a mouthful of decay"). Scruffy people like Jimmy Porter (Burton), the mean-mouthed proletarian hero, would not be welcomed within such rarefied circles of power and influence. *(Warner Brothers)*

1. They usually were made on small budgets with relatively unknown actors.
2. They emphasized social commitment (usually implied rather than overt) from a left-liberal perspective.
3. They featured young working-class heroes who are rebellious, angry, or frustrated at their lack of opportunity.
4. They were shot on actual locations, often in midland industrial cities, with many scenes set in such locales as bars, factories, amusement parks, and shabby project houses.
5. They reflected an attitude of hostility toward the ruling-class Establishment and its institutions.
6. They were almost equally disillusioned with the Welfare State, which is portrayed as drab, bureaucratic, and joyless.

7. They portrayed the vices as well as the virtues of the characters, including such traits as cynicism, narrow-mindedness, and moral expediency.
8. They avoided the King's English in favor of earthy, unliterary dialogue, including regional dialects, swearing, and slang.
9. They often contained violent scenes, such as drunken brawls, sporting events, and ritual beatings (sometimes well deserved) of the hero.
10. They depicted the sexual lives of the characters frankly—prior to this period, most English movies could have been given the title of a long-playing London stage hit, *No Sex Please, We're British*.
11. They introduced a new realistic style of acting, indebted to the American **Method,** emphasizing emotions and naturalistic gestures rather than pear-shaped tones and classical diction.

TONY RICHARDSON (1928–1992) was at the forefront of the new movement. Like several of his colleagues, he was a television and stage director as well as a filmmaker. In the mid-1950s, he also wrote occasional movie criticism for the British journal *Sight and Sound*. Most of Richardson's films were stage and literary adaptations. After the success of *Look Back in Anger,* he and Osborne produced another hit play, *The Entertainer,* which was made into a movie in 1960. Both versions starred Laurence Olivier as the seedy music hall performer, Archie Rice—Olivier's favorite role. The British music hall survived longer than its American counterpart, vaudeville, but at the time that the story takes place—the Suez crisis of 1958—the music hall was gasping its final breaths. Archie Rice is a symbol of a discredited older generation—desperate, opportunistic, morally bankrupt.

The Loneliness of the Long Distance Runner (1962) is one of Richardson's finest works. Based on a novel by Alan Sillitoe, who also wrote the script, the story revolves around a lower-class youth (Tom Courtenay) who is sent to reform school for a bungled larceny. The only time he feels really free is when he is running. The warden allows the boy to practice running in the hopes that he will win the race against a posh public school team. Throughout the movie, Richardson **intercuts** shots of the running hero with flashbacks of his earlier life—the death of his father, who was exploited and cheated by the factory where he worked; his mother's tawdry affair with an opportunistic creep; the youth's aborted burglary; and so on. During the actual race, the protagonist realizes that he's being exploited just like his father, that the reform school is just another institution of a repressive Establishment. Though he is far ahead of his competitor, the hero deliberately refuses to win the race, halting in front of the finishing line. His act of defiance against the warden and the system he represents is an exhilarating moment of triumph in defeat.

Tom Jones **(13–13)** was Richardson's most successful film, both critically and commercially. It manages to be faithful to Fielding's sprawling novel of the lusty eighteenth century while still incorporating the technical razzle-dazzle of the French New Wave. The comedy is virtually an encyclopedia of cinematic self-consciousness, including iris shots, fast-motion, wipes, freeze frames, lyrical helicopter shots, frenzied editing, and characters who speak directly to the camera. Bawdy, vibrant, and romantic, *Tom Jones* signaled a change in the British cinema, away from the downbeat, realistic films of the earlier period toward the livelier and more subjective movies of Swinging England.

Unfortunately, Richardson didn't swing with it. Not that he didn't try. For the most part, however, his subsequent films were disappointing—ill-conceived, la-

13–13. *Tom Jones* **(Great Britain, 1963),** *with Albert Finney and Joan Greenwood, directed by Tony Richardson.*
Tom Jones fuses the virtues of traditional English movies with the technical vivacity of the French New Wave. Based on the classic eighteenth-century novel of Henry Fielding, the script by John Osborne is a model of intelligent adaptation. The flawless cast includes such established luminaries as Joan Greenwood, Edith Evans, and Hugh Griffith, as well as younger performers such as Finney, Susannah York, and David Warner. Despite its high budget and its lavish **production values,** the film recovered its costs many times over, for it was a huge international hit, garnering rave reviews.   *(United Artists)*

bored, and often incoherent in tone. *The Charge of the Light Brigade* (1968) contains some brilliant scenes, but they fail to produce a unified effect. His adaptation of *Hamlet* (1969) is a respectable achievement, shot mostly in **tightly framed** closeups and **medium shots,** but it pales against Olivier's 1948 version and Zeffirelli's 1990 adaptation. Richardson later made a number of movies in America, most of which were panned by the critics and ignored by the public. His final film was *Blue Sky* (U.S.A., 1994), with Jessica Lange and Tommy Lee Jones.

LINDSAY ANDERSON (1923–1994) directed for the stage and television, but he completed only a handful of films. His first and best movie, *This Sporting Life* **(13–14),** is based on a novel by David Storey, who wrote the screenplay. The film is a powerful account of the world of professional rugby (British football) and the people who profit off the sport. The protagonist (Richard Harris) is an ex-miner who elbows his way into the big time, then becomes disillusioned when he's treated like an ape on a playing field. Anderson included several slow-motion sequences of

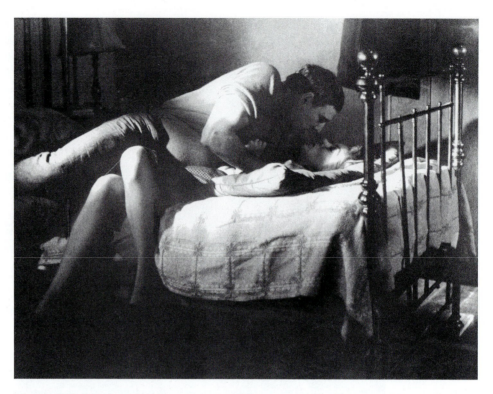

13–14. *This Sporting Life* (**Great Britain, 1963**), *with Richard Harris and Rachel Roberts, directed by Lindsay Anderson.*

Kitchen Sink realism required a new style of acting—sexier, more psychological and physical, with less emphasis on crisp diction and the beauty of the spoken word. Many of the newcomers who appeared in these films adopted the techniques of Stanislavsky and the American Method to capture the unstudied naturalism required of their roles. Harris's performance as a brutish but sensitive rugby player is reminiscent of the early performances of Marlon Brando. The actors who came to prominence during this era include, among others, such major performers as Harris, Tom Courtenay, Albert Finney, Alan Bates, Julie Christie, Rita Tushingham, Vanessa Redgrave, Lynn Redgrave, Michael Caine, Sean Connery, Glenda Jackson, Susannah York, Terence Stamp, David Warner, James Fox, Oliver Reed, Sarah Miles, Michael York, Robert Shaw, and Malcolm McDowell. Most of them are equally adept at traditional acting and have performed occasionally in the repertory classics of the British stage.   *(Continental Distributing)*

rugby matches, in which the mud-covered combatants crunch against their hulking opponents like groaning prehistoric monsters fighting to the kill.

Anderson's next important film, *If . . .* (1968), loosely based on Jean Vigo's *Zero for Conduct,* attacked the breeding grounds of the Establishment, the exclusive public school system. Its hero, Mick (Malcolm McDowell), and his pals revolt against the oppressive rules of an all-male boarding school, which is run by sadistic masters and their minions. Intercut with the realistic scenes are fantasy episodes in which the boys give vent to their anger and frustration.

O Lucky Man! (1973), also starring McDowell, represented the further adventures of Mick in the outside world. The movie is more frankly allegorical, with the good-natured hero stumbling from one way station of insanity to another in an effort to make it to the top. Interspersed with these satirical episodes are shots of Alan Price and his rock group playing appropriate music that comments ironically on the action, like a mocking Greek chorus.

KAREL REISZ (1926–2002) was the main popularizer of Kitchen Sink realism with his first feature, *Saturday Night and Sunday Morning* **(13–15),** which was a big success. Based on a novel by Alan Sillitoe, the movie was shot in Nottingham on a small budget and featured newcomer Albert Finney as a snarling, boozing factory worker, Arthur Seaton. Here was an angry young man with a vengeance—violent, cynical, and nobody's fool, yet capable of surprising tenderness.

Morgan: A Suitable Case for Treatment (1966, released in the United States as *Morgan!*) stars David Warner as a crazy Marxist artist who goes over the edge when his wife (Vanessa Redgrave) divorces him. This off-beat social comedy is filled with zany episodes that are weirdly touching. *Isadora* (1968) stars Vanessa Redgrave as the eccentric American, Isadora Duncan, a pioneer of the art of modern dance. The story is narrated in a series of flashbacks by a woman decidedly on the skids. The flashback structure contrasts the bloated, frizzy-haired egomaniac dictating her memoirs with scenes of the exquisite if somewhat pretentious young dancer who lived only for beauty. It is one of Reisz's finest works.

Like many British filmmakers, Reisz went to the United States in the 1970s, but his American movies failed to excite much popular interest: *The Gambler* (1975), *Who'll Stop the Rain?* (1978), and *The French Lieutenant's Woman* (1983) contain some impressive scenes, but they lack the vitality of his British movies.

13–15. *Saturday Night and Sunday Morning* **(Great Britain, 1960),** *with Albert Finney and Shirley Anne Field, directed by Karel Reisz.*
British filmmakers made very few attempts to smooth over the rough edges of their angry young men to render them more palatable. They are presented in all their contradictions: crude, arrogant, and sometimes downright mean, yet also shrewd and emotionally alive. *(Continental Distributing)*

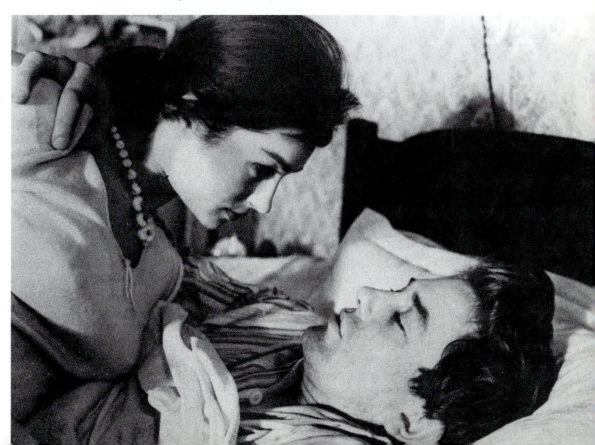

The career of JACK CLAYTON (1921–1995) follows this same downward trajectory. *Room at the Top* (1958), the story of a scheming opportunist (Laurence Harvey), based on a novel by John Braine, was a big international success. It won Simone Signoret a Best Actress Academy Award. Clayton followed this with *The Innocents* (1961), an adaptation of Henry James's *The Turn of the Screw*. *The Pumpkin Eater* (1964) is one of Clayton's best movies; it features Anne Bancroft and Peter Finch as a couple whose marriage is failing apart. Scripted by Harold Pinter in his typically mysterious, elliptical style, the story is unfolded in an elaborate series of flashbacks. Its superb cast also includes James Mason and Maggie Smith.

Our Mother's House (1967) is a sad tale of how some children secretly manage a household after their invalid mother dies. Their plan is spoiled by the sudden appearance of their disreputable father (Dirk Bogarde). As in his previous two films, Clayton's direction of children is refreshingly uncloying. *The Great Gatsby* (U.S.A., 1974), based on the novel by F. Scott Fitzgerald, contained some fine scenes, but it was seriously flawed by the miscasting of its leading roles. The film opened to scathing reviews and indifferent public response. Clayton went into a long hiatus after that, but he came back strong with the downbeat *Lonely Passion of Judith Herne* (1987), with a powerhouse performance by Maggie Smith in the title role.

JOSEPH LOSEY (1909–1984) was born and raised in the United States. After a brief period as a stage director, he went to Hollywood, where he made a number of promising movies. A victim of the political witch hunts of the 1950s (see Chapter 10), he was unable to find work. Like a number of other **blacklisted** Americans, he settled in England.

Eventually Losey teamed up with the gifted playwright Harold Pinter (b. 1930). The first Losey–Pinter collaboration was *The Servant* **(13–16),** a psychological study of how an insidious "gentleman's gentleman" (Dirk Bogarde) manages to corrupt and dominate his effete master (James Fox). Their power struggle is not conveyed in words—which are evasive, oblique—but through the mise en scène. Pinter's dialogue is seldom where the real action is. The **subtext,** or what is implied beneath the words, is what's important. Characters often talk about perfectly neutral subjects, but the manner in which they speak, their hesitations and pauses, is how we come to understand the subcurrents of emotions.

This type of emotionally repressed audiovisual communication was refined in two other Losey–Pinter collaborations, *Accident* (1967), with Bogarde as an Oxford professor who falls in love with a student; and *The Go-Between* (1971), with Julie Christie as an aristocratic woman who falls in love with a farmer (Alan Bates). Many of Losey's pictures explore the sexual and social tensions between classes.

King and Country (1964) is a World War I drama about an army captain (Bogarde again) who is assigned to defend a working-class private (Tom Courtenay), a deserter. *A Doll's House* (1973) is an excellent adaptation of Ibsen's famous feminist play, with Jane Fonda and David Warner in the leading roles.

Losey then went to France, where he directed the award-winning *Mr. Klein* (France, 1976), a political thriller about a mistaken identity during the Nazi occupation. *Don Giovanni* (France, 1979) is one of the few successful translations of opera into film. Losey's interpretation of Mozart's great work is visually sumptuous and emphasizes the dark, brooding undertones of the story rather than its elegance and wit.

RICHARD LESTER (b. 1932) was also born and raised in America and directed TV commercials before moving to England. His first feature, *A Hard Day's Night*

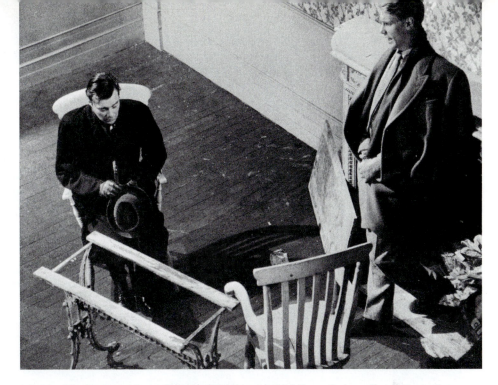

13–16. *The Servant* **(Great Britain, 1963),** *with Dirk Bogarde (seated) and James Fox, directed by Joseph Losey.*

Losey rarely states his themes outright, nor do the characters usually discuss what's really on their minds. The burden of interpretation is placed on the viewer, who must actively mine the mise en scène to arrive at an understanding of the human relationships. We infer the subtle shifts in psychology through the way that the characters are placed within the **frame:** the **angle** from which a shot is photographed, how close or far the characters stand from each other, who is higher (more dominant) in the frame, the body language of the actors, the symbolic implications of foreground obstructions, the significance of decor and lighting in revealing character. *(The Landau Distributing Company)*

(13–17), was a huge hit and introduced The Beatles to the world. It was love at first sight. Scripted by Alun Owen, the movie is an exhilarating romp—playful and energetic, with just a touch of self-mockery. Lester followed this with another Beatles comedy, *Help!* (1965). Like its predecessor, it is stylistically sophisticated in its New Wave panache and is edited at a furious pace. Its silly story is a deliberate throwaway—a pretext for the musical numbers and for the lads to demonstrate their considerable comic talents.

The Knack (1965), a charming comedy about young people based on the play by Shelagh Delaney, won the Grand Prize at Cannes. *How I Won the War* (1967) was an antiwar fantasy starring John Lennon. It fared poorly at the box office. *Petulia* (U.S.A., 1968) was almost totally devoid of comedy, though it was edited in Lester's typically fragmented style. It failed to excite much interest commercially, but it has become a favorite with many film critics.

Lester later devoted his time to directing more routine commercial assignments, primarily Anglo-American productions like *The Three Musketeers* (1974), *The Four Musketeers* (1975), *Robin and Marian* (1976), and *Superman II* (1981), all pleasant entertainments.

JOHN SCHLESINGER (1926–2003) was perhaps the most prestigious British filmmaker to divide his energies between England and America. He began his career

13–17. *A Hard Day's Night* **(Great Britain, 1964),** *with The Beatles, directed by Richard Lester.*
No one embodied the spirit of Swinging England more engagingly than those dynamic lads from Liverpool, The Beatles. Lester's movie fuses slapstick comedy with the documentary and the musical, capturing the group's irrepressible wit in an avalanche of images that whiz by at breakneck speed. The quicksilver editing and kaleidoscopic visuals are accompanied by a soundtrack of classic Beatles tunes.   *(United Artists)*

making documentaries for the BBC. His first feature, *A Kind of Loving* (1962), is a domestic drama starring Alan Bates as a working-class youth who is forced to marry his girlfriend after she gets pregnant. *Billy Liar* (1963), starring Tom Courtenay, deals with a frustrated young man who feels trapped by his boring life. Throughout the film, Schlesinger intercuts the hero's loony fantasies with the realistic episodes, producing a comic and sometimes poignant contrast. *Darling* (1965) is the story of a restless model (Julie Christie) who lives a trivial, meaningless existence. A cynical depiction of London's Swinging generation, the film was an international hit and won Christie a Best Actress Academy Award. Schlesinger followed this with an adaptation of Thomas Hardy's powerful novel *Far from the Madding Crowd* (1967), with Christie, Bates, and Peter Finch.

Schlesinger's greatest commercial success was *Midnight Cowboy* (U.S.A., 1969), with Dustin Hoffman and Jon Voight in two of their finest performances. The film won a Best Picture Oscar, and Schlesinger also won for his direction. *Sunday, Bloody Sunday* (1971) was less successful commercially, though it was praised by critics. *Marathon Man* (U.S.A., 1976), with Dustin Hoffman and Laurence Olivier, is a political thriller, edited in Schlesinger's typically jumpy style. *Yanks* (1979) deals with the complex relationships between American soldiers and British civilians during World War II. Another American project, *The Falcon and the Snowman* (U.S.A.,

1985), with a riveting performance by Sean Penn as a traitor to his country, was an undeserved box office failure.

By the late 1960s, the British film industry had become almost a subsidiary of Hollywood. Throughout the decade, as much as 90 percent of the funding for English movies had come from America. When this source of capital evaporated around 1970, the British industry shriveled. Some filmmakers turned to television and the live theater for employment. Others moved to Hollywood, where they constituted a virtual British wing of the American cinema.

Italy

The Italian cinema continued to prosper during the 1960s. Such established masters as De Sica, Visconti, and Fellini produced some of their best works during this decade, not to speak of a half dozen other filmmakers who achieved international fame, like Pier Paolo Pasolini and Sergio Leone **(13–18).** The two most prominent artists to emerge during this period were Michelangelo Antonioni, a Marxist intellectual, and Ermanno Olmi, whose films carried on the tradition of Christian humanism.

ANTONIONI (b. 1912) was a late bloomer. As a young man he wrote film criticism for the journal *Cinema* and then attended film school at the Centro Sperimentale. He began as a scriptwriter during the early 1940s, and in the later half of that

13–18. *The Good, the Bad and the Ugly* **(Italy, 1966),** *directed by Sergio Leone.*

The 1960s gave birth to the so-called spaghetti western, the creation of Sergio Leone (1929–1989), whose works in that genre include *A Fistful of Dollars* (1964), *For a Few Dollars More* (1965), and *Once Upon a Time in the West* (1969). The finest example of the genre is *Once Upon a Time in the West,* the only great western not produced in America. Leone's father Vincenzo was a film director and as a boy Sergio saw hundreds of American movies, which he adored. As a young man he was an assistant to various filmmakers, including a number of American directors working in Italy. "America is really the property of the world, and not only of the Americans," Leone once said. His westerns are strongly mythic, populated with **archetypal,** larger-than-life characters and executed in a florid, baroque style that emphasizes ritual and lyricism rather than realism. Aided in large part by the brilliant musical scores of Ennio Morricone, these works are virtually operas—like Verdi out West. The trademark features of Leone's drawn-out sequences are looming closeups of mean faces, epic widescreen panoramas, crane shots that swirl giddily above the landscape, lengthy stretches of foreboding silence, and ritualized shootouts that seem to owe more to ballet than to history. Leone's last work was *Once Upon a Time in America* (U.S.A, 1984), a gangster film with Robert De Niro. The treatment is characteristically mythic: "I am enchanted by fables, especially their dark side," Leone said.

(Paramount Pictures)

decade he made six short documentaries. He didn't direct his first fiction feature, *Story of a Love Affair* (1950), until he was thirty-eight years old. He followed with four other movies, the most respected of which are *Le Amiche* ("The Girl Friends," 1955) and *Il Grido* ("The Outcry," 1957). None of them attracted much notice at the time.

Antonioni came to international prominence in 1960 with *L'Avventura* ("The Adventure," **13–19**). At Cannes, where it premiered, the film was booed by an audience of hostile critics, who kept yelling "Cut! Cut!" at the screen. The shots were so lengthy and the pace so slow that they simply assumed Antonioni was inept at editing. But like most of his films, *L'Avventura* uses space to suggest time, to symbolize the gradual erosion of the human spirit. The protagonist (Monica Vitti) spends much of her time searching—at first for her best friend who has mysteriously disappeared, then for her lover, who was formerly the lover of her best friend.

Like most of Antonioni's mature works, *L'Avventura* is ostensibly a love story, told from the woman's point of view. But it also explores complex psychological and philosophical themes—the difficulty of preserving one's integrity in a world of easy money, the laxness with which even decent people betray their loved ones, the

13–19. *L'Avventura* **(Italy, 1960),** *with Gabriele Ferzetti and Monica Vitti, directed by Michelangelo Antonioni.*
Antonioni's scenes between lovers are a somber gauge of their alienation and ambivalence. Often they don't look at each other, but stare off into space, absorbed by private doubts. Antonioni sometimes cuts from one to the other, isolating them in separate space cubicles rather than having them share the intimate proximity of a unified mise en scène. The sexual scenes are seldom tender or affectionate. The lovers hardly speak. Their groping spasms are photographed in fragmentary details—an outstretched hand, a tensed limb, a fearful face falling off frame. *(Janus Films)*

transience of sexual passion, the spiritual sterility of the bourgeoisie, and, above all, the sense of alienation that contemporary life inflicts upon us all.

Antonioni soon became a favorite among intellectual critics, who admired his modernist solemnity and his uncompromising vision of the Age of Anxiety. His revolutionary style influenced even the mainstream commercial cinema. In movies like *La Notte* ("The Night," 1961), *Eclipse* (1962), and his first film in color, the brilliant *Red Desert* (1964), Antonioni virtually discarded plot in favor of a relatively static psychological state, which is explored in depth. Instead of dramatic confrontations, he employed lengthy sequences in which nothing much seems to be happening—except the minute-by-minute fluctuations in the emotional subcurrents of the characters.

But these must be inferred: They are seldom discussed. Antonioni exploits his mise en scène to convey most of his ideas. The characters are often positioned within constricting enclosures such as doorways or windows. They are dwarfed by towering structures, squeezed at the bottom or edges of the frame like visual afterthoughts. They are sometimes partially hidden behind foreground obstructions. Often they stream over desolate landscapes, like lost souls in search of . . . what? They hardly know. Something meaningful. Something to hold on to . . . anything. They grope and stammer, but their anxieties are too vague for verbal formulations.

13–20. *Romeo and Juliet* (**Italy/Great Britain, 1968**),
with Olivia Hussey and Leonard Whiting, directed by Franco Zeffirelli.

A former assistant and protégé of Luchino Visconti, Zeffirelli (b. 1923) has continued in Visconti's tradition of aestheticism, though without the political undertones. For Zeffirelli, visual opulence is its own justification—beauty for beauty's sake. Like Visconti, he began his career as a set and costume designer for the stage and opera. He still enjoys international fame as an opera director in Milan, London, and New York. He has made only a few films, mostly adaptations of classic plays and operas. But these are fully realized *movies,* highly fluid and kinetic, not canned stage productions. His major films include *The Taming of the Shrew* (U.S.A./Italy, 1966), with Richard Burton and Elizabeth Taylor; another Shakespearean adaptation, the surprisingly popular *Romeo and Juliet,* with a sensitive score by Nino Rota; *La Traviata* (Italy, 1983), a rich cinematic translation of Verdi's great opera; and *Hamlet* (1990) with Mel Gibson in the title role.   *(Paramount Pictures)*

They search. Rarely do they discover anything but the most fleeting consolations—usually love, that most transitory of human comforts. At best, Antonioni's movies end on a note of pity, shattered hope, or spiritual exhaustion.

Antonioni went to other countries to make movies, but what he found was always the same: moral confusion, spiritual torpor, loss of personal identity. *Blow-Up* (1966) was made in Britain, *Zabriskie Point* (1970) in America, *The Passenger* (1975) in Africa and England. All of these films are less realistic, more abstractly philosophical than his earlier works.

Not all Italian movies of this period were so grimly pessimistic. The lushly romantic works of Zeffirelli **(13–20)** and the social satires of Germi **(13–21)** were

13–21. *Divorce—Italian Style* (**Italy, 1962**), *with Marcello Mastroianni and Daniela Rocca, directed by Pietro Germi.*
Germi (1914–1974) studied film at the famous Centro Sperimentale and made his directorial debut in 1945. He was one of the earliest neorealists, concentrating on social dramas set in poverty-stricken Sicily. He did not come into his own internationally until the 1960s, with a series of Sicilian satires initiated by *Divorce—Italian Style,* which ridicules Italy's then-archaic divorce laws. (The slimy protagonist, played to perfection by Mastroianni, can rid himself of his unlovely wife only by murdering her.) Germi followed this with the hilarious farce *Seduced and Abandoned* (1963), which satirizes the sexual double standard and stereotypical Italian macho men. *The Birds, the Bees, and the Italians* (1966), another Sicilian sex comedy, won the Grand Prize at Cannes. Germi's final completed movie was the comedy *Alfredo Alfredo* (1973), with Dustin Hoffman.   *(Embassy Pictures)*

closer to the mainstream and portrayed human nature in a more positive light. Pontecorvo's celebrated political movie, *The Battle of Algiers* **(13–22),** was in the tradition of the Resistance film, pioneered by *Open City.*

Perhaps the most positive vision of humanity is found in the films of ERMANNO OLMI (b. 1931), though he hardly portrays life as a garden party. Born of peasant parents, he and his family moved to the city, where they worked in factories. During the 1950s, while Olmi was employed at an electric utility company, he made about forty short documentaries sponsored by his company, many of them centering on the lives of the workers. He made his feature debut with *Time Stood Still* (1959). Like most of his later works, it carries on the tradition of neorealism: The film was shot on actual locations, employed nonprofessional actors, and deemphasized plot in favor of capturing the slow rhythms of everyday life.

Neorealism gave birth to the two major strains of the Italian cinema—the Christian and the Marxist. Olmi is in the Christian tradition. His films are quiet celebrations of the power of faith, of the resilience of the human spirit, even under oppressive conditions. He is not concerned with remarkable heroes, but ordinary

13–22. *The Battle of Algiers* **(Italy/Algeria, 1966),** *directed by Gillo Pontecorvo.*
Throughout the 1960s, the Italian cinema remained profoundly political. Indeed, perhaps no other country has produced a body of Marxist films of such commanding international prestige. Pontecorvo (b. 1919) began as a politically committed documentarist in the 1950s. He has made only a few fiction films, the most famous of which is *The Battle of Algiers,* which won the Golden Lion Award at the Venice Film Festival. A powerful account of the Algerian rebellion against their French colonial masters, the movie looks like a documentary, with its shaky, grainy images, its nonprofessional cast, and its use of authentic locations.   *(Rizzoli Films)*

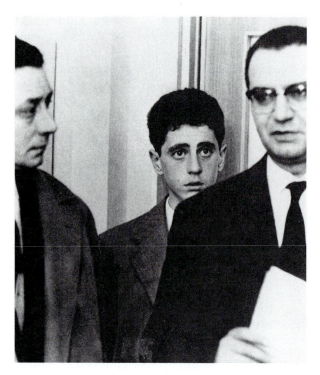

13–23. *Il Posto* ("The Job," Italy, 1961), *with Sandro Panzeri (center), directed by Ermanno Olmi.*
The sweet, sincere protagonist of this film, which is also known as *The Sound of Trumpets,* is crowded by his environment, elbowed aside by more aggressive people, and casually shunted to the rear because of his social insignificance, his youth, and his gentle nature. Despite his passivity, he is an appealing youth—decent and quietly charming. Characteristically, Olmi treats him with tenderness and respect. As the French critic Pierre Marcabru pointed out, "Olmi displays compassion for all that is fine, fragile, condemned." *(Janus Films)*

mortals—the kind of people who would be astonished if someone suggested that a movie could be made about their lives, which are simple and unassuming.

Olmi came into international prominence with *Il Posto* **(13–23),** about a shy working-class youth who gets a lower-level clerking job with a huge corporation in Milan. The film consists entirely of little things: his anxieties about taking an entrance exam, his purchase of a trenchcoat that impressed a pretty fellow worker, a slightly comical company party, and so on. The boy is especially pleased that he has a secure job "for life." Olmi is more ambivalent. The final scene of the movie presents a picture of stupefying tedium and entrapment: A closeup of the youth's sensitive face is juxtaposed with the monotonous sound of a copying machine clacking louder and louder and louder.

Olmi's few subsequent films pursued this same unpretentious course. *The Fiancés* (1963) deals with the relationship of an engaged working-class couple when a job transfer forces them to part. *A Man Named John* (1965) is a biography of "the peasant Pope," John XXIII. In *One Fine Day* (1968), the protagonist must reevaluate his life after he kills a man in an auto accident.

Olmi's masterpiece to date is *The Tree of the Wooden Clogs* (1978), which is steeped in the values of Christian humanism. Winner of the Golden Palm at the Cannes Film Festival, the film celebrates the everyday lives of several peasant families around 1900. For them, God is a living presence—a source of guidance, hope, and solace. Their faith is childlike, trusting, like that of St. Francis of Assisi. In a series of documentarylike vignettes accompanied by the majestic music of Johann Sebastian Bach, Olmi unfolds their gentle drama, extolling their patience, their tough stoicism, their dignified labor. Above all, he exalts the sacredness of the human spirit. For Olmi, they are the salt of the earth.

Eastern Europe

Dominated by the Soviet Union, the Communist countries of Eastern Europe pretty much reflected the Moscow party line, and their film industries were patterned on the Soviet model. The official style of Socialist Realism, put forth by the cultural flunkies of dictator Josef Stalin, held sway until his death in 1953. With the gradual relaxation of Cold War tensions and the de-Stalinization of the arts, the cinematic climate improved, especially in Hungary, Poland, and Czechoslovakia. (Yugoslavia had always been a special case, since its ties with the U.S.S.R. were looser.) Finally, filmmakers in these countries were allowed to go beyond the simple-minded platitudes of boy-loves-tractor stories, or stale variations on the theme of the Heroic Resistance of the People against the Nazi hoards.

Eastern European movies gradually became more individualized, reflecting a more complex morality and a more experimental technical range. Most promising young directors had been trained at the excellent state-subsidized film schools, where they had been permitted to view recent movies from the West. They were especially impressed by the achievements of the French New Wave and anxious to see what they could do with some of the same ideas and techniques.

Yugoslavia, always the freest and most independent of the Communist bloc countries, established its supremacy in **animation** as early as the 1950s. Throughout the next decade, at various international film festivals, the celebrated "Zagreb School" consistently copped the top awards in short animated movies, which were clever, sophisticated, and technically inventive. A few Yugoslavian feature films also began to draw worldwide attention, particularly those of Dusan Makavejev, whose *W.R.: Mysteries of the Organism* (1971) was lavishly praised in the West. Critics delighted in its outlandish wit, its anarchic spirit, and its Godardian technical flamboyance.

In the Soviet Union itself, the period of de-Stalinization produced some freer, more realistic studies of Soviet life, most notably Mikhail Kalatozov's *The Cranes Are Flying* (1957), but compared to the movies being produced in the West, even this sincere effort looks pretty tame. The majority of important movies from the U.S.S.R. during this era were period films and adaptations of literary classics, most notably Sergei Bondarchuk's four-part *War and Peace* and the works of Grigori Kozintsev—*Don Quixote* (1957) and his two highly praised Shakespearean adaptations, *Hamlet* (1964) and *King Lear* (1972).

In Hungary, the leading filmmaker of the 1960s was MIKLÓS JANCSÓ (pronounced **Yahn**-cho). Jancsó (b. 1921) is a superlative technician, a master of **widescreen** compositions, the lengthy take, and gracefully choreographed traveling shots. In movies like *The Round-Up* (1965) and *The Red and the White* (1967), his style is brazenly complex, with formations of people streaming over various planes of his vast exteriors while the camera relentlessly **tracks,** zooms, or **cranes** with or against their movements. Many of his movies deal with military engagements, in which civilians and soldiers alike are subjected to sadomasochistic rituals of humiliation and violence. Characters are often stripped of their clothing, subjected to torture and cruel degradations. The main problem with Jancsó's films is that most of them deal with Hungarian historical events, and the political implications of these events—which often evoke present-day analogues—are lost on many viewers who are unfamiliar with the historical details.

Poland was the most prolific film-producing nation in Eastern Europe, with an output of nearly two hundred features annually, most of which never reached

13–24. *Ashes and Diamonds* (Poland, 1958), *with Sbigniew Cybulski, directed by Andrzej Wajda.*

Like the first two films of Wajda's *War Trilogy, Ashes and Diamonds* features Cybulski as a characteristically rebellious young man, alienated by the hypocrisies of both sides in the final days of World War II. Cybulski was called the James Dean of Poland, a symbol of disaffected youth. He died in 1967—like Dean, in an auto accident.   *(Museum of Modern Art)*

the United States. The elder statesman of the Polish cinema was ANDRZEJ WAJDA (pronounced **Vai**-da). Born in 1926, Wajda was a graduate of the famous Lodz film school. His earliest movies dealt mostly with the country's traumatic Nazi experience, but his vision of war and its bitter aftermath is not heroically glorified. *A Generation* (1954), his feature debut and the first of his celebrated *War Trilogy,* explores the effects of the war on Poland's disillusioned youth. Its sister films, *Kanal* (1957) and *Ashes and Diamonds* **(13–24),** also challenged the official view of war as glory for the fatherland.

Wajda is a survivor. Throughout his lengthy career, his movies were surprisingly critical of the Polish Communist regime. In repressive times, his critiques were oblique and symbolic; in more liberal times, courageous and blunt. Because of his international prestige, he was allowed considerably more freedom of expression than the vast majority of his peers. Even during the crisis years of the late 1970s and early 1980s, Wajda continued to challenge the official wisdom of the Establishment in movies like *Man of Marble* (1977) and *Man of Iron* (see **17–19),** which openly embraced the ideas of the Solidarity movement. *Danton* (France/Poland, 1983) deals with the French Revolution and the conflict between the liberal democrat Danton and the repressive autocrat Robespierre. The film was a thinly veiled analogue to the situation in Poland at that time.

Poland's most famous filmmaker, ROMAN POLANSKI (b. 1933), has made most of his films outside his native country. His childhood was a nightmare of terror and persecution. His family was Jewish, and when he was only eight, his parents were sent to Nazi concentration camps, where his mother was murdered. Young Polanski escaped to the Cracow Jewish ghetto; when that was incinerated to rubble, he

13–25. *Macbeth* **(Great Britain, 1971),** *with Jon Finch and Francesca Annis, directed by Roman Polanski.*
Polanski's films, which are impeccably crafted, are filled with brutality, terror, and mindless cruelty. His version of *Macbeth* was criticized for its violence—derived, of course, from Shakespeare's original. Polanski is also a master of atmospheric effects, charging his scenes with a sense of anxiety and unspeakable evil. Many of his movies deal with sexual and social repression, concealed hatreds, paranoid fears, and the malignancy of the human heart. Haunted by a life strewn with violence, persecution, and personal tragedy, Polanski is one of the most deeply pessimistic of all contemporary filmmakers. His best works include *Repulsion* (Great Britain, 1965), *Cul-de-Sac* (Great Britain, 1966), *Rosemary's Baby* (U.S.A., 1968), *Macbeth*, *Chinatown* (U.S.A., 1974, see **14–6),** *The Tenant* (France, 1976), *Tess* (France/Great Britain, 1979), *Frantic* (U.S.A., 1988), and *The Pianist* (Poland/France/Britain/Germany, 2002). *(Columbia Pictures)*

once again escaped and wandered the countryside, taking refuge with a series of Catholic families. After the war, he attended film school at Lodz, where several of his short films won awards. His first feature, *Knife in the Water* (1962), a low-key psychological triangle drama, won the Critics' Prize at the Venice Film Festival and was nominated for an American Academy Award as Best Foreign Language Film.

Polanski subsequently left Poland and continued his career in France, Great Britain, and the United States. Most of his movies have been in English. Most of them have been psychological thrillers, steeped in a sense of alienation, paranoia, and terror. Tragedy continued to stalk him even after his international success as a filmmaker. In 1969, in Hollywood, while Polanski was out of town, his wife, actress Sharon Tate (who was eight months pregnant), and a group of friends were horribly mutilated and murdered by the Charles Manson cult.

The greatest surprise in Eastern Europe came from tiny, multilingual Czechoslovakia. During the 1960s, over fifteen young graduates of the Prague film school made their feature debuts. They became part of a cultural movement called the Prague Spring, which included such accomplished filmmakers as Jan Kadar, Elmar Klos **(13–26),** Jiri Menzel, Vera Chytilova, Milos Forman, and Ivan Passer. Like their French counterparts, the movies of this group were personal, often experimental, and made on low budgets with small crews and flexible equipment. Some of their films were technically audacious, like Chytilova's spritely *Daisies* (1966), which vibrates with energy and dazzling pyrotechnics. However, most of the movies of the Prague Spring were quiet, understated, and poignant.

The appealing humanism of the Prague Spring movement is best illustrated perhaps by the films of MILOS FORMAN (b. 1932). Forman lost both parents to Nazi

13–26. *The Shop on Main Street* (Czechoslovakia, 1965), *with Ida Kaminska and Josef Kroner, directed by Jan Kadar and Elmar Klos.*
The Prague Spring filmmakers rejected the phony heroics of Socialist Realism in favor of the harsher verities of Italian neorealism. The protagonists of the best Czech films of this era are flawed, sometimes weak. In this movie, for example, a lazy if good-hearted lout (Kroner) manages to exploit the Nazi occupation of his country by becoming the "Aryan Controller" of a button shop belonging to a deaf old Jewish widow (Kaminska). She is unaware of what's happening in the outside world. Their relationship begins comically, with the slightly dotty old woman coming to care for her "assistant" like a stern but loving mother. A bond develops between these two outsiders, but just as the protagonist begins to act like a human being, he panics and accidentally kills her while the Nazis are rounding up all the remaining Jews in the village. The film won the American Academy Award as Best Foreign Language Picture. *(Museum of Modern Art)*

death camps, and he was raised by relatives. After graduating from film school, he made a series of short fiction movies, which led to his first feature assignment, *Black Peter* (1964). It won the First Prize at the Locarno Film Festival. He went on to direct two charming comedies, *Loves of a Blonde* (1965) and *The Firemen's Ball* (1967).

Forman's films are realistic, low-key studies of the frailties and foibles of human nature. His themes often revolve around the generation gap and the embarrassing difficulties of preserving one's dignity without spoiling the fun of life. His satire is gentle, almost affectionate. His tone is ironic, yet warm and compassionate. He is more concerned with exploring the oddities of character than the intricacies of plot, for his narrative structures are generally loose, the episodes unforced. His films are filled with the comic incongruities of everyday life. For example, in *The Firemen's Ball*, the small-town gala celebration in honor of a dying fireman is interrupted by a fire. When the firemen return, they discover that all the food and prizes have been filched by the guests.

Alarmed by the liberal permissiveness of the popular Dubcek government in Czechoslovakia, the Soviet Union in 1968 sent in an occupying army and toppled the government, replacing it with a Soviet puppet regime. In one fell swoop, a whole cultural movement—among other things—was wiped out. Most of the members of the Prague Spring fled to the West, where they have made honorable and important contributions.

FURTHER READING

CURRAN, JAMES, and VINCENT PORTER, eds. *British Cinema History*. Totowa, N.J.: Barnes and Noble Books, 1983. Collection of essays on the art, industry, and ideology of British movies.

FUKSIEWICZ, JACEK. *Film and Television in Poland.* Warsaw: Interpress Publishers, 1976. Selective survey, well illustrated.

GRAHAM, PETER, ed. *The New Wave.* London: Secker and Warburg, 1968. Collection of articles, many from the journals *Positif* and *Cahiers du Cinéma.*

HILL, JOHN. *Sex, Class and Realism.* London: British Film Institute, 1986. British Kitchen Sink cinema, 1956–1963.

KOLKER, ROBERT PHILLIP. *The Altering Eye.* New York: Oxford University Press, 1983. Critical analysis of contemporary international cinema, with special emphasis on Italian neorealism and the French New Wave.

LIEHM, MIRA. *Passion and Defiance.* Berkeley: University of California Press, 1984. Film in Italy from 1942 to the late 1970s.

MONACO, JAMES. *The New Wave.* New York: Oxford University Press, 1976. The best study of the *nouvelle vague,* with emphasis on Truffaut, Godard, Chabrol, Rohmer, and Rivette.

RICHARDS, JEFFREY, and ANTHONY ALDGATE. *British Cinema and Society 1930–1970.* Totowa, N.J.: Barnes and Noble Books, 1983. Examination of ten key films and how they illuminate the values of their times.

SKVORECKY, JOSEF. *All the Bright Young Men and Women.* Toronto: Take One Film Book Series, 1971. A personal history of the Czech cinema by a former member of the Prague Spring movement.

WITCOMB, R. T. *The New Italian Cinema.* New York: Oxford University Press, 1983. Survey of the 1960s and after.

14

American Cinema in the 1970s

Twentieth Century–Fox

Timeline: 1970–1979

1970

U.S. military strength in Vietnam: approximately 400,000 troops (the year before: 543,000 troops)

Massive student demonstrations: 448 U.S. colleges and universities are closed or on strike

1972

All in the Family is the leading TV show in the United States

1973

Vice-President Spiro Agnew resigns amid charges of corruption; he is replaced by Gerald Ford (Republican), leader of House of Representatives

U.S. Supreme Court rules that states cannot prohibit abortion during first six months of pregnancy

1973–1974

Watergate scandal: Nixon forced to resign as result of coverup revelations; Vice-President Ford becomes U.S. President (1974–1977); he grants Nixon a pardon

1974

Gallup Poll shows that 40 percent of U.S. adults attend church services weekly

New fad: "streaking" (running naked in crowded public places)

1975

U.S. evacuates from Vietnam—South Vietnam immediately overrun by Communists; becomes a single country in 1976

1976

Jimmy Carter (Democrat) elected President of United States (1977–1981); U.S. population: 214 million

1977

Completion of 800-mile Alaska oil pipeline

1978

Egypt–Israeli Mideast Peace agreement; full diplomatic relations with the People's Republic of China

1979

U.S. miniseries on TV, *Holocaust,* viewed by more than 120 million people

The schizoid decade. Vietnam and Watergate: America in the depths. Black Power. A new cinema, dark and dangerous—Hollywood's last golden age. Revisionist genres. Sex and Violence—bigger and better than ever. Sources of fresh directorial talent. Robert Altman and the cinema of discovery. The epic dark canvas of Francis Ford Coppola. Raging Martin Scorsese. Woody Allen's *Manhattan*. *Star Wars* and other light fare. Whiz kid: Steven Spielberg. Box office paradise: Hollywood at decade's end.

HISTORY IS NOT SO TIDY as historians would wish it. The period considered in this chapter actually comprises two distinct eras, with the dividing line falling shortly after the mid-decade. The earlier 1970s—dominated by the unending war in Vietnam and the Watergate scandals—represent a continuation of the sensibility of the late 1960s. Most film historians point to *Star Wars* (1977) as the beginning of a new epoch in American filmmaking, characterized by a nostalgic longing for the simplicities of bygone days.

The Vietnam–Watergate Era

The most important movies of the Vietnam–Watergate era emphasized violence, racial and sexual conflicts, and the moral bankruptcy of public institutions. It was a pessimistic period, steeped in cynicism and paranoia. For the first time in American film history, movies with downbeat themes became the rule rather than the exception. Virtually every American institution was subjected to skeptical scrutiny and rejected as corrupt and corrupting: marriage and the family, authority, the success ethic, politics, government, the military, patriotism, the police, capitalism.

Some of the key films of the period are *Five Easy Pieces, M*A*S*H, Little Big Man, Joe, A Clockwork Orange, Mean Streets, Petulia, The French Connection, McCabe and Mrs. Miller, Klute, Carnal Knowledge, Straw Dogs, Shaft, The Godfather* films, *Serpico, Chinatown, The Conversation, Lenny, One Flew Over the Cuckoo's Nest, Nashville, All the President's Men, Taxi Driver*, and *Cabaret* **(14–1)**.

The war in Vietnam was tearing America apart. Despite the promises of our nation's leaders that there was a "light at the end of the tunnel," there was no diminishment in the savage intensity of the fighting. When President Nixon expanded the war by invading Cambodia, America's college campuses were convulsed by violent protests. At Kent State University, National Guardsmen opened fire on jeering demonstrators, killing some students and maiming others. It was not until 1975 that the United States managed to withdraw from the most unpopular war of its history. The casualties were awesome: 58,000 young Americans were killed in the jungles of Vietnam, Laos, and Cambodia. Many of those lucky enough to return suffered intense emotional anguish and a feeling that they had been cynically exploited **(14–2)**.

14-1. *Cabaret* (U.S.A., 1972), *with Joel Grey, choreographed and directed by Bob Fosse.*
The controlling metaphor of this musical is taken from the title song: Life is a cabaret. The musical numbers—raucous, tawdry, and cynical—comment obliquely on the dramatic episodes, mocking their sentiment and undermining their sincerity. *(Allied Artists)*

By 1970, the early idealism of the civil rights movement had turned rancid. Its charismatic leader, the Reverend Martin Luther King, Jr., had been assassinated in 1968 (the same year that presidential candidate Robert F. Kennedy was gunned down), and soon afterward, the movement veered sharply from nonviolence to strident militancy. Much of the violence was unfocused rage, rage at "The Man"—that is, the white folks with all the money and power. Black militant Stokely Carmichael pointed out the sham of Vietnam—ironically, a war that was increasingly being fought by black draftees. The social gains of the previous decade were slowly eroded by the economic recession that hit the United States in the early 1970s and stayed on—along with raging inflation—for the remainder of the decade. Blacks had been the last to be hired; they were also the first to be fired. The image of the FBI and its venerated leader, J. Edgar Hoover, was irrevocably tarnished when it was revealed that Hoover, the hero of many a Hollywood crime saga, was illegally persecuting the Black Panthers and other militant organizations. More disillusionment awaited.

Melvin Van Peebles's *Sweet Sweetback's Baadasss Song* (1971) popularized a new **genre,** the so-called blaxploitation picture—primarily urban melodramas and detective thrillers, reflecting the new black militancy. The early 1970s saw the release of over sixty of these films, most of them produced, directed, and acted by blacks. Most of them also vented a murderous resentment against the white majority. *Sweetback* is mean, angry, and alive. It is bursting with the vitality of ghetto culture, and its audience realized immediately that this was something truly new. It grossed a surprising $10 million and inspired many (mostly inferior) imitations. Van Peebles financed the picture himself, produced it, directed it, and played its leading

14–2. *The Deer Hunter* (**U.S.A., 1978**), *with John Savage and Robert De Niro, directed by Michael Cimino.*
Unlike previous military engagements, Vietnam inspired very few movies that dealt overtly with the war while it was actually taking place. The subject was considered box office poison until near the end of the decade, several years after the conflict had been concluded. Movies like *The Deer Hunter, The Boys in Company C* (1978), *Coming Home* (1978), and *Apocalypse Now* (1979) treated the war as an unmitigated national disaster. *(Universal Studios)*

role. He also composed the music for the soundtrack. He dedicated the movie to "All the Brothers and Sisters who have had enough of The Man." He added sassily: "This movie rated 'X' by an all-white jury."

Sweetback, Shaft, Superfly, The Mack, and other movies like them polarized the African American community. Middle-class black spokesmen, who preferred positive images like those in *Sounder* (**14–3**), expressed alarm at the negative images these films provided. Blacks were portrayed as cool and stylish, yes, but they were also shown to be violent, employed mostly in illegal professions, and as blatantly racist as their white counterparts. The antiheroes of these films were a far cry from that moral paragon of the 1960s, Sidney Poitier. Blaxploitation died out by 1975. Some of the artists and technicians who got their first break making these movies eventually found work in the mainstream entertainment industry. On the whole, television has been more receptive to black talent than the movies.

Deep in the night of June 17, 1972, five men broke into the Democratic National Committee Headquarters at the Watergate office building in Washington, D.C. While they were photographing documents and placing bugging equipment in the phones, the burglars were caught redhanded by a security guard. Thus began one of the most bizarre episodes in the history of American politics. Despite many obstacles, two *Washington Post* reporters, Bob Woodward and Carl Bernstein, doggedly investigated this "third-rate burglary." What they gradually revealed was a pattern of such hypocrisy that the nation was staggered by its impact. President

14–3. *Sounder* (**U.S.A., 1972**), *with Paul Winfield (center) and Cicely Tyson (right), directed by Martin Ritt.*
Repelled by the brutality and racism of the blaxploitation genre, middle-class African Americans were more attracted to the quiet dignity of such films as *Sounder*. The movie deals realistically with the hardships of a black family during the Depression thirties. *Sounder* appealed to white as well as black audiences—unlike blaxploitation, whose audiences were almost exclusively young, black, urban, and poor. *(Twentieth Century–Fox)*

Richard M. Nixon eventually was forced to resign from his office in disgrace. A number of his associates—who flouted the law like gangsters—served prison terms. Public confidence in politicians plunged to an all-time low. A number of Watergate-inspired movies reflected the atmosphere of paranoia and disillusionment of this era: *The Parallax View, Chinatown, Marathon Man, Three Days of the Condor, Godfather II, The Conversation, Serpico,* and of course the film based on the book written by Woodward and Bernstein, *All the President's Men* (**14–4**).

The New Cinema

Paradoxically, in the midst of all this violence, corruption, and despair, the American cinema was undergoing a renaissance. The 1968–1976 era constitutes one of the richest periods in movie history. For the first time in twenty years, film attendance began to rise, not decline. Most of this expanding audience was young (75

14-4. *All the President's Men* (U.S.A., 1976), *with Robert Redford, directed by Alan J. Pakula.*
In addition to being one of the top stars of his generation, Redford was also a distinguished producer. He exercised tight artistic control over his projects, and the results were almost invariably impressive, as can be seen in such Redford productions as *Downhill Racer* (1969) and *The Candidate* (1972), both directed by Michael Ritchie. Redford's production company, Wildwood Enterprises, also produced *All the President's Men*, an excellent adaptation of the best-selling book by Woodward and Bernstein. Redford also tried his hand at directing: *Ordinary People* (1980) not only won the Best Picture Oscar, it also won Redford the Academy Award as Best Director. He also directed the charming fable *The Milagro Beanfield War* (1988), *A River Runs Through It* (1992), a philosophical period film, *Quiz Show* (1994), an insightful dramatization of a famous 1950s television scandal, and *The Horse Whisperer* (1998), a psychological drama set in the American West. *(Warner Brothers)*

percent under age thirty) and well educated. American movies also reasserted their dominance on the international scene. Up to 50 percent of the grosses of American films were—and still are—earned abroad.

Leaders of the film industry were delighted, if somewhat confused, by their sudden good fortune. The studios were now controlled by younger men (many of them under forty) who became more receptive to innovative projects. Since many of the most profitable films of the period were made on relatively small budgets and even without important **stars,** studio executives were willing to gamble on new talent and fresh story ideas. Anyone capable of relating to "the youth market"—or anyone claiming to—was now a viable commercial possibility **(14–5).** An exceptionally large number of young directors made their debuts during this period.

Though the country was racked by runaway inflation—film production costs increased more than 200 percent between 1968 and 1976—the studios prospered. In the first place, most of their investment capital was plowed into six or seven big-budget projects with strong entertainment values. The off-beat movies were often independently produced and later distributed by the major studios. They took a hefty percentage of the grosses without risking much of their own money on pro-

14–5. *American Graffiti* (U.S.A., 1973), *with Candy Clark, Charlie Martin Smith, and Ron Howard, directed by George Lucas.*
Set in the Kennedy era of the early 1960s, this immensely popular movie was largely responsible for the nostalgia craze that swept the country in the 1970s. The film inspired two television series: *Happy Days* and *Laverne and Shirley,* both vastly inferior to the original. The movie's success defied the conventional wisdom of the industry. It was virtually plotless. It featured no big stars. And it was made on a small budget by a very young, fledging director. *(Universal Studios)*

duction. The tax-shelter laws of this period allowed outside investors to finance a film almost risk-free. If the movie failed, the investors would then receive a tax write-off. If it turned out to be a hit, everyone was on easy street. Many films during this period were presented to lay investors as package deals, which included the producer, a story property, the director, and one or more bankable stars (i.e., proven box office magnets).

Perhaps no other period in American film history represents such a radical departure from what preceded it. The time-honored conventions of **classical cinema** were increasingly regarded as old-fashioned and mechanical. The tight, well-made narrative structures that had served American filmmakers since the time of Griffith were now pretty much the province of mass-market entertainments. And even there, the dominance of classical cinema was considerably weakened. The new filmmakers tended to prefer loose, episodic structures. Their movies were more personal, more like European movies. The endings of these films are often unpredictable and inconclusive, not neatly resolved to give a sense of closure to the dramatic materials. Life goes on, even after the final fade-out **(14–6).** Besides, there was always the possibility of a sequel.

14–6. *Chinatown* (U.S.A., 1974), *with Roman Polanski, Jack Nicholson, and Roy Jenson, directed by Polanski.*

The battered hero (Nicholson) of this detective **film noir** is tough, smart, and courageous. But he's no match against the morally degenerate forces that close in on him. Nor is justice finally served at the end of the story, for the protagonist inadvertently precipitates the death of his lover. Life just goes on, sublimely indifferent to the anguish of mere mortals. No other American film of the period is so fatalistic, so immersed in a sense of impotence, defeat, and despair. *(Paramount Pictures)*

Though there were some important exceptions, filmmakers tended to be more interested in exploring the complexities of character rather than the intricacies of plot. A good many of the movies of this era employed variations of the Grand Hotel formula, so named after the 1932 MGM movie of that title. What this formula involves is a central location in which a collection of otherwise disparate characters is thrown together for a limited period of time. The major emphasis is on the interrelationships among the characters. Movies employing this formula include Bogdanovich's *The Last Picture Show,* Michael Ritchie's *Smile,* and Lucas's *American Graffiti.* Many of the films of Robert Altman also employ this formula: *M*A*S*H, Brewster McCloud, McCabe and Mrs. Miller, California Split, Nashville, A Wedding,* and *Short Cuts* **(18–14).**

Even the genre films of this era were different. Traditionally, genres tend to be conservative and resistant to change. In fact, one of the main reasons audiences enjoy them is because they are relatively predictable: They carry us into familiar aesthetic territory. But the genre films of this period were generally **revisionist—** that is, they reversed or undercut an implied classical ideal. By definition, revisionist genres are in the ironic mode, questioning many of the values of the genre in its classical phase **(14–7).**

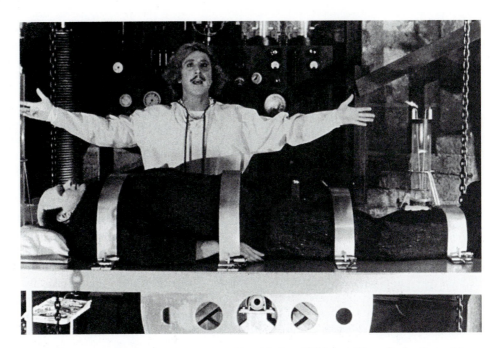

14–7. *Young Frankenstein* **(U.S.A., 1974),** *with Gene Wilder and Peter Boyle, directed by Mel Brooks.*

Film critics and scholars classify genre movies into four main cycles: (1) The *primitive* phase is usually naive, though powerful in its emotional impact, in part because of the novelty of the form. An example of this type of horror film is F. W. Murnau's *Nosferatu the Vampire* (Germany, 1922). (2) The *classical* phase of a genre's evolution is often said to be poised and symmetrical, its values assured and widely shared. There is a balance preserved between the form and the content, which is a mixture of both traditional and original **motifs.** An example of a classical horror movie is James Whale's *Frankenstein* (U.S.A., 1931). (3) *Revisionist* genres are generally symbolic, ambiguous, less certain in their values. They tend to be stylistically complex, appealing more to the intellect than the emotions. Often the genre's preestablished conventions are exploited as ironic foils to question or undermine popular beliefs. A revisionist horror film is Roman Polanski's *Rosemary's Baby* (U.S.A., 1968). (4) The *parodic* phase of a genre's development is an outright mockery of its conventions, reducing them to thumping clichés and presenting them in a comical manner, though often with affection, as in Brooks's *Young Frankenstein*. Most of Brooks's works are parodies of popular American genres. *(Twentieth Century–Fox)*

The revisionist impulse can be seen in many genre films of the period. Bob Fosse's *Cabaret* (1972) is in part a love story, like most classical musicals. But instead of the traditional boy-wins-girl finale, Fosse's bitter tale ends with the girl procuring an illegal abortion and going her solitary way, too fearful and self-absorbed to commit herself to a permanent relationship. Similarly, the detective thrillers of this era do not feature such cool sardonic heroes as Sam Spade, the hero of *The Maltese Falcon* and other films. Spade was almost always in control of his situation. But the new protagonists stumble in confusion, deceived even by their close friends, as in *The Long Goodbye* (1973). The hero of *Chinatown* (1974) is powerless to prevent the tragedy that overwhelms him. And the detective hero of *Night Moves* (1975) can't solve a single problem, professional or personal.

Prior to the Vietnam–Watergate era, the heroes and heroines of most American movies were heroic—that is, they were presented as positive role models. (Implicit in the star system was the belief that stars influence public behavior, and for this reason, most stars refused roles that conflicted with their carefully built-up positive images.) But the times were changing. The protagonists of classical cinema were goal-oriented and purposeful. The new antiheroes were often drifters. Many of them feel alienated and lack a sense of purpose. "I move around a lot," says the Jack Nicholson character in *Five Easy Pieces.* "Not because I'm looking for anything really. But because I'm getting away from things that get bad if I stay." Even those protagonists who do have a set of values and a sense of purpose are often at odds with their environment, which is portrayed as contemptuous or indifferent to their code of honor **(14–8).**

Sex has always been one of the most popular subjects of the American cinema, but never before had it been treated so explicitly as during this period. With the loosening of the censorship code in 1968, American movies soon became the freest and frankest in the world. Virtually everything on the screen was now protected by the First Amendment of the Constitution. By 1972, there were more than seven hundred theaters in the United States exhibiting only hard-core pornography. To say that these movies drained the romance out of sex would be an under-

14–8. *Dirty Harry* **(U.S.A., 1971),** *with Clint Eastwood, directed by Don Siegel.*

Throughout the 1970s and 1980s, Eastwood ranked among the top two or three box office attractions in America. He is one of the few contemporary stars who can generate the **iconic** power of such past giants as John Wayne and Gary Cooper. He rose to fame in Europe during the mid-sixties, playing the violent, tight-lipped "Man With No Name" in a trilogy of Italian-made westerns by Sergio Leone, all of which were enormously popular throughout the world. In his American movies—especially those directed by his mentor Don Siegel—he retained in his **persona** the aura of mystery, the vigilante proclivity for violence, and a profound sense of alienation. A silent, solitary man with a gun—this is the image Eastwood most frequently projects in his films. There is a touch of majesty in his solitude, his implacable single-mindedness, and his private code of honor—so often at odds with the corrupt values surrounding him. He specialized in playing westerners, big-city cops, and working-class loners, but whatever the role, he brings to it a commanding presence, usually with a minimum of dialogue. Eastwood is also an independent producer and a director of considerable accomplishment. Orson Welles described him as "the most underrated director in America." However, in more recent times Eastwood's artistic achievements have received greater critical recognition. In 1980, the prestigious Museum of Modern Art featured a retrospective of his works, an honor accorded only to major artists. In 1992, his revisionist western, *Unforgiven* **(18–12),** received the best picture Oscar, as did Eastwood for his direction. He won his second Oscar for directing *Million Dollar Baby* **(20–37).** *(Warner Brothers)*

statement. In fact, porn usually presents its sex scenes rather clinically, relatively divorced from character or believable feelings. It hardly matters who the genitals in closeup are connected *to*. It's nothing personal.

Of course, for most people the opposite is true. Nothing is more personal than the way lovers make love. Since the publication of the "shocking" books of D. H. Lawrence in the early twentieth century, novelists have known that a character's sexual behavior can reveal much about his or her psyche. Similarly, the sexual revolution in movies allowed filmmakers unprecedented freedom to dramatize an important aspect of their characters' lives. Whether lovers make love tenderly, passionately, violently, ineptly, playfully, coldly, fearfully—it makes a difference in how we view them as characters. What people reveal when they are naked can be intimately spiritual as well as physical.

Oddly enough, this was not a good period for love stories, and sexual scenes were rarely romantic. True, there were a few filmmakers, like Altman and Mazursky **(14–9)**, who explored the relations between the sexes sympathetically. It's also true that the mawkish soap opera *Love Story* (1970) was one of the biggest hits of the

14–9. *Blume in Love* **(U.S.A., 1973),** *with George Segal and Susan Anspach, directed by Paul Mazursky.*
Most of Mazursky's films explore warm, loving relationships in bittersweet tones laced with comedy. However, even the hero of this tender romantic comedy is a part of his times: He rapes rather than woos the woman he loves. Since she is his ex-wife, he feels he has the right. She sets him straight in this scene, nearly nine months later, when she refuses to marry him until he exhibits signs of real manhood, like maturity, loyalty, and consideration for others. Mazursky is an actor, writer, and independent producer as well as a major director of this period. His best works besides *Blume* are *Bob & Carol & Ted & Alice* (1969), *Harry and Tonto* (1974), *Next Stop, Greenwich Village* (1976), *An Unmarried Woman* (1978), *Moscow on the Hudson* (1984), *Down and Out in Beverly Hills* (1988), and *Enemies: A Love Story* (1989). *(Warner Brothers)*

era, but it was an isolated phenomenon, an oddity. For the most part, sex was fused with violence. Many movies of this period contained rape scenes, some in sadistic detail, like *Straw Dogs* and *Frenzy*. Violence against women was common, especially in the films of Peckinpah, Coppola, Scorsese, and Siegel.

Feminist film critics complained, for the most part correctly, that females in American movies were portrayed primarily as sexual playthings for the boys. Women were accorded no serious treatment outside the erotic realm. If they were not relegated to the periphery of the story, they were often ignored entirely. Even very gifted actresses had difficulties finding work during this period. The only female star who consistently placed in the top ten box office attractions was Barbra Streisand. Otherwise, the top ten was pretty much man's country.

The masculinization of American movies coincided with the rise of the feminist movement. Militant feminists like Jane Fonda (**14–10**) fueled the movement, which was growing more vocal in its demands for justice. Several film critics wondered if there was a correlation between the growing stridency of feminism with the increasing brutalization of women in movies like *Joe, A Clockwork Orange, Klute,*

14–10. *Coming Home* (**U.S.A., 1978**), *with Jane Fonda, directed by Hal Ashby.*
Fonda was radicalized by the war in Vietnam. Throughout that era at rallies and college campuses across the country, she was a harsh critic of American militarism, racism, and sexism. She exploited her status as a star to gain publicity and generate support for the protest movement, suffering at the box office for her outspoken views. Nonetheless, she decided to politicize her work as well as her life. Her first Academy Award–winning performance, as a prostitute in Pakula's *Klute* (1971), incorporated many of her feminist convictions. She was usually successful in fusing her political beliefs with her work and everyday life. *Coming Home* was produced by her own production company and won Fonda her second Academy Award. It is a veiled autobiography, tracing her spiritual evolution. *(United Artists)*

Straw Dogs, Lenny, Frenzy, Mean Streets, Magnum Force, Taxi Driver, Carrie, and many others. Of course, the makers of these films didn't necessarily approve of the way women are treated in their movies. Some of them are strongly sympathetic toward their female characters. However, feminist film critics pointed out that even where the treatment is sympathetic, as in Mike Nichols's *Carnal Knowledge* (1971), Cassavetes's *A Woman Under the Influence* (1974), and Scorsese's *Alice Doesn't Live Here Anymore* (1974), the heroines are usually portrayed as helpless victims, incapable of taking control over their own lives without the help of a man.

On the other hand, there were dozens of films during this period in which men got along fine without women, or in which women were simply occasional distractions: *The Dirty Dozen, Husbands, Deliverance, The Last Detail, Bad Company, Fat City, Dirty Harry, The Man Who Would Be King, Patton,* and *The Longest Yard.* In fact, one of the most popular genres of this time was the so-called **buddy film,** an offshoot of the action picture, emphasizing the camaraderie between two adventurous males. The genre is antidomestic and usually excludes important female characters. One critic called them love stories between men, though usually they contain no homoerotic scenes. The love is fraternal rather than sexual. The best buddy films of this era include *Butch Cassidy and the Sundance Kid, Midnight Cowboy, The Sting, Scarecrow,* and *Thunderbolt and Lightfoot.*

Traditionally, the power base for women in the American film industry was the star system, but now very few female stars were considered "bankable." Nor were women welcomed into directing, which would allow them to tell their stories from their own perspectives. Only a few women managed to direct a major commercial movie during this period, most notably Elaine May, whose wryly witty *Heartbreak Kid* (1972) was not successful at the box office. Working primarily out of New York as an independent, Joan Micklin Silver directed several fine movies, the best of which was *Hester Street* (1975). Otherwise, women filmmakers were working mostly in documentaries and **avant-garde** films rather than fiction.

Like virtually every other characteristic of the Vietnam–Watergate cinema, this situation concerning women's issues began to change after the mid-decade. Indeed, by 1977, four of the five Best Picture nominees dealt predominantly with women: *Annie Hall, The Goodbye Girl, Julia, The Turning Point;* and the fifth, *Star Wars,* featured a feisty, resourceful heroine.

Another characteristic of the films of this period is their technical and stylistic panache. Of course, American movies have always been among the best crafted in the world, and Hollywood was a consistent leader in advancing the technology of its art. But implicit in the ideal of a classical style was the principle of transparency. We weren't supposed to admire the camerawork, the editing, or the sound mixing because these were merely the vehicles for conveying the characters in action. European and Japanese movies were long regarded as arty by popular American audiences precisely because they often called attention to their style, sometimes at the expense of the story. This characteristic was especially true of the French New Wave movies of the 1960s—movies that exerted an enormous influence on the young American directors who came to prominence in the Vietnam–Watergate era.

The new directors were often referred to as the "whiz kids" because of their technical razzle-dazzle. Friedkin, Coppola, Lucas, Scorsese, and Spielberg—all of them are capable of exhilarating bravura flourishes. Even the works of established directors like Peckinpah, Kubrick, and Fosse were superbly crafted, with stunning photographic effects, audacious editing techniques, bold and subtle orchestrations in the soundtracks. In climactic scenes especially, these pyrotechnics are often combined simultaneously, as in the famous chase sequence of *The French Connection* **(14–11).**

Sensitive filmmakers tailored their style to suit their materials. For example, Peter Bogdanovich's *The Last Picture Show* (1971) takes place in a dying Texas town, a dead end for most of the young people who are stuck there. Nothing much happens. The future promises only more of the same—or rather, less of the same. Even the sole movie theater is closing down for lack of business. Bogdanovich shot the film in long, languorous **takes,** with very little cutting. (Fast cutting tends to energize a scene.) He often used slow **dissolves** between scenes to suggest dragging time and the boredom most of the characters feel. The style, in short, is organically related to the essential nature of the story, which was written by Larry McMurty, based on his own novel.

Where did the new directors come from? Some got their start in such traditional proving grounds as scriptwriting and television. However, the majority of

14–11. *The French Connection* **(U.S.A., 1971),** *with Gene Hackman and Marcel Bozzuffi, directed by William Friedkin.*

The chase sequence of this movie is a stylistic tour de force, brilliantly orchestrated to keep us at the edges of our seats. During most of the sequence we feel as battered as the speeding auto swerving and screeching through the big-city traffic. The **editing** is punctuated by abrupt **jump-cuts,** explosive juxtapositions, and a driving sense of urgency. The sweeping hand-held camera propels us forward, refusing to allow us to catch our breath or recover our equilibrium. The soundtrack reverberates with a cacophony of gunshots, screams of horrified bystanders, and the shrieking noises of a driverless subway car surging forward like a roller-coaster out of control. The sequence climaxes with this shot in which the detective protagonist (Hackman) finally nails his quarry.   *(Twentieth Century–Fox)*

new filmmakers came from (1) Europe, and especially England; (2) America's university film programs; and (3) the acting profession.

Of course, there was nothing odd about foreign film directors working in America, especially in the silent era. During the years dominated by Hitler's climb to power, there was another massive migration of European talent to Hollywood, most of them German and Austrian Jews who foresaw the tragedy of the Holocaust. A third wave of European migration—primarily from Great Britain—took place in the Vietnam–Watergate era and continues to our own time. In the field of rock music, a similar "British invasion" took place.

Even in the best of times, the British film industry existed in a state of constant crisis. Throughout the 1960s, the best English movies were financed primarily with American capital. By the time the 1970s came around, there wasn't much of a British industry left to finance. Having few other outlets, British filmmakers came to Hollywood to work, and many of them thrived: John Schlesinger, Alan Parker, Ridley Scott, John Boorman, and Peter Yates.

Filmmakers also immigrated from other countries: Norman Jewison from Canada; Franco Zeffirelli from Italy; Louis Malle from France; Bruce Beresford from Australia; Roman Polanski from Poland; and Milos Forman from Czechoslovakia **(14–12).** The myth of the melting pot is somewhat discredited these days, but in American movies the myth still commands credibility. Most of the works of these foreign directors are quintessentially American. They are acutely perceptive in revealing the textures and nuances of American life, the strengths as well as the limitations of the American character.

A second source of directing talent during this era came from the film programs of American universities, three in particular: New York University, the University of Southern California, and the University of California at Los Angeles. Prior to this time, very few mainstream American filmmakers received their training at film schools, which is a pattern more characteristic of the Eastern European nations. For example, both Forman and Polanski received their training at the excellent state film schools of their native countries. Though some American colleges and universities had set up cinema programs as early as the 1920s, the serious study of movies on the university level did not become widespread until the late 1960s.

By 1975, the American Film Institute reported that there were at least three thousand film courses at more than six hundred colleges and universities across the United States. By 1981, that figure had climbed to nearly eight thousand courses. This cinematic self-consciousness gave rise to an unprecedented number of serious film critics and scholars. More critical studies about movies were published during this era than in all previous periods combined. Among the film school graduates of the late sixties and early seventies were Francis Coppola and Paul Schrader (both from UCLA), George Lucas and John Milius (both from USC), and Martin Scorsese and Brian De Palma (both from NYU).

No other generation could boast so many filmmakers coming from the ranks of the acting profession. Some of these performers directed only one or a few movies: Jack Nicholson, Peter Fonda, Dennis Hopper, Jack Lemmon, Warren Beatty, George C. Scott, Robert Duvall, Ossie Davis, Alan Arkin, Elaine May, Burt Reynolds, Alan Alda, and Barbra Streisand are some. A surprising number of actors have directed major works, including Paul Newman, John Cassavetes, Robert Redford, Clint Eastwood, Kevin Costner, Mel Brooks, and Woody Allen. Brooks and Allen are writers as much as actors, but virtually all these performers are "hyphenates"—that is, they function in multiple capacities, such as actor-producer-director. Being a hyphenate guarantees creative control.

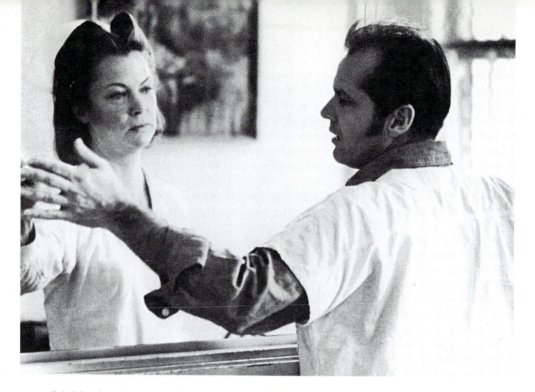

14–12. *One Flew Over the Cuckoo's Nest* (U.S.A., 1975), *with Jack Nicholson and Louise Fletcher, directed by Milos Forman.*

One of the leading filmmakers of Czechoslovakia's famous Prague Spring (see Chapter 13), Forman fled to America when Soviet tanks rumbled into his country and toppled the liberal regime of popular Premier Alexander Dubcek. Forman is not a prolific artist, but his American movies constitute some of the finest works of recent times. *Taking Off* (1971), a warm comedy reminiscent of his Czech movies, is a wry exploration of American suburbanites in panic. *Cuckoo's Nest* was a huge hit and swept the top five Academy Awards: Best Picture, Best Director, Best Screenplay (Lawrence Hauben and Bo Goldman based on the novel by Ken Kesey), Best Actor (Nicholson), and Best Actress (Fletcher). Forman's next film, *Hair* (1979), was a bold and moving adaptation of the famous stage musical of the 1960s. *Ragtime* (1981) was a sensitive translation of the great American novel by E. L. Doctorow. *Amadeus* (1984), another stage adaptation, was widely praised critically and won a Best Picture Oscar, as well as the Best Director Award for Forman. Like most of his adaptations, it differs considerably from the original. *(United Artists)*

Major Figures

ROBERT ALTMAN (b. 1925) was the elder statesman of the directors who came to prominence during this era. A failed writer as a young man, he became a busy television director in the 1960s. He repeatedly attempted to break into movies during this time, but with disappointing results. He was forty-five years old when producer Ingo Preminger offered him the job of directing *M*A*S*H* **(14–13).** Reputedly, Altman was Preminger's fifteenth choice.

The movie is his first mature work and contains many trademark characteristics: (1) the deemphasis of plot in favor of **aleatory** structures; (2) a strong concern with characterization; (3) a subversion of genre expectations (most of Altman's movies are genre films, all of them in the revisionist mode); (4) a throwaway style of acting, based on improvisation; (5) a documentary visual style; (6) the use of overlapping dialogue; and (7) an essentially pessimistic view of the human condition, though often expressed in comic form.

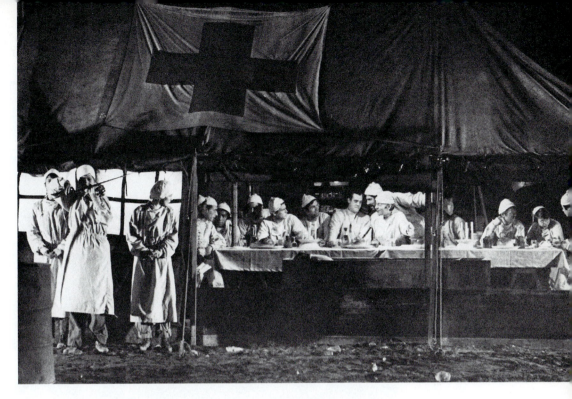

14–13. *M*A*S*H* (U.S.A., 1970), *directed by Robert Altman.*
M*A*S*H is filled with jokey sound techniques and visual gags, like this parody of Leonardo's *Last Supper.* The huge success of the movie took almost everyone by surprise. It was the most popular antiwar comedy in history, grossing an astonishing $40 million. It also won the Grand Prize at the Cannes Film Festival and established Altman as a favorite with critics, artists, and intellectuals. It inspired a popular television series, and though it was considerably laundered in comparison with the raunchy humor of the movie, it was nonetheless one of the most sophisticated sitcoms ever offered on American TV. Its final episode, aired in 1983, captured the largest viewing audience in television history. *(Twentieth Century–Fox)*

Some critics have attempted to superimpose a thematic unity on Altman's films, but he claims that they've been distorted in the process. "I don't want anybody to come out with the right answer, because I don't think there is any right answer," he insists. Mostly he's interested in exploring character. But we never have the sense that a given character can be finally summed up in an Altman movie, for there are too many surprises and too much that's left deliberately ambiguous.

Some of his characters manage to be funny, repellent, and endearing at the same time. In *Nashville* **(14–14),** for example, one of the major characters is the rich and powerful Haven Hamilton (Henry Gibson), a country-and-western singer and self-appointed city father. An unctuous egomaniac, Hamilton lards his talk with tired homilies on family, country, and God. Yet near the end of the film, when an assassin's bullet cuts down one of his dearest friends, this same strutting pipsqueak of self-importance is the only person with the presence of mind to calm a panicky audience, even though he's wounded himself.

Altman explores characters in groups that are in a state of flux, where human affections are transitory, provisional. In the harsher films, like *McCabe and Mrs. Miller* (1970), *Thieves Like Us* (1974), *Nashville, A Wedding* (1978), *The Player* (1992), and *Short Cuts* (1993), the characters are left with their dreams dispersed, the fragile strands of love and affection blasted often by a traumatizing death. The

14–14. *Nashville* **(U.S.A., 1975),** *directed by Robert Altman.*
Altman is a master at capturing privileged moments that can fuse conflicting emotions. In this scene, for example, a sweet but spectacularly untalented singer (Gwen Welles) has just learned that she is expected to perform a striptease at an all-male political smoker. To further her career, she agrees, and the subsequent performance is at once funny, touching, and sad. Altman is not concerned with scoring plot points in such scenes. He simply wants to capture the beauty and poignance of a fleeting event: "I have no philosophy. All I'm trying to do is paint a picture and show it to you. It's like a sand castle. It's going to go away." *(Paramount Pictures)*

survivors seldom have permanent roots to solace them. Almost invariably, the movies conclude on a note of loss, disintegration, and defeat.

Altman was fascinated by the element of chance in his films. His scripts were rarely written out in advance, and he encouraged his actors to improvise much of their dialogue. He sometimes used multiple cameras to capture a variety of viewpoints of the same scene. "It's like jazz," Altman explained. "You're not planning any of this that you film. You're capturing. You can't even hope to see it, you just turn on the camera and hope to capture it." By using these aleatory methods, he was able to convey a sense of spontaneity, surprise.

Throughout the 1970s, Altman averaged better than a movie a year. He was also a generous friend, producing several films of his colleagues.

Francis Ford Coppola (b. 1939) was the most prestigious filmmaker of the 1970s. He was an idol to such younger artists as Steven Spielberg, the darling of critics on several continents, and a favorite with the public, especially for his popular *Godfather* films **(14–15).** An intellectual, a media personality, and an extravagant showman, Coppola consistently dumbfounded the film industry by his artistic daring and reckless disregard for money, which he considered to be merely a work

14–15. *The Godfather* (U.S.A., 1972), *with Al Pacino, directed by Francis Ford Coppola.* Commerce and art are not necessarily the deadly enemies they're often said to be. *The Godfather* was the highest-grossing movie in history and is still among the all-time box office champions. Yet the movie, along with its sequel (most critics regard them as a single work), is also one of the most critically admired of the contemporary cinema. Critic James Monaco described it as "the most significant American film since *Citizen Kane." (Paramount Pictures)*

tool. "Caution doesn't make for good show business or good art," he insisted. Since then, he has probably tempered this view.

Coppola didn't begin his career very auspiciously. His first movie was a softcore porn film that he financed himself. His second was a cheapie horror movie produced (on a preposterously small budget) by **B-film** producer and director Roger Corman. Corman gave many young filmmakers their first break, including Martin Scorsese, Dennis Hopper, Peter Bogdanovich, and Jack Nicholson. Coppola's first important movie, *You're a Big Boy Now* (1967), was his M.F.A. thesis film at UCLA, but it failed to create much of a stir critically or commercially. His next two movies—*Finian's Rainbow* (1968) and *The Rain People* (1969)—were also flops.

It was as a writer that Coppola managed to earn credibility within the industry. He won an Academy Award for coscripting Franklin Schaffner's *Patton* (1970). Since then he scripted or coscripted all of his own movies.

When he was assigned to direct *The Godfather*, which no one expected to be an important movie, he worked on the script with Mario Puzo, who had written the best-selling novel on which the film is based. Coppola also insisted on using Marlon Brando in the leading role of an elderly Mafia chieftain. (Brando was then considered box office poison because very few of his films of the previous decade had prospered.) Coppola cast mostly unknown performers of Italian descent in the other roles, to guarantee a sense of authenticity. Because of his painstaking attention to detail, the three-hour-long film not only broke every previous box office record, it also garnered rave reviews. The movie won the Best Picture Oscar, Brando took the top prize as Best Actor, and Coppola received his second Award for writing.

The Godfather, Part II (1974) turned out to be even more astonishing. It dovetailed perfectly with the first film, adding depth and richness to the story and expanding its political implications. The movie was three hours and twenty minutes long, but nobody complained. Critic Pauline Kael called it "an epic vision of the corruption of America." The movie was compared in its romantic sweep and power to the operas of Verdi and the great epic novels of the nineteenth century. (The third *Godfather* installment was made in 1990, and it is an embarrassment.)

In all three installments, the Mafia family is used as a metaphor for corruption in all spheres of power, including big business and government. At one point, the new don, Michael Corleone (Al Pacino), says to a slimy U.S. senator, "We're both part of the same hypocrisy." In *Part II,* Coppola dramatizes how the Corleone family plans to expand its operations to Cuba, which has a "friendly government," headed by the dictator Batista. Seated on a sunny penthouse terrace, Michael and a number of corporate executives—representing such U.S. industries as communications, mining, leisure, tourism, etc.—are assured that the rebel activity (Castro's guerrillas) will soon be suppressed. A huge cake with a map of Cuba on it is wheeled out to celebrate the birthday of one of the delegates. As these fat cats discuss how they will exploit the "resources" of the country, Coppola keeps cutting back to the dwindling cake, which likewise is being sliced away and fed to non-Cubans. Coppola won three Academy Awards, for producing, writing, and directing *The Godfather, Part II.*

At the Cannes Film Festival, another of his films, the low-keyed masterpiece *The Conversation* (1974), swept the Grand Prize and established Coppola as something of a culture hero among European intellectuals. Five years later, his long-awaited *Apocalypse Now* (1979) shared the top prize at Cannes with Volker Schlöndorff's *The Tin Drum.*

Unfortunately, Coppola's subsequent films proved disappointing. The best, *Rumble Fish* (1983) and *Peggy Sue Got Married* (1986), are both stylish entertainments, but hardly major works. Throughout the 1970s, however, Coppola remained a role model for other socially committed artists, such as Hal Ashby **(14–16).**

MARTIN SCORSESE (b. 1942) grew up in an Italian American ghetto in New York City. He originally planned to enter the Roman Catholic priesthood but decided instead to study cinema at New York University. Thanks to several prize-winning short films that he had directed as a student, he managed to become an editor, specializing in rock documentaries, most notably *Woodstock* (1969). After directing a Roger Corman cheapie, he got a chance to direct his first important feature, *Mean Streets* (1973). The movie was strongly praised by critics and established Scorsese as a promising newcomer.

Like most of his films, *Mean Streets* is intensely violent and reflects his childhood environment. "There was always blood in the streets," Scorsese has recalled of his youth in New York's Little Italy. "We saw fighting as the answer to most prob-

14–16. *Being There* **(U.S.A., 1979),** *with Peter Sellers and Shirley McLain, directed by Hal Ashby.*
Like many American filmmakers who began their careers during the Vietnam–Watergate era, Ashby (1932–1988) was strongly anti-Establishment in his sentiments and often satirized the abuse of power. Based on a novel by Jerzy Kosinski (who also wrote the script), *Being There* ridicules the gullibility of people at the top, eager to embrace any scheme, however imbecilic, so long as it coincides with their selfish interests. Ashby's other major works include *The Landlord* (1970), *Harold and Maude* (1971), *The Last Detail* (1973), *Shampoo* (1975), *Bound for Glory* (1976), and *Coming Home* (1978). *(United Artists)*

lems. Violence has always been a pretty scary thing for me, but I'm fascinated by it. It's always erupting when you don't expect it." Most of his protagonists are groping, inarticulate, trying desperately to break out of the confines of their narrow lives. Often they resort to violence because they have no other outlets. The unifying thread that runs through most of Scorsese's movies—*Mean Streets, Alice Doesn't Live Here Any More* (1974), *Taxi Driver* (1976), *New York, New York* (1977), *Raging Bull* (1980), *The King of Comedy* (1982), *The Color of Money* (1986), *The Last Temptation of Christ* (1989), *GoodFellas* (1990) and *The Aviator* (2004)—is the theme of the outsider, struggling for recognition. "I realize that all my life, I've been an outsider," Scorsese has admitted. "I splatter bits of myself all over the screen. I go to shrinks. But they might as well look at the movies."

Savage as it is, Scorsese's universe is shot through with wisps of transient beauty and tenderness. *Raging Bull,* a biography of Jake La Motta, the middle-weight boxing champion of the 1940s, is visceral in its impact yet paradoxically

14–17. *Taxi Driver* (U.S.A., 1976), *with Martin Scorsese and Robert De Niro, directed by Scorsese.*

Scorsese's protagonists are often hard to like, and all of them are to some degree neurotic, but the main character of *Taxi Driver* (De Niro) is an outright psychotic. In a weird stroke of irony, the character was loosely modeled on the would-be assassin of Governor George Wallace and served as an inspiration to John Hinkley III, the would-be assassin of President Ronald Reagan. *Taxi Driver* was Scorsese's most violent film to date, and it scored a big success with the public. Despite its disjointed structure, it was hailed by critics as a major work and won the top prize at the 1976 Cannes Film Festival.   *(Columbia Pictures)*

filled with images of striking beauty **(14–18).** Several scenes are introduced or concluded with poetic still-life shots of a discarded piece of clothing, a coffee cup, an empty room. Michael Chapman's striking black-and-white cinematography is harshly contrasting, with virtually no grays to mediate between the extremes of light and dark—a tribute to the American **film noir** movies of the 1940s. The handheld camera often swirls out of control, kineticizing the **mise en scène** with a terrifying mercurial instability. At other times, the camera glides overhead, choreographed in **slow motion** to the majestically solemn music of Mascagni. Many of the camera **angles** are low and steep, the fighters towering above us like savage combatants. The staccato editing style jams the images together to produce a sense of frenzied collision. Scorsese **intercuts** brief shots of sweat pouring down torsos, blood splattering off a fighter's face as he's dealt a stupefying blow, sponges soaked in bloodied water as it pours over the boxers' overheated bodies. The soundtrack throbs with the thud of leather pounding flesh, hissing noises, and animal screeches, as though we were in a primordial jungle. The sound **fades** in and out, suggesting a diminishment of consciousness. The boxing arenas are steaming pits, suffocating in smoke and rising heat waves that ripple the surface of the images. Glaring spotlights tear up the pervasive blackness of these infernal regions, producing a sense of visual anguish. In a 1989 poll of film critics, *Raging Bull* was voted the greatest American movie of the 1980s.

14–18. *Raging Bull* (U.S.A., 1980), *with Robert De Niro, directed by Martin Scorsese.*
Although Scorsese has attempted to expand his thematic range—most notably with the underrated *King of Comedy* and the refined *Age of Innocence*—the director is best known for his movies dealing with the violent and sometimes larcenous denizens of New York's Italian-American ghettos. *Raging Bull* was voted by a panel of film critics as the greatest American movie of the 1980s. *(United Artists)*

Structurally, Scorsese's movies are seldom slick or polished. The disjointed scenes are seared together by the sheer force of the director's personality. There are frequent gaps in the continuity of the story, and instead of concluding smoothly, they often simply stop. In part this ragged quality is deliberate, paralleling the raggedness of the characters' lives. Scorsese also likes to improvise on the set, and he shoots massive amounts of footage. In the editing stage, he is forced to discard many of these scenes to confine his movie to a reasonable running time—hence the rough, jumpy sense of discontinuity.

Robert De Niro is Scorsese's most frequent collaborator, and the actor won a Best Actor Oscar for his performance in *Raging Bull.* His gallery of characters in Scorsese's films is impressive: the arrogant, slightly crazy Johnny Boy in *Mean Streets;* the scary wacko Travis Bickle in *Taxi Driver* (**14–17**); the hustling saxophonist in *New York, New York;* the boxer hero of *Raging Bull,* which is a quintessential description of him; the obnoxious egomaniac Rupert Pupkin, who yearns to be a famous stand-up comic, in *The King of Comedy;* and the cold-blooded gangster of *GoodFellas.* De Niro dares us to like him in Scorsese's movies, but he never falls back on personal charm as most stars do. De Niro *acts* that small flicker of humanity that makes these misfits morally salvageable.

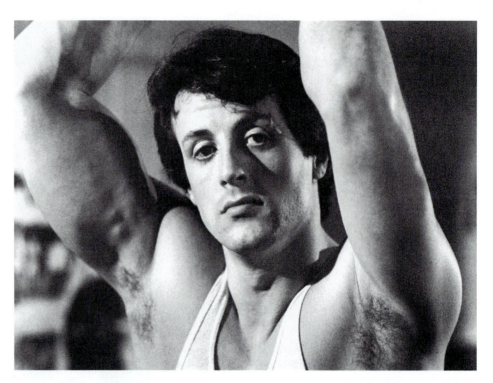

14–19. *Rocky* **(U.S.A., 1976),** *with Sylvester Stallone, directed by John Avildsen.*
Shortly after the middle of the decade, American movies—especially the blockbuster hits like
Stallone's *Rocky* series—became progressively more optimistic, less concerned with social tensions. The happy ending made a comeback, as did such traditional values as the success ethic.
The characters were less complex—straightforward and goal-oriented. Action frequently took
precedence over theme or depth of characterization. Above all, American movies after the
mid-1970s sought to uplift the spirits in an entertaining way. They did so primarily by escaping from the real world and entering the reel world, where perseverance, hard work, and sincerity always pay off.   *(United Artists)*

WOODY ALLEN (b. 1935) was born and raised in New York City—where he still
lives and works. He began his career in the 1950s while he was still in his teens,
writing for television's famous comedy program *Your Show of Shows,* starring Sid
Caesar. Three senior writers for the show were Neil Simon, Mel Brooks, and Carl
Reiner. In the early 1960s, Allen decided to try stand-up comedy at various Greenwich Village clubs. Although he was terrified by the experience, he eventually
proved to be a popular performer. Never content to rest on his laurels, he soon
turned his attention to the Broadway stage, where two of his comedies were produced and later turned into movies. The better of these is *Play It Again, Sam*
(1972), which Allen wrote and starred in, though it was directed by Herbert Ross.
Allen is also a gifted essayist and frequently contributes humorous pieces to such
prestigious literary magazines as *The New Yorker.*

His first attempt at directing his own movie was *Take the Money and Run*
(1969), which he also wrote and starred in. A parody of **cinéma vérité** documentaries, the movie—like most of Allen's early works—is disjointed and episodic, but
sprinkled with brilliant comic bits and pieces. *Bananas* (1971), a political parody

dealing loosely with a South American revolution, was a stylistic improvement over the crudities of his first film, but still far from polished. *Everything You Always Wanted to Know about Sex* (1972) was an anthology film, a series of short sketches more or less unified by the theme of sex—an obsessive preoccupation with Allen. *Sleeper* (1973) was a sci-fi parody set in the future.

Throughout these movies, Allen developed a comic **persona** that was partly based on the popular film comedian of the 1940s, Bob Hope, and partly based on Allen Konigsberg, aka Woody Allen. The Bob Hope side: Woody is not gracefully endowed by nature. Small, frail, klutzy, and slightly frazzled, he is rather cowardly when confronted by danger—usually in the form of bullies. He is also nobody's fool and knows that the better part of valor is discretion. His sotto voce cynical one-liners, muttered mostly to himself, are often ignoble, if too horribly true. He's a born kvetcher, complaining that the world does not devote itself to fulfilling his fantasies of success. Sex-obsessed, he is not very successful in wooing women, mostly because he has difficulties relating to them as people. Sex gets in the way. Despite these considerable deficiencies, he is immensely likable, perhaps because he appeals to our practical, unromantic side.

14–20. *Manhattan* (**U.S.A., 1979**), *with Diane Keaton and Woody Allen, written and directed by Allen.*
Manhattan is a contemporary comedy of manners, satirizing the self-absorbed narcissism of a group of New York intellectuals, who ought to be conducting their lives with more competence than they're willing to command. Allen's thematic emphasis is on the immorality of expediency in human relations. Though his moral code is less flabby than those of his peers, even the protagonist is not above placing self-gratification above loyalty.   *(United Artists)*

Woody Allen is Jewish, intellectual, and a New Yorker—three important aspects of his persona and his sensibility. New York Jewish might also be considered a style, since it also characterizes the comedy of Neil Simon, Elaine May, Mel Brooks, Carl Reiner, Joan Rivers, Jerry Seinfeld, and Jon Stewart. This type of comedy emphasizes ethnic clichés: guilt, neurosis, sexual obsessiveness, inadequacy anxieties, Jewish mothers, and so on. New York Jewish comedy is skeptical, understated, and wryly ironic. It is often directed at the self. Allen's humor is strongly intellectual, though it sometimes takes the form of anti-intellectualism. His gags sometimes allude to such highbrow literary figures as Franz Kafka and August Strindberg. But Allen is equally adept at slapstick. No other film artist can match the sheer breadth of his comic arsenal.

Allen's earlier films emphasized the Bob Hope side of his persona. Beginning with his first masterpiece, *Annie Hall* (1977), the autobiographical side predominated. In both substance and style, *Annie Hall* represented a new direction for

14–21. *Stardust Memories* (**U.S.A., 1980**), *with Woody Allen and Dorothy Leon, directed by Allen.*

Like Fellini's *8½*, on which this film is loosely based, *Stardust Memories* is a blend of comedy and serious ideas. Most of the ideas Allen explores revolve around his three thematic obsessions: art, love, and death. They include the search for the perfect woman; the transience of love; self-contradiction; the enervating toll of celebrity and fame; the lack of faith in "relationships"; artistic illusion versus crass reality; the inexorability of decay and death; and the search for meaning in the moral void of contemporary life. The movie also includes a number of slapstick routines. One of the most endearing episodes deals with the hero's problems with his housekeeper-cook (pictured). Flaky, jittery, and bewildered, she can barely see through her thick eyeglasses, much less perform such subtle tasks as lighting the oven without creating a conflagration in the kitchen.   *(United Artists)*

14–22. *Star Wars* **(U.S.A., 1977),** *directed by George Lucas.*
Star Wars broke every box office record in history, grossing a staggering $216 million in Canada and the United States alone. In addition, its earnings from such tie-in products as dolls, T-shirts, and toys topped the $500 million mark. The second two films of the trilogy were produced but not directed by Lucas. *The Empire Strikes Back* (1980, directed by Irvin Kershner) and *The Return of the Jedi* (1983, directed by Richard Marquand) also broke through the $200 million mark, placing them all among the top ten box office champions. The trilogy's charm and whimsy—not to speak of its superb special effects—appealed especially to teenagers, many of whom returned to see the movies again and again and again. Lucas has a special rapport with young people, and he even talks about his movies as though they were childish play rather than grownup work: "I'm very much akin to a toy-maker. If I wasn't a filmmaker, I'd probably *be* a toy-maker. I like to make things move and I like to make them myself. Just give me the tools and I'll make the toys. I can sit forever doodling on my movie." *(Twentieth Century–Fox)*

Allen. Essentially a romantic comedy, the film is bittersweet and poignant, appealing more to the emotions than his previous works, which were funny but rarely moving. The movie is also stylistically assured, the work of an accomplished directorial technician, thanks in part to the brilliant cinematographer, Gordon Willis, who photographed many of Allen's films. There are the usual Allen virtues: the droll one-liners, the comic persona, the witty literate dialogue, and a charming comedienne (Diane Keaton) as his costar.

Since then, Allen has averaged almost a movie per year, in addition to writing an occasional play and a considerable number of humorous essays. In his extraordinary self-discipline and devotion to his art, he resembles his idol, Ingmar

Bergman. Of course, not all of his movies since *Annie Hall* have been successful. Allen is seldom at his best outside the comic range, and such noncomic works as *Interiors* (1978), *September* (1987), *Another Woman* (1988), and *Shadows and Fog* (1992) can only be described as honorable failures.

But otherwise, what an embarrassment of riches he provided in the 1980s: *Stardust Memories* **(14–21),** with its striking black-and-white cinematography and complex philosophical themes; *Zelig* (1983), a parody of television documentaries, exploring the tribulations that accompany fame, a recurring theme in his **oeuvre;** *Broadway Danny Rose* (1984), a warm, poignant comedy, filled with ethnic humor and characteristically moral in its emphasis; the brilliant *Purple Rose of Cairo* (1985), a heady Pirandellian exercise in truth and illusion, set in the Depression thirties, playing with the idea of cinema as escape; *Hannah and Her Sisters* (1986), a comedy of manners, reminiscent of *Manhattan* in its Grand Hotel structure and its moral emphasis; the nostalgic *Radio Days* (1987), filled with wonderfully funny performances, especially by Mia Farrow, who has done her finest work with Allen; and *Crimes and Misdemeanors* (1989), a very dark comedy, which critics proclaimed one of his greatest works.

People didn't wake up one morning and cheerily announce, "We're in the post–*Star Wars* era." The stridently self-critical movies of the 1968–1976 period receded only gradually, and never entirely disappeared. Once the war in Vietnam had been concluded, however, Americans were forced to deal with problems closer to home—economic hard times. People wanted escape, hope, and cheer from their movies, and audiences found these qualities in such blockbuster hits as the *Rocky* films, the James Bond series (still churning after all those years), the *Superman* movies, and especially the *Star Wars* trilogy of George Lucas **(14–22).** The filmmaker most attuned to the sensibility of the new era, however, was probably STEVEN SPIELBERG (b. 1948).

Spielberg was a whiz kid par excellence. Even as a child growing up in the suburbs of New Jersey and Arizona, he knew he wanted to be a filmmaker. As a teenager, he shot several 8-mm movies, then graduated to 16-mm. A total film freak, he read widely about movies and saw as many as he could. Like many filmmakers of his generation, his own works are filled with homages and **allusions** to other movies, genres, and filmmakers. After graduating from college with a degree in English, he moved to Hollywood, where he befriended Lucas, Coppola, and other hungry young cinéastes.

On the basis of some student films he had made, the twenty-one-year-old Spielberg was hired by MCA (the parent organization of Universal Pictures) to direct episodes of various television series. Confident, charming, and clever, Spielberg soon convinced MCA to allow him to direct some made-for-TV movies. *Duel* (1971), the best of these, was released theatrically in Europe, where it was well received both critically and commercially, especially in Great Britain and France. A slightly paranoid fable of a suburbanite being stalked on the highway by an anonymous, menacing truck, the film is technically dazzling, if somewhat shallow thematically. Like several of Spielberg's other movies, it is strongly indebted to the works of Hitchcock, especially in its buildup of suspense and its taut editing style.

Spielberg's first American theatrical feature was *The Sugarland Express* (1974), a more serious chase film and one of the few movies he's directed without a happy ending. It created no big stir. When he was assigned to direct *Jaws* (1975), he was plagued by bad luck on location, but he persisted and saw the project through.

14–23. *E. T.: The Extra Terrestrial* (U.S.A., 1982), *with Henry Thomas and E. T., directed by Steven Spielberg.*
"A film is a ribbon of dreams," Orson Welles once stated. "The camera is much more than a recording apparatus, it is a medium via which messages reach us from another world that is not ours and that brings us to the heart of a great secret. Here magic begins." *(Universal Studios)*

The movie grossed $133 million and was the top money-maker of all time—for a time. (Box office precedents were shattered throughout this period: Virtually all the top ten box office champions have been released since 1970.) Since *Jaws*, Spielberg has initiated all of his own projects.

Close Encounters of the Third Kind (1977), another popular success, was a sci-fi fantasy. Though weak on character and somewhat glib thematically, the movie is sprinkled with wit and warm humor. It is clearly the work of a stylistic virtuoso, particularly in its **special effects,** its editing, and its inventive mise en scène. Like Walt Disney, another major influence on his work, Spielberg at his best is able to create an enchanted, self-enclosed universe, allowing us to suspend our disbelief, to forget the prosaic realities of everyday life. Spielberg followed this film with the comedy *1941* (1979), a mechanical, soulless exercise in contrivance that fared poorly with both the public and the press.

Spielberg's next film, *Raiders of the Lost Ark* (1981), is an homage to the weekly movie **serials** of the World War II era, complete with nefarious Nazi villains and an intrepid hero. Overflowing with verve, romance, exotic locales, and high-spirited fun, its story line is one breathless adventure piled on top of another. Its protagonist is a dashing and resourceful anthropologist–adventurer. The movie succeeds because it's both exciting and playfully tongue-in-cheek in its tone, like many of the films of Hitchcock. *Raiders* was another blockbuster hit for Spielberg. Its two sequels, *Indiana Jones and the Temple of Doom* (1984) and *Indiana Jones and the Last Crusade* (1989), provided more of the same—only in a more mechanical manner.

E. T.: The Extra-Terrestrial **(14–23)** was Spielberg's masterpiece to date. Like its sister film, *Close Encounters, E. T.* is a sci-fi fantasy, but far more powerful in its emotional impact. Less plotted than Spielberg's other movies, *E. T.* is a film of poetic textures and nuances. It puts us back in touch with the beauty and innocence of children, triggering childhood memories of imaginary best friends, scary-looking creatures, the Unknown. Spielberg contrasts the reassuring rituals of suburban America with the awesome wonders of a superior alien culture, and he manages to bridge the gap, making the future seem a little less fearful and, possibly, an enthralling adventure. *E. T.* displaced *Star Wars* as the top money-maker in history, grossing $360 million in Canada and the United States alone. Its worldwide gross is estimated to be in the range of $550–$600 million. The tie-in products based on the movie constituted a virtual empire of cottage industries, reaping hundreds of millions more.

Spielberg's somewhat Disneyesque adaptation of Alice Walker's Pulitzer Prize–winning novel, *The Color Purple* (1985), was criticized for its sugarcoated visual style as well as for virtually eliminating the lesbian theme that figures so prominently in the novel. Nonetheless, the movie was a big popular success, in part thanks to a superb performance by Whoopie Goldberg in its leading role.

With the somber *Empire of the Sun* (1987), Spielberg announced he was planning to move away from the light entertainment fare he was famous for, toward more serious stories with greater thematic complexity and richer characterizations. The style of the film is less flamboyant. The story—about World War II Japanese prisoner-of-war camps as seen through the eyes of a young boy—is episodic, slow. The editing is subdued, lyrical rather than ratta-tat-tat. The surrealistic images are haunting and poetic, but they don't grab you by the lapels, as in Spielberg's other films. In short, this is the work of a more thoughtful artist—more nuanced, darker. In more recent times, Spielberg has alternated between pop blockbuster hits like *Jurassic Park* and serious artistic projects like *Schindler's List* and *Saving Private Ryan* **(18–13),** both masterpieces.

The 1970s began in turmoil and ended in a return to traditional values, best illustrated perhaps by the conservative agenda of the Reagan years in the 1980s. For some, this symbolized a trip from darkness to light. For others, it represented the transformation of a great promise into that familiar 1980s phrase, "diminished expectations."

FURTHER READING

BISKIND, PETER. *Easy Riders, Raging Bulls*. Simon & Schuster, 1998. Subtitled *How the sex-drugs-rock-'n'-roll generation saved Hollywood,* a very shrewd assessment of the 1970s film generation.

BOGLE, DONALD. *Toms, Coons, Mulattoes, Mammies, and Bucks*. New York: Bantam Books, 1974. An interpretive history of black actors and characters in American movies.

CAGIN, SETH, and PHILIP DRAY. *Hollywood Films of the Seventies: Sex, Drugs, Violence, Rock 'n' Roll and Politics*. New York: Harper and Row, 1984.

COOK, DAVID A. *Last Illusions: American Cinema in the Shadow of Watergate and Vietnam 1970–1979*. Berkeley: Univ. of Cal. Press, 2000. Volume of the excellent series, *History of the American Cinema*.

DITTMAR, LINDA, and GENE MICHAUD. *From Hanoi to Hollywood*. New Brunswick, N.J.: Rutgers University, Press, 1990. The Vietnam war in American movies.

KEYSER, LES. *Hollywood in the Seventies*. Cranbury, N.J.: A. S. Barnes, 1981. Survey of major works.

KOLKER, ROBERT PHILIP. *A Cinema of Loneliness*. New York: Oxford University Press, 1980. A sophisticated critical analysis of the works of Penn, Kubrick, Coppola, Scorsese, and Altman.

LEV, PETER. *American Films of the 70s: Conflicting Visions*. Austin: Univ. of Texas Press, 2001. A survey of Ten key genres of the decade.

MONACO, JAMES. *American Film Now*. New York: Oxford University Press, 1979. An astute discussion of the contemporary American cinema as art and industry, and the complex interrelationships between the two.

SQUIRE, JAMES E., ed. *The Movie Business Book*. Englewood Cliffs, N.J.: Prentice-Hall, Inc., 1983. A collection of essays by various artists and industry professionals about the financing of motion pictures.

15

International Cinema in the 1970s

I seek planets that do not exist and landscapes that have only been dreamed.
—WERNER HERZOG

Warner Brothers

Timeline: 1970–1979

1970
Paris: second year of peace talks between United States and North Vietnam; no progress
Nobel Prize for Literature: Soviet novelist Alexander Solzhenitsyn, dissident

1971
Fighting in Indochina spreads to Laos and Cambodia; large-scale bombing of North Vietnam by United States
U.S.S.R. softlands a space capsule on Mars

1972
Sporadic Arab–Israeli violence throughout Mideast

1973
Number of Vietnamese civilians wounded in war: 935,000
Arab oil embargo—worldwide energy crisis; price of oil skyrockets

1974
Worldwide inflation due to huge increases in cost of energy; net profits of oil companies increase 93 percent
Drought causes famine throughout much of sub-Saharan Africa

1975
Fanatical Khmer Rouge regime embarks on murderous campaign to "reform" Cambodia's educated citizens—three million Cambodians killed by their own government
Epidemic of kidnappings by radical leftists in many countries of the world

1977
Nobel Peace Prize: Amnesty International—human rights organization

1979
Revolutions in Nicaragua (left wing) and Iran (right wing); U.S. hostage crisis in Iran
Margaret Thatcher (Conservative) becomes British Prime Minister; Nobel Peace Prize: Mother Teresa

A proliferation of ideologies—new voices. British flash: Nicholas Roeg, Ken Russell, and Monty Python for laughs. France's Bertrand Blier and Diane Kurys. *Das Neue Kino*—West Germany in the American Age. Schlöndorff, Wenders, Herzog, and Fassbinder: dark fables. Italy from the Left: Bertolucci, the Taviani brothers, and Wertmüller. The censored cinema of Eastern Europe. Andrei Tarkovsky and the Soviet Union. The lure of the past: Nikita Mikalkov. The Australian New Wave. The poetics of Peter Weir. Bruce Beresford, Gillian Armstrong, George Miller, and Fred Schepisi—fresh views. Emerging cinema—Third World voices. Senegal's Ousmane Sembene. Brazil, Argentina, and Turkey.

THE INTERNATIONAL CINEMA OF THE 1970s was characterized by national movements—*Das Neue Kino* in West Germany, the sudden Australian film boom, and the struggling cinemas of the Third World. It was also a period of "isms"—feminism, Marxism, nationalism—and an era of liberation movements—black liberation, gay lib, women's lib, and so on. Three important women filmmakers debuted during this period—France's Diane Kurys, Australia's Gillian Armstrong, and the most widely admired, Italy's Lina Wertmüller. In the Communist bloc countries, restrictions loosened somewhat, especially in Poland, Hungary, and the U.S.S.R.

Great Britain

Throughout the 1970s, the British cinema was in a state of decline. Its best directors were working in British television or live theater or in America. There were a few bright spots, however, such as the popular James Bond movies and the gleeful assaults of the Monty Python Flying Circus troupe **(15–1),** for whom no institution was beyond zapping, provided it was done in the proper spirit of grossness and bad taste.

The films of a former cinematographer, Nicholas Roeg (b. 1928), also excited some interest. The elegantly photographed *Performance* (1970), codirected by Donald Cammell, features Mick Jagger and James Fox in a story about splitting and merging identities. Like most of Roeg's movies, it is strongly ritualistic and is edited in a mysterious, elliptical style. *Walkabout* (1971) was shot in Australia and deals with forbidden sexual desires and the clash between Caucasian and aboriginal rites of passage. *Don't Look Now* (1973), starring Donald Sutherland and Julie Christie, is a supernatural tale set in Venice. *The Man Who Fell to Earth* (1976) is a sci-fi fantasy starring David Bowie.

The controversial KEN RUSSELL (b. 1927) also came to prominence during this period. He began his career as a director for BBC television specializing in documentaries about famous artists. His style became more flamboyant and personal in his biography pictures of such composers as Elgar, Prokofiev, Debussy, Bartok, Richard Strauss, and the American dancer Isadora Duncan. These television films were strongly criticized by the genteel British press for their "sensationalism"

15–1. *Monty Python's Life of Brian* **(Great Britain, 1979).**
The Monty Python troupe consisted of Terry Gilliam, Terry Jones, Graham Chapman, John Cleese, Eric Idle, and Michael Palin. Coming from the world of TV skit comedy, the troupe made its film debut with the anarchic *And Now for Something Completely Different* (1972), which combined **surrealism, animation,** live-action skits, and generous servings of truly tasteless gags. The troupe prided itself on the fact that it grievously offended every major group, regardless of color, religion, sexual preference, or national origin. In this film, for example, the boys take on Christianity and De Mille–type biblical epics. *(Warner Brothers)*

and their stylistic "self-indulgence"—charges that have been leveled at his theatrical movies as well.

Russell's first important theatrical film was *Women in Love* (1969), an adaptation of D. H. Lawrence's famous novel, starring Glenda Jackson and Alan Bates. Though it too was condemned for its flashy romanticism, it is in fact one of Russell's most stylistically restrained movies. Nearly twenty years later, Russell made another Lawrence adaptation, *The Rainbow* (1988), which was also stylistically subdued. In keeping with long-standing traditions of the British cinema, text and performance take precedence over directorial self-expression. With *The Music Lovers* (1971), a fictionalized biography of the Russian Romantic composer Tchaikovsky, Russell let loose the floodgates of his voluptuously extravagant style, fusing fantasy with reality and editing his overheated images at a frenzied pace. He further enraged the staid musical establishment by describing the movie as "a love story between a homosexual and a nymphomaniac."

Russell's style was better suited to the materials of *The Devils* (1971), based on a book by Aldous Huxley about an outburst of sexual-religious hysteria in seventeenth-century France. Nonetheless, the same adjectives were trotted out for

15–2. *Tommy* **(Great Britain, 1975),** *with Elton John (center) and Roger Daltrey (right), directed by Ken Russell.*
Style is not something you can possibly ignore in the films of Russell, who has been accused of vulgarity, garishness, and even hysteria as a stylist. His jumpy romanticism is best suited to materials that require high voltage, like this famous rock opera by The Who, which pulsates with raw, throbbing energy.   *(Columbia Pictures)*

this and Russell's subsequent movies: "vulgar," "pretentious," "appalling," "hysterical," "shrill," and inevitably, "self-indulgent." Generally speaking, Russell's style is more suited to pop rather than highbrow materials—a distinction that Russell, an aesthetic populist, likes to blur. His driving energy is more organic to the subject matter of such movies as *The Boy Friend* (1971), *Tommy* **(15–2),** *Valentino* (1977), and *Altered States* (U.S.A., 1979).

France

The French cinema also fell on hard times in the 1970s, especially when contrasted to the halcyon years of the *nouvelle vague* of the decade before. The industry was chaotic and uncoordinated as usual, and even the graying masters of the **New Wave** produced relatively little of value compared to their youthful works. True, *La Cage aux Folles* **(15–3)** and its sequel (1981) were the all-time top-grossing French films in America, but these were clearly exceptions to the rule.

The most impressive talent to emerge was BERTRAND BLIER (b. 1939), a novelist turned filmmaker. Blier's most successful movies are those subversive exercises

15–3. *La Cage aux Folles* **(France, 1978),** *with Michel Serrault (left) and Michel Galabru, directed by Edouard Molinaro.*
The two *Cage aux Folles* films (Part II was released in 1981) were immensely popular, especially in the United States, where the movies inspired a hit Broadway musical. The films' portrayal of a homosexual "marriage" is heavy on stereotypes, but the actors, and especially the brilliant Serrault as the "wife," are what make the movies enjoyable. Albin (Serrault) sings in a transvestite cabaret, La Cage aux Folles (literally, "cage of crazies"), under the name of Zaza Napoli. He is so used to thinking himself as feminine that he has to relearn how a male is supposed to behave—a thought too hideously vulgar even to contemplate, except under the most extreme duress. Albin-Zaza is a devout narcissist, emotionally volatile and subject to cruel nervous disorders, like jealousy, insecurity, and fears about growing old—in short, a perfect caricature of "the little woman" and the sensitive "artiste." Devoted to her "husband" (Ugo Tognazzi), she is the very soul of bourgeois rectitude, and every inch the lady—usually. The film was adapted by Elaine May and Mike Nichols in America in 1996 as *The Birdcage* **(18–12)** and was hugely successful.   *(United Artists)*

in comic anarchy that feature Gérard Depardieu, France's greatest film star, who also made his international debut during this era. Influenced by the American **buddy film,** Blier's turf is the world of male bonding, in which the female is almost invariably treated as an intruder, an outsider, or at least The Other. In *Going Places* (1973), *Get Out Your Handkerchiefs* **(15–4),** *Femmes Fatales* (1975), and *My Best Friend's Girl* (1982), the buddies are happiest when they're goofing off together, away from the female gaze. Often these would-be studs are incapable of satisfying a woman sexually. Like Freud, they ask in frustration: "What does a woman want?"

Blier also finds the female psyche a vaguely threatening mystery. Love between males, on the other hand, he thoroughly understands: "When two guys are always together," he said in a *Film Comment* interview, "they're not friends; they're a

15–4. *Get Out Your Handkerchiefs* **(France, 1977),** *with Gérard Depardieu, directed by Bertrand Blier.*
Depardieu might be considered France's answer to Jack Nicholson. Like his American counterpart, Depardieu has been handsome (as this photo attests) and, at other times, appallingly out of shape. They're both good as tender, erotic leading men, but they're usually better in off-beat character roles. Both can play comedy or tragedy, farce or melodrama. They have performed quiet introspective roles as well as macho blowhards, villains as well as conventional heroes. They also prefer working with world-class directors, important artists, not just the big-money boys. Above all, Depardieu and Nicholson love to take a role over the edge, to be outrageously, incredibly, triumphantly *de trops.* Both are national treasures.   *(New Line Cinema)*

team, as in a tennis team." Nor does Blier avoid the implied homoeroticism of such relationships. In *Going Places,* for example, the two heroes (Depardieu and Patrick Dewaere) are constantly horny, so when they're lonely and without women, they have sex with each other. In *Ménage* (1986), Blier goes one step further. Depardieu, in a whirlwind performance that has to be seen to be believed, plays a beefy homosexual who steals a meek, bald milquetoast (Michel Blanc) away from his bitchy wife. As usual, Blier uses this sex triangle as a way of subverting the institution of marriage, which he believes is based on coercion, manipulation, and role-playing—whether straight *or* gay.

DIANE KURYS (b. 1948) is another interesting filmmaker who debuted during this period. Most of her early works are autobiographical. Her first movie, *Peppermint Soda* (1977), takes place in 1963 and centers on the charming and often touching misadventures of a French schoolgirl. *Molotov Cocktail* (1981) captures the heady political atmosphere of the student-worker demonstrations of May 1968—an event that radicalized many young European intellectuals. *Entre Nous* (1983), the deepest and richest of her movies thus far, was inspired by Kurys's childhood. It was a period in which her mother became intensely involved with a woman friend, a friendship that eventually broke up both their marriages.

Like Wertmüller and Armstrong, her sisters in the trade, Kurys is not rigidly feminist. Her female characters are not superwomen, or even role models in some cases. Her characters can be confused, unfocused, even manipulative. For the most part, however, they are admirable women—loyal, feminine, and brave. Kurys is especially strong in capturing tender privileged moments between women—an ironic smile, a knowing giggle, a quick glance of compassion. She is also sensitive to the socioeconomic realities that largely determine what their options will be. Women don't live on love in Kurys's movies, and nothing is free, as they sadly discover.

West Germany

The British film critic Jan Dawson observed: "The New German Cinema is, for the seventies, what the *nouvelle vague* was for the sixties: a questioning of received values, an intoxicating burst of energy, a love affair with the cinema, and a love—hate relationship with Hollywood." Like the French New Wave, *Das Neue Kino* was not a tightly cohesive group, and the stylistic range of its members extends from the abstract, austere **minimalism** of Jean-Marie Straub to the cerebral meditations of Wenders, to the lusty humanism of Schlöndorff **(15–5).**

But some generalizations are possible. The New German Cinema was a movement that began in the late 1960s but did not reach its peak of prestige until the mid-1970s. It was a cinema of *West* Germany, a bulwark of American-style capitalism, and one of the most prosperous nations in Europe. It was a truly national cinema, obsessed with all things German, including Germany's "unassimilated past"—the long-forbidden topic of the Nazi era. Most of these filmmakers emphasized the forgotten people who didn't benefit much by the "economic miracle" of the postwar boom years.

15–5. *The Tin Drum* **(W. Germany, 1979),** *with David Bennent (drummer), directed by Volker Schlöndorff.* Schlöndorff (b. 1939) is one of the most commercially successful filmmakers of *Das Neue Kino*. He attended film school in Paris, then apprenticed as an assistant director to such notable figures as Louis Malle and Alain Resnais. Like them, Schlöndorff is a polished technician. Unlike them, he has always wanted to make popular, mainstream movies. His first film was *Young Törless* (1966), which won the Critics' Prize at Cannes. Schlöndorff called it "the story of a humiliation that ends with a revolt"—which could describe virtually all his movies. He often works in collaboration with his wife, Margaretha von Trotta, a writer, actress, and filmmaker. Both are concerned with social themes, often from a feminist and leftist perspective. *The Lost Honor of Katharina Blum* (1975), codirected by von Trotta, deals with the radicalization of a young German woman who is persecuted by the press, the police, and the public. Based on a novel by the Nobel laureate, Heinrich Böll, the film was a surprise success at the box office. *The Tin Drum*, a bawdy, sprawling saga of the lives of ordinary Germans during the Nazi era and the immediate postwar period, is based on a famous novel by Günter Grass. The movie was cowinner (with Coppola's *Apocalypse Now)* of the Grand Prize at the Cannes Film Festival and also won the Academy Award as Best Foreign Language Picture. Commercially it was the most successful film of the New German Cinema. *(A New World Picture)*

As in other European nations, the German film industry had—and still has—close links with television: Many of these movies were financed by the television industry and premiered on TV. Most of these filmmakers were young, left-wing intellectuals, skeptical and antiauthoritarian in their values, who grew up in the postwar era. Their movies tend to be intellectually sophisticated, more concerned with ideas than easy entertainment. They often convey a vision of deep pessimism and futility.

Ironically, most of the films were not popular in West Germany but received their greatest acclaim in France, Great Britain, and the United States. The majority of these pictures were made on low budgets, with small crews and tight schedules, and were acted by friends. They often have a home movie look. These filmmakers were obsessed with American popular culture, especially movies and rock 'n' roll. German movies of this period usually deemphasize plot in favor of mood. They deal with the human condition in broadly philosophical terms. There is a decided tendency toward allegory, with characters and situations symbolizing **archetypal** concepts. The films are relatively unconcerned with the complexities of character and human motivations—humans are enigmas.

Above all, the New German Cinema was an example of *Autorenkino*—personal movies made by serious artists, in the tradition of *le cinéma des auteurs* of the French New Wave.

WIM WENDERS (b. 1945) is perhaps the most America-obsessed of these filmmakers. He has made several movies in the United States including *Hammett* (1982), a **film noir** about the American novelist Dashiell Hammett. "All of my films have as their underlying current the Americanization of Germany," Wenders has stated. As a youth, he witnessed the "economic miracle" of Germany's postwar reconstruction, which was fueled by American capital and technology. This economic dominance also produced a form of "cultural imperialism" that virtually obliterated Germany's Nazi past: "The need to forget 20 years created a hole, and people tried to cover this by assimilating American culture," Wenders pointed out. His movies are filled with his beloved American artifacts—pinball machines, jukeboxes, movies, rock 'n' roll soundtracks. But there is also ambivalence, revulsion. West Germany's American Age is garish and materialistic. Along with the prosperity came alienation, greed, and a loss of spiritual values.

Wender's movies tend to be overtly universal, transcending narrow nationalism. *The American Friend* (**15–6**) is spoken in German and English. The brilliant *Paris, Texas* (1984), with a mysterious, intriguing script by the American dramatist and actor Sam Shepard, is spoken entirely in English and takes place in America. The charming *Wings of Desire* (1987), a bittersweet fable about two angels who hover over the divided city of Berlin, is spoken in German, French, and English. Peter Falk stars as an American movie star—himself—who is one of the few living mortals who can see the angels (he's one of them). The film was so successful that Wenders made a sequel, *Far Away, So Close* (1993), which fared less well.

WERNER HERZOG (b. 1942) is perhaps the strangest filmmaker of the New German Cinema. His art rests not with what he does with the camera—which is pedestrian and utilitarian—but with what he puts in front of it. His settings are among the most exotic in all of cinema—the Sahara, the steamy jungles of the Amazon, the otherworldly mountains of Peru. He has even made movies in that strangest of strange lands—the United States of America.

15–6. *The American Friend* (**W. Germany, 1977**), *with Dennis Hopper, directed by Wim Wenders.*

Wenders's lonely protagonists (usually males) are weirded out, drifting without purpose. Lacking a sense of identity, they generally embark on some vaguely defined quest for meaning in their lives. What they usually find is more of the same: anxiety, isolation, and empty, sterile lives. Wenders's movies tend to be abstract and sometimes obscure. Most of them are structured as road pictures, loosely unified by tone rather than story. His narratives are disjointed, improvised—like the lives of his characters. *(New Yorker Films)*

Although Herzog is a poetic landscape artist in the Romantic tradition, his interest in exotic locales is not merely picturesque or for novelty's sake alone. Locale is thematic. Like Jonathan Swift in *Gulliver's Travels,* Herzog uses elements of the fantastic as a way of exposing the superficiality of "normal" perceptions. Normal life—a frequent target of his sardonic wit—depends on where you are and who you are. For example, the cast of *Even Dwarfs Started Small* (1970) consists entirely of midgets. This shift in scale calls everything normal into question. "It's not the dwarfs who are the monsters," Herzog pointed out, "but a doorknob or a chair; they've got out of all proportion."

Herzog is the foremost **allegorist** of the New German Cinema. His concern is with the human condition in broad metaphysical terms. His movies are often structured around symbolic trials and are filled with striking rituals, myths, and metaphors. His characters are obsessives, holy fools, "freaks." But they are also vaguely familiar. "Those who people my films are often marginal, not at the center of things," Herzog has said. But he added, "They are aspects of ourselves." He is fascinated by people at the breaking point. "People under extreme pressure give you much more insight about what we are, about our very innermost being."

For example, in *Aguirre* (**15–7**), which is set in the misty mountains of Peru in the sixteenth century, the central character decides to revolt against the Spanish crown, which has financed the exploratory expedition. With a small band of

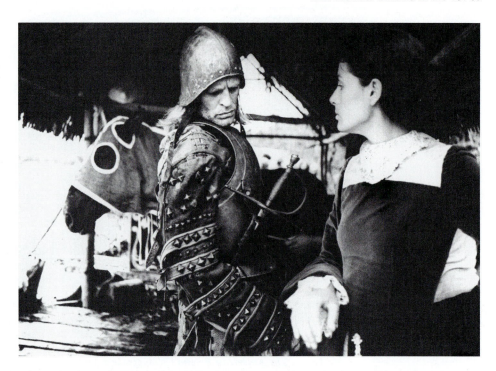

15–7. *Aguirre, the Wrath of God* (**W. Germany, 1972**), *with Klaus Kinski and Cecilia Rivera, directed by Werner Herzog.*
Formerly an obscure character actor, the late Klaus Kinski became the most famous male **star** of the New German Cinema, playing the leading role in several of Herzog's movies. The director admired the actor's "demonic" qualities—his obsessive intensity, his scariness. Like an enraged titan, his power could be awesome. His performance style in Herzog's films was usually exaggerated, conceptual rather than realistic. In *Aguirre,* for example, he played a power-crazed Spanish conquistador in a reptilian mode, his movements abrupt, mercurial. His features a frozen mask of ferocity, Aguirre can suddenly twist and coil like a cobra poised for a strike.   *(New Yorker Films)*

followers, he forges down a turbulent river and establishes his own "kingdom" on their raft, complete with an outhouse. In a demented aria of imperialistic arrogance, he proclaims all the lands within view as his own—not bothering to inquire whether others might already be living there. A hail of poisoned arrows wipes out his followers, including the daughter he plans to marry to establish his dynasty. As the staggering Aguirre rants incoherently, hundreds of chattering, spidery monkeys swarm over the raft, as if to colonize it for the mysterious jungle. So much for the indomitable human spirit.

Other movies show human beings in a more sympathetic light, though usually with equal pessimism. *Every Man for Himself and God Against All* (1974, also known as *The Enigma of Kaspar Hauser),* is based on an actual event. In 1828, in a village square in Germany, a man was discovered who had apparently grown up in solitude, confined like a brute animal. No one knew who he was or where he came from. He couldn't speak and could scarcely walk. He was very weird. (He is played by Bruno S., a former schizophrenic, who is also very weird.) In an effort to understand his mystery, the villagers subject him to various tests. A pastor wants to convert him to the "only true religion," Christianity. A professor pronounces Kaspar intellectually retarded because he fails to understand the current academic gibberish. A circus entrepreneur exploits him as a sideshow freak. An effete English lord wants to adopt him to parade his "noble savage" in the fashionable salons of Europe. And so on. Kaspar fails all these tests of civilization and is finally murdered by a mysterious assailant. However, the villagers are relieved that at least they were able to classify him as a mutant species. No need to concern themselves with the abnormal.

Herzog has a Rousseau-like veneration for such qualities as simplicity, natural dignity, and the capacity for wonder. In *Kaspar Hauser,* the protagonist is overwhelmed by ordinary events. A peasant woman who is caring for him offers to let him hold her baby. Awed, he takes the infant in his arms. Suddenly the gentle man's eyes gush in tears. "Mother," he stammers, "sometimes I feel far away from everything." Other scenes are memorable for their vulgar humor. In *Stroszek* **(15–8),** the guileless hero, once again played by Bruno S., is given a farewell present by his cell mate: He ignites his own fart and creates a fiery blast to celebrate Stroszek's release from prison.

Not all of Herzog's movies are compelling. Like other extreme artists, he sometimes fails to pull off his audacious concepts. *Fata Morgana* (1970) contains some mesmerizing images, but the film is obscure, self-consciously arty. Before shooting each day for *Heart of Glass* (1976), Herzog had his cast hypnotized to give the characters a trancelike strangeness. It sounds like a great idea, but it produced one of his dullest movies. *Nosferatu* (U.S.A./W. Germany, 1978) is a remake of Murnau's 1922 classic, with Klaus Kinski in the leading role of Dracula. The images are striking, but the dialogue contains many unintentionally funny incongruities. Its

15–8. *Stroszek* **(W. Germany, 1977),** *directed by Werner Herzog.*

Many of Herzog's movies are structured around a mythical quest. Interspersing these mock-heroic journeys are stark poetic images and occasional outbursts of black humor. In this film, for example, three endearing if none-too-bright pilgrims abandon the harshness of Berlin to seek their El Dorado in the legendary Promised Land of America—Railroad Flats, Wisconsin, to be exact. In this scene, they pour over an atlas in an attempt to locate their destination, which they know is somewhere in North America. Eva (Eva Mattes) is a sometimes hooker with a penchant for drifting off with sadistic bullies; Herr Scheitz (Clemens Scheitz) is a dear old gentleman who's spaced out in his own orbit; the strangest of them, Stroszek (Bruno S.), is a sweet innocent buried in a hulking body that doesn't seem to connect to his brain. They begin their odyssey in the dead of winter, with practically no money and even less English. They're doomed, of course. *(New Yorker Films)*

American backers switched the soundtrack from English to German in the hope that it would play better. It didn't.

Other movies have been more successful. *Woyzeck* (1978) is an adaptation of Georg Büchner's 1850 classic play, with Kinski in the leading role. *Fitzcarraldo* (U.S.A./W. Germany, 1982) stars Kinski as a fanatical opera buff who is determined to build an opera house in the wilds of the Amazon jungle. Like many of Herzog's films, the making of the movie is as interesting as the movie itself. Herzog insisted on re-creating an actual event, in which the obsessed hero has a huge steamship hauled over a steep mountain in the jungle—but Herzog wanted the boat to be bigger than the original and the mountain slope steeper. *Fitzcarraldo* is also one of his few movies with a happy ending.

Herzog has been compared to Buñuel in his use of black humor, his **surrealism,** and his tendency to be obscure. But the spirit of each artist is different. Buñuel's tone is perversely mischievous and witty. He is contemptuous of human folly but also amused by it. Herzog is more tender toward innocence. He is also more solemn, more cosmic. There is a thrilling grandeur to his fallen angels and his inexorable God of wrath. Buñuel didn't believe in God. He thought human misery was totally the product of miserable humans.

The leading filmmaker of the movement was RAINER WERNER FASSBINDER (1946–1983). He was extraordinarily prolific, completing over forty movies in fourteen years. He was also an actor, performing in his own works and those of others; and a writer-director in the live theater, radio, and television. Indeed, several critics consider his fourteen-part television series, *Berlin Alexander-platz* (1979–1980), his greatest artistic achievement. Fassbinder was an intensely unhappy man, brooding and neurotic, a demanding friend and a driven artist. When asked why he worked so hard, he replied, "to escape the loneliness." He died at thirty-six of a lethal combination of drugs and alcohol.

As a young man, Fassbinder got involved with a live theater troupe in Munich, his home base. Throughout the 1960s—a decade of student unrest and radical political movements in Germany—Fassbinder acted, wrote, and directed for the revolutionary *anti-teater* group. Most of his movies were made with the same loyal band of actors and technicians. This small company included among its regulars actresses Hanna Schygulla, who was to star in many of his later films **(15–9).**

Fassbinder began his career as a feature filmmaker with *Love Is Colder Than Death* (1969), a title that might well serve as his thematic credo. This film, along with *Gods of the Plague* (1969) and *The American Soldier* (1970), is a gangster picture, though treated in a characteristically quirky manner. In addition to the obvious Hollywood influence, these early works were also indebted to Jean-Luc Godard, especially in their odd blending of documentary techniques and stylized **genre** conventions, not to speak of their "rough draft" air of improvisation and their unevenness. Fassbinder went on to other genres as well: screwball comedies, adaptations of classical literature, film noirs, science fiction, even a western. His favorite genre was the domestic melodrama, especially the woman's picture, a staple of the Hollywood studio system.

Fassbinder's concern was always with outsiders. His is a cinema of losers—criminals, poor people, prostitutes, homosexuals, foreigners, blacks, and other despised people at the fringes of society. His characters are sad and alone. They yearn for love and acceptance in a world obsessed with status, material wealth, and bourgeois respectability. His male protagonists are generally homely, inarticulate,

15–9. *The Marriage of Maria Braun* (**W. Germany, 1978**), *with Hanna Schygulla, directed by Rainer Werner Fassbinder.*
Schygulla is the most famous female star in the New German Cinema and has acted in many of Fassbinder's works. In the grand tradition of the woman's picture, here the unhappy heroine goes on a monumental binge to drown her sorrows, like her American sisters before her—Joan Crawford, Lana Turner, Susan Hayward, and many others. The rise in Maria Braun's fortunes is symbolically likened to West Germany's postwar period of material prosperity. *(New Yorker Films)*

slightly absurd. We smile at their awkwardness even as we're touched by their unrequited passions, their desperate neediness.

Fassbinder was both a Marxist and a militant homosexual. His movies generally explore the themes of politics and sex—often the politics *of* sex. Love relationships, whether gay or straight, are usually power struggles, with a dominant and dominated lover, an oppressor and a victim. For Fassbinder, love was an affliction—"the best, most insidious, most effective instrument of social repression." In *The Merchant of Four Seasons* (1971), a gentle soul is repeatedly betrayed by the wife he adores and ends up drinking himself to death. Fassbinder used this situation again in *Bolwieser* (1977). *The Bitter Tears of Petra von Kant* (1972) explores the sadomasochistic agonies of a lesbian triangle.

Ali: Fear Eats the Soul (1973) was Fassbinder's breakthrough film on the international scene, winning the prestigious Critics' Prize at Cannes. The movie deals with the improbable love affair between a dumpy, middle-aged cleaning woman and a black Arab laborer twenty years her junior. They are socially ostracized and persecuted for their forbidden love. *Fox and His Friends* (1974) explores class conflicts within the gay subculture, which has a ruling-class elite and an underclass that's exploited sexually as well as economically. Fassbinder plays the leading role of a leather-jacketed prole who is stripped of his lottery earnings and his self-respect by a snobbish esthete. "It's incidental that the story happens

15–10. *In a Year of Thirteen Moons* (W. Germany, 1978), *with Volker Spengler (in matching pearls), directed by Rainer Werner Fassbinder.*
This parody/homage of a woman's picture and its All-for-Love theme is at once grotesque, ludicrously funny, and tragic. Spengler plays a married man named Erwin who during a casual affair with an eccentric millionaire falls hopelessly in love with him. Before disappearing, the millionaire says he could really go for Erwin, if only he were a woman. Erwin duly abandons his family, endures a sex-change operation, changes his name to Elvira, and is finally reduced to prostitution to survive. Spengler, a large man and not in the least condescending to his role, plays Elvira as a dignified matron, impeccably groomed and ladylike. In this scene, Elvira decides to visit an old teacher, Sister Gudrun, who fails to recognize him/her. "Sister, it's me, Erwin," Elvira says. Without batting an eye, Sister replies, "Oh yes, Erwin." During their conversation, neither mentions the obvious. Pure Fassbinder.   *(New Yorker Films)*

among gays," Fassbinder pointed out. "It could have worked out just as well in another milieu."

Fassbinder's films are usually melodramatic, filled with eruptions of violence and florid emotional outbursts. But the melodrama is often undercut by his campy wit. As Susan Sontag said in her celebrated "Essay on Camp," the camp sensibility is especially associated with the culture of male homosexuals, though it is hardly their exclusive province. Female heterosexuals like Mae West, Carol Burnett, and Bette Midler are strongly campy in their work. Nor is it necessarily typical of all male gays—Eisenstein, Murnau, and Cukor were homosexuals, but there is nothing campy about their films.

Camp is nostalgia-oriented. It often takes the form of a mockery of pop art that was originally intended as serious but is now outdated. For example, some of Fassbinder's favorite films were the glossy women's pictures of Douglas Sirk—movies like *Magnificent Obsession* (1954), *All That Heaven Allows* (1956), and *Imitation of Life* (1959). Commonly known as "weepies," pictures like these are emotionally overripe and luxuriantly lachrymose. Their heroines love not wisely but too well. They suffer. They survive. And they do it all in designer clothes and sumptuously appointed dwellings. Camp favors certain female stars as cult idols, especially larger-than-life figures like Joan Crawford and Judy Garland. The lives of such women are commonly associated with grotesque extremes of emotion. The camp sensibility is bitchy and malicious in its wit, delighting in the masochistic excess even while acknowledging the humanity beneath it.

As critic John Sanford has pointed out, Fassbinder was above all a humanist, hopeful of a more humane society in the future: "He has been accused of cynicism, and certainly in his bleaker moments his pessimism carries him to the borders of nihilism. But Fassbinder's despair is occasioned by the world, the society, the conditions in which people live, not by the people themselves. If his films have a message, then it is that the world must be changed."

Italy

The two most important Italian filmmakers to emerge during this era were Bernardo Bertolucci and Lina Wertmüller—both Marxist intellectuals, both concerned with the themes of sex and politics, but in other respects totally dissimilar. BERTOLUCCI (b. 1940) is the son of a poet and film critic. As a youth, Bernardo also published poetry and won a national poetry prize at the age of twenty for his volume, *In Search of Mystery*.

Bertolucci's first important film, *Before the Revolution* (1964), was made when he was only twenty-four years old. The movie centers on a young man of the upper middle class who views himself as a romantic rebel, a Marxist revolutionary in revolt against bourgeois values. But he has a "nostalgia for the present," a lingering fondness for the pleasures and comforts of his class. He is also incestuously attracted to his pretty aunt, who embodies the hedonistic allure of their class. Bertolucci's films are filled with Oedipal attractions—generally young men drawn to older women who are sexy, wise, and maternal. There is a pronounced Freudian perspective in all his movies.

Before the Revolution contains many traveling shots, which were to become a trademark in the years ahead. Often they are combined with dance scenes, which also have become a trademark. Bertolucci's traveling shots are eccentric, personal. Sometimes the camera lunges forward, sideways, or up and away even in the middle of dialogue sequences—as in *The Conformist* (1970). The famous tango ballroom sequence in *Last Tango in Paris* **(15–11)** is rapturously lyrical, a *pas de deux* between camera and dancers—a kinetic embodiment of voluptuous release. In *1900* (1976), victorious anti-Fascist partisans unfurl a huge red flag while the camera swirls up in ecstatic triumph. Bertolucci's usual cinematographer is the gifted Vittorio Storaro, famous for his mobile camera work.

Bertolucci is arguably the most lyrical and operatic of Marxist filmmakers. In addition to his elegant traveling shots, his images are often strikingly composed—like the shady art deco interiors of *The Conformist* and the mysterious de Chirico-like streets of *The Spider's Stratagem* (1970). His lush, romantic melodrama *1900* spans fifty years of Italian history from the perspectives of two families, one rich, the other poor. The movie is reminiscent of Visconti in terms of its lush production values and international cast, which includes Robert De Niro, Gérard Depardieu, Burt Lancaster, and Donald Sutherland.

Bertolucci went into a decline for the next ten years, but he came back strong with *The Last Emperor* (1987), a lavish international coproduction that won the American Academy Award as Best Picture. Spoken in English, the film recounts the improbable but true life of Pu Yi (John Lone), the last emperor of China, who was placed on the throne as a child in 1908, miraculously survived the "reeducation" prisons of the brutal Communist regime after World War II, and ended his life as a

15–11. *Last Tango in Paris* (Italy/France, 1972), *with Marlon Brando and Maria Schneider, directed by Bernardo Bertolucci.*

Last Tango was a cause célèbre, with some critics hailing it as a masterpiece and others dismissing it as pornography. It was condemned by the Italian courts as "obscene, indecent, and catering to the lowest instincts of the libido." Naturally it was a huge hit, thanks largely to this publicity. Bertolucci claimed, "I didn't make an erotic film, only a film *about* eroticism." His main concern in the movie is to show how sex is used to satisfy subconscious needs that are only superficially related to sex: "Things are 'erotic' only before relationships develop," he pointed out. "The strongest erotic moments in a relationship are always at the beginning, since relationships are born from animal instincts. But every sexual relationship is condemned. It is condemned to lose its purity, its animal nature; sex becomes an instrument for saying other things." *(United Artists)*

contented gardener during the Maoist cultural revolution in the late 1960s. The movie is filled with pageantry and panoramic vistas of the garishly overwrought palaces and courtyards of the 250-acre Forbidden City—the first western production ever allowed to be shot there. The movie is also an intimate portrait of a man who was forced to play the puppet in other people's plays—a recurrent metaphor throughout the film.

Only two of the films of the Taviani brothers, Paolo and Vittorio, have been widely distributed in the United States, *Padre, Padrone* ("My Father, My Master," 1977) and *The Night of the Shooting Stars* **(15–12)** but they are among the most strongly praised movies of their time. The Tavianis' debt to **neorealism** is obvious in their use of authentic locations and nonprofessional actors, but they also break the conventions of realism by including blatantly intrusive devices. In *Padre, Padrone,* for example, thrillingly lyrical music miraculously swells up from nowhere in otherwise realistically presented scenes. We are allowed to hear the thoughts of many of the characters and even the complaints of a goat!

LINA WERTMÜLLER (b. 1928) was an actress, playwright, and director in live theater before apprenticing as Fellini's assistant director in *8½.* Her first important

15–12. *The Night of the Shooting Stars* (Italy, 1982), *directed by Paolo and Vittorio Taviani.*
The Tavianis are fond of juxtaposing styles to produce incongruous contrasts between reality and imagination. For example, this movie deals with the lives of some Italian villagers during the final days of Fascist rule, when the American army was about to liberate their community. The tale is told by a woman who was only six at the time. In this scene we see the death of a Fascist soldier not as it occurs in reality (he is shot by partisans), but as it appears to the imagination of a six-year-old: The partisans are armor-clad gladiators who hurl their spears of wrath at the Fascist bully, impaling him like a contemptible cockroach. *(United Artists)*

movie was *The Seduction of Mimi* **(15–13),** which won her the Best Director award at Cannes. Like most of her films, it is a farce about politics and sex—and the politics of sex. Throughout the 1970s, she directed a series of comic works that were hailed and sometimes criticized, but seldom ignored: *Love and Anarchy* (1973), *All Screwed Up* (1974), *Swept Away* (1974), *Seven Beauties* (1976), and *Blood Feud* (1979). Her output radically diminished after 1980.

Wertmüller's movies were especially popular in the United States, where audiences delighted in their bawdiness, their raucous energy, and their strong entertainment values. Wertmüller is populist in her values: She makes mainstream movies, movies that ordinary working people can learn from. But she doesn't preach to her audiences, preferring them to draw their own conclusions.

Wertmüller was criticized by some feminist film critics for featuring vulgar, garrulous female characters who look like Rubens and Titian nudes—put together. Indeed, one critic headlined her review: "Is Lina Wertmüller Really Just One of the Boys?" But Wertmüller delights in irony, in paradoxes. She has been a consistent champion of the cause of women, but she's not sentimental. However funny her women characters are (and the men are just as funny), Wertmüller's females are usually strong, practical, with a surer sense of personal identity than the males.

Perhaps the most obvious influence on Wertmüller's works are the social comedies of Pietro Germi (see **13–21).** Both deal with Italian stereotypes, and both

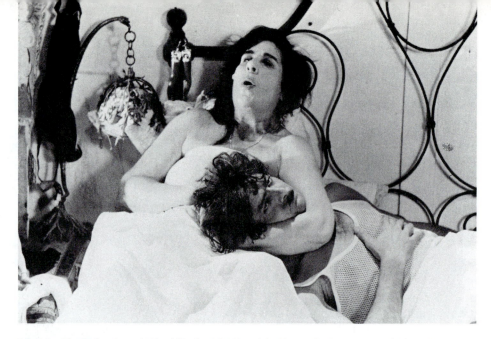

15–13. *The Seduction of Mimi* (Italy, 1972), *with Giancarlo Giannini and Elena Fiore, directed by Lina Wertmüller.*
The tone shifts in Wertmüller's movies are audacious. Mimi (Giannini), our swaggering hero in this film, regards himself as a sexually liberated man, living with his mistress and their son. The fact that he's married to another woman is an unfortunate accident of bad timing—unfortunate for the wife at any rate, who is expected to live a chaste, circumspect life. When Mimi learns that his wife is pregnant by another man, the enraged cuckold embarks upon a revenge campaign to seduce the unlovely wife (Fiore) of the man who "dishonored" him. Mimi's honor requires nothing less. After his repeated overtures, the wronged Fiore finally succumbs to his lecherous entreaties, complete with sighs and whimpers. The "seduction" is hilarious, with the cowering Mimi trembling in the corner of the bed while he gawks in awe at the gargantuan woman moving toward him, like Mt. Vesuvius about to suffocate a gnat. Pictured here, our exhausted stud contemplates the agonizing rigors of the macho code, as his fair lady sings lustily of the joys of being truly loved. When he tells her the truth of why he pursued her, she is crestfallen. The film's tone shifts again as she berates him for hypocrisy, for she considers herself an honorable woman who yielded to him out of genuine passion. By the end of the scene, our sympathies are entirely with the twice-wronged woman, and our fondness for the hero is considerably diminished.   *(New Line Cinema)*

are concerned with satirizing social and sexual hypocrisies. Like Germi, too, Wertmüller is strong on story: Her films have lots of action. In fact, her films have lots of everything—dialogue, music, noise, and above all, energy. Wertmüller can stir up the audience even with exposition scenes—as in the whirlwind opening of *Seven Beauties* **(15–14),** her most admired film. Some of her best comedy is found in her dialect humor, but of course most of this is lost to audiences who must rely on subtitles. Her dialogue is frequently peppered with swears and coarse expressions, and these generally manage to come through in some form or another.

Like Chaplin, Wertmüller is concerned with the fate of the "little fellow." Her films are usually told from the male point of view. Despite their prejudices and vanities, most of her working-class heroes deserve a better life but usually end up getting the shaft. They are frequently undone by their own blind allegiance to a "masculine" code of honor, which Wertmüller equates with the Mafia, Big Business, and Fascism—in fact, with all patriarchal structures of power.

15–14. *Seven Beauties* (Italy, 1976), *with Giancarlo Giannini, directed by Lina Wertmüller.*
Giannini was Wertmüller's favorite actor and appeared in many of her films until they parted
ways in the early 1980s. Although he is an accomplished dramatic performer, Giannini is most
famous as a farceur. Farcical acting requires an intense comic exaggeration and can easily become tiresome and mechanical if the performer is not able to preserve the humanity of the
character. In this, perhaps his greatest role, he plays a typical ethnic stereotype—a preening,
heavy-lidded lothario and small-time hood, intoxicated with his own irresistibility. He is so
caught up in his self-importance that he's unaware that World War II is taking place around
him. "How did the world get this way?" he asks when he finds himself in an appalling Nazi
concentration camp. How indeed. *(Warner Brothers)*

True equality in Wertmüller's movies is usually associated with true love—love
between equal partners. In the fablelike *Swept Away,* for example, the hero (Giannini) is a sweaty Communist crew member of a luxury yacht. He must endure the
constant insults of a spoiled rich bitch (the wondrously funny Mariangela Melato)
as she complains of his ineptitude and his rank body odor. He gets his revenge
when they are stranded alone on a desert isle. In classic macho fashion, he subjects
her to a series of indignities to show her who's boss. Finally they call a truce. Inevitably, they fall in love—which humanizes them both. They enjoy a respite from
the class antagonisms of the mainland, until they spot a rescue ship at sea. She
wants to hide, to remain in their private paradise. But he wants to test her love—to
see if it will survive the prejudices of her class. Once back on the mainland, she remains silent, pensive. Giannini's brilliance in combining comedy with emotional
power is nowhere better illustrated than in the film's conclusion. As she departs
forever in a helicopter, the camera zooms in to his stricken face—surprised and
devastated by her betrayal. This is reality, not paradise.

Eastern Europe

Compared to Western—and especially American—standards, artistic freedom was a sometimes thing in the Communist bloc countries of the 1970s. Nonetheless, conditions improved for filmmakers and for other artists in general, at least when compared to the Stalinist past. In Poland and Hungary, movies were openly critical of the political power structure, pointing out its corruptibility **(15–15).** In the Soviet Union, however, the finest films were rarely overtly political. The Soviets were still at their best with literary adaptations and period films, or movies in which the political background was kept neutral.

A sign of the relatively more tolerant atmosphere in the Soviet Union was that an artist like ANDREI TARKOVSKY (1932–1987) was allowed to work, though not without a lot of interference. Tarkovsky was an **avant-garde** artist—difficult, personal, and often obscure. He was the Godard of the Soviet cinema, and his intellectually challenging movies include such elements as dreams, visions, stream-of-consciousness techniques, surrealistic imagery, complex editing styles, newsreel footage, and

15–15. *Angi Vera* **(Hungary, 1979),** *with Veronika Papp (center), directed by Pál Gábor.*
The heroine of this ambiguous tale is a naive, earnest young nursing student who becomes a revolutionary in the 1948 period of confusion and political reorganization. At Communist party school she develops a crush on her group leader and then has an affair with him. Later, when she is under the influence of a more highly placed party member (Anna Traján, left), Vera denounces her former lover at a public meeting. She keeps her eyes and ears open, ever alert to shifts in the political climate. She's always right there when the shifts occur. A calculating opportunist or sincere revolutionary? Filmmaker Gábor doesn't say.   *(New Yorker Films)*

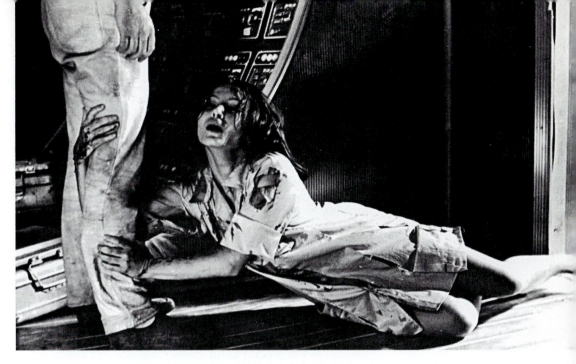

15–16. *Solaris* (U.S.S.R., 1971), *directed by Andrei Tarkovsky.*
Tarkovsky's intensely personal and individualistic style of filmmaking did not endear him to the moribund cultural establishment in the Soviet Union. Because his movies consistently won prestigious awards at various film festivals (especially at Cannes), the commissars were more or less obliged to release them in the lucrative western European market, where Tarkovsky's films were popular. He became the Soviet cinema's "bad boy"—humiliated, censured, but tolerated because of the prestige and foreign currency he brought home. In the U.S.S.R., his movies were shown only intermittently. No need to encourage others. *(Museum of Modern Art)*

special effects. He completed only seven features in twenty-five years: *My Name Is Ivan* (1962), *Andrei Rublev* (1966), *Solaris* **(15–16),** *The Mirror* (1974), *Stalker* (1979), *Nostalghia* (Italy/U.S.S.R., 1983), and *The Sacrifice* (Sweden, 1986).

Tarkovsky's themes characteristically revolve around metaphysical ideas—the problems of faith and doubt, the need to develop spiritual values. Like the American avant-garde filmmaker Stan Brakhage, he was concerned with the visionary role of the artist in society and his or her relationship with nature. His last movie, the brooding, enigmatic meditation on life and death, *The Sacrifice,* was highly praised by international critics, especially in western Europe. Tarkovsky believed that cinema is a synthesis of all the arts, and his movies often include homages to European artistic masters of the past.

Tarkovsky was constantly hassled by the Soviet authorities. Several of his films were temporarily shelved, recut, or strongly criticized by the Soviet cultural establishment. As the American critic Michael Dempsey wittily observed, "They all sound amazingly like baby moguls in Hollywood scratching their heads over this artsy wacko who, if you can believe it, doesn't like money." Largely because of the lukewarm—or nonexistent—support from the Soviet film bureaucracy, Tarkovsky went to Italy in 1983 to make *Nostalghia.* Until his wasteful death from cancer in 1987, he remained in the West.

One of the finest Soviet filmmakers is NIKITA MIKHALKOV (b. 1945), whose works are mostly period films, adaptations of classic literary texts. Like a cinematic Chekhov, Mikhalkov is the poetic chronicler of the pathos of missed opportunities, of decent people of the prerevolutionary bourgeoisie who *want* to lead meaningful lives, who yearn to do something extraordinary with their talents yet in the end yield to the blandishments of the easy life. His is a cinema of inertia, of exquisite longueurs, of regret. *Slave of Love* (1976) is about a stranded movie crew during the confusion of the 1917 revolution. *Oblomov* (1980) is an adaptation of the celebrated tragicomic novel by Ivan Goncharov. Oblomov is a mythic character in Russo-Soviet culture—a good-hearted parasite of childlike innocence who just can't seem to get his life together. When he is depressed, he sleeps. When he is anxious, he sleeps. When he wants to avoid making a decision, he sleeps. He even takes naps shortly after rising from his morning slumbers. He is a symbol of Russian torpor and sloth.

Not surprisingly, Mikhalkov's best movie to date is an adaptation of Chekhov, *An Unfinished Piece for Player Piano* (1977), based on *Platonov,* Chekhov's first published full-length play. Mikhalkov captures the subtle tragicomic tone of Chekhov, his tenderness and comic poignance. The characters in the film philosophize endlessly, drink tea, mourn for the lost ideals of their youth, drink more tea, and vow to change their lives—but not right away. At one point, the protagonist Platonov decides to put an end to his trivial existence and jumps into a lake to drown himself. Unfortunately, the water is about two feet deep, and the chagrined hero succeeds only in covering himself in mud. "Nothing will change," a character shrewdly observes of the day's proceedings.

Australia

The sudden emergence of Australia as a world-class film-producing nation was attributed mainly to the creation of the Australian Film Commission in 1971. This government-subsidized agency offered producers tax incentives, promotional campaigns, and other attractive inducements that paid handsome dividends in the 1970s and early 1980s. The most widely praised movies resulting from this government policy were generally period films, often set around 1900. Several of them deal with Australia's British colonial heritage and the injustices perpetrated by whites against the black aboriginal population.

It is difficult to generalize about the major figures of the Australian cinema, because only two or three films by each were released in the United States. Most of their movies are well crafted and contain striking panoramas of the Australian landscape. Stylistically they are variable, ranging from the low-keyed humanism of Fred Schepisi's *The Devil's Playground* and Bruce Beresford's *The Getting of Wisdom,* to the evocative mood pieces of Peter Weir, to the flamboyant technical virtuosity of such pictures as Gillian Armstrong's *Starstruck* and George Miller's *The Road Warrior.* These five directors, in addition to the American-born actor Mel Gibson, were the most respected figures of the Australian New Wave.

PETER WEIR (b. 1944) was the best known of these filmmakers. His work is strong on social consciousness but treated from an offbeat perspective, with emphasis on the occult, myths, and legends. He is obsessed with the edges of things, suggesting feelings and ideas obliquely. *Picnic at Hanging Rock* **(15–17),** which is based on an actual event, deals with the mysterious disappearance of some girls at a British-style boarding school located in the Australian wilderness. We never find out what happened to the girls, but Weir suggests that the aborigines of the region

15–17. *Picnic at Hanging Rock* **(Australia, 1975),** *directed by Peter Weir.*
Weir is a master of atmosphere, capable of evoking an air of mystery and threat with the barest
of means—a crackling twig, the stirring of leaves, a sinister dark area in the mise en scène.
(Museum of Modern Art)

may have abducted them for encroaching on forbidden territory. The film is saturated with an atmosphere of dread, of the violation of something sacred.

Weir pursues this idea in *The Last Wave* (1977), which is more overtly supernatural. The protagonist (Richard Chamberlain), a lawyer from Sydney, is disturbed by his dreams and is told by an aborigine that "a dream is a shadow of something real." Nature goes berserk, as though on a rampage of revenge. Huge hailstones crash down from the blue skies, shattering windows and injuring children. In another scene, water gushes out from the lawyer's car radio. Black rain pours down in torrents over the city, portending a biblical flood. The movie is a symbolic allegory of the alienation of white people from nature, which they have violated, along with the aborigines who once lived in harmony with it.

Gallipoli (1981) is more realistic and deals with the rites of passage of two appealing youths (Mel Gibson and Mark Lee) during the World War I era. Stunningly photographed in **widescreen,** this **epic** work contains images of great beauty and power. An antiwar, anticolonialist film, *Gallipoli* dramatizes the folly of blind loyalty and obedience to the British mother country. In the film's climactic scene, the infamous Battle of Gallipoli in Turkey, the Australian diversionary forces are slaughtered by the enemy machine guns moments after the soldiers leave their trenches, while the haughty British main force, further up the Turkish peninsula, lands virtually without opposition.

Weir's *The Year of Living Dangerously* (Australia/U.S.A., 1982) is set in Indonesia in 1965. The film is a steamy love story of a naive but ambitious Australian journalist (Gibson again) and a British embassy employee (Sigourney Weaver). The story takes place during the political upheavals brought on by the corrupt regime of the dictator Sukarno. The images of the movie unfurl like a hallucinatory dream. Weir's evocation of an atmosphere of violence, evil, and squalor is masterful, even if his handling of the story is sometimes unfocused.

Like several other Australian filmmakers, Weir eventually went to America to make movies, with mixed results. The thriller *Witness* (1985) was a commercial success, with Harrison Ford as an American cop who lives undercover in an Amish community. *Dead Poet's Society* (1989) was also a success and is about a repressive private boy's school and the influence of a charismatic English teacher, played by Robin Williams. Weir's other Hollywood productions were less successful: *Mosquito Coast* (1986), *Green Card* (1990), and the philosophical *Fearless* (1993). However, *The Truman Show* **(18–6),** with Jim Carrey, was a huge hit.

BRUCE BERESFORD (b. 1940) is perhaps the quietest talent of this group. His most famous film, *Breaker Morant* **(15–18),** is a court-martial drama that takes place during the Boer War (1899–1902), in which the British were opposed to the Dutch Afrikaners in South Africa. The court-room scenes are interspersed with **flashbacks** of the guerrilla warfare episodes. The film is strongly anticolonial and shows how three lieutenants were used as scapegoats by a morally corrupt British government.

15–18. *Breaker Morant* (Australia, 1980), *with (wearing cross-straps, left to right) Lewis Fitz-Gerald, Bryan Brown, and Edward Woodward, directed by Bruce Beresford.*
A number of commentators have remarked upon the "manliness" of the Australian cinema, its strong feeling for male bonding and virile friendships. These qualities are especially apparent in masculine genres like war films, which rarely feature important female roles.   *(A New World Picture)*

The movie is similar to Kubrick's *Paths of Glory* in portraying the utter cynicism of politically minded career soldiers.

Since moving to Hollywood, Beresford's career has also been a series of ups and downs. His best American movies are *Tender Mercies* (1982), about a born-again country singer, superbly played by Robert Duvall. *Crimes of the Heart* (1986) is an excellent adaptation of a quirky Beth Henley play. *Driving Miss Daisy* (1989) was a surprise hit that also won many critical awards, including the Best Picture Oscar.

GEORGE MILLER (b. 1945) is arguably the noisiest of the Australian new wave. He is best known for his exciting Mad Max films—*Mad Max* (1979), *The Road Warrior* **(15–19),** and *Mad Max Beyond Thunderdome* (1985), all starring Mel Gibson in his most macho mode. The first movie is more conventional and realistic, an Americanesque revenge fantasy punctuated by frequent outbursts of violence, car wrecks, and explosions—a genre that critic David Chute wittily identified as a "crash-and-burn" film.

The Road Warrior is one of the damnedest movies ever made. Part biker film, part sci-fi, it also incorporates elements from samurai movies, comic strips,

15–19. *The Road Warrior* **(Australia, 1982),** *with Mel Gibson, directed by George Miller.*
Now a major star of the American cinema, Gibson was originally a star of the Australian cinema. He is an accomplished actor and an academy award winning director (*Braveheart*) with an unusually broad range. In this film he plays Mad Max, a hungry, marauding warrior—a cross between John Wayne and a wandering samurai, with a touch of *Shane*. *(Warner Brothers)*

spaghetti westerns, and leather S&M porn films. Max is introduced as a dissipated mythic hero, and his spiritual rebirth is presented in archetypal terms. The story is a loose adaptation of the traditional western plot in which the powerful romantic loner sides with the homesteaders against the outlaws and savages. Only here the setting is a barren, nuked landscape after the devastations of World War III. The warring nations are still fighting over petroleum, and the few remaining human communities must defend their diminishing resources from marauding outlaws.

Miller's emphasis is not on theme or character so much as style. A visually stunning film, *Road Warrior* is filled with mysterious, powerful images—at once poetic and epic. The **editing** style can sweep us up lyrically or pound us with its power-hammer vibrato. The celebrated truck race scene is brilliantly edited and was praised by that master technician, Steven Spielberg. The movie is also punctuated with outbursts of sardonic epic humor—masculine, scornful, and grisly.

Perhaps the most widely praised movie from Australia was *The Chant of Jimmie Blacksmith* (15–20), directed by FRED SCHEPISI (b. 1939). The film is based on an actual event that took place in 1900. Jimmie Blacksmith, half white and half aborigine, is rescued from a life of misery by a Caucasian missionary couple. They raise him to be docile and respectful, to admire all that is white, despise all that is black. The Reverend Mrs. advises the youth to marry a white farm girl, produce children, who in turn will produce children who would be "scarcely black at all." Jimmie tries to play the white man's game but is repeatedly cheated by his bosses, who have little to fear from the law since aborigines had no legal rights. He finally revolts in a paroxysm of rage, returning to the homes of the people who humiliated and cheated him, slaughtering their women and children. He is accompanied by his

15–20. *The Chant of Jimmie Blacksmith* (**Australia, 1978**), *with Tommie Lewis and Freddy Reynolds, directed by Fred Schepisi.*

Pauline Kael, the influential film critic of *The New Yorker,* had high praise for this epic masterpiece, which she described as "a Requiem Mass for a nation's lost honor." The roots of racism, Schepisi demonstrates, are both economic and sexual. Whites exploit Jimmie (Lewis) and other aborigines as cheap labor and fear them as sexual threats. After submitting to a lifetime of humiliation and rejection, Jimmie finally repudiates his Caucasian aspirations and declares war on his white masters. But as Kael pointed out, "he doesn't wage war directly against the men: he attacks the men's most prized possessions—their robust, well-fed women, their pink-and-white children." *(New Yorker Films)*

good-natured half brother Mort (Freddy Reynolds), who is sickened by Jimmie's mindless fury and eventually leaves him.

Schepisi (pronounced **Skep**-see) is a first-class stylist, framing his story in widescreen panoramas of tremendous force. His landscapes are awesome in their grandeur. His editing style can be so frenzied that we imagine we see more than we do. For example, there is relatively little actual gore in the movie, but the jamming together of fragmented images has an almost palpable impact. In Jimmie's initial rampage, which takes place in a ranch kitchen, we catch glimpses of tense, silent women. Hatchets. Lurching hand-held shots of Jimmie slashing. Blood splatters in milk. Raw eggs crash to the floor. Baby screams. Red. Red everywhere, smeared.

Schepisi's Hollywood career has been spotty, too. One of his most successful American movies was *Roxanne* (1987), a witty update of the classic French play *Cyrano de Bergerac,* with a winning performance by Steve Martin, who also wrote the script. *Six Degrees of Separation* (1994) is a stylish adaptation of a Broadway play by John Guare. Though critically praised, it failed to arouse much popular success.

GILLIAN ARMSTRONG (b. 1942) was the finest comic talent among Australia's New Wave. Her first important movie, *My Brilliant Career* **(15–21),** is a convincing

15–21. *My Brilliant Career* **(Australia, 1979),** *with Judy Davis, directed by Gillian Armstrong.*
Sybylla (Judy Davis) is confident and outspoken, even cocky. One reviewer called her a young Australian Kate Hepburn—independent, intelligent, a little too sure of herself. Armstrong is especially strong in creating warm, likable characters, people who can be funny and gutsy at the same time, people we can root for. Her attitude toward her heroine in this film is gently satirical, affectionate. The girl's got spirit.   *(Analysis Film Releasing Corporation)*

15–22. *In the Realm of the Senses* **(Japan, 1976),** *with Eiko Matsuda (above) and Tatsuda Fuji, directed by Nagisa Oshima.*
The Japanese cinema went into a serious decline in the 1970s. Oshima is the only world-class filmmaker to emerge from Japan during this period. He gained notoriety when this controversial film was confiscated by the U.S. Customs as obscene on the eve of its exhibition at the New York Film Festival. It was later released and, thanks to the publicity, widely shown in America. The film *is* problematical. By almost any definition, it qualifies as pornography since it presents many scenes of explicit sexuality. But it is also an attempt to explore the ideology of sex and its underlying motivations—especially the death wish, which Oshima associates with the experience of orgasm. Oshima is the most iconoclastic of Japanese filmmakers, a savage critic of traditional values, which he views as stultifying and repressive. He is a champion of individualism and a spokesman for all outsiders, especially young people.   *(Argos Films)*

evocation of the 1901 era. The film deals with a gutsy young woman from the wrong side of the outback who manages to attend a snooty British-style boarding school. Although plain and without connections, she snares the most eligible bachelor around, then turns down his proposal of marriage to devote herself to her writing career.

Jackie Mullens, the heroine of Armstrong's punk-rock musical *Starstruck* (1982), is even more appealing. Angus, her fourteen-year-old cousin and manager (he's young but he has a fertile mind), is determined to make her a big star, if only they can attract the attention of the media. Their off-the-wall schemes to gain publicity are very funny. At one point, Angus informs the press that Jackie will walk a tightrope high over one of Sydney's busiest intersections. When informed that the stunt would be no big deal, the desperate youth adds, "Topless?" Jackie balks but is persuaded to go through with it. She chickens out on the topless bit, however, and instead wears a ludicrous flesh-colored breastplate, complete with painted nipples. The breastplate has the odd effect of making her look more obscene than if she had performed the stunt *au naturel.*

In the early 1980s, the Australian cinema began to run out of steam. The country was suffering from a recession, and many of the tax breaks that had nurtured the film industry were rescinded. Period films were thought to have run their course, and television was offering stiff competition to the film industry. Most importantly, virtually all the major figures of the Australian renaissance were working for the Hollywood studios, digging in for an extended stay in the United States.

The Third World

Films of the Third World—primarily underdeveloped former colonies in Latin America, Africa, and Asia—came to international prominence as early as the 1950s, with the works of India's Satyajit Ray (see **11–1**). Throughout the next decade, the "Third Cinema" expanded sporadically, especially in Latin America. Brazil's *Cinema Novo*, spearheaded by the former movie critic turned filmmaker, Glauber Rocha (1939–1983), produced a number of important pictures, including Rocha's revolutionary *White Devil, Black God* (1964), *Land in Anguish* (1967), and *Antonio Das Mortes* (see **13–9**). In Cuba, too, the early euphoria of the revolution gave birth to such milestone works as Thomás Gutiérrez Alea's *Memories of Underdevelopment* (1969) and Humberto Solás's *Lucia* (1969).

In the 1970s, the Third Cinema survived, despite severe shortages of capital and fierce antagonism from repressive governments of both the Left and Right—usually the Right. A number of Third World filmmakers were forced to work under ground, guerrilla-style. Rejecting the escapist, plot-oriented movies of the Hollywood commercial cinema as well as the highly personal *films des auteurs* of the Europeans, the Third Cinema often blended Marxism and nationalism, characteristically devoting itself to dramatizing Marx's basic dictum: "The history of all human society, past and present, has been the history of class struggle."

But Third World Marxism differed considerably from the so-called armchair Marxism of the western European intelligentsia, which tended to be theoretical and more oriented toward analysis than action. It also differed from Soviet-style Communism in that the U.S.S.R. and its client states were relatively prosperous societies with advanced technologies and were ruled by entrenched bureaucracies that were controlled by a political elite. Third World Marxism was more pragmatic and flexible. It was concerned less with ideological abstractions than with urgent social realities—poverty, ignorance, injustice. Their filmmakers strongly identified with the oppressed masses—which wasn't just an empty phrase in the Third World.

The Marxist strain in the Third Cinema can be summarized by the following general characteristics: (1) the use of art as a tool for social change; (2) the assumption that imperialism and neocolonialism exploit the peasantry and proletariat to further the interests of a small ruling class; (3) the belief that all art is at least implicitly ideological, affirming or challenging the status quo; (4) a demystification of power, demonstrating how it's actually wielded and who it benefits; (5) an identification with oppressed groups such as women, outcasts, and racial minorities; (6) the belief that environment largely determines human behavior; (7) a rejection of religion and the supernatural in favor of a strict scientific materialism; (8) a belief in the equal worth of all human beings; and (9) a **dialectical** view of history and knowledge, in which progress is the result of a conflict and ultimate synthesis of opposites.

The Third Cinema was stylistically variable, though it tended to favor realism, for a number of reasons. In the first place, these filmmakers were concerned with exposing the injustices of the real world. Fernando Solanas and Octavio Gettino, guerrilla filmmakers from Argentina, pointed out: "Every image that documents, bears witness to, refutes, or deepens the truth of a situation is something more than a film image or purely artistic fact; it becomes something which the System finds indigestible." Realism is also cheaper. Authentic locations can be used instead of expensive studio-built sets. Rather than smooth professional actors, these films sometimes employ amateur players, often re-creating scenes they know from first-hand experience. Realistic movies also require a minimum of complex sound and optical techniques and no costly special effects.

Third World movies of this era are often powerful, even grim. But not always. The works of Senegal's Ousmane Sembene can be warm, humorous, and gently satirical **(15–23).** For example, in *Mandabi* ("The Money Order," 1970), the plump protagonist is a vain, somewhat pompous illiterate who lives in a poor village with his two wives and numerous children. Unemployed for years, the pious soul trusts that "Allah will never abandon us." He receives a money order from his nephew working in Paris, and the rest of the movie details what happens to our hero as a result of his windfall. First he charges some food at the village store, then pigs out in a gastronomical orgy, burping and rolling over to sleep like a satiated walrus. The next day, decked out in his finest habiliments, he departs for the city to cash the money order, his billowing robes swelling in the wind like a mighty schooner about to engage the open seas. In the city, this gullible naïf is cheated by a series of con artists and is subjected to endless runarounds by apathetic bureaucrats. In frustration, he turns to another nephew for help and in the process is cheated out of his money by his own city-slicker relation. In the end, the poor devil is reduced to cynicism: "Honesty is a sin in this country," he sadly concludes. Like the moral of a fable.

Some Third World filmmakers, especially those of a didactic bent, believe that realism is too restrictive a style, too objective and superficial. Realism doesn't get *beneath* the facts, it can only show their effects. The goal of demystification requires an analysis of causes too. An example of this more overtly manipulative style is *The Hour of the Furnaces* (Argentina, 1968), by Solanas and Gettino. The movie runs four hours and twenty minutes and is clearly influenced by the cinematic "essays" of Jean-Luc Godard. Fictional sequences are juxtaposed with documentary scenes. Each structural "cell" is presented in a different style. Statistics are offered. For example, 5 percent of the Argentine population keeps 42 percent of the national revenue. These scenes are contrasted with interviews of some of the victims of this maldistribution of wealth. The structure of the film is dialectical—proposing a thesis, offering a counterthesis, then arriving at a synthesis. As James Roy MacBean points out, movies like these attempt to demystify power, showing that "social and economic relations are not objective but subjective; not neutral as the ruling class would have us believe, but partisan (in *their* favor); not inevitable, but *arbitrary* (and arbitrarily *imposed*); and above all, not immutable . . . but capable of being transformed in a revolutionary way."

At its best, the Third Cinema can pack an emotional wallop by appealing directly to our sense of justice. In Yilmaz Güney's *The Father* (Turkey, 1976), for exam-

15–23. *Publicity photo of Ousmane Sembene (left) directing a scene from Xala* (Senegal, 1974).

Senegal, a former French colony that won its independence in 1960, has a population of only four million, yet it has produced the most important movies of black Africa, most notably those of Sembene, the continent's best-known filmmaker. *Xala* (which roughly translates "the curse of impotence") is spoken in French and Wolof, the native language of Senegal. The movie is an exposé of the nation's servile ruling class, whose members have eagerly embraced the culture of their white colonial predecessors. At this lavish wedding reception, for example, several Frenchified Beautiful People wonder what the English translation is for "le weekend." The cultural commentator Hernandez Arregui has observed: "Culture becomes bilingual not due to the use of two languages but because of the conjuncture of two cultural patterns of thinking. One is national, that of the people, and the other is estranging, that of the classes subordinated to outside forces. The admiration that the upper classes express for the United States or Europe is the highest expression of their subjection." Like many Third World artists, Sembene advocates the creation of a truly national culture.   *(New Yorker Films)*

ple, an out-of-work laborer (played by Güney) is not allowed to emigrate to West Germany and a waiting job because he has defective teeth. Later he is offered a proposition by a wealthy industrialist whose son is being indicted for killing a man. The father, ashamed and embarrassed, suggests that since the laborer would have to leave his family for several years to find work anyway, perhaps he could support his family by accepting the industrialist's money in exchange for confessing to the murder and serving the son's prison sentence.

While the industrialist haltingly offers this proposition, Güney looks at the camera—at us—with a steady, ironic gaze of recognition. Throughout the **lengthy take,** he remains silent, his eyes riveted on us, his features revealing a multitude of emotions. He knows the industrialist is right. However unfair, the plan would solve a lot of problems. While still looking at the camera, slowly, almost imperceptibly, as

15–24. *Bye Bye Brazil* (**Brazil, 1979**), *directed by Carlos Diegues.*
Reminiscent of the works of Fellini, this sprawling seriocomic epic explores the vacillating fortunes of a shabby road-show company of circus performers. During prosperous times, they
just barely manage to subsist on their meager earnings. During hard times, they resort to
pimping and whoring to survive. Bawdy, colorful, and often moving, Diegues's masterpiece is
a loving celebration of human endurance in the face of impossible odds.   *(A Carnival-Unifilm
Release)*

he realizes that he might be separated from his wife and children for years, a tear
escapes down his cheek. He accepts the proposition, of course.

FURTHER READING

CORRIGAN, TIMOTHY. *New German Film: The Displaced Image.* Austin: University of Texas Press,
    1983. Analysis of six key films by major figures of the New German Cinema.

ELSAESSER, THOMAS. *Fassbinder's Germany.* Ann Arbor: University of Michigan Press, 1997. The
    political and historical forces that shaped Fassbinder's works.

FORBES, JILL. *Cinema in France After The New Wave.* London: British Film Institute, 1994. The
    cultural context of film since 1968.

FRENCH, WARREN. *New German Cinema: From Overhausen to Hamburg.* Boston: Twayne Publish-
    ers, 1983. General survey of 1960s and 1970s.

GABRIEL, TESHOME H. *Third Cinema in the Third World: The Aesthetics of Liberation.* Ann Arbor:
    University of Michigan Press, 1982. Clear exposition of five themes: class, culture, reli-
    gion, sexism, and armed struggle.

LEIM, MIRA and ANTONIN. *The Most Important Art: Eastern European Film After 1945.* Berkeley:
    University of California Press, 1977. Survey of the Communist bloc countries.

NICHOLS, BILL. *Ideology and the Image.* Bloomington: Indiana University Press, 1981. Social
    representation in the cinema and other media—a demystification.

ROBSON, JOCELYN, and BEVERLEY ZALCOCK. *Australian and New Zealand Women's Films.* London: Scarlet Press, 1997. Covers films from the 1970s to the 1990s.

SANFORD, JOHN. *The New German Cinema.* New York: Da Capo Press, 1980. Perceptive survey of major figures, with excellent illustrations.

STRATTON, DAVID. *The Last New Wave: The Australian Film Revival.* Sydney: Angus and Robertson, 1980. Survey of industry and major figures.

16

American Cinema in the 1980s

*A handful of great movies, two handfuls of interesting movies and a
lot of stuff it's impossible to remember or care about.*
—Film critic RICHARD SCHICKEL about the movies of the 1980s

Twentieth Century-Fox

Timeline: 1980–1989

1980
President Carter breaks off diplomatic relations with Iran because of the continuing hostage crisis; U.S. rescue attempt of hostages fails

1981
Ronald Reagan (Republican) wins landslide victory in U.S. Presidency (1981–1989); huge cuts in taxes and social welfare spending; huge increases in military spending; country veers sharply to the Right

1983
U.S. unemployment: over 12 million—the highest since 1941; economic recession

1984
Pop singer Michael Jackson sells over 37 million copies of his album *Thriller*

1985
United States officially becomes world's largest debtor nation, with a deficit of $130 billion

1986
Museum of Contemporary Art opens in Los Angeles
Space shuttle *Challenger* explodes on takeoff, killing all seven crew members

1987
Wall Street crash—stock market loses nearly 25 percent in a single day

1987–1988
Series of sex and fraud scandals involving such televangelists as Jim Bakker and Jimmy Swaggart

1988
George Bush (Republican) elected President of United States (1989–1992)
New drug epidemic in many American inner cities—"crack," a highly addictive derivative of cocaine

1989
Tanker *Exxon Valdez* causes world's largest oil spill (eleven million gallons) in Alaskan waters

Technological explosion: the VCR revolution. Hollywood bonanza: years of plenty. Militant America—action films and the Reagan era. The studio system regained. Mainstream talents: Lawrence Kasdan, Barry Levinson, and Robert Zemeckis. Maverick talents: David Lynch, David Cronenberg, Jonathan Demme, Oliver Stone, Spike Lee, John Sayles, Terry Gilliam, and Tim Burton.

AMERICAN FILMMAKING IN THE 1980s consisted of aesthetic contraction and finan cial expansion, of experimentation in methods of production and exhibition and, for the most part, a steadfast retreat from adventurousness in content. The decade was dominated by the conservative ideology of President Ronald Reagan, a former movie star. Mainstream Hollywood films reflected many of Reagan's values, especially nationalism, winning, money, family solidarity, and militarism **(16–1)**. But cinema is never monolithic. As critic Robin Wood has pointed out, within any given epoch there will be cracks, disruptions, and countercurrents in the prevailing ideology.

Technology and the Marketplace

The advent of the videocassette recorder (VCR), as strenuously (and stupidly) resisted by the studios as television itself had been, added yet another diversion with which movies had to compete. The VCR revolution changed the way films were made and seen. For example, the number of revival movie houses, which had been an offshoot of the 1960s, declined precipitously. Why pay five dollars to see *The Maltese Falcon* if you could rent it on cassette—possibly diminished and, if "colorized," definitely distorted—for two dollars? Thus, the experience of seeing old movies on a big screen with large audiences, as they were designed to be seen, increasingly became a thing of the past or was relegated to infrequent screenings in a film festival context.

The use of **widescreen** processes declined severely also, and for similar reasons. Filmmakers reasoned that if more people were going to see their work on cassette and cable TV rather than in theaters, why bother composing images that would be cropped by as much as one half in a medium other than the theaters? Likewise, camerawork became increasingly utilitarian, because anything too crowded or visually complex tends not to "scan" on the small screen.

Against all this was the laudable fact that virtually the entire history of film was now at the right hand of anybody who lived near a well-stocked video store. By 1987, video rentals surpassed ticket sales as the industry's leading source of revenue.

16–1. *Rambo III* (U.S.A., 1987), *with Sylvester Stallone, directed by Peter MacDonald.*
Military images abound in American movies of the 1980s. The enormous worldwide success of the three *Rambo* films occasioned much sociological hand-wringing and woeful lamentations from liberals. In essence, the movies replayed the Vietnam War, with Stallone's humorless, absurdly indestructible killing machine, John Rambo, tapping into the depths of his character's and the American public's inchoate, underlying anger about America's defeat in Southeast Asia. However, it should be noted that the *Rambo* films were also successful in other countries, where the audience perceived him as just another post modern samurai fronting an elaborate action movie. *(Tri-Star)*

The marketing of movies attained a standard of excellence that sometimes overshadowed the film being marketed. The noise of the publicity machine and merchandising tie-in products often obscured the mediocrity of the films being sold. It became a commonplace occurrence for slick movies like *Batman* (1989) to be promoted into firestorm successes. By the time the blitz was over and the truth began seeping into public consciousness, it was too late.

As independent filmmakers found to their displeasure, the 1980s saw something of a return to the studio system. Organizations like Disney's Touchstone, Paramount, and Orion once again began signing box office favorites to long-term contracts: Eddie Murphy at Paramount, Bette Midler and Tom Selleck at Disney, among others. In addition, spurred on by a Republican administration that was friendly to big business, studios again began buying into theater chains, slowly rebuilding the blocks of the **vertically integrated** companies that the government had painstakingly dismantled forty years earlier. By the end of the decade, the studios owned 3,500 of the nation's 22,000 screens, according to critic Gregg Kilday.

The results were mixed. While many movie companies had never made as much money as they had at the end of the 1980s (in part because of steep rises in ticket prices), only ardent stockholders could be inclined to point with pride to the

16–2. *Commando* **(U.S.A., 1985),** *with Arnold Schwarzenegger, directed by Mark L. Lester.*
Although initially laughed at for his bulbous physique and un-melodious Austrian accent, Schwarzenegger went on to become a major action **star** in films like *The Terminator* and *Predator* and *Total Recall*. With his massive body, lantern jaw, and guttural accent, Schwarzenegger specialized in playing live-action cartoons, a friendly Frankenstein monster incapable of being damaged. His best films work off this quality, usually putting him in a comic book or science-fiction context. *(Twentieth Century–Fox)*

films that were bringing in the profits. If movies, en masse, were not worse than ever, they were certainly more mediocre than ever. True, every year still offered its quota of eight to ten excellent films. But the vast middle ground of vehicles and **programmers** that had once harbored the ferocious energy of a Cagney or the saturnine elegance of a Bogart were now given over to banal time-passers that lacked even the conviction of craft.

According to a study by *Orbit Video* magazine, the top ten box office performers of the 1980s were, in this order, Harrison Ford, Dan Aykroyd, Eddie Murphy, Bill Murray, Tom Cruise, Sylvester Stallone, Jack Nicholson, John Candy, Steve Guttenberg, and Danny DeVito. It was not a good period for female stars or women's pictures. In the same survey, Kim Basinger placed fifteenth and Sigourney Weaver ranked sixteenth as the top women earners. Five of the top ten were former TV comedians. Their movies were generally tired retreads of their earlier (and better) work on television—slickly packaged star vehicles, very much in the manner of the old Hollywood studios.

The revitalized—and highly successful—Disney studio was a good example of the new studio system. It constructed an efficient assembly line that turned out a profusion of modestly budgeted films featuring medium-range performers (Robin Williams, Tom Selleck, Bette Midler) with a high degree of likability. The scripts and direction of movies like *Stakeout* (1987), *Three Men and a Baby* (1987), and *Beaches* (1988) were indifferent at best, but the "packaging" was immaculate. Like

MGM in the 1930s and 1940s, Disney showcased popular stars as the public wanted to see them.

These were movies designed to divert you for ninety minutes and leave you with nothing afterward, movies that the mind flushed after viewing. On that limited basis, they succeeded splendidly, often bringing in enormous profits. With filmmaking like this, the commercial cinema moved closer than ever to the simple, formulaic images of routine television.

The reasons were not hard to come by. Movie studios were increasingly run by executives recruited from television and talent agencies. These people were used to providing what had already been perceived as a public demand. The old moguls, whatever their lack of social graces, were promoters, entrepreneurs who were not averse to taking chances. But in the 1980s, film budgets, rapidly ascending toward the sky, made it harder to justify financing any project that might be considered risky.

This is not to say that younger directors lacked passion for filmmaking. But increasingly it seemed that the passion was unconnected to anything deeper than the celluloid itself. Part of this creeping sterility was the result of life experience— or lack of it. Old-time directors like William Wellman came to movies after, as the

16–3. *Aliens* (U.S.A., 1986), *with Sigourney Weaver and Carrie Henn, directed by James Cameron.*
With "women's pictures" increasingly being relegated to television, strong parts for female stars became harder to find. Fine actresses like Sigourney Weaver found themselves in Arnold Schwarzenegger parts, with their femininity and humor often providing the only reason to see the picture. In *Aliens,* however, director Cameron provided a roller-coaster ride of propulsive excitement.   *(Twentieth Century–Fox)*

saying goes, having made other plans. Wellman was an aviator and flew with the Lafayette Flying Corps in World War I. Raoul Walsh rode with the Mexican revolutionary, Pancho Villa. Experiences like that can't help but broaden one's horizons beyond those of someone who grew up cruising the suburbs of Phoenix, Seattle, or Atlanta.

Many younger directors were now in the position of being lavishly costumed without having a place to go, of having technique to burn without having anything to say. Thus, a director like James Cameron, having already proved himself to be a superb orchestrator of action and reaction in films like *The Terminator* (1984) and *Aliens* **(16–3),** attempted a film like *The Abyss* (1989). In trying to venture deeper into himself than he ever had, he came up with an embarrassingly empty hand. In most cases, however, these were precisely the kinds of films that were right for the times.

The Reagan Era

President Ronald Reagan and his conservative agenda placed major emphasis on a return to what was commonly referred to as "traditional" values—that is, not the 1960s. This movement away from the social concerns that had defined the previous generation could not help but be reflected in a mass-audience art like film. The majority of audiences (and voters), exhausted by nearly twenty years of civil, social, and political strife begun by the assassination of John Kennedy and eventually encompassing Vietnam, the antiwar movement, the civil rights struggle, rampaging inflation, the Watergate scandal, and the loss of national prestige abroad, simply decided that they didn't want to hear about it anymore.

During President Reagan's administration, military spending, financed primarily with borrowed money, reached record-shattering heights. Many of the top-grossing films of the 1980s dealt with military subjects: *Top Gun; Rambo; First Blood II; Platoon; An Officer and a Gentleman; Good Morning, Vietnam; Stripes; Private Benjamin; Rambo III; Full Metal Jacket;* and *Heartbreak Ridge.*

It was an era of big money. The national debt exceeded all previous administrations combined and now had to be calculated in trillions of dollars. Enormous private and corporate fortunes were amassed. American audiences were fascinated by the lives of the rich, as illustrated by such television shows as *Dynasty, Dallas,* and *Lifestyles of the Rich and Famous,* as well as such movies as *Trading Places, Wall Street,* and *Arthur.*

Conversely, social welfare spending was radically slashed. The results: an estimated one to three million homeless—many of them women and children—wandered the streets of America's cities, where many of them still barely survive. The U.S. Census Bureau reported that by the late 1980s, the poorest one fifth of American families received only 4.6 percent of the total income, the smallest percentage since 1954. On the other hand, the richest one fifth accounted for 44 percent of the income, the biggest share ever recorded. The 1980s might be aptly summed up by Dickens's famous line: "It was the best of times; it was the worst of times."

Nevertheless, throughout the decade, good movies were made both within the mainstream framework of conventional filmmaking modes as well as in covertly subversive ways, by maverick artists with an eye on subterranean America.

16–4. *Bird* (U.S.A., 1988), *directed by Clint Eastwood*.
The slightly schizoid career of star/director (and sometimes politician) Clint Eastwood reached its height by the late 1980s. On the one hand, he could appear in *Heartbreak Ridge* (1986), a conventional tough-sergeant-turns-boys-into-men boot camp story which climaxed in an attempt to make the invasion of tiny Grenada an act of heroism on the level of raising the flag at Iwo Jima, instead of a triumph of public relations. On the other hand, he could direct the downbeat *Bird*, a sensitive, visually sophisticated biography of the great jazz saxophonist Charlie Parker, which won Forest Whitaker (left) the Best Actor award at the Cannes Film Festival. *(Warner Brothers)*

The Mainstream

Many of the best movies of the 1980s were made by veteran directors, established artists like Bruce Beresford, Peter Weir, Milos Forman, Woody Allen, Steven Spielberg, and Paul Mazursky. Most of these filmmakers came to prominence in the 1970s. Sydney Pollack's *Tootsie* (1982) was one of the hallmarks of the feminist cinema, a witty exploration of gender roles, with a brilliant performance by Dustin Hoffman in the title part. Similarly, three of John Huston's greatest works—*Wise Blood* (1980), *Prizzi's Honor* (1985), and *The Dead* (1987)—were made when the old master was in his seventies, an extraordinary achievement in itself. But there were also some newcomers who managed to create enduring works.

LAWRENCE KASDAN (b. 1947) showed in films like *Body Heat* **(16–5)**, *The Big Chill* (1983), *Silverado* (1985), and *The Accidental Tourist* (1988) an uncanny ability to mimic someone else's source material, then give it a slight twist. It didn't matter whether the subject was **film noir,** as in *Body Heat's* spinoff of *Double Indemnity* and *Out of the Past;* the western, as in *Silverado* taking off on *The Magnificent Seven; The Accidental Tourist's* mimicking of Anne Tyler's affectless prose; or *I Love You to Death* (1990), a rip-off of *Divorce—Italian Style.*

16–5. *Body Heat* **(U.S.A., 1981),** *with William Hurt and Kathleen Turner, directed by Lawrence Kasdan.*
William Hurt rapidly attained star status after his debut in *Altered States* (1980). The tall, quiet, deep-voiced Hurt clearly enjoys challenges and is not afraid of playing characters nowhere near as bright as they think they are. In *Body Heat*, Hurt played lawyer Ned Racine, a dupe enslaved and destroyed by his lust for Matty Walker (Kathleen Turner). Turner went on to become one of the primary female stars of the decade, enlivening all her films with her sensuality and indomitability. *(The Ladd Company)*

While this ability to emulate his betters stands Kasdan in good stead with those audiences unaware of just who is being stolen from, it also accounts for an odd hollowness in his films. Except for his taste for off-beat, slightly unsympathetic characters, it is possible that Kasdan, a very talented man without much of a voice of his own, would have been perfectly happy under the classic studio system, making slick commercial assignments.

BARRY LEVINSON (b. 1932) showed that it was still possible to make quality, personal movies and make money too. After a long apprenticeship spent writing in both television and motion pictures, Levinson finally got to write and direct his first film. *Diner* (1982) was a Baltimore version of Fellini's *I Vitelloni*—about a bunch of young men nervously circling around adulthood by sitting around talking. It was a success, and Levinson then began a habit of alternating apparently commercial projects with apparently personal ones. The sentimentally overstuffed, celebratory marshmallow *The Natural* (1984) was followed by the pleasant but slightly impersonal *Young Sherlock Holmes* (1985).

Then came *Tin Men* (1987), more schmoozing around in Baltimore, this time in the early 1960s. Amusingly desperate aluminum-siding salesmen, middle-aged and on the edge of burning out, stave off exhaustion by filling up their lives with ephemeral, diverting stupidities: a Hatfield–McCoy feud involving a woman (Barbara Hershey) or obsessing about the plot subtleties of the TV western *Bonanza*.

Levinson next made *Good Morning, Vietnam* **(16–6),** which was primarily several Robin Williams stand-up routines bookended by a meandering, sentimental Vietnam movie. Like *The Natural,* it was not among Levinson's most interesting films, although it was an enormous commercial hit, largely due to Williams's box office popularity.

Levinson followed that, however, with *Rain Man* **(16–7),** a painstakingly observed movie about a middle-aged autistic (Dustin Hoffman) and his slimy, opportunistic younger brother (Tom Cruise). Levinson's respect for his characters, exemplified by his unintrusive use of **telephoto lenses,** was never more apparent. He cunningly deemphasized costar Cruise and his character's predictable voyage from selfishness to decency by keeping most of the attention centered on the noncommunicative Raymond.

As the brothers journey across America, Levinson shoots their trek in an original, semiabstract manner that gives the film an unexpected element of elegant visual poetry. *Rain Man* made nearly $150 million and won the Best Picture Oscar, cementing Levinson's position as one of the most gifted talents working in American films.

Of the commercial directors of the 1980s, few had the energy, good will, or high spirits of ROBERT ZEMECKIS (b. 1952). Zemeckis and writing partner Bob Gale began as protégés of Steven Spielberg. Spielberg stuck with them even after their initial production. *I Wanna Hold Your Hand* (1978), was a complete failure and the film they wrote for him, *1941* (1979), turned out to be a critical and commercial disaster.

16–6. *Good Morning, Vietnam* **(U.S.A., 1987),** *with Robin Williams, directed by Barry Levinson.*
Like many comedians who became popular through television, Williams went on to make movies, some successful, some not. Because of his particular stream-of-consciousness manner of speed talking, it was difficult to devise a viable screen framework for him. *Good Morning, Vietnam,* with the comedian as an anti-Establishment disc jockey in Vietnam, proved to be one of his greatest hits. The actor's ambition got more satisfying challenges afterward, as he went on to work for respected directors like Peter Weir and opposite actors like Robert De Niro. *(Touchstone Pictures)*

16–7. *Rain Man* **(U.S.A., 1988),** *with Tom Cruise and Dustin Hoffman, directed by Barry Levinson.*
Rain Man is an effective mingling of the artistic and commercial. Its star, Dustin Hoffman, a major acting figure since 1967's *The Graduate,* consolidated his reputation as the screen's finest character actor with his portrayal of the autistic Charlie Babbitt. Working with heart-throb Tom Cruise gave Hoffman access to an audience that would probably never have gone to see the movie otherwise.   *(United Artists)*

Zemeckis came into his own with *Used Cars* (1980), a hilariously mean-spirited, larcenous comedy in which venality runs wild. *Used Cars* is about Rudy Russo (Kurt Russell), who delights in selling dangerously rickety "pre-owned autos" to stupid suburban families he despises. Between sales, he dreams of going into politics. He regards his moral, upright boss (Jack Warden) as a hopeless, anti-quated dupe. When his boss is murdered by his corrupt twin brother (who also sells used cars in a lot across the street), Rudy, to save the business, gets a chance to exercise his gift for duplicity and conniving. It was all very much in the manner of Preston Sturges, although this film too was a box office disappointment.

Zemeckis finally got the hit he deserved with the romantic comedy/adventure film *Romancing the Stone* (1984). Since then, he has gone from strength to strength, including the adept *Back to the Future* (1985) and its two sequels.

The big hit *Who Framed Roger Rabbit* **(16–8)** is an ingenious amalgam of live action and **animation,** which served as both a tribute to and rebirth of classical animation. Zemeckis's major fault is one he shares with his mentor Spielberg—an affection for noisy hyping within a film, a certain restlessness, an inability to trust the audience to get the point without a rude nudge in the ribs.

Zemeckis's biggest hit was *Forrest Gump* (1994), which provided Tom Hanks with one of his greatest roles. He was also the principal reason for the film's success.

16–8. ***Who Framed Roger Rabbit*** **(U.S.A., 1988),** *with Bob Hoskins (left) and Roger Rabbit, directed by Robert Zemeckis.*
Who Framed Roger Rabbit is one of cinema's great technical triumphs. During filming, Hoskins acted to nothing, while props (the handcuffs, for instance) were manipulated by wires that the camera couldn't see. After the live-action footage was shot, Richard Williams and his animators had the job of believably inserting their animation into the scenes. *(The Walt Disney Company and Amblin Entertainment)*

The Mavericks

"Established" mavericks like Martin Scorsese continued to make audacious movies during the 1980s. There were also some startling debuts, like DAVID LYNCH (b. 1946), who first drew attention with the eerie, surrealistic *Eraserhead* (1978). The movie was billed as "a dream of dark and troubling things." For once, the publicity didn't lie.

Lynch's first aboveground hit was *The Elephant Man* (1980), the story of John Merrick, a nineteenth-century victim of a horribly disfiguring disease. What made the movie remarkable was not so much the narrative as the imagery. Lynch and his cinematographer, the great Freddie Francis, photographed the film in black-and-white CinemaScope, infusing the **mise en scène** with terrifying shadows. The soundtrack throbs with weird, forbidding industrial rumblings. Gradually, Lynch enables us to perceive the distorted, tormented, yet oddly poetic creature that was John Merrick, a human being.

16–9. *Blue Velvet* **(U.S.A., 1986),** *directed by David Lynch.*
Dorothy (Isabella Rosellini) is implicated in a crime; Jeffrey (Kyle MacLachlan) is rifling her apartment looking for evidence when she catches him. She forces him to undress at knifepoint and begins a strange sexual ritual. "Don't touch me or I'll kill you," she whispers as she becomes excited. In Lynch's movies, love hurts—literally. *(De Laurentiis Entertainment Group)*

After running headlong into the brick wall of the unadaptable *Dune* (1984), Lynch made his masterpiece, *Blue Velvet* (**16–9**). It too might well have been advertised as "a dream of dark and troubling things." Taking place in the imaginary small town of Lumberton ("the town that knows how much wood the woodchuck chucks . . ."), Lynch takes his protagonist, the baby-faced Kyle MacLachlan, and the audience into a dizzying descent into perversity and death, as represented by Dennis Hopper at his most demonic.

The film's opening clearly signals what we are in for. While the sloppily romantic old Bobby Vinton title song croons on the soundtrack, Lynch **dissolves** in and out of short, bucolic images: a fire truck driving by in **slow motion,** with a fireman waving at the camera, small-town homes in the manner of Norman Rockwell, all bathed in relentlessly cheerful colors and a nostalgic, fuzzy **soft focus.** For the first minute or so, we seem to be in a soft-sell campaign commercial.

The camera moves in on a man watering his lawn. The hose gets tangled up. The man is suddenly stricken by something, grabs his neck and collapses. A neighborhood dog begins playing with the water spewing awkwardly out of the hose. The camera then moves down, past the stricken man to the ground, through the grass, into the world of the chattering, buzzing, crawling insects waging frantic battle below the conventionally pleasant surface "reality."

The rest of Lynch's movie fully lives up to the metaphoric tone of the opening scene. He continually juxtaposes the false domestic jollity seen in bad commercials with overwhelming flashes of nightmarish evil. Jeffrey, the film's main character, stares transfixed as all his naive assumptions about the nature of the universe slowly disappear. "I'm seeing something that was always hidden," he tells his girlfriend as he finds himself voyeuristically led into thrilling kinky sex and, ultimately, murder.

Blue Velvet proved conclusively that Lynch was a total original, one of those directors (Cocteau also comes to mind) who seems to work primarily from the subconscious, dredging up images and inchoate concepts with very little intervening mediation from an ordering intelligence. He is one of those rare directors who can make the irrational simultaneously seductive and terrifying. Unfortunately, he can also become mannered, as in *Wild at Heart* (1990).

The Canadian DAVID CRONENBERG (b. 1948) also produces images from horrifying nightmares. Cronenberg's early movies like *Scanners* (1981) and *Videodrome* (1983) devolved into a succession of set pieces on the subject of grotesque physical transformations. Unfortunately, they also deteriorated into narrative incoherence.

But with *The Fly* **(16–10),** Cronenberg achieved something he had only hinted at before, an elemental emotional involvement to accompany his undoubted gift at graphically demonstrating disfigurement. Based on the potboiler 1958 original—but a potboiler with a fascinating central idea—Cronenberg concentrated on the humiliation wrought on a human being gradually becoming something else . . . something less. A scientist working on the problem of matter transference unwittingly allows a common housefly into the teleporter with him. The fly's genes mix with his own, and the debilitating, ultimately horrifying transformation begins.

By tying the basic premise in with a love story of some passion and believability, Cronenberg transcended the narrow limits of the genre he was working in and created a convincing, moving metaphor: transformation as fatal illness, analogous to cancer, or AIDS. Truly, a movie for the 1980s.

JONATHAN DEMME (b. 1944) has managed to work within the mainstream conventions of commercial cinema in spite of the fact that he has never been particularly commercial. A Demme film is usually marked not by flourishes of the camera

16–10. *The Fly* **(U.S.A., 1986),** *with Jeff Goldblum, directed by David Cronenberg.*
Rather than using a conventional leading man for his film, David Cronenberg wisely cast the gangly, quirky, empathetic Jeff Goldblum, an actor the audience can relate to instantly. Because he is without the monolithic invulnerability that usually attaches to movie stars, Goldblum's portrayal made the fate of his character all the more viscerally horrifying to the audience. *(Twentieth Century–Fox)*

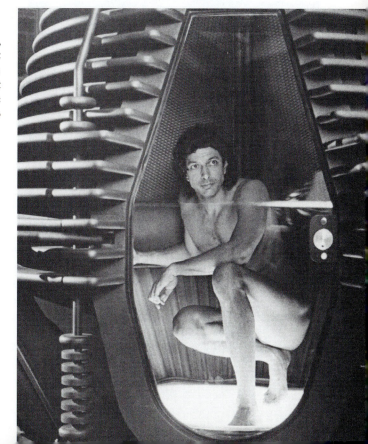

16–11. *The Silence of the Lambs* **(U.S.A., 1991),** *with Anthony Hopkins, directed by Jonathan Demme.*
This psychological thriller was Demme's breakthrough film, a huge hit which also won an Oscar as best picture. Hopkins's electrifying performance as Dr. Hannibal "The Cannibal" Lecter also won an Academy Award. Like most British-trained actors, Hopkins is extraordinarily versatile, equally at home playing Shakespeare, romantic contemporary roles, offbeat character parts, and in a variety of styles and dialects. He did not command much popular attention until his performance in this movie. Since then, he has gained a wide following and is one of the most admired actors in the world.   *(Orion Pictures)*

but by a concentration on characters on the periphery of society. His characters range from the lonely blue-collar naifs of *Melvin and Howard* to the tacky Mafia members of *Married to the Mob* (1988). Demme's métier is in films about losers whom he refuses to treat as losers. He invests even their most bizarre, illogical moments and schemes with a frayed, yearning dignity.

Demme's best movie is probably *Something Wild* (1987). It begins with the conventional premise of an uptight, middle-class bourgeois (Jeff Daniels) liberated by a sexual and socially outrageous pickup (Melanie Griffith). But into the premise, which has served as a basis of dozens of movies since the era of screwball comedy, Demme introduced a dangerous ex-boyfriend (Ray Liotta), who scarily causes events to turn very serious indeed. Unfortunately, the unnerving mix of the good-humored with the homicidal got in the way of the film's commercial success. Demme's biggest hits to date are *The Silence of the Lambs* **(16–11)** and *Philadelphia.* His biggest disappointment was *Beloved* (1999), an adaptation of the Toni Morrison novel, with Oprah Winfrey, which died at the box office.

OLIVER STONE (b. 1946) first achieved popular success with *Platoon* (1986), but he had been around for almost ten years, since winning an Academy Award for

16–12. *Salvador* (**U.S.A., 1986**), *with James Woods (center), James Belushi (left), and John Savage, directed by Oliver Stone.*
James Woods is something of a throwback to the great Warner Brothers stars of the thirties: a daring actor with a gift for embodying danger and emotional violence. Woods's gift isn't merely that he has a high degree of resistance to the common actor's need to be liked. It's that he transforms even an ordinary scene by, at the very least, his intensity, his sublimated hostility, his sarcastic charm, or, at the most, his gift for the unexpected, the off-center line reading or character revelation. His performance as photographer Richard Boyle in *Salvador*, a manic sleaze slowly but methodically redeemed by his love for a woman and for the country of El Salvador, was one of the high-water performances of the decade. *(Hemdale Releasing Corporation)*

his script to *Midnight Express. Platoon* was a powerful, elemental film positing clearly defined positions of good and evil in the persons of two competing sergeants played by Willem Dafoe and Tom Berenger. Caught between them is a callow battle virgin—the appropriately callow Charlie Sheen. This elemental—one might even say schematic—structure, and even the fact that many of the plot incidents were thin revisions of similar episodes in previous films like *Paths of Glory*, were overlooked because of Stone's passion and because the time was ripe for a reexamination of America's role in Vietnam.

The success of *Platoon* overshadowed Stone's far superior *Salvador* (**16–12**), the story of a renegade journalist (played by the edgy, compulsive, snarling James Woods) loose in an El Salvador ravaged by civil strife and American political complicity.

Stone went on to make two flashy exercises in the obvious. The first, *Wall Street*, breathlessly informed the audience that desperately climbing the greasy pole of material success leads to failure and dishonor. It's a message that needed to be stressed in the 1980s, but Stone's sober seriousness proved inadequate, superficial. The picture was redeemed in part by a zesty performance by Michael Douglas as the diabolical entrepreneur Gordon Gekko, greed incarnate. Stone's next film was the loud diatribe *Talk Radio* (1988). He returned to the subject of Vietnam in the box office hit *Born on the Fourth of July* (1989), with Tom Cruise in the leading role. The final installment of his Vietnam Trilogy was *Heaven and Earth* (1993), the least successful critically and commercially of the three movies.

Stone is a strident critic of the conservative status quo in the manner of earlier American pulp film artists like Robert Aldrich or Samuel Fuller. It's clear that Stone is unafraid to milk melodrama; he can be powerful, but he can also be heavy handed. Too often he uses his splashy tabloid style to reduce complex problems to glib, left-wing certainties, a criticism lodged by many commentators about his dazzlingly virtuosic conspiracy film, *JFK* (1992).

One of the most interesting filmmakers to emerge during the decade was SPIKE LEE (b. 1957). A black artist who proudly asserted his blackness and his roots in the Bedford-Stuyvesant area of Brooklyn, Lee produced his first feature on an absurdly small budget. *She's Gotta Have It* (1986) turned out to be a funny, spunky triangle comedy about a sexy woman who insists on her right to not commit to any one man. After a slight stumble with the insular, slightly garbled *School Daze* (1987), Lee came back strong with *Do the Right Thing* **(16–13),** a day and a night in a black ghetto neighborhood surrounding a white-owned pizzeria, culminating in an explosive race riot.

Do the Right Thing is an unsentimental critique of bigotry, both black and white. The film shows off Lee at his best: the rich sense of behavioral detail and humor, the idiosyncratic, often very funny dialogue, the ability to orchestrate and work with a large, expert group of actors. It also marked a quantum leap forward in his style. *Do the Right Thing* effortlessly utilizes the entire arsenal of film technique with a skill bordering on virtuosity.

16–13. *Do the Right Thing* **(U.S.A., 1989),** *with Bill Nunn and Giancarlo Esposito, produced, written, and directed by Spike Lee.*
The world of Spike Lee is layered, polemical, and intensely political: sex as politics, inner-city turf as politics, politics as politics. Yet for all the director's specificity about time (now) and place (Brooklyn), his films are as popular in cities like London as they are in New York. *(Universal Pictures)*

16–14. *Planes, Trains and Automobiles* (U.S.A., 1987), *with John Candy and Steve Martin, directed by John Hughes.*
The decade saw a steady stream of feather-light comedies starring the male alumni of *Saturday Night Live* and *Second City* such as Chevy Chase, John Candy, Eddie Murphy, and Dan Aykroyd. Perhaps because they were made to appeal to the same audience that had made the stars popular, these films often took the form of a loosely connected series of episodes (skits) around a central theme in which the comedians would attempt characterizations similar to those that had made them popular in the first place. Despite their cardboard parameters, these packaged films were usually successful in appealing to the TV-bred audiences for which they were made.   *(Paramount Pictures)*

Lee mixes up style and content. Three middle-aged wastrels sitting around boasting about their sexual conquests in the graphic, funny rhythms of the street are perfectly naturalistic. But behind them is a stylized red wall unlikely to be found in any inner city. Lee is also a confrontational artist, unafraid of offending racial hypocrites of any color. As the film's ethnic tensions begin to heat up, Lee suddenly fires a quick barrage of the film's characters (black, white, and yellow) screaming out racist invectives directly to the camera . . . and to us.

Someone who would have found it difficult to function under the studio system is JOHN SAYLES (b. 1948). Sayles began as a novelist and screenwriter before moving into direction. His command of the film medium gradually strengthened until, by the end of the decade, he was an assured, if low-key stylist. Sayles's first movie, *The Return of the Secaucus Seven* (1980), was a rueful, winning, slightly clumsy ensemble effort about the reunion of a group of college radicals from the 1960s.

After that critical and commercial success, Sayles next had an unhappy experience with a studio on *Baby, It's You* (1983). He returned to his independent ways with the self-financed *Lianna* (1983), a story about a married woman coming out as a lesbian. After the funny, sly parody *The Brother from Another Planet* (1984), a science-fiction parable about, among many other things, racism, Sayles made two impressive features nearly back to back: *Matewan* (1987), about a coal-mining strike in the 1920s, and *Eight Men Out* **(16–15),** another period film.

Eight Men Out was a critically successful work, an examination of the 1919 Black Sox Scandal. Sayles beautifully captured the shifting alliances on the baseball field, the alliance of the bought, and the rage of those who weren't playing along.

Both *Matewan* and *Eight Men Out* adopted a Marxist view of history. In the latter, the context for the players taking their $10,000 bribes is the disgustingly cheap, conniving owner of the White Sox, Charles Comiskey, who is explicitly equated with the corrupting gamblers.

Unfortunately, Sayles's timing could hardly have been worse. The most conservative political mind-set since the early 1920s was hardly sympathetic to Marxist analyses of capital and labor. Both movies were financial failures. The indifferent public response to these movies may hinder but not prevent Sayles from contributing more of his slyly moving morality plays about times when Americans were genuinely shocked by corruption rather than subliminally expecting it, excusing it, and, by doing so, participating in it.

Although widely thought to be English because of his years of work with the Monty Python troupe, TERRY GILLIAM (b. 1940) is in fact American. He came to directing through his work as an animator, and the cutout collage style of antic animation he devised for the Python troupe has also become the dominant mode of his live-action work. Gilliam's list of movies is short but distinctive. His first film, *Jabberwocky* (1976), was a pastiche of cruel humor and absurdist style which never quite fused. His next work, *Time Bandits* (1981), revealed Gilliam's strangely beautiful visual gift at full bore.

Brazil **(16–17)** was not a lighthearted travelogue but a slightly thin rewrite of George Orwell's *1984,* done with all of Gilliam's artistry. Unfortunately, it involved

16–15. *Eight Men Out* **(U.S.A., 1988),** *with David Strathairn, directed by John Sayles.*
A master of low-budget filmmaking, Sayles's movie is exceptionally rich in its period details. A first-class cast re-creates the notorious 1919 World Series, in which the Chicago White Sox were bribed to throw the games in exchange for cash. As usual, Sayles plays a small role in the picture, as the famous sportswriter Ring Lardner. *(Orion Pictures)*

16–16. *Ironweed* (U.S.A., 1987), *with Meryl Streep,*
directed by Hector Babenco.
In a 1989 poll of fifty-four national movie critics, conducted
by the magazine *American Film*, Meryl Streep was the easy
winner as the best actress of the 1980s. Her performance
credits during this decade include such important works as
*The French Lieutenant's Woman, Sophie's Choice, Plenty, Out of
Africa, Silkwood, A Cry in the Dark,* and *Ironweed*, among
others. A graduate of the prestigious Yale Drama School,
Streep has performed in live theater and television as well as
movies. She is best known for playing tragic and courageous
women, but she is also adept at comedy and even musicals.
Like most ambitious artists, she strives for diversity in her
roles and has worked with a wide variety of directors, including such international filmmakers as Reisz, Schepisi, and
Babenco. *(Tri-Star Pictures)*

the filmmaker in a deleterious tussle with the film's distributors over its length and
content. The movie was released in Gilliam's version, but it was a Pyrrhic victory,
for it never found a large audience.

Unfortunately, neither did *The Adventures of Baron Munchausen* (1989),
though it was Gilliam's most unified, visually inventive effort since *Time Bandits.* It
is clear that Gilliam's primary gifts are for startling imagery and the ability to create
a sense of playful wonder. His storytelling ability is something else again. Most of
Gilliam's pictures easily subdivide into sequences, some brilliant, some muddled.
Of all modern filmmakers, Gilliam is the one who can trace his lineage most clearly
to the work of the equally antic Georges Méliès.

A similarly quirky talent who emerged during this era was TIM BURTON (b.
1960). Known for his comic strip sensibility, Burton in fact was educated at the California Institute of the Arts, with a major in animation, and he served briefly as an
animator with the Disney studio. His feature directing debut was *Pee-Wee's Big Adventure* (1985), a sly children's parable with the gifted comedian Pee-Wee Herman
in the leading role.

Burton's *Beatlejuice* (1988) was more personal, a campy ghost story with flashy
special effects and a superb comic performance by Michael Keaton. *Batman*
(16–18), based on the popular comic book, was one of the biggest hits of the 1980s,

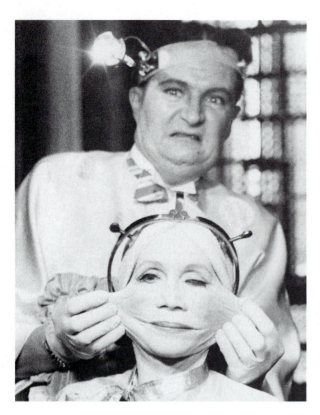

16–17. *Brazil* **(U.S.A./Great Britain, 1985),** *with Katherine Helmond and Jim Broadbent, directed by Terry Gilliam.*
Gilliam's social satire is never funnier than in the scenes involving this silly society matron and her frequent trips to her plastic surgeon.   *(Universal Pictures)*

with another tour-de-force performance by Keaton in the title role. Burton's masterpiece to date is probably the poetic *Edward Scissorhands* (1990), a bittersweet fairy tale about an artistic youth (Johnny Depp) who has cutting shears instead of hands. Depp also starred in the bizarre *Ed Wood* (1994), based on an actual film personality of the 1950s.

Burton's weird sensibility is apparent in all of these movies: a predilection for fablelike narratives; a fondness for the grotesque and the bizarre; the frequent use of black comedy and campy wit; a preoccupation with youth and childhood fears; the frequent use of special effects, often with comical intent; and a striking visual style, based on distortion and exaggeration, very much in the tradition of German Expressionism.

There could not help but be a reaction against the preponderance of impersonal, studio-style entertainments that dominated the 1980s. Many small companies rushed into production only to discover that making quality films that the public is interested in paying to see is a considerably trickier job, with far less margin for error, than taking an already completed picture and shipping it out to the marketplace. After three or four years of producing films for shrinking audiences, companies like Cannon, Atlantic, and Vestron ceased to exist.

For many of these companies, the cart of video was placed before the horse of the movie itself. A major art movie could bring as much as $700,000 for video rights alone, so even with bad distribution or indifferent response in the theaters, a

16–18. *Batman* (U.S.A., 1989), *with Michael Keaton and Kim Basinger, directed by Tim Burton.*
Batman was a huge blockbuster hit, thanks in part to its shrewd promotion and marketing. The movie established Burton as one of the foremost visual stylists of his generation. The major characteristics of his weird sensibility are a childlike sense of innocence tinged with undercurrents of dark anxiety and touches of campy malice. Production designer Anton Furst created a Gotham City that's part comic book cartoon, part **film noir,** and a lot of German Expressionism. The city's towering skyscrapers strain upward, gasping for air through the polluted skies. Sinister alleys and dark, cavelike crannies conceal unspeakable crimes against humanity. Danny Elfman's morose, Wagnerian score offers no relief from the oppressive gloom. Critic Pauline Kael marveled, "It's Manhattan gone psycho." *(Warner Brothers)*

distributor could at least break even. But as video shelves got more crowded, there was less room and less demand for "art" movies. In addition, production required far more money than just distribution did. The 1987 stock-market crash dried up a lot of venture capital, and the tax laws were altered, making film investment much less attractive.

By October 1989, when the Japanese Sony Corporation purchased Columbia Pictures from the Coca-Cola Company, it was apparent that foreign investors would become increasingly involved in studio ownership. This merely made official what had already become a standard part of the production process: considering foreign territories as well as domestic when contemplating a prospective film project. By the late 1980s, the foreign returns for movies like *Top Gun* and *Who Framed Roger Rabbit* far outstripped domestic grosses.

Only one thing was certain: D. W. Griffith's ideal of film as a "universal language" assuredly came true, not only artistically but economically as well.

16–19. *Dangerous Liaisons* (U.S.A., 1988), *with Uma Thurman, Glenn Close, and John Malkovich, directed by Stephen Frears.*
The gifted British filmmaker Stephen Frears was able to bring in this lavish costume picture for under $15 million—in an era when even run-of-the-mill Hollywood movies averaged from $17 to $20 million. Similarly, ambitious actors like Glenn Close and John Malkovich—who have performed in live theater and television as well as film—sometimes accept modest salaries to perform in such quality productions. *(Warner Brothers)*

FURTHER READING

AUSTIN, BRUCE A. *Immediate Seating: A Look at Movie Audiences.* Belmont, Calif.: Wadsworth Publishing, 1989. Sociological research on the film industry and its relation to the mass audience.

CROWDUS, GARY. "Personal Struggles and Political Issues," *Cineaste* (vol. 16, no. 3, 1988). A thoughtful interview with Oliver Stone about his political and social beliefs and his film-making philosophy.

HICKENLOOPER, GEORGE. "The Primal Energies of the Horror Film," *Cineaste* (vol. 17, no. 2, 1989). A revealing interview with David Cronenberg on the roots of the horror film, critics, and being Canadian.

JEFFORDS, SUSAN. *Hard Bodies: Hollywood Masculinity in the Reagan Era.* New Brunswick: N.J.: Rutgers University Press, 1994. A critical study of the right-wing drift of American movies of the 1980s.

KAEL, PAULINE. *State of the Art* (New York: E. P. Dutton, 1985), and *Taking It All In* (New York: Holt, Rinehart and Winston, 1984). Provocative movie reviews by the astute former film critic of *The New Yorker.*

KILDAY, GREGG, and GREIL MARCUS. "The Eighties: The Industry & the Art," *Film Comment* (November–December, 1989). Survey of the decade.

KINDEM, GORHAM, ed. *The American Movie Industry: The Business of Motion Pictures.* Carbondale: Southern Illinois University Press, 1989. A collection of essays by experts in film-related fields such as law, mass communications, and finance.

NICHOLS, BILL, ed. *Movies and Methods,* Vol. II. Berkeley: University of California Press, 1985. A collection of scholarly essays on film theory, including genre criticism, feminism, semiotics, structuralism, and psychoanalytic approaches.

PRINCE, STEPHEN. *A New Pot of Gold: Hollywood Under the Electronic Rainbow.* N.Y.: Charles Seribner's Sons, 2000. Perceptive industry survey.

PRINCE, STEPHEN. *Visions of Empire.* New York: Praeger, 1992. Political imagery in American movies of the 1980s.

17

International Cinema in the 1980s

*We must all try to be more international, to make films for a world market
rather than just the home audience.*
—JUZO ITAMI, Japanese filmmaker

Atlantic Entertainment Group

Timeline: 1980–1990

1980

U.S.S.R. military mired in Afghanistan—"the Soviet Vietnam"

Lech Walesa leads "Solidarity" strike in Polish shipyards—new union formed, demanding political reforms

Beginning of Iraq–Iran war—bloody battles continue throughout the decade with horrendous casualties

1981

Marriage of Britain's Prince Charles and Lady Diana Spencer, accompanied by a media feeding frenzy

1984

Indian Prime Minister Indira Gandhi assassinated—riots ensue

French and American teams independently discover the AIDS virus

1985

Soviet leader Mikail Gorbachev begins radical liberal reforms in U.S.S.R.

1986

World premiere of Andrew Lloyd Webber's musical *The Phantom of the Opera,* London

World's worst nuclear accident in Chernobyl, U.S.S.R.—133,000 evacuated from area

1987

Gorbachev campaigns for *glasnost* (openness) and *perestroika* (restructuring) in U.S.S.R.

1988

Widespread strikes by Solidarity Union in Poland—Communist regime on the defensive

1989

Political revolution in Czechoslovakia—rejection of Communist rule in favor of parliamentary democracy

Thousands of prodemocracy demonstrators are killed by government troops in Tianamen Square, Beijing, China

Hated Berlin Wall is demolished—East and West Germany are united in 1990 under Chancellor Helmut Kohl

1990

South African President F. W. de Klerk radically liberalizes country—general amnesty for political prisoners, including African national Congress (ANC) leader Nelson Mandela

Free elections in many formerly Communist nations of Eastern Europe

British cinema, old and new. Kenneth Branagh and the Shakespearean tradition. Masterpiece Theatre movies. Late autumn: the cinema of James Ivory. Left-wing voices: Neil Jordan, Bill Forsyth, Stephen Frears. Western Europe: Spain's Pedro Almodóvar. France: Claude Berri. Holland's Paul Verhoeven. Scandinavia. The Eastern Bloc: pre- and post-*glasnost* Poland, Hungary, and the U.S.S.R. Third World cinema. Latin America: Brazil's Hector Babenco. Turkey's Yilmaz Güney. Japan: internationalization and the world marketplace. Juzo Itami.

XCEPT FOR THE RESURGENT BRITISH FILM INDUSTRY, which enjoyed a renaissance during the 1980s, this decade produced no important new movements in the international cinema. There was no *nouvelle vague*, no Prague Spring, no *Neue Kino*. Such traditional sources of artistic fertility as Italy, West Germany, and France experienced a dramatic shrinkage in quality and output. Some technically "foreign" movies were consciously aimed at the vast American market **(17–1)**. The film industries in the Soviet Union, Poland, and Hungary—the most progressive Communist bloc countries—were in a state of radical reorganization, like their economies and governments. The Japanese and Third World cinemas continued to struggle against overwhelming obstacles, yet a few forceful film artists managed to produce masterpieces.

Great Britain

The British film renaissance was a blending of the old and new. The old: literate scripts, first-rate actors, a high level of craftsmanship, and an intense class consciousness. There were also some familiar faces, established artists who were still producing important work: directors like David Lean and Richard Attenborough, writers like Robert Bolt and Harold Pinter, and actors like Maggie Smith, John Gielgud, and Vanessa Redgrave **(17–6),** to mention only a few of the most famous.

The "new" centered on an obsession with the recent past, especially the 1950s; and a rancorous resentment on the part of intellectuals toward Prime Minister Margaret Thatcher, who dominated the 1980s in Britain just as her fellow conservative Ronald Reagan dominated the political climate in America. The new wave of films also introduced some fresh faces: actors like Bob Hoskins, Kenneth Branagh, Gary Oldman, and Daniel Day-Lewis; writers like Hanif Kureishi and Dennis Potter. The works of three directors stand out from the rest: James Ivory, Bill Forsyth, and Stephen Frears.

For the most part, however, the majority of British movies during this period were created by relatively self-effacing directors who made only three or four pictures during the decade. Many of these artists also worked in television and live theater, which explains their small output of films. These three performing arts have always been more integrated in Britain **(17–2),** unlike the United States,

17–1. *Crocodile Dundee II* **(Australia, 1988),** *with Paul Hogan, directed by Peter Faiman.*
Hogan's star vehicle, *Crocodile Dundee* (1986), and its likable sequel were the Australian box office champions in the United States, grossing over $100 million apiece. Both movies were shot in Australia and the United States, featuring Aussie and American casts. Throughout the decade, many famous movie artists from Australia emigrated to the American studios—a temptation too glamorous to resist.
(Paramount Pictures)

where established film artists rarely work in television or live theater. The best films of the 1980s were generally only modestly successful at the box office. Even *Chariots of Fire* **(17–3)** and *Gandhi* (1982), both Oscar winners, were not huge grossers, at least not by American standards.

Sex is a frequent preoccupation in many British films of this era—hardly in keeping with the English stereotype of reserve. Typical themes included prostitution, homosexuality, adultery, sadomasochism, sexual repression, and, above all, sexual hypocrisy. "I think the English are highly motivated sexually," said Alan Clarke, who wrote and directed *Rita, Sue & Bob Too* (1987). "They're doing it all over the place in England, but not until now have they been doing it all over the place in films. We didn't set out to deliberately show 'the awakening sexuality of England,' but these films have been a long time in coming, and I don't see anything shocking or consciously exploitive in them."

A number of these pictures deal with famous sex scandals in modern British history. David Leland's *Wish You Were Here* (1987) and *Personal Services* (1988) are both loosely based on the life of Cynthia Payne, a well-known brothel madam whose ritzy clientele included many top government officials. *Another Country* **(17–4)** is a fictionalized account of the origins of the Soviet spy scandals of the 1950s.

The British cinema has always been characterized by a split between the left and right wings. In the past, the traditional, conservative wing has dominated. Some waggish critics dubbed this group the "Masterpiece Theatre" school of filmmaking. In the 1980s, the left-liberal wing gained ascendancy. It was an extension of the "Kitchen Sink" movement of the late 1950s (see Chapter 13). It also commanded most of the attention of international film critics.

17–2. *Henry V* **(Great Britain, 1989),** *with Kenneth Branagh (center), directed by Branagh.*
Shakespeare's play, which is not among his greatest works, is static and talky, with relatively little poetry and few memorable characters other than the title role. Branagh's brilliant direction transformed these stagey materials into a dazzling feat of cinematic virtuosity. Shot mostly in **closeups,** with a stirring score and exquisitely modulated lighting, the movie is highly kinetic and emotionally involving, with many moving camera shots, rapid-fire **editing,** and a first-rate cast. The battle scene, clearly indebted to the works of Kurosawa (especially *The Seven Samurai* and *Ran*), is gritty, visceral, and shockingly violent—yet choreographed with an unearthly beauty. It was a stunning debut, eclipsing even Olivier's famous 1944 version. *(The Samuel Goldwyn Company)*

First, the Masterpiece Theatre tradition. Ideologically, this school of filmmaking embraced a kind of upper-class humanism, with an emphasis on conservative values, especially that privileged troika—family, country, and God. Many of these movies are period films, set in the comfortable past, with its reassuring rituals. London and picturesque rural hamlets in the south of England usually serve as the principal settings, rarely the harsh industrial north.

17–3. *Chariots of Fire* **(Great Britain, 1981),** *with Ben Cross, directed by Hugh Hudson.*
Based on the true story of two champion British runners in the 1924 Paris Olympics, this popular film signaled a change for fortunes for the long-stagnant British cinema. The movie won the Best Picture Academy Award, and the musical score by Vangelis was a best-selling recording. *(Warner Brothers)*

17-4. *Another Country* **(Great Britain, 1984),** *with Rupert Everett and Colin Firth, directed by Marek Kanievska.* This rite-of-passage film is an exposé of the corrupt values of an exclusive prep school during the 1930s. The two protagonists, roommates and best friends, are both iconoclasts, rebels. Guy (Everett) is an open homosexual who refuses to be ashamed of his sexuality. Tommy (Firth) is a Communist intellectual who is disgusted by the elitist snobbery of the headmasters and most of the students, who are "all part of the same hypocrisy," a mirror of British society. *(Orion Classics)*

The best of these movies are not knee-jerk endorsements of Establishment values but deeply felt affirmations of such traditional British virtues as civility, duty, and courage, especially in troubled times. For example, John Boorman's *Hope and Glory* (1987) is set during the London Blitz of World War II, when the city was terrorized by Nazi bombs almost every night. Instead of the usual stiff-upper-lip stoicism of British wartime lore, however, the story is told from the perspective of an eight-year-old boy—Boorman as a child. The youth sees the Blitz as a liberating festival, a playground with fireworks every night. This bittersweet comedy reaffirms the tough resilience of family and country under fire, not in the usual sentimental manner but with audacious humor and outlandish characters.

Many of the movies of this conservative wing are adaptations of respected literary works. For example, several of the novels of the Edwardian E. M. Forster were adapted for the screen: *A Passage to India, A Room With a View* **(17–5),** and *Maurice* (1987). One of the most touching adaptations is Jack Clayton's *The Lonely Passion of Judith Hearne* (1987), based on the 1955 novel by Brian Moore, with Maggie Smith and Bob Hoskins playing desperate, tragically incompatible characters.

Since most of these movies deal with well-educated people, the characters speak the King's English—the "correct" dialect that is universally taught in the so-called public schools (which of course are private, expensive, and exclusive). The characters are articulate, poised. Sometimes they are melancholy, even tragically doomed, like those in *The Shooting Party* (1984), a poignant lament for a lost era of

17–5. *A Room With a View* **(Great Britain, 1986),** *with Helena Bonham-Carter and Daniel Day-Lewis, directed by James Ivory.*
When earnest Lucy Honeychurch (Bonham-Carter) travels to Italy in 1907, she almost sheds her proper English reserve when she almost falls in love with an exciting, free-spirited young Englishman, George Emerson (Julian Sands). Terrified by her feelings, she retreats back to England, where she becomes engaged to the priggish snob, Cecil Vyse (Day-Lewis). Throughout most of the movie, she lies to her friends, her family, and even to herself, but at the last moment, she follows the dictates of her heart—much to the relief of all the sensible people in the story. *(Cinecom International)*

graciousness and decency. Unlike the Kitchen Sink wing, the movies in this more traditional school of filmmaking usually treat sex with restraint. Some explore the negative effects of a repressed sexuality. Above all, the characters are almost exclusively bourgeois, white, Anglo-Saxon, and Protestant.

JAMES IVORY (b. 1928) has been directing movies since the 1960s, but it wasn't until the surprising success of *A Room With a View* that he found a large audience. Ivory is an American and attended film school at the University of Southern California. All of his movies have been produced by his longtime partner, Ismail Merchant, who was born and raised in India but educated in America. Most of the Merchant–Ivory productions were written by novelist Ruth Prawer Jhabvala, who is German but was educated in England and is married to an Indian. Ironically, although the majority of the movies they have produced together more than thirty-five years have been British, not one of them is British.

Known for their uncompromising artistic standards, these filmmakers operate more like a family than a company. Most of their movies have been made for less than $3 million, despite the fact that a lot of them are period films, which are usually expensive. Merchant, the money man, manages to run a thrifty operation, cutting costs by shooting on location and convincing actors to work for modest salaries and a percentage of the grosses rather than their usual fees.

Their earliest movies were shot in India and usually dealt with the clash of cultures between Indians and Europeans. The most artistically successful of these was *Shakespeare Wallah* (1966). When they began adapting literary properties, they enjoyed more commercial and critical success, most notably with such movies as

17–6. *Publicity photo of James Ivory, Vanessa Redgrave, and Ismail Merchant during the production of Howards End* **(Great Britain, 1992),** *directed by Ivory.*
The greatest of Ivory's three E. M. Forster adaptations, *Howards End* is set in England's Edwardian era (1901–1910), which is regarded by many Tory conservatives as the golden age of British power and prestige. The advent of World War I in 1914 brought these glory days to an end. When the war was over in 1918, Britain was staggering, stunned, no longer Number One. Vanessa Redgrave has acted in several Merchant–Ivory films. She is considered the foremost British actress of her generation, a winner of many international acting awards. Frank Rich, drama critic for *The New York Times,* described her as "the greatest living actress in the English-speaking world." Descended from a famous theatrical family, she began her career in the late 1950s, ranging freely from stage, movies, and television, in Britain, America, and elsewhere. *(Sony Pictures)*

The Europeans (1979) and *The Bostonians* (1984), both adapted by Jhabvala from novels by Henry James.

A Room With a View was a huge hit, grossing over $50 million internationally and receiving eight Academy Award nominations in the United States. (It won three—for art direction, costumes, and screenplay adaptation.) Like most of Ivory's best works, this charming comedy-romance is beautifully mounted, with elegant camerawork, ravishing color, and subtle compositions. Unlike most of his other movies, *A Room With a View* is juicy and lyrical, complete with thrilling Puccini arias, waving fields of grain, and a swooning heroine. Silly as all this sounds, the movie has an undeniable air of enchantment.

Maurice, their next film, is about a young man trying to come to terms with his homosexuality in a genteelly repressive and homophobic society. The movie is an honest piece of work, exquisitely mounted and well acted, but suffering from an excess of good taste. Critics complained of Ivory's reverential tone, his emotional detachment, and his lack of energy. Indeed, enervated movies like *Maurice* are precisely those that originally prompted critics to deride this school of filmmaking as "Masterpiece Theatre"—too tame.

The left-wingers are more lively. And rebellious. The "Kitchen Sink" label, after all, was originally a slam. A critic complained that British working-class life, at least as portrayed in movies, novels, and plays, is coarse and nasty, containing every manner of ugliness, including the kitchen sink. Originally, this term implied a realistic style and a **Marxist** ideology. The ideology is still there, at least implicitly, but the style is more variable.

It is impossible to understand the movies of the left-wing school without having an understanding of its social context. Prime Minister Margaret Thatcher came to office vowing to dismantle the welfare state and to open up new avenues of wealth by restoring free enterprise. In large measure, she succeeded. The rich and upper-middle classes prospered in Thatcher's Britain, but blue-collar workers and others at the lower social echelons were devastated. Racial tensions became inflamed, especially in London, where many immigrants of color live in squalor. Unemployment ran as high as 20 percent in some areas of the country, especially in the industrial cities of the midlands and the north. The rate of inflation skyrocketed, wiping out the savings of many working-class families.

Virtually all the movies of the Kitchen Sink school were written directly for the screen. Set in the here and now, they explore the implications of these harsh

17–7. *A World Apart* **(Great Britain, 1988),** *with Linda Mvusi (center), directed by Chris Menges.*
British left-wing films tend to be emotionally involving, appealing to our feelings as well as our minds. This picture deals with the cruel injustices of the *apartheid* laws in South Africa. The title is a poetic metaphor, dealing not only with the forced separation of the races but the chasm between parents and children and the isolation of a small group of reform activists from the all-white power structure. Mvusi, along with her costars Barbara Hershey and Jodhi May, shared the Best Actress Award at the Cannes Film Festival.   *(Atlantic Entertainment Group)*

17–8. *Letter to Brezhnev* **(Great Britain, 1985),** *with Alexandra Pigg and Peter Firth, directed by Chris Bernard.*
A lively comedy/drama/love story, this movie centers on a spirited working-class heroine who has a brief love affair with a decent Soviet sailor on weekend leave in Liverpool. Her life before meeting him consisted of boring, low-paying jobs, long stretches of unemployment, meat-rack beer joints, and dead-end relationships with losers. (One lounge lizard crudely propositions her. "What," she asks, "when there are dogs in the streets?") When a British foreign officer discourages her from leaving the comforts of England to be with her Soviet lover, she replies: "I have nothing to give up." *(Circle Film Releasing)*

social conditions, often with rough, raunchy humor. *Mona Lisa* **(17–9),** directed by the Irish novelist Neil Jordan, is one of the finest works of this period. It was a big commercial success, establishing Bob Hoskins as an important star. The story deals with an ex-con (Hoskins) who works as a chauffeur for a beautiful black call-girl (Cathy Tyson). Disastrously, he falls in love with her and she takes advantage of his feelings in a variety of ways. Essentially a **film noir,** the movie explores the rank underworld of prostitution, blackmail, and the drug scene in a hallucinatory, glossy style. The picture is steeped in a sense of evil—of sweat, semen, stale smoke, and tawdry "girlie" shows. When the protagonist is shocked to see a whore meet a vicious pimp in a church, the call girl explains: "It's the one place no one goes to." The music, by Genesis, is throbbing and sexy, especially Phil Collins's "In Too Deep," with its fatalistic lyrics.

The movies of BILL FORSYTH (b. 1948) are much lower-keyed. In fact, they might almost be called minimalist comedies, because their narrative structures are delicate, almost improvised-looking, and the "jokes" are barely that. Forsyth never underscores his comic scenes to make sure we get the gag. The humor is understated, almost throwaway.

Forsyth is a Scot, not an Englishman. All of his British films to date have been set in Scotland, because he associates well-made narrative structures and a "grand" tradition of acting with English movies. Hence, he believes that by shooting his rambling tales in the north, using low-key, nonactorish Scottish actors, he is, in effect, rejecting English culture. The British Isles, after all, consist of Scotland, Wales, and Northern Ireland as well as England—a fact that the English often forget.

Forsyth's first movie, *That Sinking Feeling* (1979), is technically crude, in part because of its very small budget. Some of the scenes lack energy—always a danger

17–9. *Mona Lisa* **(Great Britain, 1986),** *with Bob Hoskins, directed by Neil Jordan.*
Photographed by Roger Pratt in the **expressionistic** tradition of film noir, *Mona Lisa* is a
neon poem—with garish colors, unusual **angles,** and moody, low-key lighting. A versatile
artist, Pratt also photographed the anguished **surrealism** of *Brazil,* the plain documentary
style of *High Hopes,* and the audaciously expressionistic *Batman.* Most of the films of the
Kitchen Sink school were made on low budgets and are mounted in a realistic style. The nature of the subject matter—everyday life at the frayed fringes—works against glamour. The
production values are kept deliberately matter-of-fact, nothing fancy. The domestic scenes in
this movie are photographed in such a plain style; whenever the protagonist descends into the
sleazy underworld, however, the photography becomes stylized and simultaneously sinister.
(Island Pictures)

with this kind of whimsical material. Forsyth called it "a fairy tale for the workless,"
because it deals with a group of unemployed working-class lads who decide to pull
a heist. Unfortunately, they don't plan in advance how to rid themselves of their
cumbersome loot—a hundred stainless steel sinks.

Local Hero (1983) was Forsyth's breakthrough film on the international
scene—in part because Burt Lancaster played a cameo role. The movie deals with
the culture clash between American businessmen and Scottish townspeople when
oil is discovered in their fishing village. The community is poor and could use an
infusion of capital, but Forsyth's treatment is nonideological. The movie is typically
gentle, wry, and ironic.

In *Housekeeping* (U.S.A., 1988), Forsyth brought his British love of eccentricity
to an American story, an adaptation of Marilynne Robinson's highly praised novel.
The movie is deeper than his British works, more unsettling. Forsyth is able to
show a darker, more threatening side of eccentricity; there's sting and venom lurking beneath the surface charm.

STEPHEN FREARS (b. 1942) is perhaps the most critically admired of the new
British filmmakers. Working-class in his origins, he began his career in the 1960s as
an assistant to filmmakers Karel Reisz and Lindsay Anderson. From 1971 to 1974,
Frears made more than thirty 16-mm films for British television, all of them low-

17–10. *Gregory's Girl* (**Great Britain, 1980**), *with Dee Hepburn and Gordon John Sinclair, written and directed by Bill Forsyth.*
Bittersweet and gently ironic, Forsyth's movie deals with a youth who falls in love with his school soccer team's newest member. He doesn't realize that this beautiful girl has stolen his position on the team as well as his heart. She goes on to reverse the team's losing streak—which doesn't help his deflated ego. *(Samuel Goldwyn Company)*

budget. They were shot in the streets, like **cinéma vérité** documentaries, or quickie **B films.** His two forays into theatrical features were *Gumshoe* (1971) and *The Hit* (1984), both Americanesque **genre** films, and both commercial flops.

His filmmaking career did not take off until he teamed up with the talented young writer HANIF KUREISHI (b. 1957). Their first movie, *My Beautiful Laundrette* **(17–11),** was originally made for British television. It was shot in six weeks for a mere $900,000. When it was released theatrically, the film became an international hit. It deals with ethnic and class tensions between Pakistani immigrants and working-class Brits. It also explores a variety of sexual possibilities. For example, the two young heroes, one English, the other a "Paki," are both business partners and lovers. Family tensions are explored primarily among the bicultural immigrants, especially between an authoritarian Muslim father and his English-educated, liberated daughter.

Kureishi was born and raised in England, the son of a Pakistani father and British mother. At the age of eighteen, he had a play produced by the prestigious Royal Court Theatre. More plays were produced by the Royal Shakespeare Company. In addition, Kureishi has written an autobiography, short stories, and novels. *My Beautiful Laundrette* was his first film script and garnered him an American Academy Award nomination for writing.

The next Frears–Kureishi collaboration was *Sammy and Rosie Get Laid* (1987), once again a collage of various characters, colors, ideologies, and sexual persua-

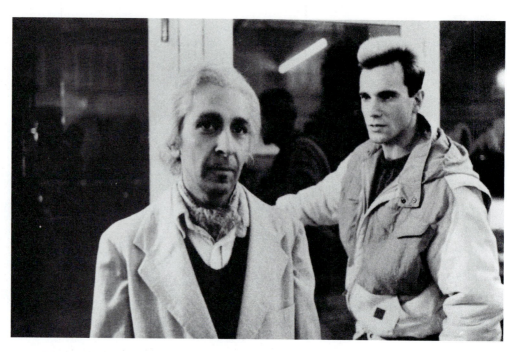

17–11. *My Beautiful Laundrette* **(Great Britain, 1986),** *with Daniel Day-Lewis (right) and Roshan Seth, directed by Stephen Frears.*
Daniel Day-Lewis is often described as the best British actor of his generation. His most impressive quality is his versatility. In *A Room With a View,* he plays the heroine's fruity fiancé, an idle twit and cultural snob. In *Laundrette* he plays a shrewd Cockney tough. His brilliant performance in *My Left Foot* (Ireland, 1989), as a tough-minded, tormented victim of cerebral palsy, garnered him an American Academy Award as best actor (see **19–15**). Day-Lewis has also performed in numerous American films, including *The Last of the Mohicans* (1992), *The Age of Innocence* (1993), and *The Gangs of New York* (2001).   *(Orion Classics)*

sions, from various walks of life, both British and Pakistani. The movie is stronger on character than on story and contains a good deal of Thatcher-bashing, rough language, political torture, allegory, lots of comedy, police brutality, street riots, and militant lesbianism.

Frears's next movie, *Prick Up Your Ears* **(17–12),** was not written by Kureishi—and it shows. Despite a superb performance by Gary Oldman as the murdered playwright Joe Orton, the film lacks the liveliness of Frears's collaborations with Kureishi.

Dangerous Liaisons (1988) features a script by Christopher Hampton, based on his own stage play, which was adapted from a "scandalous" eighteenth-century French novel about decadent aristocrats before the Revolution **(16–19).** Costume pictures are usually stately, photographed mostly in long shots, the better to display the sumptuous **production values.** Frears decided to shoot the film mostly in close-ups, with fluid camera movements—techniques that make the movie more immediate and emotionally involving. Financed with American capital, the movie features an American cast. Studio executives explained that Frears, known for his "ghetto films," was chosen because "he's great with dialogue, and he knows how to work within a budget."

17–12. *Prick Up Your Ears* **(Great Britain, 1987),** *with Gary Oldman, directed by Stephen Frears.*
Oldman was born and raised in poverty in South London. He has specialized in playing working-class outsiders, though he has also acted in classical roles as well as some American parts. Unlike most British actors, he is strongly oriented toward Stanislavsky's techniques of performance, especially the American **Method,** with its emphasis on spontaneity, emotional intensity, and living the role internally. When he played the punk rocker Sid Vicious in Alex Cox's *Sid & Nancy* (1986), Oldman was obsessed with appearing as skinny as Vicious, and he wasted away from 150 pounds to 115, which eventually landed him in the hospital. In this movie, he plays the cocky, gay playwright Joe Orton. Oldman claims that during production, he abstained from straight sex. In recent years, Oldman has worked primarily in America, most notably in *State of Grace* (1990) and Coppola's *Dracula* (1991). *(Samuel Goldwyn Company)*

Western Europe

Spain's PEDRO ALMODÓVAR (b. 1951) was the most important new filmmaker to emerge from "La Movida"—the exhilarating atmosphere of freedom after the death of the dictator Franco in 1975. Indeed, Almodóvar might almost be considered Spain's poet laureate—a debunker of all dogmas, a champion of individual freedom and autonomy. Almodóvar can be described as part Buñuel, part Fassbinder, and part Carmen Miranda.

Like Buñuel, Almodóvar is not much of a storyteller. His movies are fragmented, consisting of loosely connected comic skits rather than coherent narratives. He also shares Buñuel's love of shocking the bourgeoisie, especially with his mockery of all things Catholic. For example, *Dark Habits* (1983) is set in a Catholic convent that specializes in rehabilitating killers, hookers, and junkies. The mother superior (herself an addict) recruits sinners by shooting them up with heroin. Almodóvar also enjoys mocking stereotypical Spanish macho men, most effectively in *Matador* (1986), which features a bullfighter who faints at the sight of blood. Another Buñuelian trait is Almodóvar's matter-of-fact surrealism—weird events presented as though they were perfectly ordinary.

17–13. *Women on the Verge of a Nervous Breakdown* **(Spain, 1988),** *with Carmen Maura, directed by Pedro Almodóvar.*
Maura has appeared in most of Almodóvar's films and is a specialist in camp comedy. In this movie, she plays a jilted actress who is so furious at her ex-lover that she doesn't even have time for drugs, sex, or suicide. "Camp makes you look at our human situations with irony," Almodóvar pointed out. "In camp you sympathize with the lack of power, like the pathos of sentimental songs. This is kitsch, and you are conscious that it is, but that consciousness is full of irony, never criticism. *(Orion Pictures)*

Like Fassbinder, Almodóvar is a flaming homosexual, though not nearly so despairing and dark as Fassbinder. Both filmmakers prefer female protagonists, especially if they are lonely, abandoned, obsessive, betrayed, fragile, or hysterical, the kind of melodramatic sobsisters found in American women's pictures of the 1950s. *Women on the Verge of a Nervous Breakdown* (**17–13**) is the best example of this genre, though Almodóvar's tone is much more comic than Fassbinder's. Both directors are obsessed with sex and drugs.

Carmen Miranda was a popular performer in American musicals and comedies of the 1940s. Known as the "Brazilian Bombshell," she specialized in outlandish costumes with wax fruit cascading from her enormous headdresses, garish halter tops, platform shoes, and a rapid-fire comic delivery of mangled American idioms. Enormously popular among gay males, she is a virtual patron saint of camp—that style of comedy that delights in theatricality, excess, and trashiness. Campy comedy is especially funny when the participants are unaware of their grotesqueness, as in Almodóvar's *What Have I Done to Deserve This?!* (1985) and *Law of Desire* (1987).

The French produced a handful of first-rate movies during the 1980s. *Diva* (1982), directed by Jean-Jacques Beineix, a former film critic, was a big international hit. Part thriller, part love story, the movie is above all an exercise in style. It abounds with breathtaking chase scenes, enchanted landscapes, bizarre settings, and rhapsodically lyrical traveling shots. The offbeat characters are mysterious, funny, suddenly poignant.

Claude Lanzmann's *Shoah* (1986) is a 563-minute documentary dealing with the Holocaust and the Poles and Germans who were connected with the Nazi death camps. *Shoah,* the Hebrew word for chaos or annihilation, does not feature footage from the 1940s, when the events occurred, but mostly interviews with aged, present-day witnesses. They describe—sometimes in horrifying detail—the day-to-day mechanics of how the camps were organized and operated. Lanzmann also shows us the camps as they look now—a sinister reminder of how millions of Jews, Slavs, gypsies, homosexuals, political dissidents, and other "undesirables" were murdered in cold blood by people who were "just doing their jobs."

Two of the most successful French movies of the decade were the adaptations of Marcel Pagnol's two-volume novel, *The Water of the Hills,* originally published in 1963. Pagnol was also an important filmmaker in France during the 1930s. Adapted and directed by CLAUDE BERRI (b. 1934), the movies were titled *Jean De Florette* (1986) and *Manon of the Spring* **(17–14).** The first film features the great Gérard Depardieu as an optimistic hunchback from the city who tries to run a farm in the south of France along strictly scientific methods. The period is the 1920s. He is aided by his devoted wife and young daughter, Manon. But the good-hearted amateur is defeated by the rapacious peasant farmers of the district, who dislike him because he's an "outsider" and because he doesn't farm according to traditional customs. A greedy old fox (Yves Montand) and his moronic nephew (Daniel Auteuil) cheat Jean out of success by secretly blocking off the spring on his land, thus killing off his crop, and killing off Jean as well.

17–14. *Manon of the Spring* **(France, 1987),** *with Daniel Auteuil and Yves Montand, directed by Claude Berri.*
The romantic lyricism of this film and its companion piece, *Jean De Florette,* suggests the doomed world of nineteenth-century opera—a world of passionate emotions and cosmic ironies. A malevolently cruel Fate controls the narrative, creating elegant formal symmetries from the raw pain of human suffering.   *(Orion Pictures)*

Manon of the Spring, which takes place ten years later, deals with the revenge of his daughter against the villagers, and especially against Montand, who wants her to marry his drooling nephew—hardly an enticing prospect for a beautiful young woman. Both movies are lush and cosmically brooding, like a Verdi opera. In fact, the score is adapted from Verdi's deeply fatalistic opera *La Forza del Destino*. Both films unfold slowly, building toward their ironic conclusions with tragic inevitability.

The Netherlands produced a major talent in PAUL VERHOEVEN, who first came to prominence with the World War II Resistance film *Soldier of Orange* (1979), about a group of wealthy Dutch college students and their reaction to the Nazi occupation of Holland in 1940. The film features Rutger Hauer and Jeroen Krabbé in leading roles.

Spetters (1980) employs a similar structure but explores the lives of a group of working-class young people in contemporary Holland. Tough and unsentimental, the movie dramatizes the tensions between generations, between the sexes, and between value systems. The Netherlands is probably the most permissive society in the world, with an exceptionally high tolerance for human diversity. Verhoeven explores the down side of that liberal tolerance—the world of drug addiction, alienation, and moral drift.

The Fourth Man **(17–15),** a much flashier film stylistically, was Verhoeven's biggest international hit up to that time. A psychological thriller, the movie also explores the interrelationship between reality and imagination in an audacious editing style that constantly throws us off guard by flipping between these two worlds without warning. The protagonist is played by Jeroen Krabbé, who, along with Rutger Hauer and Verhoeven himself, is presently working in Hollywood. Verhoeven's American debut film was the popular *Robocop* (1988), which he followed with *Total Recall* (1990).

17–15. *The Fourth Man* **(Holland, 1984),** *with Jeroen Krabbé, directed by Paul Verhoeven.*
The protagonist of this movie (Krabbé) is a bisexual novelist with a shaky grasp of reality. He also has a drinking problem, a voracious sexual appetite, sporadic bouts of Catholic guilt, and a runaway imagination—all powerful sources of his artistic creativity. *(International Spectrafilm)*

The cinema in West Germany fell on hard times after the death of Fassbinder and the diminished output of such important filmmakers as Herzog and Schlöndorff. *Das Boot* **(17–16)** was a popular hit, as was Doris Dörrie's *Men* (1985), a sly feminist comedy about male attitudes toward women. In a country where comedy is not a popular genre, *Men* was a huge commercial success, outgrossing even *Rambo*, which had been West Germany's box office champion.

West German movies of the 1980s are lighter and more accessible than those of the previous decade. Percy Adlon's *Sugarbaby* (1985) is a good example. The movie is a bittersweet love story between a heroically hefty female mortician and a passive young subway worker. The eccentric, likable heroine is played by Marianne Sägebrecht, who manages to combine great innocence with sexual hunger. Sägebrecht also plays the semi-supernatural German tourist in *Bagdad Café* (1988), which is spoken in English and was shot in the United States with an American supporting cast.

The boutique film industries of Scandinavia produced several high-quality works during the 1980s. *My Life as a Dog* (1987) was the most prestigious film to emerge from Sweden after Bergman. Lasse Hallström's gentle coming-of-age story

17–16. *Das Boot* ("The Boat," W. Germany, 1982), *with Jürgen Prochnow, directed by Wolfgang Petersen.*
The taut, suspenseful story of a German submarine crew during the waning days of World War II, *Das Boot* is steeped in irony. The captain (Prochnow) realizes that he and his crew are fighting for a hopeless and corrupt cause, but his only concern is to guide his crew to safety while they patrol the dangerous North Atlantic. Petersen pays homage to the courage of those forgotten men who were skeptical of politics but were trapped in someone else's nightmare—symbolized by the claustrophobic confines of the fragile submarine. These brave men fight not for their *Führer,* but for their comrades. *(Columbia Pictures)*

is about a twelve-year-old hellion (played by the charming Anton Glanzelius) who goes to live with his eccentric country relatives in the 1950s. Full of surprises, the movie is often funny, yet it features several emotionally touching scenes as well.

Tiny Denmark produced two Oscar-winning Best Foreign Language Pictures during this era—*Babette's Feast* (1987) and *Pelle the Conqueror* (1988), both period films. The first is an adaptation of a story by Isak Dinesen (the heroine of *Out of Africa*). More impressive is the powerful *Pelle the Conqueror* **(17–17),** written and directed by Bille August, from the novel by Martin Anderssen Nexo. Set in the harsh rural world of nineteenth-century Denmark, the story has an **epic** sweep. It is exceptionally sensitive to class and ethnic antagonisms, dramatizing how lower-class Swedish hirelings were treated almost like animals by the Danish propertied class of the era. The movie contains many striking landscapes. Equally

17–17. *Pelle the Conqueror* **(Denmark, 1988),** *with Max von Sydow (right) and Pelle Hvenegaard, directed by Bille August.*

In a career capped by many majestic performances, Max von Sydow here plays an aging Swedish widower who travels to Denmark with his spirited young son in search of a new life. Though the character he plays is a weak, drunken blowhard, von Sydow manages to reveal the humanity—and even a touch of spiritual grandeur—in this rather sorry specimen of manhood. In addition to at least a half dozen great roles in the films of Ingmar Bergman, von Sydow has acted in British, German, and American movies as well. His best-known American performance was as the powerful old priest who performs the exorcism in the 1973 blockbuster hit *The Exorcist.* *(Miramax Films)*

impressive are the interior shots, with their poetic, Vermeer-like lighting. In addition to the American Oscar, *Pelle* won the Palme d'Or (grand prize) at the Cannes Film Festival.

U.S.S.R. and Eastern Europe

The Communist bloc countries were by no means uniform in their cinematic output. The Soviet Union, Poland, and Hungary produced the overwhelming majority of noteworthy movies. In the Soviet Union, there was a sharp break in policies around 1985, the beginning of the Gorbachev era of *glasnost* (openness) and *perestroika* (restructuring). The first half of the decade was still dominated by the conservative, old-style values of the Brezhnev era—the last gasp of neo-Stalinist inertia.

Even under the Brezhnev regime, however, the cultural establishment realized that the old days of simple-minded propaganda movies were dead. Filmmakers were encouraged to make their movies more accessible, more commercial. The early 1980s saw the release of many light-entertainment films, far removed from the everyday problems of Soviet citizens. Many of these movies pandered to the escapist fantasies of the public, but there were a few that went beyond the drivel of routine entertainment, movies like Vladimir Menshov's *Moscow Does Not Believe in Tears* **(17–18)**.

After 1985, the Soviet film industry began a period of restructuring. Filmmakers now enjoyed unprecedented freedom. There was no official Party Line, and in fact any form of "routine thinking" (i.e., ideological conformity) was discouraged. This "New Model" represented a long-term commitment to the ideal of pluralism and artistic freedom—freedom to criticize, to speak frankly.

As a gesture of good faith, the restructured film industry released a bevy of suppressed movies, some of them twenty years old, which had been shelved by previous regimes because they were ideologically "incorrect." Gleb Panfilov's *Theme* (originally made in 1979, released in 1986) contains some gutsy criticism of the moral and artistic bankruptcy of the Soviet cultural establishment. Alexander Askoldov's *Commissar* (originally made in 1967, released in 1988) portrays Jewish religious values in a positive light. By Western standards, these are hardly earth-shattering innovations, but by Soviet standards they represented the opening wedge of change.

The Polish cinema was intimately connected with politics, and the 1980s were years of upheaval and change in Poland. Filmmakers in this country were extraordinarily courageous in speaking out against the incompetence and corruption of the government. Andrzej Wajda, the dean of Polish filmmakers, constantly defied the Official Lie of government, both in movies like *Man of Iron* **(17–19)** and as an outspoken champion of the Solidarity Movement. Like most Polish filmmakers, Wajda is an intellectual, deeply committed to the ideals of freedom.

The Hungarian film industry—like the Polish "cinema of moral concern"—was surprisingly outspoken, individualistic, and obsessed with moral issues. Like the Poles too, the Hungarian cinema is sadly underrated in the United States, where only a handful of Hungarian movies are exhibited. In part, this is because Hungarian films are "difficult"—morally complex, slow moving, often humorless. They also tend to favor historical subjects. Nonetheless, the works of such distin-

17–18. *Moscow Does Not Believe in Tears* (**U.S.S.R., 1980**), *directed by Vladimir Menshov.*
This movie traces the lives of three provincial young women who emigrate to Moscow in 1958, following their romances and professional careers over a twenty-year period. It is a warm, compassionate portrait of ordinary people trying to cope with universal problems. The movie is surprisingly neutral politically, avoiding even the hint of propaganda. In fact, it is an endorsement of the status quo, hardly a revolutionary film. The movie was enormously popular in the Soviet Union, where 75 million viewers saw it in its first twelve months of exhibition. It also won the American Academy Award as Best Foreign Language Picture. *(IFEX Films)*

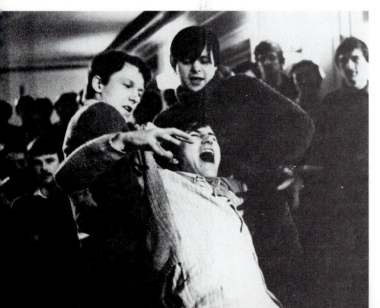

17–19. *Man of Iron* (**Poland, 1981**), *directed by Andrzej Wajda.*
A sequel to the director's courageous *Man of Marble* (1977), this picture is even more critical of the lying, corrupt regime that ruled Poland in the 1980s. The movie explores the role of the media in preserving or challenging the status quo. Despite its flaws—the film was made under intense political pressure—*Man of Iron* was the most popular Polish movie of all time. *(United Artists)*

17–20. *Mephisto* **(Hungary/West Germany, 1981),** *with Klaus Maria Brandauer, directed by István Szabó.*
The great Austrian actor Brandauer stars as an intelligent, ambitious actor who gradually compromises his ideals and political principles to make it to the top. This is one of several movies that attempts to demythologize the Nazi experience, to portray it in human, everyday terms. The actor's sellout is not a matter of grand confrontations or a theatrical bartering of his soul with the Nazi Devil. Rather, he chips away at his soul bit by bit, in ordinary transactions that seem more like minor concessions than moral betrayals. Before he realizes it, he is completely the creature of the Nazis, with nothing left to barter. *Mephisto* won the Best Foreign Language Oscar in the United States. Szabó and Brandauer went on to collaborate on another excellent film, *Colonel Redl* (1984), a drama of political corruption during the Austro-Hungarian Empire just prior to World War I. *(Analysis Film Releasing)*

guished filmmakers as Károly Makk, Márta Meszáros, and István Szabó (**17–20**) deserve a wider audience.

The Third World

Filmmakers in the Third World have it rough. Almost everything is more difficult. There is a serious shortage of capital, and priority usually goes to such essentials as food, housing, and disaster relief. Film is more expensive, more individualistic, and more difficult to control than television; so what little money remains tends to go to state-controlled media, which are usually mouthpieces for the government.

In small countries especially, Third World filmmakers have to deal with the problems of language. If the characters speak in regional dialects, which wouldn't be understood outside a small area, the filmmaker must then **dub** or subtitle the movie if it is to recover its costs, let alone show a profit. Both techniques are expensive. If the characters speak in English or French—the two most common second languages in the Third World—the movie will have a wider appeal, but it might not appeal to native audiences, many of whom are illiterate and speak no foreign languages. Besides, English and French can be ideologically incongruous, for they connote upper-class values and foreign imperialism to many Third World audiences.

And of course, there is the problem of politics. Censorship and political repression are common in the Third World. Victor Anti, a filmmaker from Ghana, in

17–21. *The Gods Must Be Crazy* (**Botswana, 1983**), *directed by Jamie Uys.*
Third World films often deal with the effects of an alien technology on native tribal traditions. They frequently contrast the cultures of whites and blacks. What's unusual about this movie is that it explores these themes humorously, often with slapstick comedy. It all begins when a Coke bottle falls from the heavens—actually from an airplane—and lands in the midst of the Kalahari bush people. They believe the bottle to be an exotic gift from the gods. On this slight premise, Uys creates a charming comic parable, full of wry observations about human nature everywhere. The film's sequel, *The Gods Must Be Crazy II* (1990), exhibits the same sense of whimsy and slapstick goofiness. *(Twentieth Century-Fox)*

western Africa, has spoken of the vicious circle many Third World artists must confront in trying to finance their movies: "Scripts have to be agreed to by the government in your country, which leads to self-censorship, which leads to stories that aren't interesting and therefore can't sell."

Astonishingly, despite all these hassles, Third World filmmakers sometimes manage to break through to the world market. A good example is the surprising success of *The Hour of the Star* (Brazil, 1985), by Suzana Amaral, a fifty-two-year-old mother of nine, who made this first movie in four weeks for $150,000. The film explores the world of a nineteen-year-old orphan girl from the provinces. With no skills or education, she emigrates to the teeming city of São Paulo, population fourteen million. The movie alternates styles, flipping magically from harsh realities to surreal fantasies, a technique typical of much of Latin American fiction.

Realism is still the style of choice for most Third World filmmakers. Realism is cheaper, allowing artists to shoot in the streets. It is also a powerful weapon of shock. Squeamish viewers are put off by the realistic depiction of squalor in such movies as Babenco's *Pixote* **(17–22),** which deals with the violent life of an orphaned street urchin. At the beginning of the movie, the ten-year-old Pixote is sent to juvenile prison, where he witnesses a gang rape of a helpless boy by some older inmates. In prison, he is taught more sophisticated methods of crime by the older youths. He also witnesses scenes of cruelty by the prison authorities.

After he and some friends escape, they engage in a variety of criminal activities to survive. When one of several crooked adults attempts to cheat the boys, Pixote panics and stabs her, running off with her gun. Later the youths team up with a drunken, diseased prostitute, whom they have "bought" from her pimp.

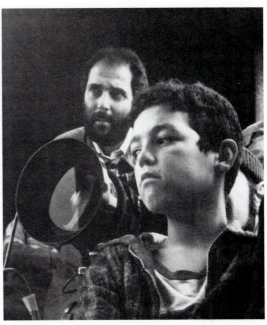

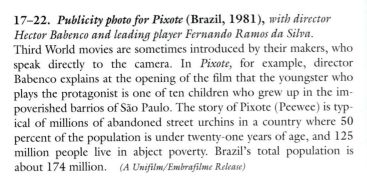

17–22. *Publicity photo for* Pixote **(Brazil, 1981),** *with director Hector Babenco and leading player Fernando Ramos da Silva.*
Third World movies are sometimes introduced by their makers, who speak directly to the camera. In *Pixote,* for example, director Babenco explains at the opening of the film that the youngster who plays the protagonist is one of ten children who grew up in the impoverished barrios of São Paulo. The story of Pixote (Peewee) is typical of millions of abandoned street urchins in a country where 50 percent of the population is under twenty-one years of age, and 125 million people live in abject poverty. Brazil's total population is about 174 million. *(A Unifilm/Embrafilme Release)*

Pixote understands the cause of her delirium after he notices the splattered remains of a bloodied fetus in a slop bucket of her filthy toilet. And so on, through a series of sordid episodes, ending with Pixote killing a man. The movie concludes with a shot of the protagonist, alone again, walking along the railroad tracks, his future as inexorably charted as the tracks that stretch into the horizon. Seven years after the film was made, Fernando Ramos da Silva, the youngster who played Pixote, was shot and killed in an attempted armed robbery. He was seventeen.

Poverty and the oppression of women go hand in hand. In India, China, and other Third World nations, female infanticide is far from unusual. International women's organizations have pointed to Muslim societies as the most oppressive to women, especially when accompanied by extreme poverty. In Pakistan, for example, forced child marriages are common. Women cannot testify in certain legal cases, like adultery. In other cases, the evidence of two women is necessary to equal that of one man. A 1985 "Report of the Pakistan Commission on the Status of Women" stated that

> the average rural woman of Pakistan is born in near slavery, leads a life of drudgery and dies invariably in oblivion. This grim condition is not fantasy, but the stark reality of nearly 30 million Pakistani citizens who happen to have been born female.

A persistent champion of women's rights was the Turkish filmmaker YILMAZ GÜNEY (1937–1984). Himself of peasant origins, Güney was a revolutionary filmmaker who served many years in Turkish prisons for his political beliefs. He was also one of the most popular actors in his country, an idol to millions. His powerful film *Yol* **(17–23)** won the top award at the Cannes Film Festival, catapulting him into international prominence.

17–23. *Yol* **(Turkey, 1981),** *with Tarik Akan (left) and Serif Sezer (upper right), directed by Yilmaz Güney and Serif Goren.*
In a society where women are sometimes treated worse than livestock, even fundamentally decent men, who are themselves victims of oppression, victimize the women they love, rarely questioning the sexist values of their culture. "Can a man's mind be his own enemy?" the Akan character asks when he is expected to kill his wife in retribution for her adultery. Everyone expects nothing less—even the members of her own family, who have kept her chained in the cellar for eight months, giving her only bread and water, not allowing her even to wash. The man still loves his wife, yet he is torn between pity and hatred, between the demands of social convention and his private anguish. He decides instead to "let God kill her," and in an agonizing trek across a vast snow-covered pass, he and their son, followed by the flimsily attired, exhausted wife, trudge through the freezing terrain.   *(Columbia Pictures)*

Yol was executed by Serif Goren, who followed Güney's instructions while the actor-director was serving an eighteen-year sentence at hard labor. (He later escaped from prison and, until his untimely death at the age of forty-seven, was working underground.) The film explores the lives of five inmates on a brief leave from a minimum-security prison. The movie demonstrates that all the people in the story are prisoners, as much of their own minds and value systems as of the state, which is run by a right-wing military junta.

Ironically, the prisoner-protagonists of the film become oppressors themselves in their treatment of their wives, sisters, and daughters. "The women I show in my films belong to the oppressed social classes," Güney pointed out. "But they suffer a second oppression since they belong to the oppressed sex. And through women we can show the contradictions, the ambiguity of men . . . men who can be courageous, heroic, who can rebel, yet at the same time can be very reactionary towards their women."

Japan

The 1980s was a decade of continued decline in the Japanese cinema—shrinking audiences, lowered artistic standards, and widespread juvenilization of subject matter. From a high of nearly one billion paid admissions in 1960, the box office issued fewer than 150 million tickets annually by the late 1980s, despite the fact that Japan's gross national product increased nearly tenfold during that same period. Other forms of entertainment were luring away potential filmgoers, most notably television and video.

Of those who did go to the movies, three quarters were under the age of twenty-one. A few genres comprised the overwhelming majority of films produced by the four **majors:** *yakuza* (gangster) pictures, *buriko* ("cutie-pie" films), wayward husband stories, soft-core pornography, installment films (sequels), **animation** features based on comic books, and movies adapted from popular television programs. Japanese film critic Nao Kisaragi summed up the general quality of these movies. "I know that they can't get any worse," she lamented, "since they're already at rock bottom."

There were a few bright spots, though. Production costs were still relatively low. The average Japanese film cost about $2 million, compared to about $20 million in the United States. Japanese audiences were perfectly willing to honor Japan's film artists—so long as foreign critics would kindly point them out first.

17–24. *The Ballad of Narayama* (**Japan, 1983**), *directed by Shohei Imamura.*
Although Imamura made his directorial debut in the 1950s, his movies were not widely known in the West until this film won the top prize at Cannes. A harsh Darwinian fable of the survival of the fittest in a primitive Japanese village, the picture is typical of his works in that it deals realistically with characters from the lower social echelons. The movie is sprinkled with earthy, rough humor, especially in the sexual scenes. *(Kino International)*

After Imamura's *Ballad of Narayama* **(17–24)** won the Grand Prize at Cannes, home audiences dutifully paid homage to their native son. Similarly, the great Kurosawa, long considered passé, created one of his most brilliant works during this era— *Ran* **(17–25).**

Another positive trend was the increasing internationalization of movie audiences. Prior to this period, Japanese filmgoers overwhelmingly preferred their own movies. Throughout the 1980s, however, foreign films accounted for about 50 percent of the total pictures exhibited in Japan. American movies were, and still are, the most popular imports. This is not surprising, considering the mania for almost anything American in contemporary Japan, which is the most profitable foreign market for American films.

Another surprising trend during this era was the success of several world-class comedies. Prior to World War II, Japan produced many excellent comic films, but in the postwar cinema, comedy was virtually a forgotten genre among important filmmakers. Yoshimitsu Morita's *The Family Game* (1983) was the opening wedge. It was a huge popular hit in Japan, in addition to sweeping several prestigious *Kinema Jumpo* awards. The movie scrutinizes that most revered of all Japanese institutions, the family, exposing the ties that bind in more ways than one. *The Family Game* also ridicules the crude materialism and worship of money that Morita and other satirical artists regard as typical of contemporary Japanese society.

17–25. *Ran* **(Japan, 1985),** *with Tatsuya Nakadai, directed by Akira Kurosawa.*
Ran (Chaos), Kurosawa's long-awaited adaptation of *King Lear*, created an international sensation when it was released. In addition to being the greatest Japanese movie of the 1980s, it is also a world-class masterpiece, one of the finest of all Shakespearean adaptations. The old master was seventy-five at the time and more pessimistic than ever about the pitiful human condition.   *(Orion Classics)*

17–26. *Tampopo* **(Japan, 1986),** *with Nobuko Miyamoto and Tsutomo Yamazaki, directed by Juzo Itami.*
The main narrative strand in Itami's mosaic structure concerns the heroic efforts of Goro (Yamazaki), a Shane/Clint Eastwood cowboy-truckdriver hybrid, to help Tampopo (Miyamoto) perfect her dismal skills as a raman noodle cook. Virtually all raman chefs are men, and the idea of a woman presuming to poach on this traditionally masculine preserve would strike many Japanese viewers as ludicrous. Hence, the film is a satire of male chauvinism as much as anything else. *Tampopo* (which means "dandelion") is a symbol of the female outsider trying to make her way in a man's world. In this scene, she listens to the urgings of Goro during their first "training session," terrified that she will not prove worthy of her sacred mission. *(New Yorker Films)*

JUZO ITAMI (1933–1998) was the most promising filmmaker to emerge during this decade. A comic humanist, he was a gentler and warmer artist than Morita, with more heart. The son of the 1930s film director Mansaku Itami (whose most respected films were also comedies), Juzo Itami was an artist of exceptional breadth and accomplishment. He began his career as an actor, performing leading roles in such important Japanese movies as *The Makioka Sisters* and *The Family Game*. In addition, Itami was a television talk show host, a translator, and a popular essayist. One collection of essays, *Listen, Women!*, sold more than one million copies. *The Family Game*, in which Itami played the father, inspired him to switch to filmmaking himself.

Itami's directing debut, *The Funeral* (1984), swept the *Kinema Jumpo* best picture, director, actor, and actress awards. The movie is a rambling, shaggy-dog story, affectionately satirizing the bumbling efforts of a middle-class family to observe all the "correct" forms of burying a recently deceased relative. What Itami ridicules is not the funeral rituals (which they have to learn about from a videocassette) but the family's pathetic eagerness to conform to them, despite the inconvenient fact that they don't remotely connect with their real feelings. These empty forms might just as easily be Druid rites. Nonetheless, being Japanese, the family members agree that correct form is, after all, correct form.

Itami's next comedy, *Tampopo* **(17–26),** was his biggest international success. Dubbed a "noodle western" by its creator, the movie is another rambling comic essay, good-naturedly satirizing the Japanese obsession with raman noodle restaurants, table manners, movies (especially American westerns), sex, and sexism. *Tampopo* features a charming female protagonist, played by Nobuko Miyamoto, Itami's widow, who starred in all of his movies.

A Taxing Woman (1988) is less overtly comical and explores the labyrinthine baroqueries of the Japanese internal revenue service. The movie features a single-minded, bloodhoundlike heroine (Miyamoto again) as a fraud-proof tax auditor. In a country where virtually everyone cheats on paying taxes, Itami scores many satirical points about the hypocrisies of everyday life in the rat race of modern Japan.

The sequel, *A Taxing Woman Returns* (1989), is less comic than the first film, darker and more sardonic. The movie broke many box office records in Japan and was credited with mobilizing public opinion against the scandal-ridden government, which eventually collapsed amidst a flurry of exposés of bribery, cronyism, and massive greed. "In trying to internationalize itself," Itami said, "Japan tried to adopt an international language and the language it happened to choose was money."

What could be more universal?

FURTHER READING

ARMES, ROY. *Third World Film Making and the West.* Berkeley: University of California Press, 1987. A comprehensive account of one half of the world's film output.

DIAWARA, MANTHIA. *African Cinema.* London: British Film Institute, 1992. Politics and culture reflected in African movies.

DOWNING, JOHN D. H., ed. *Film and Politics in the Third World.* New York: Praeger Publishers, 1988. Collection of scholarly essays.

DYER, RICHARD, ed. *Gays and Film.* New York: New York Zoetrope, 1984 revised edition. A collection of scholarly essays.

GOULDING, DANIEL J., ed. *Post New Wave Cinema in the Soviet Union and Eastern Europe.* Bloomington: Indiana University Press, 1989. Excellent anthology of scholarly essays, covering the U.S.S.R., Poland, Hungary, Yugoslavia, and other Communist and ex-Communist countries.

HARASZTI, MIKLÓS. *The Velvet Prison: Artists Under State Socialism.* New York: Basic Books, 1988. A Hungarian critic's assessment of the arts in the *glasnost* era—a skeptical view.

HILL, JOHN. *British Cinema in the 1980s.* New York: Oxford Univ. Press, 1999. Survey of the decade.

Kuhn, Annette. *Women's Pictures: Feminism and Cinema.* London and New York: Routledge and Kegan Paul, 1982. A British feminist's explorations, well written and perceptive.

Lent, John A., et al. *The Asian Film Industry.* Austin: University of Texas Press, 1990. Encyclopedic coverage of industries in China, Japan, India, and many other Asian nations.

Powrie, Phil. *French Cinema in the 1980s.* New York: Oxford University Press, 1997. A discussion of two major themes—nostalgia and the crisis of masculinity.

18

American Cinema in the 1990s

It is the end of the century now. It's the last decade. This is the art form of the century. It's American. And this whole hundred years is like a Golden Age. . . . People in 2050 are going to look back at this century as the Golden Age of Cinema, not only in America but everywhere else.
—MARTIN SCORSESE, Filmmaker

Paramount/Twentieth Century Fox

Timeline: 1990–1999

1990

Time-Warner introduces a new magazine, *Entertainment Weekly*

1991

"Operation Desert Storm"—American military crushes Iraqi invaders of tiny Kuwait in six weeks

1992

Violent race riots erupt in Los Angeles when an all-white jury acquits four white police officers of viciously beating Rodney King, an African American who was stopped for speeding and D.U.I.

Bill Clinton (Democrat) elected U.S. President (1992–2000)

1994

Ex-football hero O. J. Simpson is charged with murdering his estranged wife and a visiting friend in one of the most widely publicized trials of the century. Simpson was later acquitted

1995

U.S. Government resumes diplomatic relations with Vietnam

1996

Body piercing becomes popular with America's bored youth

1997

Ellen DeGeneres becomes the first openly gay star of a TV sitcom, *Ellen*

1998

Series of presidential sex scandals involving Bill Clinton and a variety of women, both willing and otherwise

1999

A single-engine plane, piloted by John F. Kennedy, Jr., plunges into the Atlantic a few miles off the Cape Cod shoreline, killing him, his wife, and her sister

The Hollywood Studios: *Titanic* and the blockbuster syndrome, new technologies, internationalization. The era of special effects. The decline of personal styles. A golden age of acting. The animation boom. Minority Voices: African Americans, women, and gays. Major filmmakers: Spielberg, Scorsese, Allen, and Eastwood. The Independent cinema: Tarantino, Nunez, Stillman, Crowe, Solondz, Anderson, and the Coen brothers. The future: Expanded options.

The Hollywood Studios

A S THE MOVIES ENDED THEIR first hundred years, the American motion picture industry had no economic competition. Ironically, in spite of its worldwide hegemony, the movie business no longer made a great deal of economic sense.

As of 1999, the average cost of the Hollywood film was $53.4 million, exclusive of advertising—twice what it had been at the beginning of the decade. The cost of marketing a movie had also doubled, to about $25 million. While a great many people were going to the movies—1.46 billion tickets in North America in 1998, 5 percent more than 1997—the fact that the average cost of an American picture was roughly $80 million spelled trouble.

Even pictures grossing over $100 million and widely regarded as hits could, because of costs and participation percentages owned by major stars and directors, actually return very little profit to the producing company. As one knowledgeable observer said, "the major studios' average return on investment from movies slipped to nearly nothing over the past decade."

Perhaps the most interesting thing about the worldwide success of James Cameron's *Titanic* (18–1) was that there was no attempt to replicate it in either scope or budget. The reason was that the downside risk was more catastrophic than the upside potential was tempting. Within the industry, the film was regarded as a near-death experience. Had *Titanic* failed, it wouldn't have taken down Twentieth Century Fox the way *Heaven's Gate* devastated United Artists in 1980, but it would have made things interesting. *Titanic* was a coproduction between Fox and Paramount, with the lion's share of the costs absorbed by Fox, owned by Rupert Murdoch, a multinational media baron. *Titanic* cost around $200 million but the studios were shying away from most budgets over $100 million, despite its enormous commercial success.

Hollywood responded to the Case of the Vanishing Profits by cutting the number of releases and, whenever possible, cutting costs. Disney chopped $500 million out of a total filmmaking budget of $1.5 billion by reducing the number of movies produced from 30 to 20 and collapsing three film operations—Disney, Touchstone, and Hollywood Pictures—into one. Likewise, Sony Corporation shut down TriStar Pictures and Triumph Films, the better to concentrate on name-

18–1. *Titanic* (U.S.A., 1997), *written and directed by James Cameron.*
Physical spectacle and the recreation of lost worlds have always been an exciting part of the cinema. That appeal was reinforced by the worldwide success of *Titanic,* which blended eloquent, amazingly sophisticated visuals that had an authentic grandeur with a corny and anachronistic love story. Result: over $1 billion at the box office. It was the most commercially successful movie in history. *Titanic* is also an appropriate symbol of the worldwide dominance of the Hollywood film industry, as Douglas Gomery has pointed out: "The 1990s stood as the era when Hollywood achieved an international influence, a mass-entertainment marketplace superiority, and millions in profits unparalleled in its history." *(Paramount/Twentieth Century Fox)*

brand Columbia. "If you are in a marginalized business," said one studio head, "you have to look for every margin you can."

Where was all the money going? Mostly to actors and special effects. But paying a major star like Tom Cruise **(18–3)** $20 million in the hope that he will serve as a form of insurance and give the film a leg up in its opening weeks was only part of the inflation. Then there were the perks that go with that salary: an expensive trailer, a couple of assistants (i.e., go-fers), a nanny for the kids, a special driver, personal hair and makeup people.

Because of the immense costs, it was easier and less risky to make pictures that would do well in foreign markets. With few exceptions (the British film *The Full Monty* was one), humor rarely travels well. Similarly, what is intensely dramatic in France may strike an American audience as muffled and insular. On the other hand, special effects extravaganzas, heavy on situation, light on character and theme, can be assimilated easily by any culture, in any language.

The blockbuster mentality permeated not only American cinema but world cinema as well. Indigenous French or German filmmaking became rarer on American screens and even endangered at home, as American movies got bigger, louder, more explosively garish and geared to mass audiences everywhere. In short, as a character from a Wim Wenders movie says, "The Yanks have colonized our subconscious." American movies upped the ante all over the world, raising audience

18-2. *Face/Off* (U.S.A., 1997), *with Nicolas Cage and John Travolta, directed by John Woo.* Part of the appeal of movies has always been movement for movement's sake, the principal domain of action films. It's no accident that one of the precursors of the movies were sequential photographs of a horse running. John Woo graduated from the Hong Kong school, which specializes in martial arts movies, a genre made up of equal parts deliriously over-the-top violence and male bonding. Aestheticizing what would otherwise be distasteful, or more often just plain ridiculous, Woo's *Face/Off* involves a Federal agent (Travolta) who agrees to have a criminal's face grafted onto his own in the hopes of getting the criminal's brother to divulge important information. Then things get complicated. The plot is overtly absurd, but the conviction of the two splendid actors and Woo's trademarked ballets of gunfire amidst flying doves make the film an exhilarating guilty pleasure. *(Paramount Pictures)*

expectations to a point where only companies with multinational backing could afford to make movies. And sometimes not even then.

Because of the staggering costs, the studios sought to minimize risk by taking coproduction partners on even modestly budgeted films. Financing arms such as Rysher (the filmmaking arm of Cox Communications), Village Roadshow (Australian movie theaters), and independent concerns such as Beacon Communications, Regency, and Mutual Film were partnered with the major studios. Some of these co-financing firms found out the hard way that the movie business is glamorous only on the surface.

For the independents, co-financing pictures with a major studio allows them to get into the movie business without incurring heavy start-up and overhead costs; for the major studios, it enables them to cut the risk. Co-financing also means that the studios stand to benefit far less from the occasional hit, because foreign rights are usually handed to the co-financiers in return for their investment. Rysher invested in a long series of movies, usually with Paramount. One of the few hits they were involved with was the Howard Stern film *Private Parts,* which did very well in America. But overseas, nobody had ever heard of Howard Stern. Rysher is now out of the movie business.

The tendency toward internationalization invaded the Hollywood studios. Columbia Pictures was purchased by Sony Corporation in 1989; Universal is owned

18–3. *Jerry Maguire* (U.S.A., 1996), *with Tom Cruise and Renée Zellweger, written and directed by Cameron Crowe.*
Tom Cruise is one of the most ambitious and focused of the younger stars, and he's created a screen persona for his era as traditional as John Wayne's was for his. Typically, Cruise's screen character is materialistic, manically self-absorbed, and deluded, but he eventually learns enlightenment through another, purer person, usually a pretty young woman who loves him. It's a progression that describes films as disparate as *Top Gun, Rain Man, The Firm,* and *Jerry Maguire.* What has kept Cruise's career from declining into been-there-done-that has been his willingness to work with the very best directorial talent available, culminating in Stanley Kubrick's final film *Eyes Wide Shut* in 1999. *(TriStar Pictures)*

18–4. *The First Wives Club* (U.S.A., 1996), *with Goldie Hawn, directed by Hugh Wilson.*
Even a comparatively innocuous film can deal with bedrock societal pressures. This is a raucous comedy about the phenomenon of trophy wives, the young women that successful middle-aged men have a way of acquiring after they've discarded their first wives—the partners who helped them *get* to the top. What, the movie asks, happens to those first wives? The principals, consisting of three fiftyish actresses (Diane Keaton, Bette Midler, and Hawn) belied the oft-repeated complaint that Hollywood studio executives aren't interested in roles for women over 40. The movie struck a social nerve and became one of the biggest hits of its year. *(Paramount Pictures)*

by Seagram. At the end of the century, among the major Hollywood studios, only Disney was a free-standing, independent entity. However, between the theme parks, the American Broadcasting Company that "merged" with Disney, and various cable properties, the company has survived—flourished—by becoming its own multinational **(18–5)**.

Largely because of economics, the major studios more or less opted out of the quality film business. Most studios produced only one or two pictures a year that could conceivably win critics' awards. The rest were designed for the box office, pure and simple. Thus, the nominees for the Best Picture Oscar were as likely to come from mini-majors like Miramax or New Line as they were from Paramount or Columbia; because the smaller companies spent less money, they could survive with smaller profits.

Even art films could be expensive. *Shakespeare in Love,* the Best Picture Oscar winner of 1998, cost nearly $40 million, too rich for even a quasi-independent's blood. The movie was a coproduction between Miramax and Universal. But the mini-majors were often swallowed by the major studios—Disney bought Miramax, Time-Warner owns New Line. In this way, the big studios got some reflected prestige with only a modest risk.

The changing nature of studio ownership changed the rules of the game. In decades past, studios lusted for Oscar recognition and made sure to produce a number of pictures that could bring them awards and the box office bump that accompanied them. But Time-Warner earned over 40 percent of its revenues from

18–5. *The Lion King* (U.S.A., 1994), *directed by Roger Allers and Rob Minkoff.*
In essence *Hamlet* adapted to the animal kingdom, *The Lion King* was the most successful of Disney animated films, telling a universal coming-of-age story in the guise of a cartoon. Some sophisticates sneer at Disney animated films such as this or *Tarzan* (1999), but the best of them make pop poetry out of the bond between humans and animals, not to mention implying valid truths about the difficulties of becoming an adult. *The Lion King* was a huge hit, reaping over $200 million at the box office both at home and abroad. Its soundtrack, consisting of several Elton John songs, went on to become a best-selling recording. The film also inspired an enormously successful Broadway musical, which won several Tony awards. *(© Disney)*

cable television. What happened with Time-Warner's cable operation and their relationship with AT&T was more important to them than whether or not a Warner Bros. movie won another Oscar on awards night.

Special effects movies occupied the financial high end of Hollywood filmmaking. Movies based on television shows, or teenage movies featuring actors from popular TV dramas, occupied the low end. Horror movies or gross-out comedies are cheap—they don't call it the bottom line for nothing—with a limited but built-in audience. The best that can be said of them as genres is that they might illuminate an authentic star or two before they peter out. For example, Tom Cruise first gained notice as the star of innocuous teen pictures like *Taps* (1981) and *All the Right Moves* (1983).

These categories are essentially B movies in A movie drag, Hollywood applying a BMW production over a Chevrolet chassis. Slightly disreputable genres that were once the province of exploitation companies like American-International or Hammer have been appropriated by the major studios. Even if the picture was successful, the imbalance between the material and its treatment was apparent. On occasion, the studios financed a sophisticated mature film, especially if it was the pet project of an important director or star, but these were rare. Hard-hitting, prestige social movies like *The Grapes of Wrath* or *On the Waterfront* are basically extinct, replaced by an occasional sincere and dull vanity project like *Beloved* (1998).

18–6. *The Truman Show* **(U.S.A., 1998),** *with Jim Carrey, directed by Peter Weir.*
Witty and inventive as it is, Andrew Niccol's original screenplay to this film was no guarantee of its production. The movie might never have been made had not Jim Carrey exerted his considerable clout as a star by strongly supporting its production. "Stars completely dictate which movies get made," one top talent agent says. "A studio head will come to me with six scripts and say, 'Which of these do you want for your client?' And the projects won't go forward unless the actor says yes." *(Paramount Pictures)*

18–7. *Men in Black* **(U.S.A., 1997),** *with Will Smith and Tommy Lee Jones, directed by Barry Sonnenfeld.*
Will Smith was one of the most appealing stars to reach the top during the decade of the 1990s. He began as a rap and hip-hop recording artist, then moved on to a television sitcom before making an impressive dramatic acting debut in the film *Six Degrees of Separation* (1993), directed by Fred Schepisi. Smith's main virtue as a star is his immense likability. His good looks and confident sex appeal make him a viable romantic leading man, but the public usually prefers him in a comic mode—with lots of attitude, streetsmarts, and ironic, witty flashes of self-mockery.   *(Columbia Pictures)*

The filmmaking talent of previous eras usually evolved out of other media such as literature or live theater. The generation of the 90s derived from MTV and television. A huge number of them got their training in the film schools of America's universities. In 1980, the percentage of first-time directors who attended film school was 35 percent; in the mid-1990s, it was 72 percent. Despite this university cachet, screenwriting in Hollywood was never less important, or worse, than it was in the 90s.

Many scripts were little more than thin premises for a disposable fireworks display, a long and noisy entertainment that disappears from the mind as soon as the credits roll. These are movies with virtually no character development, just scenes that clash with or even contradict each other, so long as the explosions and crashes grow ever larger. Some of these movies were done quite well, with a touch of wit and a sense of wonder, as with *Independence Day* (1996). Others were done with all the substance and style of a pounding rock video, like *Armageddon* (1998).

Filmstyle also suffered. As recently as 30 years ago, a Coppola film didn't resemble a Sam Peckinpah film, which didn't look like a Blake Edwards film; just as an earlier generation could distinguish between the look of a movie directed by Alfred Hitchcock or John Ford.

Most movies of this era were shot in an indistinguishable style. Without the credits, it would be difficult to identify the director. Closeups predominate, because they play well on television, the screen that most films are seen on by most people. Contemplative long shots, crane shots, and a smooth methodical pace largely disappeared from mainstream American movies because filmmakers worried that an audience used to the luxury of the remote control would grow restless and tune out. Even the most popular foreign films—*La Femme Nikita* (1990), *Four Weddings and a Funeral* (1994)—were, in content, tone, and style, largely indistinguishable from the American genres they were imitating (see Chapter 19).

Perhaps the most regrettable consequence of the dominance of American movies abroad was the decline of the once-thriving national cinemas of France,

18–8. *Leaving Las Vegas* (U.S.A., 1995), *with Elizabeth Shue and Nicolas Cage, directed by Mike Figgis.*

Foreign directors in Hollywood often bring with them a certain intellectual cachet, and consequently get to direct more ambitious and off-beat movies than most native-born filmmakers. The British Mike Figgis, a former jazz musician, adapted John O'Brien's bleak novel of alcoholism, prostitution, and despair. Figgis also composed the film's score (with vocals by Sting). The story of a man successfully attempting suicide via alcoholism showed the influence of John Cassavetes. The performances and overall mood of soulful regret at three in the morning carried the picture to a most unlikely commercial and critical success—the texture of an independent film in a Hollywood movie with stars. Cage won a well-deserved Best Actor Oscar. *(United Artists)*

Germany, Japan, and Italy. Young European directors used to pride themselves on making strong, idiomatic statements. The lyrical French films of Truffaut and the stark, austere chamber dramas of Ingmar Bergman served as stylish nudges that affected U.S. cinema for the better. This worldwide aesthetic conversation between filmmakers and their audiences gave movies a more interesting texture. Everybody won.

More often than not, promising foreign directors want to become Hollywood directors in the worst way. As movies like Luc Besson's *The Fifth Element* (1997) and Paul Verhoeven's *Starship Troopers* (1997) proved, they often succeeded, and in the worst way. Of course, there were always exceptions **(18–8).** This apparent decline might be just a temporary calm, symptomatic of the uneasy, slightly disengaged limbo into which the post-cold war world has fallen. Perhaps the malaise is a mental retooling, stemming from the fact that the movie business has changed more in the last two decades than it had in the previous 80 years.

The baroque downtown movie palaces gave way to multiplexes with several dozen screens. The slow release pattern was replaced by simultaneous release in 2500 theaters. A strong system of producer control evolved into catch-as-catch-can control by actors, agents, and sometimes directors, but almost never by producers. The continuity of the contract system was displaced by freelancing, with each movie's creative team assembled from scratch. And television and cable have siphoned off talent and audiences as well. Hollywood seemed to be in the midst of a transition in which only a few films were able to break through the media white noise to attain the singular cultural importance of the movies of our past.

The Bright Side

But for everything that was lost, something was gained. While we lost skill in some of moviemaking's component parts, screen acting has never been better. There is a wealth of superlative actors spanning the generations, from Clint Eastwood to Kevin Spacey to Johnny Depp and Gwyneth Paltrow. And there are more on the way—Christina Ricci, Reese Witherspoon. Even stars in the classic mode such as Tom Cruise and Leonardo Di Caprio are making choices that earn points for ambition. For many years, female performers have complained of the dearth of good women's roles, but even here, the situation improved considerably **(18–4, 18–9).**

Another bright spot was animation. It was better and more widespread than ever. Disney created mainstream films of quality and beauty with strong underlying messages such as *The Lion King* **(18–5),** just as it had for decades. But Disney was no longer the only game in town. Fox and Warners were both in the animation business, although films like *Anastasia* (1997) did not find Disney-sized audiences. Television animation such as *The Simpsons, South Park,* and *Rugrats* further broadened the styles acceptable to the mass audience.

Also contributing to the expansion of the animation business was CGI, or computer graphics imaging. This type of computer animation has a bright, plastic sheen—smoother, less organic, less obviously drawn than conventional animation. CGI made its mainstream debut in Disney's *Toy Story* (1995) and struck a chord with audiences used to the digital animation of arcade and computer games. CGI also ushered in a new era of special effects, with films like *Jurassic*

18–9. *My Best Friend's Wedding* (U.S.A., 1997), *with Julia Roberts and Cameron Diaz, directed by P. J. Hogan.* Julia Roberts was the highest-paid female star of the 1990s, and a darling of the public, especially in romantic comedies like this, and especially when she brandished her big hair and dazzling smile. Cameron Diaz, as a result of her captivating comic performance, went on to become a popular favorite in *any* comedy. Gorgeous, endearing, sexy, and funny, she recalls such classic 1930s comediennes as the great Carole Lombard. *(TriStar Pictures)*

Park (1993) displacing the stop-motion animation developed by Willis O'Brien (*King Kong*) in the early thirties and Ray Harryhausen (*Jason and the Argonauts, The 7th Voyage of Sinbad*) in the fifties. Animation of the future will almost certainly be all digital.

Most impressively, there was probably more variety in U.S. filmmaking than in any previous period. Hollywood turned into a shape-shifting culture. African American filmmakers were far more numerous, not to mention gifted, than ever before. Spike Lee, the Hughes brothers (**18–10**), John Singleton, and Forest Whitaker, to take just a few examples, could coexist comfortably and not be dependent on the success of every single film, demonstrating, in effect, that they had as much right to fail as anyone else. Likewise, the expanding Hispanic population promoted acting talent like Antonio Banderas, Jennifer Lopez, Salma Hayek, and directors like Robert Rodrigues and Alfonso Arau. From abroad, Brenda Blethyn and Katrin Cartlidge, Asia Argento, Stellan Skarsgard, Bai Ling, Djimoun Hounsou, and Michelle Yeoh all showed potential as actors and stars.

The status of women filmmakers also vastly improved. There were several dozen women directors working in mainstream filmmaking, from art movies (Jane Campion) to broad commercial comedies (Betty Thomas). As with any other grouping, women filmmakers made all sorts of movies, at all sorts of levels of accomplishment. In the real world, as opposed to theoretical wishful thinking, talent and sensitivity are more important determinations of success than gender. At times, women directors proved that they can be every bit as obvious and untalented as their male counterparts. A sad example is Amy Heckerling's lame *Look Who's Talking* (1989) and its embarrassing sequels. It's hard to believe that this was the same director who made the zesty coming-of-age comedy, *Fast Times at Ridgemont High* in 1982.

18–10. *Menace II Society* **(U.S.A., 1993),** *with Larenz Tate and Tyrin Turner, directed by Albert and Allen Hughes.*
Perhaps the most impressive film dealing with the violence of the inner city, *Menace II Society* is also the most pessimistic, offering little hope for the future. Larenz Tate's electrifying performance as O-Dog is genuinely shocking. Handsome, shrewd, and arrogant, O-Dog is also one of the most heartless swines of the contemporary American cinema, killing without remorse, insolently daring the world to do something about it.   *(New Line Cinema)*

At their best, women directors brought something new and valuable to the table. Some of them made their mark with small, personal movies that could not have been made as effectively by male directors simply because the materials required a sympathetic insider's point of view. Allison Anders's *Gas Food Lodging* (1992) as well as Martha Coolidge's bittersweet *Rambling Rose* (1991) clearly revealed a feminine sensibility at work.

Other filmmakers were relatively gender-neutral, like Barbra Streisand's *Prince of Tides* (1991) and Penny Marshall's charming *Big* (1988), although her popular *A League of Their Own* (1992) was overtly feminist. There was a growing presence of women producers—Jodie Foster, Sandra Bullock, Drew Barrymore, Randa Haines. Furthermore, women were moving into unobvious genres. Mimi Leder, who distinguished herself as a television director on the popular and critically acclaimed *E.R.,* made two action films—*The Peacemaker* (1997) and *Deep Impact* (1998)—for her feature inaugurals. Betty Thomas, a former actress, became a successful director of mainstream comedies like *The Brady Bunch Movie* (1995) and *Doctor Dolittle* (1998). With both these filmmakers, however, the movies tend to be male-centered and high concept (i.e., plot driven, with lots of action). The fact that they were women is irrelevant in terms of the movies they directed.

A few women's films even achieved blockbuster status, most notably *Sleepless in Seattle* **(18–11),** a winsome, wispy romantic comedy written and directed by Nora Ephron, and its semi-sequel, *You've Got Mail* (1998). Penelope Spheeris's *Wayne's World* (1992) was also a huge hit, despite the fact that the story materials were regarded as "too masculine" for a woman director. Stimulated by fields of long green, gender stereotypes were becoming increasingly passé.

Likewise, the gay sensibility, as represented by writers like Paul Rudnick (*Addams Family Values, In & Out*) and Don Roos (*The Opposite of Sex*), proved that

18–11. *Sleepless in Seattle* (U.S.A., 1993), *with Tom Hanks, written and directed by Nora Ephron.*
One of the most successful romantic comedies of the decade, *Sleepless in Seattle* recalls the golden age with its lush soundtrack of romantic ballads of the 1940s and 1950s, like "In the Wee Small Hours of the Morning," "When I Fall in Love," "As Time Goes By," and the great "Stardust." The movie also pays homage to the classic Leo McCarey romantic comedy, *An Affair to Remember* (1957). *(TriStar Pictures)*

18–12. *The Birdcage* (U.S.A., 1996), *with Nathan Lane and Robin Williams, directed by Mike Nichols.*
An Americanized remake of the art-house movie **(15–3)** and musical *La Cage Aux Folles,* this film posits a happily "married" gay couple (pictured), forced to play straight for the marriage of Williams's son and his conservative in-laws. Entirely stereotypical, but played with charm and energy, the mainstream success of the film showed that gay themes were no longer relegated to the fringe. The movie is a good example of how a popular star like Williams can influence public opinion, creating a sympathetic climate for a subject that Hollywood traditionally regarded as box office poison. *(United Artists)*

even the long-touchy subject of homosexuality was now commercially feasible in the mainstream cinema. Some movies about gay life—like Mike Nichols' *The Birdcage* (18–12)—were huge box office hits. Gay directors like Gus Van Sant (*Good Will Hunting*) and performers such as Ian McKellan (*Gods and Monsters*) moved beyond the early days of being ignored, the later days of being scorned, and the more recent period of being pitied. Now, gays and lesbians are just people, like everyone else.

Major Filmmakers

The sense of the 1990s as a creative holding pattern is amplified by the fact that, for the most part, the leading directors of the 1980s were the leading directors of the 1990s—older, grayer, but incontestably the leaders of the gang.

STEVEN SPIELBERG entered the decade as the oldest manchild in Hollywood and the most commercially successful filmmaker in history; he enters the twenty-first century as the foremost filmmaking talent of his generation. Still capable of turning out a delicious popcorn movie like *Jurassic Park* (1992), Spielberg's maturing evidenced itself with powerful movies like *Schindler's List* (1993), the underrated *Admistad* (1997), and the World War II epic, *Saving Private Ryan* (18–13).

Spielberg ascended to the top of his field not because he evolved out of his faults, but rather because he managed to transcend them. These faults still exist: a tendency toward bravura displays of stylistic virtuosity in excess of what the material calls for, and an over-reliance on the often sentimental music of John Williams, which hammers home every point that Spielberg's eloquent images have already made.

18–13. *Saving Private Ryan* (**U.S.A., 1998**), *with Tom Sizemore and Tom Hanks, directed by Steven Spielberg.*
While modern cinema is full of stars who could never have been stars at any other time, there are also some throwbacks. There are handsomer actors than Tom Hanks, there are actors with more range, but nobody invests his characters with the underlying sense of bedrock decency that Americans have always admired in their greatest screen heroes—iconic stars like James Stewart, Henry Fonda, and Gary Cooper. But they were always somewhat remote, larger-than-life. Hanks is more intimate, more democratic. Few contemporary stars are as beloved: He has nurtured an intimate bond with his audience by his laid-back appearances on talk shows, where he is invariably witty, charming, and unpretentious. A devoted family man, Hanks is also generous with his time and money, supporting many good causes. He is intensely conscious of the moral values of the characters he plays, and has been known to turn down juicy roles because he doesn't want to be associated with morally repugnant characters *(DreamWorks Pictures)*

But Spielberg knows that the essence of cinema is a succession of rhythmically edited, expressive, carefully composed shots. He has total command of the visual language of film. At his best, he gives the impression that he could have been a great director of silent movies—pictures without words, communicating meaning to a rapt audience. Certainly he's never found a writer as eloquent as his images.

Spielberg's gambit when dealing with an important subject is not to inflate his style, but to deflate it. He shoots an Indiana Jones movie briskly, but with a luscious, pearly sheen and sense of majesty. A story about saving Jews from the Nazis or self-sacrifice in World War II is shot neorealistically, with the camera bobbing and weaving as if it were a caught-on-the-run, you-are-there newsreel.

"I came to realize," said Spielberg at the time *Schindler's List* was released, "the reason I came to make the movie is that I have never in my life told the truth in a movie. My effort as a moviemaker has been to create something that couldn't possibly happen." The bravura opening passages of *Amistad*—a slave revolt in 1839—or the D-Day landing of *Saving Private Ryan* attained the status of instant classics.

MARTIN SCORSESE struggled through the decade with a succession of hit-and-miss films, starting off with the brilliantly executed mob drama *GoodFellas* **(18–14),** one of his most commercially successful films as well. He then lurched through the over-the-top Grand Guignol of *Cape Fear* (1991), which was clearly made to

18–14. *GoodFellas* **(U.S.A., 1990),** *with Ray Liotta, Robert De Niro, Paul Sorvino, and Joe Pesci, directed by Martin Scorsese.*
Though this film takes place on Scorsese's usual turf—the lower echelons of the Italian-American mob—the treatment is witty and occasionally exhilarating in its stylistic rapture. The story is based on the actual life of Henry Hill (Liotta) who eventually betrayed his fellow mobsters and ended up in the Federal witness protection program. Like most of Scorsese's mafia pictures, there is a good deal of violence and a great deal of cursing and swearing—it's a guy thing. Scorsese's movie was one of his biggest commercial hits in the 1990s and also received rave reviews.   *(Warner Bros.)*

maintain some commercial foothold, and provided the necessary box office bonanza.

In 1993 he adapted Edith Wharton's Pulitzer Prize winning novel, *The Age of Innocence,* starring Michelle Pfeiffer and Daniel Day-Lewis. The material—sexual repression among New York's upper social echelons in the 1870s—was a radical departure from Scorsese's usual turf. Perhaps to regain his footing from its disappointing reception, Scorsese returned to the mob with *Casino* (1995), starring his favorite actor, Robert De Niro. He ended the decade with the respectful, beautiful, but rather arty spiritual drama, *Kundun* (1997).

Even in the least of these films there were images that no other director could have imagined, and more than a few critics have referred to Scorsese as America's greatest living director. His core problem is that he has never been able to make a successful movie that isn't energized by physical or emotional violence. A movie like *Kundun,* the story of the early life of the Dalai Lama, is a succession of striking images but dramatically it's rather inert. Scorsese's career is that of a torrentially involved and frenetic seeker, deeply spiritual and conflicted, his reach often exceeding his grasp, but bravely continuing to reach all the same.

Throughout the 1990s, WOODY ALLEN continued to make about a movie a year, despite an enervating and highly publicized breakup and custody battle with actress Mia Farrow. His movies of this period probably don't rank with his extraordinary artistic accomplishments of the previous decade, but no other filmmaker can match the diversity and sheer volume of his output.

18–15. *Deconstructing Harry* (U.S.A., 1997), *with Woody Allen and Judy Davis, written and directed by Allen.*
Nearly every year for 30 years, Woody Allen released a movie, compiling a body of work few contemporary directors can approach, let alone equal. Allen's pictures can be charming or unnervingly close to the bone, like this film, a portrait of a rotten, selfish, irresponsible, unreliable, unfaithful louse who happens to be a good writer. Of Allen's two idols, Fellini and Bergman, *Deconstructing Harry* is definitely in the Bergman vein—a pitiless exploration of modern life among the spoiled sophisticates of New York City. The psychic violence inflicted in this movie is every bit as damaging as the physical violence of *GoodFellas*. Oddly, it's also one of Woody Allen's funniest movies.   *(Fine Line Features)*

Alice (1990) is a character study of a rich New York housewife (Mia Farrow) who has lost her sense of purpose in life. The film contains several fantasy scenes that are charming and funny as well as touching. Allen also directed a number of movies that were frankly third-rate: the pretentious *Shadows and Fog* (1992), the trivial *Manhattan Murder Mystery* (1993), and the overwrought *Celebrity* (1998).

Allen has always had a large appreciative audience in Europe and Japan, and in the 1990s he became something of an Orson Welles figure—more respected (and even revered) abroad than at home, where his movies have been, at best, only modestly successful, primarily with art-house audiences. His light comedies during

18–16. *Alien Resurrection* **(U.S.A., 1997),** *with Sigourney Weaver and Winona Ryder, directed by Jean-Pierre Jeunet.*
Back in 1968, Stanley Kubrick's seminal *2001: A Space Odyssey* ushered in a golden age of science fiction. Since then, a number of directors have created first-rate movies in this genre. The *Alien* Tetralogy is among the most interesting. Each of the four films is a self-sufficient movie, and each was directed by someone different. However, all of them star the powerful Sigourney Weaver as Ripley, a fierce warrior who does battle with the slimy alien in its many incarnations. The original *Alien* (1979) was directed by the sophisticated visual stylist, Ridley Scott, whose dark sinister setting—a remote half-forgotten outpost in space—established the tetralogy's smoky atmosphere and rustbelt technology, with its hissing and clanging machinery. The second installment, *Aliens* (1986), was directed by James Cameron. Its dazzling special effects won an Oscar, and its action footage was the most powerful of the four movies. *Alien³* (1992) was directed by David Fincher. It was slower, more philosophical in emphasis. The final installment, *Alien Resurrection,* picks up the story 200 years after part three, with a clone of Ripley aboard an alien-contaminated spaceship. *(Twentieth Century Fox)*

this period were especially popular in Europe: the delicious jazz-age comedy, *Bullets Over Broadway* (1994), the whimsical *Mighty Aphrodite* (1995), and the offbeat musical, *Everyone Says I Love You* (1996).

Allen also made two corrosive domestic dramas that were as painful to watch as they were psychologically insightful, the abrasive *Husbands and Wives* (1992) and the equally caustic *Deconstructing Harry* **(18–15).** "Relationship" movies like these almost certainly have influenced such pessimistic young American filmmakers as Neil LaBute (*In the Company of Men, Your Friends and Neighbors*), Doug Liman (*Swingers, Go*), and the brilliant Todd Solondz (*Welcome to the Dollhouse, Happiness*). All of these artists tend to view their characters as alienated and pathetically hollow at best, vicious and depraved at worst. Usually they're at their worst.

CLINT EASTWOOD is arguably the most inconsistent of major American filmmakers. In part, this is because he is an incorrigible risktaker. Sometimes these risks result in mediocre productions like *The Rookie* (1990), a police story with virtually no redeeming qualities; *A Perfect World* (1993), a manhunt movie with no suspense; or *Absolute Power* (1997), a thriller with no real thrills. Eastwood is a slow, ponderous director who likes to linger over his scenes, so why would he choose to direct *Midnight in the Garden of Good and Evil* (1997), a story that clearly called for a lightness of touch that's totally foreign to Eastwood's sensibility?

On the other hand, sometimes Eastwood's risks pay off. His films of the 1990s reflect a more vulnerable side of his talent, especially in his acting. His insecure, shakey CIA agent in the thriller *In the Line of Fire* (1993, directed by Wolfgang Petersen) is surprisingly poignant, much deeper emotionally than audiences are used to. Similarly, who would have guessed that Eastwood's adaptation of the

18–17. Unforgiven (U.S.A., 1992), *with Clint Eastwood, directed by Eastwood.*

The career of Clint Eastwood is a model example of how a movie star's **persona** can alter and deepen with age. Eastwood dedicated *Unforgiven* to Don Siegel and Sergio Leone, the two directors who believed in him as a young actor and from whom he learned the most as a director. *Unforgiven's* William Munny is a man who has long struggled to ignore the fact that he's really good at only one thing: killing. At the film's climax, when he once again begins practicing his bloody craft, he achieves something remarkable: catharsis at the long-withheld violence. He also experiences a sinking sense of doom, for nothing will save William Munny now. *Unforgiven* is a remarkable film: methodical, deeply felt, with a devastating emotional and moral impact. It is easily one of the best westerns since Siegel's own *The Shootist* in 1976. Eastwood's film is beautifully directed, the crowning achievement of an impressive career. Its critical and commercial success earned it the Academy Award for Best Picture—only the second western to be so honored. Eastwood also won the award for Best Director. Both Siegel and Leone would have been very proud of their pupil. *(Warner Brothers)*

mawkish novel *The Bridges of Madison County* (1995) would be so moving? Most critics ravaged the novel, lamenting its florid prose style. Meryl Streep gives one of her finest performances in this understated love story of two lonely middle-aged lovers who must give each other up. As usual with Eastwood's films, the musical soundtrack is superb, consisting of soulful ballads of the 1950s and 1960s by such fine recording artists as Johnny Hartman and the great Dinah Washington.

The 1990s was also the artistic culmination of Eastwood's work in the western, with the production of *Unforgiven* **(18–17)**. It is almost universally regarded as a masterpiece. Eastwood also gave one of his best performances in this film—funny, scary, inexorable.

The Independent Cinema

Perhaps the most significant phenomenon of the decade was the emergence of the independent cinema as the main source of artistically significant movies in America. The decade introduced new talents like Quentin Tarantino, Ben Stiller, Lili Taylor, Ben Affleck, Stanley Tucci, Tim Roth, Campbell Scott, and Parker Posey,

18–18. *Good Will Hunting* (U.S.A., 1997), *with Ben Affleck and Matt Damon, directed by Gus Van Sant.*
Affleck and Damon wrote the script to this film when they were hungry unknowns, and to save money, they played leading roles. The movie became a big box office hit and the young co-writers eventually went on to win an Oscar for Best Original Screenplay. To add to the implausibility, Affleck and Damon also became popular stars, appearing in a number of mainstream and independent films. If their story were made into a movie, not many people would believe it—much too Hollywoodish to be credible.   *(Miramax Films)*

who come to the fore out of this movement, which also made quasi-stars of older talent like Harvey Keitel.

The low-budget films they created and starred in were first seen, typically, at Sundance and other film festivals, where talent scouts for the major studios become an ubiquitous presence. As a result, the cream of the independent crop usually found a ready conduit to the mass audience. Some filmmakers, like the Coen brothers and Cameron Crowe, straddle both worlds, beginning as independents, then gradually moving to the big Hollywood studios, though usually with more artistic autonomy than most studio hired hands could command.

Many independent films aren't really good, just independent—grotty little movies about fashionably bleak, minimalist lives, a remarkable number of which seem to take place at 7-Elevens. Of course, making a good, completely realized film is very hard. A single bad choice about the script, the cast, or the director can submarine even the loftiest intentions. Most movies are inadequate to their ambition.

Also, independent movies aren't exactly new. In every sense of the word, *The Birth of a Nation* (1915) was an independent film, and John Cassavetes, Robert Altman, and Woody Allen were making films that were independent in conception and execution when Quentin Tarantino was just a gleam in his father's eye. Some of the Bright Young Things of the independent cinema sink surprisingly quickly. Edward Burns made a splash with *The Brothers McMullen* in 1995, but little has been heard from him as a director since then. Likewise Robert Townsend, who was unable to replicate the success of *Hollywood Shuffle*.

But sometimes they swim. QUENTIN TARANTINO's rise is a case in point. His first film was *Reservoir Dogs* (1992), a bloody, expert little thriller about the aftermath of a heist that owed a good deal to Huston's *The Asphalt Jungle* and a great

18–19. *Pulp Fiction* **(U.S.A., 1994),** *with Bruce Willis, directed by Quentin Tarantino.*

The contemporary American cinema has probably never been so hospitable to diverse independent talents, like the gifted Quentin Tarantino. The off-the-wall weirdness of this movie provoked a surprisingly enthusiastic response from critics and audiences. The movie also swept the top award— the Palme d'Or—at the prestigious Cannes Film Festival. *(Miramax Films)*

deal to Kubrick's *The Killing*. Tarantino exploded into the mainstream with *Pulp Fiction* **(18–19),** a lengthy neo-noir that was less interesting for its content than its style. Tarantino dared to scramble conventional storytelling chronology by interweaving a series of stories about various L.A. lowlifes in which the central character of one story plays only a glancing part in the succeeding story. The effect was of a rich, poignant, original cornucopia of dark delights.

Then in 1997 came *Jackie Brown*, an adaptation of an Elmore Leonard novel that took almost as long to watch as the novel did to read. Although it was appreciably less flashy than either of his previous films, and featured an appealing central performance by Pam Grier, the blaxploitation goddess of the 1970s, Tarantino's hipness was no longer so fresh, and the film had a muted response both critically and commercially.

Tarantino has a gift for rich, rather theatrical dialogue that can sound humorously incongruous coming out of the mouths of his crooks. He also has a voluptuous visual style that matches up surprisingly well with his bleak, nihilistic humor. One of the funniest scenes in *Pulp Fiction* involves a couple of hoods who accidentally blow someone's head off and then struggle to clean up the mess.

Tarantino also has a genuine knack for offbeat casting, specializing in mixing a few bonafide stars with a selection of talented has-beens and never-wases drawn from the exploitation films of the 1960s and 1970s that he loves. The result is a synthesis of styles and cross-references that give his films a kicky pop resonance. But there is some question as to what kind of career Tarantino is going to have. His few films show a great deal of talent, especially as a writer, but he has frittered away a good deal of his career momentum with ill-advised acting turns and some downright junky producing and writing projects, like *From Dusk to Dawn*.

Among the most original talents that have achieved some mainstream success are JOEL and ETHAN COEN. Their dark, mordant satires have brought a unique kind of humor to the screen, made up of equal parts corrosive mockery of white trash stupidity (*Raising Arizona*, 1987), or ruling class obtuseness that imagines itself to be intellectual superiority (*Barton Fink*, 1991, *The Hudsucker Proxy*, 1994). The Coen brothers are fascinated by traditional Hollywood genres, which they treat from an ironic, revisionist perspective—the gangster film in *Miller's Crossing* (1990), the private eye movie in *The Big Lebowski* (1998), an inverted send-up of Raymond Chandler's seminal *The Big Sleep*.

The Coen brothers' greatest asset, an ironic and chilly style, is also their greatest liability. For every Coen success like *Raising Arizona* and *Fargo* **(18–20),** there is a corresponding muddled failure offering little but attitude and cruelty—*Hudsucker, Lebowski*. As any number of failed Tarantino wannabes have demonstrated, attitude may get you through the door, but it won't get you a seat at the table with the adults.

CAMERON CROWE first came to notice with his screenplay for *Fast Times at Ridgemont High*, based on a book he had written. Crowe was only 24 at the time (1982), but already had several years of writing for *Rolling Stone* behind him. The young writer went undercover as a student to get beneath the surface of high school life. Although *Ridgemont High* was directed by Amy Heckerling, it set the matrix for the rest of Crowe's career: an ordinary premise redeemed by painstaking observation and character development.

Crowe has written and directed such films as *Say Anything* (1989, teenagers struggling to maintain a love affair in the face of a father's disapproval), *Singles*

18–20. *Fargo* **(U.S.A., 1996),** *with Steve Buscemi and Peter Stormare, directed by Joel Coen.* In the films of the Coen brothers, incompetence is the ruling trait. Their characters are nowhere near as slick or talented as they think they are. In this comic detective thriller, a scheming husband hires two idiot thugs (pictured) to bump off his rich wife. They bloodily botch the job and force him into a downward spiral of deceit and murder that can only end in capture. Loosely based on an actual case, the movie centers on Marge Gunderson (Frances McDormand), the very pregnant police chief of Brainerd, Minnesota. The film is often funny, interspersed with unsettling scenes of brutality and gore. Though Chief Gundersen finally solves the case, the "happy ending" is considerably undercut by its tone of sadness and pessimism concerning our pathetic species. The movie was the Coen brothers' most successful work, winning two Academy Awards: Best Actress for McDormand, Best Screenplay for Joel and Ethan Coen.   *(Gramercy Pictures)*

(1992, young unmarrieds in a Seattle apartment building), and *Jerry Maguire* (1997, the redemption of a bigtime sports agent who happens to be an acquisitive, materialistic lout). All have been sympathetically acted and painstakingly written.

Crowe is one of the few contemporary screenwriters whose work could stand with the best writer/directors of the Golden Age—Sturges, Huston, Wilder—and not seem terribly diminished. Like most writers who have become directors, Crowe's emphasis is on the words and the characters. His films are cleanly but functionally directed—nothing too flashy.

WHIT STILLMAN carved out a small clearing for his precise renderings of young urban professionals. His first film, *Metropolitan* (1990), was set in the rarified world of New York debutantes. *Barcelona* (1994) was a strange, strangled romantic comedy set during the end of the Cold War. *The Last Days of Disco* (1998) was about more or less what the title indicated, following two attractive young women trying to find Mr. Right at a succession of nightclubs. One critic called Stillman's characters "wealthy, conservative and as doomed as the clueless aristocrats in Chekhov's

The Cherry Orchard." These fretful, compulsively verbal people let the revolution drift right past. Stillman's sensibility is preppy, thoughtful, with a mordant streak of absurdism, and invariably literate. Above all, a *writer*/director.

Another gifted writer/director is the weird, subversive, and totally unnerving TODD SOLONDZ. His first important film, *Welcome to the Doll House* (1996), is a coming-of-age movie centering on dorky Dawn Wiener, a junior-high school student from a pathologically dysfunctional suburban family. (Mom and Dad dote on her "adorable" younger sister—a sibling from Hell.) There are very few movies that dramatize so painfully—and often hilariously—the humiliations of early adolescence.

Happiness (1999) explores another dysfunctional family, focusing on three adult sisters and their various neuroses, some funny, some pathetic, a few scary. Solondz is capable of extraordinary artistic courage, like showing the humanity of

18–21. *Chasing Amy* (**U.S.A., 1997),** *with Ben Affleck and Joey Lauren Adams, written and directed by Kevin Smith.*

The central problem with romantic comedy has always been creating a believable way of keeping two people that we know are meant for each other apart for 90 minutes. Kevin Smith's film created a novel central problem to divide the lovers: She's a lesbian. Then Smith went even further: After they get together, the gap between their personalities proves too much for them and they split up. It's not a plot that would have been possible in Old Hollywood, but it worked very well for a more ambiguous time. In his films (most notably *Clerks* and *Mallrats*) Smith focuses on the heretofore ignored and very unglamorous lives of blue-collar kids and young adults. Smith's profane, often very funny dialogue helps make up for a directorial style that could delicately be termed minimalist. *(Miramax Films)*

18–22. *There's Something About Mary* (U.S.A., 1998), *with Ben Stiller and Cameron Diaz, written and directed by Peter and Bobby Farrelly.*
This movie gave rise to a popular genre in the late 1990s—the gross-out comedy. The ruling characteristic is bad taste: political incorrectness and a cheesy sense of the grotesque are also much admired traits. The roots of the genre extend back at least to Preston Sturges and Billy Wilder in the 1940s and 1950s. The films of Jim Abrahams, David and Jerry Zucker—like *Airplane!* and such John Belushi vehicles as the gross *Animal House*—have contributed substantially to the slob aesthetic that rules in this type of movie. The most obvious influence is the skit comedy of such satiric television shows as *Saturday Night Live, Second City,* and *Mad TV.* Gross-out films tend to be hit-or-miss, with a rambling narrative that's often interrupted by brief skits, some of which are not very amusing, while others can be incredibly crude, if undeniably laugh-out-loud funny. Examples: racist gags, anti-jock jokes, fart jokes, yelping dog gags, anything involving genitals, especially male genitals that are attacked, whacked, or otherwise abused, cruel gags about deformities, jokes about old or fat people, and anything involving bodily fluids. In short, the genre revels in all subjects that are likely to shock or disgust respectable citizens.   *(Twentieth Century Fox)*

a compulsive child molester, a narrative line that prompted considerable criticism. *Happiness* is often bizarrely comical, even while we squirm at the disgusting specimens of humanity that are our brothers and sisters—or so Solondz seems to suggest.

Although PAUL THOMAS ANDERSON has made only three films, he is clearly an important talent. He is interested in subcultures that nobody else notices. His first film, *Hard Eight* (1997), was a little-seen picture about gambling. His second was the virtuosic *Boogie Nights* (1998), about the porn industry in the 1970s, the days when pornography came out into the open. Loosely modeled on the ensemble films of Robert Altman, and with a flamboyant visual style adapted from Scorsese, *Boogie Nights* was an ambitious pocket epic that spanned a decade. The movie gave an accurate picture of both the heavenly and hellish aspects of the skin trade and the damaged people that populate it.

Anderson created moments no one had ever seen before. One scene, in which the film's central character, the porn star Dirk Diggler (Mark Wahlberg), now desperately broke and a cocaine addict, tries to rip off an even more coked-out party-boy, is remarkable for the variety of emotions it contains. The party-boy (Alfred Molina) is ensconced in a plush Beverly Hills house, surrounded by pounding metal anthems blasting over the stereo and armed bodyguards who are constantly setting off firecrackers on the mansion's marble floor. Dirk's already tautly stretched nerves are doing trampoline jumps. Since he and his friends are attempting to pass off baking soda as cocaine, we expect a conventional scene where the ruse is discovered. But Anderson takes it in another direction. Violence erupts and people die, but the most dangerous man in the room turns out to be the party-boy. The scene is simultaneously funny, menacing, and scary, with the audience having

18–23. *Ulee's Gold* (U.S.A., 1997), *with Peter Fonda, directed by Victor Nunez.*
Movies have always been a factory of dreams, with only a nodding acquaintance with objective reality. But *Ulee's Gold* painstakingly showed the audience the life of a beekeeper—not something most people give a lot of thought to. Aside from the intrinsic value of the story of a man coming out of a self-imposed emotional exile, the daily work of harvesting honey provided the film with a fascinating grounding in the real world.   *(Orion Pictures)*

no clue where the disaster will come from. Anderson got excellent performances out of a dozen actors, including Burt Reynolds as the director, Julianne Moore as the porn queen, and Wahlberg as the sweet, dim Dirk Diggler. *Boogie Nights* is one of the most impressive pictures of the decade.

For all of the press attention given to the independents, many of them were only independent until they could get a studio deal. Among the true independents, always including the venerable John Sayles, there also emerged VICTOR NUNEZ. Nunez has been making films in his native Florida for years. Unlike Sayles, he never got much notice.

Movies as good as *Gal Young' Un* (1979, a lonely widow in Prohibition-era Florida is victimized by a fast-talking young man), *A Flash of Green* (1984, a reporter struggles with political scheming and environmental peril), and *Ruby in Paradise*

18–24. *The Thin Red Line* **(U.S.A., 1998),** *with (clockwise from left) Adrien Brody, Dash Mihok, Will Wallace, Sean Penn, and Woody Harrelson, directed by Terrence Malick.*
In the 1970s, Terrence Malick made two strikingly original masterpieces, *Badlands* (1973) and *Days of Heaven* (1978). He spent the intervening years contemplating his possibilities and writing a few scripts that didn't see the light of day. Finally, he came forward with this poetic, typically mystical adaptation of James Jones's World War II combat novel, *The Thin Red Line*. This kind of expensive comeback from a director with only two art-house films to his credit—both of them commercial failures—would have been impossible in the more monolithic industry of the 1970s. In the 90s, film producers and distributors were more willing to take a chance on unconventional material, assuming that almost any movie has an audience out there somewhere, either on the big screen, broadcast television, or on video. *(Twentieth Century Fox)*

(1993, a young woman in flight from a bleak past passes through a small Florida beach community and seeks to realize her dreams) never broke out. This is probably because, like John Cassavetes, Nunez sought to reproduce not the rhythm of movies, but the rhythms of life itself. The pace is relaxed, the story is revealed incrementally, the tone is lyrical. No dazzle, just immense dignity, depth, and richness.

It was *Ulee's Gold* (**18–23**) that finally earned Nunez the notice that had eluded him for 15 years. A quiet story of a widowed beekeeper struggling to raise his grandchildren, the movie gave Peter Fonda an opportunity for a career performance. The film encapsulated Nunez's greatest gifts—rigorous respect for his characters and his audience, a contemplative sense of day-by-day life as it's really lived, and a respect for and interest in working people that's nearly disappeared from the big screen. "The truth is that there will always be people who want to make

18–25. *Magnolia* (U.S.A., 1999), *with Julianne Moore, written and directed by Paul Thomas Anderson.*

Like many American actors, Julianne Moore paid her proverbial dues by performing on a television soap opera for several years. Her big break in feature films came when Robert Altman cast her as an unfaithful painter in 1993's *Short Cuts*. Fearless, she played one scene entirely bottomless—an act so brazen that critics remained fixated on it for years. Since then, she has amassed a roster of credits the equal of any performer of the contemporary cinema. She is extraordinarily versatile, playing an unhappy aristocrat in the Chekhov adaptation, *Vanya on 42nd Street*, directed by Louis Malle; a coked-out porn queen in Anderson's *Boogie Nights*; and a woman who's allergic to virtually everything in Todd Haynes's *Safe*. Moore has played in big budget projects like Spielberg's *The Lost World: Jurassic Park* and small indie films like the Oscar Wilde stage adaptation, *An Ideal Husband*. She is drop-dead gorgeous as the British adulteress in Neil Jordan's *The End of the Affair* but, in Altman's *Cookie's Fortune*, she plays a drab mousy spinster. She prefers roles that are unusual and difficult, like the guilt-ridden trophy wife who's constantly on the verge of hysteria in *Magnolia*, a part written expressly for her by Anderson. Driven, ambitious, and apparently indefatigable, Moore acted in a staggering five movies in 1999 alone.   *(New Line Cinema)*

independent movies and succeed," Nunez has explained. "It's not a trend. It happens one film at a time."

Miramax, the leading independent producer, was actually more of a throwback to the classic movie studio. Brothers Bob and Harvey Weinstein kept a fierce eye on the budgets (think Jack Warner), were known for carrying on conversations at high decibel levels (think Harry Cohn), and thought nothing of re-editing and, if necessary, reshooting movies at will (think every movie mogul of the Golden Age). And the Weinstein brothers added a weapon to the arsenal that never occurred to the old moguls: When a picture didn't work, they simply didn't release it. In the old days, with 50 pictures a year on the schedule, everything got released, one way or another. Miramax distributed such landmark independent films as *The Crying Game, Pulp Fiction, The Piano,* and two Best Picture Oscar winners, *The English Patient* and *Shakespeare in Love,* movies of extraordinary diversity.

What this means is that the old verities were dead. No one really knew where the next wave of hits was coming from. The industry had to be open to all sorts of possibilities, however remote. The good news is that because Hollywood's dominance in the global marketplace created so much demand, there was a constant clamor for more product. The result was that practically everybody got a chance.

The first century of film possessed more energy and innovation in its youth and middle years than in its dotage. Well, life is like that. In the next century, the gap between studio movies and the independents would grow smaller and even merge. All-digital cinema for both production and exhibition was lurking just around the corner. Technology would soon make it possible to create movies more cheaply, and cheap movies can be more adventurous movies.

Now, more than ever, anything was possible.

FURTHER READING

DIXON, WHEELER WINSTON. *Disaster and Memory: Celebrity Culture and the Crisis of Hollywood Cinema.* New York: Columbia University Press, 1999. An overlapping series of essays on how we got from then to now, with interesting chapters on the Red Scare and the pioneering woman director Ida Lupino.

FRIEDMAN, LESTER, ed. *Unspeakable Images: Ethnicity and the American Cinema.* Champaign: University of Illinois Press, 1991. Scholarly essays on ethnic stereotyping in American movies.

GUERRERO, ED. *Framing Blackness: The African-American Image in Film.* Philadelphia: Temple University Press, 1994. Critical analysis of recent black films.

LEWIS, JON, ed. *The End of Cinema As We Know It: American Film in the Nineties.* New York: U.P., 2001. A collection of essays.

MAYNE, JUDITH. *The Woman at the Keyhole.* Bloomington: Indiana University Press, 1990. Feminism and women's cinema.

NEALE, STEVE and MURRAY SMITH. *Contemporary Hollywood Cinema.* New York: Routledge, 1998. A survey of the decade.

ORWAL, BRUCE, and JOHN LIPPMAN. "Cut! Hollywood, Chastened by High Costs, Finds a New Theme: Cheap." *Wall Street Journal* (April 12, 1999). The how and why of financial retrenchment at the American studios.

RICHARDSON, JOHN H. "Dumb and Dumber," *The New Republic* (April 10, 1995). Why 1990s movies aren't much good, by a seasoned show business journalist.

WOLLEN, TANA, and PHILIP HAYWARD, eds. *Future Visions: New Technologies of the Screen*. Bloomington: Indiana University Press, 1993. Covers IMAX, virtual reality, high-definition television, interactive games, and multimedia.

WYATT, JUSTIN. *High Concept Movies and Marketing in Hollywood*. Austin: University of Texas Press, 1994. Modern industry practices in the United States.

19

International Cinema in the 1990s

European cinema is in danger of dying. My fight isn't anti-American, it's anti-industrial. The movie industry in the United States is like a war machine.
—GÉRARD DEPARDIEU, French film star

Miramax Films

Timeline: 1990–1999

1990
South African political dissident Nelson Mandela is released from prison by white Prime Minister F. W. de Klerk—three years later, they share a Nobel Peace Prize

1991
Collapse of the Soviet Empire, leaving fifteen republics in its place

1992
Era of "ethnic cleansing" begins in Yugoslavia as Muslims, Roman Catholics, and Eastern Orthodox Christians begin slaughtering each other en masse

1993
First step toward peace in the Middle East as Israel's Prime Minister Yitzhak Rabin and P.L.O. leader Yassir Arafat agree to negotiate after nearly five decades of war. Rabin was later assassinated by a Jewish religious fanatic

1994
Over one million civilians slaughtered and two million dispersed in Rwanda, Africa in brutal clashes between ethnic rivals, the Hutus and Tutsis

1997
Within three days of each other, two of the most admired women in the world, Mother Teresa (age 87) and Britain's Princess Diana (age 36) die
Dr. Ian Wilmut of Scotland's Roslin Institute announces that scientists have cloned a sheep, "Dolly"

1998
India and Pakistan both test nuclear weapons, intensifying ancient enmities
Asia's booming stock markets crumble as monetary crises cripple the economies of Indonesia, Thailand, Korea, and other developing nations

1999
NATO planes bombard Serbia in retaliation for its "ethnic cleansing" of more than 850,000 ethnic Albanians out of the Kosovo region of Yugoslavia

Hollywood Blitzkrieg. The shrinking European film industries. The spread of international co-productions. British cinema. Masterpiece Theatre masters: Kenneth Branagh, James Ivory, John Madden. Shakespeare on film. Kitchen Sink masters: Ken Loach and Mike Leigh. Irish film boom: Jim Sheridan and Neil Jordan. Continental Europe: France, Holland, Scandinavia, Spain, and Italy. Eastern Europe after the collapse of Communism. Emerging cinemas: Mexico and China. Australia and New Zealand: Jane Campion.

Hollywood Über Alles

IN THE 1990S THE HOLLYWOOD film industry virtually blitzed the international market, pulverizing the struggling cinemas of most foreign competitors. According to the American Enterprize Institute, the United States produced only 10 percent of the world's feature length films, but it accounted for about 65 percent of the global box office receipts. Europe was especially hard hit by the American blitzkrieg. American movies accounted for about 85 percent of total European box office revenues. In contrast, European pictures made up only 1 percent of the American market.

In France, where the government enacted protectionist legislation to safeguard the country's "cultural identity," over 70 percent of the entertainment dollar was spent on American movies and television. In 1998 only three of the top 20 films in France were made in France. In 1990 *Pretty Woman* was the top grosser in Germany, Sweden, Italy, Spain, Australia, and Denmark. Near the end of the decade, James Cameron's *Titanic* was the box office champion in virtually every international free market of the world.

Naturally, the resentment toward Hollywood was and still is enormous. Foreign film critics routinely described their national cinemas in mortuary metaphors. In Italy, for example, the number of native films declined from about 100 annually in the 1980s to a mere 40 in 1993. One producer complained: "If you speak about the film industry here, you must first consult a mortician!" The land of the titans, of Fellini, De Sica, Visconti, and Antonioni became deserted. Remarked Francesco Maselli, president of the Italian author's association, "Now, Italian kids know everything about American political and social systems through American films—and nothing about their own."

The American studios also dominated the international market by providing capital for new theaters, which of course gave precedence to American movies rather than the local product. According to Douglas Gomery, throughout the 1990s the Hollywood studios built new theaters in Germany, Spain, France, Australia, and even in Russia. In Great Britain, U.S. capital financed more new screens than was seen in over a generation.

How did these countries defend their industries from the American colossus? After 1991, the number of international coproductions increased dramatically,

19–1. *Shall We Dance?* (Japan, 1997), *with Koji Yakusyo, directed by Masayuki Suo.*
Japanese film critics routinely refer to their cinema as "debased," "exhausted," or, more often, "dead." The home of such giants as Ozu, Mizoguchi, Mifune, and Kurosawa—all dead—was now virtually a cinematic wasteland. Miraculously, *Shall We Dance?*, a charming and profound social comedy, sprang from this barren soil. The story centers on a 42-year-old accountant who secretly takes up ballroom dancing—a totally foreign concept in Japan, where such a hobby would be considered weird. In a society that makes a fetish of social conformity, any act of individualism is likely to be viewed as ridiculous and laughable. Nonetheless, our hero decides to take dancing lessons. He's so ashamed that he doesn't even tell his wife. Besides, they hardly speak anymore, though they're unfailingly polite. He feels that there's something pretentious about imitating "Western" oddities, something unmanly about wanting to be graceful. Yet his daily grind lacks excitement and romance. He is virtually a stranger to his family, like most Japanese fathers. And maybe—just once—he would like to stand out in a crowd. This shot embodies his double life: Above the desk, he's a conscientious accountant, but down below, he's practicing his dance steps. *(Miramax Films)*

jumping as much as 50 percent in some countries, especially in Europe. Some critics refered to these international coproductions contemptuously, as "Europuddings." But others saw no other alternative. "Coproductions are the route to survival," said Danish filmmaker Finn Gjerderum. "We Europeans have to work together or one day we'll have no choice but to watch only what is made in Hollywood."

Many countries also deregulated their television industries, which are no longer dominated by government bureaucracies. Throughout much of Europe especially, movies are financed by independent television networks and premier on TV before they are exported as feature films to foreign markets.

There are also many expatriate filmmakers who work in a variety of countries, depending on where they can raise their financing. This is a common pattern for many Eastern European filmmakers like the late Krzysztof Kieslowski **(19–3).** His fellow Pole, Agnieszka Holland, has made movies in France, England, and the United States (see **19–22).** Of course expatriate cinema is nothing new. Some leave their countries for political reasons; others for wider opportunities. Many years ago the Spaniard Luis Buñuel made most of his films in Mexico and France. The Polish

19–2. *The Sweet Hereafter* (**Canada, 1997**), *with Alberta Watson and Bruce Greenwood, written and directed by Atom Egoyan.*

Atom Egoyan is one of Canada's most accomplished fiction filmmakers. He has also written and directed for television, opera, and live theater. *Exotica* (1995) was the first Canadian movie to be invited into competition at the Cannes Film Festival in over a decade, and it won the International Prize for Best Film. *The Sweet Hereafter,* based on a novel by Russell Banks, is his most successful film to date, winner of the Grand Prize, the International Critics Prize, and the Ecumenical Prize at the 1997 Cannes Film Festival. Like most of his movies, it explores the theme of alienation, especially within families and within small communities. Russell Banks said of Egoyan's adaptation: "He takes the ordinary texture of life and mythologizes it and turns it into a larger, more universal story." *(FineLine Features)*

19–3. *Publicity photo of Red* (**France/ Switzerland/Poland, 1994**), *with writer-director Krzysztof Kieslowski and actors Jean-Louis Trintignant (center) and Irene Jacob.*

As the British critic Geoffrey Nowell-Smith observed, the collapse of Communism in 1991 was not entirely salutary for many artists working in Eastern Europe: "In cinema terms, the 'New World Order' threatens to be not just the triumph of West over East or North over South, but a specifically American victory over all competition." Many filmmakers from Eastern Europe, like Krzysztof Kieslowski (1941–1998) could no longer confine themselves to native materials and had to finance their movies like patchwork quilts. For example, his "Three Color Trilogy," consisting of *Blue* (1993), *White* (1993), and *Red* (the three colors of the French flag) derived most of their financing and casts from France, not Kieslowski's native Poland. *(Miramax Films)*

19–4. *Eat Drink Man Woman* **(Taiwan, 1994),** *directed by Ang Lee.*
Ang Lee was born in Taiwan and moved to the United States in 1978. He is a New York University film school graduate whose movies began to win international awards almost immediately. *Eat Drink Man Woman* is the third film of his "Father Knows Best Trilogy." The other two are *Pushing Hands* (Taiwan, 1992) and *The Wedding Banquet* (Taiwan/U.S.A., 1993). Lee is something of an expatriate filmmaker, directing *Sense and Sensibility* **(19–6)** in England and the stunning 1970s period piece *The Ice Storm* (1997) in the United States. Although these movies seem to have little in common, most of them explore tensions within families. For example, *Eat Drink Man Woman* is a gentle comedy about a master chef (Sihung Lung, third from left) who has lost his sense of taste and has alienated his three adult daughters. "We communicate by eating" one of his daughters observes, but, in fact, the rituals of preparing and eating food are ways of avoiding interaction. Lee has a very delicate sense of texture, of the space between the words, the glances that reveal character, as much as a brilliant line of dialogue. *(The Samuel Goldwyn Company)*

Roman Polanski has also worked in a variety of countries, most notably the United States, France, and England. In the 1990s, the most famous expatriate filmmaker was Taiwan's Ang Lee **(19–4).**

In some parts of the world, especially Asia and Latin America, the film industries are doing better, primarily by catering to native audiences. India still produces more movies than any other country in the world, but these films rarely appeal to international audiences. Perhaps the most successful foreign filmmakers in the 1990s were the Irish and the British, in part because, like the Americans, they enjoy the advantages of a massive English-speaking market throughout the world. English is also the international language of commerce, diplomacy, and the internet.

Great Britain

"There is no British cinema," proclaimed the English critic Duncan Petrie, "there is only a British input into international (American) cinema." To say the least, Petrie's observation is extreme. In fact, a good argument can be made that the decade of the 1990s represented the high point of prestige and profitability for the British cinema.

19–5. *The English Patient* (**Great Britain, 1997**), *with Ralph Fiennes and Kristin Scott Thomas, directed by Anthony Minghella.*
Based on Michael Ondaatje's celebrated novel (winner of the 1992 Booker Prize), this film's complex flashback structure is merely one of the many difficulties Minghella had to overcome in bringing this tragic tale of obsessive love to the screen. The movie attempts to reproduce the novel's haunting and poetic texture with an understated spareness. His next film, the critically acclaimed *The Talented Mr. Ripley* (1999), was also an adaptation of a prestigious novel by Patricia Highsmith.   *(Miramax Films)*

English movies routinely got nominated for American Academy Awards, especially in the acting categories. Two British films won Best Picture Oscars: Anthony Minghella's *The English Patient* (1997) and John Madden's *Shakespeare in Love* (1998). British movies also did well in terms of box office receipts. The worldwide grosses of Peter Cattaneo's *The Full Monty* (1997) exceeded $200 million. (The movie cost a piddling $3.5 million to make.) Similarly, Mike Newell's romantic comedy *Four Weddings and a Funeral* (1994) was the biggest box office hit in British film history, grossing a staggering $250 million.

The British cinema is one of the most diverse in the world. Traditionally, the Brits are at their best with classy adaptations of prestigious plays and novels. The key filmmakers in this "Masterpiece Theatre" branch are Kenneth Branagh, James Ivory, and John Madden. The left-wing "Kitchen Sink" branch of British filmmaking also prospered during the 1990s, most notably with the works of Ken Loach, Stephen Frears, and Mike Leigh.

There are also a number of remarkably versatile directors who can switch from one style of filmmaking to another, from stage work to screen (both TV and film), and from American projects to British. For example, Mike Newell's exquisite English film *Enchanted April* (1992) is a romantic, softly evocative period piece set in the post–World War I era. In the United States, Newell went on to direct the gritty *Donnie Brasco* (1997), a down-and-dirty gangster film about two low-level wiseguys played by Al Pacino and Johnny Depp (the latter an FBI agent).

British culture is profoundly literary, and among the most ambitious works of the "Masterpiece Theatre" branch of English cinema are adaptations of Shake-

19–6. *Sense and Sensibility* **(Great Britain, 1995),** *with Emma Thompson and Kate Winslet, directed by Ang Lee.*
In the 1990s, all six of Jane Austen's major novels were made into movies and television series, most of them quite fine. *Sense and Sensibility* is perhaps the finest, thanks in part to Emma Thompson's superlative screenplay, which won an Academy Award. It was her first screenplay. Thompson wrote several drafts over a period of four years. "The novel is so complex and there are so many stories in it that bashing out a structure was the biggest labor," she admitted. As an actress, she knew that some of the dialogue in the novel would not translate well to film, so she turned to Austen's letters (Miss Jane was a prodigious letter writer), which contained simpler language. "Some of the sentences in the book go on forever," Thompson said, but in the letters, "Austen's personal style was very clear and elegant. And very funny." In addition to writing the screenplay, Thompson also played one of the leading roles, superbly. *(Columbia Pictures)*

speare's plays. The leading figure in this genre is Kenneth Branagh, who directed two major works, *Much Ado About Nothing* (1993) and a full-length (i.e., over four-hour long) *Hamlet* (1996). *Much Ado* was a crossover hit, appealing to many movie-goers who never thought they'd ever enjoy a movie written by Shakespeare. And no wonder. The film fairly explodes with high energy. Shakespeare's most famous comic lovers, Beatrice and Benedick (played brilliantly by Emma Thompson and Branagh), are endearing, funny, and sexy. Their verbal duels do full justice to the Bard's wit and linguistic virtuosity.

Nobody could accuse Branagh of insufficient flash, either as a director or actor. His starring roles in *Henry V, Much Ado,* and *Hamlet* pleased purists and movie fans alike with their textual fidelity and their exuberant visual flair. These are not plodding literary genuflections, but full-bodied *movies,* peopled with virile soldiers, lusty wenches, and passionately driven characters. The camerawork is often lyrical, and the editing style can be swooning or staccato with equal ease. No boring talking heads here, but a swooping swirl of events unfolded at a zesty pace.

Although Branagh's non-Shakespearean films exhibit much of the same dazzle, the style seems overdone when grafted onto less substantial scripts such as *Dead Again* (1991) and *Mary Shelley's Frankenstein* (1994). Branagh also played a compelling Iago in a middling film version of *Othello* (1995, directed by Oliver Parker) that made you realize how much you missed him as a director. If Branagh hasn't yet surpassed *Henry V,* his first movie, his loyalty to Shakespeare and his great gifts as an actor/director make him one of the few younger directors capable of summoning the theatrical flourish of Orson Welles.

19–7. *Much Ado About Nothing* **(Great Britain, 1993),** *with Emma Thompson and Kenneth Branagh, directed by Branagh.*
An uncharacteristically quiet and tender moment as the battling Beatrice and Benedick haltingly, reluctantly, squirmingly declare their love for each other. The movie makes maximum use of the gorgeous Italian countryside, lending the story a sense of sunny enchantment. *(The Samuel Goldwyn Company)*

Other Shakespearean movies during this period include a lively *Twelfth Night* (1996), helmed by one of Britain's most gifted stage directors, Trevor Nunn, and starring Helena Bonham Carter, Ben Kingsley, and Nigel Hawthorne. A much celebrated stage production of *Richard III,* updated to the Fascist 1930s, and starring Ian McKellen as Shakespeare's most famous disciple of evil, was made into a 1995 movie directed by Richard Loncraine. However, the movie version was radically cut, and many of the sequences were so juiced up with loud sound effects and rapid editing that many audiences complained they couldn't hear the dialogue.

A stage and television director, John Madden, had made only two obscure movies before he hit it big with *Mrs. Brown* (1997), a gentle period picture about the grieving widow, Queen Victoria, starring Judi Dench as the aging monarch. Madden went on to direct the immensely popular *Shakespeare in Love,* which grossed over $100 million and won its American star, Gwyneth Paltrow, a Best Actress Oscar. Dench played another aging monarch, Queen Elizabeth I, which won this gifted artist an Oscar as Best Supporting Actress.

Young Queen Elizabeth I was the main focus of another period picture, *Elizabeth* (1998), starring the talented young Australian actress, Cate Blanchett. The movie was directed by the Indian Shekhar Kapur, and features the usual British virtues of sumptuous production values and first-rate actors. Another biography film, *Wilde* (1998) explored the final tragic years of writer Oscar Wilde, skillfully played by Stephen Fry. Written by Julian Michell and directed by Brian Gilbert, the film is an incisive exposé of British hypocrisy regarding homosexuality and Victorian England's extreme discomfort about all matters sexual.

19–8. *Shakespeare in Love* **(Great Britain, 1998),** *with Gwyneth Paltrow and Joseph Fiennes, directed by John Madden.*

Fast moving, funny, and erotically charged, this tour-de-force was cowritten by American Marc Norman and British playwright Tom Stoppard. The story (entirely fabricated) explores an illicit love affair between a betrothed aristocrat and a struggling young playwright. "It had a sense of humor and an intelligence," Madden said of the script. "And it felt so modern and potentially sexy. I thought it would be great to have a movie about Shakespeare that could be sexy." *(Miramax Films)*

Of the many excellent British movies based on famous novels and plays, *The Wings of the Dove* is one of the finest. Based on a novel by Henry James, the film was written by Hosein Amini. Oscar Wilde wittily observed that Henry James wrote "as if it were a painful duty." The movie infuses the story with passion and energy as well as an explicit sexuality that would have made the prudish Victorian novelist blush. Director Iain Softely updated the story to 1910, bringing it to the edge of the modern age, when women began to smoke publicly and automobiles were about to galvanize the languid Belle Epoque into the Jazz Age.

There were two other important adaptations, *The Madness of King George* (1994) and *Jude* (1996). Alan Bennett's witty and provocative stage play served as a basis for his script to *The Madness of King George,* which was the debut film of the celebrated stage director, Nicholas Hytner. George's main claim to fame—or infamy—is that he lost the American colonies in 1776. This was not a good year for the poor demented monarch, who was clearly not all there. He is played with great poignancy by the estimable Nigel Hawthorne. Helen Mirren, riveting as usual, plays his desperate, loyal wife, Queen Charlotte.

Jude, an adaptation of Thomas Hardy's great nineteenth-century English novel *Jude the Obscure,* was directed by Michael Winterbottom. The film is uncompromising and every bit as pessimistic and cosmically fatalistic as the original. Christopher Eccleston plays the doomed protagonist, Kate Winslet his tormented

19–9. *The Wings of the Dove* **(Great Britain, 1997),** *with Alison Elliott and Helena Bonham Carter, directed by Iain Softley.*
British actors have always been the envy of the civilized world, but in the 1990s there was a virtual explosion of brilliant performers, especially among women. In 1997, four of the five Oscar nominees for Best Actress were Brits: Helena Bonham Carter, Julie Christie, Kate Winslet, and Judi Dench. (The winner was the sole American, Helen Hunt.) Other first-rate English actresses include Kristin Scott Thomas, Miranda Richardson, Emma Thompson, Helen Mirren, Brenda Blethyn, and Emily Watson, to name only some of the most prominent. *(Miramax Films)*

lover Sue. Winslet was already an accomplished actress, playing leading roles in this film as well as *Heavenly Creatures, Sense and Sensibility, Hamlet,* and *Titanic.* Not bad for an actress still in her teens.

Of course the dean of the British Masterpiece Theatre branch of filmmaking is the American James Ivory (see Chapter 17). Working with his longtime partner, producer Ismail Merchant, Ivory directed films in the United States during the 1990s as much as he did in Britain. His finest work of the decade is the E. M. Forster adaptation, *Howards End* **(17–6).** Set in the transitional Edwardian era of the 1910s, the movie is beautifully produced and features a nearly perfect cast, headed by the ubiquitous Emma Thompson (who won a Best Actress Oscar), Vanessa Redgrave, Anthony Hopkins, and Helena Bonham Carter. The screenplay, a superlative piece of craftsmanship in its own right, was written by longtime collaborator, Ruth Prawer Jhabvala. The Merchant-Ivory team followed this film with another excellent adaptation, *The Remains of the Day* **(19–10).**

Mr. & Mrs. Bridge (U.S.A., 1990) is a little gem of a movie—intimate, funny, and poignant—with husband and wife Paul Newman and Joanne Woodward in the title roles. The film is unusual in that it focuses on an elderly couple, even more unusual in that the two leading characters are not reduced to sentimental clichés. Rather, they're presented as complex human beings in their not-so-golden years: They're constantly sniping at each other. Newman and Woodward have never been better: Both deliver tough, disciplined performances, glowing with humanity.

19–10. *The Remains of the Day* (Great Britain, 1993), *with Anthony Hopkins and Emma Thompson, directed by James Ivory.*
Like most of Ivory's best works, this film is a faithful adaptation of a distinguished literary original, Kazuo Ishiguro's prize-winning British novel of the same title. The screenplay was written by the gifted Ruth Prawer Jhabvala, who has collaborated on most of Ivory's biggest successes. As usual, the movie is impeccably mounted and superbly acted. It's hard to believe that the repressed, rigidly proper butler of this film (Hopkins) is played by the same actor who played the scary wacko Hannibal Lecter in *The Silence of the Lambs*. Similarly, the dowdy but decent housekeeper (Thompson) is performed by the same artist who created the sexy, irrepressible Beatrice in *Much Ado About Nothing.* (Columbia Pictures)

Another American-made movie, *A Soldier's Daughter Never Cries* (1998) is based on a book (with the same unfortunate title) by Kaylie Jones, the daughter of the American author James Jones, who wrote two famous novels about the World War II era, *From Here to Eternity* and *The Thin Red Line*. Once again working on a limited scale (and of course the usual limited budget), *A Soldier's Daughter* is a family saga that's tough-minded yet also sweet and touching. The cast is headed by Kris Kristofferson and Barbara Hershey as the unconventional parents.

The so-called "Kitchen Sink" brand of filmmaking had its monster hit with *The Full Monty* **(19–11),** which is British slang for totally nude. For many years writer Simon Beaufoy had observed how there were fewer and fewer mills in the once prosperous steel-producing region of Sheffield. When film producer Uberto Pasolini asked him to write a comic script about male strippers, Beaufoy used the opportunity to combine the characters with the social scourge of unemployment in Sheffield. *The Full Monty* was the result, a story of how six beefy unemployed steel workers find salvation—or at least temporary financial relief and self-respect—by stripping down to the buff in front of 400 cheering women.

The characters all speak with a thick Yorkshire accent, so director Peter Cattaneo didn't think the movie would travel well. It traveled spectacularly well, especially at the Sundance Film Festival, where it premiered in the United States. "People starting stomping their feet and clapping," Beaufoy recalled, and the movie went from there to undreamed of popularity, one of the all-time largest grossing English movies in history.

A less spectacular success was *My Name is Joe* (1999), directed by Ken Loach (b. 1936). The movie is unusual in that it features subtitles: The Scottish brogue of the characters is all but impenetrable even to native speakers of English. Loach has been making movies for over three decades, but he has never had a wide international following. Like Mike Leigh, he is a champion of the British working class, which he views from a staunchly left-wing perspective.

Loach's movies are generally about "little things"—like an unemployed blue-collar man struggling to buy his daughter a first communion dress in *Raining Stones* (1993). His characters are flawed, occasionally violent, like the unlucky protagonist of *Riff-Raff* **(19–12),** who tries hard to repudiate his shoddy past. Though clearly sympathetic to his characters, Loach never sentimentalizes them. Nor does he offer glib excuses for their rotten behavior.

19-11. *The Full Monty* (**Great Britain, 1997**), *with William Snape and Robert Carlyle, directed by Peter Cattaneo.*

Screenwriter Simon Beaufoy, who was born and raised in Yorkshire, wanted to focus on six likable working-class characters in this tale of social change in the late 1980s, when thousands of men were laid off from the steel mills of the region. "With women increasingly becoming the breadwinners and traditional roles being reversed by their newfound economic independence, men were forced to re-examine their relationships and deeply held beliefs about gender roles," said Beaufoy. "Fifteen years ago male strippers were unheard of in England. There have been huge changes in the past several decades in how men and women view each other and in *The Full Monty* we used the idea of stripping as a starting point to examine those changes." *(Twentieth Century Fox)*

The protagonist of *My Name Is Joe* is a psychologically damaged recovering alcoholic in his late thirties, Joe Kavenagh (Peter Mullan). He has been clean and sober for over a year. Unemployed and living on welfare, he throws his energies into coaching a soccer team of mean-mouthed delinquents. He falls in love with a nurse, but in his efforts to rescue a buddy who is involved with a drug lord, Joe betrays her. His life then collapses around him. Not many happy endings in the works of Ken Loach.

He began his career in television and has always favored a documentarylike realism in his films. His actors tend to employ a loose, improvisatory style, which is by no means artless. (Mullan won a Best Actor award at the Cannes Film Festival.) Loach also tends to favor a hand-held camera and on-location shooting, lending his scenes a streetwise authenticity. His tough masculine style has been compared favorably with such masters of realism as Sidney Lumet and Martin Scorsese.

In the 1980s, most of the works of Bill Forsyth were set in Scotland (see Chapter 17), and *Gregory's Girl* (1981) even had to be redubbed for American and English audiences because the Scottish burrs were considered too extreme. For the most part, however, mainstream filmmakers avoided Scottish stories—until the cult thriller, *Shallow Grave* (1994) proved an unexpected international hit. Since then, over 40 movies have been shot in Scotland, including such important works as Mel Gibson's *Braveheart* and Lars Von Trier's *Breaking the Waves*. Other Scottish films include *Eden Valley, Complicity, Women Talking Dirty, Orphans,* and *Among Giants.*

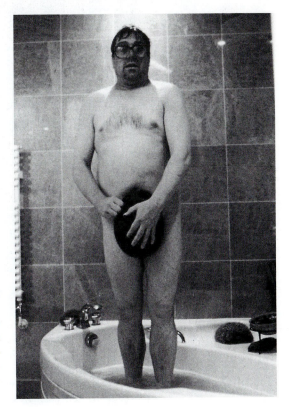

19–12. *Riff-Raff* **(Great Britain, 1991),** *with Ricky Tomlinson,*
directed by Ken Loach.
Loach's movies are often downbeat and discouraging, especially
about the eternal class struggle in Britain, but they can also be rau-
cously funny. This film explores the problems faced by a blue-collar
worker (Robert Carlyle) and his mates at a London construction
site. Some of the regional accents are so thick that Loach resorted to
subtitles so that the dialogue would be comprehensible. The screenplay was written by Bill Jesse, himself an ex-construction worker.
(FineLine Features)

By far the most interesting of these Scottish films is *Trainspotting* **(19–13).**
Adapted by John Hodge from Irvine Welsh's cult novel, the movie explores the
lives of several heroin addicts living—barely surviving—in Edinburgh. Ewan Mc-
Gregor plays Renton, the most intelligent of the group. He also narrates the story,
giving us insights into the bizarre behavior of his mates, who are drifting through
life without money, without prospects, and without any plans to change. The movie
is often very funny, with weird surrealistic episodes that stand out from the grim realism of most of the film.

The most prestigious artist of the Kitchen Sink school is Mike Leigh (b.
1943). He has been working in film, television, and live theater for nearly thirty
years, but didn't attract much international attention until *High Hopes* (1989), a
typical blend of working-class geniality and sharp-edged satire. The hilarious (and
often touching) *Life is Sweet* (1991) was also a modest international success. It's an
intimate portrait of a semifunctional working-class family, consisting of a blowsy
middle-aged couple and their two likably dorky daughters.

At their best, Leigh's characters are appealing—warm-hearted, unpretentious
good ol' boys and girls. His sympathies are unabashedly socialist, which can be
seen even in his working methods. For years he has worked with a loyal stable of actors, including the versatile Alison Steadman (Leigh's wife) and Jim Broadbent.
The actors generally improvise on their roles for weeks and even months before
they agree on a finished screenplay. Their movies are relatively plotless, bittersweet
slices-of-life that emphasize character rather than story. Leigh's visual style is usually plain: a meat-and-potatoes documentarylike functionalism. No pretty pictures
here.

19–13. *Trainspotting* **(Great Britain, 1996),** *with Ewan McGregor, directed by Danny Boyle.*
A huge international hit, this movie solidified the reputation of Ewan McGregor as an important new British actor. Extraordinarily versatile, he has performed in a wide range of styles and genres, including working-class Scottish stories like this, refined period dramas like the Jane Austen adaptation *Emma,* and even science fiction like George Lucas's *Star Wars: Episode I—The Phantom Menace. Trainspotting* was made by the same creative team that made *Shallow Grave:* director Boyle, producer Andrew Macdonald, and writer John Hodge. *(Miramax Films)*

Leigh's characters aren't always genial and likable. *Naked* (1993) features a protagonist (David Thewlis) who is mean-spirited and violent, an unemployed thug who alternates between casual cruelty (especially toward women) and surprising flashes of intelligence and sensitivity. Leigh won a Best Director award for this work at the Cannes Film Festival.

Leigh's most successful film to date is *Secrets & Lies* **(19–14),** which won the Palme d'Or (top prize) at Cannes and garnered several American Oscar nominations, including a Best Actress nod for Brenda Blethyn, Best Supporting Actress for Marianne Jean-Baptiste, and Best Original Screenplay for Leigh. The story revolves around the attempts of a young professional black woman (Jean-Baptiste) who goes in search of her birth mother, only to discover that mom is a white woman (Blethyn), a messy, weepy, cheery, hysterical factory worker who just can't seem to get her life together. Critic David Denby perceptively describes the scene in which Hortense identifies herself to Cynthia, her birth mother:

> Cynthia, refusing to believe that Hortense can possibly be her daughter, sits in a café with this amazing young woman at her side, and the camera holds steady on the two of them as Brenda Blethyn passes through stages of sweet disbelief, impacted memory, panicky denial, a slow, mortified recognition followed by incomparable dismay and then, at last, by something like pleasure. The shot, unmoving, lasts a full seven minutes without a cut.

19–14. *Secrets & Lies* **(Great Britain, 1996),** *with Brenda Blethyn (extreme right) and Marianne Jean-Baptiste (back to camera), directed by Mike Leigh.*
Mike Leigh's actors just don't look or sound like actors: They seem to be real people with real hang-ups. In this movie, the Blethyn character always manages to find the worst possible moment to embarrass or shock her family. Weepy, self-pitying, grotesquely funny, and desperately needy, she manages to repel us even while enlisting our sympathy. It is only one of several great performances in the film. The acting style is a far cry from the pear-shaped tones and precise diction of traditional British acting techniques. With Leigh's actors, you don't notice the technique, just the raw emotions. *(October Films)*

The scene, superlatively acted, is breathtaking, hovering precariously between comedy and possible catastrophe.

Ireland

Irish movies of the 1990s did not fall into a predictable style (though realism predominates), and the range of genres is extraordinarily broad, encompassing rural comedies like *The Playboys, Widows' Peak,* and *Waking Ned Devine;* biography films like *My Left Foot, Michael Collins,* and *The General;* love stories like *Circle of Friends;* stage adaptations like *Dancing at Lughnasa;* family stories like *The Snapper, The Van,* and *The Field;* coming-of-age psychological dramas like *The Miracle* and *The Butcher Boy;* and stories about teenagers and other young people, like the charming musical film, *The Commitments.*

The most important movies—both socially and aesthetically—are those dealing with "the Troubles" of Northern Ireland and the Irish paramilitary organization, the IRA (Irish Republican Army). "The Troubles" refers to the violent conflicts between the predominantly Protestant state in the northeastern corner of

19–15. *My Left Foot* **(Ireland/Great Britain, 1989),** *with Ruth McCabe and Daniel Day-Lewis, directed by Jim Sheridan.*
This is the movie that put Ireland on the international map. It was nominated for five American Academy Awards, and it won two, Best Supporting Actress for Brenda Fricker and Best Actor for Day-Lewis. The movie is based on the true story of Christy Brown (Day-Lewis), a feisty Irish writer and painter who was born with cerebral palsy and could use only his left foot to write and paint with. Based on Brown's own autobiography, the film is funny, shocking, and inspirational at the same time. We get to know a man who is passionate, witty, gifted, hard-drinking, hard-assed, and hard-as-nails when anyone crosses him or tells him what he can't accomplish. The films of director Sheridan have been strongly influenced by American culture. He was the Director of the Irish Arts Center in New York City for six years, and studied filmmaking at New York University before making his film debut with this work. His film *In America* (2004) is virtually a valentine to the country that nurtured him as a young artist. *(Miramax Films)*

the island, which is British-controlled, versus the independent Republic of Ireland, which dominates most of the island and is 95 percent Roman Catholic. The IRA is a terrorist organization that is officially outlawed, but is still widely admired by many Irish Catholics.

This conflict is as much about class as it is about religion. In Northern Ireland the Catholics have been mostly poor, while the Protestants were—and still are—generally prosperous. They also control most of the institutions of power and prestige. These are ancient enmities, extending back for centuries. The role of the IRA in Irish society has occasioned a number of film masterpieces, including *The Crying Game, In the Name of the Father, Some Mother's Son,* and *The Boxer.* Although these films are sympathetic to the goal of Irish unification, they are by no means mindless endorsements of the violent methods that the IRA employs. Quite the contrary: The secret organization is portrayed ambivalently at best, and often negatively, as thugs determined to foist their will on everyone, regardless of the human costs.

The social context of this outburst of world-class films is an unprecedented economic boom in Ireland. Until recent years, the country was isolated and predominantly rural, with chronically high unemployment. Modern Ireland is mostly urban, its citizens relatively well-educated and upwardly mobile. There is still a large blue-collar working class, but the middle class is growing rapidly. The economic boom in Ireland has also spread to the other arts, especially rock music, live theater, and Ireland's traditional artistic stronghold, literature.

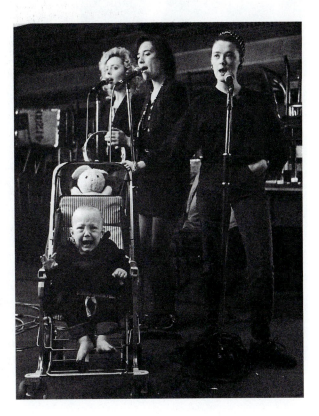

19–16. *The Commitments* (Ireland, 1991), *with Angeline Ball, Maria Doyle, Bronagh Gallagher, and one crying baby, directed by Alan Parker.*
Ireland has the largest percentage of young people under 20 of any country in Europe, and its movies are typically youthful, energetic, and sexy. This film is the first of a trilogy, written by Roddy Doyle, chronicling the life of a working-class Dublin family and their friends. The Irish actor Colm Meaney plays the father in all three movies. The other two works of the trilogy are *The Van* and *The Snapper,* both rowdy, funny, and immensely likable, like the original. The rock music throughout this film is a good example of the explosion of musical talent that put Ireland on the rock'n'roll map. Contemporary Irish music includes such musicians as U2, Sinead O'Connor, Enya, the Cranberries, and the Saw Doctors.   *(Twentieth Century Fox)*

Film critics praised the "authenticity" of the new cinema, pointing out that these movies reflect a genuinely Irish voice, not someone else's idea of what it's like to be Irish. Prior to this period, films dealing with Irish life were mostly created by foreigners, especially the British and Americans. To the Brits, the Irish were drunken buffoons and braggarts, or vicious terrorists with no regard for human life. These stereotypes have persisted in British culture for centuries. Popularized by such Irish-American filmmakers as John Ford, American movies portrayed the Irish as sentimental rustics, dressed in homespun tweedy clothes, and talking in ridiculously exaggerated brogues. Irish characters were usually pious, sexless, and comically fond of their "wee drop" of whiskey.

Contemporary Irish movies are not totally free of these corny stereotypes, but the characters and situations in the films of the 1990s are much more complex. The settings tend to be urban rather than rural. The dialogue is tough and strewn with swears and colorful colloquialisms. The role of the Catholic Church is virtually absent as a living presence in the lives of the characters. The influence of American popular culture—especially movies and rock music—is enormous. There is also a strong streak of antiauthoritarianism in these movies especially toward patriarchal figures. The women are strong and outspoken, and like the males, they're sexually active without guilt or benefit of the institution of marriage. Family life is generally validated, but there is also a good deal of tension within families, especially between generations. Contemporary urban blights like violence, unemployment, and drug addiction are commonplace in these films.

The foreign influence in the Irish cinema has not been eliminated by any means. With relatively little capital to work with, and only small government

19–17. *The Crying Game* (Ireland/ Great Britain, 1992), *with Jaye Davidson (standing) and Miranda Richardson, written and directed by Neil Jordan.*

The deceptiveness of surfaces is a thematic obsession that runs through most of Jordan's work, both literary and cinematic. Underneath the masks that people wear to appear normal, a desperate dark secret lurks. When the secret is revealed, it sends the story spinning into a totally different direction. In this cosmetic makeover scene, the Richardson character looks into a mirror to inspect the face that she will use in order to execute her IRA mission—to assassinate her former lover. (He is played by the sad-eyed Stephen Rea, who has appeared in seven of Jordan's movies.) The final irony: In Jordan's world, there are often faces behind the faces behind the masks. *The Crying Game* was nominated for an unprecedented six Oscars, including Best Picture. Jordan's dazzling screenplay won for its audacious originality. *(Miramax Films)*

19–18. *In the Name of the Father* (Ireland/Great Britain, 1993), *with Daniel Day-Lewis and Emma Thompson, directed by Jim Sheridan.*

This movie, set in Belfast, Northern Ireland in the 1970s, is based on a true story, a notorious political frame-up. The protagonist (Day-Lewis) is an Irish hippie and street punk who is arrested, beaten, and forced to sign a false confession by the British authorities. By admitting his guilt to a horrible crime committed by the IRA, he implicates his father and aunt, who are also sent to prison. The protagonist is sentenced to 30 years. An idealistic British attorney (Thompson) becomes his champion and eventually uncovers a widespread pattern of rigged cases, illegally withheld evidence, and police intimidation. The movie was an international success and received seven American Academy Award nominations. *(Universal Pictures)*

subsidies, Irish film producers have had to find their financing abroad for the most part. The majority of these movies have been bankrolled by British and American sources.

Often these foreign financiers hedged their investments by insisting on name stars to provide the movies with more box office clout. For example, the American actress Robin Wright played the main character in *The Playboys,* Mia Farrow was featured in *Widows' Peak,* Meryl Streep in *Dancing at Lughnasa,* and Hollywood heart-throb Chris O'Donnell played the romantic male lead in *Circle of Friends.* Other movies showcased well-known international stars of Irish origin, such as Albert Finney, Peter O'Toole, Gabriel Byrne, Pierce Brosnan, Richard Harris, Liam Neeson, and Kenneth Branagh. The brilliant English actor Daniel Day-Lewis (who was born and lives in Ireland) has starred in a number of important Irish movies.

Many of these films were originally produced for television, a pattern that is as commonplace in Europe as it is rare in the United States. British television has also produced many Irish movies, which were later released as feature films in America and elsewhere. English filmmakers have directed a number of these movies, most notably Stephen Frears, Alan Parker, and John Boorman (who had lived in Ireland since the 1970s).

In what sense are these movies Irish at all, one might ask. The answer: the writing, mostly. Like the British, Irish movies are much more dialogue dependent than the Continental or American cinemas. Twentieth-century Irish authors include such major figures as James Joyce, George Bernard Shaw, Lady Gregory,

19–19. *Circle of Friends* **(Ireland/Great Britain/U.S.A., 1995),** *with Saffron Burrows, Minnie Driver, Chris O'Donnell, and Geraldine O'Rawe, directed by Pat O'Connor.*
Based on the best-selling novel by Maeve Binchy, this movie is set in 1957 and explores life in a small Irish village as well as college life in Dublin. In addition to being a love story (primarily between Driver and O'Donnell), the movie explores the relationships among three girlfriends (pictured). The multiple narrative strands permit us to explore their longing for love, their secrets, and their betrayals. Several commentators have noted the "virility" and "masculine energy" of the Irish cinema, but Irish women also have True Grit. Female characters dominate not only this film, but such movies as *The Playboys, Widow's Peak,* and *Dancing at Lughnasa.* Ireland's two best-known women filmmakers are Trish McAdam (*Snakes and Ladders,* 1996) and Geraldine Creed (*The Sun, the Moon and the Stars,* 1996). *(Savoy Pictures)*

William Butler Yeats, Oscar Wilde, John Millington Synge, Sean O'Casey, Brandan Behan, Brian Friel, William Trevor, Edna O'Brien, Samuel Beckett, Maeve Binchy, and Seamus Heaney. This formidable list, which includes three Nobel laureates in literature, would be a source of pride to any world-class nation. When we consider that Ireland is a small country of fewer than 3.5 million inhabitants, its literary achievement is staggering.

Virtually all Irish movies have been written by Irish screenwriters, many of them also novelists and short story writers. Most of the new filmmakers are writer/directors, most notably Neil Jordan, Jim Sheridan, and Pat O'Connor. Shane Connaughton, co-author of *My Left Foot* and *The Playboys,* and Roddy Doyle, whose novels served as the basis for his screenplays to *The Commitments, The Van,* and *The Snapper,* are both highly respected authors who have also worked in television as well as movies.

Neil Jordan is the dean of Irish filmmakers, active since the early 1980s, and working in England and America as well as his native country. He is also the most stylistically sophisticated of Irish filmmakers, equally at home in expressionistic **film noir** styles or gritty urban realism like *Mona Lisa* (see **17–9),** epic canvasses like *Michael Collins* (U.S.A., 1996), and dreamlike poetic fables like *Interview with the Vampire* (U.S.A., 1994) and *The Butcher Boy* (Ireland, 1998). Jordan has also pub-

19–20. *Some Mother's Son* **(Ireland, 1996),** *with Helen Mirren and Fionula Flanagan, directed by Terry George.*
Cowritten by Terry George and Jim Sheridan, this movie is loosely based on the events surrounding a notorious hunger strike in 1981, in which a political prisoner, Bobby Sands, starved himself to death to protest British brutality in Northern Ireland. The story is told from the perspective of two mothers (pictured). Deeply conflicted, the two women don't even agree politically, and don't know whether they should support their sons and not intervene, or try to prevent their deaths and needless martyrdom. Brilliantly acted, the film packs a powerful impact and deals with "the Troubles" in a complex and emotionally wrenching manner. *(Castle Rock Entertainment)*

lished two novels and an award-winning collection of short stories. His themes are strongly sexual as well as political. His films often explore the conflict between politics and ethics.

Like their American cousins, Irish filmmakers tend to be storytellers, far more so than most European film artists. But Irish narratives are usually complex, unpredictable. They are not as star-driven as most American films, nor do they slavishly follow the narrative conventions of a popular genre. Irish filmmakers tend to prefer multiple narratives. *In the Name of the Father,* which has several plot lines, was coproduced by actor Gabriel Byrne, who wittily complained of the McDonaldization of world cinema, the sorry spectacle of other nations imitating American "Mc-Movies"—i.e., star-centered narratives that follow a formulaic three-act structure, concluding with an obligatory happy ending.

Irish film critics, like film critics everywhere, are constantly complaining. The so-called Irish film boom is mostly foreign, Yankee McMovies or "Europuddings" these purists scoff. Until a movie is financed, written, acted, and directed by an all-Irish company, how can anyone speak of an "authentic" Irish cinema? But these gripes are mostly spurious. Authentic Irish voices are being heard for the first time, and they are commanding the respect of film critics and audiences all over the world. In 1992, only three feature films were produced in Ireland; by the end of the 1990s, the country was averaging over twenty movies per year.

Continental Europe

The Continental European picture is grim. The French cinema is perhaps the most healthy, due largely to the country's quota system. According to critic Peter Graham, in 1991, France made more features (156), had more screens (4,531), and sold more tickets (117.5 million) than any other western country except the United States. Unfortunately, the movies produced in France rarely prospered outside their own borders. Claude Berri's $30 million spectacular, *Germinal* (1994), based on the novel by Emile Zola, is a good example of what's wrong: The subject matter is traditionally French, but the style of production is very à l'américain.

Not even the heroic talents of Gérard Depardieu could rescue the film version of another French classic, *Cyrano de Bergerac,* directed by Jean-Paul Rappeneau. Static, talky, and interminable, the movie is an exercise in literary overkill—windbag cinema at its worst. *Indochine* (directed by Regis Wargnier) is saved by a luminous performance by Catherine Deneuve, but otherwise it's a rather conventional movie, plodding compared to France's past glories.

The international coproduction of Luc Besson's *La Femme Nikita* (1990) was so Americanesque in its subject matter *and* style that the *New Yorker's* capsule review of the film wittily announced: "The end of French cinema as we know it."

In other countries the situation is desperate. Only an occasional movie achieved international fame, pictures like the Belgian *Ma Vie en Rose* (1998, directed by Alain Berliner) roughly translated as "My Life in Pink." The movie centers on a middle-class couple and their problems with their nine-year-old son who stubbornly thinks he's a girl. The film is funny, touching, and insightful in its observations about gender stereotypes and social pressures to be "normal."

In the Netherlands, *Antonia's Line* (1996), directed by Marleen Gorris, was an international success. A feminist epic, the movie follows the fortunes of a strong woman who returns to her rural village after World War II and becomes the matriarch of a line of women who don't need husbands. (As she says to a persistent suitor: "You still can't have my hand. But you can have the rest.") Lusty and comical, the film won an American Oscar as Best Foreign Language Picture.

The Scandinavian cinema had some modest successes on the international scene. Lars Von Trier, a Dane, made *Breaking the Waves* in Scotland with a British cast, but the production crew was mostly Scandinavian. It's main claim to fame was introducing the English actress Emily Watson to a wider audience. The Swedish Bille August, whose best movie is still *Pelle the Conqueror* **(17–17),** directed a number of critical successes during the decade, including *Jerusalem* (1997) and *Smilla's Sense of Snow* (1997), as well as two films scripted by the great Ingmar Bergman, *Best Intentions* (1992) and *Private Confessions* (1999).

The Spanish cinema held its own throughout the 1990s, but with the exception of the charming sex comedy, *Belle Epoque* (1993, directed by Fernando Trueba) and the deliciously trashy movies of badboy Pedro Almodóvar, most of these films were seen primarily by home audiences. Over half the Spanish films of this period were international coproductions. During the decade there were 129 film debuts, but only 38 of these new artists managed to establish a career, according to critic Barry Jordan.

The dean of Spanish film artists, Carlos Saura, directed two modestly successful dance films, *Flamenco* (1995) and *Tango* (1999). But it was the prolific Almodóvar who kept Spain on the cinematic map. According to critic Marsha Kinder, six of Spain's all-time top grossing exports to the United States were Almodóvar pictures. Several of them featured the hunky Antonio Banderas, who eventually went on to Hollywood and greater fame and much greater fortune. *Live Flesh* (1997) and *All About My Mother* (1999) were fiestas of gay theatricality, according to critic Lisa Schwarzbaum, who referred to writer-director-actor-producer-interior decorator

19–21. *Life Is Beautiful* **(Italy, 1998),** *with Roberto Benigni, Nicoletta Braschi (Mrs. Benigni in private life), and Giorgio Cantarini, directed by Benigni.*
The central theme of this Holocaust film is that people will do whatever is necessary to protect their loved ones. What is unusual is that the picture is a comedy, albeit a very dark one. Benigni has long been Italy's most beloved comedian, directing and starring in such farcical movies as *Johnny Stecchino* (1991) and *Il Mostro* (1994). He also appeared in several American movies, most notably *Son of the Pink Panther* and Jim Jarmusch's *Down by Law.* *(Miramax Films)*

Almodóvar as "the Spanish John Waters." That is, the creator of movies that are gaudy, cheery, outrageous, shamefully enjoyable, and—sometimes—oddly moving.

The mighty river that once was Italian cinema dwindled to a trickle in the 1990s. But there were two important exceptions: *Il Postino* (1995) and *Life Is Beautiful* **(19–21)**. The first, also known as *The Postman,* was directed by an Englishman, Michael Radford. The film was inspired by an incident in the life of the famous Chilean poet, Pablo Neruda, played by the French actor Philippe Noiret. When the left-wing Neruda was forced into exile in 1952, he was granted sanctuary by the Italian government on a remote island off the coast of Naples. Mario (Massimo Troisi), a simple peasant postman, becomes friends with the poet and his life is transformed as Neruda introduces him to the lyrical power of poetry. Neruda also helps our hero win the heart and hand of a beautiful young woman who inspires the lust of virtually every male on the island. The movie is funny and touching, filled with sweetness and humanity. It was a huge international success, raking in

19–22. *Europa Europa* **(Germany/France, 1991),** *with Julie Delpy and Marco Hofschneider, directed by Agnieszka Holland.*

Born in Warsaw, Poland in 1948, Holland attended film school in Prague under the tutelage of Milos Forman. She thrived in the Prague Spring era but was later arrested and jailed by the hard-line Communist thugs who took over the Czechoslovakian government. Returning to Poland, she began to work in television, the live theater, and movies, gaining a modest reputation chronicling Europe's Nazi and Communist past. She also became involved with the trade union Solidarity, which eventually brought down the Communist regime that then ruled Poland. *Europa Europa* was her breakthrough film—an improbable but true story of a Jewish youth (Hofschneider) masquerading as a Nazi during the Holocaust period. The movie is based on the life of Soloman Perel. Holland's other important works, *Olivier Olivier* (France, 1992) and *The Secret Garden* (U.S.A., 1993), also deal with abandoned children trying to survive in a hostile environment.   *(Orion Pictures)*

over $25 million in the United States alone. Troisi, who had a serious heart ailment, could only work a maximum of two hours a day. He died the day the filming was completed. He was only 41 years old.

Life Is Beautiful was the highest-grossing foreign language film in U.S. history, amassing over $50 million in North America alone. Roberto Benigni plays Guido, an Italian Jew who is sent to a Nazi concentration camp along with his wife and five-year-old son. While there, he shields his little boy from the brutality of the camp by pretending it's all a game, the source of most of the comedy in the movie. While some commentators complained of the picture's insensitivity ("You'll laugh! You'll cry! You'll smile through the evils of genocide!" mocked critic Owen Gleiberman), the majority of viewers embraced the movie. The picture won two American Oscars, Best Actor for Benigni and Best Foreign Language Film. It also won over twenty-eight international awards, including the top prize at Cannes.

The cinemas of Eastern Europe were in desperate disarray throughout the 90s. Few could have foreseen the chaos that ensued after the collapse of Communism in 1991. "Before, we were dominated by the Russians," said Polish filmmaker Krzysztof Zanussi, "now it's the Americans." In 1993 the ten most popular films in Poland were American. Producer Jacek Moczydlowski, a former dissident, noted the irony of what the new freedoms had wrought in the former Communist world:

> Under Communism, film was the freest way to express ideas. Of course there was censorship. We had to figure out a way to say what people wanted to hear without saying it specifically. It was a game of wits. Now that anything can be said in the open, there's nobody to fight against. We don't know what stories people want us to tell them.

Poland's best known filmmakers—Polanski, Zanussi, Wajda, and Agnieska Holland—work mostly outside of Poland. In the former Communist world, these artists are considered lucky. At least they're working *somewhere*.

Emerging Cinemas

Outside Europe, the international cinema was mostly geared to the home audience (i.e., it was provincial). The important movies that have emerged from China, Mexico **(19–23)**, and elsewhere did so precisely because they stood out from the crowd.

In the People's Republic of China, for example, the most promising filmmaker were often referred to as the "Fifth Generation." Obviously, there were at least four generations that came before, but very few of those filmmakers commanded much international prestige. Predictably, the most famous present-day Chinese filmmakers, Chen Kaige and Zhang Yimou, have been heavily censored and some of their works have been banned. The situation is similar to the old Soviet style of Big Brother coercion.

But China was hungry for international recognition and cultural prestige. When Chen Kaige's *Farewell My Concubine* was chosen as cowinner of the best picture award at the Cannes Film Festival, the Chinese cultural gestapo finally permitted the movie to be shown at home, but only after some severe cutting, especially of the homosexual scenes and the suggestion of political abuse by the contempo-

19–23. *Like Water for Chocolate* **(Mexico, 1992),** *with Lumi Cavazos and Marco Leonardi, directed by Alfonso Arau.*

Funny, passionate, and extravagantly whimsical, Arau's film was a surprise hit in America, a top grosser on the art-house circuit. The movie is based on Laura Esquivel's best-selling novel, and she also wrote the screenplay. Arau is an actor who has appeared in American as well as Mexican movies. Among the film's many charms are its outlandishly literalized metaphors—like a woman's unceasing tears which, when dried, provide an entire household with a plentiful supply of cooking salt! *(Miramax Films)*

rary ruling regime. Modern life in China is supposed to be happy, wholesome, and heterosexual.

Zhang Yimou is widely regarded as China's foremost film artist. Many of his movies of this era starred the beautiful Gong Li and explored the problems of women in a traditionally sexist society. Like Chen Kaige, Zhang is a virtuoso stylist, as can be seen in such films as *Red Sorghum, Ju Dou,* and *Raise the Red Lantern* **(19–24).** However, Zhang is stylistically variable, depending on his subject matter. For example, *The Story of Qiu Ju* (1993), set in contemporary provincial China, is documentarylike in its artless realism.

The cinema of Hong Kong is not exactly "emerging." In the 1970s, the martial arts films of Bruce Lee put the island nation on the map, appealing to youthful audiences especially. Hong Kong was taken over by the Chinese in 1997, but it continues to retain a separate identity and its cinema continues in its traditional mode—that is, mostly martial arts action films and crude comedies. The main characteristic of both genres is excess: breakneck speed, chaotic violence, crude jokes, and action, lots of action. The best known Hong Kong film artists—like John Woo, Jackie Chan and Chow Yun-Fat—have moved to the Hollywood studios, where their films have proved hugely popular, especially with 13-year-old males (of all ages) in a variety of countries.

19–24. *Raise the Red Lantern* **(People's Republic of China, 1991),** *with Gong Li (center), directed by Zhang Yimou.*
A visual stylist of the first rank, Zhang always tailors his visuals to fit the story. The beautiful but glacially rigid mise en scène is symbolic of the unyielding society it reflects: Humans are deprived of their spontaneity and freedom. They are merely formal pawns in a calculated pattern of someone else's design. *(Orion Classics)*

Australia and New Zealand

The Australian cinema enjoyed a mini-revival in the 1990s, though it was modest in comparison to the golden age of the late 1970s and early 1980s. Many of Australia's most gifted filmmakers continue work in Hollywood, most notably Peter Weir (*The Truman Show*), Bruce Beresford (*Paradise Road*), George Miller (*Babe: Pig in the City*), Fred Schepisi (*Fierce Creatures*), and Baz Luhrmann (*William Shakespeare's Romeo and Juliet*).

One of the most popular Australian movies of the decade was *Muriel's Wedding* (1995), directed by P. J. Hogan. This was Hogan's debut film, which he described as "a woman's courtship with her own down-trodden self-image." Our plump heroine, Muriel Heslop (Toni Collette) of Porpoise Spit Australia, dreams of being the girl in the old ABBA song—the always loved, always in-control "Dancing Queen." Her bullying father calls her "useless" because she's a secretarial school graduate who can't even type. Her bitchy friends consider her "an embarrassment" because she's so uncool she worships a 1970s band. But Muriel refuses to give up, and with the help of her cocky friend Rhonda (Rachel Griffiths), she manages to find, if not the man of her dreams, at least a strong sense of who she is and what she's worth. This endearing comedy was a huge international success, winning many awards. Hogan went on to the United States, where he directed the equally charming *My Best Friend's Wedding* with Julia Roberts.

A movie whose success surprised almost everyone was *Babe* (1995), directed by Chris Noonan. The fablelike story deals with an orphaned pig who's adopted by an eccentric farm couple. They raise him to be a sheep dog substitute. Various farmyard animals comprise the supporting cast. The movie is funny and endearing, the protagonist the sweetest little porker since Porky Pig. Sweeter even. The Oscar-winning special effects combine humans, real animals, animatronic doubles, and computer creations into a seamless whole that is utterly enchanting.

19–25. *Strictly Ballroom* (Australia, 1992), *with Paul Mercurio and Tara Morice, directed by Baz Luhrmann.*
Among the most charming Australian movies of this era, *Strictly Ballroom* is a spoof of the oddball denizens of the world of ballroom dancing. Innocent but sexy, the movie is filled with eccentric and lovable secondary characters, who are viewed from a playful and slightly ironic perspective. Luhrmann's direction is campy and spontaneous, filled with cornball bravura flourishes that are self-mocking yet undeniably thrilling. *(Miramax Films)*

   The movie's sequel, *Babe: Pig in the City* (1999), was an Australian-American coproduction. It was directed by George Miller, who produced and coscripted the first film. Inexplicably, the sequel did not do well at the box office, despite a much bigger budget and rave reviews. A number of commentators thought that the sequel was too dark and scary for children and not well promoted for adults. Both movies are rare instances of films that can be enjoyed by both kids and grownups.
   Because of their geographical proximity and common cultural heritage, Australia and New Zealand frequently coproduce movies. *The Piano* **(19–26)** was the result of such a collaboration. The movie was written and directed by New Zealander Jane Campion (b. 1954); was financed primarily with Australian capital; and starred two Americans, Holly Hunter and Harvey Keitel, and New Zealander Sam Neill. The picture was the best film cowinner (along with *Farewell My Concubine*) of the 1993 Cannes Film Festival. It also went on to gross many millions on the international circuit and won many prestigious critical awards as well, including a Best Actress Oscar for Holly Hunter.
   Campion's movies avoid politically correct feminist clichés. Her heroines are contradictory, driven. They tend to be emotionally unstable, hard to get along with, and painfully, embarrassingly needy. *An Angel at My Table* (1990) is based on the life of Australian novelist Janet Frame, who was incarcerated for mental illness for a number of years. It's a brilliant movie, constantly throwing the viewer off-guard with its unpredictable shifts and surprising spiritual revelations.
   The protagonist of *The Piano* recalls the literary heroines of the Brontë sisters, but unlike them she is unable to tell her own story because she's mute

19–26. *The Piano* **(Australia/New Zealand, 1993),** *with Anna Paquin and Holly Hunter, directed by Jane Campion.* The epic grandeur of Campion's movie owes much to the pristine wilderness of the New Zealand setting. The visual poetry of the film is achieved by the incongruous juxtaposition of this wild terrain with the vulnerable artifacts of modern (i.e., mid-1850s) civilization. *(Miramax Films)*

throughout most of the film. Holly Hunter plays the role with fierce intensity. Like all of Campion's heroines, she's an outsider, rebelling against convention, ferociously refusing to be dominated. *The Piano* is also dazzling in its stylistic virtuosity—lyrical, poetic, and rather grand.

We've seen how film movements are notoriously unpredictable. Sometimes they flower from the ashes of devastation and despair, like the post–World War II Italian Neorealist movement. Sometimes great movies are produced even in totalitarian societies. Countries with magnificent film traditions—like Italy, France, and Japan—can suddenly cease to produce important works. And, as we can see in the last decade of the twentieth century, sometimes the best movies are produced by small countries like Ireland and Australia, with tiny but fiercely creative populations.

FURTHER READING

BROWN, NICK, et al. *New Chinese Cinemas: Forms, Identities, Politics.* Cambridge: Cambridge University Press, 1996. Movies from the People's Republic, Taiwan, and Hong Kong.

BYRNE, TERRY. *Power in the Eye.* Lanham, Md. and London: Scarecrow Press, 1997. An introduction to contemporary Irish cinema.

CORNELIUS, SHEILA. *New Chinese Cinema.* N.Y. Columbia U.P., 2002. Survey of 1980s and 1990s.

"East European Film Supplement," in *Cineaste* (vol. XIX, no. 4), 1993. A collection of articles on recent films from Poland, the Czech Republic, and elsewhere.

JORDAN, BARRY, and RIKKI MORGAN-TAMOSUNAS. *Contemporary Spanish Cinema.* Manchester and New York: Manchester University Press, 1998. Spanish movies of the 1980s and 1990s.

PETRIE, DUNCAN. *Creativity and Constraint in the British Film Industry.* London: Macmillan, 1991. A rather harsh view.

POWRIE, PHIL. *French Cinema of the 1990s.* N.Y. Oxford U.P., 2000. Survey of main themes and genres.

ROCKETT, KEVIN, et al. "Contemporary Irish Cinema," Supplement, *Cineaste* (vol. XXIV, nos. 2–3), 1999. A good survey.

SCHILLING, MARK. *Contemporary Japanese Film.* N.Y. and Tokyo: Weatherbill, 1999. Survey of 1990s, with interviews and profiles of major film makers.

TEO, STEPHEN. *Hong Kong Cinema.* British Film Institute distributed by Indiana U.P., 1998. Emphasis on martial arts genres.

20

Global Cinema Since 2000

When we're talking about cinema, I think it's largely a commercial issue and not a cultural issue. Globally there is a preference for what Hollywood puts out. We have a very competitive industry; and that is certainly evidenced by the amount of film we sell worldwide.
—Peter Morici, former director of the U.S. International Trade Commission

The elements of culture are not pure business. What is at stake is the cultural identity of all our nations. It is the freedom to create and choose our own images. A society that abandons the means of depicting itself would soon be an enslaved society.
—François Mitterand, former French President

(Dreamworks Animation SKG)

European masters. Britain's Kitchen Sink and Masterpiece Theatre traditions. Internationalists: Roman Polanski and Mira Nair. France's Jean-Pierre Jeunet. Spain's Pedro Almodóvar. Eastern Europe. Islamic Cinema. Iranian masters: Abbas Kiarostami, Mohsen Makhmalbaf, Jafar Panahi. Chinese Martial Arts genres. Latin-American Film Boom: Brazil and Mexico. United States: the Hollywood Studios. Technology and the marketplace. Major Figures: Steven Soderbergh and Michael Mann. Controversial Mavericks: Mel Gibson and Michael Moore. Emerging Artists: Richard Linklater, Todd Haynes, Alexander Payne.

As the two quotes above suggest, the conflict between the powerful American film industry and the struggling cinemas of smaller countries has continued into the new millenium. American movies still dominate the world's screens, unless they are legally curtailed, as in France, or totally banned, as in Iran. Even in the United States, the films churned out by the Hollywood studios have often marginalized the more personal movies of the independent cinema, which still produces most of the artistically significant films in the United States

Nevertheless, individual masterpieces are still being produced all over the globe, and two important film movements have emerged in recent years—the poetic neorealist cinema of Iran, and the vibrant film boom of Latin America.

Europe

Europe since the new millenium has not produced any major film movements, only some interesting new filmmakers and individual movies. The British cinema has produced many of these, some from established masters like Mike Leigh (**20–1**), others from new artists.

Among the most notable newcomers is Gurinda Chada, whose popular *Bend It Like Beckham* (2003) grossed an impressive $20.6 million in the United States alone. Like most ethnic comedies, it deals with the conflict between cultures and generations, between an older generation of Indian immigrants and their English-bred children. A film in a similar vein is *East is East* (1999), about Pakistani parents and their rebellious Anglicized offspring. These stories of working-class life are in the British "Kitchen Sink" tradition, which also includes such excellent movies as *Sexy Beast* (2001), a heist film directed by Jonathan Glazer, starring Ben Kingsley in a strikingly original performance; *Billy Elliott* (2000), a spectacular dance film, directed by Stephen Daldry; and Stephen Frears' grisly film noir, *Dirty Pretty Things* (2004).

The so-called "Masterpiece Theatre" tradition also produced some fine English movies, most notably *Nicholas Nickelby* (2002), based on the novel by Dickens, adapted and directed by the American Douglas McGrath. Movies based on British literary sources, like *The Lord of the Rings* trilogy and the Harry Potter movies (**20–2**) are essentially international co-productions, made mostly with American capital, but performed primarily by British actors, who of course are the *crème de la crème* of the profession.

Another movie in this international vein is *Vanity Fair* (2004), based on the famous 19th century English novel by Thackeray. It stars the ambitious Reese Witherspoon in the central role of the scheming social climber, Becky Sharp. The film was directed by Mira Nair (rhymes with fire), who was born in India, was educated in the United States, and makes movies wherever she pleases. Nair also directed such offbeat movies as *Salaam Bombay, Mississippi Masala,* and the critically acclaimed romantic comedy, *Monsoon Wedding* (2002), which is in English, Hindi, and Punjabi. How's *that* for diversity?

Of course one of the most famous internationalists is Roman Polanski, who makes most of his movies in Europe, often with American financing. One of his greatest works, and one of his most personal, is *The Pianist* (**20–3**). The film earned him an American Academy Award as Best Director, as well as a Best Actor Oscar for Adrien Brody, a relatively unknown performer, in the leading role. Polanski, who is in his seventies, refuses to slow down or rest on his past achievement. *The Pianist* also swept the coveted Palme d'Or at the Cannes Film Festival.

The French cinema has produced a number of interesting movies since 2000, most notably the whimsical *Amèlie* (**20–4**), which was a huge international hit, grossing $174 million worldwide. The film is a romantic comedy, a playful fantasy, and a stylistic tour-de-force. Its director, Jean-Pierre Jeunet, had previously created two other visually inventive fantasies, *Delicatessen* (France, 1991) and *City of Lost Children* (France/Spain/Germany, 1995), both co-directed by Marc Caro. Jeunet also directed the final installment of the *Alien* franchise, *Alien Resurrection* (U.S.A., 1997). He teamed up again with Audrey Tautou for the big-budget World War I era epic, *A Very Long Engagement* (France, 2004), another widely-praised work.

20-1. *All or Nothing* **(Britain, 2002),** *with James Corden, Alison Garland, Lesley Manville, and Timothy Spall, directed by Mike Leigh.*

Mike Leigh is best known for his contemporary stories of working-class life, like this movie, about a painfully dysfunctional blue-collar family living in Southeast London. As this image suggests, no one in this family seems to have much to say to anyone else. In more recent years, Leigh has made several period pictures. *Topsy-Turvy* (2000) is about the tortured collaboration of the famous Victorian theatrical team, Gilbert and Sullivan, a movie that was met with rave reviews. *Vera Drake* (2004), set in the 1950s, is about a cheerful, good-hearted woman (Imelda Staunton), who secretly helps young women who are "in trouble." That is, she's an illegal abortionist. Made for under a million dollars (cheap for a period film), the movie garnered Leigh some of the most enthusiastic reviews of his long career, especially for Staunton's brilliant performance as the frumpy, grandmotherly Vera. Many critics regard Leigh as Britain's greatest living filmmmaker.   *(United Artists)*

One of Europe's most celebrated filmmakers is Spain's Pedro Almodóvar, who had a string of international hits during this period, beginning with *All About My Mother* (1999), continuing with *Talk to Her* (2002), and culminating with *Bad Education* (2004). Like many gay artists, Almodóvar has demonstrated great insight into the complexities of the female psyche. In the Oscar-winning *All About My Mother* he portrays women in all their infinite variety—passionate, tough, sexy, funny, loyal, vulnerable, endearing, resilient, and altogether fabuloso. He also pays homage to two great American works of art—the Joseph Mankiewicz film *All About Eve* and the Tennessee Williams stage drama, *A Streetcar Named Desire,* both of them iconic works of gay culture.

20–2. *Harry Potter and the Prisoner of Azkaban* (**Britain/U.S.A., 2004**), *with Daniel Radcliffe, directed by Alfonso Cuarón.*
This was the third installment of the Harry Potter series, and several critics noted that the movie was darker, more mature than the previous films. In part this was because the actor playing Harry (Radcliffe) was now fourteen years old. Steve Kloves' adaptation of J. K. Rowling's novel also goes beyond issues of childhood into concerns of adolescence and coming-of-age. As Cuarón noted: "Even though on the surface this is a story about magic and magical creatures, it was the issues about growing up, identity, relationships with friends, the lack of parental guidance, and the search within that were so interesting to me, and so relevant today. There are also issues about social class, injustice, racism—things that affect all of us around the world." *(Warner Bros.)*

Talk to Her is less overtly comical, more reflective and philosophical. It's also a weird love story of sorts—actually, two weird love stories. Two women lie in a coma at the same hospital, while the two bereft men who love them hover at their bedsides. The film focuses primarily on the men rather than the women, though the movie contains the usual assortment of gender-bending paradoxes and sexual role reversals. *Talk to Her* received rapturously glowing reviews, and won the 2002 Golden Globe as Best Foreign Language film, in addition to a slew of other international awards.

Bad Education, another non-comic work, stars the gifted Mexican actor, Gael Garciá Bernal. In this dark and complex study of human sexuality, Bernal plays multiple roles, including that of a slinky drag-queen who is hell-bent on revenge against the priest who sexually molested him as a child. While auditioning for the role, the actor said to Almodóvar: "If I look too manly, I can slim down. I'm very flexible. I can do anything." Bernal received some of his most admiring reviews for his performance.

In Eastern Europe, the film industries have been struggling, as usual since the fall of Communism, with its state-subsidized industries. But a few movies still manage to get made, even in the middle of the most horrific circumstances, like

20–3. *The Pianist* (**Poland/France/Britain/Germany, 2002**), *with Adrien Brody, directed by Roman Polanski.*

In many respects, this is Polanski's most autobiographical movie, even though it's a biography of the distinguished Polish pianist, Wladyslaw Szpilman, a preeminent interpreter of the music of Chopin. A Jew, Szpilman survived the Nazi Holocaust in the 1940s. He managed to escape the Nazi roundup, but was separated from his family and hid out in the notorious Warsaw Ghetto, where he barely survived disease and starvation. Polanski, himself a Polish Jew, was only a child during this period. He too managed to elude the Nazi death camps and lived to tell about it. But the director has not softened the pessimism that characterizes most of his films. Like Polanski, Szpilman survived not because he was stronger or more clever than the Nazis, but because of sheer dumb luck. He survived because he was still standing—though barely—when World War II finally came to an exhausted end.   *(Focus Features)*

20–4. *Amèlie* (**France, 2001**), *with Audrey Tautou, directed by Jean-Pierre Jeunet.*

This movie is about a shy Parisian waitress (Tautou) who lives in the picturesque—and digitally enhanced—neighborhood of Montmartre, where she secretly performs acts of kindness for a variety of eccentric and needy recipients. The film is edited at a breakneck pace, and adorned with charming nuggets of silliness and whimsy. *Amèlie* was a big hit in the United States, where it grossed a dazzling $33 million. It is the most commercially successful French film in American box-office history.   *(Miramax Films)*

20–5. *No Man's Land* (**Bosnia, 2001**)*, with Branko Djurić and Rene Bitorajac, written and directed by Danis Tanović.*
The situation of this political black comedy might almost have been dreamed up by Samuel Beckett, a fellow dramatist of the absurd. Both artists share a bleak comic vision of humanity. Two enemy soldiers, a Bosnian and a Serb, are trapped in a trench between enemy lines during the brutal Bosnian War. Neither trusts the other, and there's no escaping without getting shot. A wounded soldier lies nearby, collapsed on a spring-loaded bomb, set to explode beneath him if he moves, thus killing everyone else in his vicinity. Oddly, the movie is surprisingly funny. The movie won the Best Screenplay prize at the Cannes Film Festival. *(United Artists)*

the disintegration of what used to be Yugoslavia. Out of the ashes of the war in Bosnia, came the black comedy *No Man's Land*, a bleak masterpiece reminiscent of the absurdist dramas of Samuel Beckett (**20–5**).

Other directors, like the great Hungarian filmmaker, István Szabó (see **17–20**) have had to patch together their financing from a variety of sources, as in the powerful historical drama, *Sunshine* (Hungary/Britain/Germany/Canada, 2000). The movie chronicles the cruel obstacles a Jewish family must overcome in order to survive in a toxically anti-Semitic Hungary. Szabó traverses three convulsive epochs—the Austro-Hungarian empire in the pre–World War I era, the Nazi occupation of the 1940s, and the brutal Communist era of the 1945–1991 period. The excellent British actor Ralph Feinnes plays leading roles in each segment. In every period, the family is shafted, its hard-earned wealth confiscated, and its religious identity almost obliterated. No matter what they do to please the authorities, it's never enough. Everybody loses.

Islamic Cinema

Cinema in the Islamic world has long been dominated by only a handful of countries, primarily Turkey, Egypt, and Iran. Until recently, only a few Islamic filmmakers have reached a worldwide audience, most notably Egypt's Youssef Chahine and Turkey's Yilmaz Güney (see **17–23**). Egypt is one of the most prolific film producing countries in the world, its output nearly rivaling the huge industries of India and the United States. But Egyptian movies, for the most part, are light, star-driven commercial entertainments, catering to a mass Arab audience of over 300 million. Like the cinemas of most Islamic nations, Egyptian movies are subject to severe censorship, both political and religious.

Since the terrorist attack on the United States on September 11, 2001, the worldwide image of Islam has been demonized by the western media, as though the crazed actions of a relatively few religious fanatics are somehow typical of millions of decent people who happen to be Muslims. In fact, as the new cinema has demonstrated, the most deeply-wronged victims of Islamic fanaticism have been other Muslims, especially women (**20–6**).

The status of women in most—not all—Islamic societies is deplorable. Islam allows a man to have up to four wives, but it is not allowed for females to have four husbands. In effect, the law says that it takes four women to equal one man. The right to vote, drive, work, walk in public without a male family member, or even to receive a meaningful education are denied or curtailed in many Muslim societies. The most extreme form of female oppression was in Afghanistan under the iron rule of the notorious Taliban (**20–7**). Prior to their takover, 40 percent of the work force was female, including over 50 percent of the teachers and physicians. The Taliban forbade women from working anywhere but in the home. Female children were not allowed to go to school, and were frequently married off as young as 13 or 14.

If there is one overriding theme of the new Islamic cinema, it is the oppression of women. Many of these brave filmmakers have suffered considerably for dramatizing the many ways that women are shafted and devalued in Islamic societies. Religious and government censors have witheld financing or banned "unacceptable" films from public exhibition. Some film artists have been harassed, and a few have even been jailed for presuming to criticize the patriarchal status quo.

Yet they continue to make movies, stubbornly insisting on the equal value of women. Even in sub-Saharan Senegal, which is 80 percent Muslim, the grand old man of the African cinema, 81-year old Ousmane Sembene (see **15–23**) attacked

20–6. *The Day I Became a Woman* (**Iran, 2001**), *directed by Marzieh Meshkini.*
The oppression of women in the Islamic world is by no means uniform. In some societies, a woman can be stoned to death for having sex outside of marriage. Where there is more education—beyond the study of the Muslim holy book, the Quran—women tend to have more rights. In Iran, for example, over 40 percent of the work force is female, and women constitute more than 60 percent of university students. Still, the old medieval ways cling stubbornly. This movie, written by Mohsen Makhmalbaf and directed by one of his wives, tells three stories of female disenfranchisement—one of a nine-year-old girl, another (pictured) of a young married woman, and a third of an old woman. In the pictured episode, the determined wife wants to compete in a bicycle race: Absolutely forbidden by the religious authorities. She decides to defy them. As she frantically peddles her bike, she is pursued on horseback by her outraged husband and his clan, who are scandalized by her unwomanly, immodest behavior. *(Shooting Gallery)*

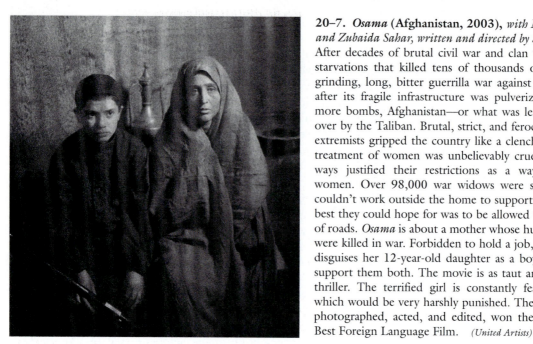

20–7. *Osama* **(Afghanistan, 2003),** *with Marina Golbahari and Zubaida Sahar, written and directed by Siddiq Barmak.*
After decades of brutal civil war and clan warfare, after mass starvations that killed tens of thousands of Afghans, after a grinding, long, bitter guerrilla war against the Soviet Union, after its fragile infrastructure was pulverized by bombs and more bombs, Afghanistan—or what was left of it—was taken over by the Taliban. Brutal, strict, and ferocious, these Islamic extremists gripped the country like a clenched iron fist. Their treatment of women was unbelievably cruel, though they always justified their restrictions as a way of "protecting" women. Over 98,000 war widows were suddenly told they couldn't work outside the home to support their families. The best they could hope for was to be allowed to beg by the sides of roads. *Osama* is about a mother whose husband and brother were killed in war. Forbidden to hold a job, in desperation she disguises her 12-year-old daughter as a boy, so the child can support them both. The movie is as taut and suspenseful as a thriller. The terrified girl is constantly fearful of discovery, which would be very harshly punished. The movie, beautifully photographed, acted, and edited, won the Golden Globe as Best Foreign Language Film. *(United Artists)*

the barbaric tradition of female genital mutilation in *Moolaadé* (Senegal, 2004). Female circumcision is practiced throughout much of Africa and the Middle East, contributing to poor reproductive health. In Africa alone, 80 million women undergo ritual circumcision, which involves removing a female's clitoris at puberty, thus depriving her of one of the main sources of sexual pleasure. Many Muslim communities regard this as a "purifying" practice, deadening a woman's interest in sex. Sexual pleasure is regarded as appropriate only in males.

When Abbas Kiarostami's *Taste of Cherry* (**20–8**) won the Palme d'Or (top prize) at the prestigious Cannes Film Festival, the movie world discovered that neorealism was alive and thriving in Iran. Actually, throughout the 1990s, Iranian movies were creating considerable interest in the film festivals of Europe. Since 2000, Iranian auteurs have cemented their position among world-class moviemakers, most notably Kiarostami, Mohsen Makhmalbaf, and Janfar Panahi, Iran's three leading film artists.

The comparison with Italian neorealism is multifaceted:

1. Both movements attempt to capture social reality as it is commonly perceived, with emphasis on ordinary people.
2. Both are strongly humanistic, with an emphasis on the spiritual life of the characters—the Italians from a Catholic, the Iranians from an Islamic, perspective.
3. Both favor a documentarylike "styleless" style, anti-Hollywood in its rejection of flashy production values.

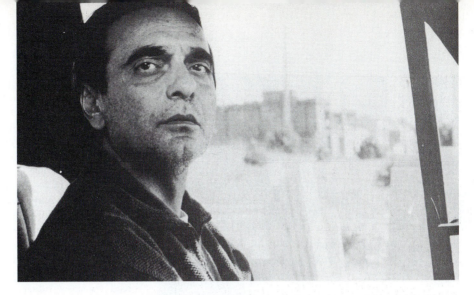

20–8. *Taste of Cherry* **(Iran, 1998),** *with Homayoun Ershadi, written and directed by Abbas Kiarostami.*
A traditional problem of film realism is how to make ordinary life, well, *interesting*. Is everyday reality dramatic enough for a movie or does it have to be heightened, juiced up with jolts of melodrama? Kiarostami often jokes about the "boring" Iranian cinema, as opposed to the explosive action-oriented movies of Hollywood. He usually prefers loose, episodic narratives, combining documentary techniques with fiction. But underlying these quiet, slow-moving stories is a profound spirituality. Kiarostami typically explores basic issues, like life and death, wisdom, social alienation, and the absence of meaningful values in the lives of people. He rarely resorts to pompous preachments, however, preferring to explore these ideas indirectly, simply, without making a big deal. Kiarostami has Soul. *(Zeitgeist Films)*

4. Both are variations of low-budget filmmaking: Almost all Iranian movies cost less than $100,000—very cheap by western standards.
5. Both favor nonprofessional performers, even for major roles—thus heightening the sense of authenticity.
6. Both prefer exterior settings—landscape is an important symbolic presence, especially the desert.
7. Both reflect a sense of sympathy and solidarity for the oppressed, especially foreigners, women, and children.
8. The films of Iran's new wave, like their Italian counterparts, are not particularly popular in their native land. The new cinema's most enthusiastic reception has been primarily in Europe and other western markets. In Iran itself, the mass audience prefers escapist entertainment.

With a population of roughly 64 million, over 50 percent of them under 25, Iran has a large filmgoing audience. Even before the 1979 Islamic revolution, the country produced from 50 to 90 movies a year. After the revolution, this number declined. Between 1979 and 1983, for example, only 40 movies were made, and 23 of them were banned by the religious censors, according to film historian David A. Cook. In more recent times, Iran's output has nearly matched its pre-revolutionary levels. But the censorship hasn't abated.

Most Iranian filmmakers complain about this censorship, pointing out that adult stories about the relation of men to women are virtually impossible to make

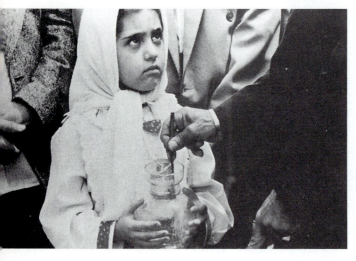

20–9. *The White Baloon* (Iran, 1995), *with Aida Mohammadkhani, directed by Jafar Panahi.*

Iranian movies are so crippled by censorship that it's virtually impossible for these artists to explore mature themes without appearing downright silly. According to Iranian Islamic codes, a woman can be intimate only with the immediate members of her family. Therefore, strict dress codes require women to cover their hair on screen and wear loose-fitting clothes to cloak their body curves, just as they must in real life. Actors playing husband and wife can't have any physical contact on the screen unless they're actually married. But even in the privacy of their home, female characters' hair must be covered, since the audience would not be intimate with the actress playing the part. Filmmakers are forced to show ridiculous scenes like female characters sleeping in bed with their head scarves still on. Even when the movie's story is set before the 1979 revolution, female characters' hair must be covered. A number of filmmakers have pointed out that they center their stories on children precisely because there are fewer restrictions than with grown women.   *(October Films)*

20–10. *Kandahar* (Iran, 2001), *written and directed by Mohsen Makhmalbaf.*

"In *Kandahar* I tried to portray the devastated, hopeless, soul of a nation," Makhmalbaf said, "particularly that of its women." An Afghan-born Canadian journalist (Nelofer Pazira, whose life the movie is based on) returns to her ravaged homeland to prevent her sister from committing suicide. Traveling undercover—literally—she manages to enter Afghanistan, which looks like a pock-marked lunar landscape, stripped of vegetation. Wearing the despised burqa that covers a woman from head to toe, the journalist surveys the degradation of women everywhere. The tented females slither anonymously, like tormented shadows in Dante's Inferno. But Makhmalbaf is a poet as well as a social critic. At a Red Cross refugee camp, we see legless war victims cajoling and begging relief workers for prosthetic legs. (Tens of thousands of live land mines still lurk beneath the Afghan landscape, a grim reminder of wars past.) Suddenly, the sky is filled with planes, dropping hundreds of small parachutes, floating down, dreamily, each with a pair of prosthetic limbs attached. The crippled veterans hop and hobble across the desert to collect the prosthetic treasure, like pilgrims on a fervant quest. The scene is poetic, surreal, and poignant.   *(Avatar Films)*

because of the restrictions of dress and behavior mandated by the all-powerful clerics. Hence, these artists often focus their stories around children, as in Panahi's *The White Baloon* (**20–9**).

Iranian filmmakers have shown an extraordinary degree of solidarity. The Makhmalbaf Film House is virtually a school and production facility, offering support—both aesthetic and financial—to aspiring young filmmakers, including numerous female artists. Makhmalbaf himself has written scripts for others (**20–10**), smoothed over censorship problems, and lent his prestige to movies that would otherwise go unproduced or unnoticed. Kiarostami is similarly generous, offering his services as a producer, writer, and international celebrity to help his fellow cineastes get their movies out to the public. In their moral commitment, their strong sense of social responsibility, and their championing the cause of oppressed people, these artists are among the most admired in the world, a shining searchlight of Islamic idealism.

Hong Kong/China

Asian martial arts movies—most of them made in Hong Kong—have long appealed to adolescent males, primarily because of their testosterone-infused emphasis on bloodletting, violence, and macho posturing. Because the narratives are pocked with wildly improbable events and the characters are reduced to cardboard

20–11. *Crouching Tiger, Hidden Dragon* (Hong Kong/Taiwan/ U.S.A., 2000), *with Michelle Yeoh (on ground), choreography by Yuen Wo Ping, directed by Ang Lee.*
Action as dance. What distinguishes movies like this and Zhang Yimou's *Hero* and *House of Flying Daggers* is a sense of magical realism, produced primarily by the dazzling audacity of the choreography. Through the use of CGI (computer generated imagery), a great stylist can sweep us into wondrous worlds of swirling motion. The masterful Yuen Wo Ping is more an artist than a technician. "I want to bring out the aestheticism of the art form," he explained, "because I really believe that this is a type of art. I want to bring out its beauty by incorporating dance movements, so that the elegance of the gestures can be seen more clearly." *(Sony Pictures Classics)*

stereotypes, this genre has had a somewhat déclassé status among serious film critics, who often refer to them as chop-socky pictures.

A few of these movies transcend the narrative crudity of the genre, most notably the action films of John Woo, a virtuoso stylist with a genius for converting conventional narratives into operatic displays of visual rapture. Woo has been employed in the United States in recent years, working on more mature material, like the excellent thriller, *Face/Off* (**18–2**). Hong Kong martial arts movies have also produced some first-rate actors, most notably Chow Yun-Fat, Michelle Yeoh, and Ziyi Zhang.

When Ang Lee made *Crouching Tiger, Hidden Dragon* (**20–11**), many critics were surprised, for Lee is best known for his subtle social dramas like *Eat Drink Man Woman* (**19–4**) and *Sense and Sensibility* (**19–6**). But *Crouching Tiger*, which stars Chow Yun-Fat, Michelle Yeoh, and Ziyi Zhang, is more complex thematically, and the characterization is rich and understated.

Not to speak of Yuen Wo Ping's spectacular martial arts choreography. Yuen is the foremost martial arts choreographer in the world, best known for his work in *The Matrix Trilogy* and the *Kill Bill* films. He makes frequent use of computer-generated special effects in his work. His style is a blending of traditional Hong Kong martial arts, acrobatics, CGI, Chinese opera, and Hollywood dance musicals. His warrior/dancers frequently "vault"—fly or swoop up walls, slither up tall trees, or flit across rooftops like graceful flying creatures. Yuen often incorporates the camera's movements into his choreographies. He also likes to use women in his action sequences, fusing the erotic with the acrobatic.

Crouching Tiger inspired other world-class filmmakers to explore the dancelike potential of the genre, most notably the great Chinese director, Zhang Yimou, whose *Hero* (2003) and *House of Flying Daggers* (2004) are both mounted in a richly kinetic operatic style. As one critic exclaimed of these movies, the eye swoons.

20–12. *The Road Home* (China, 2001), *with Ziyi Zhang, directed by Zhang Yimou.*
Ziyi Zhang (the westernized form of her name that she now prefers) is a Zhang Yimou discovery. Despite the same family name, they're not related. While still in her early twenties, the beautiful actress starred in this film as well as *Crouching Tiger, Hero,* and *House of Flying Daggers.* Her range is exceptionally broad, extending from the demure innocence of this pastoral love story, to the kickass martial arts virtuosity of her elegantly choreographed kung fu films. *(Sony Pictures)*

Latin America

The Latin-American film boom erupted in the new millenium seemingly out of nowhere, but in fact this cinematic flowering had its roots in the past, both recent and remote. Most of the new movies were made in countries that boasted the richest cinematic traditions and the healthiest industries: Argentina, Brazil, and Mexico.

The new cinema has been nurtured in part by the policies of democratically elected governments. In Brazil, film producers have been able to take advantage of recently enacted tax incentives, encouraging increased production. As in the United States and Europe, aspiring filmmakers can now receive their training in newly established film schools, especially in Argentina. Mexico privatized its film financing laws, encouraging increased international co-productions. Some of the new movies have been financed with capital from Spain, Germany, France, and the United States (**20–13**).

Especially in the 1960s and 1970s, Latin-American cinema was stridently left-wing and even revolutionary, with militant anti-imperialist and anti-United States biases (see **13–9**). The new cinema is still Marxist in its sympathies, but far less in-your-face, more nuanced and subtle. Rosa Bosch, a producer of *The Buena Vista Social Club* (Cuba/France/Germany/U.S.A., 1999, directed by Wim Wenders), pointed out that the Latin-American cinema of the previous decades "had the public perception of being dull, dour, political, and lacking in production values and hipness."

Not so the new cinema, which is more accessible, less self-consciously intellectual, funny, sexy, and raunchy (**20–14**). Some of these movies have enjoyed wide international box-office success as well as critical acclaim, beginning with Walter Salles' *Central Station* (Brazil, 1998), which was nominated for two American Academy Awards.

20–13. *Behind the Sun* (**Brazil/France/Switzerland, 2001**), *with Rodrigo Santoro, directed by Walter Salles.*
Many of the new movies coming out of Latin America explore traditional folk tales and mythic materials. This film, set in Brazil in 1910, deals with the cult of machismo. Two feuding families are headed by patriarchs who send their sons to kill off their enemy's sons in the name of masculine "honor." Like other movies of this vibrant new cinema, *Behind the Sun* contains scenes of rapturous lyricism. The camerawork is stylish and inventive, the editing energetic, and the musical score seductive and soaring. *(Miramax Films)*

20–14. *Υ Tu Mamá También* (**And Your Mother Too, Mexico, 2002**), *with Maribel Verdu, Diego Luna, and Gael Garciá Bernal, directed by Alfonso Cuarón.*
Two guys and a chick on the open road, with lots of laughs, booze, and wild sex. The movie was a huge hit in Mexico and even grossed an impressive $13.6 million in North America. A road picture, a coming-of-age film, and a shrewd commentary on male sexuality, friendship, and betrayal, the movie is also a symbolic political statement. For Cuarón, Mexico is also like a callow teenage country, trying to find its identity as a grown-up nation.   *(IFC Films)*

Gone too is the anti-Americanism. In fact, several of these young filmmakers have made movies in the United States, most notably the Mexicans Guillermo del Toro (*Mimic,* 1997 and *Blade II,* 2002), and the gifted Alfonso Cuarón (*A Little Princess,* 1995 and *Great Expectations,* 1998). Cuarón also directed the hugely popular *Harry Potter and the Prisoner of Azkaban* (**20–2**), the most critically admired of the Harry Potter films.

Guillermo del Toro divides his energies between Mexico and the United States, between art and commerce: "If I want to make big, flashy movies, I'll make them in Hollywood," he said. "If I want to do something more exotic and personal, then I'll go home to Mexico." Cuarón, on the other hand, believes that art and commerce are not necessarily at odds, nor is one language better than another: "There are very good movies in English and Spanish. And there are movies that *suck* in both languages. Audiences are responding to good movies. That's the bottom line."

Other filmmakers ashare this internationalist perspective. *Before Night Falls* (U.S.A., 2000) explores the life of the late Cuban writer Reinaldo Arena, who was persecuted in his native country both for his homosexuality and his politically dangerous opinions, which didn't sit well with the cultural gestapo of Communist Cuba. The film was directed by the American Julian Schnabel, and starred the Spanish actor Javier Bardem in the leading role, a performance that netted him an American Academy Award nomination.

A common narrative device in the new cinema is the journey motif. Many of these stories are structured around a trip of some kind, most notably *The Motorcycle Diaries* (**20–15**). Set in the 1950s, the story centers on a young Argentinian medical student, Ernesto Guevara (Gael Garciá Bernal), who was later known to the world as "Che" Guevara, an iconic figure in the world of left-wing politics. Guevara's journey is both external and internal. What the 23-year-old sees on his trip across South America is poverty, exploitation, and desperation.

20–15. *The Motorcycle Diaries* **(Brazil, 2004),** *with Gael Garciá Bernal (front) and Rodrigo de la Serna, directed by Walter Salles.*

The handsome and ambitious Bernal is the breakout star of the new Latin-American cinema. Critics almost routinely describe him as "the Mexican heart-throb," but that hardly does justice to this young artist's accomplishments. "He is the most gifted actor of his generation," Salles said of him. While still in his early twenties, Bernal played leading roles in a number of important films. His feature debut was in the brutal and bloody *Amores Perros* (Mexico, 2000, directed by Alejandro Gonzalez Inarritu), also known as *Love's a Bitch.* The young actor also played the naive but corruptible young priest in *The Crime of Father Amaro* (Mexico, 2001), directed by Carlos Carrera, a controversial exposé of the moral laxness within the Catholic Church. The movie was the biggest boxoffice hit in Mexican history. Bernal also played one of the two horny teenagers in the exuberantly sexy road picture, *Y Tu Mamá También* (**20–14**).   *(Focus Features)*

But he also experiences the color and adventure of the gorgeous landscape and the camaraderie and decency of the poeple. There's also a bit of sex along the way—one of the principal reasons Guevara and his traveling sidekick (Rodrigo de la Serna) take the epic journey in the first place.

Guevara's journey is also spiritual, as he comes to realize what a soft and spoiled life he has lived, and how much of his worldly wealth is based on exploitation of the weak. "Unlike Europe, we are societies in which the question of identity has not yet crystallized," director Salles has said. This theme of identity is at once psychological, national, ideological, and spiritual.

The population of Latin America is about 450 million, and encompasses many races, languages, and national traditions. Salles and his fellow cineastes celebrate this cultural richness: "We make films that are, like the melting pot that characterizes our cultures, impure, imperfect, and plural. This diversity pulsates throughout the continent."

Above all, the Latin-American cinema has been obsessed with the theme of poverty and the desperation that poverty breeds. One of the most harrowing movies dealing with this theme is *City of God* (**20–16**), which is set in a dog-eat-dog ghetto that's ruled over by street gangs and drug dealers. Feral children with guns roam the streets, terrorizing everyone in their way, daring the world to try to stop them. The action sequences are photographed with a hand-held camera, and the rapid-fire editing accentuates a sense of forward rush, of events spinning out of control. The movie was nominated for an unprecedented four American Academy Awards.

20–16. *City of God* **(Brazil, 2003),** *with Alexandre Rodrigues, directed by Fernando Meirelles.*

Based on actual events from the childhood of photographer Wilson Rodriguez (known as "Rocket" in the film), this story is set in a vicious slum of Rio de Janeiro, ironically known as City of God. Many of the youngsters in the cast were actually street children of the neighborhood. "Some of them worked for drug dealers," Meirelles said. "They knew much more than me about the film I was doing." Violent, brutal, and bloody, the movie offers very little hope for these lost children. Most of them will never reach adulthood. *(Miramax Films)*

A less brutal but equally scary account of economic desperation is *Maria Full of Grace* (**20–17**). The story deals with several female drug smugglers—called "mules"—who must swallow dozens of heroin-filled latex pellets before flying to New York City, where the pellets are later excreted. If one of the pellets should burst, the mule would die an agonizing death. The central character is an unemployed 17-year-old girl (Catalina Sandino Moreno), pregnant with the unwanted child of a loutish boyfriend who deserts her.

The movie is as taut as a thriller, but photographed and edited as though it were a documentary. The film won a number of international awards, and Moreno shared the top acting prize (with Charlize Theron of *Monster*) at the Berlin Film Festival.

The popularity of Latin-American films in the United States can be attributed in part to demographics. Hispanics now constitute the largest minority in America, roughly 14 percent of the population. Latino audiences account for about 15 percent of the tickets sold in the United States, the highest per capita attendance of all the ethnic groups in America, according to Nicholas Fonseca, an industry analyst.

Latino-based movies are also winning prizes at various film festivals. For example, Patricia Cardoso, who graduated from UCLA's film school, directed the charming ethnic comedy, *Real Women Have Curves* (U.S.A., 2002), about a group of Latina women working in the Los Angeles' garment district. The movie won two awards at the prestigious Sundance Film Festival.

20–17. *Maria Full of Grace* **(Columbia, 2004),** *with Catalina Sandino Moreno, written and directed by Joshua Marston.*
Winner of the prestigious Audience Award at the Sundance Film Festival, this Spanish-language movie was the debut film of its American director. The protagonist, a pregnant teenager, desperate to help her impoverished family, decides to become a "mule"—a drug smuggler who must ingest 62 latex-wrapped pellets of heroin, destined for the United States. On her tense and suspenseful journey to New York, she must navigate past the suspicious customs agents, not to speak of the vicious thugs and drug dealers who meet her in the United States. *(HBO Films/Fine Line Features)*

United States

The first years of the new century were a time of social turbulence and upheaval—a disputed election which was finally decided by the Supreme Court rather than the voters, a terrorist attack on American soil which exacerbated an economic recession that had been created by the dot.com burnout, the invasion of Afghanistan, and a loss of American prestige abroad as a result of the invasion and occupation of Iraq. When times are bad, people often opt for comfort food in their entertainment diet.

Ironically, as recently as 1999, the American movie industry seemed to be on the edge of a rebirth. Movies like Spike Jonze's *Being John Malkovich,* David Fincher's *Fight Club,* M. Night Shymalan's *The Sixth Sense,* the Wachowski brothers' *The Matrix,* and *The Blair Witch Project* achieved both critical and commercial success.

What happened? Not an awful lot. The directors' followups were less than dazzling, and in some cases, non-existent. (Daniel Myrick and Eduardo Sanchez, the directors of *Blair Witch,* have yet to make another movie.) By 2001, with pictures like *Pearl Harbor* and *Planet of the Apes,* it seemed as if the studios had abdicated any attempts to make good movies. Of the year's best films, *Training Day* was one of the very few that came from a conventional studio. The prospect of a new golden age seemed like ancient history, at least so far as the Hollywood studios were concerned. The still flourishing independent cinema was another matter **(20–19).**

20–18. *Master and Commander* **(U.S.A., 2003),** *with Russell Crowe, directed by Peter Weir.*
Russell Crowe has earned nearly as much attention for his off-screen life as for his on-screen work. Nonetheless, there's no question that he is an unusually serious and gifted actor, with the sex appeal of a leading man and the instincts of a character actor. He is skilled at accents, and eager to disappear into his parts as much as possible, in films as varied as *Gladiator*, *The Insider*, and *A Beautiful Mind*. For Peter Weir's admirably crafted adaptation of the Patrick O'Brian novel of the Napoleonic Wars, Crowe and the director avoided conventional heroics. At first as much of a mystery to the audience as to his sailors, the captain is gradually revealed to be an admirable man of action who's also capable of respect for those of a more contemplative bent. *(Twentieth Century Fox)*

20–19. *Napoleon Dynamite* **(U.S.A., 2004),** *with Jon Heder (left), written and directed by Jared Hess.*
Because independent filmmakers usually explore themes that are off-beat, eccentric, or unfashionable, few of them expect the huge grosses of mainstream Hollywood movies. But sometimes these indies turn out to be surprise hits, like *Napoleon Dynamite*. It was warmly received at the Sundance Film Festival, which is still the preferred debut venue of most indie filmmakers. The movie then went on to gross an astonishing $44 million, becoming a cult favorite in the process. The film centers on an endearingly awkward, frizzy-haired high school geek (Heder) and his equally dorky family and friends. Young audiences especially responded to the film's innocent charm and deadpan humor. *(Twentieth Century Fox)*

The Hollywood Studios

Partly, the diminishment of accomplishment of the big studios was because the old order had irrevocably changed, especially as it concerned costs and formats. Hollywood continued to place major emphasis on movies that weren't created so much as manufactured, in order to attract the widest possible audience. In part this was because costs had risen to an insupportable point. In 2004, the average movie cost $64 million to make, and another $39 million to market, according to the Motion Picture Association of America. The former president of this organization said that in the past five years, about six pictures out of a thousand had recouped their costs in theaters alone (**20–20**). Even allowing for hyperbole, it was a shocking admission.

The movie business is now dominated by six corporate entertainment empires: Viacom, Time/Warner, NBC/Universal, Twentieth Century Fox, Sony, and Disney. These companies concentrate on movies that can be reliably made for a relatively undiscerning audience: risk-adverse McMovies. In spite of the fact that the over-30 demographic accounts for nearly half of all admissions, it was—and still is—notably underserved.

The conventional industry wisdom encourages the creation and feeding of franchises to be sold on as many global platforms as possible. These include such family franchises as the *Harry Potter* and *Shrek* films, or more teen-oriented franchises like *The Lord of the Rings*, *Spider Man*, and *X-Men*. Some wannabe franchises foundered with disastrous second installments (*Lara Croft*, *Charlie's Angels*), which lost most of the money the first film had made. The public's curiosity had been

20–20. *Four disk Special Extended Edition of The Lord of the Rings: The Fellowship of the Ring* (U.S.A., 2002), *directed by Peter Jackson.*
Many film critics continue to compare what a movie grosses in theaters with what it cost, which in fact has little to do with profitability. Few movies can make money by themselves. Only by a continual series of relaunchings on a succession of platforms—cable, video, satellites, DVD, broadcast television, etc.—can a big budget film hope to recoup its cost. The popularity of DVD is partly because of the superior quality offered by the digital format, and the extras that soon became a part of the experience—commentary tracks, outtakes, and so forth. The profit margin is also considerably higher: DVDs have a 66 percent profitability compared to 45 percent for videocassettes. Peter Jackson created Special Editions for each of the *Lord of the Rings* movies, adding more than a half hour to the running time of each film. Likewise, Quentin Tarentino's *Kill Bill* movies, modest successes in their theatrical releases, will undergo various profitable permutations: a Special Edition for each film, then a boxed set, then repackaged with his other films as a collectable boxed set, with the possibility of the more violent version Tarentino edited for Japan also being offered domestically. And all of this multiplied internationally. *(New Line Home Entertainment)*

20–21. *Chicago* **(U.S.A., 2002),** *with Catherine Zeta-Jones, Richard Gere, and Renée Zellweger, directed by Rob Marshall.*

Miramax, the leader in quality filmmaking under the aegis of the Weinstein brothers, developed something of a stranglehold on the Oscars, simply because the major studios virtually abandoned upscale filmmaking. In 11 years, Miramax pictures were nominated for the Best Picture Oscar 11 times: In reverse order— *Chicago, In the Bedroom, Chocolat, The Cider House Rules, Shakespeare in Love, Life is Beautiful, Good Will Hunting, The English Patient, Il Postino, Pulp Fiction,* and *The Piano.* All of these movies had budgets under $50 million. Miramax's widely feared ex-studio chief, Harvey Weinstein, is the only contemporary studio head who could have competed with the likes of Jack Warner, Louis B. Mayer and the rest of the colorful studio moguls who essentially created the American movie industry. *(Miramax Films)*

sated the first time. Either way, impersonality reigned: Most of these films constitute corporate filmmaking at its most obvious.

Because the weekend opening of a film is so important, long runs are now rare. Even hit movies can see their second week grosses tumble by as much as 50 percent. A picture that continues in theaters for months on end because of good word-of-mouth and repeat business, such as *Titanic,* is now exceedingly rare.

The studios have developed an expertise in handling their product, even if the films are terrible. Tim Burton's remake of *Planet of the Apes* grossed $357 million worldwide, and was highly profitable. But it left such disappointment behind that nobody even mentioned a sequel. Furthermore, as a result of specializing in one kind of movie, the big Hollywood studios increasingly are having trouble marketing anything else. This has left openings for other, more nimble distributors, like prestigious Miramax Films (**20–21**).

Technology and the Marketplace

DVDs have altered the economic balance of the movie business nearly as much as television did 50 years ago. DVDs now bring in a majority of Hollywood's total revenue. According to the Motion Picture Association of America, in 2003, DVDs earned $9.4 billion, compared to theaters, which brought in $3.9 billion. Cable brought in $1.6 billion, conventional television earned $1.2 billion, and the nearly obsolete cassette brought in $1.9 billion.

The mass audience buys DVDs in a way they never did cassettes, and by doing so has rewritten the math of the movie business. Traditionally, a movie had to gross two and a half to three times its cost to show a profit. A movie like the Will Ferrell comedy *Old School* (2003) took in $73 million at the boxoffice, making it a moderate hit. But it made $143.5 million on DVD, propelling it to the status of a major success. Similarly, Pixar's *Finding Nemo* grossed $431 million in the DVD format, about $100 million more than it did in its theatrical release. In effect, theatrical exhibition has become what amounts to a loss-leader for the DVD release.

Just as entertainment values have gradually supplanted artistic values, just as DVDs have gradually become more important than theatrical exhibition, so has storytelling changed and the viability of film itself has become doubtful.

Traditionally, the structural model for movies was, and occasionally, still is, the three-act structure of theater. But increasingly, the models for movies are comic books and, especially, video games. Instead of gradually building character details and deepening the plot, most commercial American movies are built on a continuous series of confrontations building to a grand confrontation at the end.

As for film itself, the 35 mm camera has always been fairly cumbersome. Increasingly, the benefits of digital photography are beginning to seem preferable. The benefits are obvious: It's cheaper, about 20 percent the cost of film, and it's more malleable. Digital requires much lower light levels, and a minimal crew can be used. There's no processing—dailies can be viewed immediately, which means the director can correct errors immediately and accomplish more setups.

20–22. *Spider-Man 2* **(U.S.A., 2004),** *with Tobey Maguire, directed by Sam Raimi.*
A successful series of franchise movies can practically support a studio. The *Spider-Man* movies are Exhibit A. *Spider-Man 2* grossed $784 million worldwide in theaters, with much additional revenue coming from DVD and cable. While expensive to make and market, these movies can become world-wide events. What's critical to their success is a director who understands the comic book universe without condescension, can give the films gravity, yet avoid pretending they're literature. The material is pulp, but with a touch of class. It's a tough line to walk, but Sam Raimi was the perfect choice. To effect the touch of class, screenwriter Alvin Sargent (*Ordinary People, Julia*) was enlisted to work on the script. Hence the humanity and emotional richness in the characterization.   *(Sony)*

The drawbacks of digital are also obvious. It has less definition than film, muddier colors—rather like a badly tuned television set. Worst of all, there's a blurring, strobe effect during fast movement or action sequences. The advantage of film (about 4000 lines) over even high-definition digital video (about 1000 lines) remains considerable. Yet, widespread distinctions between professional and amateur equipment have been obviated by the proliferation of the technology. In 1999, only 10 percent of submissions to the Los Angeles Film Festival were on digital video; in 2001 it was 60 percent.

The attraction of digital is not primarily a matter of money among professionals. Raw stock itself is a very minor item in a Hollywood film's budget. The attraction seems to be novelty and artistic challenge. A-list directors like Jean-Jacques Annaud (*Two Brothers*) and Michael Mann (*Collateral*) want to explore the capabilities of the new technology.

Even non-digital films are regularly tweaked with digital means. A grey sky can be brightened, a muddy river can be converted to blue with a few clicks of a computer mouse. The digital revolution has also impacted film form in terms of editing. Machines such as Avid and Lightworks, where a film's rushes are entered on a hard drive, make it possible to try dozens of editing choices in the time it used to take an editor to put together a single scene on film.

This classic example of technology driving content has encouraged an MTV style of editing. As editor Tom Priestly has pointed out:

> I can spot a film that's been cut with the new technology. It tends to be over-quickly cut and uses too much material. There's an impatience about it in

20–23. *Moulin Rouge* (U.S.A., 2001), *with Nicole Kidman and Ewan McGregor, directed by Baz Luhrman.*
American movies have always been the fastest-moving films in the world, and digital technology has allowed them to move even faster. At its most extreme, as in *Moulin Rouge*, the film never stops for the audience to draw its breath, enjoy a performance, a set, or a song. The director's intent seems to disorient the audience. This style of cutting can work effectively for movies of non-stop action, but it's probably inappropriate for movies that depend on character or nuance. Anne Coates, the great editor of *Lawrence of Arabia*, as well as Steven Soderbergh's *Erin Brockovich* and *Out of Sight*, says: "I'm not against flashy cutting, it can be great. But I don't see the point of a lot of cuts where you don't see what's happening at all. I think that's going over the top with this, and it's very easy to do it on these machines." *(Twentieth Century Fox)*

terms of "we have to keep making it interesting." It's easy, you just press a button and it happens. It's like nudging the audience all the time—"Look, now are you looking? Now we're doing this," rather than just letting the audience relax and sort of go with the experience of seeing the film.

Also greatly affecting content is CGI. By 2004, entire movies, like *Sky Captain and the World of Tomorrow* (**20–24**) were being shot with actors against a blue screen, with all the sets deriving from a hard drive. The technology is so expert that even dead actors can be resurrected for special guest appearances, as with Laurence Olivier's turn as the villain, 15 years after his death.

Acting has also been affected by this new technology. Phil Tippett, an animator and special effects technician (*The Empire Strikes Back, Starship Troopers, Jurassic Park*), has pointed out the odd lifelessness that afflicts many scenes shot before a blue screen: "On the conventional shooting stage, you have props, the other three walls. But with a blue screen stage, you have 100 technicians and you're surrounded on three sides by blue. Put two and two together: The actors and director aren't bouncing off of anything."

The transition to digital imaging and editing will probably mean the death of film itself. It is certainly in the studio's self-interest to do away with it, because films are still distributed to theaters in trucks, just as they were a hundred years ago. Dis-

20–24. *Sky Captain and the World of Tomorrow* **(U.S.A., 2004),** *with Angelina Jolie, Jude Law, and Gwyneth Paltrow, directed by Kerry Conran.*
With the aid of computers, the (almost) totally artificial film is now achievable, though a good script always helps. *Sky Captain* was made by hardworking actors performing in front of a blue screen for months. The only real props were the ones they were wearing or handling—everything else was digitally created. The film's look is ravishing, an amalgam of the Max Fleischer Superman cartoons of the World War II era, and sepia memories of 1930s Moderne. But the script is a tired rehash of the bickering-couple-in-search-of-High-Adventure from *Raiders of the Lost Ark*. Nonetheless, blue screen technology has enormous potential. For example, filmmakers and their crews no longer need to travel to distant locations, nor do they have to reproduce expensive period settings if these can be created convincingly with computers. *(Paramount Pictures)*

tribution via computer disk or satellite would save hundreds of millions of dollars in print and trucking costs industry-wide. An average 35 mm print costs about $1,200. A domestic release encompassing 2000 prints would thus cost about $2.4 million. Spread that over a studio's average output of 15 or so movies yearly and the long-term savings are considerable—enough to make another movie every year.

From a commercial point of view, the main problem is who's going to pay for the installation of very expensive digital projectors. There are 35,000 projection booths in America, another 115,000 in the rest of the world. Each theater has projectors that cost about $30,000 apiece and, with proper maintenance, can last for about 30 years.

A digital projector costs well over $100,000; because the technology is new, its lifespan is uncertain. Add the cost of the satellite dishes or high-speed lines needed to receive the digital files containing the movie, and the installation costs for a national chain of theaters are intimidating. Since it is the studios that will save money and not the theaters, exhibitors believe that there's no viable reason why they should have to pay the freight.

Given the economic pressures, there can be little doubt that digital projection is just around the corner. And given the consumer pressures, there can be little doubt that the problems of color and definition will be solved. Likewise, the next generation of DVDs, offering high-definition images and sound two or three

20–25. *Star Wars Episode II: Attack of the Clones* (U.S.A., 2002), *with Hayden Christensen and Natalie Portman, directed by George Lucas.*
The problem with a lot of movies that use CGI is that they're not very interesting except from the narrow point of view of technology. The second trilogy of Lucas' *Star Wars* films are widely regarded as inferior to the first trilogy, mostly because Lucas seems to have lost interest in dialogue, character, or plot in favor of technology for its own sake. Nevertheless, Lucas remains unapologetic and now makes his movies digitally. "Film has been around for 100 years," he has said, "and no matter what you do, you're going to run celluloid through a bunch of gears. It's gotten more sophisticated over the years, but it'll never get much more than what it is right now. With digital, we're at the very bottom of the medium. This is as bad as it's ever going to be. This is like 1895. In 25, 30 years, it's going to be amazing." *(Lucasfilm Ltd.)*

20–26. *The Incredibles* (U.S.A., 2004), *written and directed by Brad Bird.*
Pixar movies generally deal with threats to a family unit, which are vanquished by dint of much effort, humor, and occasional dumb luck. What sets the films of this company apart from other CGI animation are the quality of the images, and the layered levels of verbal and visual wit. *The Incredibles* offers such subtleties as a devastating take-off on a fashionista who happens to be a midget, for no good reason other than it makes the character intrinsically absurd. It's also a delicious parody of the famous Hollywood costume designer, Edith Head. Not to speak of the basic concept of a family of superheroes sidelined by the possibility of class-action lawsuits. Pixar films make most other CGI animation look crude. *(Walt Disney Pictures/Pixar Animation)*

times better than the contemporary disks, with interactive bonus material similar to videogames, promise a visual and aural wonderland for audiences.

Now, if only filmmakers can come up with equivalently dazzling content. As Steven Soderbergh has said: "You always hope people are going to expand their minds to fit the art, instead of trying to narrow the art to fit their minds."

Major Figures and Trends

One of the most interesting developments since 2000 is the director as shape-shifter. Filmmakers can adapt easily, creating independent pictures that no major studio would get near, then sliding over to do an overtly commercial picture, but managing to instill it with an unusual degree of visual and dramatic integrity. British directors, such as Stephen Frears, have long been adept at this sort of thing. Most European directors are trained to work at whatever comes to hand—TV as well as movies, live theater as well as commercials.

In Hollywood, this artistic flexibility was less common until recently. For example, STEVEN SODERBERGH followed up mainstream hits like *Erin Brockovich* and *Ocean's Eleven* with an experimental movie shot digitally called *Full Frontal.* His next picture was *Solaris,* an opaque, esoteric science-fiction remake of a classic Russian movie. After this, Soderbergh returned to a safe haven with *Ocean's 12* (**20–27**).

For those who care to discount the collected works of John Cassavetes, Soderbergh (b. 1963) is usually given credit for starting the indie film boom with *sex, lies and videotape* (1989). This was a movie where the content was the star—women confess their sexual histories and anxieties to the camera of a central male character

20–27. *Ocean's 12* **(U.S.A., 2004),** *with George Clooney, Matt Damon, and Brad Pitt, directed by Steven Soderbergh.*
American movies have always exulted in star power, and this movie flaunts it. *Ocean's 12* is a canny sequel to a successful remake of the Frank Sinatra/Dean Martin/Sammy Davis Jr. original of 1960, a work of considerably less charm. The plot of the original was updated for the remake, but the script was never as important as the chance to gaze at beautiful people having a good time and letting the audience in on the fun.   *(Warner Bros.)*

who is sexually gratified by the emotional intimacy. The themes of sexual paranoia and impotence were particularly timely for a period when AIDS had landed hard in both the gay community and the media.

Soderbergh's breakthrough film was central to the idea of independent films' aesthetics and economics, not to mention the firm foundation on which the Weinstein brothers built Miramax Films. Miramax was to the 90s what MGM was to the 40s—an imprimatur of quality. Soderbergh's *sex, lies and videotape* cost a mere $1.1 million, earned $24 million domestically, and had a higher cost-to-earnings ratio than Tim Burton's *Batman,* which was a huge boxoffice hit.

The general tendency of other indie filmmakers was to make a critical hit, then go to Hollywood and direct a studio project. This was a path that was followed by artists like Doug Liman, who segued from *Swingers* (1996) to *Go* (1999) to the big-budget Matt Damon vehicle, *The Bourne Identity* (2002). Similarly, Bryan Singer moved from *The Usual Suspects* in 1995 to *X-Men* in 2000, not to mention its sequels, with only an unsuccessful Stephen King adaptation in between.

Unlike some of the people who came after, Soderbergh kept a wary eye on the integrity meter. He followed up *sex, lies and videotape* with a variety of pictures, some excellent like *King of the Hill* (1993), some far from excellent (*Kafka, The Underneath,* 1995), and some that were outright experimental (*Schizopolis,* 1996). Soderbergh has a lot of arrows in his quiver, but none of these movies repeated the commercial or critical success of his first film.

20–28. *The Phantom of the Opera* (U.S.A., 2004), *with Gerard Butler and Emmy Rossum, directed by Joel Schumacher.* The success and Best Picture Oscar awarded to *Chicago* did not result in a wave of new musicals. The genre is difficult and expensive, and each film has to be built from the ground up. The studios don't seem to trust the audience to turn out for anything other than a pre-sold property. Hence, the only musicals that get made are major Broadway hits, like *Phantom, The Producers,* and *Rent.* Composer Andrew Lloyd Webber financed the production of this, his most successful musical, himself. Since the stage version has always been its own star, Webber and Schumacher cast the film with comparative unknowns, and put the money up on the screen. The result is a physically sumptuous rendering of a beloved story. *(Warner Bros.)*

Mainly, Soderbergh seems to be interested in pushing the boundaries and in enjoying himself more than building a career. His flexibility has led him to experiment and try different things without apology. This fearless spirit of inquiry has led the director to serve as his own cameraman on occasion, despite his admission that "I'm not a world-class cinematographer." Many of his actors share this same spirit of adventures. "*I* had fun," he said of *Full Frontal.* "Did they?" he asked of his actors. "Uh, I *think* they did."

Perhaps his best movie of this uncertain period was *The Limey* (1999), a delicious little (nonviolent) crime thriller with '60s icons Peter Fonda and Terence Stamp as antagonists. But Soderbergh began to reinvent himself commercially with *Out of Sight* (1998), an excellent adaptation of an Elmore Leonard novel starring George Clooney and Jennifer Lopez. That film led to *Erin Brockovich* (2000), a story of a crusading woman seeking to clean up toxic waste left by an energy utility. It was the stuff of a hundred TV movies, but its star, Julia Roberts, doesn't make TV movies. Soderbergh shot it sharply, with much rougher cutting and more jagged emotion than is usually found in by-the-numbers genre pictures.

The director's string of hits continued with *Traffic* (2000), a remake of an English mini-series that was upgraded by a premium cast and Soderbergh's hand-held camera and experiments with color. Then came *Ocean's Eleven* (2001), which was followed by the inevitable sequel, *Ocean's 12.* These movies, and *Solaris* (2002), starred the admirable George Clooney, who has the features of a classic leading man, and a willingness to try almost anything, including playing the fool, which he has done very well for the Coen brothers in *O Brother, Where Art Thou* and *Intolerable Cruelty*.

MICHAEL MANN (b. 1943) has always been a splendid stylist with a distinctive ouevre, splitting his time between movies and television (*Miami Vice, Crime Story, Robbery/Homicide*). He rose through the ranks, writing episodic television, directing some TV movies, then making *Thief* (1981), a first-rate existential thriller about a safecracker. That was followed by *The Keep* (1983), a murky movie about Nazis and Ancient Evil that was as big a critical and commercial failure as *Thief* had been a success.

Mann went back to television and served as the executive producer of the stylish and influential series, *Miami Vice*. He came back to movies in 1986 with *Manhunter,* an adaptation of the Thomas Harris novel *Red Dragon*, which introduced Hannibal Lecter, in the person of actor Brian Cox, to the movies.

It was an excellent film, but Mann didn't make another movie until six years later, with *The Last of the Mohicans* (1992), an adaptation of the moss-bound James Fenimore Cooper novel. The movie version cleared away the dust, and with leading man Daniel Day-Lewis, made the material sexy and exciting, as well as demonstrating Mann's great gift for action scenes and visual voluptuousness.

Mann's movies tend to be about one or two lonely men who are defined by their professions and their pride in those professions. They can countenance being failures in love or as human beings, but not in their work. In addition, his films often exude an existential air. *Thief* was basically a heist movie, a variation on Huston's *The Asphalt Jungle,* but rigidly focused on one criminal rather than a gang. In this case, the man is a safecracker with immense pride in his craft.

The Insider (1999) is a docudrama about a producer at CBS television who turns whistleblower when the broadcaster is coerced by a tobacco company. *Ali*

20–29. *Fahrenheit 9/11* (**U.S.A., 2004**), *with Michael Moore (wearing cap) directed by Moore.* *(Lions Gate Films/IFC Films/Fellowship Adventure Group)*

20–30a. *American Splendor* (U.S.A., 2003), *with Hope Davis and Paul Giamatti, written and directed by Shari Springer Berman and Robert Pulcini.*
(*HBO/Fine Line Features*)

20–30b. *American Splendor, with Joyce Brabner and Harvey Pekar.* (*HBO/Fine Line Features*)

a.

b.

In recent years, the documentary has shed its somewhat dowdy past, and become more lively, more playful, and definitely more partisan. *Fahrenheit 9/11* won the prestigious Palme d'Or at Cannes, in addition to a slew of other awards. Moore's documentaries have carved out a surprisingly large niche for themselves. Each of his films has outgrossed the last, and *Fahrenheit 9/11* is the largest grossing documentary in history—over $220 million worldwide. Its form is quasi-journalistic, and the effect is agit-prop speaking most effectively to the already-convinced. What separates Moore from other documentarians is that he's not afraid to play the clown and go for laughs. In this scene, for example, he corners a U.S. Representative and tries to get him to enlist his son to go fight in Iraq, a military engagement the Representative voted for in Congress. Moore is also capable of being hectoring and mean-spirited on occasion. These are qualities that are usually denied to documentaries because of their traditional pretense of impartiality.

Very much in the Moore mold was *Super Size Me* (2004), an amusingly personalized story by filmmaker Morgan Spurlock, who decided to eat every meal for a month at McDonalds' restaurants. As a result, his health nosedives. On camera, one doctor warns him that his liver is turning into liver paté.

There were also films that mixed documentary techniques with fiction, or at least quasi-fiction, like *American Splendor*, about the cartoon writer Harvey Pekar. The movie juxtaposes Pekar and his wife (b) with the actors portraying them in the film (a). Often the real people comment wryly on the fictionalized characterizations. There are also animated scenes, and, of course, cartoons.

20-31. *The Passion of the Christ* (U.S.A., 2004), *with Jim Caviezel, directed by Mel Gibson.*

Self-financed by its director, *The Passion* aroused condemnation from Jews and liberals, and ardent support from conservatives and evangelical Christians. The film became an artifact of the culture wars as much as a movie. Basically a blow-by-blow (literally) account of Jesus' trial and crucifixion, Gibson's film is relentlessly visceral. It's also a good illustration of the way the portrayal of Jesus has changed over the years. In Cecil B. DeMille's *King of Kings,* made in the far more decorous year of 1927, Christ's flogging is denoted by two lines of blood on his chest, which might have come from an unfortunate encounter with a rose bush. In the Gibson film, made in a century more attuned to horror, Jesus is covered in layers of blood and flayed flesh, the result of floggings we have witnessed in detail. None of the Hollywood studios wanted to distribute the film, which they regarded as boxoffice poison. The fact that the picture's dialogue is entirely in Latin and Aramaic (the language spoken by Jews at the time), and therefore required subtitles, merely confirmed the industry consensus that the film—dubbed "Gibson's Folly"—was hopelessly uncommercial. It ended up grossing $675 million worldwide—one of the top ten all-time highest grossing films in history.   *(Newmarket Film Group)*

20-32. *Collateral* (U.S.A., 2004), *with Tom Cruise and Jamie Foxx, directed by Michael Mann.*

Although Cruise has consistently been the biggest male star in the movies for 15 years, it is only in one of his infrequent bad guy roles that he makes the critics sit up and take notice. Cruise usually plays narcissists who tumble into moral awareness by the end of the movie. The resulting chilly temperature means that villains actually seem more suited to his cool emotional qualities. He also has a tendency to come off as younger than he really is—to his professional detriment. In 2000, Cruise was 38 years old, the same age as Clark Gable when he played in *Gone With the Wind.* But there seems a world of difference between the totally adult Gable and the often slightly juvenile Cruise. In *Collateral,* aided by the tough director Michael Mann, Cruise plays a hit man with a penchant for nasty mind games. It's a sharp performance that greatly added to his street cred.   *(Paramount)*

(2001) is a biography of the great boxer Muhammad Ali. Both pictures received respectful reviews but underperformed commercially.

Collateral (**20–32**) was shot in digital video and offered some beautifully abstract images of urban isolation worthy of the great American painter Edward Hopper. The visuals went quite well with the story of a hitman who commandeers a taxi and its driver for one long night in the murky underbelly of Los Angeles.

All of Mann's movies are made for adults, with themes of compromise, integrity, and commitment. They are also stunningly photographed and often feature compelling stars at their peak—Will Smith, Daniel Day-Lewis, Al Pacino, Tom Cruise. If Mann has a fault, it's usually with script. For example, *Heat* (1995), is a film about a cop and a crook that had the epic length of three hours, draped heavily over two hour's worth of script. But *Heat,* like most of Mann's films, has a continual dramatic intensity that compels interest and has made the movie a critical and cult favorite.

Emerging Artists

There were a number of film artists who came to prominence after 2000, most of whom began their careers in the previous decade. Perhaps the most unusual is TODD HAYNES (b. 1961), who has a more academic foundation than usual. He attended Brown University and majored in art and semiotics. He is also among a new breed of gay artists who is neither militant nor apologetic. His first commercial film, *Poison* (1991), was inspired by the great French writer Jean Genet, an iconic figure in gay literature. The movie explores the theme of alienation, and won the Grand Jury Prize at the Sundance Film Festival. The film is now regarded as a seminal work of the Queer Cinema.

Safe (1995) involved a housewife who suddenly becomes allergic to her entire environment as ordinary household products become deadly toxins. It was a premise for a scifi movie, but Haynes, aided by the invaluable Julianne Moore, took it in a more allegorical direction—a metaphor for AIDS. Or something not caused by a virus—emotional instability, perhaps.

The Velvet Goldmine (1998) told the story of the rise and fall of a fictional rock star in the world of glam rock. Up to this point, Haynes was a favorite of critics and a small audience, but *Far From Heaven* (2002) was something of a breakthrough. The movie is a loving recreation and homage to the Douglas Sirk "women's pictures" of the 1950s, which explored the tensions of domestic life in suburban America. The film was directed with such meticulous attention to period detail that it can be enjoyed as a lush melodramatic throwback even if the viewer has no particular knowledge of the 1950s.

An apparently happy suburban housewife (Julianne Moore again) has her life upended when she discovers that her husband (Dennis Quaid) is a homosexual. Shortly afterwards, she finds herself drawn to her African-American gardener—the 1950s equivalent of the love that dares not speak its name. The movie is directed with exquisite attention to costuming, art direction, and camera style. At times the Sirkian homage makes the film verge on an extended paraphrase of movies like *All That Heaven Allows, Magnificent Obsession,* and *Imitation of Life,* Sirk's most famous women's pictures.

20–33. *Ray* (U.S.A., 2004), *with Jamie Foxx, directed by Taylor Hackford.*
A major trend in the new millenium was a revival of interest in the biography film, or the biopic, to use the lingo of the trade. In over 100 years, despite all the changes in the film industry, this genre has changed the least. Almost all of them tell the story of a protagonist who overcomes adversity to eventually triumph in his chosen field. *Ray,* the story of the great blues singer Ray Charles, is one of the best, thanks to a brilliant performance by Jamie Foxx. Others in this genre include Bill Condon's *Kinsey* (about the 1940s sex researcher); Martin Scorsese's *The Aviator* (about millionaire Howard Hughes); Oliver Stone's *Alexander* (the Great, that is); *Hotel Rwanda,* (about the African humanitarian Paul Rusesabagina); *Finding Neverland* (about *Peter Pan* playwright James M. Barrie); Ron Howard's *A Beautiful Mind* (about mathematician John Nash); and Kevin Spacey's *Beyond the Sea* (about pop singer Bobby Darin), to mention only the most recent.   *(Universal)*

Far From Heaven also features the last musical score of the great film composer, Elmer Bernstein, who died shortly afterwards. The movie showed that Haynes has the most valuable attribute a creative personality can have—a complete lack of fear. Haynes' gay sensibility has sensitized him to people who are outsiders. His characters are either looking through life's shop window because of intrinsic feelings of apartness, or because of changes they are forced to go through, which cause them to question their values and prior assumptions.

RICHARD LINKLATER (b. 1960) is typical of his generation of filmmakers, bouncing from one thing to another with a complete lack of self-consciousness. A Texan who once worked as an oil rigger, Linklater broke through with *Slacker* (1991) and followed it up with the similar *Dazed and Confused* (1993).

20–34. *The Bourne Supremacy* **(U.S.A., 2004),** *with Matt Damon and Franka Potente, directed by Paul Greengrass.*
The Bourne films are a sort of latter-day version of the James Bond movies. Bourne is far more vulnerable than Bond in that he has no idea of who he used to be (the old amnesia plot), but is nevertheless immensely skillful with firearms and close combat. We're never in serious doubt that Bourne will survive, but *he* is. Stylistically, the films feature a jittery editing style meant to mirror the character's uncertainty about his surroundings, and his difficulty in determining just who can or cannot be trusted. The movies are not to all tastes, but Matt Damon's ever-present likeability—he never acts like a movie star—makes them high-end entries in the commercial movie sweepstakes.   *(Universal)*

Then he did something different, a two-person comedy/drama with Ethan Hawke and Julie Delpy called *Before Sunrise* (1995), about two young people on a train in Europe who connect in the hours before she has to leave for home. As they walk through Vienna, they fall in love. *Before Sunrise* earned Linklater respectful attention from critics who had previously been indifferent to his earlier films about scruffy, stifled characters flailing around.

Linklater is often bracketed with Kevin Smith as a self-taught filmmaker whose visual sense is, at worst, lamentable, and at best indifferent. Linklater's films are nevertheless recognizable because of their idiosyncratic structure. The best of them usually take place in a limited time-frame, usually 24 hours. He also has a knack for witty dialogue and an undercurrent of romanticism. He is one of the few filmmakers who has contributed a slang term to the vocabulary: "Slacker" has become universally understood for any undermotivated citizen of the younger demographic.

After a failed experiment with a period gangster film called *The Newton Boys* (1998), and a middling experiment with animation in *Waking Life* (2001), Linklater directed *School of Rock* (2003), an exuberant comedy starring Jack Black. He

20–35. *Eternal Sunshine of the Spotless Mind* (U.S.A., 2004), *with Kate Winslet and Jim Carrey, screenplay by Charlie Kaufman, directed by Michel Gondry.*
The film industry has proved itself amenable to creators of all types, not just directors. The screenwriter Charlie Kaufman has had critical successes with movies like *Being John Malkovich, Human Nature, Confessions of a Dangerous Mind, Adaptation,* and *Eternal Sunshine of the Spotless Mind.* Though none of these movies was a big boxoffice success, Kaufman is still a respected talent in Hollywood. His scripts have a similar surreal character no matter who directs them. In that sense, he's a throwback to such highly regarded screenwriters of the classic Hollywood cinema as Ben Hecht and Dudley Nichols, whose scripts tended to sound and feel the same no matter who directed them. Kaufman's films are simultaneously gloomy and funny. There is a weak dividing line between fantasy and reality. Most of his movies are highly subjective and rely, to a great extent, on whether or not the actors are sufficiently charming to make you buy the film's wildly improbable premise.   *(Focus Features)*

then returned to his first love with *Before Sunset* (2004), a sequel that brought back Ethan Hawke, whose character is now a married novelist, and Julie Delpy, still alluring, smart, and sexy, for a long walk about Paris. They fall in love all over again.

The two Hawke/Delpy films—there will almost certainly be a third—are essentially variations on Eric Rohmer movies: attractive people talking intensely about love, sex, and life for 90 minutes. The charm comes from the fact that Linklater never shies away from the dorm bull-session aspects that are implicit in the films. In fact, he revels in all that talk. Just as the conversation is descending into repetitive verbiage, Linklater and his actors always manage to penetrate to a place of genuine emotion and insight. The films have a quiet, meandering charm, but also a surprising dramatic force. They feel more like life than movies usually do.

Linklater has no particular feel for any milieu but his own, or any period but now. His gift is for wry humor and quirky character studies. Because he is content to work cheaply, he continues to work in the industry. His movies constitute a series of on-the-run sketches of a youth culture that seems permanently betwixt and between: disinterested or distrustful of their parents' culture, as every generation surely must be, but, in the words of Bob Dylan, with "no direction home" of their own either.

20–36. *Sideways* (**U.S.A., 2004**), *with Virginia Madsen, Paul Giamatti, Thomas Haden Church, and Sandra Oh, directed by Alexander Payne.*
Paul Giamatti specializes in playing disconnected schlubs with surprising reservoirs of passion. Not prepossessing, not handsome, not sexy, he is a continuation of a strain of character-actor-as-star that began with Lon Chaney in the silent era, which led to Paul Muni and Marie Dressler in the talkie era of the 30s, continued with Dustin Hoffman beginning in the 60s, and Jennifer Jason Leigh in the 90s. Immense talent aside, these people are stars, not in spite of their ordinariness, but because of it.   *(Fox Searchlight)*

ALEXANDER PAYNE (b. 1961) was born in Omaha, and he has adopted some of the dead-pan flatness of his native state as his operative discipline. Essentially, Payne's movies involve men intimately acquainted with futility, but who work very hard to maintain a degree of delusion. By film's end, they are nudged into a semblance of self-knowledge by the crush of circumstance or, often, by women, who are almost invariably smarter and more realistic.

Election (1999) features Matthew Broderick as a sodden, prematurely aged high school teacher, and Reese Witherspoon as an oppressively cheerful agent of destruction, who plows through her senior class election (and Broderick's feeble obstructions) like a military juggernaut.

About Schmidt (2002) stars Jack Nicholson, the movies' most prominent exponent of explosiveness since the days of James Cagney, as an inhibited, alienated, retired insurance man who learns a little about life and himself while on a trip to his daughter's wedding. It also features wickedly funny performances by Kathy Bates and Dermot Mulroney. The movie is sometimes outright nasty, but also funny, bittersweet, and finally, poignant.

Sideways (**20–36**) is Payne's finest film to date. A delicious script by Payne and his usual co-writer Jim Taylor centers on two old friends—one a teacher/writer, the

20–37. *Million Dollar Baby* **(U.S.A., 2004),** *with Clint Eastwood and Hillary Swank, directed by Eastwood.*

Most filmmakers' careers peter out as they age. Changing audience tastes and their own de-clining energies make it hard for them to get work, let alone mesh with the current moviego-ing public. But Clint Eastwood's directing career has had a far more effective third act than his first or second acts. He has consistently taken great risks with downbeat, basically uncommer-cial material, like *A Perfect World, Bird,* and *Mystic River.* With *Unforgiven,* he made a majestic summing-up of a beloved genre, the western, producing a masterpiece of that genre. With *The Bridges of Madison County,* he invigorated inferior material with his own passion and com-mitment. *Million Dollar Baby* is equally daring and unexpected, a conflation of the boxing movie and the family drama. As an actor, Eastwood has pushed his aging alter-ego to reveal a naked vulnerability that's extremely unusual for a great movie star.   *(Warner Bros.)*

other an actor—on a road trip they take to the California wine country before the impending wedding of the actor. Paul Giamatti plays a middle-school teacher whose marriage has failed and who can't sell his novel. He's a self-absorbed oenophile who only comes alive when talking about or drinking wine, which substi-tutes for the enriching artistic experience he hungers to create but can't. The two men meet women (Virginia Madsen and Sandra Oh) who, in their own way, bring the men to a smattering of self-realization.

Payne's subject is the indigenous American drab, and the catastrophes that are often necessary to spark a sense of life's bounty. He's essentially a screen-writer who directs, so he doesn't do much with the camera: "Functional" would describe

20–38. *Madagascar* (U.S.A., 2005), *with Melman the Giraffe (voiced by David Schwimmer), Marty the Zebra (Chris Rock), Alex the Lion (Ben Stiller), and Gloria the Hippo (Jada Pinkett Smith), directed by Eric Darnell and Tom McGrath.*
We live in a golden age of animation, a genre dominated in the U.S. by four major organizations: Disney, Pixar, Fox, and DreamWorks. One reason for the success of many of these movies is due to the voiceover talent, which is often provided by well known stars with unique vocal personalities. Many of them are parents themselves, and enjoy the idea of performing in movies their children will enjoy. The best animated features also appeal to adults as well, thanks to their witty scripts and wryly comic characters. *Madagascar* is about four friends (pictured) who were born and raised in New York's Central Park Zoo. Provided with cozy dens, regular meals, and a constant stream of adoring admirers, they enjoy all the perks of *la dolce vita*. But soon there's trouble in paradise. Marty the Zebra (Rock) longs to see the outside world. He escapes and is pursued by his frantic friends. After a series of bizarre twists, they end up on the tropic isle of Madagascar. Now these native New Yorkers must learn to survive in the real wilds of nature. They learn the true meaning of the phrase, "It's a jungle out there." *(DreamWorks Animation SKG)*

his visual style. But that's a fair exchange for his unrelenting eye for character and what seems to be a gradual warming toward the weaknesses of humanity.

Haynes, Linklater, and Payne are only three of the many gifted artists now working in movies. Never has the American cinema been so varied, and so open to new possibilities. Established auteurs like Clint Eastwood (**20–37**), who is now in his seventies, are doing the best work of their careers. Thanks to a new technology that is cheaper and more accessible, who knows how many aspiring Spielbergs or Scorseses are waiting in the wings, waiting to add their voices and unique images to the American experience.

FURTHER READING

Biskind, Peter. *Down and Dirty Pictures: Miramax, Sundance and the Rise of Independent Film* (New York: Simon & Schuster, 2004). A lively account of the indie movement.

Caldwell, John Thornton, ed. *Electronic Media and Techno-Culture* (New Brunswick: Rutgers University Press, 2000). The digital revolution.

Hayes, Dade, and Jonathan Bing. *Open Wide: How Hollywood Box Office Became a National Obsession* (New York: Miramax Books/Hyperion, 2004). The marketing apparatus of the Hollywood studios.

Issa, Rose, and Sheila Witaker, eds. *Life and Art: The New Iranian Cinema* (London: National Film Theatre, 1999).

Martin, Michael T., ed. *New Latin American Cinema.* 2 vols. (Detroit: Wayne State University Press, 1997). A collection of scholarly essays.

Miller, Toby, et al. *Global Hollywood* (British Film Institute, distributed by Indiana University Press, 2001). The contemporary Hollywood studios.

Perkins, Roy, and Martin Stollery. *British Film Editors: The Heart of the Movie* (London: BFI Publishing, 2004).

Tapper, Richard, ed. *New Iranian Cinema: Politics, Representation and Identity* (London and New York: I.B. Tauris Publishers, 2002). A collection of scholarly essays.

Washington, Julie. "Soderbergh and Clooney: Like-Minded Odd Couple," *Cleveland Plain Dealer* (November 24, 2002).

Waxman, Sharon. "Studios Rush to Cash in on DVD Boom," *New York Times* (April 19, 2004).

Glossary

(C) predominantly critical terms   (T) predominantly technical terms
(I) predominantly industry terms   (G) terms in general usage

actor-star. See **star.**

A-film (I). An American studio era term, signifying a major production, usually with important stars and a generous budget.

aleatory techniques (C). Techniques of filmmaking which depend on the element of chance. Images are not planned out in advance but must be composed on the spot by a director who often acts as his or her own camera operator. Usually employed in documentary or improvisatory situations.

allegory (C). A symbolic technique in which stylized characters and situations represent rather obvious ideas, such as Justice, Death, and Society. A popular **genre** in the German cinema.

allusion (C). A reference to an event, person, or work of art, usually well known.

angle (G). The camera's angle of view relative to the subjects being photographed. A high angle shot is photographed from above; a low angle from below the subject.

animation (G). A form of filmmaking characterized by photographing inanimate subjects or individual drawings **frame** by frame, with each frame differing minutely from its predecessor. When such images are projected at the standard speed of twenty-four frames per second, the result is that the objects or drawings appear to move, seeming "animated."

archetype (C). An original model or type after which similar things are patterned. Archetypes can be well-known story patterns, universal experiences, or personality types. Myths, fairy tales, **genres,** and cultural heroes are generally archetypal, as are the basic cycles of life and nature.

art director, also production designer (G). The individual responsible for designing and overseeing the construction of sets for a movie, and sometimes its interior decoration and overall visual style.

aspect ratio (T). The ratio between the horizontal and vertical dimensions of the **frame.**

available lighting (G). The use of only that illumination that actually exists on a location, either natural (sun) or artificial (house lamps). When available lighting is used in interior locations, generally a sensitive **fast film stock** must be used.

avant-garde (C). From the French, meaning "in the front ranks." Those minority artists whose works are characterized by an unconventional daring and by obscure, controversial, or highly personal ideas.

back lot (I). During the studio era in the United States, standing exterior sets of such common locales as a frontier town, a turn-of-the-century city block, a European village, and so on.

B-film (G). A low-budget movie usually shown as the second feature during the big studio era in America. B-films rarely included important stars and took the form of popular **genres,** like thrillers, westerns, horror films, etc. The major studios used them as testing grounds for the raw talent under contract and as their filler product.

blacklist (G). During the anti-Communist hysteria of the late 1940s and 1950s, many writers, actors, and directors were forbidden employment in the American studios because of their political beliefs or former beliefs. Blacklisted artists were **left-wing** in their values.

blind booking (I). A marketing strategy, common in the big studio era, in which theater owners were required to rent studio movies before they were produced. Generally these promised pictures were identified by **genre**—a western, a musical—or by **star**—a Clark Gable picture, etc.

block booking (I). A marketing strategy, common in the American studio era, in which a production company's movies were rented as a package rather than individually. This practice was declared illegal in the late 1940s.

blocking (T). The planned movements of the actors within a given playing area.

box office (G). Literally, the ticket office at a movie theater. Figuratively, the drawing power of a performer, **genre,** or individual movie.

buddy film (G). A male-oriented action **genre,** especially popular in the 1970s, dealing with the adventures of two or more men, usually excluding any significant female roles.

character roles (G). Secondary roles in a movie, usually lacking the glamour and prominence of the leading parts.

chiaroscuro lighting (C). Dramatic use of light and dark, with little use for midrange grays. Often used for intense, dramatic subjects or by particularly visual directors.

cinéma vérité (C). A method of documentary filmmaking using chance elements that don't interfere with the way events are taking place in reality. Such movies are made with a minimum of equipment, usually a hand-held camera and portable sound apparatus.

cinematographer, also director of photography, lighting cameraman (G). The artist or technician responsible for the lighting of a shot and the quality of the photography.

classical cinema (C). A vague but convenient term used to designate the mainstream of fiction films produced in America, roughly from the maturity of Griffith in the mid-1910s to the late 1960s. The classical **paradigm** is a movie strong in **story, star,** and **production values,** with a high level of technical achievement and **edited** according to the conventions of **classical cutting.** The visual style is functional and rarely detracts from the characters in action. Movies in this style are structured narratively, with a clearly defined conflict, complications that intensify to a rising climax, and a resolution that emphasizes formal closure.

classical cutting, *découpage classique* **(C).** A style of editing developed by Griffith, in which a sequence of shots is determined by a scene's dramatic and emotional emphases rather than by its physical action alone. The sequence of shots represents the breakdown of the event into its psychological as well as logical components.

closeup, close shot (G). A detailed view of a person or object, usually without much context provided. A closeup of an actor generally includes only his or her head.

continuity (I). The kind of logic implied between edited shots, their principle of coherence. Cutting to continuity emphasizes smooth transitions between shots, in which time and space are unobtrusively condensed. More complex, **classical cutting** is the linking of shots according to an event's psychological as well as logical breakdown. In radical **montage,** the continuity is determined by the symbolic association of ideas between shots rather than any literal connections in time and space. Continuity can also refer to the time-space continuum of reality before it's broken down into fragments (shots).

convention (C). An implied agreement between the viewer and artist to accept certain artificialities as real in a work of art. In movies, **editing**—or the juxtaposition of shots—is accepted as "logical" even though a viewer's perception of reality is continuous and unfragmented. **Genre** films contain many preestablished conventions. In musicals, for example, characters express themselves most forcefully through song and dance.

crane shot (T). A shot taken from a special device called a crane, which resembles a huge mechanical arm. The crane carries the camera and the cinematographer and can move in virtually any direction.

creative producer (I). A producer who supervises the making of a movie in such detail that he or she is virtually its artistic creator. During the studio era in America, the most famous creative producers were David O. Selznick and Walt Disney.

cross-cutting (G). The alternating of shots from two sequences, often in different locales, suggesting that they are taking place at the same time.

Dadaism (C). An **avant-garde** movement in the arts stressing unconscious elements, irrationalism, irreverent wit, and spontaneity. Dadaists films were produced mostly in France in the later 1910s and 1920s.

deep focus (T). A technique of photography which permits all distance planes to remain clearly in focus, from **closeup** ranges to infinity.

dialectical (C). An analytical methodology, derived from Hegel and Marx, that juxtaposes pairs of opposites—a thesis and antithesis—to arrive at a synthesis of ideas.

dissolve, lap dissolve (T). The slow fading out of one shot and the gradual fading in of its successor, with a superimposition of images, usually at the midpoint.

distributor (I). Those individuals who serve as middle men in the movie industry, who arrange to book the product in theaters.

dolly shot, tracking shot, trucking shot (T). A shot taken from a moving vehicle. Originally tracks were laid on the set to permit a smoother movement of the camera. Today even a smooth hand-held traveling shot is considered a variation of the dolly shot.

double exposure (T). The superimposition of two literally unrelated images on film.

double feature, double bill (G). The practice, common primarily in the 1930s and 1940s in America, of exhibiting two feature-length movies for a single admission, usually an **A production** followed by a **B-film.**

dubbing (T). The addition of sound after the visuals have been photographed. Dubbing can be either **synchronous** with an image or **nonsynchronous.** Foreign-language movies are often dubbed in English for release in the United States.

dupe (T). A positive print made from a negative that was in turn struck from a positive, resulting in inferior visual quality. During the **nickelodeon** era, most successful films were duped and bootlegged by unscrupulous promoters.

editing (G). The joining of one shot (strip of film) with another. The shots can picture events and objects in different places at different times. Editing is called **montage** in Europe.

epic (C). A film **genre** characterized by bold and sweeping themes, usually in heroic proportions. The protagonist is usually an ideal representative of a culture—national, religious, or regional. The tone of most epics is dignified, the treatment larger-than-life. The western is the most popular epic genre in the United States.

establishing shot (T). Usually an **extreme long** or **long shot** offered at the beginning of a scene, providing the viewer with the context of the subsequent closer shots.

expressionism (C). A style of filmmaking that distorts time and space as ordinarily perceived in reality. Emphasis is placed on the essential characteristics of objects and people, not necessarily on their superficial appearance. Typical expressionist techniques are fragmentary **editing,** extreme **angles** and lighting effects, and the use of distorting lenses and **special effects.**

extreme closeup (G). A minutely detailed view of an object or person. An extreme closeup of an actor generally includes only his or her eyes or mouth.

extreme long shot (G). A panoramic view of an exterior location, photographed from a great distance, often as far as a quarter-mile away.

fade (T). The **fade-out** is the snuffing of an image from normal brightness to a black screen. A **fade-in** is the slow brightening of the image from a black screen to normal.

faithful adaptation (C). A movie based on another medium (usually a work of literature) which captures the essence of the original and uses cinematic equivalents for specific literary techniques.

fast-forward (G). An **editing** technique that suggests the interruption of the present by a shot or series of shots representing the future.

fast motion, accelerated motion (T). If an action is photographed at a slower rate than twenty-four **frames** per second, when the film is projected at the standard rate of twenty-four frames per second, the action will appear to be moving at a faster rate than normal and will often seem jerky.

fast stock, fast film (T). Film stock that is highly sensitive to light and generally produces a grainy image. Often used by documentarists who wish to shoot only with **available lighting.**

feature, feature-length film (G). A movie of over an hour's duration, and generally under two.

film noir (C). A French term—literally, "black cinema"—referring to a kind of urban American **genre** that sprang up after World War II. Archetypal film noirs revolve around an existentially despairing universe where there is no escape from mean city streets, loneliness, and death. Stylistically, film noir emphasizes **low-key** and **high-contrast lighting,** complex compositions, and a strong atmosphere of dread and paranoia.

final cut, also release print (T). The sequence of shots in a movie as it will be released to the public.

first cut, also rough cut (I). The initial sequence of shots in a movie, often constructed by the director.

first run (I). A film's initial release pattern, in which most of its profits are earned. After its first run, the movie is then rented to second-run "neighborhood" theaters, television, cable stations, etc.

flashback (G). An **editing** technique that suggests the interruption of the present by a shot or series of shots representing the past.

focus (T). The degree of acceptable sharpness in a film image. "Out of focus" means that the images are blurred and lack acceptable linear definition.

frame (T). The dividing line between the edges of the screen image and the enclosing darkness of the theater. Can also refer to a single photograph from the filmstrip.

freeze frame, freeze shot (T). A shot composed of a single **frame** that is reprinted a number of times on the filmstrip which, when projected, gives the illusion of a still photograph.

full shot (T). A type of **long shot** which includes the human body in full, with the head near the top of the frame and the feet near the bottom.

gauge (T). The width of the filmstrip, expressed in millimeters (mm). The wider the gauge, the better the quality of the image. The most common gauges are 8 mm, 16 mm, 35 mm, and 70 mm. The standard in theatrical exhibition is 35 mm.

genre (C). A recognizable type of movie, characterized by certain preestablished conventions. Some common American genres are westerns, musicals, thrillers, comedies.

go-fer, also gopher (I). A minor functionary or assistant whose job is mainly to assist a major functionary. A go-fer "goes for" coffee, sandwiches, and so on.

high-angle shot (T). A shot in which the subject is photographed from above.

high contrast (T). A style of lighting emphasizing harsh shafts and dramatic streaks of lights and darks. Often used in thrillers and melodramas.

high key (T). A style of lighting emphasizing bright, even illumination, with few conspicuous shadows. Used generally in comedies, musicals, and light entertainment films.

homage (C). A direct or indirect reference within a movie to another movie, filmmaker, or cinematic style. A respectful and affectionate tribute.

iconography (C). The use of a well-known culture symbol or complex of symbols in an artistic representation. In movies, iconography can involve a star's **persona,** the preestablished conventions of a **genre,** the use of **archetypal** characters and situations, and such stylistic features as lighting, settings, costuming, props, and so on.

independent producer (G). A producer not affiliated with a studio or large commercial firm. Many stars and directors have been independent producers to insure their artistic autonomy.

intercutting (T). See **cross-cutting.**

iris (T). A **masking** device that blacks out portions of the screen, permitting only a part of the image to be seen. Usually the iris is circular or oval shaped and can be expanded or contracted.

jump-cut (T). An abrupt transition between shots, sometimes deliberate, which is disorienting in terms of the continuity of space and time.

key light (T). The main source of illumination for a shot.

Kinetoscope (G). An early device for viewing films under a minute in length. The film was a continuous loop encased in a cabinet which could be used only by one person at a time.

leftist, left-wing (C). A political term used to describe the acceptance, at least in part, of the economic, social, and philosophical ideas of Karl Marx.

lengthy take, long take (C). A shot of lengthy duration.

long shot (G). Includes an area within the **frame** which roughly corresponds to the audience's view of the area within the proscenium arch in the live theater.

low-angle shot (T). A shot in which the subject is photographed from below.

low key (T). A style of lighting emphasizing diffused shadows and atmospheric pools of light. Often used in mysteries, thrillers, and so on.

majors (I). The principal production studios of a given era. In the golden age of the Hollywood studio system—roughly the 1930s and 1940s—the majors consisted of MGM, Warner Brothers, RKO, Paramount Pictures, and Twentieth Century-Fox.

Marxist (G). A person who subscribes to the economic, social, political, and philosophical theories of Karl Marx. Any artistic work reflecting these values.

masking (T). A technique whereby a portion of the movie image is blocked out, thus temporarily altering the dimensions of the screen's **aspect ratio.**

matte shot (T). The process of combining two separate shots on one print, resulting in an image that looks as though it had been photographed normally. Used mostly for **special effects,** such as combining a human figure with giant dinosaurs, and so on.

medium shot (G). A relatively close shot revealing a moderate amount of detail. A medium shot of a figure generally includes the body from the knees or waist up.

Method acting (G). An interior style of acting derived from the theories of Constantin Stanislavsky, emphasizing emotional intensity, psychological truth, ensemble playing, and the illusion of spontaneity. Since the 1950s, the Method has been the dominant American style of acting.

miniatures, also model or miniature shots (T). Small-scale models photographed to give the illusion that they are full-scale objects—for example, ships sinking at sea and giant dinosaurs.

minimalism (C). A style of filmmaking characterized by austerity and restraint, in which cinematic elements are reduced to the barest minimum of information.

mise en scène (C). The arrangement of visual weights and movements within a given space. In the live theater, the space is usually defined by the proscenium arch; in movies, by the **frame** which encloses the images. Cinematic mise en scène encompasses both the staging of the action and the way that it's photographed.

montage (T). Transitional sequences of rapidly **edited** images, used to suggest the lapse of time or the passing of events. Often employs **dissolves** and **multiple exposures.** In Europe, "montage" means the art of editing.

motif (C). Any unobtrusive technique, object, or thematic idea that is systematically repeated throughout a film.

multiple exposure (T). A special effect produced by the **optical printer,** which permits the superimposition of many images simultaneously.

negative cost (I). What the film itself actually costs to make, not counting prints or advertising.

neorealism (C). An Italian film movement that produced its best works between 1945 and 1955. Strongly realistic in its technical biases, the movement emphasized documentary aspects of film art, stressing loose episodic plots, natural lighting, actual location settings, nonprofessional actors, and a preoccupation with poverty and social problems.

New Wave, *nouvelle vague* **(G).** A group of young French filmmakers who came to prominence during the late 1950s. The most widely known are François Truffaut, Jean-Luc Godard, and Alain Resnais.

nickelodeon (G). An evolutionary step that followed the crude storefront theaters, nickelodeons were not grandiose movie palaces but functional bare-bones movie theaters. Primarily in the 1910s in America.

nonsynchronous sound (T). Sound and image are not recorded simultaneously, or the sound is detached from its source in the film image. Music, for example, is usually nonsynchronous in a movie.

oblique angle, tilt shot (T). A shot photographed by a tilted camera. When the image is projected on the screen, the subject seems to be tilted on a diagonal.

oeuvre (C). From the French "work." The complete works of an artist, viewed as a whole.

optical printer (T). An elaborate machine used to create special effects in movies. For example, **fades, dissolves, multiple exposures,** etc. Now becoming obsolete.

pan, panning shot (T). Short for *panorama,* this is a revolving horizontal movement of the camera from left to right or vice versa.

parallel editing. See **cross-cutting.**

persona (C). From the Latin "mask." An actor's public image, based on his or her previous roles and often incorporating elements from his or her actual personality as well. A form of precharacterization.

personality-star. See **star.**

point-of-view shot, also pov shot, first person camera (T). Any shot that is taken from the vantage point of a character in the film: what he or she sees.

process shot, also rear projection (T). A technique in which a background scene is projected onto a translucent screen behind the actors so it appears that the actors are on location in the final image.

producer (G). An ambiguous term referring to the individual or company that controls the financing of a film and often the way it is made. The producer can be concerned solely with business matters or with putting together a package deal (such as script, stars, and director), or he or she can function as an expeditor, smoothing over problems during production.

producer-director (I). A filmmaker who finances projects independently to allow maximum creative freedom.

Production Code, also Motion Picture Production Code (I). The American film industry's censorship arm. The Code was introduced in 1930 but not enforced until 1934. It was revised in the 1950s and was scrapped in favor of the present rating system in 1968.

production values (I). The box office appeal of the physical mounting of a film, such as sets, costumes, and **special effects.** Spectacle pictures are generally the most lavish in their production values.

program films, also programmers (G). See **B-films.**

reaction shot (T). A cut to a shot of a character's reaction to the contents of the preceding shot.

realism (G). A style of filmmaking which attempts to duplicate the look of reality as it's ordinarily perceived, with emphasis on authentic locations and details, an unobtrusive camera style, and a minimum of **editing** and **special effects.**

rear projection. See **process shot.**

reverse angle shot (T). A shot taken from an angle 180 degrees opposed to the previous shot. That is, the camera is placed opposite its previous position.

revisionist (C). The latter phase of a **genre**'s evolution in which many of its values and conventions are challenged or subjected to skeptical scrutiny.

rough cut (T). The crudely **edited** footage of a movie before the editor has tightened up the slackness between shots. A rough draft.

rushes, dailies (I). The selected footage of the previous day's shooting, which is usually evaluated by the director and cinematographer before the start of the next day's shooting.

scene (G). An imprecise unit of film, composed of a number of interrelated shots, unified usually by a central concern—a location, an incident, or a minor dramatic climax.

script, screenplay, scenario (G). A written description of a movie's dialogue and action, which occasionally includes camera instructions.

sequence (G). An imprecise structural unit of film, composed of a number of interrelated **scenes** and leading to a major climax.

sequence shot, also *plan-séquence* **(C).** A single **lengthy take,** usually involving complex staging and camera movements.

serials (G). A now extinct **genre,** used as a prelude to the main feature. Serials were installments of a continuous story (usually a melodrama or fantasy), strung out for twelve or fifteen weeks, one chapter (twenty minutes) per week. Each chapter concluded with a cliff-hanger ending.

setup (T). The position of the camera and lights for a specific shot.

shot (G). Those images that are recorded continuously from the time the camera starts until the time it stops. That is, an unedited strip of film.

slow motion (T). Shots of a subject photographed at a faster rate than twenty-four frames per second, which when projected at the standard rate produce a dreamy, dancelike slowness of action.

social realism (C). A loose term encompassing films that point out flaws in the social structure. Examples include the Warner Brothers films of the 1930s, the **neorealist** films of post-World War II Italy, and the British "Kitchen Sink" school of the late 1950s.

soft focus (T). The blurring out of focus of all except one desired distance range. Can also refer to a glamourizing technique that softens the sharpness of definition so that facial wrinkles can be smoothed over.

special effects (G). Trick photography and optical effects, usually employed in fantasy films, especially science fiction.

star (G). A film actor or actress of great popularity. A **personality-star** tends to play only those roles that fit a preconceived public image, which constitutes his or her **persona.** An **actor-star** can play roles of greater range and variety. Will Ferrell is a personality-star; Robert DeNiro an actor-star.

star system (G). The technique of exploiting the charisma of popular players to enhance the box office appeal of films.

stock (T). Unexposed film. There are many types of movie stocks, including those highly sensitive to light **(fast stocks)** and those relatively insensitive to light **(slow stocks).**

stop-motion photography (T). A staple of trick and **animation** photography, the method used to make King Kong move. Models are shaped over metal armatures and photographed one **frame** at a time, with the model being moved slightly between exposures. When the filmstrip is projected at the standard rate of twenty-four frames per second, the models seem to move realistically.

storyboard, storyboarding (T). A previsualization technique in which shots are sketched in advance and in sequence, like a comic strip, thus allowing the filmmaker to outline the **mise en scène** and construct the **editing** continuity before production begins.

story values (I). The narrative appeal of a movie, which can reside in the popularity of an adapted story, the high craftsmanship of a script, or both.

studio (G). A large corporation specializing in the production and/or distribution of movies, such as Paramount, Warner Brothers, etc. Any physical facility equipped for the production of movies.

subtext (G). A term used in drama and film to signify the dramatic implications beneath the language of a play or movie. Often the subtext concerns ideas and emotions that are totally independent of the language of the text.

surrealism (C). An **avant-garde** movement in the arts stressing Freudian and Marxist ideas, unconscious elements, irrationalism, and the symbolic association of ideas. Dreamlike and bizarre, surrealist movies were produced roughly from 1924 to 1931, primarily in France, though there are still surrealistic elements in the works of many directors.

synchronous sound (T). The agreement or correspondence between image and sound, which are recorded simultaneously, or seem so in the finished print. Synchronous sounds appear to derive from an obvious source in the visuals.

take (T). A variation on a specific shot. The final shot is often selected from a number of possible takes.

telephoto lens (T). A lens that acts as a telescope, magnifying the size of objects at a great distance. Two side effects are to flatten perspective and to cause the foregrounds and backgrounds to blur out of focus.

tight framing (C). Usually in close shots. The **mise en scène** is so carefully balanced and harmonized that the people photographed have little or no freedom of movement.

tilt shot (T). See **oblique angle.**

titles (G). In silent films, titles were used to set a scene, create a mood with language, as well as give the dialogue for the characters.

tracking shot, trucking shot. See **dolly shot.**

two-shot (T). A relatively close shot (usually at **medium** distance) containing two people within the same **frame.**

underscoring (T). Music behind film action was a staple of silent films, usually a live orchestra or, in more modest circumstances, an organist or piano player. Talkies took a few years to adjust, but by 1933, composers like Max Steiner were using music the way silent movies used titles—to create mood or indicate emotion.

vertical integration (I). A system in which the production, distribution, and exhibition of movies are all controlled by the same corporation. Vertical integration was declared illegal in the late 1940s.

Vitascope (G). A projector invented by Thomas Armat that was a progenitor of the modern movie projector. The film was fed and taken up by large spools, and for the first time a loop was used at the top and bottom of the film gate to lessen the strain on the film and allow pictures of greater length to be exhibited.

voice-over (T). A **nonsynchronous** spoken commentary in a movie, often used to convey a character's thoughts or memories.

widescreen, also CinemaScope (G). A movie image which has an **aspect ratio** of approximately 5 by 3, though some widescreens possess horizontal distances that extend as wide as 2.5 times the vertical dimension of the screen.

wipe (T). An **editing** device, usually a line that travels across the screen, "pushing off" one image and revealing another.

zoom lens, zoom shot (T). A lens of variable focal length that permits the cinematographer to change from wide angle to telephoto shots (and vice versa) in one continuous movement, thus suggesting the camera's plunging into or withdrawing from a scene.

Index

Macbeth, 199, 349
Macdonald, Andrew, 516
MacDonald, Jeanette, 135
MacDonald, Peter, 421
Mack, The, 356
Mackendrick, Alexander, 264
MacKenzie, Donald, 24
MacLachlan, Kyle, 430
MacMurray, Fred, 195
Madagascar, 569
Madame Bovary, 331
Madden, John, 508, 510, 511
Made in U.S.A., 327
Mad Max, 409
Mad Max Beyond Thunderdome, 409
Madness of King George, The, 511
Madsen, Virginia, 567, 568
Mad Wednesday, 193
Maggiorani, Lamberto, 225
Magic Flute, The, 280
Magician, The, 280
Magnani, Anna, 222
Magnificent Ambersons, The, 22, 199, 200–201
Magnificent Obsession, 398
Magnificent Seven, The, 269
Magnolia, 499
Maguire, Tobey, 553
Mairesse, Valerie, 320
Major and the Minor, The, 195, 197
Major Barbara, 216
Major Dundee, 307
Makavejev, Dusan, 347
Makhmalbaf, Mohsen, 539, 540, 542, 543
Making a Living, 48
Makioka Sisters, The, 469
Makk, Károly, 463
Malamud, Bernard, 298
Malden, Karl, 244
Malick, Terrence, 498
Malkovich, John, 440
Malle, Louis, 321, 367, 391, 499
Mallrats, 495
Malraux, André, 106
Maltese Falcon, The, 185, 186, 189, 361
Maltz, Albert, 239
Mamoulian, Rouben, 135
Man, Women, and Sin, 67
Manchurian Candidate, The, 297

Mandabi, 414
Mandela, Nelson, 443, 503
Man, Escaped, A, 285
Man for All Seasons, A, 249, 250, 331
Mangano, Silvana, 230
Manhattan, 377, 380
Manhattan Murder Mystery, 489
Manhunter, 560
Mankiewicz, Herman, 198
Mankiewicz, Joseph L., 246, 247, 248, 292, 535–536
Mann, Daniel, 222, 247
Mann, Delbert, 242, 243
Mann, Michael, 554, 560, 562, 563
Mann, Thomas, 230
Man Named John, A, 346
Man of Iron, 348, 461, 462
Man of Marble, 348, 462
Manon of the Spring, 457–458
Manson, Charles, 349
Manvell, Roger, 210
Manville, Lesley, 535
Man Who Fell to Earth, The, 386
Man Who Knew Too Much, The, 254
Man Who Laughs, The, 86
Man Who Shot Liberty Valance, The, 155, 156–157
Man Who Would Be King, The, 187, 188, 365
Man With the Golden Arm, The, 241
Mao Zedong, 207
Marathon Man, 340, 357
March, Fredric, 115, 139, 204, 298
Marconi, Guglielmo, 3
Maria Full of Grace, 548, 549
Marie Antoinette, 105
Marion, Frank, 24
Marius, 166
Mark of Zorro, The, 56, 58
Marquand, Richard, 379
Marriage, Italian Style, 227
Marriage of Maria Braun, The, 397
Married to the Mob, 432
Married Woman, A, 327
Marsh, Mae, 26, 34
Marshall, Herbert, 108
Marshall, Penny, 484
Marshall, Rob, 552
Martin, Dean, 103
Martin, Steve, 411, 435